Save Time, Improve Results! Over 200,000 students use the award-winning MyLanguageLabs online learning and assessment system to succeed in their basic language courses. If your instructor has required use of MyLatinLab, you will have online access to an eText, an interactive Student Activities Manual, audio materials, and many more resources to help you succeed. For more information or to purchase access, visit www.mylanguagelabs.com.

A GUIDE TO *DISCE!* ICON

	Text Audio Program	This icon indicates that recorded material to accompany *DISCE!* is available in MyLatinLab, on audio CD, or on the Companion Website.

Disce!

An Introductory Latin Course

Kenneth F. Kitchell, Jr.
University of Massachusetts Amherst

Thomas J. Sienkewicz
Monmouth College

Historical Consultant: Gregory Daugherty
Randolph Macon College

Prentice Hall
Boston Columbus Indianapolis
New York San Francisco Upper Saddle River
Amsterdam Cape Town Dubai London
Madrid Milan Munich Paris Montréal Toronto
Delhi Mexico City São Paulo Sydney
Hong Kong Seoul Singapore Taipei Tokyo

Library of Congress Cataloging-in-Publication Data

Kitchell, Kenneth.

Disce! / Kenneth Kitchell, Thomas Sienkewicz.—1st ed.

p. cm.

ISBN 0-13-158531-2

1. Latin language—Study and teaching. 2. Latin language—Textbooks for foreign speakers.
3. Latin language—Grammar—Problems, exercises, etc. I. Sienkewicz, Thomas J. II. Title.

PA2087.5.K54 2010

478.2'421–dc22

2010022509

Executive Acquisitions Editor: Rachel McCoy
Editorial Assistant: Noha Amer Mahmoud
Executive Marketing Manager: Kris Ellis-Levy
Marketing Coordinator: William J. Bliss
Senior Managing Editor for Product Development: Mary Rottino
Associate Managing Editor: Janice Stangel
Production Project Manager: Manuel Echevarria
Project Manager: Assunta Petrone, Preparé, Italy
Audio-Visual Project Manager: Gail Cocker
Development Editor for Assessment: Melissa Marolla Brown
Media Editor: Meriel Martínez
Executive Editor, MyLanguageLabs: Bob Hemmer
Senior Media Editor: Samantha Alducin
Senior Art Director: Pat Smythe
Interior/Cover Designer: Wanda España
Cartographer: Peter Bull Art Studio
Line Art Studio: Peter Bull Art Studio
Senior Manufacturing and Operations Manager, Arts and Sciences: Nick Sklitsis
Operations Specialist: Brian Mackey
Publisher: Phil Miller

Cover image: ML Sinibaldi/CORBIS

This book was set in 12/14 Times New Roman.

Prentice Hall
is an imprint of

PEARSON

www.pearsonhighered.com

	ISBN 10:	ISBN 13:
Disce! An Introductory Latin Course, Volume 1	0-13-158531-2	978-0-13-158531-7
Disce! An Introductory Latin Course, Volume 2	0-205-83571-6	978-0-205-83571-3

Brief Contents

DEDICATION

Omnibus discipulīs nostrīs docentibus doctūrīsque.

Table of Contents

IPSISSIMA VERBA

For a brief description
of this anthology of authentic
Latin readings, see MyLatinLab under
Online Resources in the Preface.

Note on abbreviations used in *Disce!*:
A list of abbreviations used in this book
can be found on pg. A27 at the
beginning of the *Verba Omnia*.

Preface

Disce! is a fully integrated Latin program designed expressly for classrooms and students of the 21st century. It consciously seeks to combine the best of pedagogical theory and classroom practice to produce a single textbook that serves students with varying abilities and learning styles as well as instructors who teach in a wide range of institutions and curricula. The unwavering goal of the book is to bring students to the point where they can read Latin fluently and readily and to guide them in a gradual and controlled manner toward reading original Roman authors and their texts.

Philosophy

Disce! is based on the belief that both the "reading first" and the "grammar first" approaches have pedagogical value and thus combines the best features of both.

- The guiding principle at any moment is what is best for the student and for the particular items being studied. Some grammar is readily learned by induction whereas other concepts are best learned through prior explication of the grammar.

- *Disce!* makes use of many of the pedagogical techniques found in modern foreign language books, especially combining language and culture, integrating the student's own experiences into the learning process, and providing a wide variety of practice exercises (grammatical, cultural, conversational, written, etc.).

- From the reading method approach *Disce!* uses a unified story line with controlled introduction of vocabulary and grammar in context. *Disce!* is committed to the belief that students are better able to follow, and will profit more from, stories with rich and fully developed characters than they will from a series of unconnected practice sentences or readings.

- *Disce!* is committed to exposing students to authorial Latin as soon as possible.

- From the grammar first approach *Disce!* maintains a belief that many students profit from a structured explication of the grammar and periodic review. Thus, grammatical charts are given in the body of the text as an aid for such students, but never as a primary goal in and of themselves.

As a hybrid text, *Disce!* presents the material in a carefully structured way. In each chapter, students are first exposed to the basics of a grammatical concept—just enough grammar is explained to enable students to read the *lectiō* that immediately follows the explanation. In this *lectiō* each instance of the target grammar is indicated by a special typeface. Following this exposure through reading, the grammar is explained in more depth. The story line, as well as the cultural materials in each chapter, are designed to serve the single purpose of engaging and readying students to read advanced Latin.

The Standards for Classical Language Learning[1]

Disce! has been carefully created according to the *Standards for Classical Languages* established by the American Classical League and the American Philological Association. A thoughtful Latin teacher at any level should have these "5Cs" in mind over the course of his or her class-

[1] Richard Gasoyne et al. *Standards for Classical Language Learning. A Collaborative Project of The American Classical League and The American Philological Association and Regional Classical Associations.* (Miami, OH: American Classical League, 1997).

es: Communication, Culture, Connections, Comparisons, and Communities. As the original document states, "Each goal is one strand·in a fabric that must be woven into curriculum development."

COMMUNICATION. From the earliest chapters students are communicating directly with the ancient Romans and with each other. *Disce!* strives to ensure that this communication involves four skills: reading, listening, writing, and speaking.

CULTURE. The culture of the Romans is not relegated to specific little niches, but is woven directly into the narratives the students read and is reinforced by written discussions and extensive visual aids (photographs of ancient sites, artifacts, maps, etc.).

CONNECTIONS AND COMPARISONS. From the *Quid Putās?* and *Latīna Hodierna* sections through the constant stress on the role of Classical culture in the world today, links are made between Latin and modern languages and between Roman practices and modern culture. *Disce!* encourages students at all times to learn from other languages and to see the ways in which Classical culture has evolved into significant portions of today's multicultural world.

COMMUNITIES. *Disce!* makes frequent reference to the cultures of ancient Rome and the diverse people in its empire. It also makes cultural comparisons between Roman and modern life and regularly draws attention to modern foreign languages derived from Latin. Such exposure encourages students to think about and to explore the communities of the world, both ancient and modern.

The Story Line

The story is set in Rome c. 9 B.C. and follows the lives of two families, one well-to-do, and one working class. The patrician family is that of Marcus Servilius Severus, who lives on the Viminal Hill and hopes for social and political advancement within the Augustan bureaucracy. He has two children by a previous marriage that ended in divorce (Marcus, age 21, and Servilia, age 16), and one son with his current wife, Caecilia (Lucius, age 10). This family's plot line takes us through elections, a literary banquet designed to curry favor with Augustus, the young Marcus' trip to Greece to study rhetoric, Lucius' adventures as a young child in school, and Servilia's attempts to marry the young man of her dreams (Cordus) rather than her father's chosen mate (Iullus Antonius). Also in the house is the titular *pater familiās* (the *avus,* or grandfather), and a full panoply of slaves, upon whom the story often focuses to give a more rounded picture of urban life in Rome.

The plebeian family is headed by a matriarch named Valeria. She was living in Verona on a farm and her son Licinius was serving in the army in Germany under Tiberius when her husband died, leaving her unable to run the farm on her own. Now in Rome, she runs a snack shop near the Forum, aided by her very pregnant daughter named Licinia, who is married to Aelius, a blacksmith, and by a German slave girl named Flavia. Having put all her money into the store, Valeria and her family (which also includes Plotia, Valeria's mother, and Socrates, a pet monkey) are strapped for cash and live in the Subura, providing a glimpse into a frequently overlooked area of Roman life. Their story line includes childbirth, the terrors of urban fire, worries about money and lodging, street life, fortune tellers, and, ultimately, a patron-client relationship with the Servilius family.

Grammar

From the grammar first method the authors provide orderly and clear grammar explanations that are presented in every chapter. It is a fact based upon our experience that not all grammar is best (or most quickly) learned by induction. Charts and short, clear grammar explanations are helpful to many learners and learning styles, and are used accordingly.

Disce! is unique in offering, in each chapter, both "core" grammar/morphology and a "More on the Language" section entitled *Angulus Grammaticus.* The core grammar, presented in the body of each chapter, offers students just enough explanation to enable them to read and comprehend the language as quickly as possible. But for those teachers and students who desire more, each chapter also has an *Angulus Grammaticus* where more traditional and in-depth explanations and terminology are presented.

The order of the grammar presented in the book is in accordance with the frequency with which given forms or usages appear in the Latin authors.[2]

Vocabulary

Vocabulary is also presented in order of occurrence in the major authors, following a list created by the authors based on previous studies.[3] This vocabulary is divided into *Verba Ūtenda*, which are to be used while reading, but not committed to memory, and *Verba Discenda*, which are for memorization. Where appropriate, *Verba Discenda* are accompanied by English derivatives. *Verba Ūtenda* are always given the first time they appear but gradually disappear if used frequently enough. The *Verba Discenda* are introduced according to the frequency rules discussed in the previous section, and whenever feasible, a word is used as a *Verbum Ūtendum* prior to its becoming a *Verbum Discendum*. The *Verbum Omnia*, a comprehensive list of all the Latin words used in *Disce!*, is also provided in the appendix.

Macrons are used throughout on the principle that students learn vocabulary faster and more accurately when they say and hear the words pronounced properly. Choices had to be made constantly between different theories of where to indicate long vowels (especially over internal vowels long by nature, e.g., *rōstrum* vs. *rostrum*), and the authors chose to follow the *Oxford Latin Dictionary* in such cases.

Chapter Structure

Disce! consists of two volumes with 20 chapters in each volume. In these chapters all the grammar and syntax needed for a student to begin to read authentic Latin is introduced. Each chapter is divided into two sections, each centered on a reading of approximately 250 Latin words in a connected narrative about one of our two families. Each chapter contains the following sections:

Antequam Legis (Before You Read)

This section provides students with the information needed to read the following *lectiō*. This can include cultural material, a short explanation of the new grammar being presented, pre-reading questions, and an exercise designed to reinforce the new grammatical material. The focus is on getting the student directly into the chapter with the minimum preparation possible, and thus the exercise is commonly done just prior to or in conjunction with the reading.

---

[2]Paul Distler. *Teach the Latin, I Pray You.* (Chicago: Loyola University Press, 1962, reprinted 2000, Wimbledon Publishing Co.) offers a convenient survey of this information.

[3]The vocabulary frequency lists used in *Disce!* are based on: (1) "300 Most Frequent Latin Words" from Paul Diederich's "The frequency of Latin words and their endings" (1938 University of Chicago dissertation; http://www.users.drew.edu/jmuccigr/latin/diederich/); (2) "*Tolle, lege!* The Fourteen Hundred" by Vojin Nedeljkovic (http://dekart.f.bg.ac.yu/~vnedeljk/TL/apropos/wordlist.html), a list of 1400 most common Latin words based on *Grund- und Aufbauwortschatz Latein* by E. Habenstein, E. Hermes and H. Zimmermann (Stuttgart: Ernst Klett Schulbuchverlag, 1990); (3) the entire mastery list for elementary Latin contained in the New York State Syllabus in Latin for 1956, available in the Latin-English Vocabulary of *Our Latin Heritage II* by Lillian M. Hines, Edward J., and Joseph W. Hopkinson (New York: Harcourt, Brace and World, Inc., 1966); and (4) frequency of use in *Fabulae Faciles* by Francis Ritchie (Chicago: Longman, Green and Co., 1914).

Lectiō Prīma (First Reading) and *Lectiō Secunda* (Second Reading)

In each *lectiō* the target grammar and/or usage is used in context. Moreover, the target grammar for each reading is set typographically to enable students to see it in action and in context as they read. In many cases, adapted passages from authentic Latin authors have been worked into the narratives. For example, audience members at a production of Plautus' *Amphitruō* hear a modified version of its prologue. In another, a lovesick girl consoles herself with words from a Catullus poem, and later, the menu at a banquet is taken directly from Petronius.

Postquam Lēgistī (After You Have Read)

This section, immediately following the *lectiō*, consists of a series of comprehension questions about the reading. Some of these are to be answered in English, others in Latin.

Grammatica (Grammar)

This grammar section follows each *lectiō* and provides a more detailed presentation of the target grammar introduced in *Antequam Legis*. Each *Grammatica* includes exercises on the material introduced. Exercises in the textbook are designed for classroom use, whereas those in the Student Activities Manual are designed for work outside of class.

Mōrēs Rōmānī (Roman Customs)

This section presents cultural material appropriate to the chapter *lectiōnēs*. An attempt has been made to address all levels of Roman life: the privileged and the disenfranchised; male and female; urban and rural; free and enslaved. The goal is to encourage students to see the broad span of Roman culture. Usually in this section (but sometimes in one of the next two sections), passages from ancient Roman authors are introduced in abbreviated or simplified form. These readings are always connected to the cultural material presented in the chapter.

Latīna Hodierna (Latin Today)

Here the influence of Latin in today's world is demonstrated by discussing etymologies, Latin borrowings, and the connection between Latin and living Romance languages.

Orbis Terrārum Rōmānus (The Roman World)

Addressing the fact that the narrative of the readings is largely confined to the Rome of 9 B.C., this section offers students a broad geographic introduction to Rome, Italy, and the Roman Empire. Each topic is somehow linked to the chapter readings.

Quid Putās? (What Do You Think?)

Following the three cultural sections, this section encourages students to put Roman civilization in meaningful contexts.

Exerceāmus! (Let's Practice!)

Every chapter contains a number of exercises offering pre-readings, comprehension, grammar and vocabulary review, composition, and oral drills intended for in-class work. These exercises always include some practice with the *Verba Discenda*. In addition, *Scrībāmus* exercises facilitate composition, and *Colloquāmur* exercises encourage basic oral work in Latin. The goal here and in the Student Activity Manual is to present a wide variety of types of exercises to alleviate boredom and predictability while appealing to various learning styles.

Angulus Grammaticus (The Grammar Corner)

This section offers an in-depth explanation of a point of grammar of interest to many students and instructors. The information contained in this section is confined to explanations that are not necessary to enable the student to read Latin.

Program Components

Innovative supplements provide ample opportunities for practicing lexical and grammatical features while extending the breadth and depth of the cultural presentation and the introduction to the Roman world. New and sophisticated electronic components build on *Disce!*'s pedagogical and cultural presentations in interesting, creative ways.

Student Resources

AUDIO CDs. Each chapter's two *lectiōnēs* are on the Audio CDs and can also be found in the MyLatinLab and Companion Website. Additional recorded materials include: the *Verba Ūtenda* and *Verba Discenda* from all the chapters, the vowel and diphthong charts, the stress chart, and the first four exercises from Chapter One. This additional audio can be found exclusively in the *MyLatinLab*. Recorded material is indicated by an icon in the textbook, making it easy to find selections and incorporate them into class activities or assign as homework.

STUDENT ACTIVITIES MANUAL (SAM). The Student Activities Manual consists of written exercises providing meaningful and communicative practice, incorporating the vocabulary and structures introduced in each chapter, a review of previous material, and additional process-oriented activities. Each chapter of the SAM concludes with a **How Closely Did You Read?** section offering a review of major themes, terms, and concepts covered in the chapter.

ANSWER KEY TO ACCOMPANY THE SAM. A separately bound **Answer Key** is available for optional inclusion in course packages. It includes answers for all discrete and short-answer exercises in the SAM.

Instructor Resources

INSTRUCTOR'S RESOURCE CENTER (IRC). The IRC provides password protected instructor access to the Instructor's Resource Manual and Testing Program, in downloadable format. The IRC is located at *www.pearsonhighered.com*

INSTRUCTOR'S RESOURCE MANUAL (IRM). An extensive introduction to the components of the *Disce!* program is included in the Instructor's Resource Manual (IRM). The IRM is available in downloadable format via the Instructor's Resource Center and MyLatinLab. Sample syllabi for two- and three-term course sequences are outlined, along with numerous sample lesson plans. The extensive cultural annotations are a unique feature of this IRM, providing further information about topics introduced in the textbook. Information-gap activities, ready for classroom use, are also provided for each chapter.

TESTING PROGRAM. A highly flexible testing program allows instructors to customize tests by selecting the modules they wish to use or by changing individual items. This complete testing program, available in downloadable format via the Instructor's Resource Center and MyLatinLab, includes quizzes, chapter tests, and comprehensive examinations that test reading and writing skills as well as cultural knowledge. For all elements in the testing program, detailed grading guidelines are provided.

Online Resources

MYLATINLAB™. Save Time, Improve Results! Over 200,000 students use the award-winning MyLanguageLabs online learning and assessment system to succeed in their basic language courses. If your instructor has required use of MyLatinLab, you will have online access to an eText, an interactive Student Activities Manual, audio materials, and many more resources to help you succeed. For more information or to purchase access, visit www.mylanguagelabs.com.

IPSISSIMA VERBA (THE VERY WORDS). This section of *Disce!* presents an anthology of authentic Latin readings that can serve as the beginning of the students' reading of unadapted Latin, or it can be used as a class progresses through the book. *Disce!* is unique in that much of this material has already been seen by the student. Most chapters contain bits of original Latin adapted for the current reading level of students. Some are in the *lectiōnēs,* others appear in the *Mōrēs Rōmānī* section. Selections of such readings are provided online in the section entitled *Ipsissima Verba,* which contains the unchanged, original text accompanied by full lexical assistance and notes. The *Ipsissima Verba* can be found in MyLatinLab.

COMPANION WEBSITE. The Companion Website (CW) is organized by chapter and offers open access to the *lectiōnēs* audio recordings.

To the Student

Why did you choose to study Latin? Many students of Latin do so to improve their English vocabulary, to improve their knowledge of grammar, and to read ancient Roman authors in their own words. *Disce!* is designed to help you meet these goals. Using this program will enable you to:

- Understand the Latin language well enough to read major Latin authors with the help of a dictionary.
- Gain an understanding of the structure of the Latin language: its pronunciation, grammar, and vocabulary. In the process you many even learn to understand your native language better!
- Become familiar with many features of everyday life and culture in ancient Rome. You will have the opportunity to reflect on how your life in North America and your values compare with those of ancient Romans.
- Understand the Latin basis of English vocabulary.
- Recognize the ties between Latin and Romance languages like Spanish, Italian, and French.
- Write simple sentences in Latin.
- Understand basic phrases spoken in Latin.
- Hold simple conversations in Latin.

Assuring Your Success

Use What You Already Know

Whether or not you have already studied Latin, you already have a head start on learning it. Many words of Latin origin are used in English. For example, of the 52 words in the Preamble to the Constitution of the United States, 27 (marked in bold below) are directly derived from Latin:

> We the **People** of the **United States**, **in Order** to **form** a more **perfect Union,** **establish Justice, insure domestic Tranquility, provide** for the **common defense, promote** the **general** Welfare, and **secure** the Blessings of **Liberty** to ourselves and our **Posterity,** do **ordain** and **establish** This **Constitution** for the **United States** of **America.**

Such a high percentage of English words derived from Latin is not unusual.

Some people say that Latin is a dead language. Although it is true that no one today is a native speaker of the language of ancient Rome, anyone who speaks or understands one of the Romance languages such as French, Spanish, Italian, Portuguese, and Romanian is speaking a language based on Latin. So if you know any of these languages, you will find many similarities with Latin.

You also bring to the study of Latin your knowledge of general human activities, the world in general, and of specific events, which you can use to anticipate what you read in Latin. You can use your knowledge of a particular topic, as well as accompanying photos, drawings, or titles, to anticipate what will come next. Finally, the reading and listening skills you have learned for your native language will also prove useful as you study Latin.

Take the Long View

The study of any language, including Latin, is like building a house. If you start with a solid foundation, the rest of the structure will be stronger and more solid. So, if you learn carefully as you go along, you will build an ever stronger foundation for learning later materials.

Think like an athlete in training. Before going to class prepare each lesson carefully as directed by your instructor. Be sure to complete assignments required by your instructor and review regularly, not just for an exam. It is the daily practice in the language that ensures success.

Acknowledgements

We owe great debts of thanks to many people for their gracious help in creating *Disce!* First is Rachel McCoy, our Executive Acquisitions Editor who first saw the need for such a book and was its most constant advocate. Likewise, a virtual army of editors and support team at Pearson did help guide us through the maze of publishing such a complicated project. Our thanks to all of them, including Phil Miller, Publisher; Noha Amer Mahmoud, Editorial Assistant; Mary Rottino, Senior Managing Editor; Janice Stangel, Associate Managing Editor; Manuel Echevarria, Project Manager; Gail Cocker, Line Art Manager; Melissa Marolla Brown, Development Editor for Assessment; Meriel Martínez, Media Editor; Samantha Alducin, Senior Media Editor, and Bob Hemmer, Executive Editor for MyLanguageLab, for their assistance in creating the state-of-the-art MyLatinLab; Kris Ellis-Levy, Executive Marketing Manager and Bill Bliss, Marketing Coordinator. The copyeditor, Patricia Ménard, did a tremendous job in assuring accuracy of the copy, and the keen eyes of Keith Woodell (PhD student at the University of New Mexico) and Amy Chamberlain proved to be an invaluable resource to ensure that nothing slipped through the cracks. Any remaining errors, however, are our own.

The generosity of our colleagues all across the world was fathomless. First, thanks to Greg Daugherty, our historical consultant. His advice helped formulate the story line, and his constant passion for accuracy shows on every page. Likewise, the eventual format of *Disce!* was shaped in great part by the thoughts of those who attended sessions at professional meetings (CAAS, 2005; CANE, 2007; CAMWS, 2006, 2008) and shared their advice and encouragement. Special thanks to the members of the 2008 CAMWS panel Barbara Hill, Wilfred Major, and Cynthia White.

During the writing of the actual text, countless people offered their expertise on a wide variety of areas. Surely we will omit some names in the following list and we begin with our apologies to any generous person we may inadvertently omit: Brian Breed, Stephen Brunet, Lawrence Crowson, Eric DeSena, Nick Dobson, Debbie Felton, Hans Gluecklich, Nicholas Gresens, John Gruber-Miller, Virginia Hellenga, Melissa Henneberry, Liane Houghtalin, Elizabeth Keitel, Donald Kyle, Andrew McPherson, Anne Mahoney, Thomas Mann, Eric Poehler, Teresa Ramsby, Anna Dybis Reiff, Carl Springer, Dawn McRoberts Strauss, John Traupman, Stephen L. Tuck, Tony Tuck, Rex Wallace, and Vicki Wine.

Special thanks to our family, colleagues, and students who gave us permission to use their photographs in this book and who sometimes even took a photo specifically for *Disce!*: Susan Bonvallet, Marilyn Brusherd, Nelson Eby, Robert Hellenga, Leigh Anne Lane, Victor M. Martinez, Daniel McCaffrey, Hunter Nielson, Julia A. Sienkewicz, William L. Urban, and Thomas Watkins.

It is only fitting that thanks should go to the many students who helped form *Disce!* in many ways. First, thanks to students in our own introductory Latin classes who helped us improve this book in many ways. Thanks also to the many students who participated in the field testing of *Disce!* across the country. Special thanks to University of Massachusetts MAT students Ryan Williamson, Wade Carruth, and Simon Desantis, and to all the other MAT students who taught from the book and contributed to its improvement in many ways. Dennis Mui did crucial work as a fact checker for vocabulary.

The following teachers arranged field testing at their schools, endured the imperfections of a preliminary edition, and provided valuable feedback: Monica Cyrino and Keith Woodell of the University of New Mexico; Eddie Lowry of Ripon College; Stephen Brunet, Anna Newman, and Richard Clairmont of the University of New Hampshire; Jeremy Miranda and Cynthia White of the University of Arizona; Ronnie Ancona, Tamara Green, Yvonne Bernardo, and William Mayer of Hunter College; Benjamin Haller of Virginia Wesleyan University; John Gruber-Miller and Eric Ross at Cornell College; and our colleagues at Monmouth College and the University of Massachusetts, Amherst.

Countless thanks to Andrea Crum at Monmouth College and Lisa Marie Smith at the University of Massachusetts for their cheerful support with scanning, faxing, copying, and mailing manuscripts.

Finally, and most importantly, to Theresa Kitchell and Anne Sienkewicz for their patient acceptance of *Disce!*—a demanding stepchild in their lives who consumed the time they so richly deserved.

Reviewers

Joseph McAlhany, *Carthage College*
Andrew S. Becker, *Virginia Tech*
James Brehany, *St. Bernard's Central Catholic High School, MA*
Steven M. Cerutti, *East Carolina University, NC*
Catherine Connors, *University of Washington, Seattle*
Gregory N. Daugherty, *Randolph-Macon College, VA*
Sally Davis, *VA*
Ed DeHoratius, *Wayland High School, MA*
Thomas Dinsmore, *University of Cincinnati - Clermont College, OH*
Mary C. English, *Montclair State University, NJ*
George Edward Gaffney, *Montgomery Bell Academy, TN*
Maria Giacchino, *Cambridge Rindge & Latin School, MA*
Judith P. Hallett, *University of Maryland, College Park*
Brian McCarthy, *Newington High School, CT*
T. Davina McClain, *Scholars' College at Northwestern State University*
Pauline Nugent, *Missouri State University*
Claude Pavur, *Saint Louis University*
Emma Scioli, *University of Kansas*
Janice Siegel, *Hampden-Sydney College, VA*
Linda Mitchell Thompson, *University of Maryland*
Maureen Toner, *Boston College High School*
Elizabeth Tylawsky, *Norwich Free Academy, CT*
Rose Williams, *TX*
Eliot Wirshbo, *University of California, San Diego*

21

Speculum Aēneum

Lectiō Prīma

Antequam Legis

Aelius tells his wife more about the labors of Hercules, which he will engrave on a mirror for her. Aelius also promises to make for their child a *bulla*, or amulet that Roman children wore for good luck.

In this reading you have an opportunity to consolidate your knowledge of various kinds of pronouns and adjectives. They are marked in bold in the reading. You have seen many of these words before, and you will learn a few more in this chapter.

Pronouns and Adjective Consolidation

A number of these pronouns and adjectives belong to a special group of pronouns and adjectives we call UNUS NAUTA words. You already know some of them, including *hic, haec, hoc; ille, illa, illud; quī, quae, quod*; and more. Remember that they basically work like 2-1-2 adjectives that have special genitive and dative singulars.

CASE AND NUMBER	ENDING	EXAMPLES
genitive singular	*-ius*	*eius, huius, illīus, cuius*
dative singular	*-ī*	*eī, huic, illī, cuī*

...so watch in *Lectiō Prīma* for singular forms of this irregular 3rd declension noun: *vīs, vis* f. strength, power. These are marked in **bold italics** in the reading. More on this noun after you read!

DeAgostini / SuperStock

Nero cum Bullā

21-1 Personal and Reflexive Pronouns, Possessive Adjectives, and UNUS NAUTA Words

Scan the words marked in bold in *Lectiō Prīma* to find the Latin equivalent for each of the English words listed below. Give the line number of the Latin word. Then look at the grammatical context of the *lectiō* to give the GNC for each Latin word in your list. Use the *Verba Ūtenda* as a vocabulary aid. Watch out! Some words appear more than once. Follow the model.

English Word	Latin Word	Line	Gender	Number	Case
→ herself	*ipsa*	1	feminine	singular	nominative

1. this; 2. something; 3. my; 4. which; 5. you; 6. those; 7. alone; 8. certain; 9. himself; 10. the same; 11. that; 12. me; 13. our; 14. I

🔊 NOSTER HERCULĒS NOVUS

Licinia, verba marītī audiēns, **ipsa** quoque rīdet. "Ita," inquit, "**tū** vēra dixistī! Parāre **nōs** fīliolō novō et **hunc** 'novum Herculem' honōrāre dēbēmus. Nōmen **eī** Maximus erit. **Vim** Herculis habēbit. Aelī, potesne **aliquid** fabricāre, fortasse bullam **quae** labōrēs Herculis dēmonstrābit?
5 Tālis bulla fīliō **nostrō** dōnum bonum erit!"

Aelius "Cāra," inquit, "**Meus** amor **tuī** vērus est, sed **illōs** magnōs labōrēs Herculis nōn facile possum dēmonstrāre in **hāc** bullā parvā **quam** nostrō fīliō fabricābō. Sed **ego ipse tibi sōlī** speculum aēneum fabricābō, in **quō** Herculem et aprum Erymanthium efficiam. **Tū mea**
10 Alcmēna semper eris et **noster** fīlius **meus** Herculēs. Audī nunc dē **illō** labōre aprī Erymanthiī **quem** in speculō pōnam:

"Ōlim, ut **quīdam** narrant, Eurystheus Herculem aprum **quendam, quī illō** tempore agrōs Erymanthiōs vastābat et incolās **huius** regiōnis magnopere terrēbat, capere iussit. Herculēs ergō in Arca-
15 diam, in **quā** regiōne agrī Erymanthiī erant, iter fēcit. Postquam in silvam paulum intrāvit, aprō **ipsī** occurrit. **Ille** autem simul atque Herculem vīdit, statim refūgit; et timōre perterritus in altam fossam **sē** prōiēcit. Hērōs igitur laqueum, **quem sēcum** attulerat, iniēcit, et summā cum difficultāte et magnā **vī** aprum ē fossā extrāxit. Aper, quamquam
20 fortiter repugnābat, nūllō modō **sē** līberāre potuit. Herculēs nōn aprum in **agrīs** Erymanthiīs relīquit sed cum **eōdem** aprō ad rēgem Eurystheum rediit.

"Eurystheus perterritus, cum aprum ingentem vīdit, statim in urnam magnam insiluit et **sē** abdidit."
25 Licinia "Euge, mī marīte!" inquit. "Hic labor Maximō nostrō idōneus est—**id** speculum **quod** fabricābis **mihi** semper cārissimum erit!"

Herculēs et Aper

🔊 VERBA ŪTENDA

aēneus, -a, -um bronze
afferō, afferre, attulī bring to
Alcmēna Alcmena, Hercules' mother
aper, aprī m. boar
Arcadia, -ae f. Arcadia, a region in Greece
bulla, -ae f. bulla, a locket worn around a child's neck
dēmonstrō (1) show, depict
difficultās, difficultātis f. trouble, difficulty
efficiō, efficere, effēcī execute, render
Erymanthius, -a, -um Erymanthian, pertaining to Erymanthos, a mountain in Greece
Euge! Terrific!
extrahō, extrahere, extraxī draw out, drag out
fabricō (1) make

fīliolus, -ī m. little son (affectionate)
fossa, -ae f. ditch
hērōs, hērōos m. hero (note the Greek case endings)
honōrō (1) esteem, honor
idem, eadem, idem the same
idōneus, -a, -um suitable
incola, -ae m./f. inhabitant
ingens, ingentis huge, great
iniciō, inicere, iniēcī throw in
insiliō, insilīre, insiluī/insilīvī leap into
iter facere to make a journey
laqueus, -ī m. snare, noose
līberō (1) free
magnopere greatly, especially
modus, -ī (m.) way, manner
nōs, nostrum/nostrī, nōbīs, nōs, nōbīs we, us

occurrō, occurrere, occurrī, (+ dat.) encounter, run into
paulum a little, somewhat
perterritus, -a, -um very frightened
postquam after, since
prōiciō, prōicere, prōiēcī throw down
quamquam although
quīdam, quaedam, quoddam a certain (indefinite, as in "a certain person")
quisque, quaeque, quodque/quicque/quidque each, every
redeō, redīre, redīvī/rediī, reditum come back, return
refugiō, refugere, refūgī run away
regiō, regiōnis f. region, district

relinquō, relinquere, relīquī, relictum leave, leave behind
repugnō (1) fight back, resist
silva, -ae f. woods, forest
simul atque as soon as
speculum, -ī n. mirror
suī, sibi, sē, sē himself, herself, itself, themselves
tālis, tāle such, of such a kind, of such a sort
terreō, terrēre, terruī frighten, terrify
timor, timōris m. fear
tū, tuī, tibi, tē, tē you (sing.) yourself
urna, -ae f. large water jug
vastō (1) plunder, lay waste
vīs, vis f. strength, power, force; vīrēs, vīrium pl. strength, troops, forces

POSTQUAM LĒGISTĪ

Answer each question in English and list the Latin words from the *lectiō* that support your answer.

1. Why does Licinia laugh at the beginning of this *lectiō*?
2. What name does Licinia give her child and why?
3. What scene does Aelius plan to engrave on the mirror for his son?
4. Why is it necessary for the Erymanthian boar to be captured?
5. How does Hercules capture it?
6. What humor do you notice in the story?

Grammatica A

Personal and Reflexive Pronouns

Personal Pronouns

These words refer to the "person" involved and you know them in English as "I, you, he, she, it, we, you, they." You have been using some of these Latin forms for a while now, but, by way of consolidation, here are all the forms.

CASE	1ST SINGULAR I, ME	1ST PLURAL WE, US	2ND SINGULAR YOU	2ND PLURAL YOU ALL
Nominative	ego	nōs	tū	vōs
Genitive	meī	nostrum/ nostrī	tuī	vestrum/ vestrī
Dative	mihi	nōbīs	tibi	vōbīs
Accusative	mē	nōs	tē	vōs
Ablative	mē	nōbīs	tē	vōbīs

- Latin personal pronouns are not commonly found as the subject of verbs (as they are in English) unless they are used to show emphasis:

Quis hoc fēcit?	Who did this?
Fēcī.	I did it.
Ego fēcī.	*I* did it.

- The genitive of the 1st and 2nd person pronouns is used either as an objective or partitive genitive, but not to show possession.

	TYPE	USAGE
amor meī	objective	His **love of/for me** drove him to it.
timor nostrī	objective	**Fear of us** made them surrender.
pars tuī	partitive	**A part of you** wants to do this, another doesn't.
nēmō nostrum	partitive	**None of us** wants that!

- The preposition *cum* is attached to the end of the 1st and 2nd person pronouns:

  mēcum, tēcum, nōbīscum, vōbīscum

Reflexive Pronouns

You first met reflexive pronouns in Chapter 9, but in limited fashion. Here is the complete story:

- Reflexive pronouns refer back to the subject of the sentence, as in "Mary sees **herself** in the mirror" or "We liked hearing **ourselves** on the record."
- In Latin the reflexive and personal pronouns are identical in the 1st and 2nd person.

1st	*Mē laudat.* He praises **me**.		*Nōs laudat.* He praises **us**.
	Mē laudō. I praise **myself**.		*Nōs laudāmus.* We praise **ourselves**.
2nd	*Tē laudat.* He praises **you**.		*Vōs laudat.* He praises **you**.
	Tē laudās. You praise **yourself**.		*Vōs laudātis.* You praise **yourselves**.

- But the 3rd person uses the special forms *suī, sibi, sē, sē*.

  Sē laudat.   He praises **himself**.

- As with the 1st and 2nd persons, the preposition *cum* is attached to the end of the 3rd person reflexive: *sēcum*.

Compare the uses of the 3rd person pronoun *is, ea, id* to the use of reflexive pronoun.

SUBJECT AND OBJECT ARE DIFFERENT PERSONS	SUBJECT AND OBJECT ARE THE SAME PERSON
Fēmina eam laudat. The woman praises **her.**	*Fēmina sē laudat.* The woman praises **herself.**
Vir eum laudat. The man praises **him.**	*Vir sē laudat.* The man praises **himself.**
Fēminae eōs laudant. The women praise **them.**	*Fēminae sē laudant.* The women praise **themselves.**
Virī eās laudant. The men praise **them.**	*Virī sē laudant.* The men praise **themselves.**

Review of Possessive Adjectives

- 1st and 2nd person personal pronouns (e.g., *tuī, vestrum*) are not normally used to express possession. Instead, Latin uses **personal adjectives**.

meus, -a, -um	my	*noster, -tra, -trum*	our
tuus, -a, -um	your	*vester, -tra, trum*	your
suus, -a -um	his own, her own, its own, their own		

These are all 2-1-2 adjectives.

- For the 3rd person (his, her, its, their), Latin shows possession by using the genitive of *is, ea, id*.

- Latin uses the genitive of *is, ea, id* to show possession in the 3rd person (his, her, its, their) when this person is not the subject of the sentence.

Domum eōrum videt.	He sees their house.
Domum suam videt.	He sees his (own) house.
Domum eius vident.	They see his house.
Domum suam vident.	They see their (own) house.

Irregular Adjectives and Pronouns: UNUS NAUTA Words

Latin is filled with a variety of small words that make a big difference. You have seen some of these before, but others here are new. We list them according to some categories grammarians like to use, but here is what you really need to know:

- All these words are declined like UNUS NAUTA words, meaning that they are 2-1-2 adjectives except that:

  genitive singular = *-ius*
  dative singular = *-ī*

- Many can act like either an adjective or a pronoun. Just look to see whether the word is modifying something or is working alone.

ntensives

se, -a, -um emphasizes a person or thing.

Mē ipsum laudō.	I praise **myself.**
Ego ipse id fēcī.	I did it **myself.**

At first glance these translations do not seem "emphatic" enough. But in some parts of the country, they would be translated "I'm praising my own self!" or "I did it my own self!" In this regionalism, the emphasis is quite clear.

- *Ipse* can also be used to indicate gender where it otherwise might be unclear. What is the difference between these two sentences?

*Mē ips**um** laudō*. I praise myself.

*Mē ips**am** laudō*. I praise myself.

Demonstratives

These do what their name says—they "point out" (*dēmonstrāre*). Demonstratives include words like:

- *ille, illa, illud* (that man, that woman, that thing): *Videō illās*. I see those women.
- *hic, haec, hoc* (this man, this woman, this thing): *Videō hunc*. I see this man.
- *is, ea, id* is a demonstrative too, but less emphatic than *ille* or *hic*: *Ea venit*. The woman is coming.
- *īdem, eadem, idem* (the same): *Eaedem veniunt*. The same women are coming.
- *iste, ista, istud* (that one) has a derogatory overtone: *Istī hoc fēcērunt*. Those men did this.

Remember that **m + c = nc**, which explains forms like *hanc* and *hunc*.

Indefinites

Whereas demonstratives refer to specific people or things, indefinites do just the opposite. They imply uncertainty. Compare these uses of *quīdam, quaedam, quoddam* (a certain) both as pronoun and adjective:

***Quaedam** navis advenit*. A certain ship is coming in.

***Quaedam** venit*. A certain woman is coming. *or* Some woman is coming.

aliquis, aliquid	(someone, something)
Aliquis venit.	Someone is coming.
Aliqua venit.	Some lady is coming.
Aliquae puellae veniunt.	Some girls are coming.

Relative Pronouns

Quī, quae, quod (who, which) links a subordinate clause to an antecedent noun or pronoun. Its forms are used in sentences like the following:

*Fēmina **quam** amās alma est.*   The woman **whom** you love is kind.

Interrogatives

Interrogatives ask a question about a person or thing. The interrogative pronoun is *Quis?, Quid?* (Who? What?)

- Most of these forms look like the relative pronoun *quī, quae, quod*: **Cui** *pecūniam dedit?* To whom did he give the money?
- The only different forms are the nominative forms *quis, quid* and the accusative singular *quem*, which is feminine as well as masculine.

The forms of the interrogative adjective *quī, quae, quod* are identical to the relative pronoun, but these words ask a question and modify a noun. Compare:

Quid *in domō habēs?*	What do you have in the house? (interrogative pronoun)
Quod *animal in domō habēs?*	What animal do you have in the house? (interrogative adjective)

Other Irregular Adjectives and Pronouns

- *quisque, quidque:* each, every

Quisque librum habet.	*Quaeque puella librum habet.*
Each person has a book.	Each girl has a book.

- *īdem, eadem, idem:* the same

Eandem amāmus.	*Eadem puella Cordum amat.*
We love the same woman.	The same girl loves Cordus.

  Notice how **m + d → nd**. Thus the expected form *"eamdem"* is really *eandem*. This explains forms like *eōrundem* and *quendam*.

Notā Bene:

- *Hic* and *ille* are often used together to distinguish things close by or just mentioned from things further away or mentioned earlier:

  Hic vir bonus est; ille nōn.
  This man is good; that one is not.

- *Ille* also often indicates a change in subject:

  Marcus Lūcium videt. Ille (= Lūcius) currit.

- The neuter nominative/accusative singular of many of these words ends in *-d*: *id*, *illud*, *istud*, *quod*, and *quid*.
- Unlike most neuters, the nominative and accusative plurals of some of these words do NOT end in *-a*: *haec* (these things); *quae* (which); *quae* (what things?).

The Irregular Noun *Vīs*

VĪS, VIS F.		
	Singular	**Plural**
	Strength, Power	**Troops, Forces**
Nominative	vīs	vīrēs
Genitive	vis	vīrium
Dative	vī	vīribus
Accusative	vim	vīrēs
Ablative	vī	vīribus

The 3rd declension i-stem noun *vīs, vis* f. requires your attention for several reasons:

- Some forms are irregular in the singular.
- The plural, *vīrēs*, can still mean "force," but it also takes on the sense of military forces or "troops."
- The genitive singular form *vis* is almost never used.
- Be careful not to confuse the plural forms of *vīs* with forms of *vir, -ī* m. Thus, *virī* means "men," whereas *vīrēs* means "strength."

Here are the phrases from *Lectiō Prīma* that use some of these forms. How would you translate the words marked in ***bold italics***? What cases are these words in?

Vim Herculis habēbit.
Hērōs summā cum difficultāte et magnā ***vī*** aprum ē fossā *extraxit*.

Watch for more appearances of this word in *Lectiō Secunda*.

EXERCEĀMUS!

21-2 Working with Pronouns

Substitute the words in parentheses for the word marked in **bold** in each of the following sentences. Then translate the new sentence you made. Be sure to show gender in your translation. Follow the model.

→ Licinia **Aelium** petit.
  (hunc)

Licinia **hunc** petit.
Licinia is looking for **this man**.

1. Aelius **Liciniam** amat.
   (quendam)
   (eundem)
   (aliquōs)
   (illa)
   (hanc)

2. Licinia **Aelium** videt.
   (aliquid)
   (aliquōs)
   (eadem)
   (illās)
   (haec)
   (quandam)

3. **Omnēs** Augustum honōrāre dēbent.
   (Illī)
   (Istae)
   (Eaedem)
   (Aliquī)
   (Quīdam)

4. **Aelius** Augustum honōrāre dēbet.
   (Quisquis)
   (Aliqua)
   (Īdem)
   (Quīdam)
   (Aliquis)

Lectiō Secunda

Antequam Legis

This *lectiō*, which continues the story of Hercules, is designed to help you review all the verb tenses you have learned to date. Take the time to identify each verb fully and, if needed, review the rules for identifying Latin tenses. You will need this information very soon as you learn other forms.

EXERCEĀMUS!

21-3 Treasure Hunt for Verb Tenses

Gemma

A 3rd person form of *sum* can often be translated as "There is," "There are," and the like. Do this for *erat* in line 5.

Gemma

If *spēlunca, -ae* f. means "cave," what do you think a "spelunker" means in English?

Before you read *Lectiō Secunda,* find an example of each of the forms listed among the words marked in **bold** in the *lectiō*. Then translate each verb into English. Be careful to show person, number, and tense in your translation. Follow the model.

Verb Form	Line	Verb	Translation
→ imperfect, 3rd singular	4	habitābat	he was living

1. present, 3rd singular (find two)
2. perfect, 1st plural
3. perfect, 1st singular
4. future, 1st singular
5. future, 3rd plural

6. imperfect, 3rd plural (find two)
7. perfect, 3rd plural (find two)
8. pluperfect, 3rd singular
9. perfect, 2nd singular (find two)
10. perfect, 3rd singular (find two)

🔊 VĪS HERCULIS

"Cāra Licinia," Aelius **inquit**, "dē eōdem labōre, quem iam **narrāvī**, haec alia etiam **audīvimus**:

"Herculēs, dum iter in Arcadiam **facit**, ad spēluncam dēvertit in quā centaurus quīdam, nōmine Pholus, **habitābat**. Ille Herculem benignē excēpit
5   et cēnam parāvit. In spēluncā erat amphora magna plēna vīnō optimō.

"Hērōs postquam **cēnāverat**, aliquid vīnī **petīvit** et amphoram ā Pholō postulāvit. Pholus 'Hoc vīnum,' inquit, 'aliōrum centaurōrum est. Sī igitur hoc tibi **dabō**, centaurī mē **interficient**.' Herculēs tamen pōculum vīnī dē amphorā hausit.

Herculēs et Centaurus

10   "Simul atque amphoram aperuit, aliquī centaurī nōtum odōrem sensērunt et convēnērunt ad spēluncam.

"Ubi ad spēluncam **pervēnērunt**, magnopere īrātī **erant** quod Herculēs vīnum suum biberat. Tum magnae vīrēs centaurōrum arma sua ràpuērunt et Pholum interficere **volēbant**.

"Herculēs ipse tamen in ōre spēluncae stetit et impetum vīrium fortissimē sustinēbat. Ibi multōs centaurōs sagittīs suīs **vulnerāvit**. (Hae sagittae eaedem erant quās ōlim sanguis venēnātus Hydrae imbuerat.) Omnēs aliōs cen-
15   taurōs, igitur, quī ad spēluncam **cucurrērunt**, statim necāvit.

"Postquam reliquae vīrēs fūgerant, Pholus ē spēluncā exiit. Quendam centaurum mortuum invēnit. Sagittam ē vulnere traxit sed haec sagitta ē manibus eius cecidit, et pedem leviter vulnerāvit. Ille statim dolōrem gravem per omnia membra sensit, et post breve tempus vī venēnī mortuus iacuit."

"Tanta," fīniit Aelius, "erat vīs Herculis et tanta erit vīs fīliī nostrī."
20   "Bene dictum, Aelī!" inquit Licinia. "Tū fābulam bene **narrāvistī** et omnēs meōs timōrēs **āmōvistī**."

🔊 VERBA ŪTENDA

amphora, -ae f. amphora
aperiō, aperīre, aperuī open
Arcadia, -ae f. Arcadia, a region of Greece
arma, armōrum n. pl. arms, weapons
benignē kindly
cadō, cadere, cecidī, cāsum fall; be slain; end
cēnō (1) dine
centaurus, -ī m. centaur, half-human and half-horse
dēvertō, dēvertere, dēvertī turn aside, stop to visit
dictum said
dolor, dolōris m. pain, grief
excipiō, excipere, excēpī receive, welcome
exeō, exīre, exīvī/exiī, go out
hauriō, haurīre, hausī drink

hērōs, hērōos m. hero; note the Greek case endings
Hydra, -ae f. a many-headed serpent-like monster with poisonous blood
iaceō, iacēre, iacuī lie, lie still, lie dead
ibi there
īdem, eadem, idem the same
imbuō, imbuere, imbuī wet, soak
impetus, -ūs m. attack, assault
iter, itineris n. road, journey
leviter lightly
magnopere greatly, especially
manus, -ūs f. hand
membrum, -ī n. limb
mortuus, -a, -um dead
necō (1) kill, slay
nōs, nostrum/nostrī, nōbīs, nōs, nōbīs we, us

nōtus, -a, -um known, familiar
odor, odōris m. scent, odor
pēs, pedis m. foot
perveniō, pervenīre, pervēnī, perventum arrive at, reach
petō, petere, petīvī/petiī, petītum seek; look for; attack; run for political office
Pholus, -ī m. Pholus the centaur
pōculum, -ī n. cup
postquam after, since
postulō (1) ask for, demand
plēnus, -a, -um (+ abl.) full, full of
quīdam, quaedam, quoddam a certain (indefinite, as in "a certain person")
reliquus, -a, -um remaining

sagitta, -ae f. arrow
sanguis, sanguinis m. blood
sentiō, sentīre, sensī, sensum feel, hear, see, perceive
simul atque as soon as
spēlunca, -ae f. cave
sustineō, sustinēre, sustinuī, withstand
trahō, trahere, traxī drag
tū, tuī, tibi, tē, tē you (sing.); yourself
venēnātus, -a, -um poisoned
venēnum, -ī n. poison
vīs, vis f. strength, power, force; pl. vīrēs, vīrium troops, forces, strength
vōs, vestrum/vestrī, vōbīs, vōs, vōbīs you (pl.); yourselves
vulnerō (1) wound
vulnus, vulneris n. wound

Amphorae

Centaurus

Herculēs et Hydra

POSTQUAM LĒGISTĪ

Answer the question in English, but then select the Latin words from the text that support your answer.

1. Describe the character of Pholus the Centaur.
2. Describe the character of Hercules in this story.
3. How is the wine special?
4. What draws the other centaurs to Pholus' cave?
5. Why are the centaurs angry at Hercules?
6. How does Pholus accidentally die?

Grammatica B

Synopsis of All Active Tenses

The word "synopsis" comes from Greek and means "overview." Here it refers to a certain kind of exercise where the student writes out forms of the verb in the same person and number in several tenses. It saves you from having to write out all six forms for each tense.

SYNOPSIS PRINCIPAL PARTS: VIDEŌ, VIDĒRE, VĪDĪ, VĪSUM PERSON AND NUMBER: 1ST PERSON PLURAL		
Tense	**Latin**	**English Translation**
Present	vidēmus	we see
Imperfect	vidēbāmus	we were seeing
Future	vidēbimus	we will see
Perfect	vīdimus	we saw
Pluperfect	vīderāmus	we had seen
Future Perfect	vīderimus	we will have seen

Before you try the next exercise, review the following "recipes" for forming the tenses. Then, using the synopsis as a guide, do Exercise 21-4.

Formulae for Forming the Active Tenses

USE PRESENT STEM (PS) OR SHORT PRESENT STEM (SPS) PS = 2nd principal part minus *-re* SPS = 1st principal part minus *-ō*				USE PERFECT ACTIVE STEM (PERF. ST.) Perf. St = 3rd principal part *-ī*			
Present				**Perfect**			
1, 2	PS	+	ō mus s tis t nt	1, 2, 3, 4	Perf.St. +	ī imus istī istis it ērunt	
3, 4	SPS	+	ō imus is itis it unt	**Pluperfect**			
(**N.B.:** i + i = i; i.e. *capis*, not *capiis*.)				1, 2, 3, 4	Perf.St. +	eram erāmus erās erātis erat erant	
Imperfect				**Future Perfect**			
1, 2	PS	+	bam bāmus bās bātis bat bant	1, 2, 3, 4	Perf.St. +	erō erimus eris eritis erit erint	
3, 4	SPS	+	ēbam ēbāmus ēbās ēbātis ēbat ēbant				
Future							
1, 2	PS	+	bō bimus bis bitis bit bunt				
3, 4	SPS	+	am ēmus ēs ētis et ent				

EXERCEĀMUS!

21-4 Making Synopses

Use the the synopsis of *videō* provided above as a guide to create synopses for the following verbs.

dō, dare, dedī, datum	1st singular
currō, currere, cucurrī, cursum	3rd plural
dūcō, dūcere, duxī, ductum	2nd plural
audiō, audīre, audīvī, audītum	2nd singular

SYNOPSIS		
Principal Parts: **Person and Number:**		
Tense	**Latin**	**English Translation**
Present		
Imperfect		
Future		
Perfect		
Pluperfect		
Future Perfect		

Mōrēs Rōmānī

Hospitium Rōmānum

Romans listening to the story of Hercules and Pholus would have especially noticed the theme of *hospitium, -iī* n. (guest friendship). This custom, widely practiced in the Mediterranean world, is based on courteous treatment of a stranger (*hospes, hospitis* m./f.). The concept was so ingrained that *hospes* is the Latin word not only for "stranger" but also for "guest" as well as "host." Pholus is a good host who treats his guest well, but Hercules is a poor guest who demands more than his host can give. The irony of the story is that the good host dies.

Watch for the appearance of a poorly behaved guest of Servilius at an important banquet later in the narrative.

Roman tradition is filled with stories about guest friendship. One of the best known is told by Ovid in his *Metamorphōsēs* (Book VIII). In this tale, Jupiter and Mercury come down to earth in disguise to see how they will be treated by mortals. A poor, elderly couple named Philemon and Baucis are the only humans who are good hosts. Though poor, they offer their guests all the food in their home. The gods reveal themselves and offer Philemon and Baucis their hearts' desire. Instead of asking for great riches or a prolonged life, the couple requests only that they die together. The gods grant their wish. When Philemon and Baucis die, they are turned into two trees whose trunks wind around each other.

Here is how Ovid describes the final moments of Philemon and his wife Baucis, just as the tree covers them over. The selection has been modified into prose to make it easier to read.

> Iamque dum frutex super vultūs geminōs crescēbat et dum licuit, mūtua dicta reddēbant et "Valē, ō coniunx" dixērunt simul, simul frutex ōra abdita texit.

Ovid. *Metamorphōsēs* VIII.716–719

🔊 VERBA ŪTENDA

abditus, -a, -um hidden
coniunx, coniugis m./f. spouse
crescō, crescere, crēvī grow
dictum, -ī n. word
dum as long as

frutex, fruticis m. bush, shrub
geminus, -a, -um twin
licet, licēre, licuit (impersonal verb) it is permitted

mūtuus, -a, -um shared, mutual
Philemōna acc. sing it.
reddēbant "they uttered in reply"

simul together, at the same time
tegō, tegere, texī, cover
vultus, -ūs m. face; *vultūs =* acc. pl.

Latīna Hodierna

Hospitium and Hospitality

You have probably already guessed that the English word "hospitality" is derived from *hospitium*. *Hospitium* could also mean "inn" and, through French, this led to the English words "host," "hostel," "hotel," "hospital," and "hospice," which are all places to take in guests or lodgers. The English word "hostage" is also derived from *hospes,* in the sense that "hostages" are the "guests" of their captor hosts.

Here is how *hospes* and *hospitium* have been transformed in some of the modern Romance languages:

	HOSPITAL	HOTEL	HOST	GUEST
Spanish	hospital	hotel	huésped	huésped
French	hôpital	hôtel	hôte	hôte
Italian	ospedale	hotel	ospite	ospite

Orbis Terrārum Rōmānus

Graecia

Hercules is the Greek national hero and this is exemplified by the fact that his journeys take him all over Greece. He was born in the city of Thebes, where his father Amphitryon was king and where, as an infant, he wrestled with the snakes sent by a jealous Juno. (You will also read about his conception and birth in this book.) Eurystheus was king of Mycenae, a city in the Argolid, and Hercules' first six labors all take place in the Peloponnesus. In this chapter you have read about two of these labors, the Erymanthian boar and the Hydra. In a later chapter you will read about two more, the Stymphalian birds and the Augean stables.

Graecia

The adventure of Hercules and Pholus takes place in Arcadia, a mountainous region of the Peloponnesus in Greece. The region's mountainous geography, suitable mostly for grazing animals like goats and sheep, results in the English word "Arcadian" (pastoral, bucolic). The region was also associated with the woodland god Pan, half-human and half-goat, who was very popular in Rome and Italy. The Latin equivalent of Pan is Faunus, like the bronze statue of a dancing Faun found in Pompeii. European painters sometimes created Arcadian landscapes entitled *Et in Arcadia Ego,* "And I too, in Arcadia." The source for this phrase is debated.

In 146 B.C., Greece came under Roman control and was organized in two provinces, Achaea in southern Greece, and Macedonia to the north.

QUID PUTĀS?

1. Compare the ancient custom of guest friendship to customs in your own family. How important are guests in your family? What are the expectations of your guests and of your family?
2. Do you think that Philemon and Baucis made the right request of their divine guests? Why or why not? Why is the form of their metamorphosis especially appropriate?
3. Why might *hospes* have come to mean both guest and host?
4. How has the meaning of the English word "hospital" changed from the meaning of its source, the Latin *hospitium*?

Faunus Saltāns

Faunus Saltāns Pompēiīs

Arcadia

EXERCEĀMUS!

21-5   Scrībāmus

This model sentence shows how *hic, haec, hoc* and *ille, illa, illud* are used to mean "this" and "that." Replace *sella* (chair) in this sentence with each of the following words. Follow the model.

Haec sella mea est; illa tua.

→ *liber* (book) *Hic liber meus est; ille tuus.*

1. *stilus* (pen or pencil)
2. *mensa* (table, desk)
3. *saccus* (wallet, purse)
4. *pecūnia* (money)

5. *amīcus* (friend)
6. *amīca* (friend)
7. *māter* (mother)
8. *pater* (father)

21-6   Colloquāmur

With a partner practice speaking the sentences you created in Exercise 21-5. Since *hic, haec, hoc* and *ille, illa, illud* are demonstrative words, be sure you point to or show the object you are talking about. In addition to the words used in the *Scrībāmus*, you can add the following:

crēta, -ae f. chalk
fenestra, -ae f. window
hōrologium, -ī n. clock
mūrus, -ī m. wall

21-7   Verba Discenda

Group the *Verba Discenda* in columns by parts of speech. List the first form of the word along with its English meaning. The number in parentheses tells you how many words to find in that part of speech. We have started this list for you.

Nouns (6)	Pronouns (4)	Verbs (8)	Adjectives (6)	Adverbs (1)	Conjunctions (2)
silva woods, forest	*suī* himself	*cadō* fall	*quīdam* certain		*postquam* after, since

🔊 **VERBA DISCENDA**

cadō, cadere, cecidī, cāsum **fall; be slain; end** [cadence]

dolor, dolōris m. **pain, grief** [dolorous]

iaceō, iacēre, iacuī **lie, lie still, lie dead**

ibi **there**

īdem, eadem, idem **the same**

iter, itineris n. **road, journey** [itinerary]

necō (1) **kill, slay**

nōs, nostrum/nostrī, nōbīs, nōs, nōbīs **we, us** [inter nos]

odor, odōris m. **scent, odor** [odorous]

perterritus, -a, -um **very frightened**

perveniō, pervenīre, pervēnī, perventum **arrive at, reach**

petō, petere, petīvī/petiī, petītum **seek; look for; attack; run for political office** [petition]

postquam **after, since**

quīdam, quaedam, quoddam **a certain (indefinite, as in "a certain person")**

quisque, quaeque, quodque/quicque/quidque **each, every**

redeō, redīre, redīvī/rediī, reditum **come back, return**

regiō, regiōnis f. **region, district** [regional]

relinquō, relinquere, relīquī, relictum **leave, leave behind** [relinquish, derelict]

reliquus, -a, -um **remaining** [reliquary]

sentiō, sentīre, sensī, sensum **feel, hear, see, perceive** [sentient, sensory]

silva, -ae f. **woods, forest** [sylvan, Pennsylvania]

simul atque **as soon as**

suī, sibi, sē, sē **himself, herself, itself, themselves** [per se]

tālis, tāle **such, of such a kind, of such a sort**

tū, tuī, tibi, tē, tē **you (sing.) yourself**

vīs, vis f. **strength, power, force; vīrēs, vīrium** pl. **strength, troops, forces** [vim]

vōs, vestrum/vestrī, vōbīs, vōs, vōbīs **you (pl.); yourselves**

Angulus Grammaticus

The Former and the Latter

As noted earlier, *hic* and *ille* are often used together to distinguish things close by, or just mentioned, from things further away, or mentioned earlier.

> *Marcum et Lūcium videō; hic vir bonus est; ille nōn.*
> I see Marcus and Lucius; this man (Lucius) is good; that one (Marcus) is not.

This sentence can also be translated into English in the following ways:

To show location:

I see Marcus and Lucius; this man here is good; that one over there is not.

To indicate order of reference (former/latter):

I see Marcus and Lucius; the latter [Lucius] is good; the former [Marcus] is not.

Notice that in English we generally say it the other way around. We would say, "I see Marcus and Lucius; the former [Marcus] is not good, the latter [Lucius] is." Consider this Latin sentence where the difference is clear:

> *Habeō mālum et ōvum: hoc album est, ille rūbeum.*
> I have an apple and an egg: the former is red, the latter white.

Whether showing location or order of reference, the word "this" means "closer" and "that" means "farther away." *Hic* and *ille* are paired in the same way in Latin and are used much more frequently than we use "the former" and "the latter" in English.

Gladiātōrēs Pugnantēs, Samnīs (ā sinistrā), rētiārius (ā dextrā), lanista (ā tergō)

GRAMMATICA
Passive Voice
Ablative of Agent and Ablative of Means
Imperfect Passives

MŌRĒS RŌMĀNĪ
Dē Gladiātōribus

LATĪNA HODIERNA
Semper Fidēlis

ORBIS TERRĀRUM RŌMĀNUS
Italia

ANGULUS GRAMMATICUS
Defective Verbs

LECTIŌNĒS:
PUGNA!
and
FĪNIS PUGNĀRUM
We witness the games and their aftermath.

22

Harēna Purgātur

Lectiō Prīma

Antequam Legis

As you read about the games that Lucius and Marcus are attending, watch out for verbs with a completely different set of personal endings. These endings indicate **passive voice**.

Passive Voice

In introducing verbs to you, so far we have talked about **tense** (present, imperfect, perfect, etc.) and **mood** (indicative, infinitive, imperative, participle). It is time to talk about **voice**.

Voice is a term that grammarians use for a concept you know quite well, even if you do not know its name—**active** and **passive**.

Traditionally, a verb is described as **active** if the subject of the verb does the action. A **passive** verb is one where the subject receives the action of the verb.

Active	The bestiarius **wounds** the lion.
Passive	The lion **is wounded** by the bestiarius.

Many active verbs are made passive in English simply by adding **-ed** to the verb (= past participle of the verb) and by preceding it with an appropriate form of "be."

I	**am**	wound**ed**
you	**are**	robb**ed**
he	**is**	kill**ed**

But many other active English verbs form the passive differently.

we	**are**	**heard**
you	**are**	**seen**
they	**are**	**caught**

It is a good idea to make sure you can distinguish active and passive voice in English before you do it in Latin. The following exercise will help you do this.

EXERCEĀMUS!

22-1 Passive Practice

Convert each English sentence from the active voice to the passive voice. Follow the model.

→   The baseball breaks the windshield.
    The windshield is broken by the baseball.

  1. Bonnie and Clyde are robbing the bank.
  2. They are shooting people with guns.
  3. They steal bags of money.
  4. They make their escape in that car!
  5. A teller rings the alarm.
  6. The sheriff catches them.
  7. The judge puts them in prison.
  8. He gives them each a sentence of forty years.

In Latin the present, imperfect, and future passive voice is formed with the following **passive endings**:

-r	*-ris*	*-tur*	*-mur*	*-minī*	*-ntur*
I am X-ed	you are X-ed	he/she/it is X-ed	we are X-ed	you (all) are X-ed	they are X-ed

Present passive infinitives end in *-ī* instead of *-e*; for example, *ferīrī* (to be hit) and *vincī* (to be conquered).
    Watch for verbs with these endings marked in **bold** in *Lectiō Prīma*.

Ablative of Means and Ablative of Agent

Consider these sentences:

*Leō **gladiō** vulnerātur.*   *Leō **ā bestiāriō** vulnerātur.*
The lion is wounded **with a sword**.   The lion is wounded **by the animal fighter**.
The lion is wounded **by a sword**.

The thing by which something is done (the means or instrument) is indicated in Latin by the ablative without a preposition (*gladiō*) and is translated using "by" or "with." Remember BWIOF! This construction is called the ablative of means. In a sentence with the verb in the passive voice, **the person by whom something is done** (the agent) is indicated in Latin by *ā* or *ab* + the ablative (*ā bestiāriō*). This is called the ablative of agent. Look for ablatives of agent and means marked in *italics* in *Lectiō Prīma*.

EXERCEĀMUS!

22-2 Cultural Awareness

As you read answer the following questions. Answer questions 1–8 in both Latin and English. Respond to question 9 in English only.

1. What is the signal for the games to begin?

2. How many *bestiāriī* are dressed like Hercules? How is one different from the others?

3. How many lions do these *bestiāriī* face? How do the spectators react?

4. What happens to the lions in this fight? What about the *bestiāriī*?

5. What kind of animals do the dwarves fight?

6. What happens in the arena during intermission? What do Marcus and Lucius do while this is happening?

7. What sorts of contests occurs when they get back?

8. Which gladiator has the most victories?

9. What is your reaction to this sort of entertainment?

🔊 PUGNA!

Vēnātiō *ā Marcō* et *Lūciō* avidē **exspectātur**. Subitō sonitus tubārum **audītur** et sex bestiāriī, quī omnēs vestem Herculis gerunt—ūnus Oscus parvulus fustem ferēns, aliī hastās ferentēs—in harēnam intrant. Sex terga sua appōnunt et in circulō stant. Dum animālia *ā bestiāriīs* **exspectantur**, decem leōnēs ferōcissimī intrant et populī clāmant
5 rīdentque.

"Tū! Osce," clāmat Lūcius, "minimus Herculēs in orbe terrārum es! Vōs omnēs ad mortem **dūciminī**!" Marcus "St!" inquit, "Nōlī crūdēlis esse! Praetereā, nōs *ā bestiāriīs* nōn **audīmur** quod vōcēs leōnum maximae sunt. Ecce! Leōnēs ad hominēs ruunt!"

Ūnus leō *hastā* **vulnerātur** et paulum recēdit. Mox duo aliī *ā bestiāriīs* **vulnerantur**
10 sed plūrēs leōnēs quam bestiāriī sunt et mox omnēs hī infortūnātī bestiāriī **necantur**.

Tunc multī hippopotamī et crocodīlī ferōcēs in harēnam **dūcuntur** et *ā nānīs nūdīs* **oppugnantur**. Intereā aliī nānī gregem gruum *parmīs* oppugnant.

Post multās aliās vēnātiōnēs, in quibus plūrima animālia plūrimīque hominēs **necantur**, harēna sanguine et corporibus plēna est. Dum harēna **purgātur**, Marcus et Lūcius aliquid cibī emunt.
15 Cum ad sēdēs reveniunt, duo gregēs fēminārum inter sē ad missiōnem pugnant. Posteā gladiātōrēs ipsī, prīmus inter quōs est Probus, gladiātor plūrimārum palmārum, pugnant. Astacius, quī Probī amīcus est, quoque adest. Ambō de ludō Aemīliī sunt sed Probus murmillō et Astacius rētiārius est. Hodiē Probus et Astacius, hic adversus Thrācem et ille adversus rētiārium, pugnant. **Vincī** *ab illīs* nōlunt. Vincere volunt!

Rētiārius Probō appropinquat et rēte, quod pedēs Probī capit, iacit. Cum Probus cadit, rētiārius tridentem iacit.
20 Probus paene *tridente* **ferītur** sed effugit.

"Salvusne es?" clāmat Astacius. "**Vulnerārisne**, Probe?"

"Nōn **vulneror**!" respondet Probus. "Nullō modō *ab hōc inānī rētiāriō* **ferīrī possum**! Sed tū, mī amīce, cavē! Thrāx ad tē ruit."

Diū **pugnātur** dōnec tandem missiō **datur**. Neque Probus neque Astacius **necātur** et multī *ā Probō Astaciōque*
25 **vincuntur**.

Ille fustem ferēns minimus Herculēs in orbe terrārum est!

🔊 VERBA ŪTENDA

ā, ab (+ abl. and passive verb) by

adversus (+ acc.) opposite to, against

alius...alius one...another

ambō both

appōnō, appōnere, apposuī put to (also see *terga sua appōnunt*)

avidē eagerly

bestiārius, -iī m. animal fighter

circulus, -ī m. circle

crocodīlus, -ī m. crocodile

crūdēlis, crūdēle cruel

dōnec until

effugiō, effugere, effūgī escape, flee

feriō, ferīre strike, hit

fustis, fustis m. staff, club

grex, gregis m. flock; company, group

grūs, gruis m./f. crane (a bird)

harēna, -ae f. sand; arena

hasta, -ae f. spear

hippopotamus, -ī m. hippopotamus

iaciō, iacere, iēcī, iactum throw

inānis, ināne poor, useless, vain

infortūnātus, -a, -um unlucky, unfortunate

intereā meanwhile

iocō (1) joke

ita so, thus; yes

medius, -a, -um midway, in the middle of, the middle of

missiō, missiōnis f. permission to cease fighting; *ad missiōnem* "to a draw"

murmillō, murmillōnis m. mirmillo, a heavily armed gladiator

nānus, -ī m. dwarf

nūdus, -a, -um naked, nude; unarmed

oppugnō (1) attack

Oscus, -a, -um Oscan

palma, -ae f. palm frond (of victory)

parma, -ae f. small shield

parvulus, -a, -um tiny, very small, little

paulum a little

plaudō, plaudere, plausī applaud

plēnus, -a, -um (+ abl.) full, full of

praetereā moreover

purgō (1) clean, cleanse

rēte, rētis n. net

rētiārius, -iī m. gladiatorial fighter with a net

recēdō, recēdere, recessī retire, withdraw

ruō, ruere, ruī, rutum rush, rush at; fall to ruin

sanguis, sanguinis m. blood

simul together, at the same time

sonitus, -ūs m. sound

St! Hush!

tergum, -ī n. back; *terga sua appōnunt* "they stand back to back"

Thrax, Thrācis m. Thracian; a gladiator with lighter armor, including a helmet and greaves on both legs

tridens, tridentis m. trident

tuba, -ae f. trumpet

vēnātiō, -iōnis f. hunt

vestis, vestis f. garment, clothing

vulnerō (1) wound

Gemma

Did you notice the phrase *diū pugnātur*, in *Lectiō Prīma?* It is translated impersonally, literally, "it is fought for a long time." This means "the fight went on for a long time," or even "they fought for a long time." More on impersonal verbs later.

POSTQUAM LĒGISTĪ

Before you read the following *Grammatica*, go back through *Lectiō Prīma* and find one passive form from each category. Follow the model.

Form	Line	Word	English Translation
→ 3rd person singular	1	*expectātur*	he/she/it is awaited
1st person singular			
2nd person singular			
1st person plural			
2nd person plural			
3rd person plural			
Infinitive			

Gemma

Battles between Pygmies and cranes were a popular motif in Greco-Roman mythology and art.

Nānus et Grūs

Grammatica A

Passive Voice

Formation of the Passive

Basically, Latin merely substitutes the **passive personal endings** for the active ones. Study these charts and find the forms that have slight variations on this rule.

	1ST CONJUGATION		2ND CONJUGATION		3RD CONJUGATION	
	Active	Passive	Active	Passive	Active	Passive
Singular						
1st	voc**ō**	voco**r**	mone**ō**	mone**or**	dūc**ō**	dūc**or**
2nd	voc**ās**	voc**āris**	mon**ēs**	mon**ēris**	dūc**is**	dūc**eris**
3rd	voc**at**	voc**ātur**	mone**t**	mon**ētur**	dūc**it**	dūc**itur**
Plural						
1st	voc**āmus**	voc**āmur**	mon**ēmus**	mon**ēmur**	dūc**imus**	dūc**imur**
2nd	voc**ātis**	voc**āminī**	mon**ētis**	mon**ēminī**	dūc**itis**	dūc**iminī**
3rd	voc**ant**	voc**antur**	mone**nt**	mone**ntur**	dūc**unt**	dūc**untur**
Infinitive	voc**āre**	voc**ārī**	mon**ēre**	mon**ērī**	dūc**ere**	dūc**ī**

	3RD -IŌ CONJUGATION		4TH CONJUGATION	
	Active	Passive	Active	Passive
Singular				
1st	capi**ō**	capi**or**	audi**ō**	audi**or**
2nd	capi**s**	cap**eris**	aud**īs**	aud**īris**
3rd	capi**t**	capi**tur**	audi**t**	aud**ītur**
Plural				
1st	cap**imus**	cap**imur**	aud**īmus**	aud**īmur**
2nd	cap**itis**	cap**iminī**	aud**ītis**	aud**īminī**
3rd	capi**unt**	capi**untur**	audi**unt**	audi**untur**
Infinitive	cap**ere**	cap**ī**	aud**īre**	aud**īrī**

Notā Bene:

- In the 3rd conjugation, the 2nd person singular changes its vowel from *-i* to *-e*. Note that it is *caperis*, not *capieris*.
- 3rd -iō and 4th conjugation verbs have identical endings in the present passive EXCEPT for the 2nd person singular. Compare *caperis* and *audīris*.
- The present passive infinitive is formed in the 1st, 2nd, and 4th conjugations by dropping the final *-e* on the present active infinitive and adding *-ī*; e.g., *amāre* (to love) becomes *amārī* (to be loved).
- The present passive infinitive of all 3rd conjugation verbs, including *-iō* verbs, is formed by dropping the *-ere* ending of the present active infinitive and adding *-ī*; for example, *mittere* (to send) becomes *mittī* (to be sent).

Formulae for Making Present Passives

1ST AND 2ND CONJUGATIONS USE PRESENT STEM (PS)			3RD AND 4TH CONJUGATIONS USE SHORT PRESENT STEM (SPS)		
PS = 2ND Principal Part minus -re			**SPS = 1ST Principal Part minus -ō**		
PS +	or ris tur	mur minī ntur	SPS +	or ris tur	mur minī ntur

Note: a + o = ō

Note: a) i + i = ī
b) caperis not capieris (3rd –io verbs)

Passive Facts

Transitive verbs: Only transitive verbs (i.e., verbs that take a direct object) can be passive. Notice how the direct object of a transitive verb becomes the subject of the passive verb:

I broke the **vase.**   vs.   The **vase** was broken by me.

Verbs that do not take a direct object rarely go into the passive. Such verbs are "be," "become," "happen," "go," etc.

Videō in the passive: You would think that *vidētur* would mean "he is seen," but it more commonly means "he seems" or "he appears." Consider this short dialogue:

"Marce," Lūcius inquit, "maestus vidēris!"
"Maestus videor?" Marcus respondet, "Nōn maestus sum."
"Chīrōn," Lūcius rogat, "Nōnne Marcus maestus vidētur?"

Ablative of Agent and Ablative of Means

Ablative of Agent

We indicate the performer of an action with a passive verb in English with the preposition **by**:

The lion is wounded **by the animal fighter**.

In Latin the performer of the action of a passive verb is indicated in a similar fashion: the **person by whom** something is done in the passive voice is in the ablative case with the preposition *ā* or *ab*. This construction, called an **ablative of agent**, is used for both people and animals. The result is a lot like English.

*Thrax **ā rētiāriō** vulnerātur.*
The Thracian is wounded **by the retiarius**.

Ablative of Means

If the action is performed **by means of a thing** (a tool or instrument), Latin uses an ablative without a preposition with either an active or passive verb. Remember BWIOF!

Passive   *Thrax **tridente** vulnerātur.*
The Thracian is wounded **by a trident**.

Active   *Rētiārius **tridente** Thrācen vulnerat.*
The retiarius wounds the Thracian **with a trident**.

In both sentences *tridente* is an ablative of means.

Both the ablative of means and the ablative of agent can appear in the same sentence:

> *Leō ā bestiāriō gladiō necātur.*
> The lion is killed with a sword by the animal fighter.

EXERCEĀMUS!

22-3   Ablatives of Agent and Means

Look back to the passive sentences you created in English in Exercise 22-1. Underline the phrase indicating the performer of the action. (HINT: In English the phrase begins with "by.") Then indicate whether this phrase would be an ablative of agent or an ablative of means in Latin. Follow the model.

→ The windshield is broken <u>by the ball.</u> ablative of means

22-4   Ablative of Agent or Means?

Go back to *Lectiō Prīma* and find the ablative used with each of the passive verbs listed below. These ablative phrases are marked in *italics*. Indicate whether each ablative is an ablative of agent or an ablative of means. Then translate verb with the ablative. Follow the model.

	Line	Passive Verb	Ablative	Agent or Means?	Translation
→	1	expectātur	ā Marcō et Lūciō	agent	It is expected by Marcus and Lucius
1.	9	vulnerātur			
2.	9	vulnerantur			
3.	12	oppugnantur			
4.	19	Vincī			
5.	21	ferītur			
6.	23	ferīrī			

Lectiō Secunda

Antequam Legis

The games provided more than entertainment for the masses. Some scholars believe that after the games the bodies of the slain animals were butchered and distributed to the poor. And, as with any production, there was a good deal of "post-production" work to be done. After the games the gladiators Probus and Astacius talk about their experiences in the arena.

Imperfect Passives

As you read, see if you can recognize the forms of the **imperfect passive verbs** that this reading introduces (they are in **bold**). If you remember your passive personal endings, they will be fairly easy to spot. Translate these imperfects as "were being X-ed;" for example, *necābantur* would be "they were being slain."

EXERCEĀMUS!

22-5   Imperfect Passives

All of the passive verbs marked in **bold** in *Lectiō Secunda* are either 3rd person singular or 3rd person plural imperfect passives. Find five singular verbs and five plural verbs and translate them into English. (Remember that *-tur* is singular and *-ntur* is plural.) Follow the models.

	Line	Verb	Number	Translation
→	1	pugnābātur	singular	it was being fought = there was fighting
	2	necābantur	plural	they were being killed

Gemma

Note that *lībertīnus* is used as a noun, "a freedman" whereas *lībertus* is the form used in inscriptions with the genitive of the former owner.

Gemma

Puticulī was the name of an area outside the Esquiline Hill, where bodies were left in pits (*puteī*) to rot because no one would pay for their proper burial.

🔊 FĪNIS PUGNĀRUM

Multās hōrās **pugnābātur** et nōnnullī gladiātōrēs **necābantur**. Lūcius ā frātre Marcō domum **dūcēbātur** et aliī Rōmānī quoque
5 domum ambulābant. In mediā harēnā multum ā servīs **agēbātur**. Harēna, sanguine et corporibus plēna, **purgābātur** et corpora animālium **trahēbantur** ad locum

Potesne Astacium rētiārium invenīre?

10 in quō corpora **secābantur** et carō populīs **dabātur**.

Hīc sanguis permaximus novā harēnā **operiēbātur**. Leviōra vulnera aliōrum gladiātōrum **cūrābantur** in harēnā, sed aliī, quī gravissima vulnera habēbant, ad medicum **portābantur**. Gladiātōrēs mortuī ad lanistam, quī eōs sepelīre dēbēbat, ā servīs **portābantur**.

In aliō locō Probus et Astacius de pugnīs dīcēbant. Probus Germānicus est, Astacius Umbricus. "Hodiē fortūnātī
15 erāmus, mī Probe. Sacrāmentum iūrāvimus—ūrī, vincīrī, verberārī, ferrōque necārī—tamen vīvimus."

"Ita, rectē dixistī," respondit Probus. "Pugnāvimus bene et sine vulneribus gravibus. Sed aliī infortūnātī quoque bene pugnāvērunt et illī nunc mortuī sunt."

Dum tālia dīcunt, spectābant illōs mortuōs quī ā servīs lentē **ferēbantur** ad plaustra. Inter quōs mortuōs cadāver parvulum bestiāriī, adhūc fustem Herculis gerentis, **spectābātur**. Hic bestiārius Oscus, Celsus nōmine, ab amīcīs
20 Probō et Astaciō **lūgēbātur**. Oscus amīcus semper fidēlis fuerat.

Haec plaustra nōn omnēs gladiātōrēs mortuōs portābant sed solum illōs malefactōrēs et egēnōs quī in harēnā mortuī erant. Illī mortuī quī līberī aut lībertīnī erant, ad familiās suās **remittēbantur**. Malefactōrēs, quī multa scelera ēgerant, ad locum quī "Puticulī" **nōminābātur**, **afferēbantur**.

Ad hunc locum egēnī, malefactōrēs et aliī quī nullīus mōmentī erant semper **portābantur** et in puteōs **iaciēbantur**.

🔊 VERBA ŪTENDA

afferō, afferre, attulī carry toward

cadāver, cadāveris n. corpse, dead body

carō, carnis f. flesh; meat

egēnus, -a, -um **in need of, in want of, destitute**

ferrum, -ī **n. iron; sword**

fortūnātus, -a, -um **lucky, fortunate**

fustis, fustis m. staff, club, stick

gerō, gerere, gessī, gestum **bear, carry**

harēna, -ae **f. sand; arena**

iaciō, iacere, iēcī, iactum **throw**

infortūnātus, -a, -um **unlucky, unfortunate**

ita **so, thus; yes**

iūrō (1) swear

lanista, -ae m. trainer, manager of a gladiatorial troop

lentē slowly

lībertīnus, -ī m. freedman

lūgeō, lūgēre, luxī mourn, lament

malefactor, -ōris m. criminal

medicus, -ī m. doctor, physician

medius, -a, -um **midway, in the middle of, the middle of**

mōmentum, -ī n. importance

mortuus, -a, -um **dead**

nōminō **(1) name**

operiō, operīre, operuī cover

Oscus, -a, -um Oscan

parvulus, -a, -um tiny, very small, little

permaximus, -a, -um very much

plaustrum, -ī n. cart, wagon

plēnus, -a, -um **(+ abl.) full, full of**

pugna, -ae **f. fight**

pugnābātur imp., "there was fighting"

purgō **(1) clean, cleanse**

puteus, puteī m. pit, well

Puticulī, -ōrum m. pl. an area outside the

Esquiline Hill used for mass burials

sacrāmentum, -ī n. oath

sanguis, sanguinis **m. blood**

secō, secāre, secuī cut

sepeliō, sepelīre, sepelīvī/sepelīī bury

trahō, trahere, traxī, tractum **drag, haul, draw, remove**

ūrō, ūrere, ussī burn

verberō (1) assail, flog, batter

vinciō, vincīre, vinxī tie up, bind

vulnus, vulneris **n. wound**

POSTQUAM LĒGISTĪ

Try to answer these questions in both Latin and English. The Latin part of your answer can be just a few key words. Full sentences are not necessary.

→ How long did the fighting in the arena last?

multās hōrās   The fighting lasted for many hours.

1. Where did Lucius and Marcus go after the games?
2. Where were the bodies of the dead animals taken?
3. Where did the wounded gladiators go?
4. Who had to bury the dead gladiators?
5. What were Probus and Astacius talking about?
6. What did Probus and Astacius watch while they were talking?
7. By whom were the dead put on wagons?
8. Where were the bodies of the freeborn or freedmen brought?
9. Where were bodies of the dead criminals brought?

Grammatica B

The Imperfect Passive

Formation of the Imperfect Passive

Did you recognize the new tense of the passive as imperfect? If you remember that the imperfect tense is formed by added *-ba-* between the verb stem and the personal ending, you should have little difficulty with imperfect passive verbs. Compare these two forms:

*portā**bat***	he was carrying
*portā**bā**tur*	he was being carried

Formulae for Making Imperfect Passives

1ST AND 2ND CONJUGATIONS USE PRESENT STEM (PS)		3RD AND 4TH CONJUGATIONS USE SHORT PRESENT STEM (SPS)	
PS= 2ND Principal Part minus *-re*		SPS = 1ST Principal Part minus *-ō*	
PS + bar bāmur bāris bāminī bātur bantur		SPS + ēbar ēbāmur ēbāris ēbāminī ēbātur ēbantur	

Notā Bene:

- Note that there is a macron over the *-ā-* in the 3rd person singular. Otherwise the macrons appear in the same positions as the active forms.

EXERCEĀMUS!

22-6   From Imperfect Active to Passive

Change each of the following imperfect active verbs to passive. Follow the model.

→ pugnābant: pugnābantur

1. purgābant	4. trahēbātis	7. audiēbāmus	10. pugnābāmus
2. nōminābam	5. vulnerābat	8. vocābātis	
3. iaciēbāmus	6. dūcēbat	9. capiēbam	

Mōrēs Rōmānī

Dē Gladiātōribus

After the games the gladiator Astacius reminds his colleague Probus of the powerful oath they had sworn when they became gladiators. This oath is based on one sworn by several characters comparing themselves to "real gladiators" in Petronius' *Satyricon* (117). Use the *Verba Ūtenda* on pg. 282 to translate it:

> In verba Eumolpī sacrāmentum iūrāvimus: ūrī, vincīrī, verberārī, ferrōque necārī, … tamquam lēgitimī gladiātōrēs dominō corpora animāsque religiōsissimē addīcimus.

Sacrāmentum is the word Romans used for the oath sworn by new enlistees in the Roman army. Use of this word for gladiators emphasizes the strong military associations of the gladiators who lived in a highly regimented, military environment. This oath was only sworn by gladiators who were not slaves.

Romans had a fondness for battles between unusual gladiators such as dwarves and, later in the Empire, women. We have taken the liberty of inserting some female gladiators into this story set earlier, in the time of Augustus.

Gladiators lived in a *lūdus*, in what would best be described as a military camp. There were many such *lūdī* throughout Italy and even in Rome in the early empire. The most famous of these *lūdī* is probably the *Lūdus Magnus*, which was built in Rome long after our story and was located next to the Flavian Amphitheater (completed in 80 A.D. and known better today as the Colosseum).

The *Lūdus Magnus* was a square building with a practice space modeled on that of the Colosseum. Around the perimeter of the arena were storage and training rooms, as well as bedrooms for the *familia* (troop) of gladiators and their trainers (*lanistae*). An underground passageway led from the *Lūdus Magnus* into the Flavian Amphitheater.

Tombstone inscriptions suggest that, despite their military lifestyle and a law prohibiting gladiators to marry, gladiators often had women they called their wives (*coniugēs*) and children. Consider, for example, this funerary inscription of a *murmillō* named Probus who was the inspiration for the Probus you met in the narrative. This Probus died in Spain in the first or second century A.D. His name (*probus, -a, -um* "good, clever, honest") may have been a stage name, similar to those adopted by American professional wrestlers.

Probus Murmillō (Corpus Inscriptiōnum Latīnārum, II2/7, 363)

TRANSCRIPTION OF INSCRIPTION	EXPANDED TEXT
MVR.>R	Mur(millō) (contrā) r(ētiārium)
PROBUS	Probus
PAVIL.LXXXXIX	P(ublī) A(urēliī) Vī(tālis) l(ībertus) LXXXXIX (victōriārum)
NATIONE.GERMA	nātiōne Germā(nicus)
H.S.E.S.T.T.L	h(īc) s(itus) e(st). S(it) t(erra) t(ibi) l(evis)
VOLVMNIA.SPERA	Volumnia Spērā(ta)
CONIVCI.PIO	coniugī piō
MERENTI	merentī (fēcit).
P. VOLVMNIVS	P(ublius) Volumnius
VITALIS.PATRI.PIO	Vītālis patrī piō (fēcit)
S.T.T.L.	S(it) t(erra) t(ibi) l(evis)

The inscription may still seem a bit tricky to read with all those parentheses. See if it makes more sense to you this way. Notice how the tombstone speaks directly to the deceased (*tibi*)! Probus was a freedman and had a wife and child who put up this monument to him.

> Probus, murmillō contrā rētiārium, Publī Aureliī Vītālis lībertus,
> LXXXXIX victōriārum, nātiōne Germānicus, hīc situs est.
> Sit terra tibi levis.
> Volumnia Spērāta coniugī piō merentī fēcit.
> Publius Volumnius Vītālis patrī piō fēcit.
> Sit terra tibi levis.

🔊 VERBA ŪTENDA

addīcō, addīcere, addixī consecrate
anima, -ae f. breath, soul, life
contrā (+ acc.) opposite, against
Eumolpus, ī m. Eumolpus, a character in the *Satyricon*
ferrum, -ī n. iron, sword
iūrō (1) swear

LXXXXIX victōriārum "of 99 victories"
lēgitimus, -a, -um real, lawful, right
levis, leve light
mereō, merēre deserve
murmillō, murmillōnis m. murmillo, a heavily armed gladiator

necō (1) kill
nātiōne "by nationality"
pius, -a, -um pious, devout
religiōsissimē most piously
sacrāmentum, -ī n. oath, sacred obligation (especially one sworn by soldiers)
sit "may (the earth)"

situs, -a, -um located, buried
tamquam just as, just like
ūrō, ūrere, ussī burn
verberō (1) lash, scourge, beat
vinciō, vincīre, vinxī tie up, fetter
victōria, -ae f. victory

Latīna Hodierna

Semper Fidēlis

Semper Fidēlis

Did you notice *Semper Fidēlis*, the Latin motto of the United States Marine Corps, in *Lectiō Secunda*? This motto is quite well known, but many other military organizations also bear Latin mottoes. Here are just a few:

ORGANIZATION	LATIN MOTTO	COMMON LATIN TRANSLATION
U.S. Marine Corps	*Semper Fidēlis*	Always Faithful
U.S. Coast Guard	*Semper Parātus*	Always Prepared
U.S. Air Force Security Force	*Dēfensor Fortis*	Defender of the Force
U.S. Navy (unofficial)	*Nōn sibi sed patriae*	Not for self but for country
U.S Naval Academy	*Ex scientiā tridens*	From knowledge, sea power
U.S. Air Force Special Tactics Combat Controllers	*Prīmus eō*	First there
The Royal Canadian Infantry	*Dūcimus*	We lead
Royal Air Force	*Per ardua ad astra*	Through difficulties to the stars
Canadian Air Force	*Sīc ītur ad astra*	Such is the pathway to the stars

Orbis Terrārum Rōmānus

Italia

Many different peoples inhabited ancient Italy in its earliest days, including Greeks, Etruscans, Messapians, Ligurians, and the Italic peoples of central and southern Italy.

Ancient Italy was a cultural and linguistic melting pot, and the unification of the Italian peninsula under Roman rule, culture, and language took centuries.

The Italic peoples (including the Latins) spoke linguistically related languages now classified as ancient Italic or Sabellic languages, including Latin, Oscan, and Umbrian. Much of central and southern Italy was inhabited by these non-Latin-speaking Italic peoples. By the Augustan period, both the Oscan and Umbrian languages were dying out and being replaced by Latin. Celsus, the short retiarius dressed like Hercules who dies in the amphitheater, is Oscan. His friend Astacius is Umbrian. Plautus, one of the earliest authors of Roman comedy, was Oscan.

Samnium and Umbria were two of the eleven administrative regions of Augustan Italy. Umbria is also one of the twenty regions of modern Italy. Other Oscan-speaking regions were Picenum (modern Marche) and Apulia (modern Puglia).

The modern Italian city of Benevento (ancient *Beneventum*) was originally Oscan, and Assisi (ancient *Assisium*) was Umbrian.

Beneventum Hodiē

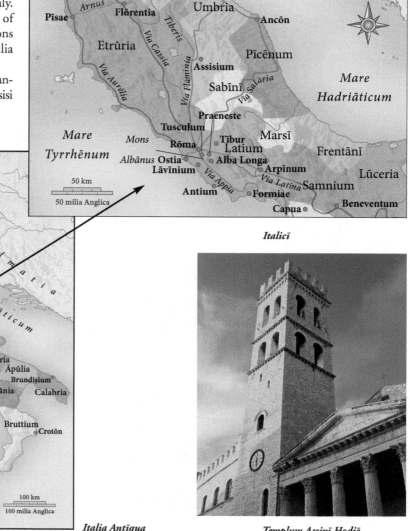

Italicī

Italia Antīqua

Templum Assīnī Hodiē

QUID PUTĀS?

1. In what contexts might Americans be asked to swear an oath similar to the one sworn by Roman gladiators? How are these oaths similar or different?
2. How does the information on the tombstone of the mirmillo Probus compare to the information on modern tombstones of Americans who are also in the entertainment industry? Use the Internet to find some examples.
3. Summarize the private life of gladiators like Probus. Where did they live? Is there evidence of a family life?
4. Why do you think it took so long for the Romans to incorporate the Italian peoples into their empire? Why was there such resistance to Roman rule?
5. Modern use of Latin of mottoes can lead to some strange translations. Can you spot these "errors" in the list on pg. 282? How would you translate them?

EXERCEĀMUS!

22-7 Colloquāmur

Read this dialogue aloud with another member of your class. Take turns with the roles, each person inserting the missing verb from the *Thēsaurus Verbōrum* that makes the most sense.

Thēsaurus Verbōrum

cavē	ferīris	sum
es	ruit	vulnerārisne
ferīrī	vulneror	

Astacius: _____, Probe?
Probus: Nōn _____, Astacī!
Astacius: Salvusne _____?
Probus: Salvus _____.
Astacius: _____, Probe?
Probus: Minimē, Astacī! Nōn ab hōc inānī rētiāriō _____ possum!
Astacius: Sed mī amīce, cavē! Thrax ad tē _____.
Probus: Et tū, mī amīce, _____!

22-8 Scrībāmus

Now rewrite this dialogue as if someone is asking about Probus and Astacius in the 3rd person. Follow the model. See if you can add a bit more at the end.

→ Vulnerāturne Probus?

22-9 Verba Discenda

Find the *Verbum Discendum* from which each of the following English words is derived. Use the meaning of the Latin word to define the English word. If you are unfamiliar with the English word, look it up in the dictionary! Follow the model.

→ gestation: *gerō, gerere, gessī, gestum* bear, carry the act of carrying

1. arena	5. repugnant	9. mortuary
2. tractor	6. unfortunate	10. plenary
3. consanguineous	7. ferrous oxide	11. nomination
4. purgatory	8. intermediary	12. invulnerable

🔊 VERBA DISCENDA

egēnus, -a, -um in need of, in want of, destitute [indigent]

ferrum, -ī n. iron, sword [ferrous]

fortūnātus, -a, -um lucky, fortunate

gerō, gerere, gessī, gestum bear, carry [gestation]

harēna, -ae f. sand; arena

iaciō, iacere, iēcī, iactum throw [ejaculate]

infortūnātus, -a, -um unlucky, unfortunate

ita so, thus; yes

medius, -a, -um midway, in the middle of, the middle of [intermediary]

mortuus, -a, -um dead [mortuary]

nōminō (1) name [nominate]

plēnus, -a, -um (+ abl.) full, full of [plenary]

pugna, -ae f. fight [pugnacious]

purgō (1) clean, cleanse [purgative]

ruō, ruere, ruī, rutum rush, rush at; fall to ruin

sanguis, sanguinis m. blood [sanguinary, consanguineous]

tergum -ī n. back

trahō, trahere, traxī, tractum drag, haul, draw, remove [tractor]

vulnerō (1) wound [vulnerable]

vulnus, vulneris n. wound

Angulus Grammaticus

Defective Verbs

In the *Angulus Grammaticus* to Chapter 11, we talked about verbs like *meminī* (I remember) and *ōdī* (I hate), which are perfect in form but are translated into English in the present tense.

Because these verbs lack present forms they are sometimes called defective verbs. Another verb that has only perfect forms is *coepī* (I begin). You can recognize such verbs in the dictionary because they have only two principal parts, both with perfect endings:

> *coepī, coepisse* begin
> *meminī, meminisse* remember
> *ōdī, ōdisse* hate

Other verbs are defective because they have no perfect forms. These include:

> *āiō* say
> *inquam* I say
> *feriō, ferīre* strike
> *quaesō, quaesere* ask for

English has some defective verbs, too. Some examples include:

- The verb "beware," which we only use in the present tense (we can't say "bewared").
- Modal verbs like "can/could," "may/might," and "will/would." We can say "I can" but not "I am canning" or "to can." So it is awkward for us to express the Latin infinitive *posse* in English with the verb "can." We can only say "to be able."
- The verb "used to" which is only used in the past, as in "I used to play the piano."
- The verbs "rumored" and "reputed," which are only used in the passive, as in "He is rumored to be out of the country."

Consilia

Mīlitēs Labōrantēs

LECTIŌNĒS:
IN INSULĀ VALERIAE
and
EPISTULA Ē CASTRĪS

Valeria and her family discuss the coming birth of a child to Licinia and Aelius and the changes it will cause in their lives. Then they receive a letter from Valeria's son, Licinius, who is serving in the army on the German border under Tiberius, the future emperor.

Lectiō Prīma

Antequam Legis

Licinia's baby will be born soon. In *Lectiō Prīma,* Licinia talks with her husband, Aelius, and her mother, Valeria, about how the baby's birth will change their lives. As you read about their hopes and worries, watch how Latin expresses passive voice in the future tense.

In this *lectiō* you also hear about Hephaestus, Aelius' lame slave, who works in Aelius' blacksmith shop. As is the case of many slaves, Hephaestus spends the night locked into the shop where he works. Unlike many others, Hephaestus was not chained to the wall at night, as Aelius trusted him. The slave Hephaestus shares his name with the lame blacksmith god of the Greeks (known as Vulcan to the Romans). The god Hephaestus made Zeus' thunderbolts, and according to some traditions, his workshop was beneath Mt. Aetna, a volcano on Sicily. In the drawing at the top of pg. 287, based on a painting by the 17th-century Spanish artist Velasquez, Apollo, the god of the sun, is visiting the forge of Vulcan.

Future Passives

Now that you have seen how present and imperfect passive verbs are formed in Latin, you can easily recognize the future passive. Just look for the passive instead of active endings at the end of the future forms. All future passive verbs are marked in **bold** in *Lectiō Prīma.*

Notā Bene: Remember to add "will be" when you translate the future passive into English, as in "will be captured" or "will be done."

EXERCEĀMUS!

23-1 **Comprehension Questions**

Before you read *Lectiō Prīma,* scan the text and try to answer these questions. Answer them in both Latin and English.

1. In lines 1–2, why does Licinia's family need to make lots of plans?
2. In lines 1–4, what does Licinia's family need to do to avoid difficulties?

3. To whom is Aelius speaking in lines 5–7? What does he call this person?
4. Why does Licinia tell her mother not to worry in lines 8–10?
5. Why does Plotia begin to cry in line 11–12?
6. What plan of Aelius do we hear about in lines 15–17?
7. What does everyone do after Aelius finishes speaking in line 18?

Fig. 56. The Forge of Vulcan

Fornax Vulcānī *ā*
Velasquez (1599–1660)

IN INSULĀ VALERIAE

Sērō est et familia Valeriae sedet et colloquium inter sē habet. Familia multa consilia facere dēbet quod mox, in hāc ipsā mense, infans, quem Licinia gerit, **pariētur**.

Valeria "Aelī et Licinia," inquit, "Vōs moneō—mox plūs pecūniae invenīre dēbēbimus. Sī plūs pecūniae nōn **inveniētur**, difficultātēs habēbimus." Aspicit
5 Aelius ad ventrem Liciniae et, tangēns ventrem, infantī futūrō dīrectē dīcit: "Certē, dulcissime, ā mātre **nūtriēris** et ā nōbīs omnibus **amāberis**. Sed vērum est—infantem novum habēre pretiōsum est."

Labōrābō dīligenter

Licinia "Māter," inquit, "Nōlī timēre! Bene nōs monēs, sed negōtium Aeliī cōtīdiē maius crescit et, dum domī cum infante maneō, paulum labōrāre poterō.
10 Ego et Aelius et Hephaestus omnēs dīligentius labōrāre **cōgēmur**."

Plōtia, māter Valeriae et avia Liciniae, lacrimāre incipit. "Vae mihi! Nam certē forīs **pulsābor** quod infans novus plūs quam ego **amābitur**. In viās sīcut canis **agar**! Et vōs omnēs magnopere improbī **vidēbiminī**."

Valeria suspīrāns mātrem leviter lēnit, "Matercula, nullō modō in viīs vīvere **cōgēris**. Sī tū in viīs vīvere **cōgēris**, nōs omnēs **cōgēmur**, nam ūna familia sumus!"

15 Aelius manum Plōtiae leviter tangit et "Avia," inquit, "Nōlī dēspērāre, nam consilium habeō! Ego et Hephaestus dīligentius quam aliī fabrī labōrābimus et mox, cum hominēs nova opera nostra vīderint, dēsīderiō illa opera emere **cōgentur**."

Omnēs rīdent et silentium tenent, sed quisque intrā sē dīcit, "Modo quid nōbīs **agētur**?"

VERBA ŪTENDA

aspiciō, aspicere, aspexī, aspectum look at
avia, -ae f. grandmother
canis, canis m./f. **dog**
certus, -a, -um sure, certain
cōgō, cōgere, coēgī, coactum force
colloquium, -iī n. talk, conversation
consilium, -iī n. plan, counsel
crescō, crescere, crēvī grow, increase
cum when
dēsīderium, -iī n. desire, wish

dēspērō (1) despair (of)
difficultās, -tātis f. trouble, difficulty
dīligentius more carefully, more diligently
dīrectē directly
dulcis, -e sweet
faber, fabrī m. artisan, smith
forīs out of doors
improbus, -a, -um disloyal, shameless, morally unsound
intrā (+ acc.) within
lēniō, lēnīre, lēnīvī/lēniī put at ease
levis, leve light, gentle

magnopere much, greatly, especially
maneō, manēre, mansī, mansum stay, remain, endure
manum hand
matercula, -ae f. dear mother
mensis, mensis m. month
modo but, only, just now
moneō, monēre, monuī, monitum warn
nam for
nūtriō, nūtrīre, nūtrīvī/nūtriī nurse, nourish, raise
opus, operis n. work, effort; structure, building; (pl.) goods

pariō, parere, peperī bring forth, bear
paulum a little
pretiōsus, -a, -um valuable, expensive
pulsō (1) strike, beat; push, drive
sērō late, too late
silentium, -iī n. stillness, silence, tranquility; silentium tenēre to keep silent
suspīrō (1) sigh
tangō, tangere, tetigī touch
vae alas, woe
venter, ventris m. belly, abdomen
vidēbiminī you will seem

POSTQUAM LĒGISTĪ

1. Are the worries of Licinia and Aelius similar or dissimilar to those of expectant parents today?
2. What kinds of assistance are available to such families today but not to their ancient Roman counterparts?
3. Why do you think Plotia is so worried? Would a woman in her position and social class have the same concerns today?
4. How do members of her family try to make Plotia feel better?

Grammatica A

The Future Passive

The formulae for making future passives are the same ones you learned for future actives. Just use passive rather than active personal endings. Here is how it works:

1ST AND 2ND CONJUGATIONS USE PRESENT STEM (PS)			3RD AND 4TH CONJUGATIONS USE SHORT PRESENT STEM (SPS)		
Present Stem = 2nd Principal Part minus -*re*			Short Present Stem = 1st Principal Part minus -*ō*		
PS +	bor beris bitur	bimur biminī buntur	SPS +	ar ēris ētur	ēmur ēminī entur

Now compare the future passive of *vocō* with the future passive of *dūcō*:

PERSON	FUTURE PASSIVE OF *VOCŌ*		FUTURE PASSIVE OF *DŪCŌ*	
Singular				
1st	vocā**bor**	I will be called	dūc**ar**	I will be led
2nd	vocā**beris**	you will be called	dūc**ēris**	you will be led
3rd	vocā**bitur**	he/she/it will be called	dūc**ētur**	he/she/it will be led
Plural				
1st	vocā**bimur**	we will be called	dūc**ēmur**	we will be led
2nd	vocā**biminī**	you (all) will be called	dūc**ēminī**	you (all) will be led
3rd	vocā**buntur**	they will be called	dūc**entur**	he/she/it will be led

Notā Bene:

- In the 1st and 2nd conjugations, the future passive ending in the 2nd person singular is -*beris*. You might expect -*biris* but the -*bi*- here becomes -*be*-; so *portā**beris***.

EXERCEĀMUS!

23-2 Translating 2nd Conjugation Future Passives

Use your knowledge of the future active to translate each of the following future passive verbs. HINT: All these verbs appeared in *Lectiō Prīma*.

1. amābitur
2. cōgentur
3. pariētur
4. amāberis
5. inveniētur

6. cōgēmur
7. agētur
8. pulsābor
9. cōgēris
10. agar

Lectiō Secunda

Antequam Legis

Letters and Numbers

In this day and age of e-mail and text messaging, it is important to stop and consider how important and difficult sending a letter was in antiquity. Although Roman roads were a marvel of engineering and ensured relatively fast travel times, it still could take weeks for letters to reach some parts of the Roman Empire.

In *Lectiō Secunda,* Valeria receives a rare letter from her son, Licinius, who is serving in the army under Tiberius near the German border. The future emperor Tiberius will use this campaign to earn a fine reputation as a general and will be awarded a triumph upon his return to Rome. You will witness this triumph later in the book.

We take the opportunity of this letter to formalize your knowledge of Latin numbers, so look out for some Roman numerals in this *lectiō*.

The Irregular Verb *Ferō*

Also look for forms of the irregular verb *ferō*, a very important verb meaning "carry," "bear," and a number of other things. *Ferō* has distinctly irregular principal parts: *ferō, ferre, tulī, lātum*. It is also an irregular 3rd conjugation verb in the present tense, but these forms use familiar personal endings. Watch for forms of *ferō*, marked in **bold**, in the *lectiō*, and see if you can identify where the verb is regular in the present system.

EXERCEĀMUS!

23-3 Recognizing Forms of *Ferō*

Before you read *Lectiō Secunda*, find the Latin forms of *ferō* for each of the following English verbs. Remember that all the forms of *ferō* are marked in **bold** in the *lectiō*. HINT: Pay attention to personal endings.

1. he carries
2. I carry
3. we carry

4. they carry
5. I carried
6. you (all) carry

7. you carried
8. you (sing.) carry

🔊 EPISTULA Ē CASTRĪS

Dum familia inter sē dīcit, aliquis portam pulsāns audītur. Aliquis portam pulsat—semel, bis, ter. Aelius ad portam festīnat et, portam aperiēns, videt mīlitem fessum, quī epistulam **fert.**

Mīles "Avē!" inquit. "Nōnne invēnī domum Valeriae, cuius fīlius C. Licinius est? Quaerō hanc Valeriam."

5   "Valeriae domum invēnistī, amīce. Quae fortūna tē ad nōs **fert**?"

"Nōmen mihi est M. Vērus. Modo Rōmam ā Germāniā advēnī dē legiōne XVII. Bonum nuntium ā Germāniā **ferō**. Hanc epistulam Liciniī mēcum **tulī**."

Haec verba audiēns, Valeria laeta ad portam currit et epistulam grātissimē accipit. "Mīlle grātiās," inquit Valeria, "tibi agō quārē epistulam ad mē **tulistī**. Nōbīs optimum dōnum **fers**. Sitiensne es? Iēiūnusne?"

10   "Alma es, sed missiōnem honestam mēcum quoque **ferō** et nunc stīpendiō meō in mātrimōnium uxōrem dūcere poterō. Plūs quam XL annōs nātus sum et magnopere quiētem cupiō! Valēte omnēs."

Postquam Vērus abiit, Valeria signum epistulae frangit et omnēs silentium tenent dum legit:

OSPD Licinius SVBEEV. Iam dūdum ad fīnēs Germānōrum sum, sed bellum in Germānōs gerere nōn iam parātī sumus. Multās difficultātēs et labōrēs **ferimus**. Nunc castra fortissima pōnimus et viās novās struimus.

15   Cōtīdiē, cum tempestās bona est, arborēs magnās in silvā secāmus et eās ad castra **ferimus**. Et cōtīdiē centuriō clāmat: 'Estisne mīlitēs Rōmānī an nōn? Onus quod **fertis** leve est—levius pennā! Celerius! Fortius!' Et, cum centuriō clāmat, omnēs fortius onera sua **ferunt**. Herī pars viae novae vī flūminis **ferēbātur** sed hodiē pluit et nōn labōrāmus. Hoc centuriōnī displicet sed nōbīs maximē placet! Crās **ferēmur** ad viam et tunc magnus labor nōbīs erit!

Advēnitne infans quem Licinia **fert**? Estne puer aut puella?

20   Vīta dūra est sed quoque bona, nam labōrāre nōn mihi displicet. Mīles sum et dulce est prō patriā labōrāre et pugnāre! Mox in Germāniā pugnābitur! KAL IŪN.

Videt mīlitem quī epistulam fert

🔊 VERBA ŪTENDA

almus, -a, -um nourishing, kind, dear

an or

aperiō, aperīre, aperuī open

arbor, arboris f. tree

bellum, -ī n. war; **bellum gerere** wage war

bis twice, two times

C. = Gaius

castra, -ōrum n. pl. camp

centuriō, -ōnis m. centurion (roughly like a sergeant today)

cum when

difficultās, -ātis f. trouble, difficulty

displicet impersonal (+ dat.) "it is displeasing"

dōnum, -ī n. gift

dūdum just now, a little while ago

dulcis, dulce sweet

dūrus, -a, -um hard, rough

epistula, -ae f. letter

ferēbātur it was carried away

ferēmur we will proceed, we will go (literally, "we will be carried")

ferō, ferre, tulī, lātum bear, carry

fīnēs, fīnium m. pl. country, territory

flūmen, flūminis n. river

frangō, frangere, frēgī break

grātus, -a, -um pleasing, thankful

honestus, -a, -um honorable

in Germānōs (remember that *in* + acc. means "into, against")

KAL IŪN "on the June Kalends," i.e., June 1

legiōne XVII = legiōne decimā septimā = the 17th legion

levis, leve light, gentle

XL = 40

M. = Marcus

magnopere much, greatly, especially

mātrimōnium, -iī n. matrimony

mīles, mīlitis m. soldier

mille 1,000

missiō, -ōnis f. discharge (military); *missiōnem honestam* "an honorable discharge"

modo only, just now

nam for

onus, oneris n. load, burden

opus, operis n. work, effort; structure, building; (pl.) goods

patria, -ae f. country, fatherland

penna, -ae f. feather, wing

pluit (impersonal) "it is raining"

porta, -ae f. door, gate

pulsō (1), strike, beat; push, drive

pugnābitur "there will be fighting"

quārē for

quiēs, quiētis f. quiet, calm, rest

Rōmam "to Rome"

secō, secāre, secuī cut, cut off, cut up

semel once, one time

signum, -ī n. seal

silentium, -iī n. stillness, silence, tranquility; *silentium tenēre* to keep silent

sitiens, sitientis thirsty

stīpendium, -iī n. pay

struō, struere, struxī build, construct

ter three times

POSTQUAM LĒGISTĪ

Answer questions 1–6 in both Latin and English. Answer question 7 in English only.

1. What happens while the family is talking about their plans?
2. Who is M. Verus?
3. Why is Valeria happy in line 8?
4. Why does Verus leave so quickly?
5. How does Licinius spend most of his time in the army?
6. What is his attitude toward his work?
7. How does his work compare to the duties of a modern American soldier?

Grammatica B

The Irregular Verb *Ferō*

Ferō is irregular only in the present tense, where some vowels drop out. These irregular forms are marked in **bold** in the chart below. Note, however, that the regular personal endings are used with this verb. The present passive forms of *ferō* are made by changing the active personal endings to passive ones.

PERSON	PRESENT ACTIVE		PRESENT PASSIVE	
Singular				
1ˢᵗ	ferō	I bear, carry	feror	I am borne, carried
2ⁿᵈ	**fers**	you bear, carry	**ferris**	you are borne, carried
3ʳᵈ	**fert**	he/she/it bears, carries	**fertur**	he/she/it is borne, carried
Plural				
1ˢᵗ	ferimus	we bear, carry	ferimur	we are borne, carried
2ⁿᵈ	**fertis**	you (all) bear, carry	feriminī	you (all) are borne, carried
3ʳᵈ	ferunt	they bear, carry	feruntur	they are borne, carried
Infinitive				
	ferre	to bear, carry	**ferrī**	to be borne, carried
Imperative				
	Fer!	Bear! Carry!		
	Ferte!	Bear! Carry!		

Remember! "*Dīc, dūc, fac,* and *fer,* lack the *e* that ought to be there."

All the other forms of *ferō* are regular:

Imperfect	*ferēbam, ferēbās,* etc, and *ferēbar, ferēbāris,* etc.
Future	*feram, ferēs,* etc, and *ferar, ferēris,* etc.
Participle	*ferēns*

The perfect system (perfect, pluperfect, future perfect) is formed normally from the perfect stem *tul-*. Thus:

tulī	I have carried
tuleram	I had carried
tulerō	I shall have carried

Translating Ferō

When you find a form of *ferō* in a sentence, the first meanings you should try to use are either "bear" or "carry."

*Mīles epistulam **fert**.*	The soldier is carrying a letter.

Although this gives you the basic meaning, *ferō* can often be better translated with different English words, depending on context. Most of the following examples come from *Lectiō Secunda*:

- carry away, dispel

  Heri pars viae novae   Yesterday part of the new road was
  *vī flūminis **ferēbātur**.*   carried away by the force of the river.

- go, proceed

  *Crās **ferēmur** ad viam.*   Tomorrow we will proceed to the road.
                                                  (Literally, this means "we will be carried")

- lead

  *Omnēs viae Rōmam **ferunt**.*   All roads lead to Rome.

- endure

  *Multās difficultātēs et labōrēs **ferimus**.* We endure many hardships and labors.

- bring, report

  *Bonum nuntium ā Germāniā **ferō**.*   I bring news from Germany.

These are just a few examples. So when you see *ferō* in a sentence, be ready to consider other possible translations besides "bear, carry." A good Latin dictionary often will list some of these possibilities for you.

Compounding Ferō

Ferō is frequently compounded. Note where assimilation of the consonants and change of meaning occur in the following forms:

ad- + *ferō* = **afferō, afferre, attulī, allātum**	carry to, bring to
ab- + *ferō* = **auferō, auferre, abstulī, ablātum**	carry off, carry away
con- + *ferō* = **conferō, conferre, contulī, collātum**	carry together, compare
dis- + *ferō* = **differō, differre, distulī, dīlātum**	put off, delay
ex- + *ferō* = **efferō, efferre, extulī, ēlātum**	carry out, produce
in- + *ferō* = **inferō, inferre, intulī, illātum**	bring into, bring against, inflict
ob- + *ferō* = **offerō, offerre, obtulī, oblātum**	bring before, offer, present
re- + *ferō* = **referō, referre, rettulī, relātum**	carry back, tell

Watch for some of these compounds of *ferō* in upcoming *lectiōnēs*.

Gemma

English words derived from *ferō* compounds can help you sort out this assimilation. For example: con**fer**, col**late**; **differ**, di**late**; re**fer**, re**late**.

EXERCEĀMUS!

23-4   ***Ferō*: From Active to Passive**

Change each of the following active forms of *ferō* into the passive. Then translate the passive form into English. Follow the model.

→ ferō   *feror*   I am carried

1. fert	5. feram	9. ferimus
2. ferēmus	6. ferēbāmus	10. ferre
3. ferēbam	7. fers	
4. ferunt	8. fertis	

Counting Like a Roman

You have seen numbers and translated them without effort prior to this. This section puts all the information in one place for you. You just need to know a few words and remember a few rules.

- A cardinal number is the regular number used for counting.
- An ordinal puts something in order or tells the rank of something, as in "fifth" or "twentieth."
- The basics of Roman numerals are:
  - **I** = 1 **V** = 5 **X** = 10 **L** = 50 **C** = 100 **D** = 500 **M** = 1,000
  - A smaller letter to the left of a larger letter means subtract. Thus **XC** = 90
  - A smaller letter to the right of a larger letter means add. Thus **CX** = 110
- These rules for Roman numerals were often broken by the Romans themselves, and the system was flexible.

Abacus Rōmānus

	ROMAN NUMERAL	CARDINAL NUMBER			ORDINAL NUMBER	NOTES
1	I	M. ūnus ūnīus ūnī ūnum ūnō	F. ūna ūnīus ūnī ūnam ūnā	N. ūnum ūnīus ūnī ūnum ūnō	prīmus, -a, -um	
2	II	duo duōrum duōbus duōs duōbus	duae duārum duābus duās duābus	duo duōrum duōbus duo duōbus	secundus, -a, -um	These three cardinal numbers are declinable.
3	III	trēs trium tribus trēs tribus	trēs trium tribus trēs tribus	tria trium tribus tria tribus	tertius, -a, -um	
4	IIII or IV	quattuor			quartus, -a, -um	
5	V	quinque			quintus, -a, -um	
6	VI	sex			sextus, -a, -um	
7	VII	septem			septimus, -a, -um	
8	VIII	octō			octāvus, -a, -um	
9	VIIII or IX	novem			nōnus, -a, -um	
10	X	decem			decimus, -a, -um	
11	XI	undecim			undecimus, -a, -um	"one and ten"
12	XII	duodecim			duodecimus, -a, -um	"two and ten"
13	XIII	tredecim			tertius decimus, -a, -um	"three and ten"
14	XIIII or XIV	quattuordecim			quartus decimus, -a, -um	Notice how both parts of these compound ordinals have adjectival endings.
15	XV	quindecim			quintus decimus, -a, -um	
16	XVI	sēdecim			sextus decimus, -a, -um	
17	XVII	septendecim			septimus decimus, -a, um	

(continued on next page)

18	XVIII	duodēvīgintī	duodēvīcēsimus, -a, -um	"two from twenty"
19	XVIIII or XIX	undēvīgintī	undēvīcēsimus, -a, -um	"one from twenty"
20	XX	vīgintī	vīcēsimus, -a, -um	
21	XXI	vīgintī ūnus	vīcēsimus prīmus, -a, -um	
22	XXII	vīgintī duo	vīcēsimus secundus, -a, -um	Just follow the pattern for higher numbers.
30	XXX	trīgintā	trīcēsimus, -a, -um	
40	XL or XXXX	quadrāgintā	quadrāgēsimus, -a, -um	
50	L	quinquāgintā	quinquāgēsimus, -a, -um	
60	LX	sexāgintā	sexagēsimus, -a, -um	
70	LXX	septuāgintā	septuāgēsimus, -a, -um	
80	LXXX	octōgintā	octōgēsimus, -a, -um	
90	XC	nōnāgintā	nōnāgēsimus, -a, -um	
100	C	centum	centēsimus, -a, -um	
500	D	quingentī	quingentēsimus, -a, -um	
1000	M	mille	millēsimus, -a, -um	*Mīlia* is an indeclinable adjective: *cum mille hominibus* (with a thousand men).
2000	MM	duo mīlia mīlia mīlium mīlibus mīlia mīlibus	bis millēsimus, -a, -um	*Mīlia* is a declinable noun used with a partitive genitive: *duo mīlia librōrum* (two thousand books). One form for all three genders.

Notā Bene:

- *Ūnus* only has singular forms. *Duo* and *trēs* only have plural forms.
- Remember that *ūnus* forms its genitive and dative singulars like *sōlus* or *nullus* (i.e., *ūnīus* and *sōlīus*). As such it is an UNUS NAUTA word.
- All ordinals are declined as 2-1-2 adjectives.
- *Ambō, ambae, ambō* (both) is declined like *duo, duae, duo*.
- You can also count by the number of times something happens. In this case the cardinal number has become an adverb instead of an adjective: *semel* (one time, once); *bis* (two times, twice); *ter* (three times, thrice); *quater* (four times). Look back in *Lectiō Secunda* and find where some of these adverbs are used.

EXERCEĀMUS!

23-5   Counting in Latin

Rearrange the following numbers in numerical sequence from one to twenty.

decem; duo, duae, duo; vīgintī; duodecim; duodēvīgintī; novem; octō; quattuor; quattuordecim; quindecim; quinque; sēdecim; septem; ūnus, ūna, ūnum; septendecim; sex; tredecim; trēs, trēs, tria; undecim; undēvīgintī

Mōrēs Rōmānī

Epistulae Rōmānae

Letter-writing was an important vehicle for communication in the Roman world. Portions of the correspondence of several famous Romans survive, especially the letters of Cicero from the 1st century B.C. and the letters of Pliny the Younger from the end of the 1st century A.D. Both Cicero and Pliny wrote personal letters to their families and more formal, business letters to their colleagues. Even some letters between Cicero and Julius Caesar survive. Wealthy Romans would typically dictate their letters to their personal scribes.

There was no governmental postal system, so letter-writers had to arrange for their own transport. If they were wealthy enough, they had their own runners to carry their letters. Otherwise, they tried to find someone going the right way, as Licinius did. Obviously, then, the delivery of such letters could take many days or even weeks and was quite unreliable.

Licinius' letter could have been written on a wax or wooden tablet. Either wax or wood was a much less expensive and durable writing material than the other alternative, papyrus.

Even if Licinius knew how to read and write, he probably would have hired a scribe (scrība, -ae m. secretary, clerk, scribe) to write his letter for him. The expense of writing materials and hiring a scribe encouraged the practice of abbreviating formulaic expressions like the following used by Licinius:

OSPD	*Omnibus salūtem plūrimam dīcit.*
SVBEEV	*Sī valētis, bene est. Ego valeō.*

SVBEEV was often further abbreviated to SVV or *Sī valēs, valeō.*

Let's take a look at an actual letter that has been uncovered at Vindolanda, a fort near Hadrian's Wall in England. Written on a wooden writing tablet, it was preserved due to the special climatic conditions that are found at Vindolanda. In this letter, Claudia Severa is inviting Sulpicia Lepidina, the wife of the garrison commander, to a birthday party in c. 100 A.D.

Claudia's letter is particularly interesting because we can tell from the handwriting that the scribe started the letter, then Claudia herself wrote a brief personal greeting, and then the scribe finished the letter. This letter is one of the earliest pieces of writing in Latin in a woman's hand. Unfortunately, we do not know whether Sulpicia accepted the invitation and came to visit.

At right is the actual wooden tablet which Claudia sent. Below you see a transcription of what is written on the tablet. [*Vacat*] indicates a lacuna, or missing part of the text. A slash indicates the end of a line. A letter in square brackets is missing in the fragmentary original and has been added by the editors. The part in **bold** was written by Severa.

Ita valeam, karissima, et havē

cl · seuerá · lepidinae [suae] / [salu]tem / jiijdusseptemb[res]sororaddie[m] sollemnemn[a]talemmeumrogo / libenter[f]aciásutuenias / adnosi[u]cundioremmihi [diem]jnteruentútuofacturásj / [*vacat*] / cerial[emtu]umsalutáaeliusmeus / etfiliol[u]ssalutant [*vacat*] / [*vacat*] **sperabotesoror / ualesoro[r]anima / meaitau[al]eam / karissimaethaue**

The handwritten letter is difficult to read without training. You can tell from the transcription that there are lots of words understood or missing and that there are no spaces between many of the words. Here is the letter in a more readable version.

Claudia Sevēra Lepidinae suae salūtem dīcit. III Īdūs Septembrēs soror ad diem sollemnem nātālem meum rogō libenter faciās ut veniās ad nōs. Iūcundiōrem mihi diem interventū tuō factūra sī…

Ceriālem tuum salūtā. Aelius meus et fīliolus [eum] salūtant.

Spērābō tē, soror. Valē, soror, anima mea. Ita valeam, karissima, et havē

On the front of the tablet the scribe also wrote the following by way of an address:

Sulpiciae Lepidinae, Ceriālis Sevēra

🔊 VERBA ŪTENDA

III Īdūs Septembrēs "three days before the Ides of September" i.e., September 11th
Aelius Claudia's husband
anima, -ae f. soul, breath
Ceriālis Sulpicia's husband
faciās ut veniās "make that you come"

factūra (es) "you will make"
havē = avē Hail. Hi.
Īdus, Īduum f. pl. the Ides of a month (either 13th or 15th day)
interventus, -ūs m. arrival, coming
iūcundus, -a, -um pleasing, pleasant

karissima note spelling of *carissima*
nātālis, nātāle birth
salūtem dīcit says *Salvē*, says hello, greets
sī…The rest of this sentence is missing from the letter.

sollemnis, sollemne solemn, holy
soror "sister" may not mean sibling here, but a term of affection among friends
spērābō tē "I will hope for you," i.e., "I will expect you"
valeam may I flourish, may I be well

Latīna Hodierna

Numerī Rōmānī

Now look at some of the many English words derived from Latin numbers.

CARDINAL NUMBER	ENGLISH DERIVATIVE	ORDINAL NUMBER	ENGLISH DERIVATIVE
ūnus, -a, -um	**un**ique, **un**it, **un**iverse	**prīm**us, -a, -um	**prim**al, **prim**er, **prim**ary
duo, -ae, -o	**du**al, **du**et	**secund**us, -a, -um	**second**, **second**ary
trēs, -ēs, -ia	**tri**ennial, **tri**centennial	**terti**us, -a, -um	**terti**ary, **ter**centenary
quattuor	**quat**rain	**quart**us, -a, -um	**quart**, **quart**et
quinque	**quinqu**ennial	**quint**us, -a, -um	**quint**et, **quint**uplet
sex		**sext**us, -a, -um	**sext**et, **sext**uplet
septem	**Septem**ber	**septim**us, -a, -um	**sept**et, **sept**uplet
octō	**Octo**ber	**octāv**us, -a, -um	**octav**e, **oct**uplet
novem	**Novem**ber, **nov**ena	**nōn**us, -a, -um	
decem	**Decem**ber, **dec**ennial	**decim**us, -a, -um	**decim**ate, **deci**gram, **deci**liter, **deci**meter
sexāgintā	**sexagen**arian		
septuāgintā	**Septuagin**t, **septuagen**arian		
octōgintā	**octogen**arian		
nōnāgintā	**nonagen**arian		
centum	**cent**ennial, **cent**ury, **centi**gram, **centi**liter, **centi**meter, **cent**urion		
mille	**mil**e, **milli**gram, **milli**liter, **milli**meter		

A Note on Roman Numerals

Roman numerals are used instead of Arabic numbers in a number of contexts today:

- Lower-case Roman numerals are used for page numbering in the front matter of books.
- In outlining
- Upper-case Roman numerals are used (sometimes) for:

  I. Numbering book chapters
  II. Numbering kings and queens (Queen Elizabeth II)
  III. On cornerstones of buildings
  IV. Numbering Superbowls
  V. The hours on fancy watches

LII super portam Amphitheātrī Flāviānī

As you can see in the photo at right, the 80 entrances of the Flavian amphitheatre were all marked with numerals over the arches to facilitate the entry and exit of large numbers of people.

EXERCEĀMUS!

23-6 Roman Numerals

1. What was the number of the last Superbowl? What will be the number of the next one? Write them out in Roman numerals.

2. Write the current year in Roman numerals.

3. Write the year you were born in Roman numerals.

4. Write the number of this book chapter in Roman numerals.

Orbis Terrārum Rōmānus

Britannia

Claudia Severa's letter to Sulpicia was written in Britain about 100 years after the time of our story. During the reign of Augustus, Britain was not part of the Roman Empire. The island was not conquered until 43 A.D. under the reign of Claudius.

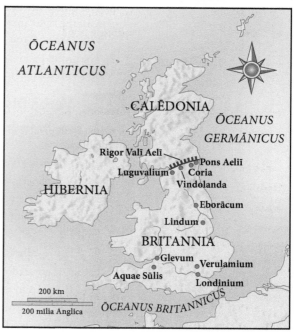

Britannia Rōmāna

In 60–61 A.D. the British queen Boudicca led a major but unsuccessful revolt against the Romans. Following the suppression of Boudicca's revolt, Rome's rule was firmly established on the island for centuries. Romans gradually expanded their sphere of influence beyond what is now southeastern England into Wales and north toward Scotland. The Scottish tribes were never fully conquered by the Romans, who built walls across the island to control and monitor movement across the border. The first of these walls, perhaps called *Rigor Valī Aelī* (the line of Hadrian's frontier) and known today as Hadrian's Wall, was built of stone and turf after 122 A.D. This wall ran from Luguvalium (modern Carlisle) to Coria (modern Corbridge) and was defended by a series of forts, including Vindolanda, where Claudia Severa's letter was found. The Antonine Wall, a series of earthen walls on stone foundations stretching from what is now Clyde on the west coast of Scotland to the Firth of Forth on the east, was built after 142 A.D., during the reign of the emperor Antoninus Pius, in an attempt to bring southern Scotland under Roman control. The Antonine Wall was abandoned by Antoninus Pius' successor, Marcus Aurelius, who established the northern boundary of the Roman province along Hadrian's Wall.

Rigor Valī Aelī

Boudicca cum fīliābus Londiniī

Many major modern cities in England were originally Roman army camps or cities, including:

Londinium (London)   Eborācium (York)
Verulamium (St. Albans)   Lindum (Lincoln)
Glevum (Gloucester)   Aquae Sūlis (Bath)

Modern English city names ending in -chester come from the Latin *castra* and indicate that the site was a fort in Roman times: Chichester, Worcester, Gloucester, etc.

QUID PUTĀS?

1. Do you think Sulpicia Lepidina accepted Claudia Severa's invitation to visit for her birthday? Why or why not?
2. Compare the way Claudia Severa invited Sulpicia to the way you might extend a similar invitation today. How are the technology and social customs different? How are they the same?
3. Explain to a friend what all these English words have in common and why: centennial, century, centigram, centiliter, centimeter, centurion. If you don't know the answer, look the words up in an English dictionary.
4. In what other parts of the world have massive protective walls similar to Hadrian's Wall been built?

EXERCEĀMUS!

23-7 Scrībāmus

Using the letter from Claudia Severa to Sulpicia Lepidina as a model, write a letter in Latin to a relative or friend inviting them to your birthday party.

23-8 Colloquāmur

This game can be played in a number of variations:

1. Line up with a number of other students or sit in a circle. The *dux gregis* (the leader of the group) picks a number and says it aloud. The next person has to say aloud the next number in sequence.
2. The group sits in a circle and each person counts by twos or threes, having to come up with the right answer within five seconds. Say it correctly and you stay in the game. Make a mistake and you are out. Last person remaining is the winner.
3. The group counts off using ordinals. Ordinals have declinable forms, so remember to use the form that matches your gender.

23-9 Verba Discenda

Use the *Verba Discenda* to answer each of the following questions. Watch for Roman numerals in the questions.

1. Find **IV** *verba discenda* related to military life.
2. Find **V** *verba discenda* that are 2nd declension neuter nouns.
3. Find **III** words in the 3rd declension.
4. Find **I** i-stem noun of the 3rd declension.
5. Find **I** 2-1-2 adjective.
6. Find **II** two-termination adjectives of the 3rd declension.
7. Find **I** noun used only in the plural.
8. Find **II** nouns in the 1st declension.
9. Find **I** 1st conjugation verb, **I** 2nd conjugation verb, and **I** 3rd conjugation *-iō* verb.
10. Give **I** additional English derivative for **V** different *verba discenda*.

🔊 VERBA DISCENDA

aspiciō, aspicere, aspexī, aspectum look at [aspect]

bellum, -ī n. war; **bellum gerere** wage war [bellicose]

canis, canis m./f. dog [canine]

castra, -ōrum n. pl. camp

centuriō, -ōnis m. centurion

certus, -a, -um sure, certain [certitude]

cōgō, cōgere, coēgī, coactum drive together, force [cogent]

consilium, -iī n. plan, counsel, reason, judgment

difficultās, -ātis f. trouble, difficulty

dōnum, -ī n. gift [donation]

dulcis, dulce sweet [dulcet, dulcimer]

epistula, -ae f. letter [epistolary]

ferō, ferre, tulī, lātum bear, carry [refer, relate, confer, collate]

grātus, -a, -um pleasing, thankful [gratitude]

improbus, -a, -um disloyal, shameless, morally unsound [improbity]

levis, leve light, gentle [levity]

magnopere much, greatly, especially

maneō, manēre, mansī, mansum stay, remain, endure, await

mīles, mīlitis m. soldier [militant]

modo only, just now, but

nam for

opus, operis n. work, effort; structure, building; (pl.) goods [magnum opus, operate]

porta, -ae f. door, gate [portal]

pulsō (1) strike, beat; push, drive [pulsate]

silentium, -iī n. stillness, silence, tranquility

Angulus Grammaticus

The Roman Calendar

Although we are essentially still using the Roman calendar as revised by Julius Caesar and officially enacted on January 1, 45 B.C., you need to understand a few important differences and points of grammar in order to know how to read and to make calendar days in Latin.

First of all, the names of the Roman months will look quite familiar, although the forms Romans used to make calendar dates are all adjectives.

Iānuārius, -a, -um	*Māius, -a, -um*	*September, -bris, -bre*
Februārius, -a, -um	*Iūnius, -a, -um*	*Octōber, -bris, -bre*
Martius, -a, -um	*Iūlius, -a, -um*	*November, -bris, -bre*
Aprīlis, -e	*Augustus, -a, -um*	*December, -bris, -bre*

The original Roman calendar was lunar and only had ten months, beginning with *Martius* and ending with *December*. That is why *September* is named the seventh month, *Octōber* is the eighth month, etc. As various reforms tried to regularize this calendar, two months, *Iānuārius* and *Februārius*, were added at the beginning of the year. *Iānuārius* is appropriately named after Janus (*Iānus, -ī* m.), the two-faced Roman god of doorways, of entering and leaving. *Februārius* is related to *febris* and is the "Fever Month." After the death of Julius Caesar, *Quinctīlis*, the fifth month, was renamed *Iūlius* in his honor. Later *Sextīlis*, the sixth month, was renamed *Augustus* in honor of the emperor.

In the Julian Calendar the number of days in each month is the same as in our modern calendar, but Romans used three fixed points in the month that dates are defined by:

Iānus

- **Kalends:** The first day of the month was called *Kalendae, -ārum* f. pl. and gives us our word "calendar."

- **Nones:** The second fixed day was the fifth day of the month and was called *Nōnae, -ārum* f. pl.

- **Ides:** The third fixed day was the thirteenth day of the month and was called *Īdūs, Īduum* f. pl.

> BUT ... in March, May, July, and October the Nones fell on the seventh day and the Ides fell on the fifteenth. That is why the assassination of Julius Caesar in 44 B.C. took place *Idibus Martiīs* (ID MAR) "on the Ides of March," i.e., March 15th.

Here are some other dates following the same format:

Kalendiīs Iānuāriīs, "on the January Kalends"	KAL IAN	Jan. 1
Nōnīs Iānuāriīs, "on the January Nones"	NON IAN	Jan. 5
Īdibus Iānuāriīs, "on the January Ides"	ID IAN	Jan. 13
Kalendiīs Māiīs, "on the May Kalends"	KAL MAI	May 1
Nōnīs Māiīs, "on the May Nones"	NON MAI	May 7
Īdibus Māiīs, "on the May Ides"	ID MAI	May 15

The days before the Kalends, Nones, and Ides were introduced by *prīdiē* (the day before) in this manner:

prīdiē Kalendās Februāriās the day before the February Kalends	(*prīdiē* + acc.) pri. KAL FEB	Jan. 31
prīdiē Nōnās Aprīlēs the day before the April Nones	pri. NON APR	Apr. 4
prīdiē Īdūs Iūniās the day before the June Ides	pri. ID IUN	June 12

To refer to all other days of the month, Romans **counted ahead** to the next Kalends, Nones, or Ides. Here they used the formula *ante diem* "before the day" followed by a number and the words for the Kalends, Nones, or Ides, and the appropriate month in the accusative plural. **As they did this, they counted both the day they were counting from and the day they were counting to.** Thus:

> *ante diem III Kalendās Iūliās* three days before the July Kalends

- Kalends of July = July 1
- Three days before this, counting Roman style → July 1, June 30, June 29
- So, a.d. III KAL IUL = June 29

EXERCEĀMUS!

23-10   The Roman Calendar

Read these Roman dates in Latin, then convert them into our calendar format. Use the *Angulus Grammaticus* as your guide and remember to count like a Roman! You may well find a conversion engine online to help you, but try it the hard way first, and use the converters to check yourself.

1. ID DEC
2. a.d. III NON OCT
3. a.d. IV ID IVL
4. a.d. X KAL OCT
5. NON MAI

6. pri KAL OCT
7. pri NON FEB
8. a.d. III KAL MAI
9. a.d. VIII KAL IAN
10. a.d. VII KAL APR

24

In Theātrō

Persōna Rōmāna

Lectiō Prīma

Antequam Legis

Going to the Theater

Romans had many opportunities to go to theatrical productions. In this chapter both families attend a revival of *Amphitruō*, a play by Plautus, one of Rome's comic playwrights. Plautus died in 184 B.C., but his plays were frequently performed after his death. The Roman theater was open to all classes, and the audiences were often rowdy. Even Mendax could have attended, as admission was free. But seats were often saved for the more influential Romans, and class-conscious Romans would know what section of the theater was reserved for their class. In *Lectiō Prīma* you will read about people arriving at the theater and their anticipation before the performance begins. Notice how Marcus summarizes for Lucius the plot of the play they are going to see. Such a plot summary, called an *argūmentum* (*-ī* n.), was often given by an actor at the beginning of the play. As you read this *lectiō*, watch out also for a special group of verbs called deponents.

Deponent Verbs

An extremely common class of Latin verbs is called **deponent**. Such verbs have passive forms but active meanings. To translate deponent verbs you only need to remember the dictum:

"Looks passive, isn't."

Regular passives and deponents are intermingled in *Lectiō Prīma*. To help you distinguish them, the deponents are in **bold** and the regular passives are in ***bold italics***. Remember to translate the deponents actively and the regular passives passively. Be careful of tenses as you read—watch especially for 3rd and 4th conjugation futures.

GRAMMATICA
Deponent Verbs
"PUFFY" Verbs
The 4th and 5th Declensions

MŌRĒS RŌMĀNĪ
Theātra Rōmāna

LATĪNA HODIERNA
Rēs and *Diēs* in Modern Usage

ORBIS TERRĀRUM RŌMĀNUS
Geōgraphia Italica

ANGULUS GRAMMATICUS
Oh No, Not Semi-Deponents, Too!

> **LECTIŌNĒS:**
> **IN THEĀTRŌ**
> and
> **ALCMĒNA ET LICINIA PARIUNT**
>
> Both families attend a revival of a play of Plautus, and life imitates art.

EXERCEĀMUS!

24-1 Translating Deponent Verbs

Below is a list of some of the deponent verbs which appear in *Lectiō Prīma*. Since these are all new vocabulary words, we provide their meanings and conjugations. Use what you know already about Latin verbs to determine whether the tense of the verb is present or future. Then use the personal endings to translate the words. Remember to translate them ACTIVELY. Follow the model.

HINT: You do not even need to look at the *lectiō* to do this exercise, but you will find the *lectiō* a lot easier to understand if you do this exercise first.

	Line	Verb	Meaning	Conjugation	Tense	Translation
→	1	colloquuntur	speak together	3rd	present	they speak together
1.	1	ingrediuntur	enter	3rd		
2.	7	fruentur	enjoy	3rd		
3.	8	sequitur	follow	3rd		
4.	13	polliceor	promise	2nd		
5.	14	mentior	lie	4th		
6.	17	patitur	suffer	3rd *-iō*		
7.	18	prōgreditur	advance	3rd *-iō*		
8.	21	loquitur	speak	3rd		

🔊 IN THEĀTRŌ

In theātrum multī spectātōrēs **ingrediuntur** et inter sē **colloquuntur** dum fābula Plautī, "Amphitruō" nōmine, ab omnibus avidē *exspectātur*.

Novum theātrum Marcellī omnēs **intuentur** et valdē **admīrantur**. Patriciī sīcut Marcus et Lūcius et amīcī suī sēdēs in prīmīs gradibus theātrī, post 5 senātōrēs, tenent et ab hīs fābula melius *audiētur spectābitur*que. Aliī, sīcut Valeriae familia, in altissimīs sēdibus sedent. Sed omnēs—fēminae līberīque pauperēsque dīvitēsque—mox fābulā **fruentur**.

In theātrum Lūcius Marcum **sequitur** et frātrēs sedent cum amīcīs suīs. Multī iuvenēs inter sē **sermōcinantur** sed Marcus fēminam ūnam gracilem et 10 pulchram **intuētur** et cum eā dīcere **cōnātur**, sed Marcus ā Lūciō *turbātur*. "Quālis," rogat, "haec fābula est? Quid in fābulā *agētur*? Quid vidēbimus hodiē?" Marcus "Frātercule," inquit, "modo manēre dēbēs et mox omnia **intuēberis**. Tibi **polliceor**! Haec fābula optima est et multum rīdēbis! Nōn **mentior**. Nōnne Amphitruōnem scīs?"

Actor Rōmānus

15 Lūcius respondet: "Certē, Amphitruō pater Herculis est."

"Ita vērō! Et uxor eius Alcmēna, quae gravida est, domī remanet dum Amphitruō contrā hostēs bellum gerit. Mox infans **nascētur** et Alcmēna **patitur** quod vir suus domī nōn est. Tum Iuppiter, quī Alcmēnam vīderat et (ut semper) statim eam adamāvit, ad Alcmēnam **prōgreditur**. In formam Amphitruōnis Iuppiter sē mūtat et cum Alcmēnā in Amphitruōnis lectō dormit. Sed, tunc Amphitruō vērus ā bellō revenit et uxōrem suam amāre spērat! Sed 20 Alcmēna fessa est et nōn ..."

In aliā parte theātrī, familia Valeriae quoque sedet et **loquitur**. Aelius "**Īrascor**," inquit, "quod uxor mea, tam gravida, tantōs gradūs ascendere dēbuit! Nōn aequum est! Decet nōbīs in gradibus inferiōribus nōn hīc in Alpibus aut Apennīnīs sedēre! Aliās sēdēs petere dēbēmus!"

Licinia rīdens, "Mī Aelī," inquit, "sedē hīc! Initium fābulae iam adest."

🔊 VERBA ŪTENDA

adamō (1) love passionately
admīror, admīrārī admire
Alpēs, Alpium f. pl. Alps, the mountains of northern Italy
Apennīnī, -ōrum m. pl. Apennines, the mountains along the spine of Italy
ascendō, ascendere, ascendī, ascensum climb, ascend
colloquor, colloquī talk together, converse
cōnor, cōnārī, cōnātus sum try
decet, decēre, decuit (+ dat. +inf.) imp. it is fitting
dīves, dīvitis rich, talented

forma, -ae f. shape, form; beauty; ground plan
frāterculus, -ī m. little brother
fruor, fruī, fructus / fruitus sum (+ abl.) enjoy, profit by
gracilis, gracile thin, slender, scanty
gradus, -ūs m. step, pace, tier (of a theater)
gravidus, -a, -um pregnant
inferior, inferius lower
ingredior, ingredī, ingressus sum enter
initium, -ī n. beginning
intueor, intuērī gaze at
īrascor, īrascī be angry at
Iuppiter, Iovis m. Jupiter, king of the gods

līberī, -ōrum m. pl. children
loquor, loquī, locūtus sum speak, talk, say
mentior, mentīrī, mentītus sum lie, deceive
mī = vocative of *meus*
mūtō (1) change
nascor, nascī be born
patior, patī, passus sum suffer, allow
patricius, -a, -um noble, patrician
pauper, pauperis poor
polliceor, pollicērī, pollicitus sum promise
prōgredior, prōgredī, prōgressus sum go to, move forward, proceed

quālis, quāle of what sort, of what kind
remaneō, remanēre, remansī remain, stay behind
senātor, senātōris m. senator
sequor, sequī, secūtus sum follow
sermōcinor, sermōcinārī converse, talk, chat
situs, -a, -um located
spectātor, spectātōris m. spectator, observer
spērō (1) hope
tantus, -a, -um so great, so many
theātrum, -ī n. theater
turbō (1) disorder
ut as
vērō in truth, truly

POSTQUAM LĒGISTĪ

Answer the questions in English, but also write down the Latin words in the *lectiō* that support your answer.

1. Describe the seating arrangements in the theater. Who sits where?
2. What does Marcus want to do while he waits for the play to begin?
3. What does Lucius want to do?
4. Briefly summarize the plot of the play.
5. What is Aelius angry about?

Gemma

Marcellus was the son of Augustus' sister, Octavia, and was a possible successor to Augustus. He died in 23 B.C., and Augustus had a theater built near the Tiber in his memory.

Grammatica A

Deponent Verbs

Look through the *Verba Ūtenda* and find all the deponent verbs marked in **bold**. They are easy to recognize with passive endings. Note that these deponent verbs have only three principal parts. Why? Because they (naturally) do not have the 3rd principal part, which is the perfect **active** form of regular verbs.

dīcō	*dīcere*	*dixī*	*dictum*
I say	to say	I have said	(having been) said

loquor	*loquī*		*locūtus sum*
I say	to say		I have said

For now, you only have to worry about the first two principal parts. The 3rd principal part of deponents is a perfect passive form you have not yet learned. For now, this form will only be given for deponent verbs which are *Verba Discenda*. You will only see and use deponent verbs in the present and future tenses in this chapter. It is easy to recognize deponent verbs in the dictionary for the following reasons:

- All the endings are passive.
- They have only three principal parts.
- The 3rd principal part has two words, the second of which is *sum*. You will not see this *sum* in the dictionary with non-deponent verbs.

Deponents are formed just like the passives of regular verbs. The only difference is that they have no active personal endings.

Now look at the present forms of these sample deponent verbs.

PRESENT DEPONENTS					
Person	**1st Conjugation** *cōnor* (try)	**2nd Conjugation** *polliceor* (promise)	**3rd Conjugation** *sequor* (follow)	**3rd - iō Conjugation** *patior* (suffer, allow)	**4th Conjugation** *mentior* (lie, deceive)
Singular					
1st	cōnor	polliceor	sequor	patior	mentior
2nd	cōnāris	pollicēris	sequeris	pateris	mentīris
3rd	cōnātur	pollicētur	sequitur	patitur	mentītur
Plural					
1st	cōnāmur	pollicēmur	sequimur	patimur	mentīmur
2nd	cōnāminī	pollicēminī	sequiminī	patiminī	mentīminī
3rd	cōnantur	pollicentur	sequuntur	patiuntur	mentiuntur

Unlike regular passive verbs, many deponent verbs are transitive and can take direct objects, like the words marked in bold in these sentences:

Novum theātrum Marcellī intuentur.   They look at the **new theater** of Marcellus.
Novum theātrum valdē admīrantur.   They admire very much the **new theater**.
Marcus fēminam intuētur.   Marcus looks at a **woman**.
Uxōrem suam amplectī spērat.   He hopes to embrace **his wife**.

Some deponent verbs are intransitive and thus do not take direct objects.

Iuvenēs inter sē sermōcinantur.   The youths chat among themselves.
Ad Alcmēnam prōgreditur.   He goes to Alcmena.
Mox infans nascētur.   Soon the baby will be born.
In theātrum Marcus ingreditur.   Marcus enters the theater.

EXERCEĀMUS!

24-2 Deponent Verbs in the Future Tense

Now use your knowledge of future passive forms and the chart of present forms above to translate the following deponents in the future tense. Follow the model.

→ *cōnābor*   I will try

1. cōnābuntur
2. pollicēbitur
3. sequentur
4. patiēminī
5. mentiēris

6. cōnābimur
7. patientur
8. pollicēberis
9. mentiētur
10. sequēris

Look for more deponents in the future tense in *Lectiō Secunda*.

Lectiō Secunda

Antequam Legis

In *Lectiō Secunda* the play begins and an actor gives an *argūmentum,* or introduction, to the play. He explains not only the plot but also the role of the character he is playing. He uses the 2nd person plural to talk directly to the audience. His words are taken directly from the original *argūmentum* of Plautus' play.

Besides the excitement on stage, there is also some in the audience. Watch out in this *lectiō* for a special group of deponent verbs that take ablative rather than accusative objects. You will also learn about the last two declensions, the 4th and the 5th.

Ablatives with Certain Deponent Verbs

Five deponent verbs take ablative objects instead of accusative ones. You already saw one of these verbs in *Lectiō Prīma* in the phrase *mox fābulā fruentur* (Soon they will enjoy the story.) The verb *fruentur* takes the ablative *fābulā* as its object. To help you spot these verbs in *Lectiō Secunda* we have marked them in ***bold italics***.

The 4th and 5th Declensions

In this *lectiō* you are also introduced to the last two declensions. You will find these endings relatively familiar, and you will be able to spot the declensions this way:

	HOW TO SPOT IT	EXAMPLES
4th Declension	-*u* in most of its endings	*manus, manūs, manuum,* etc.
5th Declension	-*e* in all of its endings	*rēs, reī, rērum, rēbus,* etc.

The 4th and 5th declension nouns are marked in **bold** in the *lectiō*. The case endings will not be a problem for you, as they are just variants of what you have already seen.

EXERCEĀMUS!

24-3   Finding Ablative Objects for Certain Deponent Verbs

Before you read *Lectiō Secunda*, scan it to find the ablative object(s) of the following deponent verbs. Then translate the verb with its object(s). Follow the model.

Line	Verb	Ablative Object(s)	Translation
→ 2	fruuntur (enjoy)	spectāculīs sonīsque	they enjoy the sights and sounds
1. 5	fruēminī (enjoy)		
2. 9	ūtitur (use)		
3. 12	fungar (perform)		
4. 22	potitur (possess)		
5. 23	fruitur (enjoy)		

ALCMĒNA ET LICINIA PARIUNT

Omnēs spectātōrēs, dīvitēs et pauperēs, nōbilēs et
plēbēiī, spectāculīs sonīsque theātrī *fruuntur*.
Subitō dominus actōrum prō spectātōribus stat et
silentium poscit. "Amīcī," clāmat, "Mox fābulā
5 *fruēminī*. Sī vōbīs placeat, silentium tenēte! Nōlu-
mus **sonitūs** infantium, sermōnum, **mōtuum**, aut
rixārum audīre. Ecce! Incipimus!"

Tunc actor, **habitum speciemque** deī
Mercuriī gerēns, intrat et magnā vōce *ūtitur* et
10 prōnuntiat.

"Ego, Mercurius, Iovis **iussū** veniō. Ego
fungar officiō meō et vōbīs argūmentum huius tra-
goediae ēloquar. Quid? Frontēs contraxistis quia
'tragoediam' dixī? **Faciēs** maestae mihi displicent!
15 Nōlīte verērī! Deus sum et facile **rēs** commūtābō.
Sed, deīs in cōmoediā agere nōn decet. Quid faciam? **Rem** teneō! Nunc **rēs** mixta est et tragi-
cōmoediam habēbimus.

Actōrēs in cōmoediā Rōmānā

"Haec est Amphitruōnis domus, sed Amphitruō nōn adest; immō, in castrīs cum **exercitū** suō est. Sed alius
20 Amphitruō intus est!

"Ille Amphitruō quī abest, vērus Amphitruō est. Hic Amphitruō, quī nunc in lectō Alcmēnae dormit, pater
meus est—Iuppiter ipse, rex deōrum. Pater nunc et **speciē et habitū** Amphitruōnis *potītur* et uxōre Amphitruōnis
vērī *fruitur*."

Paulō post spectātōrēs Alcmēnam et Iovem haec dīcentēs audiunt:
25 Iuppiter: "Bene valē, Alcmēna. Mihi necesse est abhinc īre."

Alcmēna: "Nōn mihi placet. Quandō revertēris?"

Iuppiter: "**Fidem** habē, cāra uxor. Mox revertar! Hoc tibi polliceor!"

Et, paulō post, quid vident spectātōrēs? Illum vērum Amphitruōnem. A **portū domum** suum aggreditur.
Alcmēna eum spectat et **manūs** ad **faciem** tollēns laetē exclāmat: "Revēnistī ad mē! Tam laeta sum! Sed nūper ē lectō
30 meō abiistī!"

Amphitruō, uxōris **manum** capiēns: "Quid dīcis?" inquit, "Ē lectō? Haec **rēs** mala mihi est! Ego mensēs multōs
iam absum. Quid agitur?"

Omnēs spectātōrēs rīdent sed, in aliā parte theātrī, aliquī nōn rīdent. Licinia quoque patitur. In **genua** cadit,
ventrem prehendēns et "Māter," inquit, "patior graviter et sīcut Alcmēna puerum mox pariam. Sed hodiē! Plūrēs **diēs**
35 mihi nōn sunt. Necesse est nōbīs simul dē **gradibus** descendere et subitō **domum** redīre."

Persōnae Rōmānae

🔊 VERBA ŪTENDA

abhinc from here

actor, actōris m. actor

aggredior, aggredī go to, approach

argūmentum -ī. n. plot

commūtō (1) change

cōmoedia, -ae f. comedy

contrahō, contrahere, contraxī draw together, gather

diēs, diēī m. day

descendō, descendere, descendī go down, descend

displiceō, displicēre, displicuī (+ dat.) displease

dīvēs, dīvitis rich, talented

domus, -ūs f. house

ēloquor, ēloquī, ēlocūtus sum speak out, declare

exclāmō (1) cry out, exclaim

exercitus, -ūs m. army

faciēs, -ēī f. face, appearance, beauty

fidēs, fideī f. faith, trust

frons, frontis f. forehead, brow

fungor, fungī, functus sum (+ abl.) perform, discharge

genū, -ūs n. knee

graviter severely

habitus, -ūs m. dress, clothing

immō rather

iussū "by order of" (+ gen.)

manus, -ūs f. hand

mensis, mensis m. month

mentior, mentīrī, mentītus sum lie, deceive

mixtus, -a, -um mixed

mōtus, -ūs m. motion

nūper recently

officium, -iī n. task, duty, office

pariō, parere, peperī bring forth, give birth to

paulō post a little later, somewhat later

pauper, pauperis poor

plēbēius, -a, -um plebian, pertaining to the common people

portus, -ūs m. port, harbor

potior, potīrī, potītus sum (+ abl. or gen.) take possession of, get, acquire

prehendō, prehendere, prehendī take hold of, seize

prōnuntiō (1) proclaim, announce

quandō when

rēs, reī f. thing, matter, business, affair; reason

rem teneō I have it!

revertor, revertī come back, return

rixa, -ae f. quarrel, brawl

sermō, sermōnis m. speech, talk

simul together, altogether, at the same time, all at once

sonitus, -ūs m. sound

spectāculum, -i n. spectacle, sight

speciēs, speciēī f. appearance, look, type

tragicōmoedia, -ae f. tragicomedy

tragoedia, -ae f. tragedy

ūtor, ūtī, ūsus sum (+ abl.) use, employ, enjoy, experience

venter, ventris m. stomach, belly

vereor, verērī, veritus sum be afraid of, fear, show reverence to

POSTQUAM LĒGISTĪ

1. What is the *dominus actōrum* and what does he tell the audience?
2. What role does the first actor play, and what does he tell the audience?
3. Why does Alcmena not want Jupiter-Amphitryon to leave?
4. What happens as soon as Jupiter-Amphitryon leaves the stage?
5. Why does the audience laugh when this happens?
6. Why is Licinia not laughing?
7. How do you think Licinia will get home?

Grammatica B

"Puffy" Verbs

There are five Latin deponent verbs that take ablative rather than accusative objects. These verbs are sometimes called "PUFFY" because of the following acronym:

P*otior, potīrī, potītus sum* (+ abl. or gen.) take possession of, get, acquire

Ū*tor, ūtī, ūsus sum* (+ abl.) use, employ, enjoy, experience

F*ruor, fruī, fructus/fruitus sum* (+ abl.) enjoy, profit by

F*ungor, fungī, functus sum* (+ abl.) perform, discharge

V*escor, vescī* (+ abl.) take food, feed, devour (referring to animals, not people)

The last of these, *vescor*, rarely appears. The four other PUFFY verbs, however, are *Verba Discenda* in this chapter.

EXERCEĀMUS!

24-4 Distinguishing PUFFY Verbs from Regular Verbs

Choose the correct case of each word marked in **bold** to be the object of the verb. Remember to choose the ablative for PUFFY verbs and accusative for all other verbs. Then translate the verb and its object into English. Follow the model.

→   **Spectāculīs/Spectācula** theātrī fruuntur.

    Spectāculīs theātrī fruuntur.   They enjoy the sights of the theater.

1. Actor **magnā vōce/magnam vōcem** ūtitur.
2. Licinia **ventre/ventrem** amplectitur.
3. Iuppiter **Alcmēnā/Alcmēnam** intuētur.
4. Ego **officiō meō/officium meum** fungor.
5. Rex deōrum **habitū/habitum** Amphitruōnis potītur.
6. Amphitruō **uxōre/uxōrem** admīrātur.
7. Iuppiter **dēliciīs/dēlicia** Alcmēnae vērī fruitur.
8. Mox **fābulā/fābulam** fruentur.
9. Amphitruō vērus **portū/portum** aggreditur.
10. **Sīmiā/Sīmiam** sequuntur.
11. Familia Servīliī **multīs servīs/multōs servōs** potītur.

The 4th and 5th Declensions

Did you have any trouble translating the 4th and 5th declension nouns marked in **bold** in *Lectiō Secunda*? Here are the declension patterns.

The 4th Declension

	MASCULINE/FEMININE		NEUTER	
Singular				
Nominative	man**us** (f.)	**-us**	gen**ū** (n.)	**-ū**
Genitive	man**ūs**	**-ūs**	gen**ūs**	**-ūs**
Dative	man**uī**	**-uī**	gen**ū**	**-ū**
Accusative	man**um**	**-um**	gen**ū**	**-ū**
Ablative	man**ū**	**-ū**	gen**ū**	**-ū**
Vocative	man**us**	**-us**	gen**ū**	**-ū**
Plural				
Nominative	man**ūs**	**-ūs**	gen**ua**	**-ua**
Genitive	man**uum**	**-uum**	gen**uum**	**-uum**
Dative	man**ibus**	**-ibus**	gen**ibus**	**-ibus**
Accusative	man**ūs**	**-ūs**	gen**ua**	**-ua**
Ablative	man**ibus**	**-ibus**	gen**ibus**	**-ibus**
Vocative	man**ūs**	**-ūs**	gen**ua**	**-ua**

The 5th Declension

MASCULINE/FEMININE			
Singular			
Nominative	rēs f. thing	diēs m. day	-ēs
Genitive	reī	diēī	-ēī
Dative	reī	diēī	-ēī
Accusative	rem	diem	-em
Ablative	rē	diē	-ē
Vocative	rēs	diēs	-ēs
Plural			
Nominative	rēs	diēs	-ēs
Genitive	rērum	diērum	-ērum
Dative	rēbus	diēbus	-ēbus
Accusative	rēs	diēs	-ēs
Ablative	rēbus	diēbus	-ēbus
Vocative	rēs	diēs	-ēs

Notā Bene:

- The 4th declension uses the vowel "*u*" to link the ending to the stem in all cases except the dative and ablative plurals, which are usually -*ibus* (but -*ubus* is also used).
- 4th declension neuters are notable for the dative singular (no -*ī*). Other than that, they have normal 4th declension endings and follow the "neuter rule."
- The 5th declension is marked by the vowel *e* throughout. You can see that most of the endings are fairly familiar.
- Note that there is no macron over the *e* in the genitive and dative singular of *rēs*.
- There are no adjectives that use 4th or 5th declension endings.

Gemma

Dē Diē et Hodiē: You can remember that the Latin word *diēs* is masculine by thinking of the word *hodiē*, a contraction for *hōc diē*, "on this day." You can see from *hōc* that *diēs* is masculine. The Spanish *Buenos días*, a plural meaning "Good day," still retains the masculine gender (buenos, not buenas).

EXERCEĀMUS!

24-5 4th and 5th Declension Nouns

Use the declension charts to identify the declension, case, and number of each of the following nouns. The number in parentheses indicates how many forms are possible (not including vocatives). Follow the model.

Noun	Declension	Case	Number
→ domū (1)	4th	ablative	singular

1. manum (1)
2. rē (1)
3. gradus (1)
4. gradūs (3)
5. faciēī (2)
6. sonituum (1)
7. diēbus (2)
8. speciēs (3)
9. sonituī (1)
10. rem (1)

EXERCEĀMUS!

24-6 Five-Declension Review

Compare the endings of the five declensions by filling in the empty boxes on the following chart. As you do this, try to spot the patterns that seem to hold true across the declensions.

DECLENSION	1ST	2ND	3RD	4TH	5TH
Singular					
Nominative	fēmina	amīcus	frāter	gradus	speciēs
Genitive					
Dative					
Accusative			frātrem		
Ablative	fēminā				
Plural					
Nominative					
Genitive				graduum	
Dative					
Accusative		amīcōs			
Ablative					speciēbus

Notā Bene:

- All masculine and feminine accusative singulars end in -*m*.
- In most declensions, the ablative singular is a long vowel, except in 3rd declension non–i-stems (e.g., *homine*).
- The genitive plural always ends in some form of -*um*.
- All masculine and feminine accusative plurals end in a long vowel followed by -*s*.
- Within a declension, the dative and ablative plurals are always the same.

Gender in the Declensions

Notice from the chart below that some genders predominate in a given declension.

DECLENSION	MOSTLY	BUT!	NEUTER?
1st	feminine	PAINS words are masculine	never
2nd	masculine	Trees are feminine	yes
3rd	all 3 genders		yes
4th	mostly masculine	*domus* (fem.) *manus* (sometimes fem.)	yes
5th	feminine	*diēs* (masc.)	never

If you don't remember the PAINS words of the 1st declension or the feminine words for trees, review the *Angulus Grammaticus* in Chapter 12.

Amīcī Falsī

You have now learned all five declensions. In the beginning you may have wondered why it was so important to learn both the nominative and genitive forms of each word in addition to the meaning. Now you know! Without this crucial information, you cannot know what case and number a word is in, as different endings in different declensions can look exactly the same.

These look-alike endings are called *amīcī falsī* or "false friends." The **only** way you will be able to tell the case and number of a word (and thus its function in the sentence) is by knowing its declension. So, if you were to see the unfamiliar word like *obsidum*, its ending might suggest that it was:

- an accusative singular from either *obsidus, -ī* (2ⁿᵈ) or *obsidus, -ūs* (4ᵗʰ).

or

- the genitive plural of *obsidēs, -is* (3ʳᵈ).

But the dictionary entry reads *obses, obsidis* m. hostage, and your choice is clear once you know both the declension and the stem.

Similarly, the ending of *frātrī* could be

- genitive singular or nominative plural of a word such as *frātrus, frātrī*

or

- dative singular from *frāter, frātris*.

The dictionary entry confirms that the form is dative singular.

Or consider the particularly tricky ending *-a*. Unless you know, for example, that *ancilla* is from *ancilla, ancillae* (1ˢᵗ f.) and *verba* is from *verbum, -ī* (2ⁿᵈ n.), you will not be able to tell which is feminine singular nominative and which is neuter plural nominative/accusative.

Remember: "When it doubt, look it up!"

Mōrēs Rōmānī

Theātra Rōmāna

Theaters were found in most Roman cities throughout the empire. Whereas the Greeks used their theaters primarily for dramatic performances, the Romans did not hesitate to mix various forms of entertainment in the same place. Comedies, tragedies, mimes, musical performances, and even the occasional acrobatic or gladiatorial contest were put on in Roman theaters. In addition to the comedies of Plautus (Ti. Maccius Plautus, c. 254–185 B.C.), the Romans liked to watch the comedies of Terence (P. Terentius Afer, c.185–159 B.C.), as well as tragedies like those of M. Pacuvius (c. 220–130 B.C.) and L. Accius (170–c. 86 B.C.). Many such works were written, but today we have only 20 comedies of Plautus (including *Amphitruō*) and six of Terence. The plots of most of these comedies are set in Greece and deal with situations from earlier Greek comedies—sons getting the better of their fathers and smart slaves deceiving their masters. Plautus' *Amphitruō* is unusual with its mythological plot.

Until the Theater of Pompey was built, c. 55 B.C., Rome had no permanent theater buildings made of stone, and these entertainments were held in temporary structures or in open spaces like the Forum.

The Theater of Marcellus, in which the two families see the performance of Plautus' *Amphitruō*, was dedicated by Augustus in 12 B.C. This building is the best preserved theater from ancient Rome, even though it was heavily changed in the medieval period and its upper levels have been replaced by modern apartments. Inside there was seating in three tiers for approximately 10,000–14,000 people. The stage (*scaena*) probably included a curtain (*vēlum*), which was dropped into a slot on the stage to start the show and not raised as it is today. Many Roman theaters were roofed over, but probably not the Theater of Marcellus, which may have had awnings (*vēla*) that could be drawn across the top to protect the audience from sun and rain, as in the Flavian Amphitheatre (the Colosseum).

Theātrum Marcellī Hodiē

Vergilius dē Marcellō Legit ā Jean-Joseph Taillasson

The Theater of Marcellus was named after Augustus' nephew, Marcus Claudius Marcellus (42–23 B.C.). Since Augustus never had a son of his own, it was natural that he would look to the son of his sister Octavia as a possible successor. Marcellus was married to Augustus' daughter Julia in 25 B.C. His untimely death at the age of 20 was apparently quite a shock and disappointment to the emperor.

Now look at two passages in which an Augustan author mentions Marcellus. We have simplified these poetic passages, mostly by changing the word order. But we have left some of the poetic phrasing, with some explanation.

Vergil refers to Marcellus twice in *Aeneid* 6 when the hero Aeneas journeys to the Underworld to see the ghost of his dead father Anchises. Anchises points out to his son all the great Romans of the future waiting to be born. Among them is Marcellus' ancestor and namesake, Marcus Claudius Marcellus (c. 268 B.C.–208 B.C.), a great general during the First Punic War. Use the *Verba Ūtenda* and note that all the words marked in **bold** refer to Marcellus. Can you find the deponent verb in these lines?

> Aspice ut **Marcellus insignis** spoliīs opīmīs ingreditur, et **victor** omnēs virōs superēminet!
>
> *Aeneid* 6.855–856

Notice how Vergil uses an imperative (*aspice*) to draw Aeneas' and your attention to Marcellus. The general is coming forward "conspicuous with his plunder" (*insignis spoliīs opīmīs*) and stands out (*superēminet*) as a victor over all men.

Vergil then writes the following lines about Augustus' nephew Marcellus, the general's descendent. Remember that the young man was dead when Vergil wrote the lines, but in the dramatic scene he is writing Marcellus is yet to be born. Be sure to use the notes and vocabulary that follow. Can you find one 4th declension and two 5th declension nouns in these lines?

> Nec puer quisquam dē gente Īliacā avōs Latīnōs in tantum spē tollet, nec Rōmula tellūs quondam ullō alumnō sē tantum iactābit. Heu pietās, heu fidēs prisca, et heu dextera manus invicta bellō! ... Heu, miserande puer, sī quā viā fāta aspera rumpās, tū Marcellus eris.
>
> *Aeneid* 6.875–879; 882–883

By tradition, when Vergil recited these lines to Augustus and his family, Marcellus' mother Octavia fainted. This scene has been a popular theme for artists, including Jean-Joseph Taillasson (1745–1809), whose painting is depicted at the top of the page.

🔊 VERBA ŪTENDA

alumnus, -ī m. foster son

avus, -ī m. ancestor

dextera manus right hand. Marcellus' right hand was never conquered in war (*invicta bellō*) because the boy had served in the army in Spain under Augustus in 25 B.C.

gens, gentis f. family, tribe

heu alas

iactō (1) (with sē) boast

Īliacus, -a, -um Trojan (Augustus claimed Trojan descent through Aeneas.)

ingredior, ingredī, ingressus enter, go in

insignis, insigne notable, famous

invictus, -a, -um unconquered

miserandus, -a, -um pitiable

opīmus, -a, -um rich, plentiful

pietās, pietātis f. reverence, respect

priscus, -a, -um ancient

quā viā by any way

quisquam, quicquam any

quondam someday

Rōmula tellūs = Rōma

Rōmulus, -a, -um of Romulus (the founder of Rome)

rumpō, rumpere, rūpī burst, break down; *sī ...rumpās* "if you should break"

spēs, speī f. hope, expectation

spolium, -iī n. spoil of war

superēmineō, superēminēre stand out over

tantum so much, to such a degree

tellūs, tellūris f. earth, land

ut how

victor, victōris m. conqueror

Latīna Hodierna

Rēs and *Diēs* in Modern Usage

Rēs and *diēs* are the two most common words of the 5th declension, and each has had quite an impact on our culture. In Latin *rēs* means basically "thing." The Latin term *rēs pūblica* literally means "the public thing, the public affair." The Romans used it to refer to their government, i.e., the "republic." *Rēs gestae* ("things done" or "deeds") refers especially to Augustus' auto-biography, *Rēs Gestae Dīvī Augustī* ("The Deeds of the Divine Augustus").

Rēs is especially common in modern legal parlance, where it has come to mean many different things. Consider these common legal terms:

res iudicata	"A matter already adjudicated."
res ipsa loquitur	"The matter speaks for itself." Used in cases where the issue seems open and shut and is so obvious that little argument is needed.
res nova	"A new thing." Something not decided before.
res nullius	"A thing of no one." "Nobody's thing." Referring to property that has no obvious owner.

Diēs appears in the expression *Carpe diem* ("Seize the day")—the motto of Epicurean philosophers—and in *Diēs Īrae* ("Day of Wrath"), the title of a medieval Christian poem/song about the day of judgment. The modern uses of *diēs* include the following legal, financial, and medical terms:

ad alium diem	"to another day," referring to the deferment of a meeting to another day
ad certum diem	"to a certain day," referring to the fixing of a meeting for a set day
ad diem	"to the day," referring to the day appointed
ante diem	"before the day," referring to the termination of a contract before the day fixed in the contract
per diem	"by day," referring especially to a daily spending allowance
post diem	"after the day," referring to after the due date
sine die	"without a day," referring to adjournment of a meeting without setting a day to reconvene. You will hear politicians pronouncing it "Sign day."
alternis diebus	"on alternate days," referring to taking a drug every other day
bis in die	"two times in a day," referring to taking a drug twice a day

Orbis Terrārum Rōmānus

Geōgraphia Italica

Did you notice Aelius' reference to the Alps and Apennine mountains in *Lectiō Prīma*? The geography of the Italian peninsula had a great impact on Rome's history, and average Romans like Aelius were well aware of basic features of their homeland. Here are some important facts about Italian geography:

- Since Italy is a peninsula (*paeninsula, -ae* f. i.e., "almost an island"), the sea (*mare, maris* n.) is never far away. Sea travel, albeit dangerous, was a fact of Roman life. The sea provided essential food for the Italian diet.

- Eventually the Romans came to call the Mediterranean Sea *Mare Nostrum* because their empire surrounded it, but the Romans also had separate names for the waters surrounding Italy. The two most important of these are: *(H)adriāticum Mare*, the Adriatic Sea, to the east of Italy, and, to the south, the *Ionium Mare*, the Ionic Sea separating Italy from Greece. To the west was the *Mare Tyrrhēnicum* (Tyrrhenian Sea).

- The Apennine mountain range (*Apennīnī, -ōrum* m. pl.) runs along the entire spine of Italy and divides the peninsula in half. Travel across these mountains from east to west was extremely difficult. This mountain range is a major reason why it took the

Italia ē Caelō

Romans so long to consolidate their control over the peninsula. The Alps (*Alpēs, Alpium* f. pl.) provide a natural barrier to the north between Italy and the rest of Europe. Hannibal's daring march across the Alps during the Second Punic War therefore took Rome by surprise.

- The Po river (*Padus, -ī* m.), flowing through the northern part of the peninsula, created a very fertile agricultural region in the area the Romans called Cisalpine Gaul.
- Rome is located on the Tiber River (*Tiberis, Tiberis* m.) at the first ford, about seven miles from the sea. The salt beds at the mouth of the Tiber were probably an important resource in the growth of the city.
- Sardinia (*Sardinia*) and Sicily (*Sicilia*), the two large islands that are part of modern Italy, were not politically part of Italy at the time of Augustus. They were provinicial areas.

QUID PUTĀS?

1. Compare the untimely death of Marcellus to that of a modern American who might have been thought of as "next in line" to succeed to some important post.
2. How does a Roman theater like the Theater of Marcellus compare in size and design to a modern American theater? What do you think it would have been like to attend a performance in such a theater?
3. Why do you think modern lawyers continue to employ Latin terms?
4. Is any part of the United States somewhat like Italy in its geography?

EXERCEĀMUS!

24-7 Scrībāmus

Use the information in the *Orbis Terrārum Rōmānus* to complete the following short essay about the geography of Italy.

Rōma in Italia est. Italia paeninsula est. Ad septentriōnēs (*north*) sunt montēs (1) _____. Ab oriente (*east*) est Mare (2) _____. Ad merīdiem (*south*) est Mare (3) _____. Ad occidentem (*west*) est Mare (4) _____. Per Italiam currunt montēs (5) _____. Per Rōmam fluit flūmen (*river*) (6) _____. Ad septentriōnēs fluit flūmen magnum (7) _____. Duo insulae magnae sunt (8) _____ et (9) _____.

24-8 Colloquāmur

The following skit has four speaking parts. You know most of the dialogue, so put your efforts into making the lines sound "real" and in adding the gestures that should go with the feelings the characters are experiencing.

Narrātor: Paulō post Mercurius abit sed Alcmēna et Iuppiter-Amphitruō haec dīcunt.
Iuppiter: Bene valē, Alcmēna. Mihi necesse est abhinc īre.
Alcmēna: Nōn mihi placet. Quandō revertēris?
Iuppiter: Fidem habē, cāra uxor. Mox revertar! Hoc tibi polliceor!
Narrātor: Et, paulō post, quid vident spectātōrēs? Illum Amphitruōnem vērum. Ā portū domum suum aggreditur. Alcmēna eum spectat et manūs ad faciem tollēns laetē exclāmat:
Alcmēna: Revēnistī ad mē! Tam laeta sum! Sed nūper ē lectō meō abiistī!
Narrātor: Tunc Amphitruō uxōris manum capiēns dīcit:
Amphitruō: Quid dīcis? Ē lectō? Haec rēs mala mihi est! Ego mensēs multōs iam absum. Quid agitur?

24-9 Verba Discenda

The words marked in **bold** in this short narrative are derived from *Verba Discenda* for this chapter. Identify these Latin words.

The **spectators** (1) only thought **it was decent** (2) to pay attention to the **sequel** (3). They were all in a rather **jovial** (4) mood as they watched the **gradual** (5) **progress** (6) of the talented lead actor, a rather **eloquent** (7) but **loquacious** (8) fellow, onto the stage. At a **uniform** (9) pace he **ascended** (10) the stage, took the instruction **manual** (11) from the table, turned to face the audience, and fell flat on his **face** (12).

🔊 VERBA DISCENDA

ascendō, ascendere, ascendī, ascensum climb, ascend [ascendant]

cōnor, cōnārī, cōnātus sum try

decet, decēre, decuit (+ dat. + inf.) imp. it is fitting

diēs, diēī m. day [per diem]

dīves, dīvitis rich, talented

domus, -ūs f. house [domicile]

ēloquor, ēloquī, ēlocūtus sum speak out, declare [eloquent]

faciēs, faciēī f. face, appearance, beauty [facial]

forma, -ae f. shape, form; beauty; ground plan [formation]

fruor, fruī, fructus/fruitus sum (+ abl.) enjoy, profit by

fungor, fungī, functus sum (+ abl.) perform, discharge [function]

gradus, -ūs m. step, pace, tier (of a theater) [gradation]

ingredior, ingredī, ingressus sum enter [ingress]

Iuppiter, Iovis m. Jupiter, king of the gods [jovial]

loquor, loquī, locūtus sum speak, talk, say [loquacious]

manus, -ūs f. hand [manumission]

mentior, mentīrī, mentītus sum lie, deceive

patior, patī, passus sum suffer, allow [patience, passion]

polliceor, pollicērī, pollicitus sum promise

·*potior, potīrī, potītus sum* (+ abl. or gen.) take possession of, get, acquire

prōgredior, prōgredī, prōgressus sum go to, advance, march forward, proceed [progressive]

rēs, reī f. thing, matter, business, affair; reason

sequor, sequī, secūtus sum follow [sequence, consecutive]

simul together, altogether, at the same time, all at once [simultaneous]

sonitus, -ūs m. sound

speciēs, speciēī f. appearance, look, type [species]

spectātor, spectātōris m. spectator, observer

·*ūtor, ūtī, ūsus sum* (+ abl.) use, employ, enjoy, experience

vereor, verērī, veritus sum be afraid of, fear, show reverence to

Angulus Grammaticus

Oh No, Not Semi-Deponents, Too!

Although deponent verbs are very common in Latin, the concept of a deponent verb is almost unique to the Latin language. Greek, both ancient and modern, is one of the few other languages with deponents. Knowing a little bit about Greek will make you feel a little better about Latin deponents, because Greek deponent verbs are even more complicated than Latin ones. Greek has not one kind of deponent, but two. In addition to passive verbs translated actively (like Latin), Greek also has another voice, called middle (in which the subject performs the action on or for himself or herself). Some of these middle verbs are translated actively. A good example is the Greek verb ἔρχομαι (*erchomai*, I come or I go), which is middle/passive in form but active in meaning.

Now that you recognize the special nature of deponent verbs, you can become a real grammar dilettante and learn about **semi-deponents**. Semi-deponents are a blend of active and deponent forms in the same verb. You will see this clearly in their principal parts. Here are four semi-deponent Latin verbs with the deponent forms marked in **bold**:

>*audeō, audēre, **ausus sum*** dare
>*fīdō, fīdere, **fīsus sum*** (+ dat.) trust in
>*gaudeō, gaudēre, **gāvīsus sum*** rejoice
>*soleō, solēre, **solitus sum*** (+ inf.) be in the habit of, be accustomed to

So *audeō* means "I dare" whereas *ausus sum* means "I dared."

What is important is that you can learn to recognize and translate forms like *fīsus est,* "he trusted in." Let the principal parts be your guide. The first two are obviously active. When the 3rd principal part is passive instead of active, you know it is deponent.

And you will soon learn about *fīō*, which is active in form but passive in meaning in the present, future, and imperfect. Just the opposite of a deponent verb!

Sepulcrum Obstetrīcis Rōmānae

GRAMMATICA

Imperfect Tense of Deponent Verbs
Infinitives, Imperatives, and Present
    Participles of Deponent Verbs

MŌRĒS RŌMĀNĪ

Birthing in the Roman World

LATĪNA HODIERNA

Latin in the Maternity Ward

ORBIS TERRĀRUM RŌMĀNUS

Alexandrīa

ANGULUS GRAMMATICUS

Bending Language: Linguistic Limitations
    and Linguistic Flexibility

LECTIŌNĒS:

MĒDĒA OBSTETRIX
and
SERVĪLIĪ CONSILIA

Licinia's family seeks a midwife to assist
in the birth of her child, while Servilius
and his family prepare for a big dinner
with an impressive guest list.

25

Parātūs Magnī

Lectiō Prīma

Antequam Legis

In this chapter you meet Medea, the midwife who will help Licinia give birth. Most neighborhoods had such midwives, many of whom were former slaves. Medea's name is ironic, since Medea, a witch from Colchis, was famous in mythology for killing her children to get even with her husband, Jason, who had left her for a young princess. Our Medea is from Thrace, another land famous for witchcraft, and her former owners undoubtedly found the name amusing.

This reading also introduces the imperfect passive of regular and deponent verbs.

Imperfect Passives and Deponents

If you remember the telltale *-ba-* as the mark of the imperfect, you will have no trouble recognizing and translating the imperfect passive of regular and deponent verbs. Here are the first imperfect passives you will find in the reading:

*nītē**bā**tur*	she was straining
*adiuvā**bā**tur*	she was being helped

Can you tell from the translations which one of these verbs is deponent?

EXERCEĀMUS!

25-1 **Deponents in the Imperfect Tense**

As you read *Lectiō Prīma*, answer the following Latin questions in complete English sentences. Each question asks you to find the subject of a deponent verb in the imperfect tense. All these deponents are marked in **bold** in the reading. Follow the model.

→ Quis nītē**bā**tur? (line 1)   Licinia was struggling.

1. Quī prōgrediē**ba**ntur? (line 2)
2. Quis prōgrediē**bā**tur? (line 11)
3. Quis cōnā**bā**tur iuvāre? (line 11)
4. Quī moriē**ba**ntur? (line 12)
5. Quis saccum intuē**bā**tur? (line 18)
6. Quis instrūmentīs ūtē**bā**tur? (lines 19–20)
7. Quis lentē proficīscē**bā**tur? (line 23)
8. Quis Mēdēam sequē**bā**tur? (line 23)
9. Quis precēs fervidās loquē**bā**tur? (lines 24)

🔊 MĒDĒA OBSTETRIX

Licinia, quae iam in dolōre magnō erat et **nītēbātur,** adiuvābātur ē theātrō ā mātre virōque. Per viās Rōmae lentē **prōgrediēbantur** et mox insulae suae appropinquābant.

Valeria "Māter!" clāmāvit, "Nōs adiuvā. Mox Licinia pariet! Flāvia, de-
5 scende et aquam nōbīs fer. Aelī, ī celeriter et Mēdēam mihi arcesse! Eam fer ad auxilium nostrum."

Aelius iānuās fortiter pulsāvit

Mēdēa obstetrix, quae Rōmam ā Thrāciā vēnerat, multōs annōs in Subūrā habitābat et multae fēminae gravidae Rōmānae multōs per annōs ab eā adiuvābantur. In Rōmā antīquā, praesertim fēminīs pauperibus, parere
10 perīculōsum erat. Saepe obstetrix per viās Rōmānās mediā nocte ad domicil-ia fēminārum gravidārum *prōgrediēbātur* et fortiter eās iuvāre **cōnābātur.** Sed gravida Rōmāna semper in perīculō erat et multae **moriēbantur.**

Aelius cucurrit per viās et, cōnāns obstetrīcem invenīre, iānuam Mēdēae fortiter pulsāvit. "Mēdēa! Mēdēa! Cūr ad iānuam nōn aggrederis? Diēs partūs adest! Nisi mēcum vēneris, uxor mea multa patiētur."
15 Mēdēa "Salvē, Aelī!" inquit. "Perturbātus vidēris. Nōlī timēre. Omnia salva erunt. Nōlī cunctārī! Tē sequar et mox uxor tua infantem sānum et salvum pariet. Postquam infantem in brāchiīs tenueris, laetior eris."

Mēdēa saccum parvum cēpit et Aeliō id dedit.

Aelius saccum **intuēbātur** et "Quid" rogāvit, "inest?"

"In saccō omnia—herbās, instrūmenta—quibus prō sānitāte uxōris tuae et infantis futūrī ūtar, habeō. Mihi
20 crēde, mī Aelī, illīs in Thrāciā **ūtēbar** et nunc cōtīdiē eīsdem ūtor. Multae fēminae in Thrāciā iam ā Mēdēā **adiuvābantur** et hodiē ūna alia adiuvābitur."

Mēdēa "Mēne," inquit, "nunc quiētē sequēris? Festīnā! Et mox omnēs mīrāculum parvum mīrābimur!"

Mēdēa, quae septuāgintā duo annōs nāta erat, lentē **proficiscēbātur.** Aelius eam **sequēbātur** et intrā sē precēs fervidās **loquēbātur.**

🔊 VERBA ŪTENDA

arcessō, arcessere, arcessīvī/
  arcessiī summon
auxilium, -iī n. help, aid;
  pl. auxiliary forces
crēdō, crēdere, crēdidī,
  crēditum (+ dat.)
  believe, trust
cunctor, cunctārī,
  cunctātus sum
  tarry, linger,
  hesitate
descendō, descendere,
  descendī go down,
  descend
domicilium, -iī n. home
fervidus, -a, -um fervent
futūrus, -a, -um future

gravidus, -a, -um
  pregnant
iānua, -ae f. door
insum, inesse, infuī be in
instrūmentum, -ī n. tool,
  instrument
intrā (+ acc.) within
intueor, intuērī, intuitus
  sum look at, gaze at;
  consider
iuvō, iuvāre, iūvī, iūtum
  help
Mēdēa, -ae f. Medea, the
  midwife
mīrāculum, -ī n. miracle
mīror, mīrārī, mīrātus
  sum wonder at, admire

morior, morī die
nisi unless
nītor, nītī exert oneself,
  struggle, strain
obstetrix, -icis f. midwife
herba, -ae f. herb
pariō, parere, peperī,
  paritum/partum bring
  forth, give birth, bear,
  create
partus, -ūs m. childbirth
pauper, pauperis poor
perīculōsus, -a, -um
  dangerous
perturbātus, -a, -um very
  frightened

praesertim especially,
  particularly
prex, precis f. prayer
proficiscor, proficiscī depart
quiētus, -a, -um calm,
  quiet
salvus, -a, -um safe, well
sānitās, sānitātis f. health
sānus, -a, -um healthy
septuāgintā seventy
Subūra, -ae f. Subura,
  a district in Rome
Thrācia, -ae f. Thrace, a
  Roman province located
  in what is now part of
  Greece, Bulgaria, and
  Turkey

POSTQUAM LĒGISTĪ

Read back through *Lectiō Prīma* and identify the speaker of each of these statements.

1. "Māter! Nōs adiuvā. Mox Licinia pariet!"
2. "Mēdēa! Mēdēa! Cūr ad iānuam nōn aggrederis? Diēs partūs adest! Nisi mēcum vēneris, uxor mea multa patiētur."
3. "Postquam infantem tuum in brāchiīs tenueris, laetior eris."
4. "Quid inest?"
5. "Illīs in Thrāciā ūtēbar et nunc cōtīdiē eīsdem ūtor."
6. "Mēne nunc quiētē sequeris?"

Grammatica A

Imperfect Tense of Deponent Verbs

The imperfect tense of deponents is formed exactly like regular imperfect passives, but remember to translate deponents like active verbs.

	PASSIVE		DEPONENT	
Singular				
1st	adiuvā**bar**	I was being helped	loquē**bar**	I was saying
2nd	adiuvā**bāris**	you were being helped	loquē**bāris**	you were saying
3rd	adiuvā**bātur**	he/she/it was being helped	loquē**bātur**	he/she/it was saying
Plural				
1st	adiuvā**bāmur**	we were being helped	loquē**bāmur**	we were saying
2nd	adiuvā**bāminī**	you were being helped	loquē**bāminī**	you were saying
3rd	adiuvā**bantur**	they were being helped	loquē**bantur**	they were saying

EXERCEĀMUS!

25-2 Deponent or Passive?

Translate each verb form marked in **bold** in a way that shows you know whether the verb is a deponent or a true passive. Follow the model.

→ Aelius et Valeria ad insulam suam **aggrediēbantur**.   (they) were approaching

1. Mēdēa ab Aeliō **adiuvābātur**.
2. Herbae et instrūmenta Mēdēae in saccum **pōnēbantur**.
3. Aelius Mēdēam per viās **sequēbātur**.
4. Fēminae Rōmānae in domibus suīs semper **pariēbantur**.
5. In Thrāciā semper **proficiscēbar** ad fēminās.
6. Mēdēa numquam adiuvāre **cunctābātur**.
7. Valeria in lectō **inveniēbātur**.

Lectiō Secunda

Antequam Legis

In *Lectiō Secunda* Servilius lays out his plans to win over Augustus' support when he runs for the office of praetor (*praetor, praetōris* m.). During the Roman Republic, the praetorship was second only to the consulship in importance. Praetors served as judges and administrators in Rome, in the military and in the provinces. Servilius is running for *praetor urbānus*, which would position him, in the traditional *cursus honōrum*, or order of offices, to run for consul eventually. A praetor had *imperium*, or power, wore a special toga called the *toga praetexta*, sat in a special chair of honor (*sella curūlis*) in the basilica or law court, and was attended by six lictors in the administration of his office. In the coin depicted at right, you can see M. Iunius Brutus, one of the leaders of the assassination of Julius Caesar, walking as consul among lictors.

Magistrātus Rōmānus Lictōrēsque

To advance his political ambitions, Servilius plans to present a copy of a rare book to C. Clinius Maecenas, Augustus' "Minister of Culture." The book is the *Aetia* (*Causes*) written by Callimachus (c. 280–243 B.C.), a poet who also served as head of the Library at Alexandria in Egypt. Callimachus was very popular with the poets of the Augustan age, and Servilius hopes the gift will help win over the support of Augustus and Maecenas for Servilius' campaign to become praetor.

As you read, look at the way the infinitives, imperatives, and present participles of deponent verbs are formed.

Infinitives, Imperatives, and Present Participles of Deponent Verbs

As you would expect, deponent infinitives are simply the present passive infinitive translated actively; for example, *cōnārī* (to try); *pollicērī* (to promise); *sequī* (to follow); *patī* (to allow); and *mentīrī* (to lie).

Deponent imperatives end in *-re* in the singular and *-minī* in the plural; for example, *Cōnāre!/Cōnāminī!* (Try!); *Pollicēre!/Pollicēminī!* (Promise!); *Sequere!/Sequiminī!* (Follow!); *Patere!/Patiminī!* (Allow! Let!); and *Mentīre!/Mentīminī!* (Lie!).

To form present participles, deponent verbs use the active endings you already know: *cōnāns* (trying); *pollicēns* (promising); *sequēns* (following); *patiēns* (suffering); and *mentiēns* (lying). This participle is an exception to the rule that deponent verbs use passive endings. Just translate the participle as you usually would, with **-ing**. So, in *Lectiō Prīma* you probably had no trouble translating the phrase ***cōnāns obstetrīcem invenīre*** as "**trying** to find the midwife."

All deponent infinitives, imperatives, and present participles are marked in **bold** in *Lectiō Secunda*.

EXERCEĀMUS!

25-3 Imperatives, Infinitives, and Present Active Participles of Deponent Verbs

You will find a number of imperatives, infinitives, and present active participles of deponent verbs marked in **bold** in *Lectiō Secunda*. Before you read, make three columns on a sheet of paper. Then sort the forms into imperatives, infinitives, and participles. Follow the model.

Line	Imperatives	Infinitives	Participles
→ 2			colloquentēs

SERVĪLIĪ CONSILIA

In aliā parte urbis Servīlius et Caecilia Metella sedentēs in peristȳliō domī et dē Servīliā **colloquentēs** inveniuntur. Perturbātī sunt quod fīlia cāra sua tam infēlix est, sed laetī quoque sunt. Servīlius cum Caeciliā dē epistulā, quae nūper ā Maecēnāte advēnit, colloquitur.

Servīlius et Caecilia sedentēs in peristȳliō

5   "Cāra," inquit, "**intuēre** hanc epistulam Maecēnātis!"

Caecilia, epistulam in manibus tollēns et magnā cum cūrā signum Maecēnātis **intuēns**, eam legit.

Paulō post **mīrāns** "Vērumne est?" uxor inquit. "Maecēnās apud nōs erit? Nōn crēdō! Vērēne prōgradiētur ad convīvium nostrum Maecēnās ipse? Ille praeclārus Maecēnās quī Augustī
10 amīcus et artium patrōnus maximus est? Sed cūr? Cūr ad nōs tam praeclārus vir **prōgredī** vult?"

Servīlius "Nōlī **oblīviscī**," inquit, "cāra uxor, meī dōnī! Annō superiōre, cum ad Aegyptum iter faciēbam, librum quī in Bibliothēcā Alexandrīnā fuerat, ēmī. Papȳrus magnī pretiī erat, et mox hic liber mē praetōrem faciet."

Caecilia: "Quōmodo rēs simplex tibi tam magnum auxilium feret?"

Servīlius: "Sed, mea uxor, **recordāre**! Hic liber nullō modō simplex, sed rārissimus est. Liber *Aetia* Callimachī
15 ōlim in Bibliothēcā Alexandrīnā erat sed nōn ab igne cōnsūmēbātur. Hunc librum invēnī et hoc est dōnum quod Imperātōrī Augustō dare volō. *Aetia* Maecēnātī apud convīvium nostrum dabō et tunc Augustus mihi auxilium feret cum praetōrem petam."

Caecilia quiēta est, multa dē convīviō futūrō **contemplāns**. "Mihi," intrā sē cōgitat, "cum servīs et coquō **colloquī** necesse est. Omnēs hospitēs apud nōs **epulantēs** cibīs vīnīsque praesertim optimīs fruentur. Illīs apud mē
20 **epulantibus** cibīs et vīnīs optimīs semper **fruī** decet!"

Caecilia ē **sellā oriēns**, ad sē Sicōnem, quī coquus Servīliōrum est, et Pardaliscam, quae "magistra ancillārum" apud Servīliōs est, convocat. Caecilia "Sicō!" inquit "Pardalisca! Mē **sequiminī** ad culīnam! Nōlīte **cunctārī**!"

Coquus et ancilla, dominam suam per iānuam **sequentēs**, intrā sē cōgitant: "Quid nunc?"

VERBA ŪTENDA

Aegyptus, -ī f. Egypt, a province of Rome

Aetia, -ōrum "The Causes," title of a book by Callimachus, a famous Greek poet who lived in the 3ʳᵈ century B.C.

Alexandrīnus, -a, -um Alexandrian, pertaining to the city in Egypt

annō superiōre "last year"

auxilium, -iī n. help, aid; pl. auxiliary forces

bibliothēca, -ae f. library

Callimachus, ī m. Callimachus, poet and chief librarian at Alexandria

colloquor, colloquī, collocūtus sum talk together, converse

cōnsūmō, cōnsūmere, cōnsumpsī consume

convīvium, -iī n. feast, banquet

convocō (1) call together

coquus, -ī m. cook

crēdō, crēdere, crēdidī, creditum (+ dat.) believe, trust

culīna, -ae f. kitchen

cunctor, cunctārī, cunctātus sum tarry, linger, hesitate

domina, -ae f. mistress (of the house), the woman in charge; ma'am

epulor, epulārī feast

hospes, hospitis m. guest

iānua, -ae f. door

ignis, ignis m. fire

imperātor, -ōris m. commander, ruler

infēlix, infēlīcis unhappy

iter facere to make a journey

intrā (+ acc.) within

intueor, intuērī, intuitus sum look at, gaze at; consider

Maecēnās, Maecēnātis m. Maecenas, Augustus' close friend and advisor

mīror, mīrārī, mīrātus sum wonder at, admire

oblīviscor, oblīviscī (+ gen.) forget

orior, orīrī rise

nūper recently, not long ago

papȳrus, -ī f. papyrus

Pardalisca, -ae f. Pardalisca, woman's name

patrōnus, -ī m. patron

paulō somewhat, by a little

peristȳlium, -iī n. peristyle, courtyard, colonnaded garden

perturbātus, -a, -um disturbed, confused

praesertim especially, particularly

praetor, -ōris m. praetor, judge

quiētus, -a, -um calm, quiet

rārus, -a, -um rare

recordor, recordārī remember

sella, -ae f. chair

Sicō, Sicōnis m. Sico, a man's name

signum, -ī n. seal

simplex, simplicis simple, naive

superiōre with *annō* "last"

POSTQUAM LĒGISTĪ

Aut Vērum Aut Falsum. Indicate whether each of the following statements based on *Lectiō Secunda* is true (*vērum*) or false (*falsum*). If you think the sentence is false, rewrite it to make it true. Don't simply add a negative word like *nōn*, but rewrite the sentence positively. Follow the model.

→ In hāc lectiōne Servīlius et Lūcius dē Lūciō colloquuntur.
　　Falsum. In hāc lectiōne Servīlius et Caecilia dē Servīliā colloquuntur.

1. Epistula nūper ā Maecēnāte ad Servīlium advēnit.
2. Parentēs perturbātī sunt quod fīlia cāra infēlix est.
3. Augustus ipse ad convīvium Servīliī prōgrediētur.
4. Maecēnās Servīliī amīcus et lūdōrum patrōnus maximus est.
5. Annō superiōre Servīlius iter ad Crētam faciēbat.
6. Maecēnās librum quī in Bibliothēcā Alexandrīnā fuerat, ēmit.
7. Hic liber cārus et rārissimus est.
8. Servīlius praetōrem petet.
9. Caecilia cum fīliīs et fīliā colloquī vult.
10. Pardalisca coqua est.
11. Servī Caeciliam ad culīnam sequuntur.

Papȳrus

Grammatica B

Infinitives, Imperatives, and Present Participles of Deponent Verbs

Here are the infinitives of deponent verbs in *Lectiō Secunda*.

　　*Cūr ad nōs tam praeclarus vir **prōgredī** vult?*
　　Why does so famous a man want **to come** to our house?

　　*Cum servīs et coquō **colloquī** mihi necesse est.*
　　It is necessary for me **to speak** with the slaves and the cook.

　　*Illīs cibīs et vīnīs optimīs **fruī** semper decet.*
　　It is fitting for them always **to enjoy** the best food and wines.

　　*Nōlī **oblīviscī**!*
　　Don't forget!

As long as you remember to translate these infinitive forms actively, you should have little difficulty understanding the infinitives of deponent verbs. You will, of course, also remember that the infinitive is the 2nd principle part of a deponent verb: for example *colloquor, **colloquī**, collocūtus sum.*

　　Three imperatives of deponent verbs appear in *Lectiō Secunda:*

　　Recordāre!　　　　　Remember!
　　Intuēre hanc epistulam!　Look at this letter!
　　Mē sequiminī!　　　　Follow me!

You have not seen these passive imperative endings before because they are fairly rare with non-deponent verbs, but you could, for example, tell quiet speakers to speak up by saying *Audīre!/Audīminī!* (Be heard!). Deponent imperatives, however, are fairly common. The patterns are not difficult. The singular imperative passive/deponent is easy to spot because it looks like an active infinitive (the *-re* is really a contraction of *-ris*).

　　Cōnare!　　Try!
　　Pollicēre!　Promise!
　　Sequere!　Follow!
　　Patere!　　Endure!
　　Mentīre!　Lie!

The plural imperative ending is same as the 2nd person singular indicative. So, depending on context, the form *sequiminī* can mean either "you follow" or "Follow!" Negative imperatives for deponent verbs are formed by using the infinitive with *Nōlī/Nōlīte*: for example, *Nōlī pollicērī/Nōlīte pollicērī!* (Don't promise!).

Here are some of the deponent verbs used as present active participles in *Lectiō Secunda*.

> *Servīlius et Caecilia Metella dē Servīliā* **colloquentēs**
> Servilius and Caecilia Metella, **speaking together** about Servilia
>
> *Caecilia ē sellā* **oriēns**
> Caecilia, **rising** from her chair
>
> *multa de convīviō futūrō* **contemplāns**
> **contemplating** many things about the upcoming dinner
>
> *Coquus et ancilla dominam suam* **sequentēs** *intrā sē cōgitant.*
> **Following** their mistress, the cook and maid servant think to themselves.

These participles act exactly like others you have seen before. They become tricky only when you think too hard and say, "Wait a minute. Deponent verbs have passive endings." Since there is no present **passive** participle in Latin, Romans had to use the present **active** participle endings to make present participles for deponent verbs.

Here is a summary of deponent forms introduced in this reading:

	1ST CONJUGATION	2ND CONJUGATION	3RD CONJUGATION	3RD CONJUGATION - *IŌ*	4TH CONJUGATION
Infinitive					
	cōnārī	pollicērī	sequī	patī	mentīrī
Imperative					
singular	Cōnāre!	Pollicēre!	Sequere!	Patere!	Mentīre!
plural	Cōnāminī!	Pollicēminī!	Sequiminī!	Patiminī!	Mentīminī!
Negative Imperative					
singular	Nōlī cōnārī!	Nōlī pollicērī!	Nōlī sequī!	Nōlī patī!	Nōlī mentīrī!
plural	Nōlīte cōnārī!	Nōlīte pollicērī!	Nōlīte sequī!	Nōlīte patī!	Nōlīte mentīrī!
Present Participle					
	cōnāns	pollicēns	sequēns	patiēns	mentiēns

EXERCEĀMUS!

25-4 Imperatives of Deponent Verbs

Change the following negative imperatives to positive imperatives; i.e., instead of saying not to do something, say "Do it!" Then translate the command into English. Follow the model. HINT: Pay attention to singulars and plurals!

→ Nōlī mīrārī!   *Mīrāre!* Be amazed!

1. Nōlīte patī!
2. Nōlī loquī!
3. Nōlī mentīrī!
4. Nōlīte pollicērī!
5. Nōlīte meī dōnī oblīviscī!
6. Nōlī hanc epistulam intuērī!
7. Nōlīte mē sequī!
8. Nōlī cunctārī!

25-5 **Present Participles of Deponent Verbs**

Choose the participle that agrees with each noun. Then translate the phrase. Follow the model.
HINT: Do not try to pick the participle until you are sure of the GNC of the noun!

→ vir (mīrantem; mīrantēs; mīrantī; mīrāns)

vir mīrāns the man wondering or the wondering man

1. māter (loquentis; loquentēs; loquēns; loquentium)
2. Maecēnātis (prōgredientis; prōgredientēs; prōgredientem; prōgrediente)
3. uxōrī (pollicente; pollicentibus; pollicentī; pollicēns)
4. servī (prōgredientēs; prōgredientium; prōgrediēns; prōgredientī)
5. Mēdēae (mīrante; mīrantibus; mīrantis; mīrāns)
6. Aeliō (loquēns; loquente; loquentēs; loquentis)
7. virōs (mentiēns; mentiente; mentientēs; mentientem)
8. mīrāculum (prōgrediēns; prōgredientium; prōgredientibus; prōgredientis)
9. ancillīs (pollicentis; pollicentibus; pollicēns; pollicente)
10. magister (loquentis; loquentēs; loquēns; loquentibus)

Mōrēs Rōmānī

Birthing in the Roman World

There were no maternity hospitals in ancient Rome, and childbirth was always difficult and dangerous for both mother and infant. Mortality rates were high, even in the upper classes. Cicero's daughter Tullia, for example, died at the age of 33 of complications related to childbirth.

Upper-class women may have had the services of both an *obstetrix* like Medea and a physician, but most women had to settle for the help of the *obstetrix* (if they could afford her services) as well as family and friends.

Ancient midwives were not schooled. Rather, they learned their craft as apprentices and from experience, taking much of their herbal knowledge from the sort of folk medicine recorded by Pliny the Elder (C. Plinius Secundus, 23 A.D.–August 24, 79 A.D.). Most midwives were probably freedwomen, but wealthy households could own slaves who served as midwives. The only surviving ancient medical treatise on childbirth is the *Gynaecology*, written in Greek by the 2nd century A.D. physician Soranus.

Roman women gave birth in chairs like the one illustrated in the tombstone at the beginning of the chapter. The midwife sat or knelt in front of the pregnant woman, who was often attended by one or two other women as well.

We know something about Roman folk beliefs and practices regarding childbirth from the *Historia Nātūrālis* of Pliny the Elder. We do not recommend that you take any of these statements as true, but they do suggest ancient Roman attitudes toward a very important stage in human life. With a little help from the *Verba Ūtenda*, you should be able to read the following three slightly modified statements from Pliny.

Vulva [hyaenae] data in pōtū cum mālī Pūnicī dulcis cortice mulierum vulvae prōdest.

HN 28.27.102

Partūs mulierum lacte suis cum mulsō adiuvantur.

HN 28.77.250

Penna vulturīna, sūbiecta pedibus, [fēminās] parturientēs adiuvat.

HN 30.44.130

In the following statement Pliny suggests that a woman pregnant with a male child (*marem ferentī*) has better color (*melior color*) and an easier labor (*facilior partus*). On what day does Pliny say she will feel a male child move in her womb?

melior color et facilior partus [fēminae] marem ferentī est; mōtus in uterō quadrāgensimō diē.

HN 7.6.41

🔊 **VERBA ŪTENDA**

cortex, corticis m./f. skin, bark, rind
ferentī "to a woman bearing"
hyaena, -ae f. hyena
lac, lactis n. milk
mālus Pūnica, -i f. pomegranate (lit., "Punic apple")
mās, maris male
mōtus, -ūs m. movement
mulier, mulieris f. woman
mulsum, -ī n. warm drink of honey and wine
parturiō, parturīre, parturīvī /parturiī be pregnant, be in labor, give birth
partus, partūs m. childbirth
pēs, pedis m. foot
penna, -ae f. feather
pōtus, -ūs m. drink
prōsum, prōdesse, prōfuī (+ dat.) be useful to
quadrāgensimus, -a, -um fortieth
sūs, suis m./f. pig, sow
subiecta "placed under"; refers to *penna*
uterus, -ī m. womb, belly
vulva, -ae f. womb
vulturīnus, -a, -um of a vulture

Instrūmenta Obstetrīcis Rōmānae

Latīna Hodierna

Latin in the Maternity Ward

LATIN WORD	MEANING	ENGLISH DERIVATIVE	MEANING
obstetrix, -trīcis f.	midwife	obstetrics obstetrician	
placenta, -ae f.	flat cake	placenta	mammalian organ which nurtures the fetus in the uterus; the afterbirth
umbilīcus, -ī m.	center, middle: a. the center of the world b. a decorative knob c. the ornamental end of a cylinder around which a scroll was wrapped d. belly button	umbilicus	belly button
gravidus, -a, -um	pregnant	gravida nulligravida primigravida multigravida	a pregnant woman All of these words refer to a woman and her history of pregnancies. Can you see the differences among them?
forceps, forcipis f.	tongs, pincers	forceps	an obstetrical tool
fētus, -ūs m. *fētus, -a, -um*	birth, offspring, produce pregnant, fertile	fetus	an unborn child
puerpera, -ae f.	a woman in labor (related to *puer, -ī* m. boy, child)	puerperal puerperal fever	related to childbirth an infection following childbirth, often fatal well into the twentieth century
parturiō, parturīre, parturīvī/parturiī	be pregnant, be in labor, give birth to	parturient parturiency	bearing/about to bear a child
partus, -ūs m.	giving birth; fetus, offspring	postpartum	after birth, as in "post partum depression"
nātālis, nātāle	being born	prenatal	before birth
pariō, parere, peperī, paritum/ partum	bring forth, bear	nullipara primipara multipara	a woman who has not borne a child bearing a firstborn bearing many children

Orbis Terrārum Rōmānus

Alexandrīa

"Columen Pompēiī" Alexandrīae

The city of Alexandria in Egypt, where Servilius found his manuscript, was a major commercial and cultural center in the Greco-Roman world. Founded by Alexander the Great in 331 B.C., the city possessed one of the best harbors in the ancient Mediterranean. It became the capital of Egypt under the Ptolemies, who ruled Egypt after Alexander's death in 323 B.C. until 31 B.C. Following the Battle of Actium and the death of Cleopatra, Egypt came under the direct control of the Roman emperor. Egypt was so strategically important that Roman senators were forbidden to travel there without imperial permission. Servilius must have obtained such a dispensation, a sign of favor in Augustus' eyes.

The ancient city included a great palace and many temples, but it was best known for its Pharos, or lighthouse (one of the Seven Wonders of the Ancient World), and for the great *Mūsēum* (Museum) or Library of Alexandria, from which the manuscript of *Aetia* was obtained.

Very little of Greco-Roman Alexandria is visible today. The best known feature is the so-called "Pompey's Pillar," depicted at right, which actually has nothing to do with the Roman general who died near Alexandria in 48 B.C. This pillar was actually erected during the reign of the emperor Diocletian (c. 244–311). Also prominent are the remains of the Roman theater depicted on the following page.

Pharos Alexandrīae

The dimensions of the Pharos, built in the 3rd century B.C. under the Ptolemies, are uncertain, but the structure was so tall that its light was said to be visible more than 30 miles from land. The Pharos collapsed in an earthquake in the 14th century. Some remains of the lighthouse were found by underwater archaeologists in 1994.

The Library at Alexandria was the largest in the ancient world. Like the Pharos, it was built in the 3rd century B.C. The early librarians at Alexandria, including the Greek epic poet Apollonius of Rhodes, were great book collectors and brought to the library written works from all over the Mediterranean world.

In *Lectiō Secunda* Servilius refers to a fire at the Library during Julius Caesar's siege, but this fire was probably not responsible for the Library's demise. It is more likely that the institution disappeared gradually due to war and plunder over the course of several centuries.

A new Library of Alexandria, known as the Bibliotheca Alexandrina, opened in Egypt in 2003. A photograph of this new library appears on the next page.

Alexandrīa Antīqua

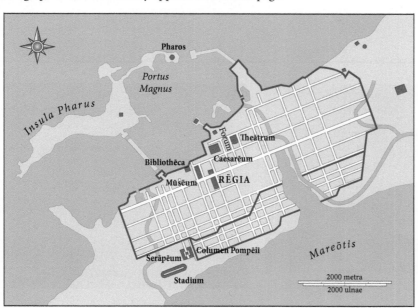

Aegyptus Rōmāna

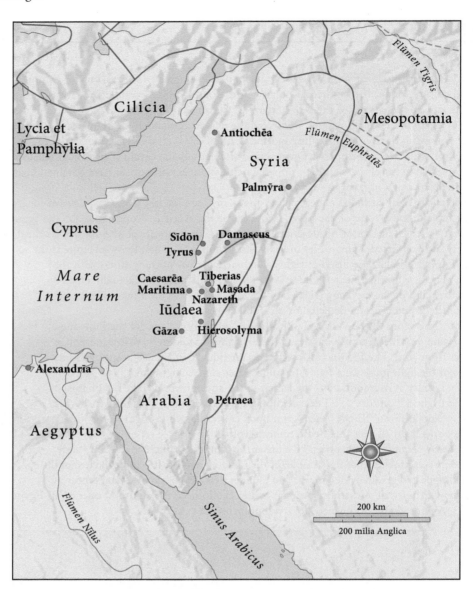

Theātrum Rōmānum Alexandrīae

Bibliothēca Alexandrīna Hodiē

QUID PUTĀS?

1. How do you think knowledge of pregnancy and birthing practices in the ancient Rome affected the lives of women?
2. Why do you think the same Latin word *umbilīcus* means "center of the world," "the knob on the rod in a book scroll," and "belly button"?
3. Pliny tells us how some Romans may have guessed the gender of unborn children. Have you heard of any similar techniques people used in the days before ultrasound?
4. To what modern city would you compare ancient Alexandria and why?

EXERCEĀMUS!

25-6 Scrībāmus

Rewrite the following section of *Lectiō Prīma* from Chapter 24 in the imperfect tense. Be careful, as not all verbs are deponent. Follow the model.

→ In theātrō multī spectātōrēs inter sē *colloquēbantur* . . .

> In theātrō multī spectātōrēs inter sē *colloquuntur* dum fābula Plautī, "Amphitruō" nōmine, ab omnibus avidē *exspectātur*.
>
> Novum theātrum Marcellī omnēs *intuentur* et valdē *admīrantur*. Patriciī sīcut Marcus et Lūcius et amīcī suī sēdēs in prīmīs gradibus theātrī, post senatōrēs, *tenent*. Aliī, sīcut Valeriae familia, in altissimīs sēdibus *sedent*.
>
> In theātrum Marcus Lūciusque *ingrediuntur* et *sedent* cum amīcīs suīs. Multī iuvenēs inter sē *sermōcinantur* sed Marcus fēminam ūnam gracilem et pulchram *intuētur* et cum eā dīcere *cōnātur*.

25-7 Colloquāmur

Use the passage you rewrote in the imperfect tense in Exercise 25-6 to ask and answer questions with other members of your class. Follow the example.

→ **Quaestiō:**   Quī in theātrō inter sē colloquēbantur?
Responsum: Multī spectātōrēs in theātrō inter sē colloquēbantur.

25-8 Verba Discenda

Find the *Verbum Discendum* that best completes each of the following statements. Then translate the sentence into English. Follow the model.

→ Caecilia _____ domī Servīliī est.
   a. domina   b. culīna   c. auxilium   d. coquus
   a. domina: Caecilia is the mistress of Servilius' house.

1. Aelius _____ Mēdēae fortiter pulsāvit.
   a. culīnam   b. iānuam   c. sellam   d. convīvium

2. Servīlius et Caecilia dē Servīliā _____.
   a. crēdunt   b. cunctantur   c. colloquuntur   d. pariunt

3. Epistula _____ ā Maecēnāte ad Servīlium advēnit.
   a. praesertim   b. nūper   c. intrā   d. paulō

4. Maecēnās ipse ad _____ prōgrediētur.
   a. culīnam   b. iānuam   c. sellam   d. convīvium

5. Aelius _____ ā Mēdēā petit.
   a. dominam   b. culīnam   c. auxilium   d. coquum

6. Caecilia in _____ in peristȳliō sedet.
   a. culīnā   b. iānuā   c. sellā   d. convīviō

7. Licinia _____ est.
   a. perīculōsa   b. quiēta   c. coquus   d. gravida

8. Sicō _____ est.
   a. domina   b. culīna   c. auxilium   d. coquus

9. Magnā cum cūrā Caecilia signum Maecēnātis _____.
   a. intuētur   b. colloquitur   c. cunctātur   d. paritur

10. Augustus _____ est.
    a. domina   b. culīna   c. imperātor   d. coquus

11. Coquī in _____ labōrant.
    a. culīnā   b. iānuā   c. sellā   d. convīviō

12. In Rōmā antīquā, praesertim fēminīs pauperibus, parere _____ erat.
    a. perīculōsum   b. quiētum   c. coquum   d. salvum

13. Et mox omnēs mīrāculum parvum _____.
    a. colloquentur   b. parient   c. mīrābuntur   d. crēdent

---

🔊 VERBA DISCENDA

auxilium, -iī n. help, aid; pl. auxiliary forces [auxiliary]

colloquor, colloquī, collocūtus sum talk together, converse [colloquial]

convīvium, -iī n. feast, banquet [convivial]

coquus, -ī m. cook

crēdō, crēdere, crēdidī, crēditum (+ dat.) believe, trust [credible, creditor]

culīna, -ae f. kitchen [culinary]

cunctor, cunctārī, cunctātus sum tarry, linger, hesitate

domina, -ae f. mistress (of the house), the woman in charge, ma'am [dominatrix]

gravidus, -a, -um pregnant [multigravida]

iānua, -ae f. door

imperātor, -ōris m. commander, ruler [emperor]

intrā (+ acc.) within [intramural]

intueor, intuērī, intuitus sum look at, gaze at; consider [intuition]

iuvō, iuvāre, iūvī, iūtum help

mīror, mīrārī, mīrātus sum wonder at, admire

nūper recently, not long ago

pariō, parere, peperī, paritum/partum bring

forth, give birth, bear, create [postpartum]

paulō somewhat, by a little

pauper, pauperis poor

perīculōsus, -a, -um dangerous [perilous]

praesertim especially, particularly

quiētus, -a, -um calm, quiet [inquietude]

salvus, -a, -um safe, well

sānus, -a, -um healthy [sanity]

sella, -ae f. chair

Angulus Grammaticus

Bending Language: Linguistic Limitations and Linguistic Flexibility

Every language has its limitations and its little tricks around these limitations. The use of participles in Latin is a good example of this.

PARTICIPLE	ENGLISH	LATIN
present active participle	saying	dīcēns
present passive participle	being said	[lacking]
perfect active participle	having said	[lacking]
perfect passive participle	having been said	dictus

You will learn about the perfect passive participle in Latin in Chapter 26.
Now think about deponent verbs and look what happens.

LATIN	PARTICIPLE	TRANSLATION
loquēns	present active participle	saying
locūtus	perfect active participle	having said

Deponent verbs should have passive endings, but Latin has no present passive participle. So the choice was never to use a present participle of such verbs or to "bend the rules." Another twist is involved in the form *locūtus*. Though passive in form, it is translated actively, and this creates the perfect active participle that is lacking for non-deponent verbs.

Another example of linguistic flexibility and limitation appears by comparing the actions expressed by Latin and English verbs.

TYPE OF ACTION	ENGLISH	LATIN
Present Tense		
simple	I say	dīcō
continuous or progressive	I am saying	dīcō
emphatic	I do say	rē vērā dīcō
Future Tense		
simple	I will say	dīcam
continuous or progressive	I will be saying	dīcam
Past Tenses		
simple	I said	dixī
continuous or progressive	I was saying	dīcēbam
present perfect	I have said	dixī
perfect continuous	I have been saying	iam dīcō
past perfect	I had said	dixeram

So an English speaker can make distinctions in the present and future tenses that a Latin speaker cannot, by showing the action is ongoing or progressive (I am saying) or by emphasizing the action (I do say). Latin speakers found other ways to express these ideas like *rē vērā dīcō* (I say indeed.).

English has its limitations, too. We long ago abandoned 2nd person singular forms (thou seest) and only use the 2nd person plural "you," even if we are speaking to only one person. Imagine what a Roman would think of that!

Moreover, many languages, including Latin and English, cannot show gender in 1st and 2nd person personal pronouns. *Ego* (I), *tū* (you), *nōs* (we), and *vōs* (you) are used for both male and female genders. Arabic, for example, uses different forms of "you" for addressing males and females.

The main point, then, is to recognize that every language has its limitations, that some things can be easily expressed in one language but not in another. At the same time, all languages are flexible and find ways around their grammatical and linguistic limitations.

Servī Labōrantēs in Epulīs

GRAMMATICA
Perfect Passive Participles
The 4th Principal Part
Ablative Absolutes
The Irregular Verb *Fīō*

MŌRĒS RŌMĀNĪ
Cibus Rōmānus

LATĪNA HODIERNA
Cornūcōpia

ORBIS TERRĀRUM RŌMĀNUS
Asia

ANGULUS GRAMMATICUS
Persons and Possession: Whose Money Bag Is It?

LECTIŌNĒS:
CONVĪVIUM
and
HOSPITĒS

This is the day of the big banquet at Servilius' house. The occasion marks his most serious attempt to date to rise in the ranks of the patricians.

26

Epulae Rēgum

Lectiō Prīma

Antequam Legis

The Banquet of a Lifetime

Many banquets like the one described in this chapter occurred in Augustan Rome. Augustus was very keen on making his new Rome the literary and cultural center of the Mediterranean. To do so he spared little time or money. Those who wanted to curry favor with the emperor often found it to their benefit to become patrons of poets, to hold readings, or to make contributions to the cultural cause. As you know from Chapter 25, the occasion for this banquet is Servilius' plan to give a copy of Callimachus' *Aetia* to Augustus. Though the emperor himself does not attend this banquet, the guest list includes a "Who's Who" of important people. You have read about several of these illustrious men already. Marcus Vipsanius Agrippa, the guest of honor, was advisor to his friend Augustus, the general who defeated Marc Antony and Cleopatra at Actium in 31 B.C., and later became the emperor's son-in-law. In 27 B.C. Agrippa built the original Pantheon, which was rebuilt, probably during the reign of the emperor Hadrian (117–138 A.D.). It is the later Pantheon, not Agrippa's, which is depicted in the photos below and on the next page. Gaius Maecenas, political advisor of Augustus and great patron of the arts in Rome, will receive Servilius' gift on behalf of the emperor. Gāius Asinius Pollio, another political advisor to the emperor and patron of the arts, built Rome's first public library. Quintus Horatius Flaccus (Horace) was a famous poet under Maecenas' patronage. Sextus Propertius and Publius Ovidius Naso (Ovid) were popular love poets of the period. Titus Livius (Livy) was the author of the monumental history of Rome called *Ab Urbe Conditā* (*From the Foundation of the City*). In creating this guest list we have taken some historical liberties. Although the date of our story is about 9 B.C., Agrippa had been dead for about three years. Horace will die in the next year, as will Maecenas.

As you read about the banquet, you are introduced to a new participle, the **perfect passive participle**.

Gemma

Note the inscription on the façade of the Pantheon. M AGRIPPA L F COS TERTIUM FECIT M(arcus) Agrippa Co(n)s(ul) L(ūciī) F(īlius) tertium fēcit. We know from ancient records that Agrippa was consul for the third time in 27 B.C. This inscription belongs to Agrippa's original Pantheon, not Hadrian's.

Pantheon Rōmae Hodiē

Perfect Passive Participles

At long last you get to use the 4th principal part of a verb. It is called the perfect passive participle (P^3). Here are its essential facts:

- P^3 is a 2-1-2 adjective, so you already know all its endings. In fact, you have been translating perfect passive participles as simple adjectives for some time now.

- As both "perfect" and "passive" you can translate these literally as "having been X-ed," although translating without "having been" is sometimes preferable.

> Caecilia cibum **coctum** inspectābat.
> Caecilia was inspecting the **having been cooked** food.

If this sounds a bit awkward to you, you can try translating this way:

> Caecilia was inspecting the **cooked** food.
> Caecilia was inspecting the food **that had been cooked**.

Look for this sentence in *Lectiō Prīma*.

EXERCEĀMUS!

26-1 **Perfect Passive Participles**

Perfect passive participles (P^3s) are marked in **bold** in *Lectiō Prīma*. Before you read, make a line-by-line list of these words and translate them following the model.

→ line 10 *coctum*   (having been) **cooked**

CONVĪVIUM

Diēs convīviī adest et tōta domus Servīliī perturbātur. In ūnā
domūs parte Caecilia servīs imperat et in aliā parte Sicōne coquus
quoque servīs in culīnam **convocātīs** imperat.

"Conservī," inquit, "hodiē diēs magnus est. Sī hodiē bene
5 labōrāverimus, fortasse aliquandō dominus noster nōbīs lībertātem
nostram dabit. Vidētis omnia **parāta**—vīnum ā villā nostrā
portātum, cibōs ad nōs trans mare **transportātōs**. Nōbīs strēnuē lab-
orāre et epulās rēgum appōnere necesse est. Agedum! Labōrēmus!"

Marcus et Lūcius et Servīlia colloquuntur.

Tōtum per illum diem servī ancillaeque strēnuē labōrābant et Caecilia cibum ā Sicōne **coctum** saepe inspectābat.
10 Dēmum omnia **parāta** sunt et in mensīs stant. Servī, **lavātī** et nova vestīmenta gerentēs, hīc et illīc astant hospitēs exspectantēs.
In aliā domūs parte, post iānuās **clausās**, Marcus, Lūcius et Servīlia dē hospitibus **invītātīs** inter sē colloquuntur.

Lūcius "Nōn," inquit, "aequum est! Cūr, Marce, tū cum hospitibus cēnāre potes, sed nōbīs hīc manēre necesse est?"

Marcus "Frātercule, tacē!" inquit. "Hospitēs nihil dē puerīs cūrant. Maecēnās ipse venit, ille Augustī amīcus et poētārum patrōnus.
Quoque venit Gāius Asinius Polliō, alius patrōnus quī bibliothēcam Rōmae aedificāvit. Polliō modo revēnit ab Asiā ubi urbēs magnās
15 Trōiam et Ephesum vīsitāvit. Maecēnās et Polliō papȳrum ā patre **emptam** accipient et mox pater Augustī amīcus novissimus erit!"

"Hui! Ēn Maecēnās?" Lūcius rogāvit. "Quis alius venit? Fortasse Augustus ipse adveniet?"

Marcus respondet: "Augustus nōn adveniet, sed Vipsānius Agrippa, multō ab Augustō **honōrātus**, veniet et optimī poētae et
scriptōrēs Rōmānī advenient—poētae Propertius et Horātius et Ovidius aderunt et Līvius quī scrībit dē rēbus **gestīs** maiōrum
nostrōrum.
20 Marcus, sē ad Servīliam vertēns, "Soror," inquit, "Cordus tuus advenit hāc vespere sed iste Antōnius, cui tē pater prōmīsit,
quoque aderit."

Servīlia nihil dīcit. Nihil est quod dīcī potest!

VERBA ŪTENDA

aedificō (1) build, make
aequus, -a, -um fair
agedum Come! Well! All
right!
Agrippa, -ae m. Agrippa,
Augustus' general and
son-in-law
aliquandō sometimes,
at length, formerly,
hereafter
ante in front, before,
ahead; (+ acc.) before,
in front of
appōnō, appōnere, apposuī,
appositum serve, put to
Asia, -ae f. Asia, a Roman
province in what is now
Turkey
astō, astāre, astitī assist
bibliothēca, -ae f. library
claudō, claudere, clausī,
clausum shut, close
conservus, -ī m. fellow slave

convocō (1) call together
coquō, coquere, coxī,
coctum cook
dēmum finally, at length,
at last
ēn/ēm (in questions) really?
Ephesus, -ī f. Ephesus, a city
in the Roman province
of Asia (modern Turkey)
epulae, -ārum f. pl. food,
dishes of food;
banquet, feast
epulae rēgum "a banquet
fit for a king"
frāterculus, -ī m. little
brother
gestae from *gerō*; *rēs gestae*
= "deeds"
honōrō (1) honor
Horātius, -iī m. Horace, an
Augustan poet

hui! wow! (exclamation
of astonishment or
admiration)
imperō (1) (+ dat.) com-
mand, order, rule
invītō (1) invite
Labōrēmus! "Let's get to
work!"
lavō, lavāre, lāvī, lautum/
lavātum/lōtum wash
lībertās, -ātis f. freedom
Livius, -iī m. Livy, an
Augustan historian
Maecēnās, Maecēnātis m.
Maecenas, Augustus'
close friend and advisor
multō much, by far, long
Ovidius, -iī m. Ovid,
an Augustan poet
papȳrus, -ī f. papyrus
patrōnus, -ī m. patron
perturbō (1) disturb,
trouble

Polliō, -ōnis m. Asinius Pollio,
a wealthy advisor
of Augustus
Propertius, -iī m. Propertius,
an Augustan poet
rēs gestae "deeds"
reveniō, revenīre, revēnī,
reventum return
scriptor, -ōris m. writer
Sicō, Sicōnis m. Sico
strēnuē actively,
vigorously
Trōia, -ae f. Troy, a city in the
Roman province of Asia
Minor (modern Turkey) (1)
transportō (1) carry,
transport
vertō, vertere, vertī,
versum turn, overturn
vesper, -eris m. evening
vestīmentum, -ī n. clothing
villa, -ae f. villa, country estate
vīsitō (1) visit

POSTQUAM LĒGISTĪ

Answer these questions in both Latin and English if the question is followed by (L). Otherwise, just respond in English.

1. What status does Sico the cook seem to have in the house?
2. What do Marcus and Lucius talk about as the guests arrive? (L)
3. What do you learn about each of the following guests from Marcus: Agrippa, Pollio, and Maecenas? (L)
4. What news does Marcus tell his sister Servilia at the end of the conversation? (L)
5. If you were Servilia, how would you feel right now? Why?

Gemma

Rēs gestae: Literally, "the deeds done." These two Latin words are best translated as "accomplishments."

Culīna Pompēiīs

Grammatica A

Perfect Passive Participles

Here are some of the perfect passive participles (P³) you saw in this *lectiō*. Compare your translations with these:

convocātīs	(having been) **called together**
emptam	(having been) **bought**
clausās	(having been) **closed**

Remember that participles are verbal adjectives. Therefore they have GNC's based on their antecedents. Here are these same participles used as adjectives.

*Hic **diēs perturbātus** est.*	This day is disturbed.
*Sicō **servīs convocātīs** dīcit.*	Sico speaks to the assembled slaves.
*Servīlius **papȳrum** in Aegyptō **emptam** habet.*	Servilius has a papyrus bought in Egypt.
*Puerī post **iānuās clausās** loquuntur.*	The children speak behind closed doors.

Note how the P³ is often translated into English by adding **-ed** to the English verb (disturb**ed**, assembl**ed**, clos**ed**). Some English verbs have "irregular" P³s like "bought" from "buy."

The 4ᵗʰ Principal Part

So far you have only used the first three principal parts of a Latin verb. P³ is the 4ᵗʰ principal part. Here are the four principal parts of the verb *coquō*, which is a *Verbum Discendum* in this chapter.

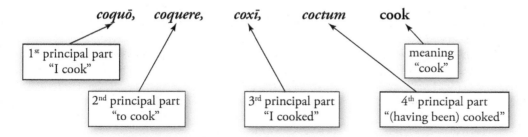

coquō, coquere, coxī, coctum   cook

- 1ˢᵗ principal part "I cook"
- 2ⁿᵈ principal part "to cook"
- 3ʳᵈ principal part "I cooked"
- 4ᵗʰ principal part "(having been) cooked"
- meaning "cook"

Notā Bene:

- Drop the *-um* from the 4ᵗʰ principal part to obtain the perfect passive stem of a verb: *coct-* from *coctum*.
- Then add *-us, -a, -um* to form the P³: *coctus, -a, -um*.

From now on, all four principal parts will be provided for verbs in the *Verba Ūtenda*.

EXERCEĀMUS!

26-2 Review of *Verba Discenda*

The 4th principal parts (P[3]) of some verbs you already know are listed in column A. Match them with the proper translation from column B.

	A		B
_____	1. vocātum	a.	asked
_____	2. crēditum	b.	believed
_____	3. audītum	c.	captured
_____	4. missum	d.	sent
_____	5. nōtum	e.	ended
_____	6. captum	f.	heard
_____	7. rogātum	g.	known
_____	8. lātum	h.	carried
_____	9. fīnītum	i.	run
_____	10. cursum	j.	called

Lectiō Secunda

Antequam Legis

Trīclīnia

Where would Servilius' banquet be held? The guests of honor eat in the *trīclīnium*, or formal dining room. As the word *trīclīnium* implies, three couches are set up in this room for the nine main diners. Other diners are served in the *peristȳlium*, where the formal presentation of the manuscript will be made.

It mattered greatly who sat where. Agrippa, as the most important man in the room, occupies the *locus consulāris* (consul's place) at the *lectus medius* (middle couch), the equivalent of our head table. With Agrippa on this couch are Maecenas and Pollio. On the couch to the right, called the *lectus summus* (highest couch) were the poets Propertius, Horace, and Ovid. On the couch to the left, called the *lectus īmus* (lowest couch) were Marcus, Livy, and Servilius, who, as host, is called *cēnae pater*. A slave stood behind each diner, ready to assist, while other

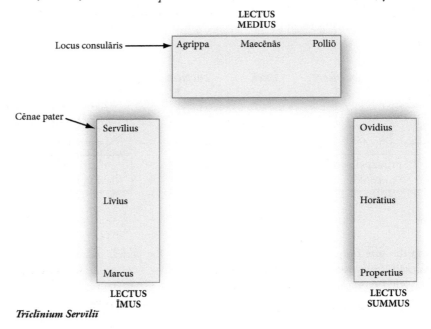

Trīclīnium Servīliī

slaves brought in the food and placed it on tables before each couch. Note that Caecilia did not eat in the room with the main guests.

The menu for this banquet is based one that found in the *Satyricon*, a 1st-century A.D. novel by Petronius. Servilius' banquet is not as lavish or pretentious as the one in the *Satyricon*, but contains several of the same dishes.

As you read about the banquet, watch for forms of the irregular verb *fīō*.

The Irregular Verb *Fīō*

Fīō, fierī, factus sum is a "mixed" verb that has both active- and passive-looking forms. Forms of *fīō* in the next reading are in ***bold italics***.

You have to be creative in translating *fīō*. Be sure to try all its basic meanings: become, happen, be made, etc.

Multī laetī fīēbant.	Many were becoming happy.
Nōs omnēs mortuī fīēmus.	All of us will become/be rendered dead.
Clāmor fīēbat.	An uproar occurred.

Lectiō Secunda also introduces you to a construction very common in Latin, but one of the most unusual for English speakers. It is called the **ablative absolute**.

Ablative Absolutes

Read this little paragraph in English:

When the food was prepared, Caecilia sighed in relief. **Because everything was fine**, she could get ready herself. Soon, **when the doors were opened**, the guests came in, hoping for a wonderful meal **since Servilius was the host**. **As the guests came in**, the children looked on from above.

Each of the English phrases marked in **bold** is a dependent (or subordinate) clause introduced by a conjunction like "when" or "after." In Latin, there is a shorthand way for doing the same thing. This is the **ablative absolute (AA)**, so named because virtually every word in it is in the ablative case.

There are two basic types of ablative absolute:

- A noun plus a participle
- A noun plus an adjective or another noun (with "being" understood)

ABLATIVE ABSOLUTE	LITERAL TRANSLATION	FREE TRANSLATION
Noun + Participle		
hospitibus ingressīs	"the guests having entered"	Once the guests had entered . . . After the guests entered . . .
hospitibus ingredientibus	"with the guests coming in"	As the guests come in . . . As the guests came in . . . (the tense depends on the general context)
Noun + Adjective or Noun		
omnibus bonīs	"everything being fine"	Because everything was fine . . . Since . . . Now that . . .
Servīliō hospite	"Servilius being host"	Because Servilius was the host . . . When . . . Because . . .

EXERCEĀMUS!

26-3 Identifying Tense and Translating Ablative Absolutes (AA)

Before you read *Lectiō Secunda,* make a line-by-line list of the ablative absolutes marked in **bold**. Indicate the tense of the participle. Then use the tense of the participle and the chart as guides to translate the ablative absolute literally. Watch out! One ablative absolute has no participle. When you find that one, don't translate it. Just say that it has no participle. Follow the model.

Line	Abl. Abs.	Tense of Participle	Literal Translation
→ 1	cibō parātō	perfect	the food having been prepared

 ## HOSPITĒS

Cibō parātō, Caecilia et fessa et laeta *fīēbat.* **Omnibus parātīs**, Caecilia ad sē ancillam, quae ornātrix sua erat, vocāvit et gradūs ascendērunt.

Mox, **iānuīs apertīs**, hospitēs adveniēbant et dē fenestrā Lūcius et Servīlia omnia, quae intrā *fīēbant,* et omnēs, quī aderant, inspicere poterant.

5   Servīlius et Caecilia hospitēs in ātrium advenientēs salūtābant et omnēs in trīclīnium ingrediēbantur.

Hospitibus plaudentibus, servī trīclīnium intrantēs lancēs maximās tulērunt. Servīlius, manūs plaudēns, clāmat: "Cēnēmus! Epulae *fīant!*"

Tālibus dictīs, hospitēs valdē admīrābantur dum servī olīvās (albās et
10 nigrās) et avēs assātās et, posteā, glīrēs melle ac papāvere sparsōs intulērunt. Aliī servī vīnum Falernum hospitibus offerunt et aliī immānem aprum et nōnnūllās speciēs piscium appōnunt. Omnēs hospitēs et aprō et piscibus avidē fruuntur—piscēs quī ōlim aut in marī aut in piscīnīs Servīliī natābant, sed nunc in condīmentīs coctī, **garō appositō**, natant.

Dēmum, **ūvīs mālīsque ōvīsque nucibusque consumptīs**, Servīlius et hospitēs, peristȳliō appropinquantēs,
15 terribilem rixam audīvērunt.

Servīlius "Ei! Quid *fit*?" rogāvit. "Quis in domō meā tālem rixam facit?"

Ecce, in mediō peristȳliō Iullus Antōnius, quī nimis vīnī hauserat et ēbrius *fīēbat,* prō hospitibus stābat. **Corōnā** in capite suō **lapsante**, Iullus carmen dē īnfāmibus fēminīs cantābat.

Servīlius īrātus "Iulle!" clāmāvit. "Mihi cantūs tuī displicent! Et ēbrius es! Discēde statim et nōlī domum meam
20 revertī! Vāh! Apage!"

Aliīs hospitibus tristibus, Servīlius quoque tristis erat. "Dominī," inquit, "mihi istum ignāvum virum ignōscite, sī vōbīs placeat! Numquam iste sub tectum meum revertētur!"

Suprā, Servīlia, dē fenestrā omnia dē Iullō intuēns et audiēns, rīdet et tunc, **Cordō** in peristȳliō **aspectātō**, suspīrat.
25 "Mī Corde," inquit, "tōta tua sum! Aliquandō uxor tua nunc certē *fīam!*"

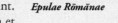
Epulae Rōmānae

POSTQUAM LĒGISTĪ

Gemma

Note that the Romans used *hospes* for both "guest" and "host."

1. What are some of the foods eaten at the banquet?
2. What does Iullus Antōnius do at the end of the banquet, and how does Servilius react?
3. How does his daughter Servilia react? Why?
4. How does this banquet compare to formal dinners you and your family may have attended or hosted? Consider not only the menu but also the goals of the host.

🔊 VERBA ŪTENDA

admīror, admīrārī,
   admīrātus sum admire,
   wonder at
albus, -a, -um here: "unripe,"
   i.e., green olives
aliquandō sometime,
   one day
apage! go! scram!
appōnō, appōnere,
   apposuī, appositum
   serve, put to
aspectō (1) gaze, look at
assō (1) roast
ātrium, -iī n. atrium, public
   greeting room of a
   Roman house
avidē eagerly
avis, avis f. bird
cantō (1) sing
cantus, -ūs m. song
caput, capitis n. head
cēnēmus! Let's dine!
condīmentum, -ī n. spice,
   seasoning
consūmō, consūmere,
   consumpsī, consumptum
   use up, eat, consume

coquō, coquere, coxī,
   coctum cook
corōna, -ae f. crown,
   garland
dēmum finally, at length,
   at last
displiceō, displicēre,
   displicuī, displicitum
   displease; displicet imp.
   (+ dat.) it is displeasing
discēdō, discēdere, discessī,
   discessum leave, depart
ei/hei ah! oh! (in fear
   or dismay)
epulae, -ārum f. pl. food,
   dishes of food;
   banquet, feast *Epulae*
   fīant! loosely: "Let the
   banquet begin!"
Falernum, -ī n. Falernian
   wine
fīō, fierī, factus sum be
   made, be done;
   happen, become
garum, -ī n. fish sauce
glīs, glīris m. dormouse
   (a great delicacy)

hauriō, haurīre, hausī,
   haustum drink, swallow
hospes, hospitis m. guest,
   host, stranger
ignāvus, -a, -um idle,
   cowardly
ignoscō, ignoscere, ignōvī,
   ignōtum (+ dat. of
   person, acc. of offence)
   pardon, forgive
immānis, immāne huge
infāmis, infāme
   disreputable
inferō, inferre, intulī, illātum
   bring, serve
inspiciō, inspicere, inspexī,
   inspectum look at, inspect
lanx, lancis f. dish, place
lapsō (1) slip
mel, mellis n. honey
natō (1) swim
niger, nigra, nigrum black
nimis too much
nux, nucis f. nut
olīva, -ae f. olive
ornātrix, ornātrīcis f.
   hair-dresser

papāver, papāveris n. poppy;
   poppyseed
peristȳlium, -iī n.
   peristyle, courtyard
piscīna, -ae f. fish pond
piscis, piscis m. fish
plaudō, plaudere, plausī,
   plausum clap, applaud
posteā afterward
Quid fit? What is going on?
   What's happening?
revertor, revertī, reversus sum
   turn back, return
rixa, -ae f. loud quarrel,
   brawl
sī vōbīs placeat "Please"
spargō, spargere, sparsī,
   sparsum sprinkle
suprā (+ acc.) over, above
suspīrō (1) sigh
tectum, -ī n. roof, house
terribilis, terribile terrible
trīclīnium, -iī n. triclinium,
   dining room
ūva, -ae f. grape
vāh/vaha ah! oh! (in
   astonishment, joy, anger)

Grammatica B

Ablative Absolutes

An ablative absolute (AA) is a combination of words (participle, noun, pronoun, adjective) in the ablative case. As you saw earlier, these words are usually translated by an English subordinate clause beginning with "when," "since," "because," or "although." To put this another way, an AA describes an event that accompanies or is **subordinate** to the main action of the sentence.

Gemma

corōnā lapsante: Note the ending on *lapsante*. In ablative absolutes, the present participle uses the alternate *-e* ending instead of the usual *-ī*.

Cibō parātō,	*Caecilia et fessa et laeta fīēbat.*
Subordinate Clause	Main action of sentence

Relative Time

If a participle is part of the AA, note the following:

- Present active participle = same time as main verb
- Perfect passive participle = time before the main verb

Consider these examples:

Gemma

mihi istum ignāvum virum ignoscite: Notice how the verb *ignoscō* takes an accusative for the offense (*virum*) and a dative for the offender; i.e., in Latin you pardon someone (in the dative) for something (in the accusative).

   Servīs intrantibus, omnēs plaudunt.
   As the slaves enter, everyone applauds.

Here both the entering and applauding happen in the present.

Servīs intrantibus, omnēs plausērunt.
As the slaves entered, everyone applauded.

Here both the entering and the applauding happened in the past (because the main verb is in the perfect tense), and the present participle shows that the entering occurred at the same time as the applauding.

In the following sentences we know that the eating happens before the applauding because the participle is perfect:

Cibō consumptō, omnēs plaudunt. Now that the food has been eating, everyone is applauding.
Cibō consumptō, omnēs plausērunt. After the food was eaten, everyone applauded.

So, before you translate an AA, be sure to check the tense of the main verb.

Ablative Absolutes without Participles

Some AAs consist of two nouns or a noun and an adjective but no participle. Here is the one example from *Lectiō Secunda*:

| *aliīs hospitibus tristibus* | Literal translation: | the other guests **being** sad |
| | Freer translation: | because the other guests **were** sad |

Note how "being" and "were" need to be added in the English translation, but are understood in Latin. So, when you find two nouns or a noun and an adjective in the ablative case, try translating them as an AA with the verb "to be" understood.

Notā Bene:

Latin does not have a perfect active participle to use in an AA. This means that, unlike English, it cannot say "Having seen him, I sighed." Instead, Latin would use a perfect passive participle:

Cordō aspectātō, Servīlia suspīrat. When Cordus was seen, Servilia sighed.

But, in English, we have a perfect active participle and can say: "Having seen Cordus, Servilia sighed."

EXERCEĀMUS!

26-4 Translating Ablative Absolutes

Translate each AA literally and then with a freer translation. Be sure to show the tense of the participle in your translation. If there is no participle, remember to understand "is" or "are." Follow the models.

| ➜ gladiātōribus necātīs: | Literal: | the gladiators having been killed |
| | Freer: | after the gladiators were killed |

| ➜ gladiātōribus pugnantibus | Literal: | the gladiators fighting . . . |
| | Freer: | since the gladiators are fighting |

1. discipulō studente
2. discipulō doctō
3. discipulīs laetīs
4. discipulīs maestīs
5. magistrō docente
6. magistrīs doctīs
7. magistrā bonā
8. magistrō malō
9. Lūciō et Servīliā colloquentibus
10. cibō devorātō
11. vīnīs ad mensās trānsportātīs
12. hospite plaudente

The Irregular Verb *Fīō*

Latin also has another irregular verb that has active forms with passive meanings in the present, imperfect, and future. In that regard, it is sort of a "reverse deponent" in that it "looks active, but isn't."

fīō, fierī, factus sum be made, become, happen

So *fīō* means "I am made, I become," whereas *factus sum* means "I was made, I became." Note that *fīō* is used as the passive of *faciō, facere, fēcī, factum* make, do, become. *Fīō* is a *Verbum Discendum* in this chapter.

The irregular forms of *fīō* are all in the present tense:

fīō	I am made, become	*[fīmus]*	we are made, become
fīs	you are made, become	*[fītis]*	you are made, become
fit	he/she/it is made, becomes	*fīunt*	they are made, become

Notā Bene:

- The forms in brackets are rarely found.
- Note the short -*i* in *fit* and *fierī*.
- In other tenses *fīō* takes fairly normal 3ʳᵈ conjugation verb forms. Thus, *fīēbam, fīēbās*, etc. (imperfect), and *fīam, fīēs* (future).

EXERCEĀMUS!

26-5 Translating *fīō*

Translate the following forms of *fīō* into English using the correct form and tense of "become."

1. fīunt	3. fīēmus	5. fit	7. fient	9. fīs
2. fīēbās	4. fīs	6. fīēbāmus	8. fierī	10. fīēs

Mōrēs Rōmānī

Cibus Rōmānus

Many of the foods we eat today, including many foods associated with modern Italy, were not known to the Romans. The coffee bean was not discovered in Ethiopia until the 9ᵗʰ century A.D. Pasta and macaroni were not eaten in Italy until after Roman times. The eggplant came from Asia and was introduced to Europeans by Arabs after 1500 A.D. The importation of tea into Europe from China and India did not begin until the 17ᵗʰ century.

Many other "Italian" foods were not known to the ancients. These foods include tomatoes, chocolate, zucchini, and many kinds of beans, including kidney, lima, butter, pole, snap, and string.

Cibus Rōmānus

What, then, did the Romans eat and drink? Some of their staples included wheat, lentils, barley, olives, broad beans, fruit, nuts, melons, milk, cheese, eggs, wine, and, if they could afford it, all sorts of meat, fowl, and seafood.

In order to illustrate how Romans prepared some of these foods, we offer you some recipes from an ancient cookbook entitled *Dē Rē Coquīnāriā* (*On Cooking*) attributed to a Caelius Apicius, who is otherwise unknown. (We do not even know when he lived.) This collection of approximately 500 gourmet recipes is divided into ten books organized according to types of food with Greek names like *Sarcoptes* ("Meats"), *Cepuros* ("Garden Vegetables"), *Aeropetes* ("Birds"), *Tetrapus* ("Quadrupeds"), and *Thalassa* ("Sea Creatures"). Many of these recipes included expensive and exotic ingredients like flamingo, which were not available to the average Roman, but the following recipes from book three on *Cepuros* could have been made in a typical Roman kitchen.

Also notice how the future tense (and, occasionally, the present) is used instead of imperatives to give directions:

faciēs	make (you will make)	*coquēs*	cook, fry, boil	*ligābis*	tie, bind
concīdēs	chop together	*eximēs*	remove	*mittēs*	put
		inferēs	serve		

Porrōs mātūrōs fierī

Pugnum salis, aquam et oleum mixtum faciēs et ibi coquēs et eximēs. Cum oleō, liquāmine, merō et inferēs.

To make mature leeks.

You will make a mixture of a pinch of salt, water, and oil. And then you will cook it and remove it (from the heat). And you will serve it with oil, fish sauce, and pure wine.

Now try translating these actual recipes, using the words above and the *Verba Ūtenda*. All the words preceded by + in the following *Verba Ūtenda* are ingredients in the recipes.

Aliter porrōs

Opertōs foliīs cōliculōrum et in prūnīs coquēs ut sūprā et inferēs.

Aliter porrōs

In aquā coctōs ut suprā et inferēs.

Bētās

Concīdēs porrum, coriandrum, cumīnum, ūvam passam, farīnam et omnia in medullam mittēs. Ligābis et ita inferēs ex liquāmine, oleō et acētō.

Aliter bētās ēlixās

Ex sināpi, oleō modicō et acētō bene inferuntur.

Carōtae seu pastinācae

Carōtae frictae oenogarō inferuntur.

Aliter carōtās

Sale, oleō pūrō et acētō.

🔊 VERBA ŪTENDA

+ *acētum, -ī* n. vinegar
aliter in another way
+ *aqua, -ae* f. water
bene "nicely"
+ *bēta, -ae* f. beet
+ *carōta, -ae* f. carrot
+ *cōliculus, -ī = cauliculus, -ī* m. small cabbage, cabbage sprout
concīdō, concīdere, concīdī, concīsum cut, chop up
coquō, coquere, coxī, coctum cook, boil, bake, fry
+ *coriandrum, -ī* n. coriander
+ *cumīnum, -ī* n. cumin

ēlixus, -a, -um boiled
eximō, eximere, exēmī, exemptum take out, remove
farīna, -ae f. flour
folium, -iī n. leaf
fricō, fricāre, fricuī, frictum rub, rub down
inferō, inferre, intulī, illātum translate here as "carry in" or "serve"
ligō (1) tie
+ *liquāmen, liquāminis* n. liquid, especially fish sauce
mātūrus, -a, -um mature, ripe

medulla, -ae f. marrow; here, the pith or inner core of the beet
merum, -ī n. pure (unmixed) wine
misceō, miscēre, miscuī, mixtum blend, mix
modicus, -a, -um a moderate amount of
+ *oleum, -ī* n. oil
operiō, operīre, operuī, opertum cover
+ *oenogarum, -ī* n. a sauce made of garum and wine

passus, -a, -um spread out, dried
+ *pastināca, -ae* f. parsnip
+ *porrus, -ī* m. leek
+ *prūnum, -ī* n. plum
pugnus, -ī m. a handful, a pinch
pūrus, -a, -um pure, plain
+ *sāl, salis* m./n. salt
+ *sināpi* (indeclinable) n. mustard
ut as
+ *ūva, -ae* f. grape; *ūva passa* dried grape, raisin

Cornūcōpia Antīqua

Latīna Hodierna

Cornūcōpia

Americans associate the cornucopia (literally, "horn of plenty") with Thanksgiving. It is actually an ancient symbol used to suggest prosperity. Since the cornucopia is traditionally filled with fruits and vegetables, let's consider how the common names for many vegetables in English and the Romance languages, as well as many scientific names for these plants, are based on Latin words. A blank box indicates that the word for the item in that language is not clearly derived from the Latin.

SCIENTIFIC TERM	LATIN WORD	ENGLISH MEANING	ENGLISH DERIVATIVE	FRENCH	ITALIAN	SPANISH
Beta vulgaris	bēta	beet	beet	bette (chard) betterave (beet)	barbabietola (beet) bietola (chard)	
Prunus cerasus (sour cherry)	cerasus	cherry	cherry	cerise	ciliegia	cereza
Malus domestica (domestic apple tree)	mālum	apple			mela	
Prunus persica	mālum Persicum (Persian apple)	peach	peach	pêche	pesca	melocoton (cotton apple)
Olea europaea	olīva	olive	olive olivaceous	olive	oliva	oliva
Pirus domestica (domestic pear tree)	pirum	pear	pear	poire	pera	pera
	pōmum	fruit	pomaceous pomade pomander	pomme (apple) pomme de terre (potato, i.e., earth apple)	pomodoro (tomato, i.e., golden apple)	
Prunus americana (wild plum tree)	prūnum	plum	prune	prune (plum) pruneau (prune)	prugna	
Vitis vinifera	ūva vītis	grape vine			uva	uva

Orbis Terrārum Rōmānus

Asia

In *Lectiō Prīma* Marcus mentions that Pollio had just returned to Rome from Asia. To the Romans, Asia (*Asia, -ae* f.) especially meant a province in what is now western Turkey, including important cities like Troy, Ephesus, and Pergamon. Troy, the site of the epic war between the Greeks and Trojans, was an important tourist location even in antiquity. Alexander the Great, for example, visited the city on his march east into Persia. The ancient Greek city of Ephesus was noted for the magnificent Temple of Artemis, one of the Seven Wonders of the Ancient World. Pergamon boasted a great Temple of Zeus (the remains of its altar are in the Pergamon Museum in Berlin) and an important library that rivaled the one in Alexandria.

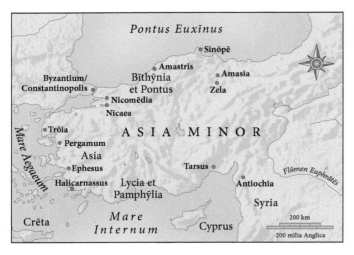

Asia Minor

Ephesus

Trōia Rōmāna

Acropolis Pergamōnis et Theātrum Magnum

The territory, strategically located along major shipping routes in the Mediterranean, was bequeathed to Rome by its ally Attalus III of Pergamon and became a Roman province in 133 B.C. This wealthy region of ancient Greek cities suffered greatly from heavy taxation, corruption, and warfare in the Late Republic. Marc Antony even gave the library of Pergamon to Cleopatra as a gift.

Many important Romans spent time in the area. The poet Catullus made a pilgrimage to Troy, where his brother died. On his way to Egypt after the battle of Pharsalus in 48 B.C., Julius Caesar also visited the city, in order to honor the homeland of his mythic ancestor, Aeneas.

Augustus followed his adopted father to Troy and traveled widely in the province, which shared the prosperity of the Augustan age. The cities of Asia grew enormously in the early Empire. Widespread public building projects, including theaters, basilicas, baths, and other public facilities resulted in a highly urbanized and prosperous region.

Under Augustus, Troy was refounded as a Roman city, and remains of Roman buildings now lie adjacent to the ruins of the city recalled in Greek legend. During the imperial period Pergamon renewed its claim as a center of learning and culture. In the 2nd century A.D., the great Roman physician Galen was born here. The ancient Greek city of Ephesus also flourished in the empire and became an early center of Christianity.

QUID PUTĀS?

1. What modern foods would you miss most if you lived in ancient Rome?
2. Which of Apicius' recipes looks the most appealing to you? Why?
3. Compare the recipes of Apicius you read in *Mōrēs Rōmānī* with the menu for Servilius' banquet.
4. Did you notice the word "pomade" in the *Latīna Hodierna*? Do you know what it means? If you don't see the relationship between the English word "pomander" and the Latin *pōmum* "fruit," look up the meaning and etymology of "pomander" in a good English dictionary.
5. List several historical and geographic reasons why the province of Asia was so important to Rome.

EXERCEĀMUS!

26-6 Scrībāmus: Composing Ablative Absolutes

Change the number in each of the following AA phrases; i.e., if the words are singular, make them plural; if they are plural, make them singular. Then translate each phrase. Follow the models.

→ *pōmō ēsō* when the apple was eaten
   pōmīs ēsīs when the apples were eaten

1. cibō parātō
2. omnibus bonīs
3. iānuīs apertīs
4. hospitibus audientibus
5. ornātrīce vocātā
6. carminibus cantātīs
7. papȳrīs emptīs
8. servō imperātō

26-7   Using *Fīō* and Ablative Absolutes

Combine AA phrases from column A and main clauses in column B to make five different sentences. Then translate these sentences into English. Follow the model.

→ Omnibus parātīs fīēbam laetus. *After everything was ready, I became happy.*

A	B
cibō parātō	fīēbam laetus/laeta
iānuīs apertīs	ūnus hospes tristis fīēbat
hospitibus plaudentibus	aeger/aegra (sick) fīēbat
corōnā lapsante	hospitēs īrātī fīēbant
Cordō aspectātō	Iullus ēbrius fīēbat
Servīs lavātīs	Lūcius iēiūnus fīēbat

26-8   Colloquāmur

This exercise is for pairs. One person says an ablative absolute from column A in Exercise 26-7 and then says the name of a character from the *lectiō*.

→ *Nucibus consumptīs Sicō*

The next person has to complete the thought with a brief statement about the person.

→ *laetus est.*

It may help to make up a list of verbs and adjectives to use before you begin.

26-9   Verba Discenda

Find the *Verbum Discendum* that best fits each statement.

1. The 1st conjugation verb that takes a dative
2. A noun that has only plural forms
3. A deponent verb
4. The opposite of *placet*
5. A 3rd declension i-stem noun
6. A 2nd conjugation verb
7. *Coxī* is the 3rd principal part of this word
8. A 2nd declension neuter noun

🔊 VERBA DISCENDA

admīror, admīrārī, admīrātus sum admire, wonder at [admiration]

aliquandō sometimes, at length, formerly, hereafter

appōnō, appōnere, apposuī, appositum serve, put to [apposition]

coquō, coquere, coxī, coctum cook [concoct]

dēmum finally, at length, at last

displiceō, displicēre, displicuī, displicitum displease; *displicet* imp. (+ dat.) it is displeasing

epulae, -ārum f. pl. food, dishes of food; banquet, feast

fīō, fierī, factus sum be made, be done; happen, become [fiat]

hospes, hospitis m. guest, host, stranger [hospitable]

imperō (1) (+ dat.) command, order, rule [imperial, imperious]

multō much, by far, long

patrōnus, -ī m. patron [patronize]

peristȳlium, -iī n. peristyle, courtyard

perturbō (1) disturb, trouble greatly [imperturbable]

piscis, piscis m. fish [piscine, Pisces]

plaudō, plaudere, plausī, plausum clap, applaud

strēnuē actively, vigorously [strenuous]

trīclīnium, -iī n. triclinium, dining room

vertō, vertere, vertī, versum turn, overturn [diversion]

Angulus Grammaticus

Persons and Possession: Whose Money Bag Is It?

In Chapter 21 you consolidated your knowledge of personal pronouns and possessive adjectives. You noted that possession is expressed by adjectives in the 1st and 2nd persons, and by either a pronoun or an adjective in the 3rd person (depending on the subject):

	POSSESSIVE ADJECTIVES VS. GENITIVE OF PERSONAL PRONOUNS			
	1st person (my, our, my own, our own)	2nd person (your, your own)	3rd person (his, her, its, their)	3rd person (his own, its own, their own)
Singular	meus, -a, -um	tuus, -a, -um	eius	suus, -a, -um
Plural	noster, nostra, nostrum	vester, vestra, vestrum	eōrum, eārum, eōrum	suus, -a, -um

Now let's consider this sentence from the *lectiō* in which Caecilia calls her hairdresser to help her get ready for the banquet:

Caecilia ad sē ancillam, quae ornātrix *sua* erat, vocāvit et gradūs ascendērunt.

The reflexive adjective *sua*, as you know, is used here to tell the reader that the *ornātrix* is Caecilia's hairdresser and not someone else's. Possessive adjectives would also be used in the 1st and 2nd person, as in *ornātrix mea* (my hairdresser), *ornātrix tua* (your hairdresser), *ornātrix nostra* (our hairdresser), and *ornātrix vestra* (your hairdresser).

Where Latin is much more precise than English is in the 3rd person, where we must distinguish *ornātrix sua*, "her own hairdresser," from *ornātrix eius* "her (someone else's) hairdresser." In order to understand the difference between *sua* and *eius* and to appreciate the precision of Latin and the ambiguity of English, consider the following sentence and try to imagine the scene in your mind (or even draw a picture):

He put **his** hand in **his** money bag.

How many people did you have involved in this scene?

- Only one? Then you understood the sentence to read "He put his own hand in his own money bag."
- But suppose scenario #2, in which "he" is a thief, and "He put his own hand in his (victim's) money bag.
- Or suppose scenario #3, in which there is actually a father and a son, and "He (the father) puts his (son's) hand in his (the father's) money bag" to get some candy?
- Or scenario #4, in which the father can put the son's hand in the son's money bag (where he hid the candy).

Are there any other possibilities you can now imagine for the original sentence? The point is that in Latin such ambiguity can be avoided:

- Scenario #1: *Is manum suam in saccō suō posuit.*
- Scenario #2: *Is manum suam in saccō eius posuit.*
- Scenario #3: *Is manum eius in saccō suō posuit.*
- Scenario #4: *Is manum eius in saccō eius posuit.*

Just remember that *suus, -a, -um* has to refer to the subject, and the rest is easy.

27

Duo Dōna

Lectiō Prīma

Antequam Legis

The banquet marks a major turning point in the lives of the *Servīliī*. If his gift is well received, Servilius will surely have Augustus' support as he runs for praetor in the upcoming elections. Servilia, with Antonius in disgrace, has some hope of fulfilling her love interest in Cordus, while, for Marcus, this represents a sort of "coming out party" in front of Rome's most influential people. After the dinner is over, the entire crowd moves to the *peristȳlium* for the presentation of Servilius' gift to the emperor.

In this *lectiō* you also get a summary of the entire **perfect passive system**.

The Perfect Passive System

It may seem like a lot of work to look at the entire perfect passive system all at once, but it is not. Remember that the **perfect active system** was so called because it contained three tenses that shared the perfect stem—the perfect, pluperfect, and future perfect.

The passive system is similar, in that all three use the perfect passive participle (P^3) and a form of *sum* to form their passive tenses. Remember the perfect passive participle is the 4th principal part.

TENSE	FORMATION	EXAMPLE	TRANSLATION
Perfect Passive	P^3 + **present** of *sum*	captus es vocāta est monitum est	you **have been** captured she **has been** called it **has been** advised
Pluperfect Passive	P^3 + **imperfect** of *sum*	audītae erāmus ductus erās capta erant	we **had been** heard you **had been** led they **had been** captured
Future Perfect Passive	P^3 + **future** of *sum*	vocātī eritis monitae erunt captum erit	you all **will have been** called they **will have been** warned it **will have been** captured

Augustus Prīmae Portae

LECTIŌNĒS:
DŌNUM PRAECIPUUM
and
INFANS NOVUS

Servilius ceremoniously presents his gift for Augustus, and Licinia's baby is born.

Note that these verb forms show gender as well as tense and number. So *captus est* means "he has been captured" and *capta est* means "she has been captured."

EXERCEĀMUS!

27-1 Practicing the Perfect Passive System

As you read *Lectiō Prīma*, be on the lookout for the forms in **bold**. These forms are passive. Your task is to find an example of the tenses asked for. Then translate the form you found. Be sure to include the line number. They do not necessarily appear in the order listed. Follow the model.

Passive Form to Find	Line	Form	Translation
→ perfect, 3rd pl. neuter	3	dicta sunt	they were said

1. perfect 3rd sing. neuter
2. perfect 3rd sing. fem.
3. perfect, 3rd pl. masc.
4. perfect, 2nd pl. masc.

5. pluperfect 3rd sing. fem.
6. pluperfect 3rd pl. neuter
7. future perfect 3rd sing. neuter

🔊 DŌNUM PRAECIPUUM

Dēsuper, per fenestram, Servīlia et Lūcius omnia quae in peristȳliō dicta et facta erant audīvērunt et vīdērunt.

Iullō Antōniō ēbriō ē iānuīs domūs Servīliī expulsō, Servīlius īrātus et vexātus ad convīvium revēnit. Postquam omnēs hospitēs in peristȳlium **vocātī sunt**, ā Servīliō haec verba **dicta sunt**:

"Hospitēs praeclārī, mihi valdē placet quod vōs omnēs apud mē hāc nocte
5 **congregātī estis**. Nunc, Augustō duce, Rōma nostra—immō tōta Italia—post illōs annōs, in quibus multī nostrōrum patrum et fīliōrum **necātī sunt**, pācem et serēnitātem habet. Nōs omnēs—dīvitēs aut pauperī, cīvēs aut mīlitēs, in Urbe aut rūrī, in Italiā aut in prōvinciīs habitantēs—Augustō nostrō, patrī patriae, grātiās maximās agere oportet. Ergō dōnum praecipuum Augustō ā mē **parātum est**.
10 "Nūper ad Aegyptum itinere factō hunc libellum rārissimum ā mē **inventum est**. Haec papȳrus, quam nunc in manibus meīs teneō, omnēs versūs carminis Callimachī, *Aetia* nōmine, continet. Antīquissima est, ut opīnor, ē bibliothēcā Alexandrīnā, cuius pars, ut scītis, in bellō **combusta est**. Haec papȳrus (nesciō quōmodo) ex igne **servāta erat** et ā mē magnī pretiī **empta** et Rōmam
15 **transportāta est**. Hanc papȳrum ipsam Augustō nostrō dōnāre volō. Sī dōnum meum, quidquid est, ab Augustō **acceptum erit**, mihi et familiae meae bonum erit."

Hīs dictīs, sē ad Maecēnātemque Polliōnemque Servīlius vertēns, "Sī vōbīs placet," inquit, "hunc libellum ducī nostrō ferte prō omnibus quae prō nōbīs fēcit!"
20 Papȳrus **recepta est** ā hīs virīs illustribus. Attonitī atque pergrātī papȳrum statim legere incēpērunt. Paulō post Servīlius perlaetus rīsit et "Fortasse papȳrus iam satis **lecta est**," inquit, "Nunc bibāmus."

Postquam, omnibus volentibus, versūs paucī praeclārōrum poētārum **audītī sunt**.

Dēsuper, per fenestram, Servīlia et Lūcius omnia quae in peristȳliō **dicta et facta erant** audīvērunt et vīdērunt.

Lūcius sorōrem rīdentem vīdit et rogāvit: "Servīlia, cūr tam perlaeta es? Quā dē causā?"
25 Servīlia respondit: "Cūr laeta sum? Audī, Lūcī, audī. Hāc nocte omnia mīrābilissima quae **dicta sunt** audīre potuimus. Ā nōbīs carmina optima optimōrum poētārum **audīta sunt**. In nūllā aliā domō Rōmānā tam praeclārus conventus poētārum scrīptōrumque hodiē **inventus est**! Et Līvius ipse dē librō novō dē historiā Rōmānā lēgit! Et, ecce! Etiam nunc Cordum meum ē hāc fenestrā clārē vidēre possum!"

🔊 VERBA ŪTENDA

attonitus, -a, -um
  astonished, amazed
bibāmus "Let's drink!"
bibliothēca, -ae f. library
Callimachus, -ī m. Callimachus, poet and chief
  librarian at Alexandria
clārē clearly
cīvis, cīvis m./f. citizen
combūrō, combūrere, com-
  bussī, combustum burn
congregō (1) gather
contineō, continēre, continuī,
  contentum contain
dōnō (1) present as a gift
dux, ducis m. leader
ēbrius, -a, -um drunk
expellō, expellere, expulī,
  expulsum throw out
immō rather, more precisely
libellus, -ī m. little book

Līvius, -iī m. Livy, the
  historian
Maecēnās, Maecēnātis m.
  Maecenas, Augustus'
  close friend and advisor
nesciō, nescīre, nescīvī/
  nesciī, nescītum
  not know
opīnor, opīnārī, opīnātus
  sum think, believe
papÿrus, -ī f. papyrus
patria, -ae f. country,
  fatherland
pax, pācis f. peace
pergrātus, -a, -um very
  agreeable
perlaetus, -a, -um very
  happy
Polliō, -ōnis, m. Asinius
  Pollio, a wealthy
  advisor of Augustus

praecipuus, -a, -um
  special, particular
prōvincia, -ae f. province
rārus, -a, -um rare, thin
recipiō, recipere, recēpī,
  receptum accept, receive
rūrī "in the country;" note
  the lack of a preposition
satis enough
scriptor, -ōris m. writer
serēnitās, -ātis f. cheerful
  tranquility
servō (1) save, protect; ob-
  serve, pay attention to
transportō (1) carry across,
  convey, transport
ut as
versus, -ūs m. verse, line of
  poetry
videor, vidērī, vīsus sum
  seem, appear; be seen

POSTQUAM LĒGISTĪ

1. Why does Servilius think that the reign of Augustus has been good for Rome?
2. How does Servilius say that the papyrus came from Egypt to Rome?
3. With what sort of entertainment does the dinner party end?
4. What does Servilia's reaction to the evening's activities tell us about her intellectual interests?
5. What does Servilia hope will happen to her personally as a result of the evening?

Grammatica A

The Perfect Passive System

Perfect passive verbs are formed by combining the perfect passive participle (P³) with forms of the verb *sum*.

Since the P³ is a 2-1-2 adjective, it must GNC with the subject. Thus:

- *Fēmina Servīlia vocā**ta** est*
- *Vir Servīlius vocā**tus** est.*
- *Animal canis vocā**tum** est.*

Papÿrus

Now note how the forms change and how the tenses are translated:

Perfect Passive	
vocātus, -a, -um sum	I have been called, I was called
vocātus, -a, -um es	you have been called, you were called
vocātus, -a, -um est	he/she/it has been called
vocātī, -ae, -a sumus	we have been called
vocātī, -ae, -a estis	you have been called
vocātī, -ae, -a sunt	they have been called
Pluperfect Passive	
vocātus, -a, -um eram	I had been called
vocātus, -a, -um erās	you had been called
vocātus, -a, -um erat	he/she/it had been called
vocātī, -ae, -a erāmus	we had been called
vocātī, -ae, -a erātis	you had been called
vocātī, -ae, -a erant	they had been called
Future Perfect Passive	
vocātus, -a, -um erō	I will have been called
vocātus, -a, -um eris	you will have been called
vocātus, -a, -um erit	he/she/it will have been called
vocātī, -ae, -a erimus	we will have been called
vocātī, -ae, -a eritis	you will have been called
vocātī, -ae, -a erunt	they will have been called

The **perfect passive infinitive** of *vocō* is *vocātum esse* (to have been called). There are no pluperfect or future perfect passive infinitives.

EXERCEĀMUS!

27-2   Practicing the Perfect Passive System

Using the chart as a guide, translate the verbs into tenses of the perfect passive system as directed. The P³ is given in parentheses to help you. Follow the model. Watch out for gender and number.

→ he has been warned (*monitus, -a, -um*)   *monitus est*
   had been warned   *monitus erat*
   will have been warned   *monitus erit*

1. we (masc.) had been led (*ductus, -a, -um*)
      have been led

2. Valeria, you will have been seized (*captus, -a, -um*)
      had been seized

3. they (neuter) had been heard (*audītus, -a, -um*)
      have been heard

4. I (fem.) was loved (*amātus, -a, -um*)
      had been loved

5. it will have been given (*datus, -a, -um*)
      had been given

6. you (pl. masc.) have been prepared (*parātus, -a, -um*)
        will have been prepared

7. you (pl. fem.) had been sent (*missus, -a, -um*)
       were sent

8. they (neuter) had been carried across (*transportātus, -a, -um*)
        will have been carried across

Lectiō Secunda

Antequam Legis

In this *lectiō* Licinia's baby is born. As you read, note how Medea the midwife cuts the umbilical cord, cleans the infant, and puts it naked on the floor. Aelius then picks the infant up. This was a formal Roman custom requiring the *pater familiās*, in this case Aelius, either to pick up the child and acknowledge it as a member of the family or to leave it on the ground. If the newborn child were not picked up, it did not legally belong to the father and had no legal rights. Such a child could be given away, abandoned, or even sold into slavery. Do you think Aelius will accept this child as his own?

As you read, you will see deponent verbs in tenses of the perfect passive system. You will also learn how the passive forms of *videō* are used in Latin.

The Perfect System of Deponent Verbs

Do you remember the saying for deponent verbs: "Looks passive, isn't"? Well, that is all there is to it. Perfect deponents in the *lectiō* are marked in **bold**. When you see one, be sure to translate it actively.

The Verb *Videor*

The passive of *videō* is rather like a deponent. *Videor* should mean "I am seen, you are seen," etc. This meaning can occur occasionally, but the more common meaning of *videor, vidērī* is to "seem" or "appear." Thus: *Servīlia! Laeta vidēris!* = "Servilia, you seem happy." When it is used in the 3rd person singular with a dative and an infinitive, this verb can mean "it seems like a good idea" as in *mihi abīre vidēbātur*, "It seemed like a good idea for me to leave." All the forms of *videor* are marked in ***bold italics*** in the *lectiō*, but try translating a few more examples in the following exercise before you start reading.

EXERCEĀMUS!

27-3 Translating Forms of *Videor*

All of the following phrases marked in ***bold italics*** in *Lectiō Secunda* use forms of *videor*. Match the phrase in column A with its translation in column B.

	A		**B**
_____	1. perlaeta vidēris	A.	He seems terrible.
_____	2. laeta videor	B.	I appear happy.
_____	3. labōrāre vīsa est	C.	The mother seems healthy.
_____	4. puer sānus vīsus est	D.	She seemed to be laboring.
_____	5. terribilis vidētur	E.	You seem very happy.
_____	6. māter sāna vidētur	F.	It seems good for me to hear everything.
_____	7. omnia quiēta vīsa sunt	G.	Everything seemed quiet.
_____	8. mihi audīre omnia vidētur	H.	The boy seemed healthy.

🔊 INFANS NOVUS

In aliā parte urbis, in cellā squālidā in Subūrā, familia Valeriae anxiē nōn carmina sed infantem exspectābat. Licinia, in sellā sedēns, dolōre terribilī **passa est**. Mēdēa, omnibus instrūmentīs et herbīs suīs ūtēns, Liciniae et infantī auxilium dare **cōnāta est**.

Multās post hōrās, vāgītus fortis infantis sānī atque fortis per insulam audītus est.
5   Infans puer erat et sānus **vīsus est**. Umbilīcus amputātus est et infans ab obstetrīce ablūtus est. Tunc, ut mōs māiōrum est, in terrā nūdus positus est et, brevī tempore sōlus iacēns, fortiter clāmābat dōnec pater infantem in manibus sublevāvit.

Aelius laetus **locūtus est**: "Mī fīlī, pater tuus sum et tū fīlius meus es. Ego tē amābō et tuēbor. Nunc, mī fīlī, dormī in gremiō mātris."

10   Hīs dictīs, Aelius infantem Liciniae dedit et ā mātre infans novus **nūtrītus est**. Valeria et Plōtia, dulciter rīdentēs, nepōtem et pronepōtem **admīrātae sunt** et Plōtia **ēlocūta est**: "Licinia, nōn multō post, quia anus sum, moriar—sed laeta moriar. Nunc quod hunc meum pronepōtem vīdī, mors nōn tam terribilis **vidēbitur**. Et tū, pater Aelī, tū quoque
15   perlaetus **vidēris**!"

Licinia, quamquam fessa est, infantem suum accipit et eī mammam offerēns eum lactāre **hortāta est**, hoc dulce et lēne carmen cantāns:

Lalla, lalla, lalla!

Ī, puer, aut dormī aut lactā.

20   Dēmum et māter et infans dormiēbant et omnia quiēta **vīsa sunt**. Nunc Mēdēae discēdere **vidēbātur**. Valeria Mēdēam ad iānuam **secūta est** et eī nummōs dedit. Mēdēa exiēns **pollicita est**: "Sī febris Liciniam nōn cēperit, salva erit. Partus facilis erat et māter sāna **vidētur**." Tunc addidit: "Sed, cavē febrem!" Tālia dīcēns, Mēdēa domum **reversa est**.

Mox silentium familiam fessam tenēbat et omnēs dormiēbant. Valeria Plōtiaque in ūnā cellā et Aelius Liciniaque
25   in aliā dormīvērunt. Flāvia, postquam omnia mundāvit, ut semper, prō iānuā cellae, in quā Aelius, Licinia et nunc parvus infans dormiēbant, iacēbat.

Pater infantem in manibus sublevāvit.

🔊 VERBA ŪTENDA

abluō, abluere, abluī, *ablūtum* wash, cleanse

amputō (1) cut off

anus, -ūs f. old woman

***cantō* (1) sing**

caveō, cavēre, cāvī, cautum beware

***dōnec* as long as, until**

febris, febris f. fever

gremium, iī n. lap

herba, -ae f. herb

Ī imperative of *eo;* here, "come now"

instrūmentum, -ī n. tool, **instrument**

lactō (1) nurse

lalla exclamation; calming sound

lēnis, lēne smooth, soft, **mild**

mamma, -ae f. breast

mundō (1) clean

nepōs, nepōtis m. **grandson, grandchild, descendant, nephew**

nummus, -ī m. coin, **money**

nūtriō, nūtrīre, nūtrīvī/nūtriī, nūtrītum nurse, nourish

partus, -ūs m. child birth

perlaetus, -a, -um **very happy**

pronepōs, -nepōtis m. great-grandson

quamquam **although, yet**

squālidus, -a, -um dirty, filthy

sublevō (1) lift, raise, support

terribilis, terribile **frightening, terrible**

tueor, tuērī, tuitus sum look at, watch over

umbilīcus, -ī m. navel, umbilical cord

ut as

vāgītus, -ūs m. cry, wail

videor, vidērī, **vīsus sum seem, appear; be seen**

vidētur imp. (+ inf.) it **seems good**

POSTQUAM LĒGISTĪ

1. Compare the description of childbirth in this reading to modern birthing customs and practices.
2. What does the midwife Medea do with the child after it is born? What does his father Aelius do? How does this compare to modern American practice?
3. Why does Plotia say she will now die happy?
4. What danger does Medea warn Aelius about as she leaves the house? Is this a concern today for women who have just given birth?

Grammatica B

The Perfect System of Deponent Verbs

Now that you know about the 4th principal part of regular verbs, you can better understand why deponent verbs like *sequor* have only three principal parts. The form *secūtus sum* includes the perfect passive participle *secūtus* ("having been followed") and means "I followed."
Here is how it works:

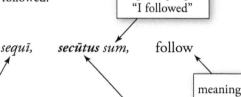

Deponent verbs form their perfect forms exactly as you would expect, by combining the P³ with the appropriate form of the verb *sum*. The only thing you have to remember is to translate this passive form in the active voice. Here is the perfect system of *cōnor* to use as a guide for all other deponent verbs.

CŌNOR, CŌNĀRĪ, CŌNĀTUS SUM			
Perfect Passive		**Pluperfect Passive**	
cōnātus, -a, -um sum	I have tried	cōnātus, -a, -um eram	I had tried
cōnātus, -a, -um es	you have tried	cōnātus, -a, -um erās	you had tried
cōnātus, -a, -um est	he/she/it has tried	cōnātus, -a, -um erat	he/she/it had tried
cōnātī, -ae, -a sumus	we have tried	cōnātī, -ae, -a erāmus	we had tried
cōnātī, -ae, -a estis	you have tried	cōnātī, -ae, -a erātis	you had tried
cōnātī, -ae, -a sunt	they have tried	cōnātī, -ae, -a erant	they had tried

Future Perfect Passive	
cōnātus, -a, -um erō	I will have tried
cōnātus, -a, -um eris	you will have tried
cōnātus, -a, -um erit	he/she/it will have tried
cōnātī, -ae, -a erimus	we will have tried
cōnātī, -ae, -a eritis	you will have tried
cōnātī, -ae, -a erunt	they will have tried

EXERCEĀMUS!

27-4 **Passive or Deponent?**

Which is the correct translation of the form? Remember, you have to know the 1st principal part of the verb in order to know if it is regular or deponent. When in doubt, use the *Verba Omnia*. Then be sure you have the right tense.

_____ 1. *cōnātus est* a. he was tried; b. he tried; c. he had tried; d. he had been tried

_____ 2. *veritī erātis* a. you were afraid; b. you had been afraid; c. you were feared; d. you had been feared

_____ 3. *secūta erō* a. I will follow; b. I will have followed; c. I will be followed

_____ 4. *missae sumus* a. we are sending; b. we have been sent; c. we sent

_____ 5. *datum erat* a. it had been given; b. it gave; c. it had given; d. it was given

_____ 6. *arbitrātus erit* a. he will have been thought; b. he will have thought; c. he is thought; d. he had been thought

_____ 7. *ausī sunt* a. they were dared; b. they are daring; c. they will dare; d. they dared

_____ 8. *secūtī sumus* a. we followed; b. we have been followed; c. we had been followed; d. we will have followed

_____ 9. *ingressum erat* a. it had been entered; b. it entered; c. it will enter; d. it had entered

_____ 10. *admīrātus es* a. you were admired; b. you are admired; c. you admired; d. you are admiring

The Verb *Videor*

As you saw in *Lectiō Secunda*, the passive forms of *videō* usually have the special meaning "seem" or "appear" in English. In a sense, then, *videor* is deponent because it has passive forms but an active meaning. Keep in mind, however, that *videor* can, at least occasionally, be translated passively as "I am seen." Here is a summary of uses of *videor*:

- With an adjective: *laetus vidētur* "He appears happy."

- With a complementary infinitive: *audīre vidētur* "He appears to be listening."

- With an infinitive and a person in the dative, the 3rd person singular can mean "it seems good": *mihi audīre vidētur* "Listening seems like a good idea to me."

It all depends on context. The forms of *videor, vidērī, vīsus sum* offer no surprises. It is conjugated like any 2nd conjugation verb. Here are some selected forms of *videor* in the perfect passive system. Note the variety of possible translations for each form.

Perfect Passive	
vīsus, -a, -um sum	I (have) seemed, appeared I have been seen, was seen
vīsī, -ae, -a sumus	we (have) seemed, appeared we have been seen, were seen
Pluperfect Passive	
vīsus, -a, -um eram	I had seemed, appeared I had been seen
vīsī, -ae, -a erāmus	we had seemed, appeared we had been seen
Future Perfect Passive	
vīsus, -a, -um erō	I will have seemed, appeared I will have been seen
vīsī, -ae, -a erimus	we will have seemed, appeared we will have been seen

EXERCEĀMUS!

27-5 Translating Forms of *Videor*

Now use the chart to expand your knowledge of *videor* by translating each of the following forms at least three ways. Follow the model. Pay attention to tense signs!

→ vidēmur we seem; we appear; we are seen

1. vidēbantur
2. vidēbor
3. vīsī sunt
4. vidēbāminī
5. videor
6. vīsae erātis
7. vidētur
8. vidēberis
9. vīsa erunt
10. vidēbuntur
11. vidēris
12. vidēbar

Mōrēs Rōmānī

Lux et Pater Patriae

Many of the guests invited to Servilius' *cēna* were members of a tightly-knit literary group. Horace, for example, addressed Iullus Antonius at the beginning of his *Ode* 4.2, and Vergil dedicated his fourth eclogue to Asinius Pollio. In Satire 1.5 Horace described a trip he took from Rome to Brundisium with Vergil and Maecenas. And, as Servilius does at the banquet, all these poets frequently sang the praises of Augustus himself.

Here is an example of such praise from Horace (*Odes* 4.5). The grammar and vocabulary are not difficult, but the poetic word order is, so here it is in a slightly less confusing form. As you read, you should know that the emperor had left the city to lead a military expedition in the Alps from 16 B.C. to 13 B.C. You should also remember that Horace is addressing the emperor directly in this poem, so look out for vocatives (marked in bold) and 2nd person singular verbs and imperatives (both in italics):

> **Orte** dīvīs bonīs, **optime custōs** gentis Rōmulae, *abes* iam nimium diū;
> Pollicitus reditum mātūrum sanctō conciliō, *redī.*
> **Dux bone**, *redde* lūcem patriae tuae;
> Enim ubi tuus vultus, instar vēris, populō affulsit, diēs grātior it et sōlēs melius nitent.

Horace *Odes* 4.5.1–8

🔊 VERBA ŪTENDA

affulgeō, affulgēre, affulsī
(+ dat.) shine on, smile on
concilium, -iī n. council = Roman senate
custōs, custōdis m. guard

dīvus, -ī m. god = *deus*
dux, ducis m. leader
gens, gentis f. family, tribe
instar indecl. (+ gen.) like, equal
lux, lūcis f. light

mātūrus, -a, -um timely, early
nimium too, excessively
niteō, nitēre, nituī shine
orior, orīrī, ortus sum rise, be born
reditus, -ūs m. return

Rōmulus, -a, -um of Romulus = Roman
sōl, sōlis m. sun = day
vēr, vēris n. springtime
vultus, vultūs m. face

Augustus Pater Patriae

When Horace refers to Augustus in his ode as *lux patriae tuae*, he is alluding to one of the titles Octavian assumed after he became the emperor Augustus, *pater patriae* "father of the country." The same title had previously been bestowed not only on Cicero but also on Julius Caesar. A succession of Roman emperors following Augustus bore the title, which was often abbreviated "P.P." on coins. You can see the full title on the coin of Augustus depicted at left. Around the edge of the coin is written the following:

DIVI F PATER PATRIAE CAESAR AUGUSTUS

Roman devotion to the rights belonging to the father, be it of the country or the *familia*, was a well-established part of the *mōs māiōrum*. Both Marcus and Servilia were raised on the *mōs māiōrum* and are aware of its obligations. For Servilia this means that she would have to accept the husband chosen for her by her father even if she liked Cordus better.

Latīna Hodierna

Pater Patriae Americānus

The Founding Fathers were often identified with the great leaders of ancient Rome. As the first president of the United States, George Washington, like Cicero, Julius Caesar, and Augustus before him, was called "Father of His Country." For this reason, Horatio Greenough depicted George Washington in a classical pose for a statue originally installed in the U.S. Capitol Rotunda in 1841 and now in the Smithsonian Museum of American History.

Pater Patriae Americānus

This Roman view of the country and its leaders as **pater**nalistic comes into English in words like **patri**ot, **patri**otism, and **patri**otic (showing respect for the fatherland), which are all derived from *patria, -ae* f.

Greenough represents George Washington handing his sheathed sword back to the country as he retires as general and returns to his farm in Mt. Vernon, Virginia. When he was later called back to be the first president of the United States, he was compared to the famous Roman Cincinnatus, who in 457 B.C. was called from his plow to serve as dictator in the Romans' war against their neighbors. After the war, like Washington, Cincinnatus put aside his power to return to his farm.

In honor of Washington and in order to preserve the ideals of the American Revolution, the Society of the Cincinnati was founded in 1783. In 1790, the city of Cincinnati, Ohio, was named in honor of this society.

Orbis Terrārum Rōmānus

Viae Rōmānae

The term *umbilīcus*, as you have seen, refers to the navel as well as to the umbilical cord. It is also surprising to find that Rome had an *umbilīcus*. The Romans built a network of excellent roads that allowed government officials and armies to move quickly throughout the empire.

With military precision, they measured their roads from the *Milliārium Aureum* (Golden Milemarker) established under Augustus. All the roads of Rome were said to start here, and the monument recorded the distance in miles to various cities in the Empire. In the reign of Septimius Severus (193–211 A.D.) or later, the monumental column called the *Umbilīcus Urbis Rōmae* was erected in the Roman Forum to mark the center of the city and of the empire and may have replaced the *Milliārium*.

One of these roads was the *Via Flāminia,* which ran north and east from Rome to the Adriatic Sea. The road was built by Gaius Flaminius in 220 B.C. Romans tended to name roads after their builders. Mile markers (*milliāria*) such as the one depicted at right usually marked distance along these roads.

Prima Porta, where the famous statue of Augustus shown at the beginning of this chapter was located, was an important stop on the Via Flaminia. At Prima Porta Augustus' wife, Livia, had a country villa, known today as Villa Liviae. Besides the statue of Augustus, the most famous finds in the excavation of this villa were some garden frescoes now on display in the Palazzo Massimo in Rome.

Umbilīcus Urbis Rōmae

Milliārium Rōmānum

QUID PUTĀS?

1. In his ode, Horace addresses Augustus as the "best guardian of the Roman state" and "light of the fatherland." Would Americans address their presidents in this way? Why or why not?
2. Horace writes his ode as a request that the emperor return home quickly from a stay abroad. In what media besides a poem might Americans discuss the travels of their president today?
3. Many Americans did not like Horatio Greenough's statue of George Washington. What do you think their objections were? Could such a statue be created today for a modern president? Why or why not?
4. Do you think Americans today look upon their country and government as a parent? Why or why not? If so, is it more like a father or a mother?
5. Are there any modern equivalents of the Romans' *Milliārium Aureum* or the *Umbilīcus Rōmae*? Why is it so important to have a standard distance marker?
6. Why do you think this chapter is called *Duo Dōna*?

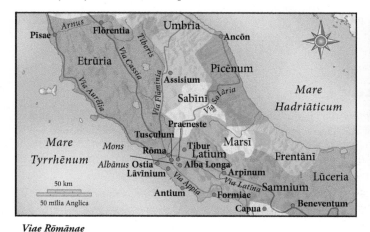

Viae Rōmānae

Via Rōmāna in Hispāniā

EXERCEĀMUS!

27-6 Scrībāmus

The following passage is from Chapter 22. Change all the present passives to perfect passives.

> Ūnus leō hastā **vulnerātur** (1) et paulum recēdit. Mox duo aliī ā bestiāriīs **vulnerantur** (2) sed plūrēs leōnēs quam bestiāriī sunt et mox omnēs hī infortūnātī bestiāriī **necantur**.
>
> Tunc multī hippopotamī et crocodīlī ferōcēs in harēnam **dūcuntur** (3) et ā nānīs nūdīs **oppugnantur** (4). Intereā aliī nānī gregem gruum parmīs oppugnant.
>
> Post multās aliās vēnātiōnēs, in quibus plūrima animālia plūrimīque hominēs **necantur** (5), harēna sanguine et corporibus plēna est. Dum harēna **purgātur** (6), Marcus et Lūcius aliquid cibī emunt.

27-7 Colloquāmur

This speaking exercise requires groups of three. Using the adjectives from the *Verba Ūtenda* below, follow these steps:

1. Student #1 makes up a question about Student #2. The sentence has to use *vidētur* and an adjective from the list below.

2. Student #2 makes a face or strikes a pose that is either what Student #1 said or its opposite. Thus, if Student #1 said that Student #2 looked happy, Student #2 could choose to look either happy or sad.

3. Student #3 then responds to the original question, saying that Student #2 does or does not look the way Student #1 suggested.

> → Classmate #1: Tristisne Robertus **vidētur**?
> Classmate #2: (smiles broadly)
> Classmate #3: Nōn, Robertus nōn tristis sed laetus **vidētur**.

Ideally each group will have both male and female participants to allow for good GNCing practice. Students take turns being #1, #2, or #3.

🔊 VERBA ŪTENDA

tristis, triste	*dormiēns*	*improbus, -a, -um*
laetus, -a, -um	*maestus, -a, -um*	*dulcis, -e*
malus, -a, -um	*fēlix, fēlīcis*	*dīves, dīvitis*
sānus, -a, -um	*fortis, forte*	*mortuus, -a, -um*
terribilis, terribile	*territus, -a, -um*	*lēnis, lēne*

27-8 Verba Discenda

Find the *Verbum Discendum* that is the source of each of the following words and phrases. Then use the meaning of the Latin word to define the English one. Follow the model.

→ Cantor: *Cantō*; one who sings

1. observatory
2. versify
3. anile
4. pacification
5. inscription
6. nepotism
7. incantation
8. inebriation
9. repatriate
10. lenient
11. civilization
12. rarify

🔊 VERBA DISCENDA

anus, -ūs f. old woman
[anile]
bibliothēca, -ae f. library
cantō (1) sing [incantation]
cīvis, cīvis m./f. citizen
[civility]
dōnec as long as, until
dux, ducis m. leader
[il Duce]
ēbrius, -a, -um drunk
[inebriation]
gremium, iī n. lap

instrūmentum, -ī n. tool,
instrument
[instrumentation]
lēnis, lēne smooth, soft,
mild [lenient]
nepōs, nepōtis m. grandson,
grandchild, descendant,
nephew [nepotism]
nummus, -ī m. coin, money
papȳrus, -ī f. papyrus
patria, -ae f. country,
fatherland [repatriate]

pax, pācis f. peace [pacify]
perlaetus, -a, -um very
happy
praecipuus, -a, -um
special, particular
quamquam although, yet
rārus, -a, -um rare; thin
[rarify]
scriptor, -ōris m. writer
servō (1) save, protect;
observe, pay attention
to [observation]

terribilis, terribile
frightening, terrible
transportō (1) carry
across, convey, trans-
port [transportation]
versus, -ūs m. verse, line of
poetry [versify]
videor, vidērī, vīsus sum
seem, appear;
be seen
vidētur imp. (+ inf.) It
seems good

Angulus Grammaticus

Personal Pronouns in the Genitive Case

In Chapter 21 you consolidated your knowledge of Latin personal pronouns and noted that possession is expressed by adjectives in the 1st and 2nd persons and by either a pronoun or an adjective in the 3rd person (depending on the subject), as in *domus eius* (his/her house) but *domus mea* (my house). In the *Angulus Grammaticus* to Chapter 26 we talked more about using a 3rd person personal pronoun in the genitive case to express possession. This is unique to *eius, eōrum, eārum*.

The 1st and 2nd person pronouns (*meī, tuī, nostrum/nostrī, vestrum/vestrī*) can only be used as objective and partitive genitives (genitives of the whole). They cannot be used to express possession.

1. Use any form ending in *-ī* as an **objective genitive**:

   memor meī (mindful of me)
   amor tuī (love for you)
   timor nostrī (fear of us)
   odium vestrī (hatred for you)

2. Use *meī, tuī, nostrum*, and *vestrum* to express the **partitive genitive** (genitive of the whole):

   pars meī (part of me)
   nēmō nostrum (no one of us)

3. Use *nostrum* and *vestrum* instead of the possessive adjective when modified by *omnium*:

   noster amor (our love)
   amor omnium nostrum (the love of all of us)

Notā Bene: The phrases *noster amor* (our love) and *amor omnium nostrum* (the love of all of us) both mean that "we" are doing the loving. But compare *amor tuī* and *tuus amor*. In the former, "you" are being loved and in the latter "you" are doing the loving. Big difference! Perhaps *tuus amor tuī* (your love for yourself) will help you remember how this works.

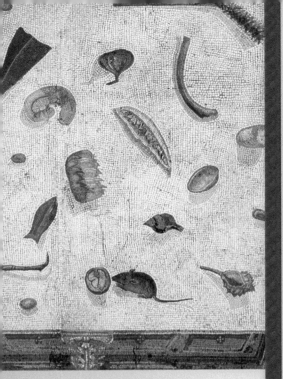

28

Labōrēs Herculis

Lectiō Prīma

Antequam Legis

An Augean Task

Xanthus and Rufus, two slaves, are cleaning up the Servilian peristyle after the big feast. Xanthus compares the enormity of this task to Hercules' fifth labor, the cleaning of the Augean stables in Elis, near Olympia. Rufus is German (his name means "reddish," referring to his hair) and Xanthus, whose name means "Blondie," is a Greek from Sicily.

Hercules, you may remember, went mad and killed his family. The Delphic oracle told him that he could atone for this by completing labors for King Eurystheus of Mycenae. In this labor he has to clean out, in a single day, an enormous pile of waste from the stables of King Augeas who lived in Elis, a city in the Peloponnesus area of Greece. He devised an ingenious way to do this, as you will see.

Passive Review

This chapter provides a review of all passive tenses. Remember that passives, deponents, and semi-deponents can look alike, so be sure what kind of verb you are dealing with before you translate.

Pavīmentum in Trīclīniō
Heracleitus. "The Unswept Floor," mosaic variant of a 2nd-century B.C. painting by Sosos of Pergamon. 2nd century A.D. Musei Vaticani, Museo Gregoriano Profano, ex Lateranense, Rome. Studio Canali, Milano, Italy, NY

GRAMMATICA
Review of All Passive Tenses
Reflexive Verb Expressions
Review of Deponent Verbs: All Tenses

MŌRĒS RŌMĀNĪ
Deī Opificēs: Vulcānus et Minerva

LATĪNA HODIERNA
Scītisne?

ORBIS TERRĀRUM RŌMĀNUS
Aetna et Sicilia

ANGULUS GRAMMATICUS
More on Voice

LECTIŌNĒS:
OPERA SORDIDA
and
AVĒS UBĪQUE

Servants in the Servilian household clean up from the feast and compare their tasks with two labors of Hercules.

Review the following formulas for forming the passives:

PRESENT							
1, 2 PS	+	or ris tur	mur minī ntur	3, 4 SPS	+	or eris itur	imur iminī untur
				3rd: i + i = i *caperis*, not *capieris* (3rd *-iō*) 4th: i + i = ī			
IMPERFECT							
1, 2 PS	+	bar bāris bātur	bāmur bāminī bantur	3, 4 SPS	+	ēbar ēbāris ēbātur	ēbāmur ēbāminī ēbantur
FUTURE							
1, 2 PS	+	bor beris bitur	bimur biminī buntur	3, 4 SPS	+	ar ēris ētur	ēmur ēminī entur
PERFECT							
1, 2, 3, 4	P³	+	sum es est	sumus estis sunt			
PLUPERFECT							
1, 2, 3, 4	P³	+	eram erās erat	erāmus erātis erant			
FUTURE PERFECT							
1, 2, 3, 4	P³	+	erō eris erit	erimus eritis erunt			

Notā Bene:
- PS = present stem = 2nd principal part minus *-re*
- SPS = Short Present Stem = 1st principal part minus *-ō*
- P³ = 4th principal part with *-us*, *-a*, *-um* endings. (Remember that it GNC's with the subject of the sentence.)

All regular passive verbs are marked in **bold** in *Lectiō Prīma*.

Reflexive Idioms

As you read this *lectiō*, watch for a number of verbal idioms that use the reflexive pronouns you learned earlier (especially *mē/nōs*, *tē/vōs*, and *sē*). These idioms are marked in ***bold italics*** in the *lectiō* and are explained briefly in the *Verba Ūtenda* and in more detail after the *lectiō*.

EXERCEĀMUS!

28-1 Pre-Reading Exercise

Before you translate *Lectiō Prīma*, just scan it to get the gist, then try to answer the following questions. You will find you can then translate the *lectiō* more quickly.

1. Which rooms in Servilius' house particularly require cleaning after the banquet?

2. Why is the slave Rufus unfamiliar with the labors of Hercules?

3. Why was cleaning the Augean Stables such a difficult task?

4. Why was Eurystheus eager to give Hercules such a task?

5. In what way does Hercules clean out the stables?

6. What joke does Rufus make after the story is finished?

7. Find ten passive or deponent verbs marked in **bold** and translate them into English.

🔊 OPERA SORDIDA

In colle Vīminālī, apud Servīliōs, Servīlius et Caecilia bene dormiunt sed servī per domum labōrant. Aliī culīnam aliī trīclīnium purgant et multī in peristȳliō labōrant, sed omnēs fessī et īnfēlīcēs fīunt. Rē vērā īrascuntur. Duo servī inter sē colloquuntur.

"Herculēs in Stabulō Augēō" *ā Francisco Zurbarán (1598–1664) picta.*

5   Rūfus "Dī immortālēs!" clāmat, "Hoc peristȳlium sordidissimum est. Ecce! Cibus et pōcula ubīque! Sīc semper est—homō dīves, pavīmentum sordidum! Dominī epulantur et nōs servī squālōrem magnum purgāre **cōgimur**!"

Xanthus: "*Tē gere* placidē, amīce. Nōn sōlum ā servīs sed etiam ā
10   deō opus sordidum **agitur**. Mementō Herculis! Locus sordidissimus ab illō ōlim **purgātus est**!"

Rūfus: "Hercule! Dīc mihi dē hōc labōre! Ut scīs, Germānicus sum et paulum dē hīs tuīs fābulīs Graecīs sciō. Narrā! Tē narrante, tempus celerius fugiet!"

15   Xanthus: "Scīsne nihil dē deīs nostrīs? Terribile est!"

Hīs dictīs, Xanthus narrāre incipit:

"Ōlim labor Herculis gravissimus ā rēge malō Eurystheō **impositus est**. Augēās quīdam, quī illō tempore regnum in Ēlide obtinēbat, tria mīlia bovum habēbat. Hī in stabulō ingentis magnitūdinis **inclūdēbantur**. Stabulum autem stercore ac squālōre **obsitum erat**, neque enim ad hoc tempus umquam **purgātum erat**. Hoc Herculēs intrā
20   spatium ūnīus diēī purgāre **iussus est**."

"Eurystheus, 'Nūllō modō,' inquit, 'tanta stabula ab ūnō virō in diē singulārī **purgārī** possunt! Tantus labor numquam et ab Hercule **conficiētur**.'

"Herculēs, etsī rēs erat difficilis, *sē gessit* bene et negōtium suscēpit. Prīmum, magnō labōre et Minervā adiuvante, fossa XVIII pedum **ducta est**, per quam flūminis aqua dē montibus ad mūrum stabulī **perdūcēbātur**. Tum
25   mūrō ruptō, aqua in stabulum **immissa est**. Tālī modō contrā opīniōnem omnium opus cōnfēcit."

Fābulā narrātā, Xanthus "Intelligisne?" inquit. "Herculēs numquam dīxit 'Cur hoc agere **cōgor**?' Et nunc ille dīvus est!"

Rūfus, labōris dēsinēns, rīsit. "Manē hīc, Xanthe! Mox revertar! Mē flūmen magnum invenīre oportet! Tunc facilius hoc peristȳlium Augēum purgāre poterimus!" Tunc ad cisternam *sē contulit*.

🔊 VERBA ŪTENDA

Augēās, -ae m. Augeas, king
　of Elis in Greece
bōs, bovis m./f. cow, bull, ox
cisterna, -ae f. cistern, well
collis, collis m. hill
conferō, conferre, contulī,
　collātum bring together,
　collect; sē conferre go
　(betake oneself); talk
　together
conficiō, conficere, confēcī,
　confectum do,
　accomplish, complete
dēsinō, dēsinere, dēsīvī/
　dēsiī, dēsitum (+ gen.)
　cease, desist (from)
Dī = deī
epulor, epulārī, epulātus sum
　feast, dine
et here: "even"
etsī although, even if
flūmen, flūminis n. river
fossa, -ae, f. ditch
gerō: sē gerere act
　(conduct oneself)
Graecus, -a, -um
　Greek
Hercule By Hercules!
immittō, immittere, immīsī,
　immissum send to
immortālis, immortāle
　immortal

impōnō, impōnere, imposuī,
　impositum (+ dat.)
　assign, impose upon
inclūdō, inclūdere, inclūsī,
　inclūsum enclose
infēlix, infēlīcis unhappy,
　unfortunate
ingens, ingentis huge
īrascor, īrascī, īrātus sum
　be angry
iubeō, iubēre, iussī, iussum
　order
magnitūdō, -inis f.
　greatness
mementō! Remember!
mīlia thousands
Minerva, -ae f. Minerva,
　goddess of wisdom
mons, montis m.
　mountain
mūrus, -ī m. wall
neque and not; neque ...
　neque neither ... nor
obserō, obserere, obsēvī,
　obsitum cover
obtineō, obtinēre, obtinuī,
　obtentum hold, support
opīniō, -ōnis f. belief,
　opinion
paulum a little, somewhat
pavīmentum, -ī n. ground,
　floor

perdūcō, perdūcere, perduxī,
　perductum lead through,
　conduct
prīmum first, at first
regnum, -ī n. kingdom
revertor, revertī, reversus sum
　turn back, return
Rūfus, -ī m. Rufus, one of
　Servilius' slaves
rumpō, rumpere, rūpī,
　ruptum break, burst,
　break down
sciō, scīre, scīvī/sciī,
　scītum know, know
　about
singulāris, singulāre,
　single
sordidus, -a, -um filthy
spatium, -iī n. space
squālor, squālōris m. filth
stabulum, -ī n. stable
stercus, stercoris n. dung,
　excrement
suscipiō, suscipere, suscēpī,
　susceptum accept
tantus, -a, -um so great
ubīque everywhere
umquam ever
ut as
Xanthus, -ī m. Xanthus, one
　of Servilius' slaves

POSTQUAM LĒGISTĪ

1. This *lectiō* describes the clean-up process after Servilius' banquet. Compare this task with the way such clean-ups occur today in your house, in a hotel room or after a catered banquet. Which of these clean-ups is most like the one in the *lectiō*? Why?
2. Use this *lectiō* to describe the relationship between master and slave in ancient Rome.
3. Explain the expression *homō dīves, pavīmentum sordidum.* In what way is this expression true in the story? In what way(s) might this expression still be true today?
4. Hercules had to clean the Augean Stables in a single day. Can you think of similar assignments from the world of fairy tales?

Grammatica A

Review of All Passive Tenses

The following chart contains all the passive forms of the 1st conjugation verb *vocō*:

1ST CONJUGATION					
Present System			**Perfect System**		
Singular					
Person	Present	Imperfect	Future	Perfect	Pluperfect	Future Perfect

Person	Present	Imperfect	Future	Perfect	Pluperfect	Future Perfect
1st	vocor	vocābar	vocābor	vocātus, -a, -um sum	vocātus, -a, -um eram	vocātus, -a, -um erō
2nd	vocāris	vocābāris	vocāberis	vocātus, -a, -um es	vocātus, -a, -um erās	vocātus, -a, -um eris
3rd	vocātur	vocābātur	vocābitur	vocātus, -a, -um est	vocātus, -a, -um erat	vocātus, -a, -um erit
Plural						
1st	vocāmur	vocābāmur	vocābimur	vocātī, -ae, -a sumus	vocātī, -ae, -a erāmus	vocātī, -ae, -a erimus
2nd	vocāminī	vocābāminī	vocābiminī	vocātī, -ae, -a estis	vocātī, -ae, -a erātis	vocātī, -ae, -a eritis
3rd	vocantur	vocābantur	vocābuntur	vocātī, -ae, -a sunt	vocātī, -ae, -a erant	vocātī, -ae, -a erunt

EXERCEĀMUS!

28-2 Passive Synopses

Write the same person and number of a verb (e.g., 1st plural) in the tenses indicated. This exercise, called a "synopsis," will help you practice the passive forms of verbs in many conjugations. We tell you the person and number to use. Gender is indicated by the subject supplied. Use the completed first synopsis as a model.

3RD PLURAL OF *VOCŌ* (1) "FĒMINAE"		
Tense	**Latin**	**English Translation**
Present	vocantur	they are called
Imperfect	vocābantur	they were being called
Future	vocābuntur	they will be called
Perfect	vocātae sunt	they have been called
Pluperfect	vocātae erant	they had been called
Future Perfect	vocātae erunt	they will have been called

2ND SINGULAR OF *MONEŌ, MONĒRE, MONUĪ, MONITUM* "MARCUS"		
Tense	**Latin**	**English Translation**
Present	monēris	you are warned
Imperfect		you were being warned
Future	monēberis	
Perfect		you have been warned
Pluperfect		
Future Perfect		you will have been warned

1ST PLURAL OF *DŪCŌ, DŪCERE, DUXĪ, DUCTUM* "VALERIA ET LICINIA"		
Tense	Latin	English Translation
Present	dūcimur	we are led
Imperfect		
Future		we will be led
Perfect		
Pluperfect		we had been led
Future Perfect		

2ND PLURAL OF *AUDIŌ, AUDĪRE, AUDĪVĪ, AUDĪTUM* "XANTHUS ET RŪFUS"		
Tense	Latin	English Translation
Present		
Imperfect		
Future		
Perfect		
Pluperfect		
Future Perfect		

Reflexive Verb Expressions

As you review passive and deponent verbs in this chapter, this is a good opportunity to consider verbs in which the subject performs the action on himself or herself. These are called **reflexive verbs**. Some reflexive verbs are always used with reflexive pronouns as objects, and others can either have a noun or a reflexive pronoun for an object. Consider the verb *lavāre*:

- *Servī pōcula lavant.* The slaves wash the cups.
- *Marcus sē lavat.* Marcus washes up (washes himself).

Now consider these two reflexive verbs in the *lectiōnēs* in this chapter:

sē conferre go (betake oneself)
sē gerere act (conduct oneself)

All three are based on verbs you already know (*ferō* and *gerō*) but have special meanings when used with reflexive pronouns. Such expressions are also called **idioms**. Notice how the reflexive pronoun can accompany all persons of the verb. Consider the expression: *sē conferre*.

mē conferō	I go (betake myself)
tē confers	you go
sē confert	he/she/it goes
nōs conferimus	we go
vōs confertis	you (all) go
sē conferunt	they go

While *mē ferō* literally means "I carry myself," this expression is not translated reflexively in English. We say simply, "I go." Now go back to *Lectiō Prīma* and find the reflexive expressions used there.

Lectiō Secunda

Antequam Legis

In this section Xanthus continues telling Rufus about the labors of Hercules. Here Xanthus describes the hero's sixth labor, his encounter with the Stymphalian birds.

The Stymphalian Birds

In this labor Hercules must drive away the brass-beaked, man-eating birds that are devouring the inhabitants of a town called Stymphalus. He asks for help from Vulcan (Greek: Hephaestus), the blacksmith of the gods. You will remember that Aelius' slave is named Hephaestus.

Use this *lectiō* as an opportunity to consolidate what you have learned about deponent verbs.

Deponent Verb Review

Remember! "Looks passive, isn't." Just translate deponent verbs actively.
How can you tell a verb is deponent?

- **Principal parts** can help. If the 1st principal part ends in *-or*, it is deponent. If there are only three principal parts, the verb is probably deponent or semi-deponent.
- **Usage and context** can also help. For example, look at these two phrases from *Lectiō Prīma*:

Dominī **epulantur**.
Labor ā rēge **impositus est**.

You can tell at a glance that both *epulantur* and *impositus est* are passive in form, but consider their meanings and usage.

- The **ablative of agent** in *Labor ā rēge impositus est* shows you that the sentence is passive.
- Then there is common sense. Which translation makes more sense for *Dominī epulantur*: "The masters are dined upon." (passive meaning) or "The masters dine." (active meaning)?

So let context, usage, and common sense be your guides in identifying and translating deponent verbs.

EXERCEĀMUS!

28-3 Deponent or Regular Passive?

All verbs with passive endings in *Lectiō Secunda* are marked in **bold**. Some are deponents and some are regular passives. Use usage and context to find five deponent verbs and five regular passive verbs. Give the 1st principal part of each verb. Then translate the verb into English. Follow the model.

Line	Verb	1st PP	Type	Translation
1	verritur	verrō	regular passive	it is being swept
2	loquitur	loquor	deponent	he says

🔊 AVĒS UBĪQUE

Herculēs avēs Stymphālidēs transfīgit.

In angulō peristȳliī pavīmentum ā Xanthō **verritur.** Subitō fortiter cachinnat et **loquitur:** "Rūfe, ecce! **Admīrābar** ossa avium ubīque in pavīmentō. In mentem fābula dē aliō Herculis labōre vēnit. Audī."

5 "Ōlim Eurystheus Herculī **allocūtus est.** 'Labor sextus tuus facillimus erit! Populī oppidum Stymphālum habitantēs paucās avēs **verentur.** Tē hās avēs dispergere iubeō. Sī tē gesseris bene et sī ad mē cum hīs avibus mortuīs **reversus eris,** dīmidium labōrum tuōrum **conficiētur.** Tibi **polliceor.'** Post

10 paucōs diēs Herculēs ad oppidum Stymphālum **profectus est.** Hae avēs rostra aēnea habēbant et carne hominum **vescēbantur.** Ille, postquam ad locum **aggressus est,** lacum **intuitus est;** in hōc autem lacū, quī nōn procul ab oppidō erat, avēs habitābant. Sed avēs nōn facile **appropinquābantur;** lacus enim nōn ex aquā sed ē līmō consistere **vīsus est.** Herculēs igitur ad avēs neque pedibus neque nāviculā **aggredī** potuit.

"Herculēs 'Quid,' inquit, 'faciam? Quōmodo illae avēs ā mē **capientur?** Avēs prīmum dē **līmō agī** dēbent! Sed

15 quōmodo? Auxilium **requīritur!'**

"Tālibus **dictīs,** Herculēs ad Vulcānum sē contulit, et auxilium ab eō petīvit. Vulcānus (quī ā fabrīs maximē **colēbātur**) crepundia quae ā deō ipsō ex aere **fabricāta erant** Herculī dedit. Herculēs ad lacum sē tulit et hīs instrūmentīs **ūtēns** ācrem crepitum fēcit. Statim avēs ē lacū perterritae **actae sunt.** Ille autem, dum āvolant, magnum numerum eārum sagittīs transfixit et cum avibus mortuīs ad Eurystheum **reversus est.**"

20 Fābulā fīnītā, Rūfus **pollicitur:** "Hercule! sīcut hērōes Graecī, nōs ipsī hunc gregem maximum avium vincere **cōnābimur.** Et nōbīs Vulcānus Minervaque ipsī auxilium dabunt. Ossa avium et alia scrūta relicta in focō exūrāmus."

🔊 VERBA ŪTENDA

ācer, ācris, ācre sharp

aēneus, -a, -um bronze

aes, aeris n. metal, especially copper or bronze

aggredior, aggredī, aggressus sum approach

angulus, -ī m. corner

avis, avis f. bird

āvolō (1) fly away

cachinnō (1) laugh loudly

carō, carnis f. meat, flesh

colō, colere, coluī, cultum worship

conferō, conferre, contulī, collātum bring together, collect; *sē conferre* **go (betake oneself); talk together**

conficiō, conficere, confēcī, confectum do, accomplish, complete

consistō, consistere, constitī, constitum consist of

corpus, corporis n. body

crepitus, -ūs m. rattling

crepundia, -ōrum n. pl. rattle

dīmidium, -iī n. half

dispergō, dispergere, dispersī, dispersum scatter, disperse

exūrāmus "Let us burn"

faber, fabrī m. craftsman, artisan; smith; workman

fabricō (1) make

ferō: *sē ferre* **go (betake oneself)**

focus, -ī m. hearth

gerō: *sē gerere* **act (conduct oneself)**

grex, gregis m. flock

iubeō, iubēre, iussī, iussum order

lacus, -ūs m. lake

līmus, -ī m. mud, slime

nāvicula, -ae f. little boat

neque and not; *neque … neque* **neither … nor**

numerus, -ī m. number

oppidum, -ī n. town

os, ossis n. bone

perferō, perferre, pertulī, perlātum convey

pēs, pedis m. foot

prīmum first, at first

procul far, far away

proficiscor, proficiscī, profectus sum set out, depart

requīrō, requīrere, requīsīvī/ requīsiī, requīsītum need, require

referō, referre, rettulī, relātum carry, bring back

revertor, revertī, reversus sum return

rostrum, -ī n. beak

sagitta, -ae f. arrow

scrūta, -ōrum n. pl. trash

sextus, -a, -um sixth

Stymphālus, -ī m. Stymphalus, a Greek lake and town of the same name

transfīgō, transfīgere, transfīxī, transfixum pierce through

ubīque everywhere

ut as

verrō, verrere, verrī, versum sweep clean

vescor, vescī (+ abl.) take food, devour

POSTQUAM LĒGISTĪ

Answer in both English and Latin.

1. Why does Xanthus laugh while he is sweeping the floor of the peristyle?
2. What does Eurystheus promise Hercules?
3. What are the unusual characteristics of the Stymphalian birds?
4. What obstacle does Hercules face in dealing with these birds?
5. How does the god Vulcan help Hercules?
6. Who does Rufus suggest can help the servants in their task?

Grammatica B

Review of Deponent Verbs: All Tenses

The following chart provides all the forms of the 1st conjugation deponent verb *cōnor*.

	PRESENT SYSTEM			PERFECT SYSTEM		
	Singular					
Person	**Present**	**Imperfect**	**Future**	**Perfect**	**Pluperfect**	**Future Perfect**
1st	cōnor	cōnābar	cōnābor	cōnātus, -a, -um sum	cōnātus, -a, -um eram	cōnātus, -a, -um erō
2nd	cōnāris	cōnābāris	cōnāberis	cōnātus, -a, -um es	cōnātus, -a, -um erās	cōnātus, -a, -um eris
3rd	cōnātur	cōnābātur	cōnābitur	cōnātus, -a, -um est	cōnātus, -a, -um erat	cōnātus, -a, -um erit
	Plural					
1st	cōnāmur	cōnābāmur	cōnābimur	cōnātī, -ae, -a sumus	cōnātī, -ae, -a erāmus	cōnātī, -ae, -a erimus
2nd	cōnāminī	cōnābāminī	cōnābiminī	cōnātī, -ae, -a estis	cōnātī, -ae, -a erātis	cōnātī, -ae, -a eritis
3rd	cōnantur	cōnābantur	cōnābuntur	cōnātī, -ae, -a sunt	cōnātī, -ae, -a erant	cōnātī, -ae, -a erunt

EXERCEĀMUS!

28-4 Deponent Synopses

This exercise is exactly like 28-2. Remember that in some of the forms gender will be an issue!
Fill in all the missing pieces.

3RD SINGULAR OF *CŌNOR, CŌNĀRĪ, CŌNĀTUS SUM* "PUELLA"		
Tense	**Latin**	**English Translation**
Present	cōnātur	she tries
Imperfect	cōnābātur	
Future		she will try
Perfect	cōnāta est	
Pluperfect		she had tried
Future Perfect		

3RD PLURAL OF *POLLICEOR, POLLICĒRĪ, POLLICITUS SUM* "LICINIA ET VALERIA"

Tense	Latin	English Translation
Present	pollicentur	
Imperfect		
Future	pollicēbuntur	
Perfect		they have promised
Pluperfect		
Future Perfect		they will have promised

1ST PLURAL OF *SEQUOR, SEQUĪ, SECŪTUS SUM* "TŪ ET EGO" (masc.)

Tense	Latin	English Translation
Present		we follow
Imperfect	sequēbāmur	
Future		
Perfect		we followed
Pluperfect		
Future Perfect		

2ND PLURAL OF *PRŌGREDIOR, PRŌGREDĪ, PRŌGRESSUS SUM* "PUERĪ"

Tense	Latin	English Translation
Present		
Imperfect		
Future		
Perfect		
Pluperfect		
Future Perfect		

Mōrēs Rōmānī

Deī Opificēs: Vulcānus et Minerva

Both gods who help Hercules in the labors narrated by Xanthus were patrons of arts and crafts. *Vulcānus, -ī* m. was the god of fire known to the Greeks as Hephaestus. *Minerva, -ae* f. was the goddess of arts and crafts known as Athena in Greece. Vulcan's forge was said to be in Mt. Aetna in Sicily. Here Vulcan made thunderbolts for Jupiter, the god of the sky, thunder, and lightning. Here Vulcan also made new armor for Aeneas at the request of Venus, the hero's mother. You can read about Aeneas' armor in Vergil's *Aeneid* 8. The Romans celebrated the feast of *Vulcānālia* on August 23. Vulcan was especially worshipped by craftsmen like Aelius. The "Steel City" of Birmingham, Alabama, celebrates Vulcan with a giant statue by Giuseppe Moretti (1857–1935), dedicated in 1904 and depicted at right.

Vulcānus Super Alabamam *statua aēnea ā Giuseppe Moretti (1857–1935)*

Minerva in Tennessee

Minerva was the goddess of wisdom, poets, actors, and physicians. Her most important temple was located on the Aventine Hill in Rome, but she was also worshipped along with Jupiter and Juno on the Capitoline Hill. A colossal statue of Minerva-Athena stands in the Parthenon in Nashville, Tennessee, a city which considers itself the "Athens of the South." Through her association with the Greek goddess Athena, Minerva was also associated with crafts, especially women's crafts like weaving. Ovid's tale of Minerva's competition with the mortal Arachne is told in his *Metamorphōsēs* 6.5–145. Here, Ovid describes how Minerva challenges Arachne to a weaving contest. The mortal woman works so well that, in the end, the goddess draws the contest to a close by transforming Arachne into the first spider. Here is how Ovid describes the transformation. Read the story in this simplified version with less poetic word order. All the words in bold are parts of Arachne's human body. Watch how they are changed into something else.

> **comae** dēfluxērunt, et cum comīs et **nārēs** et **aurēs** (dēfluxērunt),
> et **caput** fit minimum; quoque tōtō **corpore** parva est:
> **digitī** exīlēs in **latere** pro **crūribus** haerent;
> **venter** alia membra habet; dē ūnō tamen illa stāmen remittit
> et arānea tēlās antīquās exercet.

Ovid *Metamorphōsēs* 6.141–145

🔊 VERBA ŪTENDA

arānea, -ae f. spider
auris, auris f. ear
coma, comae f. hair
crūs, crūris n. shin, leg
dēfluō, dēfluere, dēfluxī, dēfluxum disappear
digitus, -ī m. finger

exerceō, exercēre, exercuī, exercitum practice
exīlis, exīle thin, small
haereō, haerēre, haesī, haesum cling to
latus, lateris n. side
membrum, -ī n. body part

nārēs, nārium f. pl. nostrils
remittō, remittere, remīsī, remissum send back
stāmen, stāminis n. thread
tēla, -ae f. loom, web
venter, ventris m. belly, abdomen

Latīna Hodierna

Scītisne?

Did you know that…

- The English word "volcano" is derived from *Vulcānus*? Why is this so?
- "Vulcanization" is a process named after the god? What is it and how did it get its name?
- Arachne gives her name to the scientific term for spiders? What is the name for the genus?
- A "ventriloquist" speaks (*loqu-*) from the stomach (*ventris*)? Is this true?
- A flower's stamen comes from the Latin word for "thread" (*stāmen*)? Why?
- Numbers are called "digits" because we count with our fingers (*digitī*)? Why then are we living in the digital age?
- The world's largest cast iron statue, representing Vulcan, can be found in Birmingham, Alabama?
- A replica of Phidias' statue of Athena was built to celebrate the 200th anniversary of Tennessee statehood and was placed in the Parthenon in Nashville in 1996?
- The largest active volcano in Europe is not Mt. Vesuvius but Mt. Etna in Sicily?
- The best preserved ancient Greek temples are in Sicily, not in Greece?

Orbis Terrārum Rōmānus

Aetna et Sicilia

Mt. Aetna (*Aetna, -ae* f.), in Sicily (*Sicilia, -ae* f.), is the largest active volcano in Europe. The Romans considered it to be the forge of the god Vulcan.

Sicily first came under Roman control in 242 B.C. as a result of the First Punic War, which Rome fought against Carthage. Rome's first province, however, was not fully subdued until the end of the Second Punic War (218–201 B.C.). Sicily was an important agricultural center (especially for grain) for the Roman world, but the island continued to be a province of Rome (rather than part of Italy) until the end of the empire in the West.

During a siege of Syracuse in 212 B.C., Roman soldiers killed the Greek mathematician and inventor Archimedes (*Archimēdēs, -is* m.), who is said to have run out of his bath shouting "Eureka!" ("I found it!" in Greek) when he discovered the theory of water displacement. Archimedes is famous not just for sophisticated mathematical discoveries but also for such wonders as devices that could lift entire ships out of the water and set attacking ships on fire from afar. While a quaestor in Sicily, Cicero visited the tomb of Archimedes.

Many cities in Sicily were originally Greek and preserve impressive pre-Roman ruins, such as the temple depicted at right. The most important cities in Sicily during the Roman period were:

- *Syrācūsae, -ārum* f. pl. (modern Siracusa)
- *Agrigentum, -ī* n. (modern Agrigento)
- *Catana, -ae* f. (modern Catania)
- *Messāna, -ae* f. (modern Messina)

Ēruptiō Aetnae

Agrigentum Hodiē

Archimēdēs dīcēns "Eurēka!" in balneō

Sicilia et Italia

QUID PUTĀS?

1. Why do you think the people of Birmingham, Alabama, chose a statue of the god Vulcan to overlook their city?
2. Why was Arachne's transformation into a spider both suitable and ironic?
3. What tombs or graves of famous people are visited in the United States? Why do you think people do this?
4. Why do you think Archimedes was killed by Roman soldiers during the Siege of Syracuse in 212 B.C.? Does this sort of thing happen in war today?
5. Make five more "Did You Know?" (*Scītisne?*) questions based on information you have learned about ancient Rome and Latin in this chapter.

EXERCEĀMUS!

28-5   Scrībāmus

Here is a simplified version of the story of Hercules and Pholus that you read in Chapter 21. Retell the story in the passive voice. Here is what you have to do.

- Marked in **bold** are all of the verbs you need to change from active to passive voice; e.g., **necāvit** would become **necātus est**.
- Marked in ***bold italics*** are the accusative objects of the active verbs you need to convert to the subjects of passive verbs; e.g., ***Pholum* necāvit** would become ***Pholus* necātus est**.
- Marked in *italics* are the subjects you need to turn into *ā/ab* + abl. to express the agent by whom the action of the passive verb is done; e.g., *Herculēs* ***Pholum* necāvit** becomes ***Pholus* ab Hercule necātus est**.

Follow the model and change each of the words numbered in the following paragraph accordingly.

Original

Herculēs, dum *iter* in Arcadiam **facit**, ad spēluncam Pholī vēnit. *Pholus* (1) ***eum*** (2) benignē **excēpit** (3) et ***cēnam*** (4) **parāvit** (5). At *Herculēs* (6) ***vīnum*** (7) **postulāvit** (8). Sed *Pholus* (9) ***hoc vīnum*** (10) nōn **dedit** (11). "Sī ***hoc vīnum*** (12) **dederō**, (13) *centaurī* (14) ***mē*** (15) **interficient** (16)." *Herculēs* (17) tamen ***pōculum*** (18) vīnī dē amphorā **hausit**. (19).

Modified

→ Dum *iter* in Arcadiam **facitur** *ab Hercule*, vēnit ad spēluncam Pholī.

28-6   Colloquāmur

Practice reading this dialogue between Rufus and Xanthus with a partner. Read with good intonation, as if these were lines from a play or a real conversation.

Rūfus: Dī immortālēs! Hoc peristȳlium sordidissimum est.

Xanthus: Sīc, vērē! Ecce! Cibus et scrūta ubīque!

Rūfus: Sīc semper est—homō dīves, pavīmentum sordidum! Magistrī epulantur sed relinquunt squālōrem magnum quī semper ā servīs—ā nōbīs!—purgātur.

Xanthus: Nōn solum ā servīs, amīce, sed etiam ā deō opus sordidum agitur. Mementō Herculis! Locus sordidissimus ab illō ōlim purgātus est!

Rūfus: Dīc mihi dē hōc labōre! Ut scīs, Germānicus sum et paulum dē hīs tuīs fābulīs Graecīs sciō.

Xanthus: Narrābō! Mē narrante, tempus celerius fugiet!

28-7 Verba Discenda

Find the *verbum discendum* that lies behind or is related to each word marked in **bold** in the following narrative. Look up the meaning of each English word if you have to.

As he walked through the museum, Dr. Osgood Littleworth, professor of **aviation** (1), was not pleased with the progress being made on the **mural** (2). Clearly, the date of completion the foreman had promised during their last **conference** (3) was a total **fabrication** (4). Angry, he ran outside, hopped on his bicycle, and **pedalled** (5) to the **prefabricated** (6) hut where the foreman had his office. The professor knew he would find the foreman there, eating donuts as usual, with **confectioner's** (7) sugar all over his shirt, and reading the paper. Well, he would just **interrupt** (8) him!

Dr. Littleworth should have been more attentive. He had forgotten about the **ubiquity** (9) of potholes in this area. His bicycle hit a **spacious** (10) pothole and he fell, fracturing his skull near the **sagittal** (11) crest. As he fell, it is reported, he uttered a **sordid** (12) word that must be expurgated here. Alas, the poor man died and his bones now reside in an **ossuary** (13) in the museum, next to the unfinished mural.

🔊 VERBA DISCENDA

avis, avis **f. bird** [avian, aviary]

conferō, conferre, contulī, collātum **bring together, collect;** *sē conferre* **go (betake oneself); talk together** [confer, collate]

conficiō, conficere, confēcī, confectum **do, accomplish, complete** [confection]

faber, fabrī **m. craftsman, artisan; smith; workman**

ferō: sē ferre **go (betake oneself)**

gerō: sē gerere **act (conduct oneself)**

Hercule! **By Hercules!**

iubeō, iubēre, iussī, iussum **order**

lacus, -ūs **m. lake** [lacustrine]

mūrus, -ī **m. wall** [intramural]

neque **and not;** *neque… neque* **neither…nor**

oppidum, -ī **n. town**

os, ossis **n. bone** [ossify]

paulum **a little, somewhat**

pēs, pedis **m. foot** [pedestrian]

prīmum **first, at first**

proficiscor, proficiscī, profectus sum **set out, depart**

rumpō, rumpere, rūpī, ruptum **break, burst, break down** [rupture]

sagitta, -ae **f. arrow** [Sagittarius]

sciō, scīre, scīvī/sciī, scītum **know, know about** [science]

sordidus, -a, -um **filthy** [sordid]

spatium, -iī **n. space** [spatial]

tantus, -a, -um **so great**

ubīque **everywhere** [ubiquitous]

umquam **ever**

Angulus Grammaticus

More on Voice

As you know already, **voice** indicates the relationship between the subject and the action of the verb. In active voice, the subject performs the action.

*Pater infantem ad uxōrem **gessit**.*   The father **carried** the infant to his wife.

In passive voice, the subject receives the action.

*Infans ā patre ad uxōrem **gessus est**.*   The infant **was carried** by his father to his wife.

Latin deponent verbs require attention because they use passive endings but have active meanings:

*Pater infantem gerēns ad uxōrem **profectus est**.*   The father, carrying the infant, **set off** to his wife.

In this chapter you saw these three Latin words in which the subject both performs and receives the action.

> *sē conferre* go (betake oneself)
> *sē ferre* go (betake oneself)
> *sē gerere* act (conduct oneself)

As you have already seen, both Latin and English express reflexion by using **reflexive pronouns**.

> *Pater **sē** cum dignitāte **gessit**.*   The father **conducted himself** with dignity.

Such **reflexive** verbs are somewhat unusual in Latin but are very common in the modern Romance languages. Here are a few examples. Pay attention to where the reflexive appears in the modern verbs:

FRENCH	SPANISH	ITALIAN	LITERAL TRANSLATION	ENGLISH TRANSLATION
se marier	casarse	sposarsi	marry oneself (to)	marry, get married
s' habiller	vestirse	vestirsi	dress oneself	get dressed
s'appeler	llamarse	chiamarsi	call oneself	be called, be named, "My name is…"

Note that the best English translation for these reflexive verbs is usually active (get dressed) rather than the literal reflexive one (dress oneself).

As we pointed out in Chapter 24, ancient Greek had a separate voice, called the middle (between active and passive), to express actions done on oneself or in one's own interest. Occasionally, in Latin, a passive verb can be used reflexively. For example, *sē fert* and *fertur* can both mean "he goes." Here is an example from Caesar:

> *Aliīque aliam in partem perterritī **ferēbantur**.*
> And, terrified, some **were going off** in one direction, others in another.

> Caesar *Dē Bellō Gallicō* 2.24

Note how the passive *ferēbantur* is translated like *sē ferēbant*, i.e., "they were going," even "they were rushing." Due to the influence of Greek on the Latin language, some Latin authors, like Vergil, occasionally used the passive voice as a **reflexive** (or Greek middle). Here are two examples from the *Aeneid*:

> *Et formīdātus nautīs **aperītur** Apollō.*
> And Apollo, dreaded by sailors, **shows himself**.

> Vergil *Aeneid* 3.275

Note how the passive form *aperītur* is translated reflexively (shows himself) rather than passively (is shown).

> *Hic torre **armātus** obustō.*
> He having **armed himself** with a burnt stick.

> *Aeneid* 7.506

Here the perfect passive participle *armātus*, used reflexively, is translated "having armed himself" rather than "having been armed."

But don't worry (yourself)! This middle use of the passive is mostly poetic and was not part of the everyday language of the Romans. You will not see such constructions until you move on to more advanced Latin readings, and, even then, you will not see them very often.

29

Avus Cārus

Lectiō Prīma

Antequam Legis

Servīlius Avus

In this *lectiō* you meet Servilius' 82-year-old father, who lives with his son and his family. The elder Servilius is hard of hearing but enjoys being around his son and his grandchildren. Because of his hearing problem, he misunderstands many things he is told, and has to have things repeated to him by the slave who personally attends him.

Future Active Participles and Infinitives

This chapter introduces you to the final participle and infinitive you have to learn. It also provides an overview for both verb forms.

Participles

Latin has a **future active participle (FAP)** formed by adding *-ūrus, -a, -um* to the stem of the perfect passive participle:

vocāt- + *-ūrus* = *vocātūrus* (being) about to call, going to call

Present active	*vocāns*	calling
Perfect passive (P³)	*vocātus, -a, -um*	(having been) called
Future active (FAP)	*vocātūrus, -a, -um*	(being) about to call

The FAP of *sum* is *futūrus, -a, -um* (about to be, going to be).

Infinitives

The future active infinitive = FAP + *esse*.

vocātūrum + *esse* = *vocātūrum esse*   to be about to call

Pater familiās

LECTIŌNĒS:
PATER ET FĪLIUS
and
AVUS ET NEPŌTĒS

Members of the Servilius family talk over last night's banquet with grandfather Servilius. A major topic, of course, is Servilia's arranged marriage to Iullus Antonius—or is it to be Cordus after all?

This now completes your list of infinitives.

Present active:	*vocāre*	to call
Present passive	*vocārī*	to be called
Perfect active	*vocāvisse*	to have called
Perfect passive	*vocātum esse*	to have been called
Future active	*vocātūrum esse*	to be about to call

The future active infinitive of *sum* is *futūrum esse* (to be about to be).

Watch in this *lectiō* for participles marked in ***bold italics*** and for infinitives marked in **bold**.

EXERCEĀMUS!

29-1 Recognizing Different Kinds of Participles and Infinitives

As you read, find one example of each of the following kinds of Latin participles and infinitives. Then translate the word into English. For this exercise, "passive" includes deponent verbs. Follow the model.

present active participle	present active infinitive
perfect passive participle	present passive infinitive
future active participle	perfect active infinitive
	perfect passive infinitive
	future active infinitive

Line	Latin Word	Type	Translation
→ 2	*esse*	present active infinitive	to be

In Peristȳliō

🔊 PATER ET FĪLIUS

Māne est et, ut solet, avus M. Servīlius Sevērus in peristȳliō sedet. Ōlim senātor et pater familiās erat sed nunc avus benignus **esse** et in peristȳliō **sedēre** māvult. Surdus est et, cum avus adest, familia omnia **repetere** dēbet.

Servīlius, patrem ***sedentem vidēns***, intrat et "Avē, pater," inquit, "quid agis hodiē?"

5   Avus, manum post aurem ***ponēns***, rogat: "Quid? Quid dīxistī?"

Famulus, avum ut semper ***tuēns***, magnā vōce clāmat: "Dominus dīxit: 'Quid agis hodiē?!!!'"

Avus "Bene," inquit, "hodiē! Bene! Sed, convīviō ***confectō***, quaestiōnēs habeō. Bonumne convīvium erat? Oportuit mē **adesse** et cum hospitibus **colloquī**, sed senēs quoque multum **dormīre** oportet! Sed, nōn mē **querī** decet—vīta, quamquam paene ***confecta***, bona est. Nōn mē vītam longam **vixisse** paenitet et bonum est ōtium
10   **habēre**. Sed, dē convīviō dīcēbāmus—eratne bonum?"

Servīlius: "Nōlī anxius **esse**, pater. Vidētur convīvium optimum **fuisse** et omnēs hospitēs ***exeuntēs*** laetī **esse** vidēbantur, praesertim Maecēnās Polliōque. Sed iste Iullus Antōnius ēbrius et valdē molestus fīēbat. Necesse erat eum, carmina ***cantūrum***, forās **ēicī**. Certum est: ille nōn rursus hospes meus erit!"

Avus: "Quid? Nōlī submissā vōce **ūtī**! Quid dīxistī?"

15   Famulus, "Iullus Antōnius," clāmat "ēbrius fīēbat!"

Avus: "Vae! Vērum est. Iullus dīcitur frequenter apud convīvia ēbrius atque molestus **factus esse**. Illō ad convīvium ***adventūrō***, pater cēnae semper cautus esse dēbet."

Servīlius "Ita," inquit. "Vidētur nunc ille Servīliam nostram in mātrimōnium nōn **ductūrus esse**. Servīliā ***nuptūrā*** Caecilia laetissima erat, sed nunc, nuptiīs ***ruptīs***, maesta est. Marītum fīliae Servīliae aptum **invenīrī**
20   necesse est. Quid, pater, dē Quīntō Naeviō Cordō intellegis?"

Avus "Familiam," inquit, "eius bene cognōvī. Adulēscens probus et honestus vidētur et . . ."

Avō subitō fessō et dormītūrō, Servīlius nihil aliud rogat. "Pater," inquit, "nunc ad Forum **īre** dēbeō. Hāc nocte dē Cordō plūs loquēmur." Et, hīs ***dictīs***, abiit.

🔊 VERBA ŪTENDA

anxius, -a, -um uneasy, anxious

aptus, -a, -um suitable, fit

auris, auris f. ear

Avē! Greetings!

avus, -ī m. grandfather, ancester

cognoscō, cognoscere, cognōvī, cognitum learn, get to know, observe; (perfect) know

ēiciō, ēicere, ēiēcī, ēiectum throw out

famulus, -ī m. servant, attendant

forās outdoors, out

frequenter often, frequently

honestus, -a, -um worthy, decent, of high rank

mātrimōnium, -iī n. marriage, matrimony

molestus, -a, -um troublesome, tiresome

nūbō, nūbere, nupsī, nuptum marry

oculus, -ī m. eye

oportuit mē adesse "I ought to have been there"

ōtium, -iī n. leisure

paenitet, paenitēre, paeni- tuit (imp.) it gives rea- son for regret; mē paenitet I am sorry

pater familiās, patris familiās m. pater famil- ias, head of the family

queror, querī, questus sum complain

repetō, repetere, repetīvī/ repetiī, repetītum repeat

senātor, -ōris m. senator, member of the senate

senātus, -ūs m. senate

senex, senis m. old man

soleō, solēre, solitus sum be accustomed (to)

submissus, -a, -um low

surdus, -a, -um deaf

tueor, tuērī, tuitus sum look at, watch over, look after, protect

vae! woe! alas!

vigil, vigilis m./f. sentry, guard; firefighter; pl., fire brigade

vīvō, vīvere, vixī, victum live

POSTQUAM LĒGISTĪ

Answer these questions in English (E) or Latin (L) as directed.

1. How is the life of Servilius' father different than it used to be when he was younger? (E)
2. Why didn't Servilius' father attend the banquet? (L)
3. What does Servilius tell his father about the banquet? (L)
4. What gossip has Servilius' father heard about Iullus Antonius? (L)
5. Do you think that Servilius' father approves of a possible match between Servilia and Cordus? Why or why not? (E)

Gemma

Because the Romans equated age with wisdom, there was a minimum age requirement for membership in the senate. So both *senātus* and *senātor* are derived from *senex*.

Grammatica A

Participle Review and Consolidation

The future active participle (FAP) is the last participial form you need to learn in Latin. Here is a list of all the Latin participles for the verb *audiō*:

Present active:	*audiēns*	hearing
Perfect passive:	*audītus, -a, -um*	(having been) heard
Future active:	*audītūrus, -a, -um*	about to hear, going to hear

Here are the participles for the deponent verb *cōnor*:

Present active:	*cōnāns*	trying
Perfect passive:	*cōnātus, -a, -um*	(having) tried
Future active:	*cōnātūrus, -a, -um*	about to try, going to try

Notā Bene:

- The present active participle is a 3rd declension adjective.
- The FAP and P³ are 2-1-2 adjectives.
- English has participles that Latin lacks:

  "being heard" (present passive)
  "having heard" (perfect active)

- As you might expect, the perfect passive participle of deponent verbs is translated actively.

- The present active and future active participles of deponent verbs are **exceptions** to the deponent rule. They are active in form and are translated actively.

As a **verbal adjective**, a participle has grammatical features of both an adjective and a verb.

As an **adjective**, a participle has gender, number, and case and GNCs with a noun or pronoun (either expressed or understood): *virīs audientibus* (the men listening); *fēminae audītae* (the women having been heard); *avus audītūrus* (grandfather about to hear).

As a **verb**, a participle has tense and voice and can take an object: *avus **verba** audītūrus* (grandfather about to hear the words).

The FAP adds another possibility to the ablative absolute. Consider the ablative absolutes in the following sentences.

Cordō dīcente, *Servīlia laeta est.*	When Cordus is speaking Servilia is happy.
Cordō vīsō, *Servīlia laeta est.*	Because Cordus was seen, Servilia is happy.
Cordō dictūrō, *Servīlia laeta est.*	When Cordus is about to speak, Servilia is happy.

EXERCEĀMUS!

29-2 Participle Review

In each of the following sentences identify the participle and the noun with which it GNC's. Give the tense and voice of the participle. Then translate the two words. Follow the model.

→ Avum in peristȳliō sedentem vīdī.
   Avum sedentem (present active)   grandfather sitting

1. Avus sedēns in peristȳliō multa dixit.
2. Avus cum fīliō collocūtus nunc dormit.
3. Avō habitante in fīliī dōmō, familia laeta est.
4. Servus avō in peristȳliō sedentī cibum dat.
5. Dē avō fessō et dormītūrō servī anxiī erant.
6. Puerī avum dē convīviō audientem vīdērunt.
7. Avō dormiente famulus ē peristȳliō currit.
8. Avō dormītūrō famulus ē peristȳliō currit.
9. Cordō vīsō Servīlius nōn laetus est.
10. Servīlia, Cordum vīsūra, laeta est.

Infinitive Review and Consolidation

The future active infinitive is the last infinitive form you need to learn in Latin. Here is a list of all the Latin infinitives for the verb *dūcō*:

Present active	*dūcere*	to lead
Present passive	*dūcī*	to be led
Perfect active	*duxisse*	to have led
Perfect passive	*ductum esse*	to have been led
Future active	*ductūrum esse*	to be about to lead

Here is a list of all the infinitives for the deponent verb *sequor*:

Present passive	*sequī*	to follow
Perfect passive	*secūtum esse*	to have followed
Future active	*secūtūrum esse*	to be about to follow

Notā Bene:

- Unlike regular verbs, deponent verbs have only one present and perfect infinitive.
- As you might expect, the present passive and perfect passive infinitives of deponents are translated actively, e.g., *cōnārī* (to try).
- Like the present and future active participles of deponent verbs (e.g., *cōnāns* or *cōnātūrus*), the future active infinitive is an **exception** to the deponent rule. It is an active form translated actively, e.g., *cōnātūrum esse* (to be about to try).

As a **verbal noun**, an infinitive has grammatical features of both nouns and verbs.

As a **noun**, an infinitive

- is neuter.

    Vīvere bonum est.   It is good to be alive.

- can function as either the subject or object of a verb.

Amāre bonum est.	To love is good.	(subjective infinitive)
Volō amāre.	I wish to love.	(objective infinitive)

As a **verb**, an infinitive

- has voice and can be active or passive.

    *Vidētur **amāre**.* He seems to be in love.
    *Vidētur **amārī**.* He seems to be loved.

- has tense.

    ***Amāre** bonum est sed numquam **amāvisse** malum est.*
    To love is good but never to have loved is bad.

- can take a subject (usually in the accusative case).

    ***Tē** adesse volō.* I want **you** to be here.

- can take an object.

    *Vidētur **mē** amāre.* She seems to love **me**.

- can also **complement** or "complete" the action of another verb.

    Possum amāre. I can love.

EXERCEĀMUS!

29-3 Infinitive Review

Choose the answer that best translates the following infinitives.

1. sessūrum esse: a. to sit   b. to be sat   c. to have sat   d. to be about to sit
2. collocūtum esse: a. to talk   b. to have talked   c. to be talked   d. to be about to talk
3. factūrum esse: a. to be done   b. to have been done c. to be about to be done   d. to be about to do
4. invenīre: a. to find   b. to be found   c. to have found   d. to be about to find
5. ductum esse: a. to be led   b. to have led   c. to have been led   d. to be about to lead
6. futūrum esse: a. to be   b. to have been   c. to be about to have been   d. to be about to be
7. potuisse: a. to be able   b. to have been able c. to be about to have been able   d. to be about to be able
8. tuērī: a. to see   b. to be seen   c. to have seen   d. to have been seen
9. cognitum esse: a. to know   b. to be known   c. to have known   d. to have been known
10. confectūrum esse: a. to complete   b. to be completed   c. to have been completed   d. to be about to complete

Lectiō Secunda

Antequam Legis

At the time of our story, there was no public fire brigade in Rome despite the great danger and frequency of fires in the city. There were private fire companies, the most notorious of which, perhaps, had belonged to M. Licinius Crassus (c.115–51 B.C.), who was said to have acquired some of his great wealth by purchasing buildings as they burned and then having his private firefighters put out the blaze. Augustus did not establish public *cohortēs vigilum*, or fire brigades, until 6 A.D. Q. Naevius Sutorius Macro, the historical figure upon which Servilia's Cordus is based, eventually became prefect of these *vigilēs*. Cordus' interest in fires, as well as his wealth, comes from his father's investment with Crassus in these "fire sales."

In *Lectiō Secunda*, the grandfather's deafness affects the grammar of the sentences as you enounter indirect statement.

Direct and Indirect Statement

These sentences are in direct statement, reporting the exact words of the speaker.

> Kate said, "I will do this for you."
> Kate said, "I did this for you."

Often, however, the words of a speaker are told to us by **indirect statement** as in these examples.

> Kate said **that she would do this for you**.
> Kate said **that she had done this for you**.

Now let's look at direct and indirect statements in Latin.

Direct Statement:	*Servīlia dixit, "Vīdī Cordum."*	Servīlia said, "I saw Cordus."
Indirect Statement:	*Servīlia dixit* **sē Cordum vīdisse**.	Servīlia said that she had seen Cordus.

In Latin, an indirect statement consists of:

- An introductory verb (also called a "head verb") (*dixit*)
- An accusative subject + infinitive construction (*sē vīdisse*)

How do you translate this type of construction?

- The word "that" is optional to begin the indirect statement in English.

  a) Servilia said that . . . or b) Servilia said . . .

- Translate the infinitive as a regular verb.

  sē Cordum vīdisse. ⟶ she had seen Cordus

Translating an indirect statement takes some practice. For now, these general examples will suffice:

Direct Statement: *Caesar venit.*   Caesar is coming.

Indirect Statements:

Sciō Caesarem venīre.	I know that Caesar is coming. (same time as main verb)
Sciō Caesarem vēnisse.	I know that Caesar came. (time before)
Sciō Caesarem ventūrum esse.	I know that Caesar is going to come. (time after)
Scīvī Caesarem venīre.	I knew that Caesar was coming. (same time)
Scīvī Caesarem vēnisse.	I knew that Caesar had come. (time before)
Scīvī Caesarem ventūrum esse.	I knew that Caesar was going to come. (time after)

This is all you need to get started with indirect statements. To help you recognize them in *Lectiō Secunda*, we have marked the following words:

- The *verb* that introduces the indirect statement is in *italics*.
- The **infinitive construction** is in **bold**.
- The *accusative* subject of the infinitive is in ***bold italics***.

Servīlius *dīcit* **sē** Iullum ēbrium **vīdisse**.

EXERCEĀMUS!

29-4 Relative Time in Indirect Statements

Gemma

Macrons matter! What is the difference between *Avē* and *Ave*?

Before you begin, translate these indirect statements. Pay attention to the tenses of the main verb and of the infinitive. All the sentences refer to Servilia loving Cordus. Follow the model.

→ Servīlia dīcit sē Cordum amāre. Servilia says that she loves Cordus.

1. Servīlia dixit sē Cordum amāre.
2. Servīlia dīcit sē nullum alium amāvisse.
3. Servīlia dixit sē nullum alium amāvisse.
4. Servīlia dīcit sē Cordum semper amāvisse.
5. Servīlia dīcit sē Cordum semper amātūram esse.
6. Servīlia dixit sē Cordum semper amātūram esse.

Avus manum post aurem pōnit.

🔊 AVUS ET NEPŌTĒS

Postquam Servīlius exiit, nepōtēs in peristȳlium ruērunt.
Servīlia avum osculāvit. "Avē, ave. Quid avus meus agit hodiē? Laeta avum meum videō!"
Avus: "Quid? Quid dixit? Quid lātum est?"
Famulus, clāmāns in aurem: "Nihil lātum est! Servīlia *dixit sē* 'laetam' avum suum **vidēre**!"
5   Servīlia: "*Sciō tē* cum patre dē Cordō **locūtum esse**. Paterne tibi *dixit mē* Cordum **amāre**?"
Avus: "Quid? Dē corde meō dīcis? Cor meum, quamquam vetus, iam forte est. Fortasse moritūrus sum, sed nōn hodiē!"
Famulus, rīdēns, clāmat: "Servīlia nōn dē corde tuō sed dē adulescente Cordō dīcit. *Dixit sē* Cordum **amāre** et **Cordum** bonum adulescentem **esse**."
Avus: "Ita, Cordus bonus adulescens est. *Spērō tē* laetam **futūram esse**."
10 Lūcius quoque avum osculat et avus respondet: "Lūcī! *Audīvī* **sīmiam** ferōcem ā tē in Forō **captum esse**. Vērumne est?"
Lūcius: "Iam tibi *dixī* nōn **mē**, sed **paedagōgum** sīmiam **cēpisse**. Iam tibi *dixī* illum **sīmiam** nōn ferōcem sed sagācem **esse**, quod in ārā Dīvī Iūliī sēdit et sīc salvus erat!"
Avus: "Nōn, nōn, puer! Nōn licet tālia dīcere! Dīvus Iūlius nullus sīmia est. Hmmph! Nōlī nūgās dīcere!"
15 Famulus clāmat: "Nōn *dixit* **Caesarem** sīmiam **esse**! *Dixit sīmiam* in ārā Caesaris **sēdisse**! Āra! Āra!"
Avus respondet: "Ah, vērum est. Aura sub arbore bona est! Sed, tū, Marce. Quid tū, studiīs rhētoricīs confectīs, actūrus es?"
Marcus "Ave cāre," inquit, "*in animō habeō mē* in Graeciā rhētoricīs **studēre**. Sīcut tū senātor fīam!"
Avus: "Quid? Quid dixistī? 'Quandō fīēs vēnātor'? 'Vēnātor'? Sīmiās captūrus es? Nōn bene audīvī."
20 Marcus respondēre incipit, sed famulus, rīdēns, sē inclīnat ad aurem avī et clāmat: "Marcus *dixit sē* 'senātōrem,' nōn 'vēnātōrem,' **futūrum esse**. Domine, sitiens et fessus vidēris. Ecce! Pōtum bibe et, fortasse, paulisper resquiesce."

🔊 VERBA ŪTENDA

animus, -ī m. mind	*famulus, -ī* m. servant,	**morior, morī, mortuus**	*requiescō, requiescere,*
arbor, arboris f. tree	attendant	**sum die**	*requiēvī, requiētum,* rest
aura, -ae f. breeze	*in animō habēre* "to have in	*nūgae, -ārum* f. pl. trifle,	*sagax, sagācis* wise, sharp
auris, auris f. ear	mind, intend"	nonsense	*sitiens, sitientis* thirsty
Avē! Greetings!	*inclīnō* (1) bend, tilt	*osculō* (1) kiss	**vēnātor, -ōris m. hunter**
avus, -ī m. grandfather	**licet, licēre, licuit, licitum**	*paulisper* for a little while	*vetus, veteris* aged, old
dīvus, -a, -um divine	**est (+ dat.) imp. it is**	**pōtus, -ūs m. (a) drink**	
	permitted		

POSTQUAM LĒGISTĪ

1. What does *Avus* hear when Servilia says, "*Laeta avum meum videō!*"?
2. What did Servilia know her father had been talking about to her grandfather?
3. From his conversation with Lucius, what signs exist that *Avus* might be losing his memory?
4. Why might *Avus* be so defensive about Julius Caesar?
5. What story did *Avus* hear about Lucius? What details did *Avus* get wrong?
6. What news does Marcus give his grandfather?

Grammatica B

Indirect Statement

As you saw in reading *Lectiō Secunda*, Latin marks an indirect statement much more clearly than English does. So, in line 2 Servilia speaks directly to her grandfather and says:

*Laeta avum meum **videō**.* Happily I see my grandfather.

Whereas in line 4 the *famulus* tells *Avus*:

*Servīlia dixit sē 'laetam' avum suum **vidēre**!* Servilia said that she sees her grandfather happily.

Note the changes:

Direct		*Laeta avum meum **videō**.*
Indirect	*Servīlia dixit*	*sē 'laetam' avum suum **vidēre**!*

- 1st person ⟶ 3rd person
- The implied *ego* ⟶ *sē*
- *laeta* ⟶ *laetam* because the subject of an infinitive (*sē*) is accusative.

Why an accusative subject? This all makes some sense if you think about this sentence:

"I saw Iullus drinking."

What did you see? You saw both Iullus and the act of drinking. So, in Latin, "Iullus" becomes an accusative "subject" and the "drinking" a verbal noun called the infinitive.

Vīdī Iullum bibere.

Eum vs. Sē

Consider this English sentence:

"Iullus knows that he is drunk."

In English, depending on context, the "he" could be Iullus or someone else. Latin has a way to avoid this confusion:

*Iullus scit **sē** ēbrium esse.*   ⟶   *sē* = same as subject
*Iullus scit **eum** ēbrium esse.*   ⟶   *eum* = someone other than the subject

Head Verbs

One way to know that an indirect statement is coming is to pay attention to the main verb of the sentence. Verbs of speaking, thinking, knowing, hearing, feeling, and the like are called "head verbs" and often introduce indirect statements. Here is a list of head verbs you have already seen as *Verba Discenda*:

dīcō	*spērō*	*monstrō*
respondeō	*intellegō*	*sentiō*
clāmō	*narrō*	*loquor*
videō	*crēdō*	
audiō	*sciō*	

Do you remember what these verbs mean? Why do you think they are called "head verbs"?

Now let's talk a little about word order in indirect statement. When the infinitive in an indirect discourse takes a direct object, two accusatives occur in a row, but the first is the subject and the second is the object. Compare:

Vīdī gladiātōrem leōnem interficere.
Vīdī leōnem gladiātōrem interficere.

In the first sentence the lion is dead, but not in the second one. So, in summary,

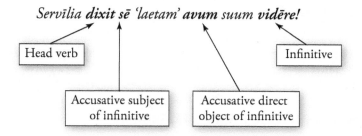

Relative not Real Time

When translating infinitives and participles, it is important to keep in mind that their tense indicates **relative time**, not real time. Remember this basic equation concerning participles and infinitives.

- The present tense of the infinitive or the participle shows **same time** as the main verb.
- The perfect tense shows **time before** the main verb.
- The future tense shows **time after** the main verb.

Consider the participles in these sentences.

Videō fēminam **canentem**.	I see the singing woman.
Vīdī fēminam **canentem**.	I saw the singing woman.
Vidēbō fēminam **canentem**.	I will see the singing woman.

The participle stays the same in each Latin sentence because as a present participle it shows that the singing is going on exactly at the same time as the seeing (no matter its tense).

Even in ablative absolutes, the tenses of the participles are relative rather than real. Here are some examples in which the main verb is in the past. Notice how the tense of the participle indicates when the action in the ablative absolute takes place relative to the action of the main verb.

Cordō dīcente, Servīlia laeta erat.	When Cordus was speaking Servilia was happy.
Cordō dictūrō, Servīlia laeta erat.	Since Cordus was about to speak, Servilia was happy.
Cordō vīsō, Servīlia laeta erat.	Because Cordus was seen, Servilia was happy.

Now consider these sentences with infinitives.

Servīlia laeta **esse** vidētur.	Servilia seems to be happy.
Servīlia laeta **esse** vidēbātur.	Servilia seemed to be happy.
Servīlia laeta **esse** vidēbitur.	Servilia will seem to be happy.

In each case the present infinitive is indicating that, at the very time of the main verb, Servilia is happy.

Infinitives in indirect statement also show relative, not absolute, time. Compare these sentences:

SAME TIME	*Dīcit sē avum vidēre.*	She says she sees her grandfather.
	Dixit sē avum vidēre.	She said that she was seeing/saw her grandfather.
TIME BEFORE	*Dīcit sē avum vīdisse.*	She says she saw her grandfather.
	Dixit sē avum vīdisse.	She said that she had seen her grandfather.
TIME AFTER	*Dīcit sē avum vīsūram esse.*	She says she will see her grandfather.
	Dixit sē avum vīsūram esse.	She said that she was going to see her grandfather.

The infinitive should be translated, therefore, based on the relationship it shows with the head verb that introduces it.

EXERCEĀMUS!

29-5   Relative Time in Indirect Statement

Indicate the tenses of both the main (head) verb and the infinitive in indirect statement in each of the following sentences. Then translate the sentence into English. Your translation can be a little loose, but be sure to show the time relationship between the head verb and the infinitive. Follow the model.

→   Marcus dixit sē in Graeciā habitātūrum esse.

Main (head) verb	*dixit*	perfect tense
Infinitive	*habitātūrum esse*	future tense

"Marcus said that he would live/was going to live in Greece."

1. Marcus dīcit sē in Graeciā habitāre.
2. Marcus dixit sē in Graeciā habitāre.
3. Marcus dīcit sē in Graeciā habitātūrum esse.
4. Marcus dīcit sē in Graeciā habitāvisse.
5. Marcus dixit sē in Graeciā habitāvisse.
6. Marcus dīcet sē in Graeciā habitāvisse.
7. Audiō sīmiam in forō captum esse.
8. Audiō sīmiam in forō capī.
9. Audiō tē sīmiam in forō captūrum esse.

Mōrēs Rōmānī

Pater Familiās

Do you remember from Chapter 16 that the Latin word *familia* refers not only to a biological family, but to a legal one? To a Roman, *familia* technically and legally meant all those individuals under the *potestās* (legal control) of the *pater familiās*, or head of the family, including servants and slaves that belonged to the household. In fact, very often when you see the word *familia* in Latin you should try translating it first as "my household" rather than "my family" (as we understand it).

The individuals in the *familia* included one's own children as well as the children of one's son and grandson. Under certain circumstances a wife was also under the legal control of her husband or her father- or grandfather-in-law.

This legal control was called *patria potestās*. The word *potestās* is important here. It refers to the kind of absolute legal authority held by the head of a Roman family. In other words, a *pater familiās* had the same total power over his children and relatives that he held over his slaves. This was considered to be a power of life and death. Originally a *pater familiās* could even sell his children into slavery or kill them with legal impunity, but this was certainly no longer the case by the time of Augustus. Nevertheless, even under Augustus, anyone who was not *pater familiās* had no individual legal rights separate from the *pater familiās*; that is, they could acquire property, but it came under the control of the *pater familiās*; they could marry and divorce, but only with the consent of the *pater familiās*.

Iustiniānus Imperātor

It was possible for a *pater familiās* to cede some of this authority to his son. This was called, legally, *maxima* or *media capitis dīminūtiō* (maximum or partial decrease of rights). This is what Servilius' father has done. Because of his advanced age, *Avus* has passed *patria potestās* over to his son Servilius, who is now *pater familiās*. If he had not done this, Servilius, Servilia, Marcus, and Lucius would all still be under the legal authority of *Avus*.

Here is how the power of *pater familiās* is described in the *Institūtiōnēs* 1.9 of the emperor Justinian (527–565 A.D.), which is the most comprehensive Roman law code surviving today. Notice how the law is written in the 1st person plural and addresses individual male citizens in the 2nd person singular. This selection is only slightly simplified.

Dē Patriā Potestāte

In potestāte nostrā sunt līberī nostrī, quōs ex iustīs nuptiīs prōcreāverimus. Nuptiae autem sīve mātrimōnium est virī et mulieris coniunctiō, indīviduam consuētūdinem vītae continēns. Iūs autem potestātis quod in līberōs habēmus proprium est cīvium Rōmānōrum:
5   nullī enim aliī sunt hominēs quī tālem in līberōs habent potestātem quālem nōs habēmus. [Is] quī igitur ex tē et uxōre tuā nascitur, in tuā potestāte est: item [is] quī ex fīliō tuō et uxōre eius nascitur, id est nepōs tuus et neptis, aequē in tuā sunt potestāte, et pronepōs et proneptis et deinceps cēterī. [Is] quī tamen ex fīliā tuā nascitur, in tuā
10 potestāte nōn est, sed in [potestāte] patris eius.

Justian *Institūtiōnēs* 1.9

Gemma

Look at the use of *id est* in line 7. This phrase is carried over into English in the abbreviation "i.e." (that is = *id est*).

🔊 VERBA ŪTENDA

coniunctiō, -iōnis f. joining together, union
consuētūdō, -inis f. companionship
contineō, continēre, continuī, contentum contain, hold
deinceps in succession
id est "that is"
indīviduus, -a, -um indivisible
item similarly
iūs, iūris n. law

iustus, -a, -um legal
līberī, -ōrum m. pl. children
mātrimōnium, -iī n. marriage, matrimony
nascor, nascī, nātus sum be born
neptis, neptis f. granddaughter
nuptiae, -ārum f. pl. marriage
potestās, -tātis f. power, authority

prōcreō (1) procreate, create
pronepōs, -pōtis m. great-grandson
proneptis, -neptis f. great-granddaughter
proprius, -a, -um unique
quālis, quāle See *tālis*.
sīve or
tālis, -e . . . quālis, -e of such a sort . . . as

Latīna Hodierna

Vēnātiō Verbōrum

In this word hunt, all of the English words marked in bold are based on Latin words you have seen as *Verba Discenda*. Identify these Latin words and use them to define the English words. If you do not know the meaning of these English words or do not recognize the Latin word on which they are based, look up the English word in a good college dictionary.

1. **Potatory** immoderation may lead to **inebriation**.
2. The **illicitness** of his behavior and his **fraternization** with **fugitives** led to his incarceration.
3. The stereotype of **anile** behavior is **loquaciousness**.
4. **Intramural** sports can be more **competitive** than **intermural** activities.
5. The original **ossuary** was full, and the cemetery attendants had to find an **alternative depository**.
6. **Lacustrine** creatures tend to be amphibian.
7. The classroom seemed more like a **scriptorium** as the students took the exam.
8. The politician was not re-elected due to serious charges of **nepotism**.

Orbis Terrārum Rōmānus

Urbs Rōma et Vigilēs

Vigilēs Ostiensēs

In 6 A.D. Augustus used a tax on slaves to establish and fund the *vigilēs urbānī* to serve as a fire brigade within the city of Rome. A cohort of vigiles was organized into seven centuries (*centuria, -ae* f.) of 70–80 men, always *lībertīnī*, who were housed in seven barracks (*statiōnēs*), one for every two of the fourteen city regions indicated on the map below. Each century was commanded by a centurion and each cohort by a tribune. The tribunes answered in turn to the *praefectus vigilum* (of equstrian rank).

Regiōnēs Urbis

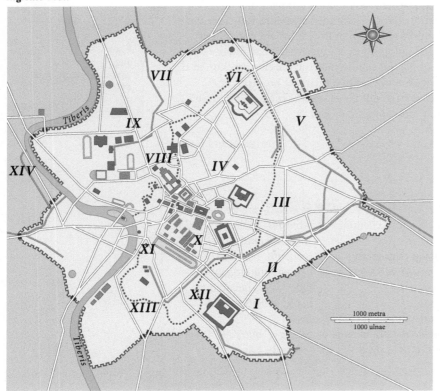

There was little elaborate equipment. Instead the *vigilēs* used blankets, buckets of water, sand, etc., to put out the fires. They also had ladders, ropes, and tools to tear down burning buildings and rescue people caught in fires. Like modern firefighters, the *vigilēs* were helmeted but carried no weapons.

The city of Ostia provides important evidence for the organization and lives of *vigilēs*, with a well-preserved barracks that was a model of efficiency. This rectangular, multi-storied building consisted of a series of small rooms built around a central courtyard. The *vigilēs* lived and stored their gear in these small rooms, most of which open onto the central courtyard.

The size of the building, its prominent location, and its decoration with mosaics all point to the central role that the *vigilēs* played in the life of ancient Ostia. The building included an imperial shrine with the dedication to Marcus Aurelius depicted below. Notice how, in the transcription, all the words marked in **bold** are dative, referring to Marcus Aurelius, who is honored as the son, the grandson, the great grandson, and the great-great grandson of emperors. With the help of this bolding you should be able to understand this inscription without a *Verba Ūtenda*.

M. AVRELIO CAESARI
IMP(eratoris) CAESARIS T. AELI HADRIANI
ANTONINI AVGVSTI PII **FILIO**
DIVI HADRIANI **NEPOTI** DIVI TRAIANI
PRONEPOTI DIVI NERVAE **ABNEP(oti)** CO(n)S(uli)
OPTIMO AC PIISSIMO

M. Aurēliō Caesarī

QUID PUTĀS?

1. How does the legal definition of marriage found in the Justinian Law code compare to the legal definition in your state? What is your opinion of the Justinian definition?
2. How does the legal role of *pater familiās* compare to the way your own family is run? How does it compare to the role of the chief male in other countries?
3. Compare the barracks of the *vigilēs* at Ostia to a firehouse in a modern American city.

EXERCEĀMUS!

29-6 Look for the Head Verbs

Here is a list of *Verba Discenda*. Which ones, based upon their meanings, are probably head verbs? HINT: Remember that a head verb is a word of speaking, thinking, knowing, hearing, or feeling. Follow the models.

Verb	Meaning	Head Verb?
→ sciō	know	yes, head verb
→ vertō	turn	no, not a head verb
1. sentiō	5. dōnō	9. pulsō
2. loquor	6. ingredior	10. sequor
3. audiō	7. servō	11. plaudō
4. spērō	8. narrō	12. admīror

29-7 Scribāmus

Use each of the numbered words or expressions below with **one** of the infinitives in the pool. You can use an infinitive only once, but you have more infinitives than you need. Then translate the sentence you made. Follow the model.

The Infinitive Pool
amāre/monēre/abīre/mittere/inspicere/revertere/ēloquī/emere/habitāre/imperāre/purgāre/
sedēre/lacrimāre/mīrārī/narrāre/parcere/quiescere/proficiscī/salīre/recumbere/scrībere

→ Bonum est **quiescere**. "It is good to be quiet."

1. Videor	5. Audeō	9. Studeō
2. Licet	6. Dēsinō	10. Solet
3. Oportet	7. Discō	11. Decet
4. Volō	8. Mē paenitet	

29-8 Colloquāmur

With two partners, practice speaking this dialogue out loud. There are three parts: *Avus*, *Famulus*, and *Servīlia*. Words have been left out. Try to supply them without looking, but they are in the *Thēsaurus Verbōrum* if you get stuck. Thesaurus words can be used more than once.

Thēsaurus Verbōrum

adulescens	cor	puella
amāre	dixit	stultus
aquam	esse	velle
audīre	fessus	vigilibus
avum	moritūrus	vīnum
canis	pōtum	

Servīlia: Avē, ave. Quid agis hodiē? Laeta _____ meum videō!
Avus: Quid? Nōn eam _____ possum! Quid lātum est?
Famulus: (clāmāns in aure avī) Nihil lātum est! Servīlia _____ sē "laetam" _____ suum vidēre!
Servīlia: Sciō tē cum patre dē Cordō locūtum esse. Pater tibi dixit mē Cordum vehementer _____! Vērum est! Cordus bonus _____ est.
Avus: Quid? Dē corde meō dīcis? _____ meum, quamquam vetus, iam forte est. Fortasse _____ sum, sed nōn hodiē!
Famulus: (rīdēns et clāmāns) Servīlia nōn dē corde tuō sed dē adulescente Cordō dīcit. Dixit sē Cordum _____ et Cordum bonum adulescentem _____.

29-9 Thinking About the *Verba Discenda*

Use the *Verba Discenda* to translate the following phrases into English.

1. animī anxiī
2. arborēs vīventēs
3. oculī aurēsque senātūs
4. senātōribus honestīs
5. senex molestus
6. vigilibus tuentibus
7. Pater familiās mortuus est.
8. Avē, ave!

🔊 VERBA DISCENDA

animus, -ī m. mind [animation]
anxius, -a, -um uneasy, anxious [anxiety]
arbor, arboris f. tree [arboreal]
auris, auris f. ear [aural]
Avē! Greetings!
avus, -ī m. grandfather, ancestor
cognoscō, cognoscere, cognōvī, cognitum learn, get to know,
observe; in perfect, know [cognition]
dīvus, -a, -um divine [divinity]
honestus, -a, -um worthy, decent, of high rank
licet, licēre, licuit, licitum est (+dat.) imp. it is permitted
molestus, -a, -um troublesome, tiresome [molest]
morior, morī, mortuus sum die [mortuary]
oculus, -ī m. eye [ocular]
paenitet, paenitēre, paenituit (imp.) it gives reason for regret; mē paenitet I am sorry
pater familiās, patris familiās m. pater familias, head of the family
pōtus, -ūs m. (a) drink [potable]
quandō when
senātor, -ōris m. senator, member of the senate [senatorial]
senātus, -ūs m. senate
senex, senis m. old man [senile]
soleō, solēre, solitus sum be accustomed (to)
tueor, tuērī, tuitus sum look at, watch over, look after, protect [tutor]
vēnātor, -ōris m. hunter
vigil, vigilis m./f. sentry, guard; firefighter; pl., fire brigade [vigilant]
vīvo, vīvere, vixī, victum live [vivacious]

Angulus Grammaticus

Archaisms

Did you wonder about the ending of *pater familiās*? The *-ās* in *familiās* is actually an archaic genitive singular, where you might expect *familiae*. The same form is preserved in phrases like *māter familiās*, *fīlius familiās*, and *fīlia familiās*. This is an example of archaism in language, i.e., a grammatical form or spelling that is no longer current.

For the words *dea* and *fīlia*, the archaic dative and ablative plurals, *deābus* and *fīliābus*, were sometimes used, especially to provide specifically feminine alternatives to the generic *deīs* and *fīliīs*. Other archaic forms include *honōs* and *colōs* instead of *honor* and *color*.

Toward the end of the Republic, shortly before the time of our story, there were some significant sound/spelling shifts in Latin. For example,

> *antīquos, -a, -om* → *antīquus -a, -um*   *saevos, -a, -om* → *saevus, -a, -um*
> *relinquont* → *relinquunt*

In some Latin words *o* became *u*, as in

> *voltus* → *vultus*   *volt* → *vult*   *quom* → *cum*

And sometimes a *u* became an *i*:

> *optumus* → *optimus*   *lubet* → *libet*

You will find many of these early forms used in the plays of Terence and Plautus, and some of the characters in our narrative may well have held onto many of the older forms. But the later forms are more commonly accepted, and they are the ones you will generally find used in Latin books like this one.

The fact that Romans continued to use older forms like *pater familiās* even in later periods illustrates how important the word was to them and how linguistically conservative they were.

English speakers occasionally use archaic phrases for special effect, for example, "thee" and "thy" in prayers. Other archaisms in English include "naught" for "nothing," "albeit" for "although," and "ere" for "before."

Tepidārium Pompēiīs

GRAMMATICA
Gerunds
Double Datives
Gerundives
Future Passive Periphrastic and
    Dative of Agent

MŌRĒS RŌMĀNĪ
Thermae Rōmānae

LATĪNA HODIERNA
Memorandum

ORBIS TERRĀRUM RŌMĀNUS
Carthāgō

ANGULUS GRAMMATICUS
Periphrasis

LECTIŌNĒS:
IN THERMĪS
and
PARUM SPATIĪ

Ten months have passed. Servilius, preparing to run for *praetor,* has a chat with Cordus in the public baths. Meanwhile, the family of Valeria is finding space tight at home.

30

Rēs Agendae

Lectiō Prīma

Antequam Legis

A Few Months Later in the Servilian Family . . .

Several months have passed since Servilius' party and his gift to Augustus. As our story resumes, Cordus has been invited by Servilius to discuss his future during a visit to the public baths, a place where a great deal of business was conducted. Pay careful attention to the variety of things wealthy Romans could do at a bath and compare it to today's health clubs and spas. Also look for a new grammatical construction called the gerund.

Gerunds: "Noun-ing the Verb"

In English, a gerund is a verb with an **-ing** ending that is used as a noun.

> I learn Latin by **reading**!   *Linguam Latīnam **legendō** discō!*

Legendō is a gerund in Latin and is, like the infinitive, a neuter verbal noun. For now, here is what you need to know:

- The gerund declines like *pōculum.*
- When you see gerunds marked in **bold** in the *lectiō* translate them

Watch also for two special uses of the gerund that show **purpose**:

- In the **genitive case**, used with **causā** (on account of) or **grātiā** (for the sake of):

  *Lūcius ad lūdum **discendī causā** vēnit.*
  *Lūcius ad lūdum **discendī grātiā** vēnit.*

  Translate both sentences as "Lucius came to school **to learn (for the sake of learning)**."

- In the **accusative case**, with **ad**:

  *Advēnī **ad discendum**.*
  I have come **for learning/to learn**.

Double Datives

Finally, as you read, watch for a construction called the **double dative**. Consider this sentence in which the datives are marked in **bold** in both the Latin sentence and its translations.

> *Spērō tē **mihi auxiliō** futūrum esse.*
> I hope you will be **to me for help**.
> I hope you will be **a help to me**.

Double datives are marked in *italics* in *Lectiō Prīma*.

EXERCEĀMUS!

30-1 **Gerunds**

As you read, take notice of the gerunds (marked in **bold**) in *Lectiō Prīma*. Identify the case of each gerund. (Keep in mind that all gerunds are neuter singular, 2nd declension, and have no nominative.) Then list them under the appropriate case heading. Follow the model.

→ Genitive   Dative   Accusative   Ablative
   exeundī (line 3)

Tepidārium Herculaneō

🔊 IN THERMĪS

Servīlius et Cordus, thermīs appropinquantēs, multa dē multīs colloquēbantur. Balneās intrantēs prīmum in apodytērium ingressī sunt **exuendī causā**. Tum, vestīmentīs dēpositīs in apodytēriō apud servōs custōdēs, nūdī in tepidāriō sedēbant
5 **sūdandī causā**.

Cum satis calidī erant, in caldārium intrāvērunt. Dum hīc manent, Servīlius "Corde," inquit, "tē vocāvī ad thermās **ad loquendum**. Spērō tē *mihi auxiliō* futūrum esse. Ego praetūram petītūrus, auxilium quam maximum in proximīs comitiīs habēre
10 dēbeō. Sciō tē et dīvitem et probum virum paucōrum hostium esse, quī multa in urbe āctūrus est, et tū *mihi auxiliō magnō* esse potes. Praetereā, ut scīs, fīlia mea Servīlia, sēdecim annōs nāta, mox virō nuptūra est et tē opīnor marītum optimum futūrum esse. Sed iam saepe dē hīs rēbus dīximus. Quid in animō habēs?"
15 Cordus, sē aspergēns aquā frīgidā, "Servīlī," inquit, "intellegō bene tē virum magnae auctōritātis in Urbe futūrum esse. Cognōvī fīlium tuum Marcum et Servīlia benigna vidētur. Sī tibi aliquid auxiliī in comitiīs afferre potuerō, libenter tibi gener erō! Semper *tibi auxiliō* erō! Adsum **ad adiuvandum**!"

"Optimē! Fīat! Sed nunc, hīc in caldāriō manēre mihi displicet. Redeāmus in tepidārium."
20 In tepidāriō virī duo dē multīs rēbus colloquēbantur—nōn sōlum dē comitiīs sed etiam dē Servīliā, dē rē pūblicā, et dē Cordī futūrō.

Servīlius "Quōmodo," rogāvit, "mī Corde, *Rōmae beneficiō* esse vīs? Quās difficultātēs habēmus? Cupidus **audiendī** sum."

Cordus statim respondit: "Ignēs! Ignēs quī semper urbem combūrunt et semper combūrent nisi quis aliquid
25 faciet! Dēbēmus vigilēs pūblicōs in urbe cōnstituere. Volō urbem ab ignibus cōnservāre et sīc ūtilis et urbī et nostrō imperātōrī Augustō esse. Fortasse Augustus adnuet coeptīs nostrīs. **Labōrandō** et **vigilandō** prō Rōmā ūtilis ac clārus fīam."

Servīlius adnuit et "Habēs," inquit, "rēctē. Ignēs semper *nōbīs perīculō* fuērunt. Sed ignēs hārum thermārum
30 quoque fortissimī sunt! Eāmus ad frīgidārium **refrīgerandī grātiā**, et posteā in bibliothēcā plūs loquāmur quārē ibi spatium plūs idōneum **loquendō** est."

Servīlius et Cordus multa dē multīs colloquēbantur.

Gemma

auxilium quam maximum = as much help as possible. "As much as possible" is the standard translation of *quam* with a superlative.

Gemma

nisi quis = *nisi aliquis* Following *nisi*, forms of *aliquis* are always written without the *ali-*.

POSTQUAM LĒGISTĪ

1. How many rooms do Servilius and Cordus visit in the bath complex? What is the name of each room, and what is each room used for?
2. What is Servilius' opinion of Cordus?
3. What propositions does Servilius put before Cordus?
4. How does Cordus respond, and what do you learn about Cordus' feelings for Servilia from his response? What is your reaction to this?
5. What are Cordus' plans for the future?

Annuit coeptīs

VERBA ŪTENDA

ac and, and besides

adnuō, adnuere, adnuī, adnūtum nod, nod assent

apodyterium, -iī n. dressing room

aspergō, aspergere, aspersī, aspersum sprinkle

auctōritās, -tātis f. authority, power

balneae, -ārum f. pl. bath

beneficium, -iī n. benefit

caldārium, -iī n. hot bath

***calidus, -a, -um* warm, hot**

***causa, -ae* f. cause, reason; *causā* (+ gen.) on account of, because of**

clārus, -a, -um famous, illustrious

coepī, coepisse, coeptum begin (perfect in form, present in meaning)

***combūrō, combūrere, combussī, combustum* burn, burn up**

comitia, -iōrum n. pl. elections

conservō (1) preserve, keep safe

constituō, constituere, constituī, constitūtum establish

cupidus, -a, -um (+ gen.) longing for, eager for

***custōs, custōdis* m./f. guard**

eāmus "let's go"

exuō, exuere, exuī, exūtum strip, undress

fāmōsus, -a, -um famed, well-known

fiat "let it happen"

frīgidārium, -iī n. cold-water bath

***gener, generī* m. son-in-law**

***grātiā* (+ gen.) for the sake of, for the purpose of**

idōneus, -a, -um (+ dat.) suitable, fit

libenter willingly

loquāmur "let's talk"

***nisi* unless**

nūdus, -a, -um naked, nude

nūbō, nūbere, nupsī, nuptum marry

***opīnor, opīnārī, opīnātus sum* think, believe**

***posteā* afterward, then**

praetereā besides

praetūra, -ae f. praetorship, judgeship

***probus, -a, -um* good, honest**

***proximus, -a, -um* nearest, next**

***pūblicus, -a, -um* public, common**

quam + superlative = as . . . as possible

quārē because

redeāmus "let's return"

refrīgerō (1) make cool

rēs pūblica, reī pūblicae f. republic

***satis* enough, sufficient**

sūdō (1) sweat, perspire

tepidārium, -iī n. warm bath

thermae, -ārum f. pl. public baths

***ūtilis, ūtile* useful**

vestīmentum, -ī n. clothing

vigilō (1) keep watch

Gemma

Adnuet coeptīs: When Cordus uses this phrase he is referring to a line in Vergil's *Aeneid.* The phrase is based upon Vergil's *Aeneid* 9.625:

> Iuppiter omnipotens, audācibus adnue coeptīs
>
> Omnipotent Jupiter, nod approval to these daring undertakings.

Note how this is one of two Latin mottos on the second Great Seal of the United States on the dollar bill: *Annuit coeptīs*, "He has given his approval to (our) undertakings."

Gemma

Cordus is loosely based on a historical figure, Quintus Naevius Cordus Sutorius Macro. This Naevius was one of the earliest known prefects of the *vigilēs*, a group formed by Augustus to serve as a combination fire and police force for Rome. Macro, as he is known in the sources, went on, under Tiberius, to be head of the the praetorian guard, the force that protected the emperor. He lasted into the reign of Caligula, but was forced to commit suicide shortly thereafter. Our Cordus has a much brighter future ahead of him.

Grammatica A

Gerunds

In *Lectiō Prīma*, you saw how similar Latin and English gerunds are. Once you know that the Latin verbal suffix *-nd-* is equivalent to the English suffix **-ing**, you can easily translate most Latin gerunds. Note that:

- The gerund is 2nd declension, neuter singular.
- It is not used in the nominative, so there are only four endings to remember.

Here are examples of gerunds in each case from the reading:

Genitive	**exuendī** causā	for the sake of **undressing**
Dative	idōneum **loquendō**	suitable for **speaking**
Accusative	ad **loquendum**	for **talking/to talk**
Ablative	**labōrandō**	by **working**

Notā Bene:

- Watch the change in vowels from conjugation to conjugation. There are no surprises here:

1st conjugation:	*vocandī*	of calling
2nd conjugation:	*monendī*	of warning
3rd conjugation:	*dūcendī*	of leading
3rd conjugation *-iō:*	*capiendī*	of seizing
4th conjugation:	*audiendī*	of hearing

- Deponent verbs form gerunds like regular verbs:

1st conjugation:	*cōnandī*	of trying
2nd conjugation:	*pollicendī*	of promising
3rd conjugation:	*sequendī*	of following
3rd conjugation *-iō:*	*patiendī*	of suffering
4th conjugation:	*mentiendī*	of lying

- There is no nominative form of the Latin gerund. Instead, Latin uses a subjective infinitive. English, however, can use a gerund as the subject of a sentence.

    *Linguam Latīnam **discere** iūcundum est!*
    Learning Latin is fun!

Gerunds of Purpose

- Gerunds in the **genitive case** with *causā* (on account of) or *grātiā* (for the sake of) show purpose.

    *Lūcius ad lūdum **discendī causā** vēnit.*
    Lucius came to school **to learn (for the sake of learning)**.

- Gerunds in the **accusative case** with *ad* also show purpose.

    *Advēnī **ad discendum**.*
    I have come **to learn (for learning)**.

Note: *Causā* and *grātiā* always follow the gerund, whereas *ad* precedes it.

EXERCEĀMUS!

30-2 Making Gerunds

Use the gerunds of *labōrō* in the following chart to form a gerund phrase in the case indicated for each of the following verbs. Then translate the gerund phrase. Follow the model.

Gen.	*labōrandī causā*	to **work**
Dat.	*idōneum labōrandō*	suitable **for working**
Acc.	*ad labōrandum*	to **work**
Abl.	*labōrandō*	by **working**
→ discō (gen.)	*discendī causā*	to learn

1. ambulō (dat.)   4. dūcō (gen.)   7. custōdiō (abl.)

2. respondeō (acc.)   5. ūtor (dat.)   8. moveō (gen.)

3. capiō (abl.)   6. lūdō (acc.)   9. opīnor (dat.)

Double Datives

In *Lectiō Prīma*, Servilius said to Cordus:

Spērō tē mihi auxiliō futūrum esse!

Although this can be translated literally as

I hope you will be to me for help.

you can see how we are more likely to express this idea in English as "I hope you'll be of help to me."

Notā Bene:

- **Double datives** are most commonly used with a form of the verb *sum*.
- One of these datives refers to the person or thing concerned:

Tū es mihi maximō auxiliō!

- The other refers to the role something serves:

Tū es mihi maximō auxiliō!

Consider these other double datives:

Canere mihi voluptātī est.	Singing is a pleasure for me.
Hoc mālum tibi dōnō erit.	This apple will serve as a gift for you.
Cui dōnō?	For whom is it (for) a good?
	(a legal term that asks who will benefit from a certain event or deed)

Gemma

Grammarians have various names for the parts of a double dative. The dative referring to the person can be called **dative of the person affected**, the **ethical dative**, or (more simply) **dative of reference**. The dative referring to the role something serves is called **dative of object for which** or **dative of purpose**.

Lectiō Secunda

Antequam Legis

A Few Months Later in the Valerian Family ...

Licinia's baby, Maximus, is now several months old. The infant was named nine days after his birth, at a special ceremony called the *Nōminālia*. This naming ceremony traditionally took place eight days after birth for females and nine for males. On this day, amid some festivity, Licinia's baby received the name Aelius Maximus A. f. (Aelius Maximus, son of Aelius). The newly named child wore a necklace of rattles called *crepundia* to scare away evil. It was also on this occasion that his *pater familiās* gave the child a *bulla*, a locket worn by male children until they came of age (between fourteen and seventeen at a toga ceremony) and by female children until they were married.

In *Lectiō Secunda* the family goes for a stroll in Rome and considers ways to deal with their over-crowded apartment. The mirror Aelius made for Licinia becomes an important topic of conversation.

As you read, watch how gerunds become gerundives.

From Gerunds to Gerundives

This is fairly simple, so don't be troubled! A gerundive is exactly like a gerund, and does everything a gerund does, but instead of being a verbal noun, it is a verbal adjective. Think of it this way:

A gerundIVE . . . is an adjectIVE

This means that it will GNC with the noun it is joined to. What does this mean? Compare the following:

GERUND	GERUNDIVE
*Veniō **videndī causā**.* I am coming for the sake **of seeing**.	*Veniō **urbis videndae causā**.* I am coming for the sake **of seeing the city**.
*Vīcimus **oppugnandō**.* We won **by attacking**.	*Vīcimus **hostibus oppugnandīs**.* We won **by attacking the enemy**.

For now, just translate these gerundives like gerunds (i.e., add **-ing** to the English verb) and you will be fine.

Gerundives can be used to express worthiness or obligation. For example, *servus laudandus* is "a slave worthy to be praised" or "a praiseworthy slave." Obligation is expressed by the gerundive + form of *sum* = "must be"

> *Imperātor Augustus **timendus** est.*   The emperor Augustus must be feared.

The person **by whom** the action must be done is in the **dative** case.

*Augustus **hostibus suīs** timendus est.*	Augustus must be feared **by his enemies**.	or	**His enemies** must fear Augustus.

This use of the gerundive is called the **future passive periphrastic**.
All gerundive phrases are marked in **bold** in *Lectiō Secunda*.

EXERCEĀMUS!

30-3 Gerundives

As you read, make a line-by-line list of the gerundives marked in **bold**. Identify the word with which the gerundive GNCs. Then give the GNC of the gerundive. Follow the model.

Line	Gerundive	Word	Gender	Number	Case
→ 3	solvendae	difficultātis	feminine	singular	genitive

Sōcratēs fortiter garrīre incipit.

🔊 PARUM SPATIĪ

In aliā urbis parte Valeria, Aelius et Licinia per viās Subūrae ambulant. Ancilla Flāvia et avia Plōtia infantem cūrant dum parentēs novī et Valeria anxia inter sē colloquuntur **difficultātis suae solvendae causā**. Sōcratēs, clāmāns et garriēns, in umerīs Aeliī sedet. Sīmiīs magnopere āerem dulcem spīrāre placet.

5   Valeria "**Aliquid**," inquit, "**nōbīs faciendum est**. Parum spatiī habēmus et sex hominēs habitāre in duōbus conclāvibus difficile est! Mox **plūs spatiī inveniendum est**, sed quōmodo? Plūrimōs hominēs sed minimam pecūniam habēmus."

Aelius "Rectē habēs," inquit. "Aut **familia nostra nova movenda est** aut **plūs pecūniae inveniendum est**! Ego et Hephaestus, **servus laudandus**, dīligenter labōrāmus sed **opus**
10 **novum nōbīs accipiendum est**. Opīnor **novās rēs** in officīnā meā **faciendās et vendendās esse**. Valeria, quid opīnāris? Aliquās rēs, quās in officīnā meā fabricābō, vendere in tabernā potes? Vīdistīne speculum quod Liciniae fabricāvī? Tāle vendere potes?"

Valeria "Profectō," inquit, "tālia vendere possum! **Speculum mīrandum** fabricāvistī! Sī **tālia plūra mīranda aut ūtilia** fabricāveris, ea vendam!"

15 Respondet Aelius: "Bene, sed **exemplum** in tabernā **monstrandum est** et nihil promptum habēmus."

Licinia, quae adhūc nihil dīxit, "Accipe, māter," lacrimātūra inquit, "speculum meum ad monstrandum. Sed, tē obsecrō, **id** nūllō modō **tibi vendendum est**. Speculum mihi cārum est quārē Aelius id mihi dōnō fabricāvit. Et quoque hās inaurēs meās, dōnum nuptiāle, accipe monstrandī causā, dōnec Aelius aliās inaurēs fabricāverit."

Valeria: "Nōlī tē perturbāre, Licinia. Hominēs tuās rēs spectābunt sed nōn ement. Sciō **speculum mihi custōdi-**
20 **endum esse et inaurēs prōtegendās esse**! Aelī, abī nunc et strēnuē labōrā **ad multās variāsque rēs fabricandās**!"

Subitō Sōcratēs, quī semper studiōsus **familiae suae defendendae** est, puerōs in viā lūdentēs vidēns, fortiter garrīre incipit et ex umerīs Aeliī **ad puerōs persequendōs** salīre vult.

Aelius "Tacē," inquit, "sīmia! Sī nōn tacueris, **aēneum sīmiam vendendum** habēbimus!!"

Sōcratēs, timēns, **suī servandī grātiā** nihil dīcit et quiētus sedet. Ut dīcitur—"**Sīmiae videndī sed nōn audi-**
25 **endī sunt!**"

🔊 VERBA ŪTENDA

adhūc to this point, still, yet
aēneus, -a, -um bronze
āēr, āeris m. air
avia, -ae f. grandmother
causa, -ae f. cause, reason; causā (+ gen.) on account of, because of
conclāve, conclāvis n. room
custōdiō, custōdīre, custōdīvī/custōdiī, custōdītum watch, guard
defendō, defendere, defendī, defensum defend

dīligens, dīligentis careful, diligent, frugal
exemplum, -ī n. sample
fabricō (1) forge, make, shape, build, construct
garriō, garrīre, garrīvī/garriī, garrītum chatter
gratiā (+ gen.) for the sake of, for the purpose of
Hephaestus, -ī m. Hephaestus, the slave who works with Aelius in the blacksmith shop

inaurēs, inaurium f. pl. earrings
lūdō, lūdere, lūsī, lūsum play, tease
moveō, movēre, mōvī, mōtum move, affect
obsecrō (1) implore, beg
officīna, -ae f. workshop
parum too little, not enough
persequor, persequī, persecūtus sum pursue
profectō without question, undoubtedly
promptus, -a, -um ready

prōtegō, prōtegere, prōtexī, prōtectum protect
quārē because, for
solvō, solvere, solvī, solūtum loosen, unbind
speculum, -ī n. mirror
spīrō (1) breathe
studiōsus, -a, -um (+ gen.) eager (to)
umerus, -ī m. shoulder
varius, -a, -um various, changeable, mixed
vendō, vendere, vendidī, venditum sell

POSTQUAM LĒGISTĪ

1. Where is Socrates the monkey as this narrative begins?
2. What problem are Valeria, Aelius, and Licinia discussing?
3. What plan do they make to solve this problem?
4. How do modern couples tend to deal with the same issues?
5. How does Socrates misbehave at the end of the narrative?
6. What does Aelius threaten to do to Socrates for misbehaving?

Grammatica B

Gerundives

Latin gerunds and gerundives are usually easy to pick out because of the *-nd-* added before the ending. Remember that the gerund is a **verbal noun**, whereas the gerundive is a **verbal adjective**. Here are the main features of the gerundive:

- The **gerundive** is an adjective that uses the same endings as a 2-1-2 adjective.
- Like the **participle**, the **gerundive** is a kind of **verbal adjective**. Whereas the participle is simply descriptive, the gerundive expresses obligation or necessity.
- As a verbal adjective, the gerundive is also sometimes called a **future passive participle**, translated into English as "going to be [verbed], deserving to be [verbed]."

vir admīrātus	perfect passive participle	an admired man
vir admīrāns	present active participle	an admiring man
vir admīrandus	gerundive	a man who ought to be admired / an admirable man

Notā Bene: Gerundives are the **only** forms of deponent verbs that can have a passive meaning!

arbitrandus	worthy **to be** thought
recordandus	worthy **of being** remembered
loquendus	worthy **to be** spoken
ūtendus	worthy **of being** used

And here is an example from *Lectiō Prīma*:

> *Speculum **mīrandum** fabricāvistī.*
> You have made a mirror **worthy of being marvelled at**.

Future Passive Periphrastic and Dative of Agent

Gerundives in the nominative case with a form of *sum* are used to express **necessity**. Such phrases are called **future passive periphrastic** constructions. If you do not like that name, think of it as the "gerundive of gottabe." The formal term is very descriptive:

- **Future** because the action hasn't happened yet.
- **Passive** because it is done to someone/something.
- **Periphrastic** because it needs a form of *sum*. (More on the term **periphrastic** in the *Angulus Grammaticus*.)

Consider this famous Latin phrase that uses a future passive periphrastic:

> *Carthāgō dēlenda est!*   Carthage must be destroyed.

Now here is the same phrase with the identity of the destroyer added:

> *Carthāgō **nōbīs** dēlenda est!*   Carthage must be destroyed **by us**.

NotāBene:

- The *nōbīs* is called a **dative of agent** and is found only with the future passive periphrastic.
- If it helps to remember that it is a dative, not ablative, of agent, think of this literal translation—"To us there is something that must be done."
- You can always translate these phrases actively: "it must be done by us" = "we must do."

The title of this chapter is also a gerundive phrase. How would you now translate it?

EXERCEĀMUS!

30-4   Gerunds and Gerundives

Which gerund(ive) construction is the correct one for the underlined words? Do not let the translation fool you—they are all gerund(ive) constructions. Be careful of GNC when using gerundives!

1. <u>In order to make a new mirror</u>, Aelius worked harder.
   - a. ad speculum novum fabricandam
   - b. ad novī speculī fabricandī
   - c. novī speculī fabricandī causā
   - d. novum speculum fabricandum est

2. Aelius survives <u>by working</u> hard.
   - a. labōrandum
   - b. labōrandī
   - c. labōrandō
   - d. labōrāre

3. All the women in the neighborhood came <u>to see Maximus.</u>
   - a. Maximum vidēre
   - b. Maximī videndī grātiā
   - c. Maximum videndum
   - d. Maximus videndus est

4. Valeria, too, will work in the house <u>to get money.</u>
   - a. pecūniam obtinēre
   - b. pecūniae obtinendī causā
   - c. ad pecūniam obtinendum
   - d. ad pecūniam obtinendam

5. Socrates gets in trouble <u>by playing.</u>
   - a. lūdendō
   - b. lūdendī
   - c. lūdendus
   - d. lūdere

6. They were speaking together <u>to solve their difficulties</u>.
   a. difficultātum suārum solvendārum causā
   b. difficultātis suae solvendae causā
   c. difficultātēs suās solvendās causā
   d. difficultātum suōrum solvendōrum causā

30-5   Dative of Agent and the Future Passive Periphrastic

Find the dative of agent in each of the following future passive periphrastic constructions. Then translate each construction two ways (actively and passively). Follow the model.

Future Passive Periphrastic	Dative of Agent	Translations
➤ Aliquid nōbīs faciendum est.	nōbīs	Passive: Something must be done by us. Active: We must do something.

1. Plūs spatiī familiae inveniendum est.
2. Familia nova mihi nōn videnda est.
3. Plūs pecūniae virō inveniendum erat.

4. Opus novum nōbīs accipiendum est.
5. Novae rēs Aeliō fabricandae sunt.

Mōrēs Rōmānī

Thermae Rōmānae

Public baths like the one visited by Servilius and Cordus were an important feature of Roman daily life. Very few Roman homes, even among the wealthy, had private bathing facilities in the first century B.C. Rather, both men and women would visit the public baths. Sometimes there were separate bath complexes for men and women, and sometimes they had separate hours in the same facility. Men and women never bathed together publicly.

A typical bath complex included the following parts:

- *apodytērium, -iī* **n.** undressing room
- *tepidārium, -iī* **n.** warm-water room
- *caldārium, -iī* **n.** hot-water or steam room
- *lābrum, -iī* **n.** basin with cool water in the *caldārium*
- *frīgidārium, -iī* **n.** cold-water room
- *palaestra, -ae* **f.** exercise space

- *bibliothēca, ae* **f.** library (occasionally)
- *piscīna, -ae* **f.** swimming pool (occasionally)
- *lātrīna, -ae* **f.** public latrine, usually a row of benches with holes in the seats and flowing water underneath

Lābrum

Hypocauston Thermārum Stabiānārum Pompēiīs

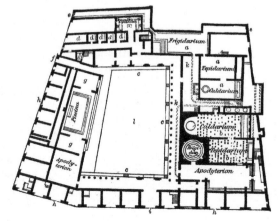

Forma Thermārum Stabiānārum Pompēiīs

An extensive aqueduct system was essential to these baths. Water from an aqueduct fed into a large reservoir and from there into the appropriate rooms. It was heated by means of a sophisticated heating system called a hypocaust (*hypocauston, -ī* n), which took heat from the furnace and ran it under the raised floor of the rooms and in between its walls. Having gone through the rooms, the water often then passed through the latrines before flowing into the sewer.

These bath facilities were not just places to get cleansed. Massages and rub-downs using olive oil were also available. The baths were also important social meeting places. The conversation between Servilius and Cordus shows how serious business could also be conducted in the baths.

Latīna Hodierna

Memorandum

You may remember that you saw a future passive periphrastic phrase used by Chiron the schoolmaster in Chapter 6:

Nunc est bibendum!

Chiron was quoting the first words of Horace's drinking song celebrating Octavian, the future Augustus, and his victory over Marc Antony and Cleopatra at the Battle of Actium in 31 B.C. Here is the first stanza of Horace's poem in simplified word order. See the *Verba Ūtenda* for help. Note that it actually contains two periphrastic constructions.

> Nunc bibendum est.
> nunc pede līberō tellūs pulsanda est;
> nunc Saliāribus dapibus ornāre pulvīnar deōrum tempus est,
> Ō sodālēs.

Horace *Odes* 1.37.1–4

Gemma

Notice how Horace repeats the word *nunc* three times. This is a poetic figure of speech called **anaphora**.

🔊 VERBA ŪTENDA

daps, dapis f. sacrificial feast, offering
līber, lībera, līberum free
ornō (1) decorate

pulsō (1) strike, beat;
pede . . . tellus
pulsanda "strike the ground with feet, "i.e., dance

pulvīnar, -āris n. cushioned couch (used for a religious statue)
Saliāris, -e of the Salii (priests of Mars, god of war)

sodālis, sodālis m. companion
tellūs, tellūris f. earth, ground

Gerundive forms should look familiar to you because we have been using them throughout the book as titles:

Verba Discenda   words that must be learned
Verba Ūtenda   words that must be used

Here are two gerundive names for girls:

Amanda   she who must be loved
Miranda   she who must be admired

A number of gerundives have been borrowed by English:

memorandum	something that must be remembered
referendum	something that must be carried back
addendum	something that must be added
corrigendum	something that must be corrected

Although some people (who do not know Latin) will make the plural of these words by adding a final -s (memorandums, referendums, etc.), these words traditionally use Latin neuter plural endings in English: memoranda, referenda, addenda, and corrigenda.

Note that English only uses the "plural" form of "agenda," and some other erstwhile gerunds have lost their endings:

legend	something that must be read
reverend	one that should be revered
tremendous	that which should be feared

Orbis Terrārum Rōmānus

Carthāgō

The great Punic city of Carthage, located in what is now Tunisia on Africa's northern coast, was Rome's bitter rival for control of the western Mediterranean. The two cities fought a series of three wars, known as the Punic Wars, which lasted from 264 B.C. to 146 B.C. The conflict did not end until Rome completely conquered Carthage and the city and its territory became the Roman province of *Āfrica*. During the imperial period, Carthage was an important commercial area, producing much grain and sending many wild beasts to circuses throughout the Roman Empire.

Cato the Elder (234–149 B.C.) was the sworn enemy of Carthage. It is said that when he spoke in the Senate, no matter the nature of the speech, he always worked in the phrase:

Carthāgō dēlenda est! Carthage must be destroyed!

Cato did this in the years following the Second Punic War (218–201 B.C.), which Rome almost lost to the Carthaginian general, Hannibal. Cato's point was that Rome would never be completely secure until it had destroyed its rival. Although several ancient authors, including Pliny the Elder and Plutarch, refer to Cato's practice, Cato's exact words are unknown today. An alternative ancient version survives in indirect statement:

Censeō Carthāginem dēlendam esse.

Thermae Rōmānae Carthāgine

Carthāgō Nova et Antīqua

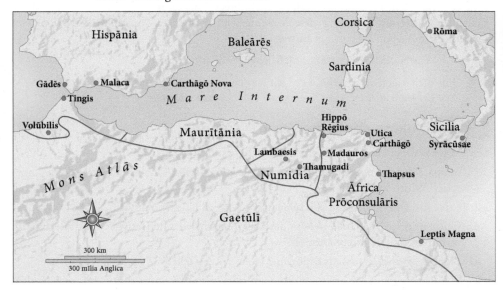

Carthāgō in Āfricā

QUID PUTĀS?

1. What does a Roman bath facility tell you about ancient Roman society?
2. What facilities in American society would serve social purposes similar to those of the ancient Roman baths?
3. What aspects of the ancient Roman bath facility would not be agreeable to Americans? What aspects might we like?
4. Horace's *Nunc est bibendum* ode is a drinking song about a major political event and naval battle. What poems or songs have been written to celebrate similar events in U.S. history?
5. Use the Latin word *referendum* to explain how a referendum works in the U.S. law.
6. Translate the two Latin mottoes on the Great Seal of the United States: *Annuit coeptīs* and *Novus Ordō S(a)eclōrum*. Then explain why you think these mottoes were chosen.
7. Look at the map of the Mediterranean in the endpapers of this book and explain how geography may have made a conflict between Rome and Carthage inevitable.

EXERCEĀMUS!

30-6 Scrībāmus

Rewrite the following passage, based on *Lectiō Secunda*, as indirect statement. Begin each sentence with *Flāvia dīcit*. Then change the main verb to an infinitive and make its subject accusative. Remember to use passive infinitives for the deponent verbs. Follow the model.

→ Valeria et Aelius et Licinia per viās Subūrae ambulant.
   Flāvia dīcit Valeriam et Aelium et Liciniam per viās Subūrae ambulāre.

1. Ancilla infantem cūrat.
2. Parentēs novī et Valeria anxia inter sē colloquuntur.
3. Sīmia, clāmāns et garriēns, in umerīs Aeliī sedet.
4. Puerī in viā lūdentēs ā sīmiā videntur.
5. Familia Valeriae paucum spatiī habet.
6. Sex hominēs in duōbus conclāvibus habitant.

30-7 Colloquāmur

Now use *Quis dīcit?* to introduce each of the indirect statements you made in Exercise 30-6. Take turns asking and answering these questions with a classmate. You can make up your own answers. Here is a pool of possible answers:

Flāvia dīcit/dīcō/narrātor dīcit/magister dīcit/dīcimus

→ Quis dīcit Valeriam et Aelium et Liciniam per viās Subūrae ambulāre?
   Dīcō Valeriam et Aelium et Liciniam per viās Subūrae ambulāre.

30-8 Thinking about the *Verba Discenda*

Use the *Verba Discenda* to answer the following questions.

1. Compare the meaning of *adhūc* with the meaning of *hūc*. One is temporal and the other spatial. Which is which?
2. If *avia* is grandmother, can you remember the word for grandfather?
3. Which principal part of *combūrō* provides English with derivatives? Give one English derivative other than "combustion."
4. Which *verbum discendum* is deponent? How can you tell?
5. What Latin verb is the origin of the noun *speculum*? What does this verb mean? Explain the relationship between the meanings of this verb and noun.

6. Use a *verbum discendum* to explain the English word "satisfaction."

7. Find the words in the following narrative that derive at least in part from the *verba discenda* below. List the English word and its Latin source. Follow the model.

→ custodian: *custōs*

The diligent school custodian moved slowly through the halls, speculating about who (or what) might have caused the internal combustion engine in his car to die so quickly. He opined that the culprit was young Mr. Sullivan, because the ludicrous story the young man had told was a mere fabric of various lies. He'd get to the bottom of the story and have the satisfaction of hearing the principal call the young man down to her office over the public address system!

🔊 VERBA DISCENDA

adhūc to this point, still, yet

aēneus, -a, -um bronze

avia, -ae f. grandmother

calidus, -a, -um warm, hot

causa, -ae f. cause, reason; *causā* (+ gen.) on account of, because of [causation]

combūrō, combūrere, combussī, combustum burn, burn up [combustion]

custōdiō, custōdīre, custōdīvī/custōdiī,

custōdītum watch, guard [custody]

custōs, custōdis m./f. guard [custodian]

dīligens, dīligentis careful, diligent, frugal [diligence]

fabricō (1) forge, make, shape, build, construct [fabricate]

gener, generī m. son-in-law

grātiā (+ gen.) for the sake of, for the purpose of

lūdō, lūdere, lūsī, lūsum play, tease [ludicrous]

moveō, movēre, mōvī, mōtum move, affect [movable, motion]

nisi unless

opīnor, opīnārī, opīnātus sum think, believe [opinion, opine]

posteā afterward, then

probus, -a, -um good, honest [probity]

proximus, -a, -um nearest, next [proximate]

pūblicus, -a, -um public, common [publication]

quārē because, for

satis enough, sufficient [satisfactory]

speculum, -ī n. mirror

ūtilis, ūtile useful [utilitarian]

varius, -a, -um various, changeable, mixed [variegated]

vendō, vendere, vendidī, venditum sell [vendible]

Angulus Grammaticus

Periphrasis

The grammatical term "future passive periphrastic" sounds quite strange and intimidating in English, but we actually use periphrastic constructions all the time, probably more than Romans did. **Periphrasis** is a Greek word that means "speaking around," and its Latin equivalent, *circumlocūtiō*, gives us the English word "circumlocution."

You have seen at least one example previously. Remember that Latin uses *nōlī* or *nōlīte* + infinitive to create a negative command: *Nōlī tangere!* (Don't touch!). This is a periphrasis because it literally says, "Be unwilling to touch!"

Another example involves the FAP, future active participle. In English we have a tense with which to say things like, "I'm about to do this," or, in dialect, "She's fixing to leave." Such a tense does not exist in Latin but it can be said via periphrasis: *Id factūrus sum* or *Abitūra est*.

Seen another way, the whole perfect passive system in Latin is periphrastic, as it is in English:

Perfect	*vocātus sum*	I have been called
		Literally, "I am having been called"
Pluperfect	*vocātus eram*	I had been called
		Literally, "I was having been called"
Future Perfect	*vocātus erō*	I will have been called
		Literally, "I will be having been called"

So what is "periphrastic" about the **future passive periphrastic**? As you saw above, a form of *sum* needs to accompany the gerundive to create this expression: *Carthāgō dēlenda est!* Literally, this says "Carthage is having to be destroyed."

This construction is part of what is sometimes called the **periphrastic conjugation**, consisting of the future active participle or the gerundive with forms of *sum*:

TENSE	ACTIVE PERIPHRASTIC	PASSIVE PERIPHRASTIC
Present	*vocātūrus sum* I am about to call	*vocandus sum* I must be called
Imperfect	*vocātūrus eram* I was about to call	*vocandus eram* I had to be called
Future	*vocātūrus erō* I will be about to call	*vocandus erō* I will have to be called
Perfect	*vocātūrus fuī* I have been about to call	*vocandus fuī* I have had to be called
Pluperfect	*vocātūrus fueram* I had been about to call	*vocandus fueram* I had had to be called
Future Perfect	*vocātūrus fuerō* I will have been about to call	*vocandus fuerō* I will have had to be called

31

Fīat

Lectiō Prīma

Antequam Legis

This narrative takes place the morning after Servilius' conversation with Cordus in the baths. Servilius tells his wife that the wedding plans are fixed, and Caecilia decides to go shopping for possible wedding presents for her daughter. This scene illustrates the two-tiered organization of an upper-class Roman household as the slaves rush to prepare breakfast for the master and his family.

Are You in the Right Mood?

In this chapter, you will learn to recognize and use one more grammatical mood, the **subjunctive**. Whereas indicative verbs "indicate" an action that actually happens, and an imperative is an order or command, a subjunctive generally refers to an action that is not as "real" as an indicative verb. That is, the subjunctive (its name means something like "subordinate") indicates not so much fact as potential, possibility, or probability. It often helps to think of it this way: The subjunctive is the mood of "lesser reality."

In the *lectiō*, you will see the **present subjunctive** and some of its uses. You will learn names for these uses later, but for now just concentrate on recognizing subjunctives and how to translate them.

Recognizing Present Subjunctives

Present subjunctives are identical to present indicatives, except for a change in the vowel that links the ending to the stem.

You can remember the vowel changes between indicative and subjunctive with this time-honored acronym:

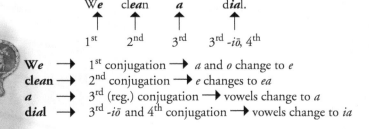

We*e*   cl*ea*n   *a*   d*ia*l.

| | 1st | 2nd | 3rd | 3rd -*iō*, 4th |

We → 1st conjugation → *a* and *o* change to *e*
clean → 2nd conjugation → *e* changes to *ea*
a → 3rd (reg.) conjugation → vowels change to *a*
d*ia*l → 3rd -*iō* and 4th conjugation → vowels change to *ia*

LECTIŌNĒS:
MĀNE
and
CAECILIA ET VALERIA

In this chapter Caecilia goes shopping to prepare for Servilia's wedding. The lives of our two families begin to intersect when Caecilia stops at Valeria's shop for a snack.

Now compare these subjunctive forms to their indicative equivalents:

CONJUGATION	MOOD	FORM	TRANSLATION
1st	Indicative	Labōrāmus.	We work.
	Subjunctive	**Labōrēmus!**	Let's work!
2nd	Indicative	Vidēmus.	We see.
	Subjunctive	**Videāmus!**	Let's see!
3rd	Indicative	Loquimur.	We are talking.
	Subjunctive	**Loquāmur!**	Let's talk!
3rd -iō	Indicative	Facimus.	We are doing.
	Subjunctive	**Faciāmus!**	Let's do!
4th	Indicative	Dormit.	She is sleeping.
	Subjunctive	**Dormiat!**	Let her sleep.

Translating Present Subjunctives

The subjunctive can be used independently or as part of a subordinate clause. All the subjunctives, marked in **bold** in *Lectiō Prīma*, are used independently. For now:

- If the verb is in the 3rd person, try "Let 'em" or "let him" or "let them." Thus: *inveniat* = Let him/her come in. *Fīat!* = Let it be done!
- If the verb is in the 1st person plural, try "Let's." Thus: *Eāmus!* = Let's go. *Bibāmus* = Let's drink.
- If the verb is anything else, choose what sounds best from the typical "subjunctive words": should, would, could, might, may.

EXERCEĀMUS!

31-1 Subjunctives

Which translation for the subjunctive (in **bold**) is best? Since these sentences are from your reading, this exercise will be of use to you as you read *Lectiō Prīma*.

1. Ientāculum **appōnātur.**   a. is served   b. will be served   c. let it be served
2. Nē **dormiāmus**!   a. let's not sleep   b. we have not slept   c. we are not sleeping
3. **Labōrēmus**!   a. we are working   b. we work   c. let's work
4. Ligna in focō **impōnantur**!   a. they will be placed   b. let them be placed   c. they were placed
5. Fīcī **ferantur**!   a. they are brought   b. let them be brought   c. they will be brought
6. Pānis **pōnātur**!   a. let it be laid out   b. it is laid out   c. it has been laid out
7. Quid **faciāmus**?   a. are we doing?   b. might we do?   c. did we do?
8. Dī mē **iuvent**!   a. may they help   b. they are helping   c. let's help
9. **Abeat**!   a. he will go away   b. let him go away   c. he goes away
10. Tranquillior **sit**!   a. He may be calmer   b. He will be calmer   c. He is calmer
11. Tranquillitās in culīnā **regnet**!   a. it reigns   b. let it reign   c. it will reign
12. **Fīat**!   a. it will be done   b. it is done   c. let it be done
13. Rēs aptae **fabricentur**!   a. let them be made   b. they will be made   c. let us make
14. **Nōlim** nostram fīliam nuptūram esse sine rēbus optimīs pulcherrimīsque.   a. I do not wish   b. I wouldn't want   c. let's wish
15. "Servī meī," inquit, "cibum meum **edant**!"   a. they will eat   b. let's eat   c. let them eat

Gemma

Prōgrediendum est in lines 1-2 of *Lectiō Prīma* is an example of an impersonal use of the gerundive. *Forum* is the object of *ad*, not the subject of *prōgrediendum est*.

The expression is literally translated "there must be a going to the Forum by Servilius," but we would say "Servilius must go to the Forum."

MĀNE

Māne est sed iam diēs aestuōsus est. Mox ad Forum Servīliō prōgrediendum est, sed priusquam abit, clientēs suī recipiendī sunt in ātriō. Rōmae cōtīdiē māne quisque patrōnus clientēs suōs recipit et eīs aut pecūniam aut sportulam dat. Post hanc "salūtātiōnem" patrōnus ad Forum ad rēs suās agendās abit.

Domina lectīcam suam ascendit.

5   Dum Servīlius et clientēs salūtātiōnem agunt, Caecilia expergiscitur, sē lavat et ientāculum in peristȳliō exspectat. Ancillae cuidam imperat et "Ientāculum quam celerrimē **appōnātur**! Iēiūna sum! Celerrimē!"

In culīnā Sicō ancillīs imperat et īrātus fit. "Anna! Pallas! Scybalē! Cūr ientāculum nōn iam parātum est? Nē **dormiāmus**. Celerius **labōrēmus** omnēs! Ligna in focō **impōnantur**. Fīcī **ferantur**! Pānis in mensā **pōnātur**! Mel et
10   vīnum **effundantur**!"

Pallas "Sicō," inquit, "ubīque quaesīvī sed nullum mel invenīre possum! Vēnitne heri mel dē apiāriīs?"

Sicō, dēspērāns, clāmat: "Quid **faciāmus**? Mel inveniendum est! Dī mē **iuvent**!" Tālibus clāmātīs, Sicō ē culīnā currit.

Scybalē Annam "Quō," rogat, "Sicō vādit?"

Anna respondet: "Sentiō coquum nostrum ad mel inveniendum abīre! Utinam aequiōris animī **sit**. **Abeat**! Postquam
15   reveniet, tranquillior **sit** et nē semper, sīcut Vesuvius, ēruptūrus **sit**! Interim, tranquillitās in culīnā **regnet**!"

Caecilia, dum ientāculum exspectat, ad coniugem vocat. "Marce," inquit, "Quid dē Cordō heri accidit? Generne noster fīet?"

"Ita, vērō," respondit Servīlius, "generum novum habēmus! Sed nunc mihi in Forō multae rēs agendae sunt. Quid tū, cāra uxor, in animō hodiē agere habēs?"

20   "Volō quāsdam rēs īnspectāre. Dōna fīliae nostrae nuptūrae apta invenienda sunt! Sī rēs aptās invēnerō, licēbitne eās fabricārī?"

Servīlius "Ita, vērō," inquit, "**fīat**! Sī rēs aptās invēneris, **fabricentur**! **Nōlim** nostram fīliam nuptūram esse sine rēbus optimīs pulcherrimīsque."

Tālibus dictīs, Servīlius abiit. Tunc, melle inventō, Sicō, cibum portāns, peristȳlium intrat. "Domina," inquit,
25   "tempus est ientāculī edendī. Ecce, mel novum habēmus!"

Caecilia "Servī meī," inquit, "cibum meum **edant**! Nunc mihi abeundum est! Nullum tempus edendō habeō! **Eāmus**!"

Quam īrātus Sicō est! Sed coquus nihil dīcēns in culīnam abit. Sicō prūdentissimus servus est et numquam id quod in mente habet dīcit. Quid aliud servī facere **possint**!? Interim domina celeriter domō abit et lectīcam suam ascendit. Tunc statim ā servīs ad dōna fīliae emenda fertur.

VERBA ŪTENDA

aequus, -a, -um level, even
aestuōsus, -a, -um hot
apiārius, -iī m. beekeeper
aptus, -a, -um suitable, fit
cliens, clientis m. client
coniunx, coniugis m./f. spouse
dēspērō (1) despair
dī = deī m. nom. pl. "gods"
effundō, effundere, effūdī,
    effūsum pour out
ērumpō, ērumpere, ērūpī,
    ēruptum erupt
expergiscor, expergiscī,
    experrectus sum wake up
fīcus, -ī f. fig
focus, -ī m. fireplace, hearth

ientāculum, -ī n. breakfast
impōnō, impōnere, imposuī,
    impositum put on
interim meanwhile
lavō, lavāre, lāvī, lautum/
    lavātum/lōtum wash
lignum, -ī n. wood, firewood
mel, mellis n. honey
mens, mentis f. mind;
    reason; mental
    disposition
nē not, in order that
    not, lest
nūbō, nūbere, nupsī,
    nuptum marry
pānis, pānis m. bread

prūdens, prūdentis prudent
quō (to) where?
recipiō, recipere, recēpī,
    receptum accept,
    receive, take back; **sē**
    recipere retreat (take
    oneself somewhere)
regnō (1) reign, hold
    power over
reveniō, revenīre, revēnī,
    reventum come back,
    return
Rōmae at/in Rome
salūtātiō, -ōnis f. greeting,
    formal morning visit by
    a client to a patron

Scybalē, -ēs f. a female name
    (Note Greek case endings.)
sportula, -ae f. gift of money
    or food from patron to
    client, lit., "little basket"
tranquillitās, -tātis f.
    calmness, stillness;
    fair weather
    [tranquility]
tranquillus, -a, -um calm,
    still, peaceful
    [tranquil]
utinam (+ subj.) would that,
    how I wish that!
vādō, vādere, vāsī go,
    advance

POSTQUAM LĒGISTĪ

1. What obligation does Servilius have at home every morning before he goes to the Forum?
2. The cook Sico gets angry twice in this narrative. What are the two things that upset him?
3. Why does Sico leave the kitchen?
4. How does Anna feel the mood in the kitchen will be while Sico is absent?
5. Where does Caecilia wait for her breakfast? To whom does she talk while she waits?
6. What news does Caecilia learn?
7. What does she decide to do as a result of this news?

Grammatica A

Mood Consolidation

As you know, every Latin verb form has tense, voice, and mood. There are three moods in Latin:

Mood	Examples	Characteristics
Indicative	amat, amābit, amāvit	fact
Imperative	Amā! Amāte! Nōlī amāre!	command, order
Subjunctive	amem, amēmus, ament	wish, possibility, polite command

Mood indicates the manner in which the action is expressed: as fact, as command, or as "less real" or subordinate. In addition to these three moods, you should also remember that verbs can become **verbals**:

Infinitive	amāre, amāvisse, amātum esse	verbal noun
Participle	amāns, amātus, amātūrus	verbal adjective
Gerund	amandī	verbal noun
Gerundive	amandus, -a, -um	verbal adjective

Translating the Subjunctive

There are no hard and fast rules as to how you should translate a Latin subjunctive into English. It all depends on context, but it may help you to study these examples to distinguish indicative, imperative, and subjunctive in English.

Indicative	**Subjunctive**
I praise my students.	I might praise my students.
Imperative	**Subjunctive**
Don't praise the lazy.	If you should praise the lazy . . .

However, there are many situations in which the subjunctive will have a very different meaning. You will learn these as you go along. It is useful to memorize these "subjunctive words" and use them when context seems to allow it: **should, would, could, might, may**.

The subjunctive mood is occasionally used as the main verb in the sentence. This is called an **independent** subjunctive. In this part of the chapter we introduce you to several uses of this kind of subjunctive. More frequently, subjunctive forms are found in dependent clauses, so called because they depend on and further elucidate the action of a main verb. In *Lectiō Secunda* you will see a **dependent** use of the subjunctive.

Present Subjunctives

As you saw in *Lectiō Prīma*, the subjunctive forms of the verb use regular personal endings but distinctive connecting vowels. Compare here the present active indicative and present active subjunctive forms of all conjugations.

INDICATIVE				
1st Conjugation	2nd Conjugation	3rd Conjugation	3rd Conjugation *-iō*	4th Conjugation
vocō	moneō	dūcō	capiō	audiō
vocās	monēs	dūcis	capis	audīs
vocat	monet	dūcit	capit	audit
vocāmus	monēmus	dūcimus	capimus	audīmus
vocātis	monētis	dūcitis	capitis	audītis
vocant	monent	dūcunt	capiunt	audiunt

SUBJUNCTIVE				
1st Conjugation	2nd Conjugation	3rd Conjugation	3rd Conjugation *-iō*	4th Conjugation
vocem	moneam	dūcam	capiam	audiam
vocēs	moneās	dūcās	capiās	audiās
vocet	moneat	dūcat	capiat	audiat
vocēmus	moneāmus	dūcāmus	capiāmus	audiāmus
vocētis	moneātis	dūcātis	capiātis	audiātis
vocent	moneant	dūcant	capiant	audiant

Notā Bene:

- The 1st person singular active ending in the subjunctive is always *-m* instead of *-ō*.
- The connecting vowel in the present subjunctive follows the pattern in the sentence "We clean a dial."
- Passive verbs and deponents follow the same vowel pattern to create their present subjunctives.

Conjugation	Passive Indicative	Passive Subjunctive
1st	cōnor, cōnāris, etc.	cōner, cōnēris, etc.
2nd	vereor, verēris, etc.	verear, vereāris, etc.
3rd	sequor, sequeris, etc.	sequar, sequāris, etc.
3rd *-iō*	ingredior, ingredieris, etc.	ingrediar, ingrediāris, etc.
4th	mentior, mentīris, etc.	mentiar, mentiāris, etc.

- **False Friends:** A handful of forms in the 3rd and 4th conjugations are identical in the 1st person of the future indicative and the present subjunctive. Thus *dūcam* is either future indicative or present subjunctive. *Audiar* can be translated "I will be heard" or "Let me be heard." Don't worry too much about this. The form is usually clear in context.

Present Subjunctives of Irregular Verbs

Latin verbs that are irregular in the present indicative are typically irregular in the present subjunctive as well. These forms require special attention.

SUM	POSSUM	EŌ	FĪŌ	VOLŌ	NŌLŌ	MĀLŌ
sim	possim	eam	fīam	velim	nōlim	mālim
sīs	possīs	eās	fīās	velīs	nōlīs	mālīs
sit	possit	eat	fīat	velit	nōlit	mālit
sīmus	possīmus	eāmus	fīāmus	velīmus	nōlīmus	mālīmus
sītis	possītis	eātis	fīātis	velītis	nōlītis	mālītis
sint	possint	eant	fīant	velint	nōlint	mālint

Independent Subjunctives

In *Lectiō Prīma* all the subjunctives you saw were independent, i.e., they were used as main verbs in the sentence. Independent subjunctives fall into three groups:

- **Commands:** Often called the **hortatory** (1st person) or **jussive** (3rd person) subjunctive

Eāmus!	Let's go!	*Nē dormiāmus!*	Let's not sleep!
Abeat!	Let him go away!	*Nē abeat!*	Let him not go away!
Fīat!	Let it happen!	*Nē fīat!*	Let it not happen!
Tranquillior sit.	Let him be calmer.	*Nē tranquillior sit.*	Let him not be calmer.

- **Possibility or Wish:**

Utinam aequiōris animī sit.	Would that he were of calmer mind.	*Nē aequiōris animī sit.*	Would that he were not of calmer mind.
Velim . . .	I would want	*Nōlim . . .*	I would not want
Tranquillior sit!	May he be calmer!	*Nē tranquillior sit.*	May he not be calmer!

- **Deliberation:** (1st person only)

Quid faciam?	What should/might I do?

Notā Bene:

- Independent subjunctives expressing commands, possibilities, or wishes use the negative *nē* instead of *nōn*.
- *Utinam* is optional: *Utinam aequiōris animī sit* and *Aequiōris animī sit* both mean "Would that he were of calmer mind."

Don't worry too much about distinguishing among commands, possibilities, wishes, and deliberation. Just keep these possibilities in mind, and see which one fits best in context.

EXERCEĀMUS!

31-2 Translating Independent Subjunctives

Here are some independent subjunctives. Translate each of them according to the samples in the previous section. Follow the model.

→ Audiāmus!   *Let's listen.*

1. Strēnuē cōnēmur!
2. Servī dūcantur!
3. Fīcī appōnantur!
4. Prōgrediantur!
5. Quid aliud faciam?
6. Celerius currant!
7. Quid agāmus?
8. Utinam sedeat.
9. Nē abeant.

Lectiō Secunda

Antequam Legis

In *Lectiō Secunda* Valeria and Licinia meet Caecilia at the snack shop while Caecilia is out shopping in preparation for the upcoming wedding of Servilia and Cordus. Caecilia sees the mirror and earrings Aelius made and is so impressed with his craftsmanship that she suggests that Aelius meet her husband. This will lead to a formal patron-client relationship between the two families. Such alliances were a common type of interaction in the ancient Roman world.

Gemmae Rōmānae

Introduction to Purpose Clauses

You have learned that the subjunctive can be used independently, but verbs in this mood are more commonly found in clauses introduced by conjunctions. The first of these conjunctions is *ut*. You have aleady seen *ut* used with indicative verbs to mean "as" in phrases like *ut opīnor*, "as I think."

Now you meet *ut* + the subjunctive in what is called in Latin the **purpose clause**, which, as its name implies, shows the purpose of the subject's action. If the clause is negative, the formula is *nē* + the subjunctive.

For now, these pattern sentences will give you all you need to know to translate purpose clauses. Note the various translations of *ut* + subjunctive verb (in **bold**).

*Veniō **ut pōtum emam**.*

> I come in order that I might buy a drink.
> I come so that I might buy a drink.
> I come (in order) to buy a drink.

*Hominēs cibum habēre dēbent **nē moriantur**.*

> Humans must have food lest they die.
> Humans must have food so that they do not die.
> Humans must have food (in order) not to die.

Each sentence is translated three different ways so that you can see the wide range of options to express purpose in English.

EXERCEĀMUS!

31-3 Translating Purpose Clauses

As you read, list the purpose clauses and give the appropriate English translation. All of these purpose clauses in *Lectiō Secunda* are marked in **bold**. Follow the model.

Line	Purpose Clause	Translation
→ 9	Ut … inveniam	in order to find

CAECILIA ET VALERIA

Caecilia, in lectīcā ā servīs lātā sedēns, dōnōrum Servīliae emendōrum causā ad multās tabernās multōrum fabricātōrum adīvit, sed nulla dōna idōnea vīdit. Alia dōna nōn satis pulchra sunt, alia nimium ostentātiōnis habent. Haec dōna turpia sunt, illa parum artis exhibent. Quid faciat?

5   Ubi dōna idōnea invenienda sunt?

Nunc quinta hōra est—et Caecilia et illī servī lectīcam in umerīs lātīs portantēs iēiūnī sitientēsque sunt.

Caecilia servīs imperat: "Servī, sistite prope illam tabernam! Descendam **ut** pōtum cibumque **inveniam**. Aliquid edere pōtāreque
10 dēbeō **nē** fame sitīque **moriar!**"

Lectīcā in terrā dēpositā, Caecilia descendit et tabernae Valeriae appropinquat **ut** aliquid **pōtet**.

Caecilia Līciniam videt et "Salvē," inquit. "Maximē sitiō. Dā mihi vīnum, pānem, et mel. Sed, manē! Nōn vīnum, sed calidum volō, sī
15 tibi placeat!"

Dīc mihi dē hōc speculō.

Licinia "Certē, domina," inquit. "Aliquid aliud vīs? Fortasse servī tuī quoque sitientēs sunt? Licetne eīs aquam dare?"

Caeciliā assentiente, Flāvia, **ut** aquam **arcessat**, urnam portāns ad fontem abit. Valeria, quae infantem Maximum portat, Caeciliae appropinquat **ut** cum eā **sermōcinētur**.

20 Valeria "Salvē," inquit, "Calidumne tibi placet? Vīnum Falernum est et hoc mel apiāriī optimī rusticī quī mel suum mihi sōlī vendit **ut** in tabernā meā calidum optimum **fīat**."

Caecilia "Rectē habēs," inquit. "Hoc calidum est optimum quod pōtāvī et hodiē mihi vīnum bibendum est! Sed, dīc mihi dē hōc speculō quod in mūrō videō."

Hoc speculum idem est quod Aelius Līciniae fabricāvit et Valeria, rīdēns, speculum dē mūrō tollit et Caeciliae,
25 **ut** illa id **inspectet**, dat. "Aelius," inquit, "gener meus hoc fabricāvit uxōrī et huic infantī suō quem vidēs. Quoque hās inaurēs fabricāvit."

Caecilia: "Ars magna in ambābus rēbus est. Hodiē frustrā multās hōrās circumiēns **ut** dōna nuptiālia fīliae **inveniam** nihil idōneum vīdī. Velim fīliae aliquid hīs simile dare. Hic Aelius hās rēs argenteās quoque fabricāre potest?"

Valeria "Potest," inquit, "sed argentum nōn habēmus. Egēnī sumus et pecūniam argentō Aelius nōn habet."

30 Caecilia: "Marītus meus vir dīves et senātor est et opīnor eum praetōrem mox futūrum esse. Aeliō ad marītum meum crās māne adveniendum est **ut** ab eō auxilium **petat**. Sī marītō placuerit, argentum Aelius habēbit et tum Aelius faber et cliens marītī et argentārius fīet. Consentīsne?"

"Consentiō, domina," respondet Valeria. "Gener meus ad senātōrem crās adveniet."

Gemma

Watch for two versions of "please" in this reading. *Sī placet*, which you have seen before, is indicative and is a simple "please." *Sī placeat* is subjunctive and is more polite: "if it should be pleasing."

POSTQUAM LĒGISTĪ

1. How does Caecilia travel around the city?
2. Why doesn't she buy anything?
3. What does Caecilia order from the menu?
4. Why is Valeria's honey special?
5. What does Caecilia think about the mirror and earrings that Aelius made?
6. What does she suggest Aelius do in the morning?

🔊 VERBA ŪTENDA

alius . . . alius one . . .
   another; pl. some . . .
   others
***ambō, ambae, ambō* both**
   (of two); note the
   irregular dat./abl. pl.,
   ambōbus/ambābus
apiārius, -iī m. beekeeper
arcessō, arcessere,
   arcessīvī/arcessiī,
   arcessītum fetch
***argentārius, -a, -um* of**
   silver, pertaining to
   silver
argenteus, -a, -um silvery,
   of silver
***argentum, -ī* n. silver;**
   money

assentior, assentīrī, assensus
   sum approve
circumeō, circumīre,
   circumīvī/circumiī,
   circumitum go around
consentiō, consentīre,
   consensī, consensum
   consent, agree
descendō, descendere,
   descendī, descensum
   go down, descend
exhibeō, exhibēre, exhibuī,
   exhibitum show, exhibit
Falernus, -a, -um Falernian,
   referring to a region in
   Italy producing an
   excellent wine
faber argentārius silversmith

famēs, famis f. hunger
fons, fontis m. spring,
   fountain
frustrā in vain
idōneus, -a, -um fit, suitable
inaurēs, inaurium f. pl.
   earrings
***lātus, -a, -um* wide, broad**
lectīca, -ae f. litter
morior, morī, mortuus
   sum die
nuptiālis, nuptiāle nuptial,
   for a wedding
parum little, too little,
   not enough
***pōtō* (1) drink**
praetor, -ōris m. praetor,
   judge

quintus, -a, -um fifth
rusticus, -i m. peasant
sermōcinor, sermōcinārī,
   sermōcinātus sum
   converse, talk, chat
similis, simile like, similar to
***sitiō, sitīre, sitīvī/sitiī* be**
   thirsty
sitis, sitis f. thirst; *sitī* (Note
   the alternative abl. sing.
   i-stem ending.)
turpis, turpe ugly, foul,
   loathsome
umerus, -ī m. shoulder
urna, -ae f. large water jar
***ut* in order that, so that;**
   how; as; when

Grammatica B

Purpose Clauses

Earlier you saw subjunctives used independently as the main verbs in the sentence. Subjunctives in purpose clauses are dependent. That is to say, they appear in subordinate clauses that depend on or hang from the main clause in the sentence. Consider this sentence:

*Veniō **ut** pōtum **emam**.*

Veniō can stand alone as a sentence by itself. But *ut pōtum emam* cannot do this and is thus "dependent."

This, then, is the formula for a sentence with a purpose clause:

main clause   +   *ut / nē*   +   verb in the subjunctive

*Veniō **ut** pōtum **emam**.*   I come in order that I buy a drink.
*Veniō **nē** vīnum **bibās**.*   I am coming so that you don't drink wine.

And remember: *ut* + the indicative = as, when

***Ut** tibi iam **dixī**, calidum*   As I already told you, we have
   optimum habēmus!   the best warm wine drink!

The main verb must be in the present or future tense in order to use a present subjunctive.

Notā Bene: You now know four ways to express purpose in Latin.

- *ut* + subjunctive: *ut pōtum emam*
- gerund(ive) in the genitive + *causā: pōtī emendī causā*
- gerund(ive) in the genitive + *grātiā: pōtī emendī grātiā*
- *ad* + accusative gerund(ive): *ad pōtum emendum*

All of these phrases can be translated "to buy a drink."

Gemma

Another case in which the macron makes all the difference: *māne* "in the morning" versus *manē* "wait!"

EXERCEĀMUS!

31-4 **Purpose Clauses with *ut* + Subjunctive**

Change the following underlined gerund(ive) purpose phrases into purpose clauses using *ut* + subjunctive. Then translate the purpose clause into English at least two different ways. Follow the model.

→   Labōrō <u>familiae meae movendae causā</u>.   *ut familiam meam moveam*
in order that I move my family
to move my family

1. Caecilia <u>ad dōna invenienda</u> venit.
2. Valeria speculum in tabernā <u>ad id monstrandum</u> pōnit.
3. Caecilia tabernae <u>calidī poscendī causā</u> appropinquat.
4. Licinia <u>ad aquam servīs dandam</u> venit.
5. Aelius ad senātōrem <u>auxiliī petendī grātiā</u> veniet.
6. Servīlius pecūniam Aeliō <u>ad argentum emendum</u> dabit.

Mōrēs Rōmānī

Salūtātiō

Before Servilius leaves for the Forum in the morning, he performs a daily task called the *salūtātiō, -iōnis* f. The *salūtātiō* is a formal greeting ceremony or morning call by a Roman client (*cliens, clientis* m. client) at the house of his patron (*patrōnus, -ī* m.). The patron-client relationship formed the heart of Roman political and commercial enterprise. The wealthy and ambitious sought to have as many clients as possible. A Roman like Cicero would have boasted of hundreds. These clients were expected to come to the home of the patron every day to greet him. The homes of many wealthy Romans had benches along the outside wall of the house where clients could wait until the patron was ready to receive them in the atrium (*ātrium, -iī* n.), the formal greeting room. You can see one of these benches outside a house in Pompeii in the photograph at the beginning of this chapter.

The patron would strive to greet each client individually and ask about his family and situation. If the client needed help, this was the time to ask. Often, the patron might give his clients *sportula, -ae* f., little gifts of money or food. The *sportula* Servilius gave his clients that morning consisted of food left over from a recent banquet. If private matters needed to be discussed, the patron might ask the client to step into the office or *tab(u)līnum, -ī* n., behind the atrium.

In return for these favors and patronage, clients were obligated to support their patron's commercial and political activities. If a patron were running for political office, clients would escort him as he campaigned. Clients were also expected to vote as the patron wished at the public assemblies and to campaign for him as well.

The system was complicated. Many clients of rich people had their own clients. The wealthiest and most powerful Romans were only patrons, not clients, and the poorest citizens, like Aelius, were lucky to have any patron at all.

In a famous poem Martial suggests that he left Rome for his native Spain because he did not enjoy the early morning salutation in his patron's atrium. Here is how he explains his position to a more ambitious fellow client, who obviously enjoys the custom more than Martial does. Martial would much rather sleep late and write poetry in Spain than get up early for a *salūtātiō* in Rome. As usual, we provide a simplified version.

Ō mātūtīne cliens, quī mihi es causa urbis reliquendae, sī sapiās, ātria ambitiōsa colās. Ego nōn sum causidicus. Nec amārīs lītibus aptus sum. Sed piger et senior comes Mūsārum sum. Ōtia somnusque, quae magna Rōma mē negāvit, mē iuvant. Rōmam redībō sī et hīc in Hispaniā dormīre nōn possum.

Martial *Epigrammata* 12.68

🔊 VERBA ŪTENDA

amārus, -a, -um bitter
ambitiōsus, -a, -um ambitious, ostentatious
causidicus, -ī m. lawyer
colō, colere, coluī, cultum pay court to, haunt

comes, comitis m./f. companion
et here; "even" or "also"
līs, lītis f. lawsuit
mātūtīnus, -a, -um of or belonging to the early morning
negō (1) deny

ōtium, -iī n. leisure
piger, pigra, pigrum low, sluggish, lazy
Rōmam to Rome
sapiō, sapere, sapīvī/sapiī show good sense
somnus, -ī m. sleep, rest

Latīna Hodierna

Latin in the Periodic Table of the Elements

In the readings you encountered *argentum*, the Latin word for silver. This leads us to the periodic table of the elements. For centuries following the fall of the Roman Empire, Latin continued to be the international language of communication among scientists. The periodic table of the elements reflects the influence of Latin. The abbreviations for several elements are based on the actual Latin name for the element:

Abbreviation	Latin Name	English Name	English Derivatives
Au	*aurum, -ī* n.	gold	auriferous, aurous, aureate, aureole
Ag	*argentum, -ī* n.	silver	argent, argentiferous, Argentina
Pb	*plumbum, -ī* n.	lead	plumber, plumbiferous
Fe	*ferrum, -ī* n.	iron	ferric, ferrite, ferriferous

Some elements derive the names from Graeco-Roman mythology:

Ir	iridium	from *Īris -idis* f. goddess of the rainbow
Ur	uranium	from a Latinized form of the Greek *Ouranos,* the first god of the sky, father of the Titans
Pm	promethium	from *Promētheus, Promētheī* m. Titan fire giver
Np	neptunium	from *Neptūnus, -ī* m. god of the sea
Pu	plutonium	from *Plūtō, -ōnis* m. god of the underworld
Ta	tantalium	from *Tantalus, -ī* m. great sinner

Many other elements were given Latinized names based on an important fact surrounding its discovery. Here are just a few examples:

Sc	scandium	from Scandinavia
Am	americium	from America
Es	einsteinium	from Albert Einstein

All these elements are formed as 2nd declension neuter nouns.

Au = Aurum

Ag = Argentum

Orbis Terrārum Rōmānus

Pompēiī et Vesuvius

At the time of our story in c. 9 B.C., Vesuvius had been quiet for more than 200 years, and the famous eruption of August 24, 79 A.D., was still 80 years in the future. So we used some poetic

license when we had Anna, in *Lectiō Prīma*, compare the unpredictable Sico to Vesuvius. At the base of this mountain lay the city of Pompeii, a small but prosperous town in southern Italy that would not be so well-known today if the eruption of 79 A.D. had not preserved the city under piles of volcanic ash. We know a lot more about everyday Roman life because of what was found in the excavation of Pompeii (as well as Herculaneum, her sister-city in destruction).

If you compare the photo of Vesuvius and Pompeii today at left with the ancient wall painting of Vesuvius below, you can see how much of the mountain fell on Pompeii in the eruption. Also notice Bacchus, the Roman god of wine, in the wall painting. Bacchus is wearing a bunch of grapes. Look closely at this picture and you will see that Vesuvius is covered with vineyards. The rich volcanic soil of the mountain was (and still is) excellent for agricultural use.

Vesuvius Nunc

Vesuvius Tunc

Pompēiī et Vesuvius in Campāniā

QUID PUTĀS?

1. Use the names of elements in the periodic table as guides to five new elements named after yourself or people you know or admire.
2. How does the Roman patron-client relationship compare to the way that politics and commerce are practiced in the United States today?
3. The patron-client relationship is an important element in the opening wedding scene of the movie *The Godfather*. Compare that relationship to one in ancient Roman practice.
4. Do you agree think that Martial had good reasons to leave Rome for Spain? What would you have done if you had been in his position? Why or why not?
5. Martial's comment that something might make him return to Rome gives an indication of what he really values in life. What is it?

EXERCEĀMUS!

31-5 Scrībāmus

Use the word pool to fill in the blanks with appropriate purpose clauses.

HINT: You will have to make the infinitives from the word pool into subjunctives. Then translate your sentence. Follow the model.

multam pecūniam habēre	vīnum bibere	auxilium petere
laetus esse	fratrem vidēre	vītā fruī
difficultātem fugere	pōtum cibumque invenīre	dē infante audīre
bene edere	artem inspectāre	mel emere

→ Labōrō strēnuē ut   *multam pecūniam habeam.*
    I work hard to have much money.

1. Epistulam scrībit ut
2. In Italiā habitāmus ut
3. Caecilia dē lectīcā descendit ut
4. Licinia Caeciliae speculum dat ut
5. Aelius ad Servīlium advenīre dēbet ut
6. Sicō abit ut

31-6 Colloquāmur

Now ask a classmate one of the following questions. Your classmate can use the sentences from Exercise 31-5 to reply. Follow the model.

→ Cūr strēnuē labōrās?   *Labōrō strēnuē ut multam pecūniam habeam.*

1. Cūr epistulam scrībit?
2. Cūr in Italiā habitātis?
3. Cūr Caecilia dē lectīcā descendit?
4. Cūr Licinia Caeciliae speculum dat?
5. Cūr Aelius ad Servīlium advenīre dēbet?
6. Cūr Sicō abit?

31-7 Vēnātiō Verbōrum

Use the following hints to identify words in the *Verba Discenda*. A word can be used only once. Follow the model.

→ "Ineptitude" is a derivative of this word. *aptus*

1. *Bibō* is a synonym for this word.
2. This is an i-stem of the 3ʳᵈ declension.
3. This word has irregular dative and ablative plurals.
4. This is a neuter noun of the 3ʳᵈ declension.
5. This word is deponent.
6. This word is a metal.
7. *Calidus, -a, -um* is a synonym for this word.
8. This word refers to a Roman custom.
9. This word is used instead of *ut* in a negative purpose clause.
10. A calm person experiences this.
11. This word is a meal.
12. This word describes what you do to dirty dishes.
13. This word refers to the opposite of being hungry.
14. This word describes what Servilia will do soon.
15. This word is the antonym of *patrōnus*.
16. This word could describe a day with no wind.
17. This word is a 3ʳᵈ conjugation *-iō* verb.

🔊 VERBA DISCENDA

aequus, -a, -um even, equal; fair, just; patient, calm [equitable]

aestuōsus, -a, -um hot

alius . . . alius one . . . another; pl. some . . . others

ambō, ambae, ambō both (of two); note the irregular dat./abl. pl., **ambōbus, ambābus** [ambidextrous]

aptus, -a, -um attached to, connected to; suitable, fit [aptitude]

argentārius, -a, -um of silver, pertaining to silver

argentum, -ī n. silver; money [Argentina]

cliens, clientis m. client

descendō, descendere, descendī, descensum go down, descend [descent]

ientāculum, -ī n. a light meal; breakfast; lunch

lātus, -a, -um wide, broad [latitude]

lavō, lavāre, lāvī, lautum/lavātum/lōtum wash [lavatory]

mel, mellis n. honey [mellifluous]

mens, mentis f. mind; reason; mental disposition [demented]

nē not, that not, in order that not, lest

nūbō, nūbere, nupsī, nuptum marry [nubile, nuptials]

pānis, pānis m. bread

pōtō (1) drink [potion]

recipiō, recipere, recēpī, receptum accept, receive, take back; **sē recipere** retreat (take oneself somewhere) [reciprocate, reception]

reveniō, revenīre, revēnī, reventum come back, return

salūtātiō, -ōnis f. greeting, formal morning visit by a client to a patron [salutation]

sermōcinor, sermōcinārī, sermōcinātus sum converse, talk, chat

sitiō, sitīre, sitīvī/sitiī be thirsty

tranquillitās, -tātis f. calmness, stillness; fair weather [tranquility]

tranquillus, -a, -um calm, still, peaceful [tranquil]

ut in order that, so that; how; as; when

Angulus Grammaticus
More on the Independent Uses of the Subjunctive

The independent uses of the subjunctive are sometimes divided into the following four categories:

Volitive (expressing a wish, from volō)

Eāmus!	Let's go!	*Nē eāmus!*	Let's not go!
Eat!	Let him go!	*Nē eat!*	Let him not go!

Notā Bene:

- Volitive subjunctives are the equivalent of mild imperatives, but in the 1st or 3rd person.
- The 1st person volitive is sometimes called **hortatory** (from *hortor*), because it urges "us" to do something. You can think of it as a "salad subjunctive" because it has "lettuce" in it, as in "Let us not go!"
- The 3rd person volitive is sometimes called **jussive** (from *iubeō*) because it is a polite order.
- Some grammar books do not use the term "hortatory" and classify forms like *Eāmus!* as jussives.
- The volitive subjunctive uses the negative *nē* instead of *nōn*.

Optative (wished for, from optō)

(Utinam) eāmus!	Would that we were going!
Utinam nē eāmus!	Would that we were not going!

Notā Bene:

- The optative subjunctive can be introduced by the word *utinam* (would that).
- The optative subjunctive uses the negative *nē* instead of *nōn*.
- *Eāmus* can equally be translated "Let's go!" or "Would that we were going!"

Potential (possible, from possum)

Velim ...	I would wish ...	*Nōn eam.*	I would not go.

Notā Bene:

- The potential subjunctive uses the negative *nōn*.

Deliberative (deliberating, from dēlīberō)

Quid faciam?	What should I do?	*Quid nōn faciam?*	What should I not do?

Notā Bene:

- The deliberative subjunctive uses the negative *nōn*.

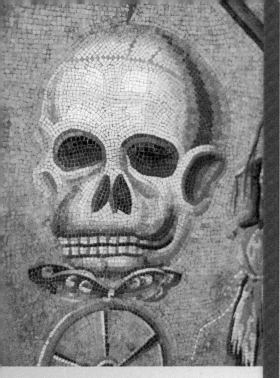

32

Mementō Morī

LECTIŌNĒS:
INCENDIUM!
and
EFFUGIUM!

The Servilius family deals with the death of their *avus*. Cordus' worst fears about fires are realized and Valeria's family is put into dire straits.

Lectiō Prīma

Antequam Legis

Rome at Night

The city of Rome was noisy and dangerous, especially at night. There were no street lights and only the bravest or most desperate went out at night without protection. Wheeled traffic was prohibited in the city center in Rome during the day, so much of this commercial traffic took place at night. The noise from this traffic could be deafening and ancient Romans often complained about the racket. The night on which *Lectiō Prīma* takes place proves to be a fatal one for many inhabitants.

Result Clauses

Result clauses tell just that—a result. Consider these English result clauses:

> Marcus is **so** naughty *that his teachers don't like him.*
> Julia is **so** smart *that her teachers always love her.*

Note how the main clause contains a "so" word (marked in **bold**) followed by the result clause (marked in *italics*). Latin result clauses are very similar. The main clause contains a "so" word like *tam* followed by a result clause in the subjunctive. Here is how the same sentences would be written in Latin:

> Marcus **tam** improbus est *ut magistrī eum nōn ament.*
> Iūlia **tam** intellegens est *ut magistrae semper eam ament.*

We have marked the Latin result clauses in *Lectiō Prīma* in the same way that the result clauses were marked above:

- "so" word in **bold**
- result clause in *italics*

Simply translate these clauses "so . . . that . . ."

Here are the most common "so" words in Latin:

ita	so, thus; yes
tam	so, so much (as)
tantus, -a, -um	so great, so much
tot	so many

EXERCEĀMUS!

32-1 Practicing Result Clauses

Find the "so" word in each of the following Latin sentences. Then translate the sentence. Use the *Verba Ūtenda* following *Lectiō Prīma* for help with vocabulary.

→ Tam sērō est ut paucī in viīs Rōmae sint.   Tam: It is so late that few people are in the streets in Rome.

1. Servī tam molliter labōrant ut dominī bene dormiant.

2. Avus tam aeger est ut familia Servīliī dormīre nōn possit.

3. Tot medicī adsunt ut domus plēna sit.

4. Rēs tantum perīculum habet ut familia deōs precētur.

32-2 Prereading for Content

Do this exercise before you try to translate the reading. For each question fill in the answer with the relevant Latin words from the reading. The line numbers indicate where you can find the answer. Follow the model.

→ Describe the streets of Rome at night. (lines 1–3) *dēsertae*

1. Who sleeps well this night? (lines 1–3)

2. Why isn't the Servilius family sleeping? (lines 4–7)

3. Who is Artorius? (lines 4–7)

4. What is Artorius' diagnosis? (lines 4–7)

5. What causes so much noise in Subura at night? (lines 8–10)

6. Why can't Licinia sleep? (lines 11–14)

7. Why can't Felix sleep? (lines 11–14)

8. Why does Mendax get drunk? (lines 11–14)

9. Why does Mendax push over the lamp? (lines 15–17)

10. What does Socrates do? (lines 18–21)

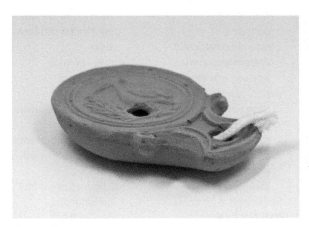

Lucerna Rōmāna

🔊 INCENDIUM!

Sērō est et paucī in viīs Rōmae sunt. In Colle Vīminālī, prope domum Servīliōrum, viae dēsertae sunt et **tanta** est tranquillitās *ut omnēs dīvitēs in cubiculīs bene dormiant.* Servī molliter labōrant

Mendax sīcut mortuus dormit.

ut dominī bene dormiant. Familia Servīliī autem nōndum dormit quod avus aeger est. Multī medicī, inter quōs
5 quīdam Artōrius est, multa temptant ut avum sānent. Servīlius Artōrium ad sē vocat et eum rogat: "Quid dē patre meō?" Artōrius "Pater tuus" inquit, "**tam** aeger est *ut haec nox eī ultima sit.* Cum febrēs senēs tenent, rēs perīculōsa est. Nihil agendum, sōlum precandum est."

In Subūrā, autem, viae numquam omnīnō dēsertae sunt. **Tanta** est paupertās in Subūrā *ut hominēs interdiū noctūque semper cibum quaerant.* Noctū plaustra per viās urbis prōgrediuntur et **tantum** clāmōrem faciunt ut *multī*
10 *incolae insulārum frequenter dormīre nōn possint.*

In ūnā insulā Subūrae trēs nōn dormiunt. Infans Liciniae **tam** fortiter flet *ut Licinia expergiscātur* et nunc sedet, infantem nūtriēns. Mox, infante nūtrītō, fortasse Licinia iterum dormiet. Infrā Fēlix fēlēs quoque, propter Mendācem stertentem, difficultātem dormiendī habet. Mendax hodiē **tantam** pecūniam ā transeuntibus habet *ut multum vīnum emere possit.* Vīnō consumptō, Mendax nunc sīcut mortuus dormit et **tam** fortiter stertit *ut Fēlix nōn dormiat.*

15 Fēlix valdē īrātus est et prīmō ūnō pede faciem Mendācis tangit ut eum excitet et sonitum sistat. Mendax autem nōn expergiscitur! Fēlix īrātior fit et nunc faciem Mendācis ambōbus pedibus haud lēniter pulsat! Mendax fēlem removēre cōnātur sed manus lucernam pulsat. Ignis lucernae pannōs, quī Mendācī lectō sunt, incendit.

Fēlix ignem metuēns Mendācem iterum excitāre cōnātur sed ignis **tam** celeriter crescit *ut fēlī fugiendum sit.* Suprā, Licinia, quamvīs adhūc infantem Maximum nūtriēns, dormit. Sōcratēs, autem, quī in angulō dormit, fūmum
20 sentit et nunc fortiter clāmāre incipit. Subitō Licinia expergiscitur et fūmum sentiēns perterrita est. Perīculum adest! Ignis in insulīs Rōmae semper rēs gravissima est!

"Aelī!" clāmat. "Aelī! Expergiscere! Incendium!"

🔊 VERBA ŪTENDA

aeger, aegra, aegrum sick
angulus, -ī m. corner
Artōrius, -iī m. Artorius, a man's name
collis, collis m. hill
consūmō, consūmere, consumpsī, consumptum consume
crescō, crescere, crēvī, crētum grow, arise, appear, increase
dēserō, dēserere, dēseruī, dēsertum desert
excitō (1) awaken, excite, raise
expergiscor, expergiscī, experrectus sum awake, wake up
febris, febris f. fever
fēlēs, fēlis f. cat

frequenter frequently
fūmus, -ī m. smoke
haud not, by no means
incendium, -iī n. fire, conflagration
incendō, incendere, incendī, incensum set fire to, inflame, burn
incola, -ae m./f. inhabitant
infrā below, underneath, under
interdiū by day
lucerna, -ae f. (oil) lamp
medicus, -ī m. physician, doctor
metuō, metuere, metuī, metūtum fear, be afraid of

molliter softly
mortuus, -a, -um dead
Nihil agendum, sōlum, precandum est: Literally, "nothing must be done; there must only be praying." But we would say, "There is nothing to do except pray."
noctū at night
nōndum not yet
nūtriō, nūtrīre, nūtrīvī/ nūtriī, nūtrītum nurse, nourish, raise
omnīnō utterly, altogether, completely
paupertās, -tātis f. poverty
plaustrum, -ī n. cart, wagon
precor, precārī, precātus sum pray

prīmō at first
quamvīs although
removeō, removēre, remōvī, remōtum remove
Rōmae at Rome
sānō (1) restore to health
sērō late
stertō, stertere, stertuī snore
suprā above; (+ acc.) over, on top of
tangō, tangere, tetigī, tactum touch; reach; affect; move; mention
temptō (1) feel; try; test
transeō, transīre, transīvī/ transiī, transitum go over, go across

POSTQUAM LĒGISTĪ

Respond to all the following statements or questions in English. Then answer those marked with (L) in Latin.

Gemma

The Artorius of this story is based on a real Artorius, a Greek physician and friend of Augustus early in his career. He died ca. 30 B.C.

1. Describe the neighborhood on the Viminal hill at night. (L)
2. Describe the Subura at night. (L)
3. Why do you think there is such a difference between the two neighborhoods?
4. How did Mendax spend the day? (L)
5. How does the fire in the *insula* start? How is such a fire likely to start today?
6. Why do you think that the lower floors in a Roman *insula* were more expensive than higher floors? Is this still true today? Why or why not?

Grammatica A

Subordinate Clauses: Purpose and Result

Both purpose and result clauses use *ut*, but they are different in meaning. Compare the relationship between the main and subordinate clauses in the following sentences:

Purpose

Indicative (or imperative) main verb + *ut* + **subjunctive subordinate** verb

> *Servī molliter **labōrant ut** omnēs dīvitēs in cubiculīs bene **dormiant**.*
> The servants work softly so that all the rich people might sleep well in their bedrooms.

Here the action of the main clause is performed with the intent or purpose that the action of the subordinate clause will happen. In this case Latin puts the main clause into the indicative mood, because this action actually happens. The verb of the subordinate clause is put into the subjunctive mood because this action is contingent on the action of the main verb. It is, if you will, "less real."

Result

Indicative main verb (or imperative) + "so" word + *ut* + **subjunctive subordinate** verb

> ***Tanta est** tranquillitās **ut** omnēs dīvitēs in cubiculīs bene **dormiant**.*
> There is such great tranquility that all the rich people sleep well in their bedrooms.

Here the action of the main clause leads to or results in the action of the subordinate clause. Latin puts the verb in the main clause into the indicative mood because this action is quite real, but puts the verb of the subordinate clause into the subjunctive mood, because this action is contingent on the main verb.

Compare the formulas for the two clauses:

Purpose: *ut/nē* + subjunctive

> Servī molliter labōrant **ut** omnēs dīvitēs in cubiculīs bene **dormiant**.
> Servī molliter labōrant **nē** omnēs dīvitēs in cubiculīs male **dormiant**.

Result: "so" word (*tantus, tam*) + *ut/ut nōn, ut nēmō,* etc. + subjunctive

> Servī **tam** molliter labōrant **ut** omnēs dīvitēs in cubiculīs bene **dormiant**.
> Servī **tam** molliter labōrant **ut** dīvitēs eōs **nōn audiant**.
> Servī **tam** fortiter clāmant **ut nullī** dīvitēs in cubiculīs **dormiant**.

Notā Bene: The negative forms of each clause can easily be distinguished. Negative purpose clauses are introduced by *nē* whereas negative result clauses are introduced by *ut* + *nōn* (or *ut* + other negatives like *nēmō, nullus,* etc.).

> Tantus est clāmor **ut** omnēs dīvitēs in cubiculīs suīs **nōn** bene dormiant.
> Tantus est clāmor **ut nullus** dīves in cubiculō suō bene dormiat.
> Tantus est clāmor **ut nēmō** in cubiculō suō dormiat.

EXERCEĀMUS!

32-3   Distinguishing Purpose and Result Clauses

The subordinate clauses in the following sentences are marked in bold. Identify each as purpose or result. Follow the model.

→   <u>result</u>   Tanta est tranquillitās **ut omnēs dīvitēs in cubiculīs suīs bene dormiant**.

1. Servī molliter labōrant **ut omnēs dīvitēs in cubiculīs bene dormiant**.
2. Pauperēs in Subūrā noctū nōn dormiunt **ut cibum quaerant**.
3. Tanta est paupertās in Subūrā **ut hominēs interdiū noctūque semper cibum quaerant**.
4. Fēlēs celeriter currit **ut incendium fugiat**.
5. Ignis tam celeriter crescit **ut fēlī fugiendum sit**.
6. Fēlī fugiendum est **nē igne moriātur**.
7. Fēlēs tam celeriter currit **ut nōn igne necētur**.
8. Pater tuus tam aeger est **ut haec nox eī ultima sit**.

Lectiō Secunda

Antequam Legis

Larēs

Pietās

As Valeria's family struggles to escape from the fire, watch for a literary allusion to a famous scene in Vergil's *Aeneid,* when the Trojan hero Aeneas escapes from his doomed city at the end of the Trojan War. He carries his father Anchises on his shoulder and has his son Ascanius (Iulus) at his side. Anchises holds in his hands the *Larēs* or household gods of the family. A similar scene is represented at left on a coin issued by Julius Caesar in 47–46 B.C. Even the poorest family, like that of Valeria, would have its own household gods for protection. The *Larēs* of Valeria's family have a major challenge on this particular night.

Notā Bene: If you look carefully in *Lectiō Secunda,* you will also find the mottoes of several U.S. states.

Faciō ut . . . (Subjunctive Noun Clauses)

Also watch out in this reading for forms of *faciō* followed by *ut / nē* and the subjunctive ("see to it that"). These clauses are marked in ***bold italics*** in *Lectiō Secunda.*

Imperfect Subjunctives

In this reading you are introduced to the imperfect subjunctive, which is very easy to recognize and form:

present active infinitive + personal endings ⟶ imperfect subjunctive

Active

clamāre + m ⟶ clamārem

vidēre + s ⟶ vidērēs

Passive

capere + tur ⟶ caperētur

audīre + mur ⟶ audīrēmur

Deponent

cōnāre + minī ⟶ cōnārēminī

sequere + ntur ⟶ sequerentur

Notā Bene: Deponent verbs do not really have a present active infinitive, but one is "invented" in order to make the imperfect subjunctive.

Look for imperfect subjunctives in *Lectiō Secunda* marked in **bold**. For now, just translate them as you would present subjunctives, i.e., with a "subjunctive" word like "should, would, could, might, may" or as part of a purpose or result clause.

EXERCEĀMUS!

32-4 *Faciō ut . . .*

Each of the following sentences contains a form of *faciō* + *ut*. Translate each sentence using an appropriate variation on "I see to it that. . ." Use the *Verba Ūtenda* following *Lectiō Secunda* for help with vocabulary.

1. Facit ut bene agant.

2. Fac ut familia bene agat.

3. Facite nē sīmia ā tabernā currat.

4. Facient ut novam vītam incipiant.

5. Faciēmus ut incendium exstinguātur.

6. Fac nē omnēs in incendiō pereant.

32-5 Reading Questions

As you read the *lectiō*, find the Latin words that answer these questions. Partial sentences are fine.

1. How does Valeria's family try to protect themselves from smoke and flames as they escape from the burning building?

2. What item(s) does each family member carry out of the building: Aelius, Licinia, Valeria, Flavia?

3. Which family member takes the lead in getting the family to safety?

4. How much damage does this fire cause?

5. To whom does Licinia attribute the family's safety? Why?

6. What addition does the family gain as a result of this fire?

7. What plan does Valeria propose for getting the family through the night?

EFFUGIUM!

Vōce Liciniae audītā, Aelius statim experrectus est et cucurrit ad uxōrem ut dē nātūrā difficultātis sē certiōrem **faceret** et uxōrem **adiuvāret.**

Aelius tōtam familiam excitāvit et vōce fortissimā eīs imperāvit: "Valeria, tū et Flāvia pannōs invenīte et **facite ut** illī pannī super ōra omnium **sint**! Celeriter! Licinia, tū **fac ut**
5 pannōs madefactōs super tōtum corpus Maximī **pōnās**! Ego Plōtiam Larēsque arcessam! Et Valeria, **fac nē** pecūniam familiae **āmittās**!"

Per fūmum Aelius Plōtiam petīvit et anum umerīs posuit ut eam ad salūtem **ferret**. *Aelius anum et Larēs portat.* "Valeria," inquit, "**fac ut** tōta familia mē **sequātur**!"

"Dīrigō," Aelius clāmāvit et, Aeliō duce, familia scālās timidē descendit. Aelius Plōtiam atque Larēs portāvit et
10 **fēcit ut** Valeria familiae pecūniam **portāret**, Licinia infantem Maximum, et Flāvia Sōcratem. Āēr in insulā incendentī tam calidus erat ut familia vix spīrāre **posset**. Tandem ad salūtem in viīs pervēnērunt et āera pūriōrem spīrāre incipiēbant.

In viā multī accurrēbant ut familiās **iuvārent** et fortasse incendium **exstinguerent**. Sed tantus erat aestus incendiī ut adiuvantēs nihil efficere **possent** et mox nōn sōlum haec insula sed etiam duae aliae combustae sunt. Tam
15 celeriter ignis per insulam extendit ut sēdecim, inter quōs Mendax, **perīrent**.

Paulō post, sedēns fessa in viā, familia Valeriae diū nihil dixit. Quid dīcendum erat? Dēnique Valeria "Vōs consōlēminī!" inquit. "Saltem neque mortuī neque vulnerātī sumus. Sīmia profectō servātor noster est! **Facite ut** vōs **consōlēminī nē**que **timeātis**. Dum spīrāmus, spērāmus!"

Valeriā haec dīcente, Fēlīx, nunc fūmōsus et lēniter ustus, familiae appropinquāvit et sē in crūre Liciniae
20 fricābat. Licinia, fēlem intuēns, eum mulsit et "Vīvis!" inquit. "Nōmen aptum habēs, fēlēs—vērē 'fēlīx' es. Opīnor tē nōbīs ōminī bonō esse! Dīs grātiam habeāmus!"

Tunc Valeria, cuius nātūra fortissima est, stetit et prōnuntiāvit: "Aelī, Licinia! Nōn hīc in viā nunc manēre possumus! Multa agenda sunt! Surgite omnēs! Viam inveniēmus! Labor omnia vincit. Hāc nocte in tabernā et in officīnā Aeliī dormiēmus et crās **faciēmus ut** novam vītam **incipiāmus**. Fortasse ōlim et haec meminisse nōs iuvābit!"
25 Tālia dīcēns et Fēlīcem tollēns, Valeria Liciniam et Maximum ad tabernam, Aelius Plōtiam Flāviamque cum sīmiā ad officīnam duxit.

VERBA ŪTENDA

accurrō, accurrere, accurrī/ accucurrī, accursum run, hasten to
āēr, āeris m. air, atmosphere; Greek acc. sing., *āera*
aestus, -ūs m. heat
arcessō, arcessere, arcessīvī/arcessī, arcessītum fetch; call for; summon; procure
certiōrem facere make more certain, inform; with *sē*, make oneself more certain, to learn about
consōlor, consōlārī, consōlātus sum console
crūs, crūris n. leg, shin
dēnique finally, at last; in fact

dīrigō, dīrigere, dīrexī, dīrectum direct, guide
efficiō, efficere, effēcī, effectum execute, accomplish, do
excitō (1) awaken, excite, raise
exstinguō, exstinguere, exstinxī, exstinctum extinguish
extendō, extendere, extendī, extentum / extensum stretch out, extend
fēlēs, fēlis f. cat
fricō, fricāre, fricuī, frictum rub
fūmōsus, -a, -um smokey
fūmus, -ī m. smoke
Lar, Laris m. household god

madefaciō, madefacere, madefēcī, madefactum make moist, soak
meminī, meminisse remember; *Mementō!* (imp.) Remember!
mortuus, -a, -um dead
mulceō, mulcēre, mulsī, mulsum stroke, pet
nātūra, -ae f. nature, character
officīna, -ae f. workshop
ōmen, ōminis n. sign, omen
pannus, -ī m. cloth, garment, rag
pereō, perīre, perīvī/ periī, peritum perish, vanish

profectō without question, undoubtedly
prōnuntiō (1) proclaim, announce, say, recite, report
pūrus, -a, -um pure, plain
Put aera
saltem at least
salūs, salūtis f. health, safety
scālae, -ārum f. pl. stairs, staircase
servātor, -tōris m. savior
spīrō (1) breathe
surgō, surgere, surrexī, surrectum get up, rise up
timidē timidly
ūrō, ūrere, ussī, ustum burn
vix scarcely, hardly

POSTQUAM LĒGISTĪ

1. How does Aelius' advice about the rags compare with what modern fire fighters would recommend?
2. What does the list of things the family saves suggest about what is important to them? What would you take under a similar situation? What would your parents take? Think about what victims of hurricanes or tornados search for in the rubble.
3. What factors do you think helped the fire spread so quickly?
4. Looking ahead, what do you think will happen to Mendax's body?

Grammatica B

Forming Imperfect Subjunctives

As you can see, the imperfect subjunctive is easy to recognize by the active or passive personal endings added directly to the present active infinitive. The only trick is to pay attention to macrons. Here is the full conjugation of *vocō* in the imperfect subjunctive:

PERSON	ACTIVE	PASSIVE
Singular		
1ˢᵗ	vocārem	vocārer
2ⁿᵈ	vocārēs	vocārēris (or vocārēre)
3ʳᵈ	vocāret	vocārētur
Plural		
1ˢᵗ	vocārēmus	vocārēmur
2ⁿᵈ	vocārētis	vocārēminī
3ʳᵈ	vocārent	vocārentur

Deponents act the same way, but they "invent" a present active infinitive on which to put their passive endings.

sequerer   sequerēmur
sequerēris   sequerēminī
sequerētur   sequerentur

Notā Bene: The macrons of the imperfect subjunctive are not hard if you remember two rules.

- Vowels long in the infinitive are long in the imperfect subjunctive. So, for *vocāre*, the *-ā-* is long throughout the imperfect subjunctive.
- The final *-e-* of the present active infinitive becomes long, regardless of conjugation, in the 2ⁿᵈ person singular (active and passive), in the 3ʳᵈ person singular passive, and in the 1ˢᵗ and 2ⁿᵈ person plural (active and passive).
- Pronouncing the forms out loud is the best way to remember the vowel pattern.

Based on these rules, you can easily form the imperfect subjunctive of any verb, no matter the conjugation. Even irregular verbs follow the regular pattern:

essem, essēs, esset, etc. (sum)
possem, possēs, posset, etc. (possum)
vellem, vellēs, vellet, etc. (volō)
nōllem, nōllēs, nōllet, etc. (nōlō)
māllem, māllēs, māllet, etc. (mālō)
īrem, īrēs, īret, etc. (eō)
fierem, fierēs, fieret, etc. (fīō)

Gemma

insulā incendentī: Remember that when a present active participle acts like an adjective, the ablative singular often ends in *-ī*, not *-e*.

Gemma

Valeria's words of consolation are based upon Aeneas' advice to his men after they are shipwrecked in Vergil's *Aeneid* I.203: *forsan et haec ōlim meminisse iuvābit* (Perhaps someday it will be pleasing to remember even these things.)

Gemma

While *fēlēs, fēlis* is feminine in Latin, *Fēlix* the cat is male.

Why Imperfect Subjunctives? Sequence of Tenses

Why does Latin need an imperfect subjunctive? The answer lies in something grammarians call the **sequence of tenses**. What does this mean?

Your knowledge of the sequence of tenses will grow as you learn more subjunctive forms, but for now you only need to know that the tense of the **main** verb of the sentence determines the choice of the subjunctive tense that follows it in a subordinate clause.

The sequence follows a simple rule:

- If the main verb is **primary**, the subjunctive has to be **primary**.
- If the main verb is **secondary**, the subjunctive has to be **secondary**.

Which tenses are primary or secondary?

PRIMARY AND SECONDARY TENSES		
	Indicative	**Subjunctive**
Primary	Present, Future, Future Perfect	Present
Secondary	Imperfect, Perfect, Pluperfect	Imperfect

Now compare these sentences. As you do, compare the tenses of the main and subordinate verbs.

	PRIMARY SEQUENCE	**SECONDARY SEQUENCE**
Purpose	Omnēs celeriter **currunt** ut incendium **fugiant**.	Omnēs celeriter **cucurrērunt** ut incendium **fugerent**.
Result	Incendium tam forte **est** ut omnēs **fugiant**.	Incendium tam forte **erat** ut omnēs **fugerent**.

Subjunctive Noun Clauses

In *Lectiō Secunda* you saw several examples of *ut* + subjunctive following a form of *faciō*, such as:

Facite ut vōs consōlēminī!	See to it that you console yourselves.
Facite nē timeātis!	See to it that you fear not.

These subjunctive clauses function as the objects of the verb: Aelius can make a mirror or can "make it that" something happens. For this reason this kind of subjunctive clause is called a **noun clause** rather than a purpose clause.

The formula for this use of the subjunctive is simple:

verb of endeavoring or accomplishing + *ut / nē* + subjunctive
faciō I see to it that
efficiō I accomplish that
nītor I endeavor that

Also note how these clauses follow the rules of sequence of tenses discussed earlier:

Primary Sequence
*Aelius **facit** ut Flāvia Sōcratem **portet**.*
Aelius sees to it that Flavia carries
Socrates.

Secondary Sequence
*Aelius **fēcit** ut Flāvia Sōcratem **portāret**.*
Aelius saw to it that Flavia carried
Socrates.

EXERCEĀMUS!

32-6 Using the Imperfect Subjunctive

Identify each sentence as primary or secondary sequence and translate it. Follow the model.

→ Fugiēbam nē ignis mē caperet.
   Secondary. I was fleeing so that the fire would not get me.

1. Aelius omnēs duxit ut familia salūtem invenīret.
2. Mendax tam ēbrius est ut nōn expergiscātur.
3. Fēlēs tam fēlix est ut post ignem vīvat.
4. Aelius tam fortiter nōs duxit ut fugerēmus.
5. Deī facient ut familia Valeriae salva sit.
6. Labōrāre possumus ut domum novam habeāmus.
7. Labōrāre poterāmus nē iēiūnī essēmus.
8. Tū facere poterās nē ignis fieret.
9. Tam territus eram ut fugere vellem.

Mōrēs Rōmānī

Prōvinciae Rōmānae

Rome's first province was the island of Sicily, which became Roman territory at the end of the First Punic War in 241 B.C. Most provinces were acquired by conquest, but others came by bequest, like Bithynia, which became a Roman province in the will of its last king, Nicomedes IV in 74 B.C.

Originally, a province was managed by a governor (*prōpraetor, -ōris* m.) appointed by the senate. Becoming a governor was usually considered an important step in advancing one's political career. Julius Caesar, for example, conquered Gallia (France) while governor of *Gallia Cisalpīna* (northern Italy). Cicero was governor of Cilicia (modern Turkey).

In the imperial period, some provinces, especially ones in which large armies were stationed, were under direct control of the emperor, who sent a deputy (*lēgātus, -ī* m.) to represent him in the province. These were called imperial provinces. Senatorial provinces were still governed by propraetors appointed by the senate.

Here is a short list of some important provinces, their years of acquisition and status as imperial or senatorial provinces. Consult the endpaper map of the Roman Empire as you look at this list. The countries in parentheses are the approximate modern equivalents.

Sicilia (Sicily)	241 B.C.	Senatorial
Hispānia (Spain)	197 B.C.	Imperial
Macedonia (northern Greece)	148 B.C.	Senatorial
Āfrica (Tunisia)	146 B.C.	Senatorial
Asia (western Turkey)	133 B.C.	Senatorial
Gallia Transalpīna or *Narbōnensis* (southern France)	121 B.C.	Senatorial
Bīthȳnia-et-Pontus	75/74 B.C.	Senatorial
Gallia (France)	59 B.C.	
Aquītānia		Imperial
Belgica		Imperial
Celtica		Imperial
Achaea (Greece)	27 B.C.	Senatorial
Britannia (England)	43 A.D.	Imperial

Egypt is not on this list because, technically, it was not a province. Rather, it was the personal property of the emperor.

Pliny served as governor of Bithynia-and-Pontus as *lēgātus Augustī prō praetōre consulārī potestāte ex senātūs consultō missus*. Usually a *lēgātus Augustī prō praetōre* (deputy of the Augustus in the place of a praetor) was sent to govern an imperial province, but *Bīthȳnia-et-Pontus* was a senatorial province. That is why Pliny's title also included the phrase *ex senātūs consultō missus* (sent by decree of the senate). He also governed with consular power (*consulārī potestāte*).

Latīna Hodierna

Latin Mottoes in the Modern World

Some states have Latin mottoes. In fact we incorporated versions of the following four into *Lectiō Secunda*:

Deō grātiam habēamus	Kentucky
Dīrigō	Maine
Dum spīrāmus, spērāmus	South Carolina
Labor omnia vincit	Oklahoma

Many other modern organizations have Latin mottoes, including these fire departments:

Ad serviendum dēdicātus	Springfield, PA
Ut aliī vīvant	Buffalo, NY
Nōn sibi sed omnibus	Cottage Grove, MN
Semper parātus	Long Beach, CA
Vēnī, vīdī, vīcī	Douglas, MA
Vēritās ex cineribus	New York City, Bureau of Fire Investigation
Audax et promptus	Metropolitan Fire and Emergency Services Board, Melbourne, Australia

Here is a small sample of Latin mottoes of colleges and universities:

Vēritās	Harvard University
In Hōc Signō Vincēs	College of the Holy Cross
Lux	Monmouth College
Lux et Vēritās	Yale University
Nūmen Lūmen	University of Wisconsin, Madison
Ense Petit Placidam Sub Lībertāte Quiētem	University of Massachusetts, Amherst
Vēritās et Ūtilitās	Howard University
Quaecumque Sunt Vēra	Northwestern University
Deī Sub Nūmine Viget	Princeton University
Mens et Manus	Massachusetts Institute of Technology
In Lūmine Tuō Vidēbimus Lūmen	Columbia University

Dīrigō

Sigillum Collēgiī Monmouthiensis

Sigillum Ūniversitātis Massachusettsiensis

Orbis Terrārum Rōmānus

Bīthȳnia-et-Pontus

Pliny the Younger is one of our sources about how ancient fire brigades were organized. When he was governor of the province of *Bīthȳnia-et-Pontus* from 109 through 111 A.D., Pliny had a correspondence with the emperor about the need to establish *vigilēs* in his province. This region, now part of northern Turkey, was first organized as a Roman senatorial province by Pompey the Great after 74 B.C. The area was settled by veterans of armies led by several generals or emperors, including Julius Caesar and Augustus.

The south coast of the Black Sea was a prosperous area during the Roman Empire and was dotted by Roman and/or Greek cities, including Amasia and Zela in Pontus, and Sinope, Nicaea, and Nicomedia in Bithynia. Nicomedia (modern Izmit) became a major imperial city under the emperor Diocletian (284–313 A.D.).

What follows is a simplified excerpt from a letter to Trajan in which Pliny describes a fire in the city of Nicomedia, tells the emperor about precautions he has taken, and asks the emperor's advice about setting up a public fire brigade in the city.

Plīnius Trāiānō Imperātōrī

Cum dīversam partem prōvinciae circumīrem, in Nīcomēdiā vastissimum incendium multās prīvātōrum domōs et, quamquam viā interiacente, duo pūblica opera (Gerūsiam et Īsēon) absumpsit. [Incendium] autem lātius sparsum est prīmum violentiā ventī, deinde inertiā hominum quōs, satis constat, ut spectātōrēs tantī malī ōtiōsōs et immōbilēs perstitisse; et aliōquī in pūblicō nullus sīpō usquam, nulla hama, nullum dēnique instrūmentum ad incendia compescenda. Et, ut iam praecēpī, haec quidem parābuntur; tū, domine, dispice an putēs collēgium fabrōrum (dumtaxat hominum CL) instituendum esse . . .

Pliny the Younger Epistulae 10.33

Trāiānus Imperātor

In his response, which survives in Pliny's correspondence (10.34), the emperor reminds Pliny about the dangers of setting up an official corporation of firefighters. Such organizations, the emperor warns, have sometimes become dangerous political organizations in Pliny's province and have disturbed the peace. Instead, Trajan advises Pliny instead to make available the equipment needed for fighting fires, but to encourage the inhabitants themselves to serve as volunteer firefighters when needed.

🔊 VERBA ŪTENDA

absūmō, absūmere, absumpsī, absumptum ruin, lay waste
aliōquī besides
an whether
circumeō, circumīre, circumīvī /circumiī, circumitum go around
collēgium, -iī n. club, group
compescō, compescere, compescuī confine, restrain
constat See *satis*
cum when (introducing a subordinate clause with an imperfect subjunctive)

dispiciō, dispicere, dispexī, dispectum consider
dīversus, -a, -um different
dumtaxat only up to
faber, fabrī m. workman
gerūsia, -ae f. a council building for elders, senate house
hama, -ae f. fire bucket
interiaceō, interiacēre, interēcī, interiactum/ interectum lie between (The fire jumped the road.)

immōbilis, immōbile immovable, unmoving
inertia, -ae f. idleness
Īsēon, -ēī n. temple of the goddess Isis
ōtiōsus, -a, -um useless, unoccupied
praecipiō, praecipere, praecēpī, praeceptum order
perstō, perstāre, perstitī, perstātum stand around
prīvātōrum of private (citizens)

pūblicus, -a, -um; in pūblicō in public, readily at hand
quidem certainly
satis constat "it is generally agreed (that)"
sīp(h)ō, -ōnis m. water hose
spargō, spargere, sparsī, sparsum spread, scatter
ut as
vastus, -a, -um huge
ventus, -ī m. wind
violentia, -ae f. force, violence

Bīthȳnia-et-Pontus

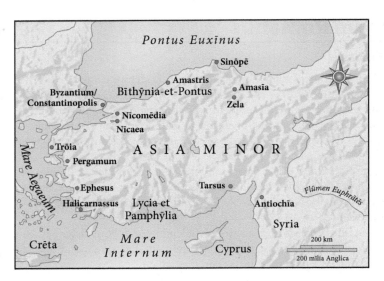

Theātrum Rōmānum Nicaeārum

QUID PUTĀS?

1. Does your school, college, or university have a Latin motto? If so, find out what it means. Why you do you think this motto was chosen? If your school does not have a Latin motto, create one for it and explain why you consider this motto appropriate.
2. What is the motto of your state? If it is a Latin motto, translate it into English. If the motto is in English, try translating it into Latin.
3. Based upon his letter to Trajan, how would you evaluate Pliny's performance as governor of Bithynia?
4. Why do you think that the Romans developed a double system of government for their provinces? How efficient does this system sound?

EXERCEĀMUS!

32-7 Scrībāmus

Convert each sentence in primary sequence into a sentence in secondary sequence and then translate it. Follow the model.

→   Fugiō nē ignis mē inveniat.
    Fugiēbam nē ignis mē <u>invenīret</u>.
    I fled lest the fire get to me.

1. Aelius dūcit ut familia salūtem inveniat.
    Aelius duxit ut familia salūtem _____.

2. Mendax tam ēbrius est ut nōn expergiscātur.
    Mendax tam ēbrius erat ut nōn _____.

3. Fēlēs tam fēlix est ut post ignem vīvat.
    Fēlēs tam fēlix erat ut post ignem _____.

4. Aelius tam fortiter nōs dūcit ut fugiāmus.
    Aelius tam fortiter nōs duxit ut _____.

5. Deī faciunt ut familia Valeriae salva sit.
    Deī fēcērunt ut familia Valeriae salva _____.

6. Labōrāre possumus ut domum novam habeāmus.
    Labōrāre potuimus ut domum novam _____

7. Labōrāre poterimus nē iēiūnī sīmus.
   Labōrāre potuimus nē iēiūnī _____.

8. Tū facere potes nē ignis fīat.
   Tū facere poterās nē ignis _____.

9. Tam territus sum ut fugere velim.
   Tam territus eram ut fugere _____.

10. Tam ēbrius est ut nōn fugere possit.
    Tam ēbrius erat ut nōn fugere _____.

32-8 Colloquāmur

Use the first paragraph in *Lectiō Prīma* to answer the following questions in a complete Latin sentence. One student asks the question and another answers it. Follow the model.

→ Quī bene dormiunt in cubiculīs quod tanta est tranquillitās in viīs?
  Omnēs dīvitēs bene dormiunt.

1. Cūr familia Servīliī nōn quiescit?
2. Quis avum aegrum adiuvāre nōn potest?
3. Quid nōmen est ūnī medicōrum?
4. Quem Servīlius ad sē vocat?
5. Quis aegerrimus est?
6. Quem febris saevissima tenet?
7. Quid agendum est?

32-9 Verba Discenda

Identify the *Verbum Discendum* to which each of the following English words is linked. It need not be a direct derivation. Then use the meaning of the Latin word to define the English word. If you need help, use a dictionary. Follow the model.

→ aerodynamics: from *āēr*; "dynamics related to **air** or gases"

1. attempt
2. excitable
3. incendiary
4. incense
5. increase
6. infrared
7. inspiration
8. insurrection
9. memorabilia
10. remote
11. salutatory
12. supernatural
13. supraorbital
14. tactile
15. temptation
16. transitory

VERBA DISCENDA

āēr, āeris m. air, atmosphere; Greek acc. sing., **āera** [aerial]
arcessō, arcessere, arcessīvī/arcessī, arcessītum fetch; call for; summon; procure
collis, collis m. hill [colline]
crescō, crescere, crēvī, crētum grow, arise, appear, increase [crescent]
dēnique finally, at last; in fact
efficiō, efficere, effēcī, effectum execute, accomplish, do [efficient, effective]

excitō (1) awaken, excite, raise
expergiscor, expergiscī, experrectus sum awake, wake up
incendium, -iī n. fire, conflagration [incendiary]
incendō, incendere, incendī, incensum set fire to, inflame, burn [incensed]
infrā below, underneath, under [infrared]
meminī, meminisse remember; *Mementō!* (imp.) Remember! [memento]

nātūra, -ae f. nature, character [naturalistic]
nōndum not yet
omnīnō utterly, altogether, completely
pereō, perīre, perīvī/periī, peritum perish, vanish
prīmō at first
profectō without question, undoubtedly
removeō, removēre, remōvī, remōtum move back; remove [removable, remote]
salūs, salūtis f. health, safety [salutary]
spīrō (1) breathe [respirate]

suprā above; (+ acc.) over, on top of [suprarenal]
surgō, surgere, surrexī, surrectum get up, rise up [surge]
tangō, tangere, tetigī, tactum touch; reach; affect; move; mention [tangible, tactile]
temptō (1) feel; try; test [temptation]
transeō, transīre, transīvī/transiī, transitum go over, go across [transient, transitory]
vix scarcely, hardly

Angulus Grammaticus

Confusing Pairs: Latin Homonyms and Heteronymns

As you may remember from Chapter 14, words that are spelled and pronounced the same are often called **homonyms**. For example, in English, we have the "bark" of a dog and the "bark" of a tree. If words have the same spelling but different pronunciation and meaning, they are sometimes called **heteronyms.** For example, the word "row" can be used to "row" a "boat" and to have a "row" (argument). Or consider this sentence: "I refuse to pick up the refuse left behind after the party."

In Latin there are many examples of such confusing pairs that require special attention. Here are some confusing pairs you have seen earlier in this book. Keep in mind that Romans did not use macrons to distinguish long vowels in writing. They only "heard" the difference between these words:

anus	*ānus*	Which one means "old woman" and which means "ring"?
hic	*hīc*	Which means "here" and which "this fellow here"?
liber	*līber*	Which means "book" and which means "free"?
malum	*mālum*	Which means "apple" and which means "bad"?

If you do not remember how the macrons change the meanings of these words, look them up in a dictionary.

Especially important in Latin are homonyms and heteronyms created by verb tense change. We have the problem in English as well. Consider the sentence "I read the book." Am I doing it now or did I already do it? Notice how English changes the pronunciation to indicate the tense change, rather like the difference between *venit* and *vēnit*. But some verbs are not as helpful.

Homonyms are especially common in 3rd conjugation verbs with the same stem in present and perfect active. Here are just a few examples. There are many more.

vertit	he turns or he turned
ascendit	he climbs or he climbed
defendit	he defends or he defended

Some 3rd conjugation verbs have present and perfect stems that create **heteronyms**:

Present	Perfect
venit	vēnit
edit	ēdit
emit	ēmit
legit	lēgit
fugit	fūgit

There are several other confusing pairs in other parts of speech; for example, the dative singular of *lex* (law) is *lēgī* and the present passive infinitive of *lego* (I read) is *legī*. Usually it is not difficult to distinquish such lookalike words in context, even when you don't have macrons to guide you:

Liber celeriter legī potest.	The book can be read quickly.
Cēdō lēgī.	I yield to the law.

Finally, try to read this sentence with a triple play of heteronyms!

Eō eō nē ab eō invenιar.	I go there lest I be found by him.

33

Post Mortem

Augustus Togātus

Lectiō Prīma

Antequam Legis

Lectiō Prīma takes place the morning after the fire. The family of Valeria meets at the *taberna* to discuss their situation. Their home is destroyed. Aelius' assistant Hephaestus is dead, and the shop severely damaged. Under these circumstances, Caecilia's suggestion that Aelius pay a visit to her husband, Servilius, becomes even more imperative.

Giving Commands

In this *lectiō* you encounter several more ways to express commands in Latin.

Indirect Commands

These clauses are commands or requests introduced by words like *imperō* (command), *hortor* (urge), and *ōrō* (pray) followed by *ut/nē* and the subjunctive.

Imperō ut sedeās.	I command that you sit.
	I command you to sit.
Hortor nē sedeās.	I urge you not to sit.

Iubeō / Vetō + *Infinitive*

Some Latin verbs of commanding use an objective infinitive to express the command.

Tē sedēre iubeō.	I order you to sit.
Tē sedēre vetō.	I forbid you to sit.

Cavē (te) nē + *Subjunctive*

The imperative of *caveō* (take care, beware) is used with *nē* + subjunctive to express a negative command.

Cavē nē sedeās!	Take care not to sit./Don't sit.

GRAMMATICA
Giving Commands in Latin
Indicative Temporal Clauses

MŌRĒS RŌMĀNĪ
Vestīmenta Rōmāna: Vestis Virum Facit

LATĪNA HODIERNA
Vested in English

ORBIS TERRĀRUM RŌMĀNUS
Via Appia

ANGULUS GRAMMATICUS
Command Performances

LECTIŌNĒS:
CONSILIA NOVA
and
FŪNERA

The family of Valeria deals with the aftermath of the fire while the family of Servilius mourns the death of *Avus*. The bodies of *Avus*, Mendax, and Hephaestus are prepared for burial.

Gemma

sōle oriente = "when the sun was rising." Since the sun rises in the east, the Latin participle led to the English "Orient," a traditional name for the "East."
sōle occidente = "when the sun was setting." So "Occident" refers to "the West" in English.

Future Imperatives

Future imperatives are used in Latin to emphasize that an event will take place sometime in the future or that the event will occur repeatedly. Watch for these imperatives with the endings *-tō* in the singular and *-tōte* in the plural. Future imperatives are marked in ***bold italics*** in *Lectiō Prīma*.

> *Sedētō!*   Sit! Keep on sitting!   *Sedētōte!*   Sit! Keep on sitting (all of you)!

EXERCEĀMUS!

33-1 Classifying Commands

Make a line-by-line list of all the new command constructions in *Lectiō Prīma*. The verbs governing each construction are marked in **bold**. Classify each by type (indirect command, *iubeō/vetō* command, *cavē(te) nē* command, or future imperative). If the command includes an infinitive or a subjunctive, list this form as well. Follow the model.

Line	Command	Type	Infinitive or Subjunctive
→ 4	imperat	indirect command	expergiscātur/arcessat

🔊 CONSILIA NOVA

Posterō diē Valeria in tabernā suā experrecta est et longē hiāvit quārē nōn bene in pavīmentō sine lectō dormīverat. Nunc, sōle oriente, consilium cēperat et adventum Aeliī exspectābat. Liciniae appropinquat et, fīliam pede lēniter fodicāns, eī **imperat** ut expergiscātur et aquam arcessat.

5   "Ego," inquit, "exībō ut pānem emam. Licinia, tē **ōrō** ut ignem accendās. **Cavē** nē diūtius dormiās! Et, cum Aelius adveniet, **iubē** eum hīc manēre dōnec redībō."

Sērius, Aeliō adveniente et ientāculō confectō, familia dē futūrīs cōgitābat dum Licinia infantem nūtrit. Valeria "Quamdiū," inquit, "in tabernā aut in
10   officīnā habitāre possumus? Aliud domicilium nōbīs inveniendum est."

Aelius "Rēs," inquit, "gravior est quam opīnāris. Officīna igne graviter laesa et lapsūra stat et Hephaestus servus meus fūmō necātus est. Proximā nocte in officīnā dormīvī ut instrūmenta custōdīrem. Hodiē Flāviam et Plōtiam illīc manēre et omnia custōdīre **iussī**. **Vetuī** eās officīnam dēserere
15   hodiē. Sed mox mihi officīna in spatium tūtius movenda est. Quid faciāmus?"

Valeria: "Omnēs mē audīte! Nōlīte dēspērāre! Spem ***habētōte***! Rēs nōn tōta perdita est. Habēmus adhūc tabernam et pecūniam quam hūc dē insulā tulī. Et, mī Aelī, ***mementō*** uxōrem M. Servīliī Sevērī herī ad tabernam advēnisse et speculum ā tē fabricātum diū admīrātam esse. Plūrēs tālēs rēs—sed argenteās!—dēsīderābat. Cum eī dixī nōs nullum argentum emere posse, illa **hortāta est** ut tū ad marītum eius advenīrēs et cliens eius fīerēs. Sī cliens
20   eius fīēs pecūniam habēbis ad officīnam novam condendam et ad argentum emendum—posteā mox faber argentārius eris! Nunc ut ad Servīlium adveniās tibi **persuādēre** volō. **Moneō** nē occāsiōnem optimam abīre sinās. ***Estō*** bonae speī! Fortūna fortēs iuvat!"

Aelius "Certē," respondet, "hoc facere velim, sed togam nōn habeō et crēdō clientem togātum ad salūtātiōnem adīre dēbēre."

25   Licinia, pannōs infantis mūtāns, "Marīte," inquit, "togam ā fullōne in diem condūcere potes. **Fac** ut togam ab eō postulēs."

Aelius ad fullōnicam festīnāvit et **postulāvit** ut fullō eī togam locāret. Pecūniā acceptā, fullō, strēnuē Aeliō **imperāns** nē togam āmitteret aut eam laederet, vestem trādidit.

Licinia infantem nūtrit.

🔊 VERBA ŪTENDA

accendō, accendere, accendī,
   accensum light, burn
argenteus, -a, -um silver, of
   silver
caveō, cavēre, cāvī, cautum
   take care, beware of
condō, condere, condidī,
   conditum build, found
condūcō, condūcere,
   condūxī, conductum rent
dēserō, dēserere, dēseruī,
   dēsertum desert, abandon
dēspērō (1) despair (of)
domicilium, -iī n. home
fodicō (1) nudge, prod
fortūna, -ae f. fortune,
   chance, luck; wealth,
   prosperity

fullō, -ōnis m. launderer
fullōnica, -ae f. laundry
fūmus, -ī m. smoke
hiō (1) yawn
hortor, hortārī, hortātus
   sum urge
hūc here, to this place
lābor, lābī, lapsus sum fall
   down
laedō, laedere, laesī, laesum
   hurt, damage
locō (1) contract for, rent
moneō, monēre,
   monuī, monitum warn,
   advise
mūtō (1) alter, change
nūtriō, nūtrīre, nūtrīvī/nūtriī,
   nūtrītum nourish, nurse

occāsiō, -iōnis f. opportunity
officīna, -ae f. workshop
orior, orīrī, ortus sum rise,
   get up, be born
ōrō (1) pray
pannus, -ī m. cloth, garment
pavīmentum, -ī n. floor,
   pavement
perditus, -a, -um ruined, lost
persuādeō, persuādēre,
   persuāsī, persuāsum
   (+ dat.) persuade
posterus, -a, -um following,
   next
postulō (1) ask for, beg, de-
   mand, require, request
praetereā besides,
   moreover

quamdiū how long
sinō, sinere, sīvī/siī, situm
   allow, permit
sōl, sōlis m. sun; day
spēs, speī, f. hope,
   expectation
toga, -ae f. toga
togātus, -a, -um dressed in
   a toga
trādō, trādere, trādidī,
   trāditum hand down,
   entrust, deliver
vestis, vestis f. garments,
   clothing
vetō, vetāre, vetuī,
   vetitum forbid,
   prohibit

POSTQUAM LĒGISTĪ

Answer the following questions in English. Also answer in Latin if the question is followed by (L).

1. Why did Valeria not sleep well? (L)
2. How do Valeria's actions this morning indicate that she is the dominant member of her family?
3. Why does Aelius say the situation is worse than Valeria and Licinia imagine? (L)
4. What hope does Valeria offer to improve the family's circumstances? (L)
5. What is Licinia doing while talking to her husband and mother? (L)
6. Where can Aelius find a toga? (L)

Gemma

Fortūna fortēs iuvat.
Valeria is using a saying first found in Terence' *Phormio* (line 203). Vergil uses a slight variation: *Audentēs fortūna iuvat* (*Aeneid*, 10.284). The phrase has become the motto of many modern organizations.

Grammatica A

Giving Commands in Latin

You have already learned several ways to express commands in Latin:

Imperative	*Illīc manē!*	Stay there!	*Nōlī manēre illīc!*	Don't stay there!
Hortatory Subjunctive	*Illīc maneāmus!*	Let's stay there!	*Nē maneāmus illīc!*	Let's not stay there!
Subjunctive Noun Clause	*Fac ut maneās!*	See to it that you stay!	*Fac nē maneās!*	See to it that you do not stay!

Depending on the verb of commanding used, Latin can express commands in a number of other ways.

Indirect Command (ut / nē + subjunctive)

Most Latin verbs of commanding or ordering take a subjunctive construction called the **indirect command**.

    Imperō ut maneās illīc.   *Imperō nē maneās illīc.*
    I order you to stay there.   I order you not to stay there.

An indirect command looks a lot like a purpose clause. Both constructions use *ut* or *nē* and the subjunctive, but the verb of commanding is the hallmark of an indirect command.

Notā Bene:

- Formula: verb of commanding + *ut* or *nē* + subjunctive
- Be on the lookout for the case a given verb of commanding governs. When in doubt, check the dictionary entry.

*Imperō **tibi** ut maneās illīc.*	I command you to stay there.
	I command that you stay there.
*Hortor **tē** ut maneās illīc.*	I urge you to stay there.

- The rules for sequence of tenses apply to indirect commands.

Primary sequence:	*Imperō ut maneās illīc.*	I order you to stay there.
Secondary sequence:	*Imperāvī ut manērēs illīc.*	I ordered you to stay there.

Here is a list of Latin verbs of command that are followed by an indirect command (*ut* or *nē* + subjunctive):

> **hortor, hortārī, hortātus sum** urge [33]
> *imperō* (1) (+ dat.) command [26]
> *moneō, monēre, monuī, monitum* warn, advise [33]
> *ōrō* (1) pray [33]
> *persuādeō, persuādēre, persuāsī, persuāsum* (+ dat.) persuade [33]
> *petō, petere, petīvī/petiī, petītum* seek to, ask for, beg [21]
> *postulō* (1) demand, require, request [33]
> *quaerō, quaerere, quaesīvī/quaesiī, quaesītum,* seek, ask [18]
> *rogō* (1) ask [10]

All of these verbs either are already *Verba Discenda* or become *Verba Discenda* in this chapter.

Object Infinitive + Subject Accusative

Remember the formula for an indirect statement in Latin:

> head verb + infinitive with subject accusative

Direct Statement:	*Illīc manēs.*	You stay there.
Indirect Statement:	*Illīc **tē** manēre sciō.*	I know (that) you stay there.

Certain head verbs expressing commands work the same way. These include *iubeō* (order) and *vetō* (forbid):

Imperative:	*Illīc manē!*	Stay there!
With *iubeō*:	*Illīc **tē** manēre iubeō.*	I order you to stay there.
With *vetō*:	*Illīc **tē** manēre vetō.*	I forbid you to stay there.

Cavē(te) + nē + Subjunctive

You have already seen how Latin can express commands with a subjunctive noun clause following the imperative of *faciō*:

Facite ut illīc maneātis.	See to it that you stay there.

A negative command can be expressed by using *cavē(te)* + *nē* + subjunctive.

Cavēte nē illīc maneātis.	Beware lest you stay there.
	Take care not to stay there.

The Future Imperative

All imperatives technically refer to the present or immediate future time. If someone tells you to stand up, he or she intends for you do it after they have spoken. Latin has a special imperative that stresses the future nature of the act or that the action is one that should keep on going. For example, when a mother tells her children "Be good!" as they go off for a visit, she does not mean "just once." The endings for this future imperative are:

Singular	Plural
-tō	*-tōte*

Here is the future imperative of *sum*:

Singular	Plural
estō	*estōtē*

Notā Bene:

- A handful of verbs regularly use the future imperative instead of the regular present forms:

  Mementō meī!
  Habētōte spem!
  Scītō parentēs tē amāre!
  Estōte bonī!

- There is a 3rd person future imperative, but it is rare.
- The negative of the future imperative is *nē*; e.g., *Nē estōte malī!* "Don't be bad. Don't misbehave!"

EXERCEĀMUS!

33-2 Commands

Determine whether each of the following verbs is likely to be followed by an infinitive with subject accusative or by *ut* + subjunctive. Then complete the sentence in Latin, telling the "you" addressed (either singular or plural) to "guard everything." Follow the models.

→ iubeō (vōs) *Iubeō vōs omnia custōdīre.*   I order you to guard everything.

→ imperō (tū) *Imperō tibi ut omnia custōdiās.*   I command you to guard everything.

1. vetō (tū)	4. rogō (vōs)	7. persuādeō (tū)
2. moneō (vōs)	5. petō (tū)	8. iubeō (tū)
3. ōrō (tū)	6. hortor (vōs)	9. imperō (vōs)

Lectiō Secunda

Antequam Legis

In this *lectiō* you read about the funerals following the night of the fire. Funeral rites in ancient Rome varied every bit as much as funerals do today. Bodies were both interred and cremated. After cremation, the ashes would probably be placed in a family tomb located outside the city walls. The city's poor received hasty burials, and the poorest or most despised were often simply dumped into public pits outside of the city gate on the Esquiline Hill. A common burial, or *fūnus plēbēium*, probably evoked little notice in ancient Rome, but, when a former senator like *Avus* passed away, a more public and elaborate display was called for. As much as he loved his father, Servilius also understood the political leverage a lavish public funeral could bring. You will also hear about the *imāginēs māiōrum* in this reading. These are the death masks of ancestors that adorned the walls of the atria of noble Roman houses. This tribute to ancestors demonstrated the importance of family among the patricians at all times, but especially at the time of a death.

Indicative Temporal Clauses

As you read *Lectiō Secunda,* also watch out for **indicative temporal clauses** introduced by conjunctions like *postquam* (after), *dum* (while), and *antequam* (before). All these conjunctions are marked in **bold** in the *lectiō.* You have seen most of these words before, but this is an opportunity to look at them as a group. In particular, pay attention to *cum,* which is not only a preposition (+ abl. meaning "with"), but also a temporal conjunction (when, whenever).

EXERCEĀMUS!

33-3 *Cum* the Preposition vs. *Cum* the Conjunction

Indicate whether the *cum* in each of the following sentences is a preposition or a conjunction. Then translate the sentence. The last five are based on sentences in the *lectiō.*
HINT: Look for an ablative with *cum* the preposition. Follow the model.

→ **Cum** avus mortuus est, fēminae flēbant.
   conjunction: *When the grandfather died, the women wept.*

1. Fēminae flent magnā **cum** clāmōre.
2. **Cum** Servīlia et māter flent, servī flent.
3. Sīmiae **cum** celeritāte cucurrērunt.
4. **Cum** sīmiae currunt, puerī rīdent.
5. Sīmiae mē**cum** currunt.
6. Parentēs **cum** servīs plōrāvērunt.
7. **Cum** avus mortuus est, familia plōrāvit.
8. Magnā **cum** dolōre oculōs parentis clausit.
9. Fēminae corpus **cum** cūrā lāvērunt.
10. **Cum** plaustrum ad insulam vēnit, servī mortuōs in plaustrō dēposuērunt.

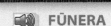

🔊 FŪNERA

Cum Marcus Servīlius Avus mortuus est, tōta familia—parentēs et līberī cum servīs—plōrāvērunt. Corpus senis in terrā positum est et Servīlius, nōmen patris vocāns, magnā cum dolōre oculōs parentis cārī clausit. Fēminae domūs, quārum hoc opus est, corpus cum cūrā lāvērunt, et **dum** ululant, libitīnārius nummum sub linguā senis

5   posuit ut umbra senis pecūniam Charōnī, flūminis Stygis transeundī causā, dare posset. Tunc corpus, togā praetextā vestītum, in ātriō **ubi** imāginēs māiōrum in mūrō erant, positum est. In illō locō, māiōribus intuentibus, corpus avī in lectō fūnebrī iacuit.

Aelius corpus Hephaestī ad plaustrum ferēns

   Priusquam corpus combustum est et cinerēs in sepulcrō positī sunt, multa agenda erant. Servīlius libitīnāriō imperāvit ut, trēs post diēs, fūnus senātōrī idōneum ageret et eum ōrāvit nē
10 pecūniae parceret.

   Simul ac Servīlius abiit, libitīnārius servīs imperāvit ut rāmus cupressī in foribus domī pōnātur et rogāvit ut tībīcinēs, cornicinēs, et praeficae invenīrentur. Fēcit ut per viās Rōmae nuntius clāmāret, "Ollus Servīlius Quirīs lētō datus est! Ollus Servīlius lētō datus est!"

   Tālibus factīs Servīlius, nunc togam pullam gerēns, ad sē fīlium Marcum vocāvit. "Fīlī," inquit, "nōmen
15 Servīliōrum tibi tuendum est. **Cum** pompa fūnebris fīet, rogō ut tū in Forō ōrātiōnem fūnebrem habeās. Fac ut dē omnibus avī cārī honōribus dīcās et familiam laudēs."

   In aliā urbis parte fūnera alia fīēbant. **Postquam** incendium exstinctum est, plaustrum sordidum, mūlīs tractum, per viās Subūrae lentē prōgrediēbātur. **Cum** plaustrum ad insulam combustam vēnit, servī mortuōs, inter quōs erat Mendax, in plaustrō dēposuērunt. Aelius ipse, corpus Hephaestī ferēns, ad plaustrum advēnit et nummō sub
20 linguā servī fidēlis positō, cadāver in plaustrum posuit. "Valē!" inquit cum maestitiā. "Valē, serve fidēlis! Dormītō bene. Ōrō ut dī tē benignē recipiant!"

   Plaustrum ad collem Esquilīnum prōgrediēbātur et per Portam Esquilīnam ad Campōs Esquilīnōs iter fēcit. Paulō post, **ubi** plaustrum constitit, cadāvera in puteō ā servīs iacta sunt. Hīc, in perpetuum, nullīs plōrantibus, Mendax Hephaestusque tandem dormient.

🔊 VERBA ŪTENDA

ac and, and besides; than
ātrium, -iī n. atrium, public greeting room of a Roman house
cadāver, cadāveris n. dead body, corpse
campus, -ī m. field
Charōn, Charōnis m. Charon, the ferryman of the Underworld
cinis, cineris m./f. ash
claudō, claudere, clausī, clausum shut, close
consistō, consistere, constitī, constitum stop, halt
cornicen, -cinis m. horn blower
cupressus, -ī f. cypress tree
cūra, -ae f. care
dī nom. pl. gods = *deī*
dolor, dolōris m. pain, grief
dum while, as long as; until

Esquilīnus, -a, -um Esquiline, one of the seven hills of Rome
exstinguō, exstinguere, exstinxī, exstinctum quench, extinguish
fidēlis, fidēle faithful, trustworthy
flūmen, -inis n. river
foris, foris f. door, gate
fūnebris, fūnebre funereal
fūnus, fūneris n. burial, funeral
imāgō, imāginis f. image, likeness
lētum, -ī n. death
līberī, -ōrum m. pl. children
libitīnārius, -iī m. undertaker
lingua, -ae f. tongue, speech
maestitia, -ae f. sadness, grief

mortuus, -a, -um dead
mūla, -ae f. mule
nuntius, -iī n. messenger, news
occidō, occidere, occidī, occāsum set (of the sun)
Ollus archaic form of *ille*: that (man)
ōrātiōnem habēre give/deliver a speech
perpetuus, -a, -um uninterrupted; *in perpetuum* forever
plaustrum, -ī n. cart, wagon
plōrō (1) weep, cry
pompa, -ae f. ceremonial procession
praefica, -ae f. hired female mourner
praetextus, -a, -um bordered; *toga praetexta*

a toga bordered with a purple stripe
pullus, -a, -um dingy, somber; *toga pulla* a dark gray toga worn in mourning
puteus, -ī m. pit
Quirīs, Quirītis m. (archaic) word for citizen
rāmus, -ī m. branch
sepulcrum, -ī n. tomb
Styx, Stygis f. river Styx, river bordering the Underworld
tībīcen, -cinis m. piper
ululō (1) wail, weep
umbra, -ae f. shade, soul
ut (+ indicative) as
vestiō, vestīre, vestīvī/ vestiī, vestītum dress, clothe

POSTQUAM LĒGISTĪ

Answer the following questions in English. Also answer in Latin if the question is followed by (L).

1. What is the duty of each of the following after *avus* Servilius dies? His son? The women of the household? The *libitīnārius*? (L)
2. What instructions does Servilius give the *libitīnārius*? What instructions does he give his son? (L)
3. What motivations do you think Servilius has for giving his father an extravagant funeral?
4. How does this funeral compare to modern funeral practices in the United States?
5. Describe how the bodies of Mendax and Hephaestus are disposed of. (L)
6. How does Aelius show his affection for his deceased slave? (L)

Charōn Portitor Infernus

Grammatica B

Indicative Temporal Clauses

The following chart summarizes the use of indicative temporal clauses in Latin. Pay special attention to the tenses used with each conjunction.

CONJUNCTION	TENSE	USE	TRANSLATION
cum (temporal)	Any tense, although perfect and present are most common	Describes the actual time something occurred	when
cum (conditional or frequentative)	Any tense	Describes the situation	whenever
dum	Present	Describes simultaneous action	while
postquam, ubi, ut, simul ac/atque	Usually perfect	Tells the time when something happens	
antequam, priusquam	Present, perfect or future perfect	"Before" action	before

EXERCEĀMUS!

33-4 Indicative Temporal Clauses

All of the conjunctions marked in **bold** in *Lectiō Secunda* introduce indicative temporal clauses. Make a line-by-line list of these conjunctions. Then find the verbs they introduce and translate both conjunction and verb into English. Follow the model.

Line	Conjunction	Verb	Translation
→ 1	cum	mortuus est	when he died

Mōrēs Rōmānī

Vestīmenta Rōmāna: Vestis Virum Facit

The Romans were very dress conscious. Indeed, it was usually easy to determine the status and power of a Roman by the kind of clothing he or she wore. The basic garment for both men and women of all ranks and classes was a tunic (*tunica, -ae* f.) consisting of two rectangular pieces of cloth sewn together. Men wore tunics down to the knee. Women's tunics were longer. A wide purple stripe (*clāvus, -ī* m.) on a tunic indicated that the wearer was a senator. Equestrians had a narrower stripe. A victorious general celebrating a triumph would wear a *tunica palmāta*, i.e., a tunic embroidered with palm leaves.

The toga (*toga, -ae* f.) was worn only by male Roman citizens. Originally the toga was worn over a naked body, but by classical times it was usually worn over a tunic. A toga was not everyday attire. It was worn only on formal occasions.

Young boys and certain public officials wore a *toga praetexta*, which had a purple stripe at its edge. In a special ceremony a Roman boy put on an unstriped, off-white *toga cīvīlis* (also called *toga virīlis* or *toga pūra*) and entered the world of adult manhood at the age of sixteen. When running for office, a Roman would wear a special whitened toga called the *toga candida* (white toga), from which the English word "candidate" is derived. Finally, a Roman male mourning the loss of a family member would wear a dark colored toga called the *toga pulla* (dingy toga).

On their marriage day, Roman women would begin wearing a *stola*, a long rectangular cloak considered the female equivalent of a toga.

The procession of members of the Augustan family, depicted in the *Āra Pācis Augustae* (Altar of Augustan Peace) on the right, is important evidence of Roman clothing customs and their social significance. See also the photograph of Augustus wearing a toga at the beginning of this chapter.

Such fashion sense makes Aelius reluctant to visit Servilius without a toga. This garment is a mark of Aelius' status as a Roman citizen, but it is expensive enough that he does not own one.

The toga was commonly seen as a peacetime garment. So in *Dē Officiīs* 1.77 Cicero says:

cēdant arma togae

Āra Pācis Augustae

i.e., let the military give way to civilian life, war to peace. (*Cēdant arma togae* is today the motto of the State of Wyoming.)

Martial also uses the toga to praise his friend Fronto as a paragon of both military and civilian life, as he tells Fronto his prayer for a simple life. Note how Martial speaks of himself in the third person and refers to himself as Marcus.

> Ō Frontō, decus clārum mīlitiae togaeque,
> sī breviter vōtum tuī Marcī cognoscere vīs,
> hoc petit, esse suī nōn magnī rūris arātor,
> et ōtia sordida in parvīs rēbus amat.

Martial *Epigrammata* 1.55. 1–4

Desiderius Erasmus (1466/1469–1536), a Dutch humanist, summed it all up in his *Adagia* (*Adages*):

Vestis virum facit. (3.1.60)

This adage is still heard in its English translation today.

Desiderius Erasmus Roterodamus (1466/1469–1536)

🔊 VERBA ŪTENDA

arātor, -ōris m. plower, farmer	*decus, decoris* n. glory	*rūs, rūris* f. country estate
	mīlitia, -ae f. military service	*vōtum, -ī* n. prayer

Latīna Hodierna

Vested in English

English has borrowed the Latin word for clothing (*vestis, vestis* f.) in a variety of words, including the following

di**vest**	**vest**
in**vest**	**vest**ee
in**vest**ment	**vest**ment
in**vest**iture	**vest**ry

Orbis Terrārum Rōmānus

Via Appia

The *Via Appia* is the main road from Rome south to Naples and east to Brundisium on the Adriatic. It was the first major road built by the Romans. Its construction began under the censor Appius Claudius Caecus in 312 B.C. The modern Via Appia runs parallel to the ancient road, which still exists. For hygienic and cultural reasons, burials inside the city walls were discouraged in Roman cities, and tombs were normally located just outside their walls. Wealthy families chose locations for their tombs that were very visible to travelers into and out of the city. Many such tombs were built along the Via Appia, where they can still be seen today. You should imagine the tomb of the *Servīliī* to be located here. Can you find it on the map below?

Two ancient tombs on the Via Appia are depicted on the next page. One of the largest tombs is the Tomb of Caecilia Metella, perhaps an ancestor of Servilius' wife. This Caecilia was daughter of Quintus Caecilius Metellus Creticus and the daughter-in-law of the triumvir Crassus. She died ca. 80 B.C.

Via Appia

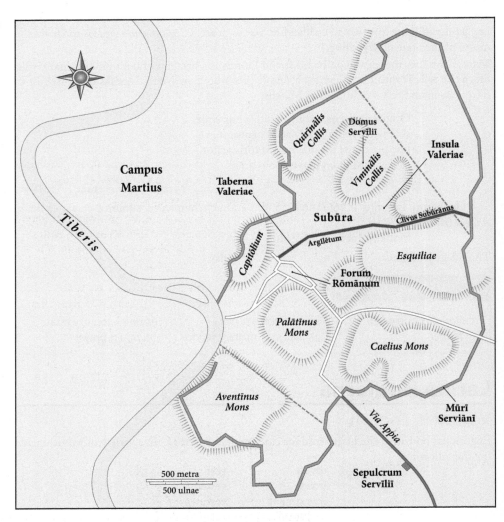

QUID PUTĀS?

1. Do you agree or disagree with Erasmus' adage *Vestis virum facit*? To what extent is this true today? By what classes or ages of people does it seem to be most believed?
2. Can you think of ways that clothing serves the same symbolic value in American society as the toga did in the Roman world? What would the American equivalent of a toga be?
3. How is the American view of togas different from Roman practice? Why do you think the difference is so great?
4. How do Roman attitudes toward clothing compare to modern American ones? Are there any kinds of clothes that indicate a person's rank or profession today? To what extent can the wealth and status of Americans be indicated by the clothes they wear?
5. Compare tombs on the Appian Way with modern American cemeteries. Think about things such as the cemetery's location, the style and the arrangement of monuments, and the need to make a social statement with the monument.

Via Appia Rōmā Brundisium

EXERCEĀMUS!

33-5 Scrībāmus

Retell these events in the present tense instead of the past. In order to do this, you need to change all the verbs marked in **bold** to the corresponding present tense form. Follow the model.

Plaustrum sordidum, mūlīs tractum, per viās Subūrae lentē **prōgrediēbātur** (1). Cum plaustrum ad insulam combustam **vēnit** (2), servī mortuōs, inter quōs **erat** (3) Mendax, in plaustrō **dēposuērunt** (4). Aelius quoque corpus Hephaestī ferēns ad plaustrum **advēnit** (5) et nummō sub linguā servī fidēlis positō, cadāver in plaustrum **posuit** (6).

Plaustrum ad collem Esquilīnum **prōgrediēbātur** (7) et per Portam Esquilīnam ad Campōs Esquilīnōs iter **fēcit** (8). Paulō post, ubi plaustrum **constitit** (9), cadāvera in puteō ā servīs **iacta sunt** (10).

→ Plaustrum sordidum, mūlīs tractum, per viās Subūrae lentē **prōgreditur**.

Sepulchrum Viae Appiae

Sepulcrum
Caeciliae Metellae

Sepulcrum Caeciliae Metellae

33-6 Colloquāmur

Use the verb *induō, induere, induī, indūtum* (put on) and the clothing vocabulary in the *Mōrēs Rōmānī* to describe Roman clothing to a classmate. Here is a sample sentence to get you started:

→ Et virī Rōmānī et fēminae Rōmānae tunicās induērunt sed virī sōlī togās induērunt.

33-7 Verba Discenda

Choose the *Verbum Discendum* that represents the **opposite** of the following definitions. Follow the model.

→ senior citizens: a. lingua   b. *līberī*   c. sōl   d. atrium

1. die:	a. orior	b. sinō	c. trādō	d. moneō
2. one who gets a message:	a. atrium	b. sōl	c. flūmen	d. nuntius
3. let one do as one pleases:	a. vetō	b. hortor	c. orior	d. sinō
4. keep in check:	a. trādō	b. vetō	c. persuādeō	d. sinō
5. ask politely:	a. moneō	b. postulō	c. caveō	d. orior
6. despair:	a. flūmen	b. spēs	c. nuntius	d. vestis
7. be reckless:	a. caveō	b. sinō	c. postulō	d. trādō
8. forbid:	a. caveō	b. vetō	c. moneō	d. sinō
9. untrustworthy:	a. ātrium	b. ōrō	c. fidēlis	d. fortūna
10. moon:	a. nuntius	b. ātrium	c. sōl	d. vestis

Gemma

veto: When presidents or governors "veto" bills, they are in effect, speaking Latin. What are they saying?

🔊 VERBA DISCENDA

ac and, and besides; than

ātrium, -iī n. atrium, public greeting room of a Roman house [atrial]

campus, -ī m. field

caveō, cavēre, cāvī, cautum take care, beware of [caution]

dum while, as long as; until

fidēlis, fidēle faithful, trustworthy [infidelity]

flūmen, -inis n. river [flume]

fortūna, -ae f. fortune, chance, luck; wealth, prosperity

hortor, hortārī, hortātus sum urge [exhort]

līberī, -ōrum m. pl. children

lingua, -ae f. tongue, speech [linguist]

moneō, monēre, monuī, monitum warn, advise [admonition]

nuntius, -iī m. messenger, news

orior, orīrī, ortus sum rise, get up, be born [orient]

ōrō (1) pray [oratory]

persuādeō, persuādēre, persuāsī, persuāsum (+ dat.) persuade [persuasive]

postulō (1) ask for, beg, demand, require, request [postulant]

sinō, sinere, sīvī/siī, situm allow, permit

sōl, sōlis m. sun; day [solar]

spēs, speī, f. hope, expectation

toga, -ae f. toga

togātus, -a, -um dressed in a toga

trādō, trādere, trādidī, trāditum hand down, entrust, deliver [trade, tradition]

vestiō, vestīre, vestīvī/ vestiī, vestītum dress, clothe [invest]

vestis, vestis f. garments, clothing [vestment]

vetō, vetāre, vetuī, vetitum forbid, prohibit

Angulus Grammaticus

Command Performances

Perhaps you are wondering why Latin needs both a present and a future imperative. The present imperative is used for a simple, immediate command, while the future imperative is especially used to refer to commands that are general rules or permanent laws, such as "Thou shall not steal." Here are some Latin examples:

- *Salūs populī suprēma lex estō.* (Let the welfare of the people be the supreme law.) This precept, the motto of the state of Missouri, is based on the following quote from Cicero's *Dē Lēgibus* 3.3.8: *Ollis salūs populī suprēma lex estō.* Note how Cicero modifies *salūs* with the archaic demonstrative *ollis* (= *illa*), which you saw in the traditional formula used to announce the death of Servilius Avus in *Lectiō Secunda*.

- *Boreā flante, nē arātō sēmen nē iacitō.* (When the north wind is blowing, do not plow or sow seed.) This is from Pliny's *Historiae Nātūrālēs* (18.334).

Latin also uses a future imperative with words or phrases that clearly refer to some point in the (distant) future, as in *crās labōrātō* or with a temporal clause clearly indicating future time, especially with the future perfect tense: *Cum bene dormīveris, labōrātō.* (When you will have slept well, work.)

Latin, like English, uses a number of adverbs to strengthen the force of a command. Here are some examples:

modo (only)	*Modo manē!* (Only wait!)
statim (at once)	*Ī statim!* (Go at once!)
proinde (well, then)	*Proinde curre!* (Then run!)
sānē (certainly)	*Sānē sequere!* (Certainly follow!)

Note also the enclitic *dum*, used in classical Latin only with *age* or *agite,* as in *agedum* or *agitedum,* to mean "Come, then!"

Latin and English can both accompany imperatives, for the sake of politeness, with words like *amābō* (please), *obsecrō* (I beg), *quaesō* (I ask), and *sīs* (if you wish, from *sī vīs*). *Mē manē, amābō!* (Wait for me, please!)

The imperative expressions *fac ut, cūrā ut, cavē nē,* which you have already seen, are actually examples of imperative **periphrasis** or circumlocution; i.e., they represent a sort of round-about command: Instead of saying *Nōlī tangere!* (Don't touch!), you can beat around the bush, so to speak, and say *Cavē nē tangās!* (Beware lest you touch!). When do you think such a periphrasis would be preferable to a direct command?

Here are some other ways Latin (and English) can express commands:

- Sometimes a question can serve as an imperative: *Nōn dīcis?* (You aren't speaking?) or (Aren't you speaking?) (*Dīc!*).

- So can a simple future indicative: *Dīcēs!* (You **will** speak!).

Indirect commands, i.e., *ut/nē* + subjunctive are sometimes called **jussive noun clauses**. "Jussive" is derived from the PPP of *iubeō*.

Officīna Fabrī

GRAMMATICA

Indirect Questions
Perfect Subjunctives
Sequence of Tenses
Pluperfect Subjunctives and
    Consolidation of Subjunctive Forms
Building the Sequence of Tenses
Consolidation of Interrogative Words
The Conjunction *Dum*

MŌRĒS RŌMĀNĪ

Commercium Rōmānum

ORBIS TERRĀRUM RŌMĀNUS

Germānia

LATĪNA HODIERNA

Latin Interrogatives in English

ANGULUS GRAMMATICUS

Macron or No Macron?

34

Patrōnus et Cliens

Lectiō Prīma

Antequam Legis

In this *lectiō* Aelius anxiously prepares to attend the *salūtātiō* at the house of Servilius. He puts on his rented toga, and he and his family worry about an appropriate gift to bring Servilius and the appropriate procedure to greet his prospective patron.

As you read about Aelius' concerns, you will see a new use of the subjunctive called an **indirect question** and a new tense of the subjunctive (**perfect**) that is used in indirect questions.

Indirect Questions

In this *lectiō* you will encounter indirect questions. They are simply reported questions. Consider this:

Direct Question:	**How** can Hermes catch the monkey?
Indirect Question:	I know **how** Hermes can catch the monkey.

Latin uses the subjunctive in an indirect question.

Direct Question:	***Quōmodo** Hermēs sīmiam capere **potest**?*
Indirect Question:	*Sciō **quōmodo** Hermēs sīmiam capere **possit**.*

The formula for an indirect question in Latin is:

main (head) verb + question word + subjunctive

As subjunctive subordinate clauses, indirect questions follow the sequence of tenses:

Primary Sequence: ***Sciō*** *quōmodo Hermēs sīmiam capere **possit**.*
Secondary Sequence: ***Scīvī*** *quōmodo Hermēs sīmiam capere **posset**.*

All the subjunctive verbs marked in **bold** in the *lectiō* are in indirect question constructions. As you read *Lectiō Prīma*, you will also see how another tense of the subjunctive, the perfect, is used in indirect questions.

Perfect Subjunctives

How can you recognize these perfect subjunctive forms? Here are some tips:

- The **perfect active subjunctive** = perfect stem + *-erim, -eris, -erit*, etc.

  vocāverim, vocāveris, vocāverit etc.   I called
  habuerim, habueris, habuerit etc.   I had
  potuerim, potueris, potuerit etc.   I was able to

- The **perfect passive subjunctive** = P^3 + present subjunctive of *sum.*

  *vocātus, -a, -um **sim***   *vocātī, -ae, -a **sīmus***
  *vocātus, -a, -um **sīs***   *vocātī, -ae, -a **sītis***
  *vocātus, -a, -um **sit***   *vocātī, -ae, -a **sint***

The perfect subjunctive is used to show **time before** the main verb. Simply adjust your English accordingly.

*Sciō quōmodo Hermēs sīmiam **cēperit**.*
  I know how Hermes caught the monkey. (time before main verb)

*Sciō quōmodo sīmia **captus sit**.*
  I know how the monkey was caught. (time before main verb)

EXERCEĀMUS!

34-1 Recognizing Indirect Questions

As you read *Lectiō Prīma*, make a line-by-line list of all the subjunctive verbs marked in **bold**. These subjunctives are all indirect questions. Find the head verb and question word that introduce the indirect question. Then identify the tense of the subjunctive. Follow the model.

Line	Subjunctive	Head Verb	Question Word	Tense of Subjunctive
→ 3	dēs	scīs	quod	present

SALŪTĀTIŌ

Paucōs post diēs, ante ortum sōlis, Aelius surgit, et togam, quam ā fullōne condūxit, induēns, sē praeparat ut salūtātiōnem apud Servīlium faciat.

Valeria "Aelī," inquit, "scīsne quod dōnum Servīliō **dēs?**"

Respondet: "Nesciō aut quid **dem** aut quid **dīcam!** Dīc mihi quid
5 dīcere **dēbeam** et quid aliī ante mē **dīxerint.**"

Valeria "Nesciō," inquit, "quālibus verbīs aliī **ūsī sint** sed hoc sciō— urbānus estō! Plānē loquere et tōta rēs bona erit."

Aelius: "Sed quid dē dōnō? Incertus sum quāle dōnum aliī **obtulerint** aut quāle **offeram.** Quālem opīniōnem tenēs?"

10 Valeria respondet: "Meministīne ānulum quod mihi duōs ante annōs dedistī? Hoc patrōnō novō da et eī dīc tē alium meliōrem ac argenteum fabricāre posse. Nunc, abī, et mementō—fortūna fortēs iuvat!!"

Aelius sōlus per viās obscūrās Subūrae ambulat facem in manū tenēns, et ad domum Servīliī sōle oriente advenit. Longam ordinem clientium prō
15 foribus domūs stantium videt et sē in novissimō ordine pōnit.

Aelius iānitōrem Servīliī appropinquantem videt. Iānitor, togā Aeliī vīsā, eī dīcit: "Salvē," inquit "cīvis. Cīvibus nōn in novissimō agmine standum est. Mē sequere et dīc mihi cūr **vēneris.**"

Aelius iānitōrī dīcit id quod Servīliī uxor Valeriae dīxit et imperāvit.

20 Iānitor "Manē hīc," inquit, et per forēs intrat.

Aelium, reditum iānitōris exspectantem, alius salūtat. "Nōnne novus es? Trepidus vidēris. Ego, prīmum trepidus ad salūtātiōnem adveniēns, nescīvī quid **agendum esset,** sed nunc sciō. Scīsne quid **agendum sit?**"

Aelius "Nihil," inquit, "sciō et ergō paulō trepidus sum. Dīc mihi vērē
25 quōmodo vōs omnēs salūtātiōnem **agātis.**"

Ille: "Fac ut tranquillus sīs! Age sīcut agō. Sed, dīc mihi, audīvistīne dē Tiberiō?"

Aelius: "Nesciō. Quid audīvistī?"

Ille: "Ut scīs, Tiberius in Germāniā est. Sed scīsne quot Germānōs **vīcerit?** Herī audīvimus, magnō proeliō factō, ducēs Germānōrum sē Tiberiō trādidisse. Omnēs in urbe … sed ecce, forēs aperiuntur."

Iānua

VERBA ŪTENDA

ānulus, -ī m. ring
argenteus, -a, -um of silver, silvery
condūcō, condūcere, condūxī, conductum rent
fax, facis f. torch
foris, foris f. (pl. forēs, -um) door, gate; forīs out of doors, outside; abroad
Germānia, -ae f. Germany

Germānī, -ōrum pl. Germans, the German people
iānitor, -ōris m. doorman, porter
induō, induere, induī, indūtum put on
nesciō, nescīre, nescīvī/nesciī, nescītum not know
obscūrus, -a, -um dark
officīna, -ae f. workshop

opīniō, -iōnis f. opinion, belief; reputation
ordō, -inis m. row, line, order; rank; class of citizens
plānus, -a, -um plane, flat; even; obvious; plānē clearly
praeparō (1) prepare
proelium, -iī n. battle

quālis, quāle? what kind of? what sort of?
quot? (indecl.) how many?
Tiberius, -iī m. Tiberius, stepson, son-in-law, and successor of Augustus
trepidus, -a, -um alarmed, anxious
urbānus, -a, -um polished, refined; witty

POSTQUAM LĒGISTĪ

Answer all the following questions in English. Also answer in Latin if the question is followed by (L).

1. In what ways does Aelius prepare himself on the morning of the *salūtātiō*? How would someone prepare himself today for a similar interview?
2. What does Aelius hold in his hand while he walks through the streets? (L) Why?
3. What does he find at Servilius' house upon his arrival? (L)
4. Where does the *iānitor* bring him? (L) Why?
5. What news does Aelius hear while he is waiting? (L) Why might he and his family be especially interested in and concerned about this news?

Gemma

In novissimō ordine literally means "in the newest line," i.e., "at the end of the line." The idea is that it is the most recent thing to pass by. Where English uses an "of" phrase, Latin here uses an adjective. Here is another example: *in summō monte* ("at the top of the mountain").

Grammatica A

Indirect Questions

Indirect questions are similar in structure to indirect statements, which you have already learned.

Direct Statement:	*Ante ortum sōlis Aelius surgit.*	Aelius gets up before sunrise.
Indirect Statement:	*Sciō Aelium ante ortum sōlis surgere.*	I know Aelius gets up before sunrise.

Here, in an indirect statement, the original verb becomes an infinitive (*surgit → surgere*) and the original subject becomes accusative (*Aelius → Aelium*).

Notice the parallels with indirect questions:

Direct Question:	*Quandō Aelius surgit?*	When does Aelius get up?
Indirect Question:	*Sciō quandō Aelius surgat.*	I know when Aelius gets up.

A direct question is an interrogative sentence and simply seeks information. We mark them in both English and Latin with question marks and with interrogative words like *quis* (who?), *quid* (what?), *ubi* (where?), *quandō* (when?), and *cūr* (why?).

However, when someone reports such a question, the resulting construction is called an **indirect question**. You can recognize an indirect question in both English and Latin because it begins with a head verb like *sciō* (know) followed by an interrogative word.

Here is the formula for an indirect question in Latin:

main (head) verb	+	interrogative word	+	subjunctive
sciō	+	*quandō*	+	*surgat*

Indirect questions follow the sequence of tenses:

Primary Sequence:	*Sciō quid Aelius **faciat**.*	I know what Aelius is doing.
Secondary Sequence:	*Scīvī quid Aelius **faceret**.*	I knew what Aelius was doing.

In both of these sentences the "doing" and the "knowing" happen at approximately the same time, at what we will now call "near time" in this book.

To show an action that happens before the main verb, the tense of the subjunctive changes. Here is how this works in primary sequence:

Primary Sequence:	*Sciō quid Aelius **fēcerit**.*	I know what Aelius did.

In this sentence the perfect subjunctive shows that this action happened before the action of *sciō*. For now, we will consider time before in primary sequence only. In the next *lectiō* we will consider time before in secondary sequence.

The Perfect Subjunctive

Here is the full paradigm of *capiō* in the perfect subjunctive.

PERFECT ACTIVE SUBJUNCTIVE	PERFECT PASSIVE SUBJUNCTIVE
cēperim	captus, -a, -um sim
cēperis	captus, -a, -um sīs
cēperit	captus, -a, -um sit
cēperimus	captī, -ae, -a sīmus
cēperitis	captī, -ae, -a sītis
cēperint	captī, -ae, -a sint

perfect active subjunctive = perfect stem (3rd PP – *ī*) + *erim, eris, erit,* etc.
perfect passive subjunctive = P^3 plus the present subjunctive of *sum*

Did you notice any similarities between perfect subjunctives and other verb forms you have learned? The perfect active subjunctive forms are very similar to the future perfect indicative.

PERFECT ACTIVE SUBJUNCTIVE	FUTURE PERFECT ACTIVE INDICATIVE
cēperim	cēperō
cēperis	**cēperis**
cēperit	**cēperit**
cēperimus	**cēperimus**
cēperitis	**cēperitis**
cēperint	**cēperint**

All the forms marked in bold are identical. But don't panic. Remember that perfect subjunctives in Latin are accompanied by word clues to warn you of their presence (in indirect questions, for example). In the *Angulus Grammaticus* to this chapter, you can read how some grammarians distinguish these forms.

Sequence of Tenses

Remember that the subjunctive does not show "real" time like indicative verbs do. When the subjunctive is used in a subordinate clause, it always shows time relative to the main verb of the sentence.

So far you have learned the present and imperfect subjunctive and know that each one shows a time that is near to the time of the main verb of the sentence—either same time as the main verb or time in the immediate future.

Purpose clause: *Ambulō ad amphitheātrum **ut** mūnera **videam**.*
    *Ambulāvī ad amphiteātrum **ut** mūnera **vidērem**.*

In each of these sentences, the seeing is expected to happen immediately after the main verb of walking. Consider the same relationship in a result clause:

Result clause: *Sōcratēs tam celer est **ut** Hermēs eum capere **nōn possit**.*
    *Sōcratēs tam celer erat **ut** Hermēs eum capere **nōn posset**.*

Here too the result (not being able to catch the monkey) is seen as either existing at the same time or shortly after the main verb of the sentence.

In order to express **time before the main verb**, Latin makes use of two other tenses of the subjunctive—the perfect (introduced here) and the pluperfect (introduced later in this chapter).

Of course, the option of **time after the main verb** also exists, and you can see this in indirect questions.

> I know what you are doing. (same time as or immediately after the main verb)
> I know what you did last summer. (time before main verb)
> I know what you are going to do next summer. (time after main verb)

Latin uses the subjunctive mood to accommodate all these options, and the tenses used follow what we call the **sequence of tenses**. See how the **perfect** subjunctive fits into this chart.

IF THE MAIN VERB IS ...	USE THIS SUBJUNCTIVE TENSE	TO SHOW
Primary Sequence		
Present		near time
Future	present	
	perfect	time before
Future Perfect		
Secondary Sequence		
Imperfect		
Perfect	imperfect	near time
Pluperfect		

We will fill in more of this chart as you learn more forms of the subjunctive.

EXERCEĀMUS!

34-2 **Changing Perfect Active Indicatives to Perfect Active Subjunctives**

Change the following perfect active indicative forms to perfect active subjunctives, without changing person and number. Follow the model.

→ vocāvī   *vocāverim*

1. duxistī
2. cēpērunt
3. fuistī
4. monuimus
5. fēcit
6. dixī
7. vēnistis
8. spectāvērunt
9. voluit

Lectiō Secunda

Antequam Legis

In this *lectiō* Aelius meets Servilius, gives him his gift, and becomes his client. As you read about this meeting you will see the **pluperfect subjunctive** in use.

Pluperfect Subjunctives

Like the perfect subjunctive, the **pluperfect subjunctive** shows **time before** the main verb. It is only used after main verbs that are in the secondary sequence. Compare:

> Sciō quid fēceris.   I know what you did. (primary)
> Scīvī quid fēcissēs.   I knew what you had done. (secondary)

Here is how you form the pluperfect subjunctive:

Active: perfect stem + *-issem, -issēs, -isset*, etc.
             fēcissem, fēcissēs, fēcisset, etc.

Passive: P³ + *-essem, -essēs, -esset*, etc.
             factus essem, factus essēs, factus esset, etc.
             Remember that the P³ GNCs.

EXERCEĀMUS!

34-3 **Pluperfect Subjunctive**

As you read, make a line-by-line list of the pluperfect subjunctive forms you see marked in **bold** in *Lectiō Secunda*. Identify the person, number, voice, and 1ˢᵗ principal part of each form. Then translate the word into English. Follow the model.

Line	Pluperfect	Person	Number	Voice	1ˢᵗ PP	English Meaning
→ 4	ēmissētis	2	pl.	active	emō	you bought

Interrogative Words

As you read *Lectiō, Secunda,* also look for interrogative words marked in ***bold italics***. We will review these words after you read.

The Conjunction *Dum*

Here is a new use of *dum*.

- *Dum* means "while" when used with the indicative, commonly with the present tense.
- *Dum* means "until" when used with the subjunctive and sometimes with the indicative.

As you read *Lectiō Secunda,* also look for uses of *dum* and decide whether you would translate them as "while" or "until."

🔊 PATRŌNUS

Foribus apertīs, Servīlius clientēs suōs salūtāvit, ūnī sportulam aliī nummōs dans. Dē morbō uxōris alicuius rogāvit, dē negōtiō aliōrum.

"Dīcite mihi," inquit, "dē negōtiō vestrō. Trepidus eram postquam revēnistis et nēmō mē certiōrem fēcit ***quot*** equōs **ēmissētis** et ***quantum*** lucrī dē illīs equīs **fēcissētis**."

Aelius Servīliō ānulum dat.

5   Et alium interrogāvit ***quandō*** nāvēs ab Āfricā Ostiam **advēnissent** et ***quālēs*** mercēs ad Italiam **tulissent**. Nōnnullī clientēs dīxērunt sē mortis avī paenitēre et ūnus, haud venustus eques, Servīlium rogāvit ***quā dē causā*** avus **mortuus esset**.

Mox Servīlius Aeliō appropinquāvit et, manum eius tenēns, rogāvit ***quā dē causā*** **advēnisset**. Aelius, vōce tremente, "Domine," inquit, "fortasse iam intellegis ***cūr*** adsim. Paucōs ante diēs uxor tua ad tabernam Valeriae,
10   socrūs meae, advēnit, et ab eā postulāvit ut hūc advenīrem. Audīvī dē morte Servīliī avī et dum tempus idōneum esset, manēbam. Nōmen mihi M. Aelius est et faber sum. Domina Caecilia pauca ex operibus meīs, quae in tabernā Valeriae exposita erant, vīdit et ea illī placuērunt. Voluit mē alia, sed argentea, fabricāre, sed nōn potuī. Uxor tua mē ut ad salūtātiōnem tuam advenīrem hortāta est et nunc adsum."

Servīlius "Ita," inquit, "uxor mihi omnia haec narrāvit. Sed mihi nōn dīxit ***cūr*** rēs argenteās nōn **fabricāvissēs**."
15   Aelius "Domine," inquit, "pauper sum et argentum nōn habeō. Praetereā, recenter incendium officīnam meam et īnsulam in quā habitābāmus dēstrūxit. Paene omnia perdita sunt, sed mēcum hunc ānulum tulī. Dōnum tibi est."

Servīlius, ānulum recipiēns, dixit: "Aelī, uxor mea, tuam artem admīrāns, mē imperāvit ut tē et familiam adiu-
vārem. Et ars tua plāna est. Patrōnus tuus erō et cliens meus eris. Quid plūra? Intrā et manē in ātriō dum omnēs aliōs
salūtō. Mox omnia necessāria habēbis—argentum, novam officīnam et novam insulam in quā familia tua habitāre
20 possit. Sērius disserēmus *quōmodo* mihi auxilium dare possīs."

Salūtātiōne confectā clientēs—aliī ad Forum, aliī ad patrōnum alium—abiērunt. Servīlius, revertēns intrā,
multa cum Aeliō dē rēbus negōtiī fabrī disseruit. Antequam Aelius abiit, Servīlius et Aelius bene intellexērunt *quantum*
lucrī Aelius Servīliō **prōmīsisset** et *quantam* pecūniam Servīlius Aeliō **pollicitus esset**.

Servīlius Aeliō abeuntī dixit: "Fac ut officīnam novam celeriter inveniās, Aelī, et strēnuē labōrā! Pecūnia mea
25 quoque prō mē semper strēnuē labōrāre dēbet!"

Âfrica, -ae f. Africa, Roman
    province in modern
    Tunisia
antequam before
ānulus, -ī m. ring
**argenteus, -a, -um of
    silver, silvery**
**destruō, destruere,
    destruxī, destructum
    destroy**
*disserō, disserere,
    disseruī, dissertum*
    discuss
**eques, equitis m.
    horseman, knight; pl.
    cavalry; order of
    knights**

equus, -ī m. horse
*expōnō, expōnere, exposuī,
    expositum* set out;
    exhibit
**foris, foris (pl. forēs, -um)
    f. door, gate; forīs adv.
    out of doors, outside;
    abroad**
**interrogō (1) ask,
    question; examine**
lucrum, -ī n. profit
merx, mercis f. a
    commodity; (pl.) goods,
    merchandise
**morbus, -ī m. illness,
    sickness**
nāvis, nāvis f. ship

*necessārius, -a, -um
    necessary, indispensible
nummus, -ī m. coin, money
officīna, -ae f. workshop
**ordō, -inis m. row, line,
    order; rank; class of
    citizens**
Ostiam "to Ostia" (the port
    of Rome)
perditus, -a, -um ruined, lost
**plānus, -a, -um plane, flat;
    even; obvious**
**praetereā besides,
    moreover**
**prōmittō, prōmittere,
    prōmīsī, prōmissum
    send forth; promise**

quā dē causā? for what
    reason? why?
quālis, quāle? what kind
    of? what sort of?
Quid plūra? "Why say more?"
quot? (indecl.) how
    many?
recenter recently
socrus, -ūs f. mother-in-law
sportula, -ae f. little basket;
    gift of money or food
    from patron to client
**tremō, tremere, tremuī
    tremble**
trepidus, -a, -um nervous,
    anxious
venustus, -a, -um charming

POSTQUAM LĒGISTĪ

Answer all the following questions in English. Also answer in Latin if the question is followed
by (L).

Nāvis Rōmāna

1. What does Servilius do and say as he greets his clients? (L)
2. How does Aelius' speech to Servilius suggest his deference to the great man and his fear of
   failure?
3. What part of Aelius' story did Servilius need more details about?
4. What evidence of Aelius' craftsmanship does Servilius have, and what is Servilius' opinion
   of Aelius' work? (L)
5. What does Servilius offer Aelius? (L)
6. What motivation does Servilius express for helping Aelius? (L)
7. Compare the way the Romans conduct business deals with modern American practices.

Grammatica B

Pluperfect Subjunctives and Consolidation of Subjunctive Forms

With the addition of the pluperfect subjunctive forms, now you have seen all four subjunctive tenses. Here is the chart for *dūcō* with the new pluperfect subjunctive forms marked in **bold**:

PRESENT	IMPERFECT	PERFECT	PLUPERFECT
Active			
dūcam	dūcerem	duxerim	**duxissem**
dūcās	dūcerēs	duxeris	**duxissēs**
dūcat	dūceret	duxerit	**duxisset**
dūcāmus	dūcerēmus	duxerimus	**duxissēmus**
dūcātis	dūcerētis	duxeritis	**duxissētis**
dūcant	dūcerent	duxerint	**duxissent**
Passive			
dūcar	dūcerer	ductus, -a, -um sim	**ductus, -a, -um essem**
dūcāris	dūcerēris	ductus, -a, -um sīs	**ductus, -a, -um essēs**
dūcātur	dūcerētur	ductus, -a, -um sit	**ductus, -a, -um esset**
dūcāmur	dūcerēmur	ductī, -ae, -a sīmus	**ductī, -ae, -a essēmus**
dūcāminī	dūcerēminī	ductī, -ae, -a sītis	**ductī, -ae, -a essētis**
dūcantur	dūcerentur	ductī, -ae, -a sint	**ductī, -ae, -a essent**

Notā Bene:

- The vowel in the pluperfect active ending is always long in the 1st person plural and the 2nd person singular and plural.

- One easy way to remember the imperfect and pluperfect active subjunctives is to note that both forms are spelled like infinitives plus personal endings.

imperfect subjunctive	=	present active infinitive	+	personal endings
dūcerem	=	*dūcere*	+	m

pluperfect subjunctive	=	perfect active infinitive	+	personal endings
duxissem	=	*duxisse*	+	m

Building the Sequence of Tenses

The pluperfect subjunctive is used to indicate **time before a main verb in secondary sequence**. These four sentences illustrate the four possibilities you have learned so far.

Primary Sequence

Rogant cūr id faciat. They ask why he is doing that.
  (present subjunctive, near time)

Rogant cūr id fēcerit. They ask why he did that.
  (perfect subjunctive, time before)

Secondary Sequence

Rogāvērunt cūr id faceret. They asked why he was doing that.
  (imperfect subjunctive, near time)

Rogāvērunt cūr id fēcisset. They asked why he had done that.
  (pluperfect subjunctive, time before)

Now see how the **pluperfect** subjunctive fits into the chart for sequence of tenses:

IF THE MAIN VERB IS ...	USE THIS SUBJUNCTIVE TENSE	TO SHOW
Primary Sequence		
Present		
Future	present	near time
Future Perfect	perfect	time before
Secondary Sequence		
Imperfect		
Perfect	imperfect	near time
Pluperfect	**pluperfect**	time before

Consolidation of Interrogative Words

At the beginning of this chapter, we reminded you of interrogative words like *quis?, quid?, ubi?, quandō?,* and *cūr?* (who, what, where, when, and why). Here are several other interrogatives you saw marked in bold italics in *Lectiō Secunda*:

quantus, -a, -um?	how much?
quālis, quāle?	what kind of? what sort of?
quā dē causā?	for what reason? why?
quōmodo?	how?
quot?	how many?

All of these words are now *Verba Discenda*. Now go back to *Lectiō Prīma* and see how many of these words you can find.

The Conjunction *Dum*

Earlier you learned that *dum* + indicative is translated "while." But *dum* can also be translated as "until" and can be used with either the indicative or the subjunctive. When it is used with the indicative, it is stating a **fact** that happened or will happen.

> *Manē hīc dum redībō.*   Wait here until I return.

When *dum* is used with the subjunctive, it is still translated as "until," but here it indicates that the anticipated event is more a possibility than a fact.

> *Manē hīc dum redeam.*   Wait here until I should return.

Here are two uses of *dum* from *Lectiō Secunda*:

> *... dum tempus idōneum esset, manēbam.*

> *Manē in ātriō dum omnēs aliōs salūtō.*

Which one indicates a fact and which one a possibility? How do you know?

EXERCEĀMUS!

34-4 Sequence of Tenses

In the following sentences, identify the subjunctive verb and its tense. Then indicate whether this verb shows same time or time before the main verb. Follow the model.

	Verb	**Tense**	**Time Sequence**
→ Scīsne quod dōnum Servīliō dēs?	*dēs*	present	near time

1. Nesciō quid dem.

2. Nesciō quid aliī clientēs Servīliō dederint.

3. Nescīvimus quid dīcerent!

4. Nescīvī quālibus verbīs aliī ūsī essent.

5. Incertus sum quāle dōnum aliī obtulerint.

6. Rogāvit quā dē causā advēnissent.

Mōrēs Rōmānī

Commercium Rōmānum

Roman society was hierarchical and plutocratic. By the time of the Empire, the ancient division between patrician (aristocratic) and plebian families had broken down a bit. However, even in the Empire, citizens were grouped by census into six classes (*ordinēs*) according to wealth. The major public offices, such as the consulship, were only open to the wealthiest group or senatorial class, of which Servilius Severus was a member. Traditionally, the wealth of the senatorial class was based on large agricultural estates called *lātifundia* (*-ōrum* n. pl.). Members of this class were not allowed to participate directly in commercial activity.

The next wealthiest group were the knights (*equitēs, -um* m. pl.) who typically made their fortunes in a wide variety of business enterprises, including trade and manufacturing. Cordus is an *eques*. As part of our story on Cordus, we imagine that his father made money by helping Crassus, who used to go to fires and buy the houses at increasingly low prices as the fire progressed. Perhaps Cordus is trying to become more respectable by starting a fire brigade at Rome.

At the bottom of this social structure were citizens called *prōlētāriī*, who owned little or no property. Aelius and his family were of this class. This social structure, however, was very mobile. It was possible for a *prōlētārius* to rise quickly to the status of *eques* through the accumulation of great wealth.

Although men of Servilius' status could not, themselves, act as merchants or traders (*mercātōrēs*) or bankers (*argentāriī*), they could, as Servilius does, seek commercial profit indirectly, by working through freedmen, clients, or agents. A skilled craftsman like Aelius was a very attractive client for a patron like Servilius, because Aelius could make money for Servilius, as well as provide Servilius with valuable support in political elections.

There were great opportunities for financial gain (*lucrum, -ī* n.) in the export of Italian wines and olive oil and the importation of grain and slaves into Italy. The luxury trade items, such as silk and spices from the East and even amber from the Baltic, were also potentially lucrative. However, the danger of severe financial loss through shipwreck, theft, and natural disaster was also very real.

Mercury (*Mercurius, -iī* m.), the Roman god of messengers and commerce, is still depicted in that role today. The god appears wearing his trademark winged helmet and sandals on the facade of Grand Central Station in New York City. Mercury is flanked by Hercules and Minerva in a group sculpted by Jules-Felix Coutan (1848–1939).

Mercurius

Orbis Terrārum Rōmānus

Germānia

The Romans used the word *Germānia* to refer to a wide geographic area in north central Europe inhabited not only by German-speaking tribes but also by Celts and others. There were two Roman provinces called *Germānia* west of the Rhine river. *Germānia Inferior* consisted approximately of what is now Belgium and the Netherlands. *Germānia Superior* included modern Switzerland and the French province of Alsace. Under the Emperor Augustus, the Romans tried to push across the Rhine river. The successful expedition of Tiberius in 9–7 B.C. was one of these efforts. For a while, the Romans controlled territory as far east as the Elbe River. However,

Porta Rōmāna Augustae Trēvirōrum

after Marcus Lollius' defeat at the hands of Germanic tribes in 17–16 B.C. and the disastrous loss in 9 A.D. of three legions under general Varus to the German leader Arminius in the Teutoburg Forest. Augustus settled the boundaries of the empire along the defendable lines of the Rhine and Danube rivers. Two of the most important cities in Roman Germany were *Colōnia Claudia Āra Agrippīnensium* (modern Cologne) and *Augusta Trēvirōrum* (modern Trier).

Suetonius' account of Augustus' reaction to Varus' defeat in Germany is quite dramatic:

> Hāc nuntiātā excubiās per urbem indixit, nē quis tumultus existeret. Vōvit et magnōs lūdōs Iovī Optimō Maximō. Adeō dēnique eum consternātum esse ferunt, ut per continuōs mensēs barbā capillōque submissō caput interdum foribus illīderet, vōciferāns: Quintilī Vare, legiōnēs redde!

Suetonius *Agustus* 23

Germānia

ac = atque and, and also, and besides

adeō so much, to such a degree

barba, -ae f. beard

capillus, -ī m. head hair

consternō (1) shock

continuus, -a, -um successive

excubiae, -ārum f. pl. guard, watch

existō, existere, extitī arise, appear

ferunt = hominēs dīcunt

foris, foris (pl. forēs, -um) f. door, gate; forīs adv. out of doors, outside; abroad

illīdō, illīdere, illīsī, illīsum strike against

indīcō, indīcere, indixī, indictum proclaim

interdum occasionally

nuntiō (1) announce, report

quis = aliquis

reddō, reddere, reddidī, redditum give back

submittō, submittere, submīsī, submissum let grow

tumultus, -ī m. uproar, disturbance

vōciferor, vōciferārī, vōciferātus sum yell, cry out

voveō, vovēre, vōvī, vōtum vow

Arminius in Germāniā

Latīna Hodierna

Latin Interrogatives in English

Use the meaning of the following Latin interrogatives and verbs of asking to define their English derivatives. Consult an English dictionary if you need help.

quaerō, quaerere, quaesīvī/quaesiī, quaesītum	**query**, **quest**, **quest**ion, **quest**ionnaire
rogō (1)	ab**rog**ate, de**rog**ate, de**rog**atory, inter**rog**ative, pre**rog**ative, **rog**atory
quantus, -a, -um?	**quant**ity, **quant**ify, **quant**um **quant**itative
quālis, quāle?	**qual**ify, **qual**ification, **qual**itative, **qual**ity
quid?	**quid**dity, **quid** prō quō
quot?	**quot**ient, **quot**a

QUID PUTĀS?

1. How do the attitudes of upper-class Romans toward commerce compare to those of upper-class Americans today? What modern American group compares to the upwardly-mobile *equitēs* in ancient Rome?
2. Are there any modern parallels to the Roman client-patron relationship?
3. Why do you think the Romans were so eager to advance into Germany? Why do you think they found this so difficult to do?
4. Can you give an example of a *quid prō quō*?
5. Describe Augustus' reaction to Varus' defeat in Germany. What does this suggest about his leadership qualities?

EXERCEĀMUS!

34-5 Scrībāmus

Find the Latin words in *Lectiō Prīma* that best answer these Latin questions. Then answer the question in Latin. Follow the model.

→ Quandō Aelius surgit?
  ante ortum sōlis (line 1):
  Aelius ante ortum sōlis surgit.

1. Quid Aelius ā fullōne condūxit?
2. Quā dē causā Aelius sē praeparat?
3. Quāle dōnum Aelius Valeriae dedit?
4. Ubi Aelius sōlus ambulat facem in manū tenēns?
5. Quandō Aelius ad domum Servīliī advenit?
6. Quid Aelius prō foribus domūs videt?
7. Quem appropinquantem Aelius videt?
8. Cūr iānitor Aelium cīvem esse scit?
9. Cui Aelius dīcit id quod uxor Servīliī Valeriae dīxit?
10. Quis trepidus vidētur?

34-6 Colloquāmur

Practice asking and answering in Latin the questions in Exercise 34-5.

34-7 Vēnātiō Verbōrum Discendōrum

Find the *Verbum Discendum* that best fits each of the following statements. HINT: Some statements have more than one answer, and a *Verbum Discendum* can be used more than once. Follow the model.

→ The opposite of *sciō*: **nesciō**

1. A 3rd declension i-stem noun:

2. An indeclinable adjective:

3. This word is used to make a list:

4. This Latin word comes to mean a maintenance person in a building in English:

5. A synonym for *iānua*:

6. A subordinate conjunction:

7. A 3rd conjugation verb:

8. A 3rd declension noun that is not i-stem:

9. A 4th conjugation verb:

10. An animal:

11. Refers to a metal:

12. This word refers to a place where crafts were made:

13. A synonym for *clārus, -a, -um*:

14. *Quaerō* is a synonym for this word:

15. A neuter noun of the second declension:

🔊 VERBA DISCENDA

antequam before
argenteus, -a, -um of silver, silvery [argenteous]
destruō, destruere, destruxī, destructum destroy [destructive]
eques, equitis m. horseman, knight; pl. cavalry; order of knights [equestrian]
equus, -ī m. horse [equine]
foris, foris f. (pl. *forēs, -um*) door, gate; *forīs*

adv. out of doors, outside; abroad
iānitor, -ōris m. doorman, porter [janitorial]
interrogō (1) ask, question; examine [interrogation]
morbus, -ī m. illness, sickness [morbid]
nāvis, nāvis f. ship [naval]
necessārius, -a, -um necessary, indispensible
nesciō, nescīre, nescīvī/nesciī, nescītum not know [nescience]

officīna, -ae f. workshop [office]
opīniō, -iōnis f. opinion, belief; reputation [opinionated]
ordō, -inis m. row, line, order; rank; class of citizens [ordination]
plānus, -a, -um plane, flat, even; obvious
praetereā besides, moreover
proelium, -iī n. battle
prōmittō, prōmittere, prōmīsī, prōmissum

send forth; promise [promissary]
quā dē causā? for what reason? why?
quālis, quāle? what kind of? what sort of? [quality]
quot? indecl. how many? [quotient]
tremō, tremere, tremuī tremble [tremor]

Angulus Grammaticus

Macron or No Macron?

When we compared the perfect active subjunctive and future perfect active indicative forms earlier in this chapter, we did so this way:

PERFECT ACTIVE SUBJUNCTIVE	FUTURE PERFECT ACTIVE INDICATIVE
cēperim	cēperō
cēperis	**cēperis**
cēperit	**cēperit**
cēperimus	**cēperimus**
cēperitis	**cēperitis**
cēperint	**cēperint**

The situation, however, is actually a bit more complex. In some grammar books you will find that the 2nd person singular and plural, and the 1st person plural have a macron over the *-ī* of the ending in the perfect subjunctive.

PERFECT ACTIVE SUBJUNCTIVE	FUTURE PERFECT ACTIVE INDICATIVE
cēperim	cēperō
cēperīs	cēperis
cēperit	cēperit
cēperīmus	cēperimus
cēperītis	cēperitis
cēperint	cēperint

This is because some Roman poets at various times used either a long or a short *-i* in these endings. It seems that there was confusion even at the time as to which was more corrrect. Such things are not uncommon, even today. Consider, for example, different American pronunciations of words like "aunt," "tomato," and "roof."

35

Lūdī Incipiant!

Lectiō Prīma

Antequam Legis

Setting the Scene

Several months have passed since the fire, and life is easier for Valeria and her family. They have moved into an *insula* at the base of the Viminal Hill, upon which, you will recall, lives their patron, Servilius. Their apartment has more rooms, and Aelius has a new workshop nearby with two slaves who help him produce silver articles of high quality. Business is good both at his shop and at Valeria's *taberna*.

Higher on the Viminal, life is also changing. Marcus is getting ready to go to Greece to continue his studies of rhetoric. Servilia and her mother are involved in planning the upcoming wedding with Cordus. Servilius himself is well into the elections for praetor. Whenever he is able, Aelius, as a good *cliens*, helps with the election.

But today is a day of festivities and not a day for work or politics. News of Tiberius' victories in Germany has spread, and the city is celebrating with chariot races.

As you read about these races, continue to consider indirect questions and the sequence of tenses.

Indirect Questions: Time After the Main Verb

So far you have learned how to use the sequence of tenses to show:

Same time or time near to that of the main verb (present or imperfect subjunctive)
Time before the main verb (perfect or pluperfect subjunctive)

Now consider this sentence, which illustrates a third option: **time after the main verb**.

> I know *what you are going to do tomorrow.*

Latin expresses this option after primary sequence verbs with a form that is very easy to recognize: FAP + *sim, sīs, sit*, etc.

> *Sciō quid crās **factūrus sīs**.*

> **LECTIŌNĒS:**
> **LŪDĪ CIRCENSĒS**
> **and**
> **NAUFRAGIUM**
>
> Marcus and his friends go to the chariot races in the Circus Maximus. They are there not only for the thrill of the races but also for socializing and flirting. In the process we learn some tips in this regard from Ovid, the famous poet-guide of love.

461

The form ***factūrus sīs*** is easy to translate by reversing the order of the FAP and the present subjunctive form of *sum*.

Sciō	*quid*	*crās*	*sīs*	*factūrus.*
I know	what	tomorrow	**you are**	**going to do**.

All the subjunctives indicating **time after** the main verb in indirect questions are marked in **bold** in *Lectiō Prīma*.

The Perfect Tense in Primary Sequence

Sometimes the perfect indicative tense expresses an action done in the past, but stresses its present consequences. When a Latin perfect is used this way, it is followed by primary rather than secondary sequence.

> *Vēnī ut tē videam.*   I have come in order to see you. = I am here to see you.

Look in *Lectiō Prīma* for two perfect indicatives marked in ***bold italics*** and followed by subjunctives in primary sequence.

EXERCEĀMUS!

35-1 **Time after the Main Verb**

Find the subject of each of the following subjunctives marked in **bold** in *Lectiō Prīma*, and translate the subject and verb together. If the subject is unexpressed, use context to determine who is performing the action. Remember that all these subjunctives express time after the main verb. Follow the model.

Subjunctive	Subject	Translation
→ adventūrī sint	hominēs	people will come

1. vīsūra sit (line 8)
2. adventūrae sint (line 10)
3. futūra sit (line 12)
4. abitūrus sīs (line 18)
5. abitūrus sim (line 19)
6. vīsūrus sim (line 25)
7. victūra sit (line 25)

Gemma

Spectātum venimus, venimus ut spectēmur! (line 22). This statement is based on Ovid's *Ars Amatoria* l. 98: *spectātum veniunt, veniunt spectentur ut ipsae*. (They come to see; they come so that they themselves will be seen.)

Agitātor Rōmānus

🔊 LŪDĪ CIRCENSĒS

Mox multī Rōmānī ad Circum Maximum libenter venient ut lūdōs spectent. Rogāsne fortasse cūr tot hominēs **adventūrī sint**?

Aelius, quī praesertim Venetae Factiōnī favet, veniet ut sponsiōnem faciat et, fortasse, plūrimōs nummōs domum ferat. Lūcius naufragiōrum
5 spectandōrum causā veniet. Cum naufragia fīunt, magnus est clāmor spectātōrum et māior est Lūciī laetitia.

Neque Servīlius neque Caecilia lūdīs fruitur, sed temporibus cessērunt et advenient quod Servīlius praetōrem petit et ā suffrāgātōribus spectārī cupit. Servīlia sē rogat utrum Cordum **vīsūra sit**.

Prīdiē lūdōrum Marcus et amīcī colloquēbantur.

10 Fabius: "Amīcī, intellegitisne quae puellae crās ad Circum **adventūrae sint**? Valdē puellās spectāre volō! Puellās formōsās . . . et multās!"

Marcus: "Nōn cūrō quis illīc **futūra sit** dummodo Aemiliam videam!"

Sextus: "Āh, dīc nōbīs plūs dē hāc Aemiliā! Estne formōsa?"

Fabius: "Estne iūcunda? Habetne sorōrem? Dīc nōbīs omnia!"

15 Marcus: "Nōlī nūgās loquī! Aemilia tōta pulchra et iūcunda est. Spērō cum eā colloquī priusquam ad Graeciam nāvigāverō. Sī nōn . . ."

Lūcius interpellat: "Graecia?! Graecia!? Nēmō mihi dixit tē mox ad Graeciam abitūrum esse! Dīc mihi quandō **abitūrus sīs**."

Marcus: "Incertus sum quandō **abitūrus sim**, sed brevī tempōre abeundum est. Abeō ut rhētoricae in terrā
20 Dēmosthenis studeam. Sed priusquam abeō, spērō mē Aemiliam spectāre et ab eā spectārī."

Sextus, quī māior nātū quam aliīs est et Ovidiī Nāsōnis amīcus est, cacchinat. "Ita vērō!" inquit. "Sīcut amīcus meus, ille poēta dē rēbus amātōriīs dixit, 'Spectātum venimus, venimus ut spectēmur!' Ovidius bene *scripsit* cūr nōs adulescentēs ad Circum veniāmus!"

Postrīdiē eius noctis, autem, dum amīcī Circō appropinquant, Lūcius, agitātus, multās quaestiōnēs habet. "Dīc
25 mihi quantōs agitātōrēs mox **vīsūrus sim**! Et dīc mihi quae factiō, omnibus certāminibus peractīs, **victūra sit**!"

Marcus: "Tacē," inquit, "frātercule! Mihi magnae rēs hodiē agendae sunt! Aemilia invenienda est!"

Sextus: "Venus," inquit, "tibi faveat! Et tū, Servīlia, Cordum tuum conspexistī?"

Servīlia nihil dīcit, sed ērubescēns turbam exāminat ut Cordum inveniat.

Postquam Marcus abiit ut Aemiliam quaereret, Fabius Sextum rogat: "***Docuit**ne nōs quoque Ovidius tuus
30 quōmodo puellīs placēre possimus?"

Sextus "Ita," inquit, "multa intellegit Ovidius dē hīs rēbus. Et libenter tē item docēbō. Sed ecce ... tubās audiō. Lūdī incipiunt."

🔊 VERBA ŪTENDA

agitātor, -ōris m. driver, charioteer

amātōrius, -a, -um loving, pertaining to love, amatory

cacchinō (1) laugh loudly

***cēdō, cēdere, cessī, cessum* go, walk; (+ dat.) yield to, give way to; succeed; allow, grant**

***certāmen, certāminis* n. contest, race**

circensis, circense pertaining to the *circus*

circus, circī m. racetrack, circle

Dēmosthenēs, -is m. Demosthenes, a famous Greek orator of the 4th century B.C.

dummodo provided that, as long as

ērubescō, ērubescere, ērubuī blush

exāminō (1) examine

factiō, -iōnis f. team

faveō, favēre, fāvī, fautum (+ dat.) favor, support, cheer for

***formōsus, -a, -um* beautiful, handsome, pretty**

frāterculus, -ī m. little brother

***incertus, -a, -um* uncertain, illegitimate**

intellegens, intellegentis intelligent

interpellō (1) interrupt

***iūcundus, -a, -um* pleasant, agreeable**

laetitia, -ae f. happiness

***libens, libentis* willing, cheerful**; *libenter* willingly

Nāsō, Nāsōnis m. Naso, Ovid's cognomen

nātū by birth

naufragium, -iī n. crash, wreck (literally, "shipwreck")

nāvigō (1) sail

nūgae, -ārum f. nonsense

peragō, peragere, perēgī, peractum finish, complete

***postrīdiē* (+ gen.) the next day**

***praetor, -tōris* m. praetor, judge**

***prīdiē* (+ gen.) on the day before**

quaestiō, -iōnis f. question

Rōmae at Rome

spectātum in order to see

sponsiō, -iōnis f. bet, wager

suffrāgātor, -ōris m. voter

temporibus cēdunt "they yield to circumstances"

***tuba, -ae* f. horn, trumpet**

***turba, -ae* f. disorder, confusion; crowd**

venetus, -a, -um blue

POSTQUAM LĒGISTĪ

Answer all of the following questions in English. Also answer in Latin if the question is followed by (L).

1. Why do each of the following individuals go to the races: Aelius, Lucius, Marcus, Servilius (and Caecilia), and Servilia? (L)
2. What U.S. event might be the equivalent of the Roman races?
3. What team does Aelius support? (L)
4. Who is Aemilia, and what does Marcus say about her? (L)
5. What poet is Sextus friends with? What observation does this poet make about the races? (L)
6. How does Sextus know that the games are about to begin? (L)

Grammatica A

Indirect Questions: Time After

As you read *Lectiō Prīma*, you saw how Latin uses the future active participle + present subjunctive forms of *sum* in indirect questions to express **time after** the main verb in primary sequence:

Fortasse rogās cūr adventūrī sint?   Perhaps you ask why they are going to go.

You would think there would be a special future subjunctive for such cases, but none exists. Instead, Latin resorts once more to periphrasis, or "around speak," to get "around" the problem. (For more information on periphrasis, see the *Angulus Grammaticus* in Chapter 30.)

All of the examples in *Lectiō Prīma* were in primary sequence. You will see examples of the FAP + *essem, essēs, esset*, etc., which is in secondary sequence, in *Lectiō Secunda*.

With these two forms you now know the entire sequence of tenses:

IF THE MAIN VERB IS ...	USE THIS SUBJUNCTIVE TENSE	TO SHOW
Primary Sequence		
Present	present	near time
Future	perfect	time before
Future Perfect	**FAP + *sim, sīs, sit*, etc.**	time after
Secondary Sequence		
Imperfect	imperfect	near time
Perfect	pluperfect	time before
Pluperfect	**FAP + *essem, essēs, esset*, etc.**	time after

The Perfect in Primary Sequence

Here are the two indirect questions in *Lectiō Prīma* where perfect verbs are followed by subjunctives in primary, rather than secondary, sequence:

*Ovidius bene **scrīpsit** cūr nōs adulescentēs ad Circum **veniāmus**!*
*Ovidius tuus nōs **docuit** quōmodo puellīs placēre **possimus**.*

These present subjunctives would seem to break the rules of sequence, until you know about what is sometimes called the **present perfect**. This is, simply put, a verb in the perfect tense that stresses the present result of its action. Compare these two purposes clauses introduced by perfect indicative verbs:

Primary Sequence	Secondary Sequence
Advēnī ut tē **adiuvem**.	*Advēnī ut tē* **adiuvārem**.
I came to save you. (in the present)	I came to save you. (in the past)
(Stresses that the saving is not yet accomplished.)	(Stresses that the saving has happened.)

Yet another case of how precise Latin can be!

EXERCEĀMUS!

35-2 From Time Before to Time After: Primary Sequence

Change the time of the subjunctive in each of the following sentences from time before to time after the main verb. Follow the model. This entails using the FAP + *sim, sīs, sit,* etc. Follow the model.

→ Fortasse rogās cūr servī advēnerint?
Fortasse rogās cūr servī adventūrī sint?

1. Intellegitisne quae puellae ad Circum advēnerint?

2. Nōn cūrō quae puellae illīc fuerint.

3. Dīcit mihi quandō abīveris.

4. Incertī sumus quandō Marcus Aemiliam quaesīverit.

5. Rogat quandō ad lūdōs advēnerimus.

6. Scīmus quī agitātor vīcerit.

Lectiō Secunda

Antequam Legis

In order to follow the race that occurs in this reading, you should know the parts of a race track. The chariots started in the starting gates (*carcerēs*, literally, "prisons") at the squared end of the track. They did six and a half laps (*sex et dīmidium spatia*) around the central barrier (*spīna*), coming as close to the turning posts (*mētae*) as they could. Each lap was counted by hoisting a dolphin and an egg at the appropriate end of the *spīna*. The finish line (*calx*) was near the rounded end of the track, where there was also the victor's gate (*porta triumphālis*), by which the winning chariot left. As you read about the race, remember that the charioteers tied the reins around their waists and steered by leaning, leaving their hands free for other things such as a whip. A significant amount of skill was required for this.

The names of the drivers and the horses in this *lectiō* are based on historical evidence, although taken from a rather broad span of time.

- Diocles, who drove for the Reds (*Russātī*), was a Spaniard of the 2nd century A.D. An inscription tells us that he won 1,462 times in his 4,257 starts before his death at age 42.

- A certain Scorpus who drove for the Greens is mentioned in an epigram of Martial (10.53) as having died aged 26. It could be a dangerous life. The Scorpus in our story is a member of the Whites (*Albī*).

- The epitaph of Fuscus tells us he won his very first race driving for the Greens (*Prasinī*) and claims he was the first charioteer ever to be victorious in his first race. Yet he died c. 35 A.D. at age 24. We have taken the liberty of making this race his first victory.

- Crescens was from Mauretania and had a nine-year career driving for the Blues (*Venetī*), ending in his death at age 22—meaning that he had begun when he was 13 years old.

Here is a chart of the drivers and teams in the *lectiō.*

Agitātor	*Factiō*
Scorpus	Albī (Whites)
Crescēns	Venetī (Blues)
Dioclēs	Russātī (Reds)
Fuscus	Prasinī (Greens)

You will also find in the *lectiō* the names of Fuscus' four horses: *Candidus, Celer, Cursor* and *Incitātus.* We know the names of hundreds of Roman race horses. See if you can translate the names of Fuscus' horses into appropriately-modern-sounding equivalents. As you read about the race, in addition to the FAP + *essem, essēs, esset* (marked in **bold**), watch out for one more new grammar feature.

Supines

Gemma

Historical Present
Latin, like English, will often slip into the present tense in the middle of a narrative set in the past. This is done for stylistic vividness and immediacy. See if you can find examples of this in *Lectiō Secunda.*

The supine is a verbal noun that looks like the P³ of the verb, but it is only used in the accusative and ablative singular with 4th declension endings. These forms are marked in ***bold italics*** in the *lectiō.* Translate them as infinitives.

EXERCEĀMUS!

35-3 **Off to the Races!**

As you read, write out in English a description of the race as if you were announcing it to fans at a modern track: "They're off! And it's X in the lead, with Y closing fast." *Et cetera.*

🔊 NAUFRAGIUM

Omnibus spectantibus, decem quadrīgae carcerēs intrāvērunt. Inter decem agitātōrēs quattuor praeclārī sunt—Dioclēs Russātae Factiōnis, Fuscus Prasinae, Crescens Venetae, et Scorpus Albae. Ille Fuscus iuvenis est—et hoc eī prīmum certāmen est.

Horribile Vīsū!—Naufragium Factum Est

5   Tubae fortiter flēvērunt et nuntius in mediō Circō clāmāvit: "Attendite omnēs. Augustus noster hōs lūdōs nōbīs libenter dedit ut urbs omnis Tiberium, lēgātum et prīvignum Augustī, laudet. Lūdī incipiant!" Tuba fremuit et quisque spectātor, victōriam spērāns, agitātōrem et equōs
10 hortātus est.

Tunc ēditor lūdōrum stetit et mappam dīmīsit ut certāmen inciperet. Scorpus prīmus est et Aelius, quī Venetīs favet, fortiter clāmāvit.

Per quinque spatia Scorpus prīmus est sed aliī prope eum sunt. Nēmō, neque agitātor neque spectātor, scīvit
15 quis victor **futūrus esset**. Tunc, quadrīgīs mētam praetereuntibus, rotae Crescentis tam fortiter spīnam tetigērunt ut quadrīga cursum āmittere inciperet.

Lūcius, haec intuēns, Marcum rogāvit quid **ēventūrum esset**, sed, priusquam Marcus respondēre potuit—horribile ***vīsū***!—naufragium factum est.

Servī et medicī ad quadrīgās fractās, inter quās Crescentis quadrīga erat, ***adiuvātum*** ruērunt, nescientēs utrum
20 agitātōrēs vīvī aut mortuī **futūrī essent**. Aelius, gemēns et pecūniam suam āmissam aestimāns, nescīvit quid Liciniae **dictūrus esset**.

Intereā octō quadrīgae supersunt et equī quam celerrimē
currunt. Mox, sex ōva et sex delphīnī in spīnā stant. Fuscus,
25 equōs suōs hortāns, clāmat: "Currite, amīcī! Currite! Age,
Candide, agite Celer et Cursor! Nōlīte cēdere! Age, mī
Incitāte!"

Equī strēnuē labōrant et—mīrābile **dictū**—prīmī ad cal-
cem veniunt. Fuscus, iuvenis, victor in prīmō certāmine suō
30 factus est et, palmā receptā, per portam triumphālem
quadrīgam ornātam lavre is ēgit.

Victōria!

Sed Fuscus nōn hodiē sōlus victor est. Marcus Aemiliam invēnit et Fabius, quem Sextus bene docuerat, duās
puellās iūcundās et pulcherrimās item cognōverat. Servīlia quoque victrix erat quod Cordum suum conspexerat. Ut
Vergilius dīcit: "Amor vincit omnia; et nōs cēdāmus amōrī." Vīsō naufragiō, Lūcius laetus domum prōgrediēbātur.
35 Servīlius et Caecilia, spectātī ā cīvibus multīs, laetī fīlium sequēbantur sed māiōre cum dignitāte. Miser Aelius,
autem, Venetīs vīctīs, et multīs nummīs āmissīs, domum lentē ambulābat.

🔊 VERBA ŪTENDA

aestimō (1) consider,
estimate
agitātor, -tōris m. driver,
chariot eer
albus, -a, -um white
attendō, attendere, attendī,
attentum listen carefully
augustus, -a, -um revered;
Augustus, "the revered
one," a title of Octavian
calx, calcis f. goal
candidus, -a, -um dazzling
white; bright
carcer, carceris m. starting
gate
cēdō, cēdere, cessī, cessum
go, walk; (+ dat.) yield
to, give way to;
succeed; allow, grant
certāmen, certāminis n.
contest, race
circus, circī m. racetrack
cognōverat "He had gotten
to know," remember that
the perfect form
cognōvī = present and
cognōveram = simple past
cursor, cursōris m. runner
cursum āmittere to go
off course

cursus, -ūs m. course,
voyage, journey, race,
march, career
delphīnus, -ī m. dolphin
dignitās, -tātis f. worthi-
ness, merit, dignity,
office, honor
dīmittō, dīmittere, dīmīsī,
dīmissum let go, send
out, dismiss, release,
divorce
doceō, docēre, docuī,
doctum teach, show
ēditor lūdōrum "the giver of
the games," i.e., the public official in charge of
the games
ēveniō, ēvenīre, ēvēnī,
ēventum come about;
happen
factiō, -iōnis f. team
faveō, favēre, fāvī, fautum
(+ dat.) favor, support,
cheer for
fleō, flēre, flēvī, flētum weep,
cry
gemō, gemere, gemuī,
gemitum moan, groan
horribilis, horribile horrible
incertus, -a, -um uncertain

incitō (1) incite; spur on
intereā meanwhile item
similarily, likewise
iūcundus, -a, -um
pleasant, agreeable
laurevs, -ī m. laurel
lēgātus, -ī m. lieutenant;
legate
libens, libentis willing,
cheerful; *libenter*
willingly, freely
mappa, -ae f. starting flag
medicus, -ī m. doctor,
physician
mēta, -ae f. turning post
mīrābilis, mīrābile
wondrous
miser, misera, miserum
wretched, miserable
naufragium, -iī n. crash
(of chariots), wreck
palma, -ae f. palm
(of victory)
praetereō, praeterīre,
praeterīvī/praeteriī,
praeteritum go past;
escape notice of;
neglect
prasinus, -a, -um green
prīvignus, -ī m. stepson

quadrīga, -ae f. chariot with
four horses
rota, -ae f. wheel
russātus, -a, -um red
spatium, -iī n. lap
spīna, -ae f. spine of the
circus
supersum, superesse,
superfuī be left over,
survive, have
strength (for)
Tiberius, -ī m. Tiberius,
Augustus' stepson,
adopted son and
successor
triumphālis, triumphāle
triumphal
tuba, -ae f. horn,
trumpet
utrum whether
venetus, -a, -um blue
Vergilius, -iī Vergil,
the poet
victor, victōris m. victor,
conqueror
victōria, -ae f. victory
victrix, victrīcis f. female
conquerer
vīvus, -a, -um alive,
living

POSTQUAM LĒGISTĪ

Answer all of the following questions in English. Also answer in Latin if the question is followed by (L).

1. How many chariots ran the race? Which one won? (L)
2. What is the signal for the race to start? (L)
3. Whose chariot crashed? (L)
4. Describe how the victorious *agitātor* is honored at the end of the race. (L)
5. How can Marcus, Fabius, and Servilia all be considered victors in this race? Why is Aelius not a winner?
6. Describe your reactions to a Roman chariot race.

Grammatica B

Supines

Like the infinitive, the Latin supine is a verbal noun. Although there is no equivalent to a supine in English, the Latin supine is easy to recognize and to translate. Here are a few tips about supines:

- The supine is based on the perfect passive participle of the verb.
- The supine belongs to the 4th declension.
- The supine appears only in the accusative and ablative cases.
- The supine is translated into English like an infinitive.

Here, then, are some sample supines:

audītum, audītū	to hear	*ductum, ductū*	to lead
clāmātum, clāmātū	to shout	*secūtum, secūtū*	to follow

Notā Bene:

- The ablative supine is used only with an adjective:

*mīrābile **dictū***	wonderous **to say**
*horribile **vīsū***	horrible **to see**

- The accusative supine is used only after a verb of motion to express purpose:

*Servī et medicī **adiuvātum** ruērunt.*	The slaves and medics rushed **to help**.
*Omnēs hī iuvenēs **spectātum** vēnerant.*	All these young people had come **to watch**.

- The accusative supine is the fourth way you have learned to express purpose in Latin.

supine	*Omnēs hī iuvenēs **spectātum** vēnerant.*
purpose clause	*Omnēs hī iuvenēs vēnerant **ut spectārent**.*
ad + gerund(ive)	*Omnēs hī iuvenēs vēnerant **ad spectandum**.*
gerund(ive) + *causā* or *grātiā*	*Omnēs hī iuvenēs vēnerant **spectandī causā**.*

All four of these sentences say exactly the same thing: "All these young people had come **(in order) to look**."

Now go back and find the supines in *Lectiō Prīma*.

EXERCEĀMUS!

35-4 Making Supines

Insert supines for each of the verbs listed below into the model sentence. Then translate the sentences you have made into English. Follow the model.

→ adiuvō Multī **adiūtum** ruērunt. Many rushed to help.

1. vincō   3. audiō   5. fīniō

2. spectō   4. respondeō   6. capiō

Mōrēs Rōmānī

Colors and Dyes in the Roman Empire

The chariot teams of ancient Rome have introduced you to four Latin color words (*prasinus, albus, russus,* and *venetus*). You have already encountered a few others, such as *niger* and *candidus.* Do you, for example, remember the name and color of Lucius' dog?

Tyrian purple, made from a type of sea snail (*mūrex, mūricis* m.), was so expensive to manufacture that it became the color of kings. Purple was also, you may remember, the color used on the *toga praetexta.*

Brightly colored clothing was often a sign of a luxury in the ancient world. The average person wore plainer clothing colored with vegetable dyes.

There was a wide range of colors and hues available for dyeing, but it is often difficult to determine the exact hue referred to by the Latin words for various colors.

Mūrex

Latīna Hodierna

Colōrēs Latīnī

"Purple" is the only English color word derived directly from Latin (*purpureus, -a, -um*), but many colors appear in various English words, especially in technical, scientific contexts. If you don't know the meaning of one of these English derivatives, look it up in the dictionary.

Latin Color Word	English Derivatives
YELLOW-ORANGE HUES	
flāvus, -a, -um	flavescent, flavin
lūteus, -a, -um	lutein, luteal
RED HUES	
ruber, rubra, rubrum	ruby, rubefacient, rubella, rubescent
BLUE HUES	
caeruleus, -a, -um (sky blue)	cerulean
cȳaneus, -a, -um (greenish blue)	cyanide, cyanogen, cyan
GREEN HUES	
prasinus, -a, -um	praseodymium
viridis, viride	virid, viridescent, viridity
BLACK HUES	
āter, ātra, ātrum	atrabilious
niger, nigra, nigrum	negritude, Negroid, Niger
WHITE HUES	
albus, -a, -um	albescent, albino, albumen
candidus, -a, -um	candid, candidate

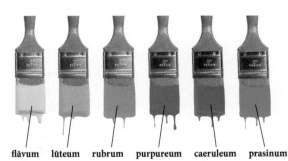

flāvum   lūteum   rubrum   purpureum   caeruleum   prasinum

Colōrēs

Orbis Terrārum Rōmānus

Circus Maximus

Located in the valley between the Palatine and Aventine Hills in Rome, the *Circus Maximus* is one of the earliest race tracks (*circus, -ī* m.) in the city. It is traditionally said that the area was first used for racing events by Tarquinius Priscus, the fifth king of Rome, in the 6th century B.C.

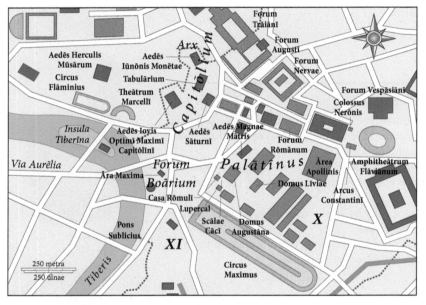

Circum Maximum invenīre potesne?

Originally there were no permanent seats or racing structures. The first permanent *carcerēs* were built in 329 B.C. By the time of Augustus, the structure included the permanent race course, *spīna*, eggs, dolphins, etc., as described in our story. The circus was primarily used for horse races, but could also be used for other events, including gladiatorial contests and animal hunts. The Circus Maximus was so large that, at one time, it probably was capable of accommodating 250,000 spectators!

Although little remains of the actual Circus Maximus, we are fortunate to have some comments by ancient Romans about the races they witnessed, including an epigram Martial wrote in memory of the historical charioteer Scorpus. The poem is written as an epitaph, in which the dead Scorpus talks directly to the city of Rome (apostrophe) and explains how envious Fate counted his victories (*palmās*) instead of his years and decided it was time to take him at the age of 27!

Circus Maximus et Palātium Hodiē

Circus Maximus Hodiē

Cursus Rōmānus in Hollywood: Charlton Heston in Ben-Hur (1959)

Here is a prose version of Martial's poem:

> Ego sum ille Scorpus, glōria clāmōsī Circī, et, Ō Rōma, ego fuī tuī
> plausūs et tuae dēliciae brevēs. Ego sum ille Scorpus quem invida Lachesis,
> crēdēns esse senem, rapuit annō vīcensimō septimō, dum Lachesis numerat
> palmās [victōriae].

> Martial *Epigrammata* 10.53

Now read a few lines from Ovid's *Ars Amātōria* (finished c. 1 B.C.), in which the poet
offers advice about how to flirt at the circus.

> Nōlī fugere certāmen equōrum nōbilium! Circus, plēnus populī, commoda
> multa habet. Nihil opus est digitīs per quōs arcāna loquāris; nec nota tibi
> accipienda est per nūtūs. Sedētō proximus ā dominā, nullō prohibente.
> Iunge tuum latus laterī eius usque quā potes.

> Ovid *Ars Amātōria* 1.135-140

🔊 VERBA ŪTENDA

arcānus, -a, -um secret
certāmen, ministo
certāmen, certāminis
clāmōsus, -a, -um noisy
commodus, -a, -um
  convenient
dēliciae, -ārum f. pl. delight,
  darling
digitus, -ī m. finger

dum while; the idea is
  that while Lachesis
  was totaling up
  Scorpus' victories, she
  thought he
  must be old
invidus, -a, -um envious
iungō, -ere, iunxī, iunctum
  join

Lachesis, -is f. the Fate who
  cut off one's life thread,
  causing death
latus, lateris n. side
nota, -ae f. sign, word
nūtus, nūtūs m. nod
opus est (+ dat.) there is
  need for
palma, -ae f. palm (of victory)

plausus, -ūs applause,
  recipient of applause;
  Scorpus is saying he was
  Rome's applause (pl.)
  and its darling
prohibeō, -ēre, -uī, -itum forbid
quā where, in so far as
usque quā as far as

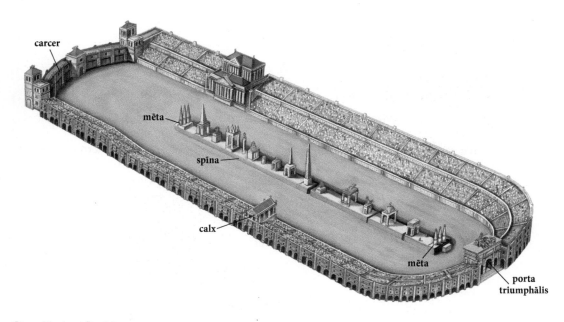

carcer

mēta

spīna

calx

mēta

porta
triumphālis

Circus Maximus Restitūtus

QUID PUTĀS?

1. Compare the career of Scorpus in Martial's poem to that of a modern athlete.
2. How would you evaluate Ovid's advice to lovers attending the races?
3. What does the size of the Circus Maximus suggest to you about the role of sports in Roman society?
4. Compare the use of colors in Roman chariot races to modern athletic practices.
5. Use your Latin to determine what color word is the origin of each of following English words: cyanide, rubric, album, flavin, caerulean, and viridian. With the help of a dictionary, explain the relationship between this color and the meaning of the English word.

EXERCEĀMUS!

35-5 Scrībāmus

Use the *Verba Ūtenda* and the information in *Lectiō Secunda* to answer the following questions in Latin. A word can be used more than once. Follow the model.

Quaestiō

→ In quā urbe Circus Maximus est?

Responsum

*Circus Maximus in urbe **Rōmae** est.*

1. Quis lūdōs dat?
2. Quot spatia equī currunt?
3. Quae nōmina factiōnibus sunt?
4. Quis quadrīgam agit?
5. Quid equī trahunt?
6. Quot equōs quisque agitātor habet?
7. Quid est in mediō Circō?
8. Ubi quadrīgae lūdum incipiunt?
9. Per quam portam agitātor victor ē Circō exit?

🔊 VERBA ŪTENDA

agitātor, -ōris m. driver, charioteer
Albī Whites
carcer, carceris m. prison; starting gate
duo two
ēditor lūdōrum, ēditōris lūdōrum m. organizer of the games

factiō, -iōnis f. team
mēta, -ae f. turning post
porta triumphālis f. triumphal gate
Prasinī Greens
Russātī Reds
quadrīga, -ae f. chariot
quattuor four

sex et dīmidium six and a half
spīna, -ae f. thorn; spine; spine of the circus
Venetī Blues

35-6 Colloquāmur

Take turns with a classmate asking and answering the questions in Exercise 35-5.

35-7 Verba Discenda

Answer the following questions about the *Verba Discenda* in this chapter. A word can be used more than once. Follow the model.

→ Which comes first chronologically, *postrīdiē* or *prīdiē? prīdiē*

1. This adjective is a synonym for *libens*:

2. This adjective is a synonym for *laetus:*

3. The opposite of *mortuus*:

4. This verb can be used in reference to both a messenger and a spouse:

5. This word refers to a musical instrument:

6. These two words come from the Latin verb *vincō*:

7. Find three concrete nouns in this list (i.e., words that refer to something you can touch).

8. Now find five abstract nouns in this list (i.e., words that refer to something you cannot touch).

9. These two words refer to something you can win:

10. These four words are adverbs:

🔊 VERBA DISCENDA

cēdō, cēdere, cessī, cessum go, walk; (+ dat.) yield to; give way to; succeed; allow, grant [cede, recess]

certāmen, certāminis n. contest, race

cursus, -ūs m. course; voyage, journey; race; march; career

dignitās, -tātis f. worthiness, merit, dignity, office, honor

dīmittō, dīmittere, dīmīsī, dīmissum send out; dismiss; release; divorce [dismissal]

doceō, docēre, docuī, doctum teach; show [docent, docile]

ēveniō, ēvenīre, ēvēnī, ēventum come about; happen [eventual]

formōsus, -a, -um beautiful, handsome, pretty

incertus, -a, -um uncertain, illegitimate [incertitude]

intereā meanwhile

item similarly, likewise

iūcundus, -a, -um pleasant, agreeable

libens, libentis willing, cheerful

miser, misera, miserum wretched, miserable

ornō (1) adorn, decorate [ornate]

postrīdiē the next day

praetereō, praeterīre, praeterīvī/praeteriī, praeteritum go past; escape notice of; neglect

praetor, praetōris m. judge, praetor

prīdiē on the day before

supersum, superesse, superfuī be left over; survive; have strength (for)

tuba, -ae f. horn, trumpet

turba, -ae f. disorder, confusion; crowd [turbid]

victor, victōris m. victor, conqueror

victōria, -ae f. victory [victorious]

vīvus, -a, -um alive, living [vivisection]

Angulus Grammaticus

Is There Really Any More to Say about Questions?

Now that you have learned the difference between direct and indirect questions, it might be useful to see an overview of ways to ask questions in Latin. First of all, remember that the Romans had no question marks, so the only way they could indicate questions in writing was by using **interrogative** words. You have learned a great number of these words already.

Some interrogative words create a question of the whole sentence:

*Perferēmus**ne** Catilīnam?*	Shall we tolerate Catiline?
***Num** Catilīnam perferēmus?*	We won't tolerate Catiline, will we?
***Nōnne** Catilīnam perferēmus?*	We will tolerate Catiline, won't we?

Other interrogative words offer choices or options:

*Perferēmus**ne** Catilīnam **an nōn?***	Shall we tolerate Catiline or not?
Utrum** perferēmus Catilīnam **an nōn?	Should we tolerate Catiline or not?
*Perferēmus Catilīnam **an nōn?***	Should we tolerate Catiline or not?

Other interrogative words ask for information:

***Quis** Catilīnam perferet?*	Who will tolerate Catiline?
***Cūr** Catilīnam perferēmus?*	Why will we tolerate Catiline?
***Quōusque** Catilīnam perferēmus?*	How long will we tolerate Catiline?

A direct question can be asked in the subjunctive, not so much to seek information, but to state a fact more strongly. This is sometimes called the **deliberative subjunctive**. It can also be considered a **rhetorical question**, i.e., a question which does not expect an answer.

Quis Catilīnam perferat?	Who would tolerate Catiline?
(Nēmō perfert.)	(No one would.)

Finally, a direct question can be introduced by *an* in order to suggest an absurdity. This is how Cicero actually asks this question in his first speech against Catiline:

An vērō Catilīnam perferēmus?	Are we really going to tolerate Catiline?

Any of these questions could be made indirect, of course, with the addition of a "head" verb as the main verb in the sentence.

Rogās utrum Catilīnam perferāmus.	You ask whether we are going to tolerate Catiline.

36

Ad Graeciam

Lectiō Prīma

Antequam Legis

Lectiō Prīma finds Lucius back in school the day after the races. He is day-dreaming and worried about his brother's imminent departure for Greece. Lucius' game with the fly is based on an incident in Suetonius' *Life of Domitian*. Apparently the emperor enjoyed stabbing flies with a sharpened stylus!

As you read about Lucius going home from school and about Marcus' journey, watch out for the following new forms and expressions.

Nē + Perfect Subjunctive

Just when you thought there could not possibly be more ways to give a command in Latin, you discover yet one more.

Nē + perfect subjunctive	Don't …!
Nē abieris!	Don't go away!

You will find several examples of this in *Lectiō Prīma*!

Cum Clauses

You have already seen *cum* used as a conjunction with the indicative to mean "when" or "whenever." In this chapter you will see it used with the subjunctive to mean "when," "since/because," or "although." To translate *cum* in this chapter:

Cum	+ indicative	when, whenever
	+ subjunctive	when, since, because, although

Notā Bene:

- If the word *tamen* (nevertheless) appears later in the sentence, translate the *cum* as "although."

All of the verbs in *cum* clauses are marked in **bold** in *Lectiō Prīma*.

Nāvis Rōmāna

GRAMMATICA
Nē + Perfect Subjunctive
Cum Clauses
Ablative of Separation and Ablative of Place from Which
Location and Direction in Latin
More *Cum* Clauses
Interjections!

MŌRĒS RŌMĀNĪ
Vōta Rōmāna

ORBIS TERRĀRUM RŌMĀNUS
Athēnae

LATĪNA HODIERNA
Acadēmīa Athēnaea

ANGULUS GRAMMATICUS
Translating and Using *Cum*

LECTIŌNĒS:
NĒ ABIERIS!
and
SĪ VALĒS, VALEŌ

Lucius is already missing his brother Marcus, who is about to leave for Greece to study with a rhetor. Some time later Lucius reads Marcus' first letter home from Greece.

Ablative of Separation

Several Latin words take an ablative without a preposition to show separation. These include:

careō, carēre, caruī, caritum be without, miss, lose
līberō (1) release, free (from)

pecūniā *carēre*	to be without money
dolōre *liberāre*	to free from pain

Watch for several examples in *Lectiō Prīma*.

Location and Direction in Latin

Latin does not always use prepositions with place names to indicate direction and location. Here are some examples:

Place	From	To	At/In
home	*domō*	*domum*	*domī*
Athens	*Athēnīs*	*Athēnās*	*Athēnīs*
Rome	*Rōmā*	Rōmam	*Rōmae*
Baiae	Bāiae	*Bāiās*	Bāiīs
Thebes	Thēbae	*Thēbās*	Thēbārum
the country	rūre	*rūs*	rūrī

The words marked in *italics* in this chart also appear in *Lectiō Prīma*, where they are similarly marked. After you read, we will explain more about how this works.

EXERCEĀMUS!

36-1 *Cum* **Indicative vs.** *Cum* **Subjunctive**

As you read, make a line-by-line list of the verbs used in *cum* clauses and indicate whether each is indicative or subjunctive. Then translate the verb with "when," "whenever," "since," "because," or "although" according to the chart and context. Follow the model.

Line	Verb	Mood	Translation
→ 4	amet	subjunctive	since he loves

Thēseus et Mīnōtaurus

NĒ ABIERIS!

Diēs proximus calidus est et Lūcius in lūdō Chīrōnis sedēbat nōn lūdum floccī faciēns, sed dē abitū appropinquantī frātris māiōris cōgitāns. Marcus iter *Athēnās* factūrus est et Lūcius, cum frātrem valdē **amet**, tristis est. Vōcem Chīrōnis audiēbat, sed vōcī nōn oper-
5 am dabat. Subitō musca prope caput puerī volāvit. Īratus, puer mus-cam stīlō necāre cōnābātur, sed musca, celerior quam puer, fūgit. Ecce! Bis, ter, quater, puer muscam necāre cōnātus est. Bis, ter, quater, musca fūgit. Lūcius opīnātus est muscam eum irrīdēre.

Puer muscam stīlō necāre cōnātur.

Post lūdum Lūcius *domum* quam celerrimē cucurrit. Marcum in peristȳliō invēnit et frātrēs collocūtī sunt.
10 Lūcius "Cūr," inquit, "tibi abeundum est? Cūr *Rōmae* remanēre nōn potes? Cum tū nōn *domī* **es**, tristis fīō. Cum *rūs* **īs**, infēlix sum et cum nūper *Bāiās* iter **fēcissēs**, infēlix eram. Heu! Tē absente socius sōlus mihi paedagōgus Hermēs est et paedagōgī malī sociī sunt! Soror et māter sōlum dē nuptiīs cōgitant. Pater sōlum dē praetūrā cūrat. Vae miserō mihi! Nē abieris!"
Marcus "Aha!" inquit. "Estō placidus, mī frātercule. Necesse est ut *Rōmā* abeam. Bene scīs mihi abeundum esse
15 ut *Athēnīs* rhētoricae atque philosophiae studeam. Ubi terrārum locum magis idōneum studendō invenīre possum?

Nē tē perturbāveris. Numquam sociīs in lūdō Chīrōnis carēbis. Praetereā, mehercle, tibi epistulās mittam et omnia quae vīderō tibi narrābō! Cum ad Crētam nāvigābō ut Labyrinthum Mīnōtaurī videam, omnia in epistulā narrābō. Cum *Thēbās* īverō, ubi Oedipus rex erat, tibi dōnum emam."

Lūcius "Eu!" inquit, "nōn tibi crēdō. Cum aliquis *domō* **abitūrus est**, semper tālia dīcit. Sed numquam scrībet,
20 nihil mittet!"

Marcus, rīdēns, "Frāatercule," inquit, "tē cūrā līberā! Cum forīs **sim**, numquam tamen tuī oblīviscar! Tibi id polliceor! Mihi, tamen, abeundum est! Cum *Athēnīs* **redierō** quaestūram petam et tunc mihi optimē ēloquendum erit. Mementō! Cum pater adulescens **esset**, *Athēnās* iter fēcit. Nunc, cum adulescens et ego **sim**, iter facere dēbeō. Ōlim cum adulescens eris, tibi *Athēnās* eundum erit!"

25 Tālibus dictīs, Marcus, Lūcium amplexus, caput eius fricat. Lūcius, rīdēns, "Hau! Dēsiste!" clāmat, "Nē id fēceris!"

Marcus "Fīat! Pax!" respondet. "Iēiūnus sum. Eia age! Eāmus ad culīnam ut servī nōbīs aliquid cibī inveniant!"

🔊 VERBA ŪTENDA

abitus, -ūs m. departure

age, agite! come! well! all right!

aha ha! (in reproof, amusement or denial)

amplector, amplectī, amplexus sum embrace

Athēnae, Athēnārum f. pl. Athens, a city in Greece

Bāiae, Bāiārum m. pl. Baiae, a resort town near Naples, Italy

bis two times, twice

caput, capitis n. **head; master**

careō, carēre, caruī, caritum (+ abl.) **lack, be without, lose**

Crēta, -ae f. Crete, an island in the eastern Mediterranean

cūra, -ae f. **worry, concern, care, anxiety**

dēsistō, dēsistere, dēstitī, dēstitum stop, cease, desist

eia!/heia! ah! ha! good! yes, indeed!; (+ *age*) quick! come on then!

eu! fine! great! (sometimes ironic)

fīat Translate here as "Okay!"

floccus, -ī m. tuft of wool; *nōn floccī facere* to consider something of no importance

frāterculus, -ī m. little brother

fricō, fricāre, fricuī, frictum rub

heu! (often + acc.) oh! (in pain or dismay)

idōneus, -a, -um (+ dat.) **fit, suitable**

infēlix, infēlīcis unhappy, unfortunate

irrīdeō, irrīdēre, irrīsī, irrīsum laugh at, mock

Labyrinthus, -ī m. maze, labyrinth, especially the one in Crete in which the Minotaur was imprisoned

līberō (1) (+ abl.) **free, free from**

mehercle by Hercules! (as an oath to express strong feeling)

Mīnōtaurus, -ī m. half-human, half-bull imprisoned in the Labyrinth

musca, -ae f. fly

nuptiae, -ārum f. pl. marriage

oblīviscor, oblīviscī, oblītus sum (+ gen.) **forget**

Oedipus, -ī m. Oedipus, king of Thebes

opera, -ae f. **work, pain, labor;** *operam dare* "to pay attention to"

pax! quiet! enough!

philosophia, -ae f. philosophy

placidus, -a, -um calm

praetūra, -ae f. **praetorship, judgeship**

quaestūra, -ae f. **quaestorship, treasurer**

quater four times

redeō, redīre, redīvī/rediī, reditum go back, return

remaneō, remanēre, remansī remain

rūs, rūris n. **country, country estate; abroad**

socius, -iī m. **partner, companion**

stīlus, -ī m. pen

Tē cūrā līberā! "Don't worry!" Literally, "free yourself from care!"

ter three times

Thēbae, Thēbārum f. pl. Thebes, a city in Greece

vae! (often + dat.) woe! (in pain or dread)

volō (1) **fly; hasten**

POSTQUAM LĒGISTĪ

Answer all of the following questions in English. Also answer in Latin if the question is followed by (L).

1. Where is Lucius, and what is he doing, as this *lectiō* begins? What is he thinking about? (L)
2. Why does Lucius not want Marcus to leave Rome? (L)
3. Why does Marcus think that Greece is the best place for him to study? What things does Marcus promise Lucius? Does Lucius believe him? Why or why not?
4. What does Marcus plan to do after he returns from Greece? (L)
5. Where do the brothers go at the end of the *lectiō*? Why? (L)
6. Describe the relationship between Lucius and Marcus. How does it compare to the relationship between brothers you have known?

Grammatica A

Nē + Perfect Subjunctive

Here are the examples of *nē* + perfect subjunctive in *Lectiō Prīma*.

Nē abieris!	Don't go away!
Nē tē perturbāveris!	Don't trouble yourself! Don't be worried!
Nē id fēceris!	Don't do that!

Compare these to other types of negative commands you have seen.

Imperative mood	*Nōlī abīre! Nōlīte abīre!*
Hortatory/jussive subjunctive	*Nē abeat! Nē abeant! Nē abeāmus!*
Commanding verb + infinitive	*Vōs nōn abīre iubeō.*
Commanding verb + *ut / nē* + subjunctive	*Imperō vōbīs nē abeātis.*
Fac nē, cūrā nē, cavē nē + noun clauses	*Fac nē abeās! Cavē nē abeās!*

Cum Clauses

As you saw in *Lectiō Prīma*, the subordinate conjunction *cum* is used with both indicative and subjunctive verbs. It is important to pay attention to the mood of these verbs, since that affects how we translate *cum* into English.

Cum	+ indicative	when, whenever
	+ subjunctive	when, since, because, although

Cum + **indicative** gives the actual time something happened or repeatedly happens.

Cum forīs sum, tē in corde meō semper ferō.
   Whenever I am abroad, I always hold you in my heart.
Cum ad Crētam iter fēcerō … omnia narrābō.
   When I will have traveled to Crete … I'll tell you everything.

Cum + **subjunctive** describes the circumstances under which something happened.

> **Cum** *nūper Bāiās iter fēcissēs, infēlix eram.*
> > **When** you recently went to Baiae, I was unhappy.
> *Nunc,* **cum** *adulescens et ego sim, iter facere dēbeō.*
> > Now, **since** I too am a young man, I must make the trip.
> **Cum** *forīs* **sim**, *numquam tamen tuī oblīviscar!*
> > **Although** I am abroad, I will never forget you! (Note the use of *tamen*.)

Ablative of Separation and Ablative of Place from Which

When a verb of motion is used with an ablative prepositional phrase beginning with *ā*, *ab*, *dē*, *ē*, or *ex*, the ablative phrase is called an **ablative of place from which**.

> **Ē Forō** *cucurrit.*
> **Ab Italiā** *nāvigāvit.*

Several Latin verbs that are not verbs of motion also take an ablative, usually without a preposition, to express separation. This ablative is called an **ablative of separation.** Here are the phrases in *Lectiō Prīma* in which an ablative of separation is used:

> *Numquam* **sociīs** *carēbis.*   You will never lack for friends.
> *Tē* **cūrā** *līberā!*   Free yourself from care!

Location and Direction in Latin

Latin uses **case without prepositions** to indicate direction with certain kinds of words:

> the NAMES of **C**ities
> **T**owns
> **S**mall
> **I**slands
> and the two words: **D**omus, *-ī* f. house, home
> **R**ūs, *rūris* n. country

With these **CTSIDR** (pronounced "kitsidder") words:

> **accusative case without a preposition** = motion toward
> **ablative case without a preposition** = motion away from
> **locative case** = location

The **locative case**, you ask? Yes, at one time Latin had a seventh case to indicate location. These case endings only survived in **CTSIDR** words. Locative endings vary according to declension and number, but the rules are fairly simple:

- The locative of plural names looks like the **ablative plural**.

    Bāiīs   at Baiae   *Athēnīs*   at Athens   *Thēbīs*   at Thebes

- The locative of 1st and 2nd declension singular names looks like the **genitive singular**.

    Rōmae   at Rome   *Ostiae*   at Ostia   *domī*   at home

- The locative of 3rd declension singular names looks like either the **ablative** or **dative**.

    Carthāgine or *Carthāginī*   at Carthage   *rūre* or *rūrī* in the country

Notā Bene:

Some forms may be confusing.

Is *Athēnīs* "in Athens" or "from Athens"?
Is *Carthāgine* "in Carthage" or "from Carthage"?

The answers depend upon context. Keep your eye on the verb. A verb of motion indicates that you should translate "from." A non-motion verb indicates "in/at."

Soror mea Carthāgine fūgit et nunc Athēnīs habitat.
My sister fled **from** Carthage and now lives **in** Athens.

Soror mea Athēnīs fūgit et nunc Carthāgine habitat.
My sister fled **from** Athens and now lives **in** Carthage.

EXERCEĀMUS!

36-2 CTSIDR

You will see the following CTSIDR words in *Lectiō Secunda*. Use the CTSIDR rules to determine whether each expresses motion toward, motion away from, or location. Then use the *Verba Ūtenda* to help you translate each word appropriately. Follow the model.

	CTSIDR	Type of Motion	Translation
→	domum (line 1)	motion toward	home

1. Brundisium (line 8);
2. Brundisiō (line 14);
3. Corcȳrae (line 19);
4. Corcȳrā (line 22);
5. Nīcopolin (line 22);
6. Cephallāniam (line 26);
7. Zakynthum (line 26);
8. Corinthī (line 29);
9. Athēnās (line 29);
10. Rōmae (line 30).

Lectiō Secunda

Antequam Legis

Three months have passed since Marcus' conversation with Lucius in *Lectiō Prīma*. Marcus has left for Greece. The wedding of Servilia and Cordus will soon take place. So will the election in which Servilius is running for praetor. When Lucius arrives home from school, he is thrilled to find a letter from his brother describing his journey to Greece. How long did such a journey take? Travel in antiquity was slow and could be made even slower by such things as bad weather, sick animals, or a shift in the wind at sea. It probably took about three weeks for Marcus to get to Athens and the same amount of time for his letter to make its way back to Rome.

As you read *Lectiō Secunda,* follow the route of Marcus' voyage on the map on pg. 483.

More *Cum* Clauses

Lectiō Secunda focuses on the use of imperfect and pluperfect subjunctives in *cum* clauses. Nothing has changed—the subjunctive stresses the events surrounding the main event, rather than fixing the actual time of the events. Subjunctives in *cum* clauses are marked in **bold** in *Lectiō Secunda.*

Indicative
*Cum ad Crētam iter **faciō**, omnia tibi narrō.*
Whenever I make a journey to Crete, I tell you everything.

Subjunctive
*Cum ad Crētam iter **facerem**, dē tē semper cōgitābam.*
When I was making the journey to Crete, I constantly thought about you.
(imperfect subjunctive = time near main verb)

*Cum ad Crētam iter **fēcissem**, Neptūnō vōtum solvī.*
When I had made a journey to Crete, I fulfilled my vow to Neptune.
(pluperfect subjunctive = time before main verb)

Interjections

Lectiō Secunda also highlights interjections, i.e., exclamations or words expressing surprise or emotion like *age* (Well!), *heu* (Oh!), and *eugae* (Terrific!).

EXERCEĀMUS!

36-3 Subjunctive Tense Review

The following subjunctive forms in *cum* clauses are marked in **bold** in *Lectiō Secunda*. Indicate the tense, voice, person, and number of each verb. Follow the model.

Subjunctive	Tense	Voice	Person	Number
→ intrāvisset (line 5)	pluperfect	active	3rd	singular

1. advēnissem (line 8);
2. quaesīvissem (line 9);
3. conscendissem (line 12);
4. dēpositae essent (line 12);
5. possem (line 14);
6. quaereret (line 20);
7. victī essent (line 24);
8. flārent (line 25);
9. nāvigārēmus (line 27);
10. stetissem (line 28)

🔊 SĪ VALĒS, VALEŌ

Lūcius domum cucurrit et servō occurrit.

Servus "Domine," inquit, "ecce epistula ā frātre tuō scripta quae ad nōs modo hodiē advēnit."

Lūcius "Eugae! Da eam mihi," inquit, "et abī! Apage!" Cum Lūcius, epistu-
5 lam tenēns, peristȳlium **intrāvisset**, sēdit et avidē legere incēpit.

"Omnibus salūtem plūrimam dīcit Marcus. Sī valētis, bene est. Ego ipse valeō. Quinque diēs in Graeciā sum et, deīs benevolentibus, salvus sum. Cum per Viam Appiam Brundisium sine difficultāte **advēnissem**, nāvem idōneam invenīre cōnātus sum. Sed, cum dīligenter **quaesīvissem**, bonā fortūnā
10 tamen carēbam. Postrēmō sōla ūna nāvis idōnea vīsa est. Illa nāvis, Amphitrītē nōmine, nāvis mercātōria erat et variās mercēs ad variōs locōs portātūra erat.

Cum nāvem **conscendissem** et meae rēs **dēpositae essent**, in puppī stetī ut melius vidērem. Āere clārō et ventō secundō magister nāvem solvit et Brundisiō abiit. Cum lītora neque Italiae neque Illyriae vidēre **possem**, nūbēs
15 subitō sōlem obscūrāvērunt et ventī fortiōrēs factī sunt. Subitō tempestās magna nāvem hūc et illūc prōpulit. Heu mē! Illō diē, mihi crēdite, Neptūnō vōtum fervidē fēcī!

Mox, Neptūnō adiuvante, mortis metū līberātī sumus et nāvis nōn fracta est. Corcȳrae diēs trēs manēbāmus dōnec tempestās quiēta
20 fieret. Cum Ulixēs Ithacam **quaereret**, regnum rēgis Alcinoī in hāc insulā vīsitāvit.

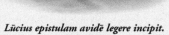

Lūcius epistulam avidē legere incipit.

Magister Corcȳrā abiēns Nīcopolin nāvem gubernāvit et hīc multa negōtia agēbat, dum ego novum oppidum Augustī, Nīcopolin, et tropaeum Actiacum videō. Cum Marcus Antōnius atque Cleopatra ab Octāviānō **victī essent**, Octāviānus (Augustus noster) prōrās nāvium illōrum Neptūnō dēdicāvit.
25 Cum ventī adversī **flārent** quinque diēs in Actiō manēre necesse erat sed mox iterum nāvem solvimus et Cephallāniam et Zakynthum magister nāvigāvit ut negōtia plūra faceret. Posteā, cum per Corinthiacum sinum **nāvigārēmus**, Delphōs procul conspicere potuī. Paulō post Corinthō appropinquāvimus et, cum in terrā firmā iterum **stetissem**, statim vōtum Neptūnō solvī.

Hodiē quintus diēs Corinthī est et crās ab hāc urbe Athēnās iter faciam ut studia incipiam.
30 Quid agitis Rōmae? Familiane mox rūs ībit? Scrībite ut omnia audiam! Cūrāte ut omnēs valeātis!"

Gemma

statim vōtum Neptūnō solvī
(line 28): It was common practice after a sea voyage, especially a difficult one, to dedicate an offering of thanks (*vōtum, -ī* n.) to Neptune, god of the sea.

POSTQUAM LĒGISTĪ

1. Whom does Lucius see when he gets home from school? What does this person have for Lucius?
2. What road does Marcus take south from Rome? What does he have to do when he arrives in Brundisium?
3. On what kind of ship does he sail? What is the name of the ship?
4. Describe his first day at sea.
5. What was the next stop after Corcyra? What famous historical event took place there?
6. What does Marcus do as soon as he sets foot in Corinth?
7. How would Marcus have traveled from Rome to Athens if he were living today? How long would the voyage take?

Iter Marcī sequī potesne?

🔊 VERBA ŪTENDA

Actiacus, -a, -um of Actium

Actium, Actiī n. Actium, site of Octavian's decisive battle with Marc Antony and Cleopatra in 31 B.C.

adversus, -a, -um adverse, contrary

Alcinous, -ī m. Alcinous, king of the Phaeacians and host of Odysseus

Amphitrīte, -ēs f. Amphitrite, wife of Neptune (a lucky name for a ship). Note Greek case endings.

apage go! scram!

Athēnae, Athēnārum f. pl. Athens, a city in Greece

avidus, -a, -um eager

benevolens, benevolentis well-wishing, benevolent

Brundisium,- iī n. Brundisium (modern Brindisi), city on the east coast of Italy, the main port city between Rome and Greece

Cephallānia, -ae f. Cephallania (modern Kefalonia), an island on the west coast of Greece

clārus, -a, -um clear, bright; loud, distinct; famous

Cleopatra, -ae f. Cleopatra, the last Ptolemaic ruler of Egypt

conscendō, conscendere, conscendī, conscensum ascend; embark

Corcȳra, -ae f. Corcyra (modern Corfu), an island on the west coast of Greece. The Greek hero Ulysses may have visited the Phaeacians here.

Corinthiacus, -a, -um Corinthian, pertaining to Corinth

Corinthus, -ī f. Corinth, a city in southern Greece

dēdicō (1) dedicate, devote

Delphī, -ōrum m. pl. Delphi, a major oracular shrine of the god Apollo in Greece

dīligenter carefully

eugae/euge/eugepae terrific! bravo!

fervidē heatedly, fervently

firmus, -a, -um firm, strong

flō (1) blow

frangō, frangere, frēgī, fractum break; crush; conquer

Graecia, -ae f. Greece

gubernō (1) steer (a ship)

heu (often + acc.) oh! (in pain or dismay)

hūc (to) here, to this place

idōneus, -a, -um (+ dat.) fit, suitable

illūc to there

Illyria, -ae f. Illyria (modern Croatia)

Ithaca, -ae f. Ithaca, island home of the Greek hero Ulysses, located in western Greece

lītus, -oris n. shore

mercātōrius, -a, -um mercantile, commercial

merx, mercis f. commodity; pl. goods, merchandise

metus, -ūs m. fear

nāvigō (1) sail

Neptūnus, -ī m. Neptune, god of the sea

Nīcopolis, -is f. Nicopolis, city in western Greece founded by Augustus after the Battle of Actium in 31 B.C.; *Nīcopolin*: note Greek accusative ending

nūbēs, nūbis f. cloud

obscūrō (1) darken, obscure, conceal

occurrō, occurrere, occurrī/ occucurrī, occursum (+ dat.) run toward; encounter, run into

postrēmō at last, finally

procul far, far away, from far away

prōpellō, prōpellere, prōpulī, prōpulsum drive, push forward

prōra, -ae f. prow

puppis, puppis f. stern; note i-stem ending

quiētus, -a, -um calm, peaceful

quintus, -a, -um fifth

regnum, -ī n. kingdom

secundus, -a, -um favorable (literally, "following", i.e., blowing from behind the ship and filling the sails)

sinus, -ūs m. gulf

solvō, solvere, solvī, solūtum loosen, unbind; fulfil, perform; pay, deliver; nāvem solvō set sail

tempestās, tempestātis f. time, weather, season, storm

tropaeum, tropaeī n. trophy, victory monument

Ulixēs, -is m. Ulysses, the hero of Homer's *Odyssey*; known in Greek as Odysseus

ventus, -ī m. wind

vīsitō (1) visit

vōtum, -ī n. vow; votive offering

Zakynthus, -ī f. Zakynthus, an island in western Greece

Grammatica B

More *Cum* Clauses

You already know these basic facts about *cum* clauses:

Cum	+ indicative	when, whenever
	+ subjunctive	when, since, because, although

Here is how you choose among possible translations:

Indicative

cum "when" (*cum* temporal clause)	refers to an absolute time, almost dating the event	past tense indicative
cum "whenever" (*cum* frequentative clause)	refers to frequent time	found with present, perfect, and pluperfect indicative

Temporal: *Cum Caesar nōs duxit, vīcimus.*
                    (That time) when Caesar led us, we won.

Frequentative: *Cum Caesar nōs duxerat, vincēbāmus.*
                    Whenever Caesar led us, we used to win.

Subjunctive

cum "when" (*cum* circumstantial clause)	refers to circumstances surrounding an event; does not date it	imperfect and pluperfect subjunctive
cum "since/because" (*cum* causal clause)	gives a reason	found with present, perfect, and pluperfect subjunctive
cum "although" (*cum* concessive clause)	tells "in spite of" something (look for a *tamen,* expressed or implied)	tense of subjunctive varies

Circumstantial: *Cum Caesar nōs dūceret, vīcimus.*
                    We won when Caesar was leading us.
                    Cum vīcissēmus fatīgātī sumus.
                    When we had won, we were tired.

Causal: *Cum Caesar nōs dūceret, vīcimus.*
                    Because Caesar was leading us, we won.

Concessive: *Cum Caesar nōs dūceret, tamen victī sumus.*
                    Although Caesar was leading us, we were beaten.

Note on relative time: The imperfect subjunctive tends to indicate time close to the main verb, whereas the pluperfect subjunctive indicates a completed action.

Interjections!

All of the following interjections appeared in the *lectiōnēs* in this chapter. Those marked in **bold** are *Verba Discenda* in this chapter.

> *apage!* go! scram!
> ***age!* come! well! all right!**
> *ecce!* see! behold!
> ***eugae! / euge! / eugepae!* terrific! bravo!**
> ***hau!* ouch! (in pain or grief)**
> ***heu!* (often + acc.) oh! (in pain or dismay)**
> ***vae!* (often + dat.) woe! (in pain or dread)**

Notice how interjections do not change their endings, although some, like *heu* and *vae*, are sometimes followed by special cases.

Now go back to *Lectiō Prīma* and see how many more of these interjections you can find.

EXERCEĀMUS!

36-4 Using *Cum* + Subjunctive

Using the chart on pg. 484 as a guide, translate the following sentences. Be sure to translate the *cum* in as many valid ways as possible in context. Follow the model.

→ Cum Lūcius lūdum intrat, sedet et legere incipit.
   When Lucius enters his school, he sits down and begins to read.
   Whenever Lucius enters his school, he sits down and begins to read.

1. Cum per Viam Appiam Brudisium sine difficultāte advēnissent, nāvem idōneam invenīre cōnātī sunt.
2. Cum dīligenter quaesīvissēmus, sōla tamen ūna nāvis idōnea vīsa est.
3. Cum nāvem conscendisset et suās rēs dēposuisset, in puppī stetit.
4. Cum nūbēs subitō sōlem obscūrent, lītora Italiae et Illyriae vidēre nōn potest.
5. Cum tempestās magna nāvem hūc et illūc prōpelleret, certī erāmus nōs moritūrōs esse!

Mōrēs Rōmānī

Vōta Rōmāna

Do you remember how Marcus made an offering to the god Neptune after his safe landing in Corinth? Such a gift to a deity is called a votive offering (*vōtum, -ī* n.). Augustus' monument at Actium is a similar offering, on a much larger scale, to the two gods, Neptune and Mars, whom Augustus credited for his victory over Marc Antony and Cleopatra in 31 B.C. Augustus commemorates Neptune, god of the sea, because Actium was a naval engagement and he honors Mars as god of war.

Vōtum Rōmānum
Musée du Louvre/RMN Réunion des Musées Nationaux, France. SCALA/Art Resource, NY

Votive offerings were common practice in the ancient world. Soldiers might leave weapons (or replicas in metal, terracotta, or marble); athletes, their sports equipment; and the sick, plaques or models of their cured body parts. Many *vōta*, like Augustus' at Actium, had inscriptions on them.

Part of the inscription on Augustus' monument at Actium survives. Some words seem to be missing at both the beginning and the end. All the words marked in **bold** are nominative and refer to Augustus. See if you can find words from this inscription on the reconstruction of the monument to the right of the Latin text on the next page.

Tropaeum Actiī Hodiē

🔊 **VERBA ŪTENDA**

bellum gerere to wage war
consacrō (1) dedicate,
    consecrate
consequor, consequī,
    consecūtus sum obtain
ēgredior, ēgredī, ēgressus
    sum march out
exornō (1) adorn
insequor, insequī,
    insecūtus sum pursue
Mars, Martis m. Mars,
    god of war
partā from *pariō*
quintum for the fifth time
regiō, regiōnis f. region,
    district
septimum for the seventh
    time
spolium, -iī n. spoils (of war)

[...] **Imperātor Caesar** Dīvī Iūlī **Fīlius**
victōriam **consecūtus** bellō quod prō rēpūblicā
gessit in hāc regiōne **consul** quintum
imperātor septimum pāce partā terrā marīque
Neptūnō et Martī castra ex quibus ad hostem
insequendum **ēgressus** est nāvālibus spoliīs
exornāta consacrāvit. [...]

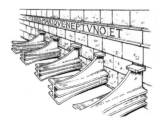

Tropaeum Actiī Restitūtum

Orbis Terrārum Rōmānus

Athēnae

In his famous Funeral Oration in Thucydides' *Histories of the Peloponnesian Wars* (Book II), the
Athenian leader Pericles boasts that Athens is "the school of Greece." This was no exaggeration
in the 5th century B.C., when Pericles' city was already known for its theater, history, and de-
mocratic government. Within the next two centuries, Athens would also become known as a
school of philosophy and rhetoric. In the early 4th century, Plato founded his Academy in
Athens, and his student Aristotle followed with his school of Peripatetic philosophy. Later,
Athens saw the founding of Epicureanism by Epicurus (341–270 B.C.), Cynicism by Crates of
Thebes (c. 365–c. 285), and Stoicism by Crates' student Zeno of Citium (334–262 B.C.).

The 4th century Athenian orator Demosthenes (384–322 B.C.), in particular, so firmly
established Athens as a center of great oratory that, even in the 1st century B.C., young Romans
flocked to Athens and other areas of Greece for their higher education, especially in public
speaking. Cicero, the poet Horace, and our Marcus were among these Romans educated in
Greece. Athens continued to be a school, not only for Greeks but also for Romans and those
who sought to become Roman, well into the 2nd century A.D. and beyond.

Athēnae Rōmānae

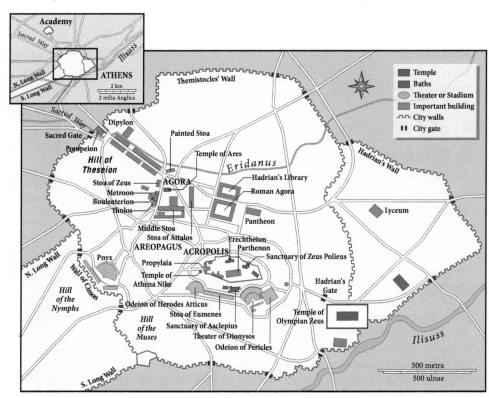

Acropolis Athēnīs

Agora Athēnīs

Latīna Hodierna

Acadēmīa Athēnaea

The Athenian schools of philosophy are the source of a number of English derivatives. Though these words were all originally Greek, the Romans borrowed them, and it is through Latin that they came into English. Note how the meanings of the English derivatives often differ from the meanings of the original Greek, and how these words have contexts outside of philosophy.

Latin Word	Greek Origin	English Derivatives	English Meaning
Acadēmīa, -ae f.	a gymnasium near Athens	academy	a school
Stōicus, -a, -um	a colonnaded building	stoic	uncomplaining or patient in enduring pain
Cynicus, -a, -um	a dog	cynic, cynical	sceptical
Epicūrēus, -a, -um	Epicurus	epicurean	fond of good food and wine
Peripatēticus, -a, -um	"walking around"	peripatetic	wandering
Platōnicus, -a, -um	Plato	platonic	spiritual (rather than physical)

If you are curious about how some of these words came to be, you might consider taking an ancient philosophy course or reading some of the philosophical works of Cicero, like *Dē Officiīs* (On Duty) and *Dē Amīcitiā* (On Friendship).

QUID PUTĀS?

1. For what reasons other than religious ones might Augustus have erected his monument at Actium?
2. Make a list of five national war monuments in the United States, and compare them to Augustus' monument at Actium.
3. If you were Marcus, what sort of votive offering would you leave for Neptune?
4. Have you ever seen anyone leave a votive offering today? If not, what might they do instead to show their gratitude to a spiritual power?
5. What kind of school is called an "academy" today? What other sorts of institutions use this word in their titles?
6. With the help of a dictionary, describe each of the following kinds of person: academic, stoic, cynical, epicurean, peripatic, and platonic. Which adjective best describes your personality? Why?

EXERCEĀMUS!

36-5 Scrībāmus!

Mindful of CTSIDR rules, describe in Latin Marcus' itinerary from Rome to Athens. Here is Marcus' itinerary in English. Use forms of the verbs *ambulō, nāvigō, eō*, and *veniō*. Follow the model.

> Rome to Brundisium
> Brundisium to Corcyra
> Corcyra to Actium (Nicopolis)
> From Actium to Cephallenia and Zakinthus
> Through the Gulf of Corinth to Corinth
> Corinth to Athens

→ Marcus est Rōmae. Rōmā Brundisium it.

36-6 Colloquāmur

Use the vocabulary marked in **bold** in the models below to practice asking and answering questions with a classmate about Marcus' journey. Go through his entire itinerary.

ubi where (at); *quō* where (to); *unde* where (from)

Quaestiō	Responsum
→ **Ubi est** Marcus?	Marcus Rōmae est.
→ **Unde** Marcus **it**?	Marcus Rōmā it.
→ **Quō** Marcus **ambulat**?	Marcus Brundisium ambulat.
→ **Unde** Marcus **nāvigat**?	Marcus Brundisiō nāvigat.

36-7 Verba Discenda

Many of the words in the *Verba Discenda* in this chapter are closely related to words learned in earlier chapters. Use the hints provided to list one other related *Verbum Discendum* for each of the following words. Follow the model.

→ *age* (make this interjection a verb): *agō, agere, ēgī, actum*

1. *cūra* (make this noun a verb):
2. *frāterculus* (remove the "little"):
3. *illūc* (make this mean the opposite):
4. *infēlix* (make this adjective mean the opposite):
5. *nāvigō* (make this the vehicle needed to perform this action):
6. *praetūra* (name the person who holds this office):
7. *quaestūra* (name the person who holds this office):
8. *regnum* (identify the Latin noun referring to the person associated with this place):
9. *ter* (change this adverb to a cardinal number):
10. *līberō* (make this verb an adjective):

Deus Ventī

🔊 VERBA DISCENDA

age, agite come! well! all right!

bis twice, two times [biennial]

caput, capitis n. head; master [capital]

careō, carēre, caruī, caritum (+ abl.) lack, be without, lose

clārus, -a, -um clear, bright; loud, distinct; famous [clarity]

cūra, ae f. worry, concern, care, anxiety

eugae/euge/eugepae terrific! bravo!

firmus, -a, -um firm, strong [firmament]

frangō, frangere, frēgī, fractum break; crush; conquer [frangible, fraction]

frāterculus, -ī m. little brother

heu (often + acc.) oh! (in pain or dismay)

hūc (to) here, to this place

idōneus, -a, -um (+ dat.) fit, suitable

illūc to there

infēlix, infēlīcis unhappy, unfortunate [infelicitious]

līberō (1) (+ abl.) free, free from

metus, -ūs m. fear

nāvigō (1) sail [navigate]

oblīviscor, oblīviscī, oblītus sum (+ gen.) forget

occurrō, occurrere, occurrī/ occucurrī, occursum (+ dat.) run toward; encounter, run into

opera, -ae f. work, pain, labor

praetūra, -ae f. praetorship, judgeship

procul far, far away, from far away

quaestūra, -ae f. quaestorship, treasurer

quater four times [quaternary]

regnum, -ī n. kingdom [interregnum]

rūs, rūris n. country, country estate; abroad [rural]

socius, -iī m. partner, companion [sociable]

solvō, solvere, solvī, solūtum loosen, unbind; fulfil, perform; pay, deliver; *nāvem solvō* set sail [solvent]

tempestās, tempestātis f. time, weather, season, storm [tempestuous]

ter three times

vae (often + dat.) woe! (in pain or dread)

ventus, -ī m. wind [vent, ventilation]

volō (1) fly; hasten [volatile]

Angulus Grammaticus

Translating and Using *Cum*

As you have seen, the Latin word *cum* can be either a preposition or a conjunction.

As a preposition, *cum* primarily means "with" and expresses accompaniment (*cum amīcīs*) and manner (*cum celeritāte*). Under certain circumstances, the position of the preposition *cum* changes, as in *mēcum, quōcum,* and *summā cum laude*. You usually know it means "with" if it is used with an ablative, but in certain expressions, *cum* is often translated without "with"; for example, *cum prīmīs* (first of all, chiefly); *iuxtā mēcum* (to the same degree as me); *sēcum cōgitat* (he thinks to himself).

As a conjunction, *cum* can mean "when," "whenever," "while," "because," "since," or "although," depending on the mood of the verb and the context.

Here are some other ways that *cum* the conjunction can be translated when used with certain words: *cum extemplō* or *cum prīmō* (as soon as, the moment that) and *cum maximē* (at the very moment that).

Occasionally, *cum* functions as an adverb, as in *cum … tum* (not only … but also) and *ut cum maximē* (as much as ever, most particularly).

Cum is also used as prefix with the meaning "with," "together," or "completely." In this case, it usually appears as *con-, com-, col-,* etc.; for example, *conferō* (carry with), *confirmō* (make completely strong), *congregō* (gather together), *colloquor* (speak together), *committō* (send with), *conficiō* (do completely), etc.

Finally, here are some Latin phrases with *cum* that are occasionally used in English.

PHRASE	LITERAL TRANSLATION	USE IN ENGLISH
cum grānō salis	with a grain of salt	Be careful, take his advice cum grano salis.
cum laude	with praise	I graduated cum laude.
vadē mēcum	go with me	Handbooks that people carry with themselves are often called vademecums.
dūcēs tēcum	you will take with you	This is a "subpoena duces tecum," so you will have to bring those documents to the deposition.

LECTIŌNĒS:
AMBITIŌ
and
AD LŪNAM
Servilius prepares to run for praetor
and enlists the help of Aelius and his
other clients.

37

Petītiō Praetōris

Lectiō Prīma

Antequam Legis

The election is near at hand, and Servilius discusses the upcoming campaign
(*ambitiō*) for praetor with Aelius. Servilius expects Aelius to show up whenever he gives a speech. He also wants Aelius to put up campaign signs and to
support the campaign of a client of his named Titus Vibius, who is running
for *Vīcī Magister, Regiōnis VI*, sort of a ward boss. As you read this *lectiō*, we
introduce you to subjunctives expressing wishes.

Wishes

Most of us have written, "Wish you were here" on a postcard or, after an
embarrassing moment, have groaned, "I wish I were dead."

It is not difficult to recognize such wishes in Latin. Look for subjunctives introduced by *utinam* ("I wish that" or "Would that") or *nē* ("I wish
that ... not" or "Would that ... not").

As you read *Lectiō Prīma*, you will find a number of wishes in the subjunctive. We have marked them in **bold** to make them easier to spot. When
you find a wish, pay attention to the tense of the subjunctive. You will see the
subjunctive in three tenses. Here is how to translate them:

Wish	Subjunctive	English Translation	Time Implied
Utinam fēlix **sīs***!*	present	May you be happy!	future
Utinam fēlix **essēs***!*	imperfect	Would that you were happy!	present
Nē infēlix **fuissēs***!*	pluperfect	Would that you hadn't been unhappy!	past

EXERCEĀMUS!

37-1 **Scanning for Details**

As you read *Lectiō Prīma*, list all the wishes marked in **bold** in three
groups according to the tense of the subjunctive they use: present,
imperfect, and pluperfect. Then use either "I wish that" or
"Would that" to translate the wishes into English. Follow the model.

M SERVILIUS

Present	Imperfect	Pluperfect	Translation
→ *sit*			*I wish that he be*

AMBITIŌ

Post salūtātiōnem Servīlius et Aelius colloquuntur in tabulāriō dē
ambitiōne appropinquantī.

Servīlius "Aelī," inquit, "ambitiō adest et sī praetūram capere poterō,
auxilium ā tē et ab omnibus clientibus meīs mihi petendum est."

5   Aelius "Certē, patrōne," inquit, "**Utinam** fortūna tua bona **sit**!"

Servīlius "Bene dictum, Aelī," inquit. "Sed labor, nōn verba,
omnia vincit. Ergō, quid tibi agendum sit dē petītiōne praetōris
cōnsīderēmus!"

Servīlius et Aelius colloquuntur in tabulāriō.

Aelius: "**Utinam** ego nōbilis aut eques dīves **essem**! **Utinam** nōbilis prō tē ōrātiōnēs in Senātū habēre **possem**. Aut,
10 **utinam** in Colle Vīminālī aut Quirīnālī familia mea **habitāret**! **Utinam** vīcīnōs tuōs hortārī ut tē ēligant **possem**!"

Servīlius: "Sed, faber argentārius es et in Subūrā familia tua habitat. Quae cum ita sint, quōmodo maximum auxil-
ium mihi offerre possēs, tibi dīcam. Prīmum rogō ut Titō Vibiō magistrātūs capiendī causā auxilium ferās. In Regiōne
Sextā multī fabrī sunt quī tibi maximē crēdunt. Dealbātor pictorque tibi quoque inveniendī sunt, quī in mūrīs prō mē
Vibiōque scrībere possunt."

15 Aelius: "Edepol, facile est omnia haec efficere, patrōne. Estne aliquid aliud?"

Servīlius: "Crās cum ōrātiōnem meam habēbō, fortiter plaude ut omnēs aliī quoque plaudant et cum aliquis mē
irrīserit, horribile dictū, fac ut ille abeat. Tālia recenter, mē aedīlitātem petente, facta sunt."

Aelius: "**Utinam**," fervidē inquit, "tunc tibi **adfuissem**! **Nē**que tālia nunc **fierent**! Sed, sī tālis aderit, celeriter
abībit! Nōlī timēre! Certē succēdēs!"

20 Servīlius "Euge, mī Aelī," inquit, "**utinam** mihi plūrēs clientēs tibi similēs **essent**!"

Aeliō abeunte, Servīlius ad sē Epaphrodītum nōmenclātōrem vocāvit. (Epaphrodītus in Campāniā parentibus
servīs nātus est et nōmenclātor in Pompēiīs factus est. Nunc Servīliī lībertīnus et cliens est.)

Servīlius "Epaphrodīte," inquit, "rogō ut mēcum ad Forum crās ambulēs. Vae! **Utinam** mihi memoria melior **esset**!
Nōmina haud facile in memoriā teneō, sed tū omnēs omniaque in memoriā retinēs. Cum alicui appropinquābimus et
25 eius nōmen nōn meminī, in aure meā nuntiā mihi nōn sōlum huius nōmen sed etiam parentum et uxōris et līberōrum
nōmina. Sī quis in familiā aeger est, sī quis recenter mortuus est, sī quis mātrimōniō coniunctus est, in aure meā nuntiā!
Tālia in ambitiōne facienda sunt! **Nē** hoc ita **esset**, sed quid aliud agam?!"

VERBA ŪTENDA

aedīlitās, -tātis f. office of
   aedile (public works)
aeger, aegra, aegrum
   sick
***ambitiō, -iōnis* f.**
   canvassing (for votes),
   political campaign
auris, auris f. ear
coniungō, coniungere,
   coniunxī, coniunctus join,
   connect, ally
cōnsīderō (1) consider,
   inspect
dealbātor, -ōris m. one who
   whitewashes walls
***Edepol!* By Pollux!**

ēligō, ēligere, ēlēgī, ēlectum
   pick, choose
***fabrica, -ae* f. workshop;**
   art, craft
fervidē hotly
factus est Take this as a
   form of *fīō*.
***horribilis, horribile* rough,**
   terrible, horrible
irrīdeō, irrīdēre, irrīsī,
   ***irrīsum* laugh at, mock**
***lībertīnus, -ī* m. freedman**
***magistrātus, -ūs* m. office,**
   magistracy; magistrate
***mātrimōnium, -iī* n.**
   marriage, matrimony

***memoria, -ae* f. memory**
nascor, nascī, nātus sum
   be born
nōmenclātor, -ōris m. a
   nomenclator, one who
   announces names of
   people
***nuntiō* (1) announce, report**
***petītiō, -ōnis* f. candidacy,**
   petition; lawsuit
pictor, -ōris m. painter,
   professional graffiti
   writer
quis after *sī* = *aliquis*
***recenter* recently**

retineō, retinēre, retinuī,
   ***retentum* hold fast,**
   retain; cling to
***sextus, -a, -um* sixth**
***similis, simile* similar,**
   like to
succēdō, succēdere,
   ***successī, successum* go**
   below, go under; come
   to; succeed (to)
tabulārium, -iī n,
   tabularium, office
***utinam* if only! would**
   that!
vīcīnus, -ī m. neighbor

POSTQUAM LĒGISTĪ

1. What is the equivalent of a *pictor* in a modern election campaign?
2. Servilius asks Aelius, as a silversmith, to help get votes from other silversmiths. What does this remind you of in modern elections?
3. Who might fulfill the role of a *nōmenclātor* in modern politics?
4. Are there any hints that Servilius doesn't like the campaign trail?
5. Do modern elections have any equivalent to the Roman practice of planting people to applaud in an audience or to usher out troublemakers?

Grammatica A

Expressing Wishes

In *Lectiō Prīma* Aelius says, "I wish I were rich" and "I wish I lived on the Viminal Hill." These sentences contain the rarely used English subjunctive, used because the thing wished for is slightly less than real. Consider this: "I wish you were here." The wishing is very real and thus is indicative in English. But you are **not** here, so as a result, this part of the sentence goes into the subjunctive in English. Wishes, basically, come down to those that are possible ("I hope you win") and those that are contrary to fact ("I wish you were here"). In Latin they are often (not always) preceded by the words *utinam* or *nē*.

Look first at this overview and then at some examples.

Type of Wish	Time Implied	English Example	Subjunctive	Translate
possible	future	May you be rich!	present	"may"
contrary to fact	present	I wish I were rich!	imperfect	"were"
contrary to fact	past	I wish I had been rich!	pluperfect	"had"

Possible Wishes

Utinam *fortūna tua bona* **sit**! — May your fortune be good!

This is a wish for the future, using the present subjunctive. It may or may not come true, but it is at least possible.

Contrary to Fact Present Wishes

Utinam *ego nōbilis aut eques dīves* **essem**! — I wish I were a nobleman or a rich "knight."

This is clearly contrary to fact, as Aelius is definitely not a noble. Note the use of the **imperfect subjunctive** referring to the present time.

Contrary to Fact Past Wishes

If Aelius had used the pluperfect subjunctive in the same phrase, he would have been referring to the past time:

Utinam *tunc tibi* **adfuissem**! — I wish I had been there for you!

The **pluperfect subjunctive** expresses a wish contrary to fact in the past, since it is clear that Aelius was not there.

Negative Wishes

Here are some examples of negative wishes. Note the use of *nē*.

Nē id fīat!	May it not happen!
Nē id fieret!	Would that it were not happening!
Nē id fēcissēs!	Would that you had not done it!

Notā Bene:

- Occasionally *nōn* is used instead of *nē* in such wishes.
  Nōn maesta essēs! — Would that you were not sad!

Sometimes these subjunctives of wish are called **optative subjunctives**. "Optative" comes from the Latin verb *optō* (1) "wish," which you will see in the next section.

EXERCEĀMUS!

37-2 Wishing in Latin

For each wish, provide the following information: the tense of the subjunctive, the time of the wish, the type of wish, and a translation. Follow the models.

	Tense	**Time**	**Wish Type**	**Translation**
→ Utinam abeās!	present	future	possible	Would that you go away!
→ Utinam abīrēs!	imperfect	present	contrary to fact	Would that you were going away!

1. Utinam mē Cordus videat.

2. Utinam mē Cordus vidēret!

3. Utinam mē Cordus vīdisset!

4. Utinam Cordus marītus meus sit!

5. Utinam hoc auxilium mihi dēs!

6. Utinam hoc auxilium mihi darēs!

7. Utinam hoc auxilium mihi dedissēs!

8. Nē aegrī essent!

9. Nē aegrae fuissent!

Lectiō Secunda

Antequam Legis

In this *lectiō* Aelius goes out at night to paint political slogans for Servilius on the walls of buildings throughout Rome. He does this with the help of Fructus, a *dealbātor* who white-washes over old political graffiti, and Florus, a *pictor* who writes new political graffiti on the wall. Fructus and Florus are based on real people known from Pompeiian graffiti.

As you read, pay attention to the sentences with *sī* clauses. These are called **conditions**.

Conditions

A condition is an if/then sentence. If A, then B. Basically, a condition either expresses (If you drop something, it falls.) or a possibility (If I were to drop this, Mother would be mad). Facts are expressed by the indicative, while possibilities and things less real are indicated by the subjunctive.

There are specific terms for the various types of conditions, but for now, just use the chart to help you translate them. The key translation words are in bold.

If you see ...	Translate as ...
1. the **indicative** in both clauses *Sī dīves **es**, multam pecūniam **habēs**.*	If A **does** B, X **does** Y. If you **are** rich, you **have** a lot of money.
2. the **present subjunctive** in both clauses *Sī dīves **fīās**, multam pecūniam **habeās**.*	If A **should** do B, X **would** do Y. If you **should** become rich, you **would** have a lot of money.
3. the **imperfect subjunctive** in both clauses *Sī dīves **essēs**, multam pecūniam **habērēs**.*	If A **were to** do B, X **would** do Y. If you **were** rich, you **would** have a lot of money.
4. the **pluperfect subjunctive** in both clauses *Sī dīves **fuissēs**, multam pecūniam **habuissēs**.*	If A **had** done B, X **would have** done Y. If you **had** been rich, you **would have** had a lot of money.

Diāna Lūnae Dea

Sī Quis

One more thing: Latin drops the *ali-* from *aliquis, aliquid* after certain words. An old school-boy's chant is a good way to remember these words:

After *sī, nisi, num,* and *nē*, all the *ali*-s run away.

Thus: *Sī quid scīs, dīc id mihi!*   If you know anything, tell it to me!

EXERCEĀMUS!

37-3 Classifying Conditions

As you read *Lectiō Secunda*, group the conditions marked in **bold** into four groups: indicative, present subjunctive, imperfect subjunctive, and pluperfect subjunctive. Follow the model.

Indicative	Present Subjunctive	Imperfect Subjunctive	Pluperfect Subjunctive
→		possēmus (line 5)	

🔊 AD LŪNAM

Nox est et Diāna Lūcifera in caelō clārō nōn lūcēbat. Aelius, Fructus dealbātor et Flōrus pictor per viās urbis ambulābant. Aelius, et duo servī armātī facēs portābant ut viam illūminārent et Aelius aliīs dixit: "**Sī** quem in viā **videāmus,** nihil scrībāmus. Opus nostrum difficile erit! **Sī** lūna plēna **esset,** melius vidēre possēmus."

Flōrus in mūrō prō Servīliō scrībit.

Sī ad mūrum in quō nōmen alīus candidātī scriptum erat **advēnērunt,** Fructus alia verba dealbāvit et Flōrus nova verba pigmentō rubrō scripsit:

M SERVILIUM SEVERUM
PRAETOREM O V F
FABRI ARGENTARII FACITE

aut in Subūrā

T VIBIUM
MAGISTRATUM
O V F
M SERVILIUM SEVERUM PRAETOREM

In ūnō mūrō proximā nocte trēs virī hoc scrīpserant:

M SERVILIUM SEVERUM PRAET

Sed, posteā, aliquis verba plūra manū dissimilī addiderat et nunc Aelius lēgit:

M SERVILIUM SEVERUM PRAET
ESSE NOLO

Aelius īrātus murmurāvit: "Edepol, **sī** illum mastīgiam quī haec duo verba addidit **invēnerō,** illum hōrum verbōrum paenitēbit! Perge, Fructe! Dealbā illa verba!"

Per noctem virī labōrāverant et fessī factī sunt. Praesertim illōs taeduit semper eadem verba iterum atque iterum scrībere. Flōrus, quī sē poētam esse arbitrātus est, "Aelī," inquit, "volō aliquid novum scrībere! Licetne?"

Aelius "Licet, mī Flōre," inquit. "Age! Fac optimum tuum! Quidquid optās!" Ita Flōrus scrīpsit:

SI PUDOR IN VITA QUICQUAM PRODESSE **PUTATUR**
SERVILIUS HIC DIGNUS HONORE BONO EST
SCR FLOR CUM FRUCTO DEALB

"Optimē, Flōre, bene factum! **Sī** quis crās hunc mūrum **legat**, poētam Catullum id scrīpsisse crēdat!"

Multās post hōrās, fessissimī erant. Aelius, quī strēnuē hōc diē in fabricā labōrāverat, domum redīre volēbat sed
30 intrā sē cōgitāvit: "**Sī** Servīlium patrōnum nōn **invēnissem**, omnia āmīsissem. **Nī** multa labōriōsa prō patrōnō **faciō,** bonus cliens nōn sum."

Virīs domum prōgredientibus, ūnus mūrus mīrābilis spectātus est. Mūrus, quī inter tabernam et lātrīnam stābat, plūs quam centum inscriptiōnēs habuit quasi omnis Rōmānus in hōc mūrō aliquid scrīpserat.

Fructus locum dealbāvit et Flōrus, rīdēns, scrīpsit:

35

ADMĪROR TE PARIES NON CECIDISSE

QUI TOT SCRIPTORUM TAEDIA SUSTINEAS

Tunc infrā addidit:

NE QUIS HOC DEALBE

Tandem, lūce oriente, quisque lectum suum quaesīvit.

🔊 VERBA ŪTENDA

addō, addere, addidī,
   additum add, give
ad lūnam by moonlight
arbitror, abitrārī,
   ***arbitrātus sum* observe,**
   perceive; think
***armō* (1) arm**
caelum, -ī n. sky
***centum* (indecl.) one**
   hundred
DEALB = dealbātor
dealbō (1) whitewash
dealbātor, -ōris m.
   whitewasher, someone
   who whitewashes walls
   either to cover up grafitti
   or to prepare the wall for
   new grafitti
Diāna, -ae f. Diana, goddess
   of the hunt and of
   the moon; the moon
   itself
dignus, -a, -um worthy,
   deserving
***dissimilis, dissimile* unlike**
facite repeats the request
   more forcefully ... "Do it!"
fax, facis f. torch
FLOR = Flōrus

Flōrus, -ī m. Florus, a male
   praenōmen
Fructus, -ī m. Fructus, a male
   praenōmen
illūminō (1) brighten
inscriptiō, -iōnis f. inscription
labōriōsus, -a, -um
   laborious, tedious
lātrīna, -ae f. public toilet
lūceō, lūcēre, luxī shine
lūcifer, -a, -um light-bearing
   (an epithet or nickname for
   the goddess Diana)
lux, lūcis f. light
M = Marcus
mastīgia, -ae m. rascal,
   someone worthy of a
   whipping
mīrābilis, mīrābile
   wondrous
murmurō (1) mutter
nī unless
***optō* (1) wish**
pariēs, parietis m. wall
pergō, pergere, perrexī,
   ***perrectum* go ahead,**
   advance, proceed
pictor, -ōris m. painter,
   professional artist

paid to write
(political) graffiti on
public walls
pigmentum, -ī n. color,
   pigment
PRAET = PRAETŌREM
prō instead of
pudor, -ōris m. shame,
   modesty, decency
***quasi* as if, practically**
quisquis, quidquid whoever,
   whatever
ruber, rubra, rubrum red
SCR = scrīpsit
sustineō, sustinēre,
   sustinuī, sustentum
   hold up, support,
   withstand
T = Titus
taedium, -iī n. boredom,
   here "boring sayings"
taedit, taedēre, taeduit,
   taesum est (+ gen. or
   + inf.) imp. be tired (of),
   be sick (of)
Vibius, -iī m. Vibius, a male
   praenōmen

Gemma

o.v.f. is a standard political abbreviation. Depending on context, expand the *o* to *ōrō, ōrat,* or *ōrant.* Here it means *ōrant vōs faciātis,* "they ask that you make ..."

Gemma

ADMĪROR TE PARIES:
This wall inscription is based on one actually found on a wall of the amphitheater in Pompeii.

POSTQUAM LĒGISTĪ

Answer all of the following questions in English. Also answer in Latin if the question is followed by (L).

1. How many people are in Aelius' party? Who are they? (L) Describe their jobs.
2. What is Aelius' wish concerning the weather that night? (L)
3. What is their plan if they see someone coming? (L)
4. What angers Aelius? (L)
5. Why does Aelius stay at the job even though he is very tired? (L)
6. What does Florus do while he writes his last message of the night? (L) Why?
7. What would be the equivalent of these activities today?

Grammatica B

Conditions

Conditions in the indicative (often called general conditions) are those that state a fact such as "If I let go, this will drop." Since they state facts, they are in the indicative, and you simply translate them as normal, indicative verbs. The tenses can vary:

Sī pecūniam habeō, laetus sum.	If I have money, I am happy.
Sī pecūniam invēnī, laetus eram.	If I found money, I was happy.
Sī Caesar nōs duxerat, vīcimus.	If Caesar had led us, we won.

One such condition has its own name, the **future more vivid (FMV) condition**, and uses the future perfect followed by the future:

Sī pecūniam invēnerō, laetus erō.	If I find money, I'll be happy.
Nisi pecūniam invēnerō, laetus nōn erō.	If I don't/Unless I find money, I won't be happy.

The first part of the condition is literally translated "If I shall have (not) found money," but we really do not speak that way. As always, the future perfect is stating that two things are going to happen, and the one in the future perfect will happen first. Feel free to translate FMVs using a present and then a future.

There are also several common kinds of conditions using the subjunctive.

Future Less Vivid (FLV)

present subjunctive in both clauses   translate: "should/would"

Note this example from *Lectiō Secunda*:

*Sī quis hunc mūrum **legat**, poētam Catullum id scripsisse **crēdat!***
If anyone **should** read this wall, he **would** believe that the poet Catullus had written it!

The subjunctive here tells the reader that this is only a possibility—hence the "should/would." Sometimes the "should/would" construction sounds odd in English, so you need to translate like this:

If anyone were to read this wall, he'd believe that Catullus had written it!

But try always to be aware of the "iffiness" of the phrase that the subjunctive indicates.

Contrary to Fact Present (CTF Present)

imperfect subjunctive in both clauses   translate: "were/would"
*Sī lūna plēna **esset**, melius **vidērēmus**.*   If the moon were full, we would see better.

Contrary to Fact Past (CTF Past)

pluperfect subjunctive in both clauses

*Sī Servīlium patrōnum nōn **invēnissem**, omnia **āmīsissem**.*

translate: "had/would have"

If I had not found Servilius as a patron,
    I would have lost everything.

Mixed Conditions

Mixed conditions do exactly that—mix the tenses and sometimes the moods. If you remember the key words associated with each tense and mood, (were/would, had/would have, etc.) mixed conditions will not be a problem.

Consider these examples:

*Sī Servīlium patrōnum nōn **invēnissem**, nulla domus, nulla fabrica mihi **esset**.*

If I had not found Servilius as a patron, I would have no house, no workshop.

The first part of the sentence (grammarians call it the protasis) is the beginning of a Contrary to Fact Past condition. The second part (apodosis) is a Contrary to Fact Present. If you remember that the first word in a CTF Past translation is "had," and the second word in a CTF Present is "would", you can easily translate the condition.

General conditions can also be mixed. In *Lectiō Prīma*, you easily translated a mixed condition in a sentence like this:

*Sī quis in familiā aeger **est**, sī quis recenter **mortuus est**, sī quis mātrimōniō **coniunctus est**, in aure meā **nuntiā**!*

If anyone in the family is sick, if anyone has recently died, if anyone has married, announce (it) in my ear!

Notice that here the present indicative is mixed with an imperative in the "then" clause.

Sī Quis

Look at this *sī* clause from *Lectiō Secunda*:

sī quem in viā videāmus

The *quem* in this clause is actually **aliquem**. If you see a "Q" word following *sī* in one of these conditions, understand it as form of *aliquis*; e.g., *sī quis = sī aliquis*. This is also a standard contraction in Latin after *nī, nisi, num,* and *nē*; for example, **Nē quis** *hoc faciat!* (Let no one do this!).

The first few times you come across a "Q" word in such a context, you may mistake it for a relative or interrogative pronoun, but if you find *sī, nī, nisi, num,* or *nē* in front of the word, you can be sure it is a form of *aliquis*. Eventually you will come to recognize this Latin contraction as readily as you do "we'll" for "we will" in English.

EXERCEĀMUS!

37-4 Translating *sī quis*

Translate the words marked in *italics* in the following sentences. Keep in mind that the word marked in ***bold italics*** is a form of *aliquis*. Follow the model.

→ **Sī** *quis* **nōs in viā videat,** fugiēmus. If anyone sees us in the road …

1. *Sī **quis** in familiā aeger est,* in aure meā nuntiā.
2. *Sī **quis** recenter mortuus est,* in aure meā nuntiā.
3. *Sī **quis** mātrimōniō coniunctus est,* in aure meā nuntiā.
4. *Sī **quis** mē irrīserit,* fac ut ille abeat.
5. *Sī **cui** appropinquābimus,* tē in aure meā nōmen susurrāre volō.
6. *Sī **cuius** nōmen nōn meminī,* tē in aure meā nōmen susurrāre volō.
7. *Sī **quem** in viā vīderimus,* quid faciendum erit?
8. *Sī **quis** nōs videat,* celeriter scrībe!
9. *Nē **quis** hoc dealbet!*

Mōrēs Rōmānī

Petītiōnēs Rōmānae

Roman elections were as important as they were complex. Only male Roman citizens were eligible to vote or to run for political office, and many positions were restricted to certain social classes. For example, only a plebeian could be elected to the office of tribune (*tribūnus, -ī* m.). As mentioned earlier, the major offices of quaestor, aedile, praetor, and consul were pursued in a set sequence called the *cursus honōrum,* with minimum ages for eligibility. First came quaestor, or treasurer, at age 30, then aedile, or public works official, at 36, then praetor at 39, and, finally, consul at 42.

Different assemblies (*comitia, -ōrum* n. pl.) elected different officials. Consuls, praetors, and censors were elected by the *comitia centuriāta,* in which the citizenry was organized into 193 groupings called centuries (*centuria, -ae* f.) based on wealth. The members of the wealthiest century voted first, and the voting stopped when a candidate had won a majority of the centuries. So the poorest citizens (at the bottom of the voting order) often missed an opportunity to vote. That is why Aelius wishes he were richer and could offer his patron more help.

Senators were not actually elected. Rather, anyone who was elected to higher political offices (typically quaestor) was automatically admitted to senatorial rank and to membership in the Senate.

Declared candidates for office wore a special white toga (*toga candidāta*). Roman politicking required "working the voters" much as modern candidates do today. Successful candidates sought support from the wealthy and powerful as well as local political leaders. Romans called the canvassing of votes *ambitiō* (*-ōnis* f.) or "currying favor." Candidates had to use their own resources to finance their campaigns and usually looked to provincial appointments after serving in office to recoup their expenses.

During the late Republic campaigns often grew violent, but, when Octavian became emperor in 29 B.C., he was determined to maintain republican institutions and offices. Armed mobs no longer ran through the city in support of various candidates, but other tactics, such as the blanketing of city walls with political graffiti, continued. The political slogans written by Aelius and his comrades in *Lectiō Secunda* are based on graffiti written on walls in Pompeii and Herculaneum. Here are three examples:

C CVSPIUM PANSAM AED AVRIFICES VNIVERSI ROG.
C. Cuspiam Pansam Aed(īlem) Aurificēs Ūniversī Rog(ant)

VERVM AED O V F VNGVENTARII FACITE ROGO
Verum Aed(īlem) Ō(rō) V(ōs) F(aciātis), Unguentāriī, Facite Rogō

HOLCONIUM PRISCUM VERECUNDISSIMUM D R P AED O V F
DIGNISSIMUM
Holconium Priscum Verēcundissimum D(ignum) R(eī) P(ūblicae) Aed(īlem)
Ō(rō) V(ōs) F(aciātis) Dignissimum

The first two (CIL IV. 710), dealing with goldsmiths (*aurificēs*) and perfume makers (*ungentāriī*) were written on the same wall. Below you can see the original inscription for the third (CIL IV. 309), dealing with a "very modest" (*verēcundus*) Holconius Priscus.

Holconius Priscus

Latīna Hodierna

Latin in Modern American Political Language

The language of American government, politics, and electioneering is based in large part on Latin words.

LATIN WORD	MEANINGS OF LATIN WORDS	ENGLISH DERIVATIVES
toga candidāta	whitened toga worn by a political candidate	candidate, candidacy, candid
senātor, -ōris m.	member of the Senate	senator
senātus, -ūs m.	the supreme council of the Roman state	senate
ambitiō, -iōnis f.	currying favor, canvassing for votes, a political campaign	ambition, ambitious
petītiō, -iōnis f.	attack, petition, candidacy, lawsuit	petition
ēlectiō, -iōnis f.	choice, selection	election
lēgis lātiō f.	the putting forward of a law	legislation, legislature
vōtum, -ī n.	vow, prayer, desire, hope	vote, voter
gubernātor, -ōris m.	helmsman or pilot (of a ship)	governor, government

Orbis Terrārum Rōmānus

Magna Graecia

Epaphroditus, Servilius' *nōmenclātor*, came from Campania, a region in southern Italy. His name suggests his Greek ancestry. This part of Italy was originally inhabited by Samnites (of Oscan origin), but so many coastal regions were settled by Greek-speaking peoples in the 8th

Magna Graecia

Templum Crotōnae Hodiē

century B.C. and later that the Romans referred to the whole region as *Magna Graecia*. The Greek influence was especially felt around the Bay of Naples (Greek "Neapolis," "New-town"), near Mt. Vesuvius and on Sicily.

Pompeii, Herculaneum, and the other cities destroyed in the eruption of Mt. Vesuvius in 79 A.D. were also located in *Magna Graecia*. Though Pompeii was originally a Samnite settlement, it was eventually taken over by Greeks. Herculaneum and Oplontis were founded by Greeks. By the Augustan Age, however, the entire region was fully Romanized, and a Campanian like Epaphroditus would have been fluent in both Greek and Latin.

Magna Graecia included the regions of Campania, Calabria, Bruttium, and the island of Sicily. The most important of Greek cities in this part of Italy were Neapolis (modern Naples), Capua, Syracusa (Syracuse), Taras (Taranto), Rhegion (Reggio), Croton (Crotone), and Ankon (Ancona).

Sinus Neāpolis

QUID PUTĀS?

1. What does the term *Magna Graecia* suggest about the cultural heritage of southern Italy?
2. How do Roman election practices compare to modern American ones?
3. What aspects of Roman electoral practices do you think we might do better to emulate?
4. Which ones do you think are not worthy of emulation?

EXERCEĀMUS!

37-5 Scrībāmus

Use the model and the *Verba Ūtenda* to write five inscriptions in which a group of people in the same profession supports a modern politician in his or her run for a modern office.

→ OBAMAM PRAESIDEM TONSORES ROGANT

🔊 VERBA ŪTENDA

argentārius, -iī m. banker	*lanius, -iī* m. butcher	*praefectus, -ī urbis* m. mayor
astrologus, -ī m. fortune teller	*medicus, -ī* m. physician	*praeses, -idis* m. president
	obstetrix, -īcis f. midwife	*saltātrix, -īcis* f. dancing girl
gubernātor, -ōris m. governor	*tonstrix, -īcis* f. hairdresser	*senātor, -ōris* m. senator
	pistor, -ōris m. baker	*tonsor, -ōris* m. barber

37-6 Colloquāmur

You are helping your patron run for office. Based on the inscriptions you have read, greet someone from your class (*Avē, cīvis!* or *Avēte, cīvēs!*) and ask that they support your candidate. Choose the candidate and an office from the chart. Your teachers can give you some background on who these people were. Follow the model.

→ Cicerōnem consulem ōrō tū faciās/vōs faciātis.

CANDIDATE	OFFICE
Cicerō, -ōnis	aedīlis, aedīlis m.
Catō, -ōnis	quaestor, -ōris m.
Pompēius, -ēī	praetor, -ōris m.
Lepidus, -ī	censor, censōris m.
Catilīna, -ae	consul, -is m.

37-7 Verba Discenda

Answer the following questions about the *Verba Discenda*.

1. From what Latin verb is *petītiō* derived?
2. What verb is *ambitiō* derived from?
3. What Latin adjective is *lībertīnus* derived from?
4. What Latin word for a family member is the basis of the word *mātrimōnium*?
5. The word *quasi* is borrowed directly by English. What does this word mean in English?
6. What is the Latin word for the person who perfoms the action expressed by the verb *nuntiō*?
7. Find an interjection.
8. What preposition is combined with *rīdeō* to create the word *irrīdeō*?
9. What Latin noun is related to *armō*?
10. What Latin verb is related to *memoria*?

🔊 VERBA DISCENDA

aeger, aegra, aegrum **sick**
ambitiō, -iōnis **f. canvassing (for votes), political campaign** [ambition, ambitious]
arbitror, abitrārī, arbitrātus sum **observe, perceive; think** [arbitrate]
armō **(1) arm** [armament]
centum **(indecl.) one hundred** [centennial]
dissimilis, dissimile **unlike** [dissimilar]
Edepol! **By Pollux!**

fabrica, -ae **f. workshop; art, craft** [fabricate]
horribilis, horribile **rough, terrible, horrible**
irrīdeō, irrīdēre, irrīsī, irrīsum **laugh at, mock**
lībertīnus, -ī **m. freedman** [libertine]
magistrātus, -ūs **m. office, magistracy; magistrate**
mātrimōnium, -iī **n. marriage, matrimony** [matrimonial]
memoria, -ae **f. memory** [memorial]

nuntiō **(1) announce, report** [annunciation, denounce]
optō **(1) wish** [optional]
pergō, pergere, perrexī, perrectum **go ahead, advance, proceed**
petītiō, -iōnis **f. candidacy, petition; lawsuit**
quasi **as if, practically** [quasi-stellar]
recenter **recently**
retineō, retinēre, retinuī, retentum **hold fast, retain; cling to** [retention]

sextus, -a, -um **sixth** [sextet]
similis, simile **similar to, like** [similarity]
succēdō, succēdere, successī, successum **go below, go under; come to; succeed (to)** [successive]
sustineō, sustinēre, sustinuī, sustentum **hold up, support, withstand** [sustainable]
utinam **if only! would that!**

Angulus Grammaticus

Greek in Latin

From early in their history, Romans were conscious of the superiority of Greek culture. They were exposed to Greek culture from their neighbors, not only, to the south, the Greek cities in *Magna Graecia,* but also, to the north, the Etruscans, who imported a great deal of their pottery and culture from Greece. The Greek language was the lingua franca of the eastern Mediteranean as well as of *Magna Graecia.*

The earliest Roman literature consisted of loose translations from Greek, such as the *Odyssey* of Livius Andronicus and adaptations like the comedies of Plautus. Even the greatest works of Latin literature, including the *Aeneid* of Vergil and the *Odes* of Horace, were based on Greek literary forms and topics.

The Romans became so enamored of things Greek that they even abandoned their traditional, stress-based poetry (called Saturnian verses) for the more quantity-based system used by the Greeks.

Greece became a Roman province in 146 B.C., but the Romans knew that Greek culture had conquered its conquerors. Horace himself says:

> *Graecia capta ferum victōrem cēpit.*
> Horace *Epistulae* 2.1.156

Notice whom Horace calls *ferum* (wild, savage) in this sentence. (It is not the Greeks.)

The Greek influence on Latin is also illustrated by the large number of Greek words borrowed directly by Latin. Many of these words, through Latin, then became English words. Here are just a few examples:

bibliothēca, -ae f.	geōgraphia, -ae f.	philosophia, -ae f.
camēlus, -ī m.	geōmetria, -ae f.	poēta, -ae m.
colossus, -ī m.	hērōs, hērōis m.	symphōnia, -ae f.
cōmoedia, -ae f.	historia, -ae f.	theātrum, -ī n.
delphīnus, -ī m.	metallum, -ī n.	thermae, -ārum f. pl.
elephans, -antis m.	paedagōgus, -ī m.	tragoedia, -ae f.
epigramma, -atis n.	peristȳlium, -iī n.	tyrannus, -ī m.

Most of these Greek words were given Latin declension endings. But some words, and most proper names borrowed from Greek, retain Greek case endings in Latin:

Nom.	hērōs
Gen.	hērōis
Dat.	hērōī
Acc.	hērōa
Abl.	hērōe (Greek has no ablative)

38

Nuptiae

Lectiō Prīma

Antequam Legis

As our story continues, we come at last to the day of Servilia's marriage to Cordus. Prior to the wedding, Servilius and Cordus agreed on the dowry and on Cordus' financial support for Servilius' run for the praetorship. After that the couple was publicly engaged and exchanged rings. We join the story on the day before the actual wedding with all its wishes, worries, and fears. As you read, you will see the ways that Latin can express fear.

Expressing Fear

"I am **afraid to** go there, because I **fear that** he will be there also!"

This simple English sentence shows two different ways to express "fear": "I am afraid to X" and "I am afraid that X will happen."

Like English, Latin has two basic ways to show fear:

Latin Fear Construction	English Translation
1. verb of fearing + **infinitive**	be afraid **to**/fear **to**
*Timeō Rōmam **īre**.*	
*Vereor Rōmam **īre**.*	I am afraid **to go** to Rome.
2. verb of fearing + **subjunctive**	
*Vereor **nē** hostēs Rōmam **eant**.*	I'm afraid **that** the enemy **are coming** to Rome.
*Timeō **ut** Augustus Rōmam **eat**.*	I am afraid **that** the Augustus **is not coming** to Rome.
or	
*Timeō **nē** Augustus Rōmam **nōn eat**.*	

Look for fear constructions marked in **bold** in *Lectio Prīma*.

Dextrārum Iunctiō
DeAgostini / SuperStock

GRAMMATICA
Fear Constructions
Subjunctives in Relative Clauses
Consolidation of Purpose Clauses

MŌRĒS RŌMĀNĪ
Nuptiae Rōmānae

LATĪNA HODIERNA
The Latin Vocabulary of Marriage Today

ORBIS TERRĀRUM RŌMĀNUS
Etrūria

ANGULUS GRAMMATICUS
The Force of the Subjunctive

LECTIŌNĒS:
PRĪDIĒ NUPTIĀRUM
and
TALASSIŌ!

Servilius' household buzzes with preparations for the upcoming wedding while Cordus and Servilius discuss the need for a fire department in Rome. After much anticipation and preparation, Servilia and Cordus are finally married.

Gemma

ānulum in quartō digitō:
Cordus is wearing his
engagement ring. Romans
exchanged rings at
engagement rather than at the
wedding ceremony. This
finger, also called the *digitus
medicīnālis,* was chosen
because it was long believed
that a nerve ran directly from
it to the heart. The custom
remains today in our ring
finger.

EXERCEĀMUS!

38-1 Skimming the *Lectiō* for Expressions of Fear

Various worries and concerns emerge in *Lectiō Prīma.* Before you read, find the answers to these
questions. Use the range of lines provided to look for the answers. Give the answers in both English
and Latin. Use the chart on Latin fear constructions on pg. 503 as a guide, and follow the model.

→   What is Caecilia worried about in lines 5–6?
   ut cēna idōnea sit (that the dinner will not be suitable)

1. What other two worries does Caecilia have in lines 5–6?
2. What two concerns does Servilia have in lines 6–8?
3. What fear does Lucius have in lines 9–11?
4. What fear does Servilius have in lines 13–14?
5. What worries Cordus in line 15?
6. What concern does Cordus have in lines 21–22?
7. What does Servilius tell Cordus he is not afraid to do in lines 23–26?

🔊 PRĪDIĒ NUPTIĀRUM

Prīdiē diēī nuptiārum est. In domibus et Servīliī et Cordī servīs multa agenda sunt—
ubīque aliī alia faciunt. Herī multī clientēs ad patrōnum cibōs opulentōs et vīna optima
mīserant. Aelius, novissimus cliens, quoque placentās dulcēs ā Valeriā et Liciniā coctās
tulerat. Et sīmiam Sōcratem Aelius mīserat ad hospitēs dēlectandōs.

Cordus anxius ānulum versat.

5   Et Caecilia et Servīlia anxiae sunt—Caecilia **timet ut** cēna idōnea **sit** et **ut** servī
strēnuē **labōrent.** Praesertim **pertimescit ut** dignitās familiae **ostendātur.** Servīlia
verētur nē amīcae rūre Rōmam **nōn adveniant** et **nē** ille patruus quī semper est ēbrius ad-
veniat.

Lūcium, autem, nullae cūrae afflīgunt. In culīnā sedet et cibum opulentum avidē
10 spectat. Gaudēns intrā sē "Ecce," inquit, "mox optimum cibum consūmam! Utinam iam crās esset! Sed **timeō** cibum
nunc consūmere. Sī autem paucī ad cēnam advēnerint, tunc plūs cibī mihi erit!"

Intereā Cordus Servīliusque in tepidāriō thermārum dē negōtiīs mūtuīs colloquuntur. Cordus, dum loquitur,
ānulum in quartō digitō manūs sinistrae anxius versat. Hōc vīsō, Servīlius rīdet et "Corde," inquit, "**vereor nē**
anxius **sīs.** Nōlī **timēre** uxōrem **dēdūcere!** Quid timēs?"

15 Cordus: "**Timeō nē** tibi, praetōrī factō, gener inūtilis **sim!** Quid beneficiī tibi offerre poterō?"

Servīlius: "Mehercle! Tibi ūnicam fīliam meam nōn dedissem nisi tē virum honestum atque ūtilem esse aesti-
māvissem! Et, praetūrā captā, magnum beneficium mihi atque urbī offerre poteris!"

Cordus: "Certē! Quid agendum est?"

Servīlius: "Ānulus ille, quem geris in manū suā, ab Aeliō cliente meō factus est. Nōnne insulam in Subūrā
20 incendiō destructam esse audīvistī? Fabrica tōta eius quoque destructa est!"

Cordus: "Audīvī! Ut semper, **vereor nē** tāle ācre incendium urbem tōtam **destruat.** Vigilēs constituendī sunt!
Nisi Augustus hoc faciat, **pertimescō nē** pācem et quiētem urbs umquam **habeat!**"

Servīlius: "Ita est. Meminī proavum tuum Crassum quī aedificia flagrantia ab incolīs emēbat. Incolae, **veritī nē**
nihil prō aedificiō destructō **acciperent,** venditiōnī accessērunt. Negōtiō factō, Crassī servī flammās ācrēs
25 exstinguēbant. Tālia negōtia multōs vexābant! Praetūrā captā, ego prō tē et prō vigilibus constituendīs in Senātū
alloquar. Hoc, mī gener, tibi prōmittō—nōn **timēbō** id **facere!**"

Iungentēs dextram dextrae, gener et socer concordant.

Tunc Cordus: "Ita. Mē Crassī pudet. Sed nunc, hīc in tepidāriō manēre quoque mihi displicet. Eāmus in
caldārium!"

🔊 VERBA ŪTENDA

accēdō, accēdere, accessī, accessum agree; assent, approach; attack

ācer, ācris, ācre sharp, violent, eager, swift

aedificium, -iī n. building

aestimō (1) value, estimate, consider

afflīgō, afflīgere, afflīxī, afflictum bother

ānulus, -ī m. ring

avidē eagerly

beneficium, -iī n. kindness, benefit, favor

caldārium, -iī n. hot bath

concordō (1) be in agreement

consūmō, consūmere, consumpsī, consump- tum use up, eat, consume

dēdūcō, dēdūcere, dēduxī, dēductum lead down, draw down; bring away, bring off; conduct, escort; derive; uxōrem dēdūcere take a wife, marry

dēlectō (1) amuse, delight, charm

dexter, dext(e)ra, dext(e)rum right; dext(e)ra (manus), -ae f. right hand

dextram dextrae iungere shake hands

digitus, -ī m. finger

exstinguō, exstinguere, exstinxī, exstinctum quench, extinguish

flagrans, flagrantis glowing, blazing, ardent

flamma, -ae f. flame

gaudeō, gaudēre, gavīsus sum rejoice, be glad

gener, generis m. son-in-law

incola, -ae m./f. inhabitant

inūtilis, inūtile useless, profitless

iungō, iungere, iunxī, iunctum join

mūtuus, -a, -um mutual, shared

nuptiāe, -ārum f. pl. wedding

opulentus, -a, -um rich

ostendō, ostendere, ostendī, ostentum/ ostensum show, display

patruus, -ī m. uncle

pertimescō, pertimescere, pertimuī become very scared

placenta, -ae f. a flat cake

proavus, -ī m. great- grandfather

prōmittō, prōmittere, prōmīsī, prōmissum promise

pudeō, pudēre, puduī, puditum be ashamed; *mē pudet* (imp.) I am ashamed

quartus, -a, -um fourth

quiēs, quiētis f. quiet, calm, rest

sinister, sinistra, sinistrum left; sinistra (manus), -ae f. the left hand

socer, soceris m. father-in-law

tepidārium, -iī n. warm bath

thermae, -ārum f. pl. public baths

ūnicus, -a, -um one and only

venditiō, -ōnis f. sale

versō (1) keep turning around, spin, whirl

vexō (1) agitate, harry, upset, disturb

POSTQUAM LĒGISTĪ

Answer the following questions in English. Answer in Latin if the question is followed by (L).

1. How do the concerns of the following characters in *Lectiō Prīma* compare to those of members of a modern wedding party on the day before the wedding: Caecilia, Servilia, Lucius, Servilius, and Cordus?

2. How do Servilius' clients prepare for the wedding? (L) How would mod- ern business and political associates acknowledge a wedding today?

3. How did Cordus' great-grandfather Crassus make his fortune? (L) Can you think of any parallels in today's world?

4. How does Cordus feel about Crassus' business methods? Do you agree or disagree with Cordus? Why?

5. Use evidence from this *lectiō* to describe the relationship between Servilius and Cordus. How does this relationship between father-in-law and son-in- law compare to modern situations you have known?

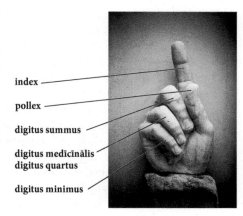

index
pollex
digitus summus
digitus medīcīnālis
digitus quartus
digitus minimus

Manus et Digitī

Grammatica A

Fear Constructions

There are two ways to express fear in Latin:

LATIN	ENGLISH
verb of fearing + **infinitive**	fear to
verb of fearing + **subjunctive** 　Positive:　**nē + subjunctive** 　Negative: **ut** or **nē … nōn + subjunctive**	fear that fear that … not

Here are the two infinitive expressions of fear from *Lectiō Prīma*:

*Nōlī timēre uxōrem **dēdūcere!***　　Don't be afraid to get married!
*Hoc, mī gener, tibi prōmittō—nōn timēbō id **facere.***　　My son-in-law, I promise you—I will not be afraid to do this!

Remember that infinitives are verbal nouns. The infinitive here is acting like a direct object. What do you fear? You fear to get married.

　　Subjunctive fear clauses are more "iffy," expressing a fear of something that may or may not happen. Notice the various ways you can translate a fear clause.

I am **afraid that** he did that.
I am **afraid that** he might do that.
I am **afraid lest** he do that.

　　The rules of sequence of tenses you have learned will also help you translate. Look at the following sentences, and notice how the subjunctives show the kind of relative time you have grown used to. Note, too, the many ways to translate fear clauses.

Primary Sequence

*Timeō nē illud **faciat**.*　　I fear that he is doing that. (present subjunctive, time near main verb)

*Timeō nē illud **fēcerit**.*　　I fear he may have done that. (perfect subjunctive, time before main verb)

*Timeō nē illud **factūrus sit**.*　　I fear lest he do that. (FAP + *sim, sīs,* etc., time after main verb)

Secondary Sequence

*Timuī ut illud **faceret**.*　　I feared that he wasn't doing that. (imperfect subjunctive, time near main verb)

*Timuī nē illud nōn **fēcisset**.*　　I feared he had not done that. (pluperfect subjunctive, time before main verb)

*Timuī ut illud **factūrus esset**.*　　I was afraid he was not going to do that. (FAP + *essem, essēs,* etc., time after main verb)

EXERCEĀMUS!

38-2 Making Fear Clauses

Convert the following sentences into fear clauses using the subjunctive. Begin your sentence with the words *timeō nē* and *timuī ut*, and pay attention to the sequence of tenses. Then translate each sentence. Follow the model.

→ Anxius es.
Timeō nē anxius sīs.   I'm afraid you are nervous.
Timuī ut anxius essēs.   I was afraid you weren't nervous.

1. Anxia erat.
2. Patruus ēbrius veniet.
3. Caecilia īrāta in peristȳliō stat.
4. Lūcius in culīnā cibum omne cōnsūmit.
5. Aeliī insula destructa est.
6. Sōcratēs hospitibus nocēbit.

Lectiō Secunda

Antequam Legis

The events of *Lectiō Secunda* occur on the day of the wedding. Before you read about Servilia's wedding, you may want to read the description of the Roman marriage ceremony in the *Mōrēs Rōmānī* section of this chapter.

You will meet a new character in *Lectiō Secunda*: Publius Quinctilius Varus. Recently (in 13 B.C.), Varus had served as consul with Tiberius and, at the time of our story, was married to Claudia Pulchra, a grand niece of Augustus. Servilius would have known him, at least in passing, since they both sat in the Senate. His presence as *auspex* is a sign of Augustus' favor toward Servilius and his campaign to become praetor. This is the same Varus you read about in Chapter 34, the general who lost three Roman legions in the Teutoburger Forest in Germany.

Subjunctives in Relative Clauses

As you read about the wedding, notice how the subjunctive mood is sometimes used with relative clauses introduced by *quī, quae, quod.*

For now, as you read *Lectiō Secunda*, just be very careful to check to see if the verb in the *quī* clause is indicative or subjunctive. If subjunctive, translate it with one of the now familiar "subjunctive words": should, would, could, might, may. This should get you through the passage in fine shape.

EXERCEĀMUS!

38-3 Relative Pronouns + Subjunctive

All the relative pronouns are marked in **bold** in *Lectiō Secunda*. As you read, list them line by line. Find the verb(s) they introduce and indicate whether the verb is indicative or subjunctive. Then translate the relative clause accordingly (using "subjunctive words" with the subjunctive). Follow the model.

Line	Relative Pronoun	Verb	Mood	Translation
→ 2	*quī*	*emeret*	subjunctive	who would buy

TALASSIŌ!

Diēs nuptiārum adest et in culīnā Sicō, omnibus servīs imperāns sīcut dux exercituī imperāns, perturbātur quod mīsit servum **quī** plūs mellis emeret et ille nōn iam rediit. Clientēs Servīliī mīsērunt servōs **quī** Sicōnem adiuvent et hī Sicōnī nōn placent.

Amīca ad Caeciliam ornātrīcem, **quae** crīnēs Servīliae hastā caelibārī ordināret et
5   eōs vittīs fīgeret, mīsit. Sed Servīlia sollicita est nē vittae crīnēs turpēs faciant. "Māter," inquit, "cūr crīnēs meī sīc ornandī sunt?"

Caecilia "Cūr," inquit, "hastā et vittīs ūtimur? Nesciō, fīlia. Hodiē multa, **quōrum** orīgō obscūra est, agēmus et nēmō, **quī** illa explicāre potest, Rōmae hodiē habitat."

Servīlia adhūc anxia est sed eī māter haec verba dīcit: "Fīlia, nōlī anxia esse. Cordus
10   bonus vir est. Cordus mihi vidētur vir mansuētus **quī** tē lēniter atque aequē tractet." Hīs verbīs dictīs, Servīlia, cum nōn iam puella sit, Laribus bullam, signum puellāre, relinquit et fēminae signum, tunicam rectam, **quam** ancilla cingulō **cingit**, induit.

Caesia intereā Servīliae consōbrīna, **quae** cupida nuptiārum videndārum Vēiīs Rōmam advēnit, intrat cum mātre Lucillā, **quae** Servīliae mātertera et prōnuba est.
15   Caesia **quae** modo sex annōs nāta est et numquam prius nuptam vīdit susurrat: "Mātercula, quae vestīmenta illa sunt? Numquam tālia antehāc vīdī." Māter respondet: "Servīlia sīcut nuptae omnēs vestīmenta nuptiālia, flammeum et lūteōs soccōs, induit."

Mox turba laeta audītur et Cordus, togā splendissimā indūtus, multīs cum cognātīs et amīcīs ad domum Servīliī advenit. Nunc est tempus auspiciōrum et Varus, viscera intuēns, "Ōmina," inquit, "bona sunt!"
20   Tunc prōnuba Lucilla Servīliam ad Cordum dūcit et manūs dextrās iungit. Tunc Servīlia, Cordum intuēns, haec verba prisca dīcit: "Ubi tū Gāius, ego Gāia."

Caesia "Sed, māter," susurrat, "nōmen eī Servīlia, nōn Gāia, est!"

"Tacē, Caesia! Sīc omnēs nuptae dīcunt. Mōs māiōrum est!"

Tunc Cordus et uxor nova farreum lībum consūmunt, et omnēs, "Fēlīciter!" clāmantēs, plaudunt. Post cēnam,
25   diē vesperascente, tempus dēductiōnis ad Cordum adest et Caesia "Māter," rogat, "cūr Servīlia nummum in soccō posuit?"

Respondet māter, "Nupta habet trēs nummōs: ūnum in manū, alium in saccō et tertium in soccō. Prīmum virō novō dabit, secundum Laribus in domō novā, et tertium Laribus Compitālibus in triviīs."

Tunc ad Cordum, **quī** iam domum rediit, nova uxor dūcitur. Tībīcinibus servīsque cum taedīs prōsequentibus,
30   omnēs rīdent et "Talassiō!" aut "Hymēn Hymenaee!" clāmant. Omnēs comitantēs nucēs **quās** antehāc eīs Servīlius dedit, ad turbam laetam iaciunt. Sōcratēs, quī in umerīs Lūciī sedet, quoque nucēs iacit!

Tandem domum adveniunt. Servīlia in postibus adipem et vittās pōnit. Tunc Cordus Servīliam trans līmen portat nē Larēs novam invideant. Marītus uxōrī novae aquam et ignem offert et iterum Servīlia: "Ubi tū Gāius," inquit, "ego Gāia." Foribus clausīs, Servīlia vītam novam intrat.

Servīlia Nupta

POSTQUAM LĒGISTĪ

Answer the following questions in English. Also answer in Latin if the question is followed by (L).

1. Describe the scene in the kitchen on the day of the wedding. Why is Sico so upset? (L)
2. How does the *ornātrix* fix Servilia's hair? What is Servilia worried about? (L)
3. What is Caecilia's advice to her stepdaughter on her wedding day? (L) How does this compare to what a mother might say to a bride today?
4. Use *Lectiō Secunda* to compare and contrast Roman and American wedding customs.
5. Why is *Lectiō Secunda* entitled *Talassiō!*

🔊 VERBA ŪTENDA

adeps, adipis m./f. fat
aequē fairly
antehāc before this time, earlier
auspicium, -(i)ī n. sign, omen, auspices
bulla, -ae f. locket worn around a child's neck
caelibāris, caelibāre unmarried. See *hasta*
cingō, cingere, cinxī, cinctum tie, put a belt around
cingulum, -ī n. belt
claudō, claudere, clausī, clausum shut, close
cognātus, -a, -um relative, kinsman
Compitālis, Compitāle of the crossroads
consōbrīna, -ae f. female first cousin (on the mother's side)
crīnis, crīnis m. hair
dēductiō, -ōnis f. leading away, escorting
exercitus, -ūs m. army
explicō (1) explain
farreus, -a, -um of grain, grain
fēlīciter luckily, with luck

fīgō, fīgere, fīxī, fixum fasten in place
flammeum, -eī n. bridal veil
Gāia, -ae f. Gaia, ceremonial name of a Roman bride
Gāius, -iī m. Gaius, ceremonial name of a Roman bridegroom
hasta, -ae f. spear; *hasta caelibāris* "the unmarried spear," traditionally used to set a bride's hair
Hymēn Hymenaee a traditional cry to the god of marriage
induō, induere, induī, indūtum put on
invideō, invidēre, invīdī, invīsum (+ dat.) envy, hate, grudge; refuse
iunctiō, -ōnis f. joining
Lar, Laris m. Lar, a household god
lēniter gently
lībum, -ī m. special holiday cake or pancake
līmen, līminis n. threshold
lūteus, -a, -um yellow

mansuētus, -a, -um gentle
mātertera, -ae f. aunt, mother's sister
nupta, -ae f. bride
nuptiae, -ārum f. pl. wedding
nuptiālis, nuptiāle nuptial, marriage
nux, nucis f. nut
obscūrus, -a, -um dark, shady; gloomy; uncertain
ōmen, ōminis n. omen, sign
ordinō (1) put in order
orīgō, orīginis f. origin, beginning, source
ornātrix, ornātrīcis f. hair dresser
postis, postis f. doorpost
priscus, -a, -um old, ancient
prius before
prōnuba, -ae f. matron of honor
prōsequor, prōsequī, prōsecūtus sum accompany
puellāris, puellare pertaining to a girl

signum, -ī n. mark, token, sign, seal
soccus, -ī m. loose-fitting slipper
sollicitus, -a, -um uneasy, apprehensive, anxious
susurrō (1) whisper
taeda, -ae f. pine-torch
Talassiō! an ancient wedding cry
tertius, -a, -um third
tībīcen, -cinis m. piper
tractō (1) treat
trivium, triv(i)ī n. an intersection, a place where three roads meet
tunica, -ae f. tunic
turpis, turpe ugly, foul, loathsome
Vēiī, Vēiōrum m. pl. Veii, a very old Etruscan city north of Rome
vesperascō, vesperascere, vesperāvī grow toward evening
vestīmentum, -ī n. clothing
viscera, viscerum n. pl. internal organs, entrails
vitta, -ae f. ribbon

Grammatica B

Subjunctives in Relative Clauses

In Latin, the relative pronoun *quī* + the subjunctive can be a purpose clause or can indicate something about the character of the subject of that clause.

Relative Clause of Purpose

*Sicō perturbātur quod mīsit servum **quī** plūs mellis **emeret** et ille nōn iam rediit.*
Sico is worried because the slave he sent (who was) to buy more honey has not yet returned.

*Clientēs Servīliī mīsērunt servōs **quī** Sicōnem **adiuvent** . . .*
Servilius' clients sent slaves to help Sico . . .
Servilius' clients sent slaves who were to help Sico . . .

Notā Bene: This construction is mostly found after verbs like "send", "choose", and "delegate".

Relative Clause of Characteristic

*Cordus mihi vidētur vir mansuētus **quī** tē lēniter atque aequē **tractet**.*
Cordus seems to me to be a gentle man who would treat you gently and fairly.

A regular *quī* clause in the indicative is stating a fact.

> *Mēdēa est fēmina quae līberōs suōs necāvit.*
> Medea is the woman who killed her children.

But a *quī* clause with the subjunctive can indicate something about the character of the person involved.

> *Tullia est fēmina quae līberōs suōs necet.*
> Tullia is the kind of woman who would kill her own children.

Consolidation of Purpose Clauses

You have now seen that **purpose** can be expressed in Latin using several different grammatical constructions:

- *ut/nē* + subjunctive

Augustus vigilēs **ut incendia exstinguant** *constituit.*	Augustus established fire brigades to put out fires.

- *ad* + accusative gerund(ive)

  Augustus vigilēs **ad incendia exstinguenda** *constituit.*

- genitive gerund(ive) + *grātiā/causā*

  Vigilēs **incendiōrum exstinguendōrum causā** *Augustus constituit.*

- *quī* + subjunctive

  Augustus vigilēs **quī incendia exstinguerent** *constituit.*

- supine in the accusative

Vigilēs **adiūtum** *vēnērunt.*	The fire brigade came to help.

EXERCEĀMUS!

38-4 Purpose Clauses

Change each purpose clause into the construction indicated in parentheses. Follow the model.

→ Caecilia in peristȳliō stat ut servīs imperat. (*ad* + acc. gerundive)
   Caecilia in peristȳliō stat ad servōs imperandōs.

1. Sīmiam Sōcratem Aelius mittit ad hospitēs dēlectandōs. (*quī* + subjunctive)
2. Varus vēnit ut ōmina acciperet. (gerundive + *causā*)
3. Servīlius hospitibus nucēs dabat ut eās iacerent. (*ad* + gerund)
4. Lūcius in culīnam intrat ad cibum videndum. (*ut* + subjunctive)
5. Cordus vigilēs mīsit ad ignēs exstinguendōs. (*quī* + subjunctive)

Mōrēs Rōmānī

Nuptiae Rōmānae

There were many kinds of wedding cermonies (*nuptiae, -ārum* f. pl.) in ancient Rome, ranging from the very formal to the very informal. These ceremonies also varied according to the historical period, social level, political intent, and other factors. The wedding ceremony of Servilia and Cordus illustrates many aspects of a typical upper-class wedding.

Rings were exchanged by the bride and groom at the engagement, not at the wedding. The Latin word for "bride" (*nupta, -ae* f.) is probably derived from *nūbō, nūbere, nupsī, nuptum* "veil oneself." The verb *nūbō* could be used only in reference to the bride. To refer to a man marrying, Romans used the phrase *uxōrem dūcere*, similar to the English "to take a wife," indicating that the groom led the bride away from her home to his. The groom was called *novus marītus* (new husband).

Marriage festivities usually took place at the homes of both the bride and the groom. Servilius' and Cordus' friends and relations sent gifts, especially food, for the *cēna nuptiālis* (the marriage feast at the bride's house) and the *repōtia* (the party at the groom's house on the day after the wedding). Many guests were often invited to both events.

In addition to the *nupta* and *novus marītus*, other important participants included:

- The *auspex, auspicis* m., the diviner, serving as both priest and best man, read omens at the ceremony and also witnessed the marriage contract.
- The *prōnuba, -ae* f., the "matron-of-honor" was typically a *ūnivira, -ae* f., that is, a woman who was still married to her first husband.

The preparations for the bride were elaborate and included:

- A ceremonial bath on the morning of the wedding
- A special hairdo, in which the hair was combed with a *hasta caelibāris* into six braids kept in place by *vittae* (woolen ribbons); the bride also wore flowers in her hair
- A solemn putting aside of her *bulla* at the shrine to her father's household gods
- A special garment called *tunica recta* (a woolen tunic woven on an archaic loom and fastened with a belt (*cingulum, -ī* n.) tied with the Herculean knot; the groom later solemnly unties this knot in the wedding chamber
- Yellow slippers (*lūteī soccī*)
- A flame-colored veil (*flammeum, flammeī* n.)
- Three coins, as described in the *lectiō*

The formal marriage ceremony consisted of:

- The procession (*pompa, -ae* f.) of the groom with his relatives to the house of the bride
- The reading of the religious signs (*auspicium, -iī* n.)
- The joining of right hands (*dextrārum iunctiō*) of the bride and the groom by the *prōnuba*
- The bride says to her new husband *Ubi tū Gāius, ego Gāia* (Where you are Gaius, I am Gaia); this was the most solemn moment of the ceremony and did not change to fit the real names of the couple
- The ratification of the marriage contract (*tabulae nuptiālēs* or *dōtālēs*)

Nupta

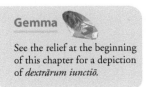

Gemma

See the relief at the beginning of this chapter for a depiction of *dextrārum iunctiō*.

- The marriage banquet (*cēna nuptiālis*)
- The procession of the bride to the home of the groom (*dēductiō in domum marītī*), as described in the *lectiō*

The bridegroom did not participate in this procession but returned earlier to his home and waited there for the arrival of his new bride.

At the home of the groom:

- The bride anointed doorposts with fat and and decorated them with woolen ribbons.
- The groom carried the bride over his threshold.
- The groom offered his wife water and fire. This was called *aquae et ignis commūnicātiō*. Water and fire were considered the basic needs of life. When a person was sent into exile from Rome, the formula used was "to deprive him of water and fire."
- There was a symbolic marriage bed (*torus, -ī* m.) in the *ātrium* of the house.
- The bride was led to the marriage chamber, where she was ceremonially undressed.
- The next day there was a festive meal (*repōtia, -ōrum* n. pl.) at the groom's house.

In one of his longer poems (#61) Catullus celebrates a wedding. Some of these verses inspired the description of Servilia's wedding. Note how one line, addressed to Hymen, the god of marriage, is repeated as a refrain. The rest of the lines are addressed to the bride. Here is a simplified version of part of this poem.

> iō Hymēn Hymenaee iō, iō Hymēn Hymenaee.
> nupta, tū quoque cavē nē negēs quae tuus vir petet, nī petītum aliunde eat.
> iō Hymēn Hymenaee iō, iō Hymēn Hymenaee.
> ēn tibi! sine ut virī tuī domus quae tibi serviat sit potens et beāta.
> iō Hymēn Hymenaee iō, iō Hymēn Hymenaee.
> usque dum anīlitās cāna tremulum tempus movēns omnia omnibus annuit.
> iō Hymēn Hymenaee iō, iō Hymēn Hymenaee.
> fer pedēs aureolōs cum bonō ōmine trans līmen et subī rāsilem forem.
> iō Hymēn Hymenaee iō, iō Hymēn Hymenaee.
> aspice intus ut accubāns tōtus tuus vir in Tyriō torō tibi immineat.
> iō Hymēn Hymenaee iō, iō Hymēn Hymenaee.
>
> Adapted from Catullus 61.143–175

🔊 VERBA ŪTENDA

aliunde elsewhere, from another person
anīlitās, -tātis f. old age (of a woman)
annuō, annuere, annuī nod (in approval) to, agree with
aureolus, -a, -um golden (because she is wearing yellow slippers)
cānus, -a, -um white-haired
ēn (+dat.) come on!

Hymēn, Hymenis m. Hymen, the god of marriage; also, the wedding song or the marriage itself
Hymenaeus, -ī m. Hymenaeus = Hymen
immineō, imminēre (+ dat.) be on the watch for
līmen, līminis n. threshold
nī = nisi unless
ōmen, -inis n. omen, sign
petītum (a supine) "in order to seek"

rāsilis, rāsile smooth, well-polished
serviō, servīre, servīvī/ serviī, servītum serve, be a slave to
tempus, temporis n. forehead
torus, -ī m. marriage bed
tōtus tuus "totally yours"
tremulus, -a, -um trembling (here, from old age)
Tyrius, -a, -um from Tyre (= purple)

Latīna Hodierna
The Latin Vocabulary of Marriage Today

Many words related to marriage in English and the modern Romance languages are derived from Latin. Here are a few examples. Look up the words in a dictionary if you are unfamiliar with what they mean in particular languages.

Latin	*caelibāris, caelibāre* unmarried	*mātrimōnium, -iī* n. marriage	*marītus, -ī* m. husband	*nuptiae, -iārum* f. pl. wedding	*sponsa, -ae* f. betrothed, married partner
			novus marītus, -ī m. bride-groom	*nuptiālis, nuptiāle* pertaining to a wedding	*sponsus, -ī* m.
			marītō (1) marry		
English	celibate	matrimony	marriage, marry	nuptials, nuptial	spouse
Italian	cèlibe	matrimoniale	marito	nuziale	sposa, sposarsi, sposalizio
Spanish	célibe	matrimonio	marido	nupcial	esposo, esposa
French	celibataire	matrimonial(e)	mari, marié(e), mariage, se marier	nuptial(e)	l'épouse, l'époux, épouser

Orbis Terrārum Rōmānus
Etrūria

Servilia's relatives, Lucilla and Caesia, come to the wedding from Veii, a city of Etruria, located to the north of Rome. The Etruscans had a major influence on Roman culture and history. Etruscan civilization began to flourish in northern Italy from about 1100 B.C. The heartland of the Etruscans was an area on the west coast of Italy, from the Tiber River in the south to the Arno River in the north. This area is known in Italy today as *Toscana* (Tuscany in English).

Etruria consisted of a collection of powerful, wealthy, and independent cities, the most important of which included:

Etruscan Name	Latin Name	Modern Italian Name
Tarchna	Tarquiniī	Tarquinia
Felathri	Volāterrae	Volaterra
Cisra	Caere	Cerveteri
Veio?	Vēiī	Veio
Phersna	Perusia	Perugia
Felsina	Bonōnia	Bologna

The proximity of Etruria to Rome and the advanced culture of the Etruscans resulted in significant Etruscan influence on Roman politics, history, and religion. Not only did the Etruscan Tarquinian family rule Rome for more than a century, but Roman efforts to subdue the independent Etruscan cities absorbed Roman attention for an additional four hundred years.

Fascēs Americānī

Etruscans built elaborate tombs for their dead, in which have been found many wall paintings, Greek painted pottery, and other artifacts. The Etruscans gave the Romans many of their religious beliefs (including the practice of augury, which you read about in Servilia's wedding) and political symbols like the *fascēs* carried by lictors at the side of consuls and praetors. By the Augustan Age, the region was fully Romanized and the Etruscan language was disappearing.

Mūsicus Tuscus

Sarcophagus Tuscānicus

Etrūria Antīqua

QUID PUTĀS?

1. Use the *Mōrēs Rōmānī* to summarize the main features of a Roman wedding. Which ones would you consider suggesting for a modern American wedding? Which would you definitely not use? Why?
2. Reread the excerpt from Catullus' Poem #61, and write your own poem celebrating a wedding you have recently attended.
3. Use the vocabulary chart in *Latīna Hodierna* to explain how Latin has influenced the English vocabulary related to weddings.
4. Summarize the relationship between the Romans and the Etruscans.

EXERCEĀMUS!

38-5   Scrībāmus

Write a letter to a friend as if you had been a guest at Servilia's wedding. Pick any part of the ceremony and write a simplified version of events in five sentences. Change all the verbs to past tense. Follow the model.

→ Tunc Servīlia nummōs trēs in soccōs posuit.

38-6   Colloquāmur

Working with a classmate, ask questions about the wedding ceremony. Take turns asking and answering the questions. Follow the model.

→   *Quaestiō: Quis est Lucilla?*
   Responsum: Lucilla prōnuba est.

38-7   Verba Discenda

Countdown. Use the *Verba Discenda* to answer the following questions.

Decem. Find ten verbs.
Novem. For nine *Verba Discenda* find an English derivative in addition to the one provided.
Octō. Find eight words that begin with prepositions used as prefixes.
Septem. Find seven adjectives.
Sex. Find six adjectives that have different nominative endings for the three genders.
Quinque. Find five 3rd conjugation verbs that form the 3rd principal part by adding *-s-* to the stem.
Quattuor. Find four 2nd declension nouns.
Tria. Find three neuter nouns.
Duo. Find two 1st conjugation verbs.
Ūnum. Find a noun that can be either masculine or feminine.

> **Gemma**
>
> *sinister vs. dexter.* The Romans believed that the left was unlucky. Hence, the English word "sinister." Can you use the English word "dexterous" to explain the Roman prejudice about *dexter*?

🔊 VERBA DISCENDA

accēdō, accēdere, accessī, accessum agree; assent, approach; attack [accessible]

ācer, ācris, ācre sharp, violent, eager, swift [acrid]

aedificium, -iī n. building [edifice]

aestimō (1) value, estimate, consider [estimable]

beneficium, -iī n. kindness, benefit, favor [beneficial]

claudo, claudere, clausī, clausum shut, close [inclusive, occlusion]

consūmō, consūmere, consumpsī, consumptum use up, eat, consume [consummation]

dēdūcō, dēdūcere, dēduxī, dēductum lead down, draw down; bring away, bring off; conduct, escort; derive; *uxōrem dēdūcere* take a wife, marry [deducible, deduct]

dēlectō (1) amuse, delight, charm [delectable]

dexter, dext(e)ra, dext(e)rum right; *dext(e)ra (manus), -ae* f. right hand [dexterous, ambidextrous]

digitus, -ī m. finger [digit]

exercitus, -ūs m. army

gaudeō, gaudēre, gavīsus sum rejoice, be glad

incola, -ae m./f. inhabitant

invideō, invidēre, invīdī, invīsum (+ dat.) envy, hate, grudge; refuse [invidious]

iungō, iungere, iunxī, iunctum join [juncture]

obscūrus, -a, -um dark, shady; gloomy; uncertain [obscure]

orīgō, orīginis f. origin, beginning, source [originate]

ostendō, ostendere, ostendī, ostentum/ostensum show, display [ostensible, ostentatious]

quartus, -a, -um fourth [quartile]

signum, -ī n. mark, token, sign, seal [signify]

sinister, sinistra, sinistrum left; *sinistra (manus), -ae* f. the left hand [sinister]

tertius, -a, -um third [tertiary]

turpis, turpe ugly, foul, loathsome [turpitude]

Angulus Grammaticus

The Force of the Subjunctive

Relative clauses of characteristic and purpose are a good place to stop and think about the subjunctive. One way to view the subjunctive is to look at it as the mood of "lesser reality." If the indicative expresses absolute fact, the subjunctive removes the statement from fact to the realm of lesser reality. Consider these sentences:

Lūcius est puer **quī** *placentam tōtam* **dēvorāvit**.
This *quī* clause states a fact. Lucius did indeed eat the entire cake, so *dēvorāvit* is in the indicative.

Lūcius est puer **quī** *placentam tōtam* **dēvoret**.
This *quī* clause is stating a tendency rather than a fact. Here Lucius is **the kind of boy** who might eat an entire cake, so *dēvoret* is in the subjunctive.

Now compare these two sentences:

Caesar mīlitēs **quī** *hostēs* **necāvit** *heri mīsit.*
Yesterday Caesar sent the troops who killed the enemy.
fact = indicative

Caesar mīlitēs **quī** *hostēs* **necārent** *heri mīsit.*
Yesterday Caesar sent troops to kill (who might kill) the enemy.
potential rather than fact = subjunctive

Here are some famous movie lines that use the English subjunctive to express lesser reality.

When the Scarecrow in the Wizard of Oz sings, "If I only had a brain … I'd be smarter than a wizard," he is stating something that is not quite true. He doesn't have a brain … yet.

In *Fiddler on the Roof,* Tevye sings, "If I were a rich man …" He isn't, hence the subjunctive.

As you go through the day, listen for subjunctives in English and see if they state absolute or lesser reality in English. May the Force be with you.

39

Nuntiī Bonī Malīque

Lectiō Prīma

Antequam Legis

Tiberius in Germany

Before you read further you should know a bit of background. Augustus became very ill in 23 B.C. and was near death. Lacking a son of his own, he knew he needed an heir. His first choice, Marcellus, the son of his sister Octavia, died prematurely, also in 23 B.C. Augustus promptly gave his daughter Julia to his old friend Agrippa in marriage, hoping for heirs. From their children he chose his grandsons Gaius and Lucius as successors and adopted them as his sons. But Lucius died in 2 A.D. and Gaius in 4 A.D.

Augustus also had hopes for Drusus, a son born to his third wife, Livia, just before she married him in 38 B.C. Livia already had an older son, Tiberius, but Augustus preferred Drusus and clearly had him in line to succeed him. Unfortunately Drusus died while fighting in Germany in 9 B.C. Tiberius rushed to Germany from his command in Pannonia to be with his dying brother and eventually took over the command in Germany, where he fought successfully. The coin depicted at right commemorates one of these victories. You will remember that Valeria's son, Licinius, is fighting in Germany with Tiberius at the time of our story.

It is against this background that we begin this *lectiō*. News of a great victory by Tiberius over the Germans has reached Rome and is the cause of a wide variety of reactions. As the news spreads, notice how the speakers express their doubts and concerns in Latin. It will come as no surprise to you that clauses expressing doubt, hindering, and prevention often use the subjunctive.

Clauses of Doubting and Hindering/Preventing

The formulas for these clauses (marked in **bold** in the *lectiō*) are straightforward, but the word that introduces the clause varies, depending on whether the phrase controlling the sentence is positive or negative.

Germānī Obsidēs Trādentēs

LECTIŌNĒS:
NUNTIĪ Ē GERMĀNIĀ
and
PECŪLIUM

Rome is excited about the good news of Tiberius' victory in Germany, but Valeria's family receives less welcome news from an old family friend.

517

Doubting

Positive phrase of doubting + *num* or *an* + subjunctive

> ***Dubitō num (an)*** *Tiberius*   I doubt that Tiberius will
> *imperātor **fīat**.*   become emperor.

Negative phrase of doubting + *quīn* + subjunctive

> ***Nōn dubitō quīn*** *Tiberius*   I don't doubt that Tiberius will
> *imperātor **fīat**.*   become emperor.

Hindering/Preventing

Positive verb of hindering/preventing + *quōminus* or *nē* + subjunctive

> *Sicō Lūcium **impedit quōminus***   Sico prevents Lucius
> ***(nē)*** *placentās **consūmat**.*   from eating the cakes.

Negative verb of hindering/preventing + *quīn* + subjunctive

> *Sicō **nōn** Lūcium **impedit quīn***   Sico doesn't keep Lucius
> *placentās consūmat.*   from eating the cakes.

For translating, we recommend that you memorize these four phrases as models.

Dubitō num/an	I doubt **that** … I hesitate **to**
Nōn dubitō quīn	I do not doubt **that** …
Impediō nē/quōminus	I keep someone **from** … **Xing**
Nōn impediō quīn	I don't keep someone **from** … **Xing**

EXERCEĀMUS!

39-1 Doubting and Hindering

Before you read, make a line-by-line list of all the clauses of doubting, hindering, or preventing in *Lectiō Prīma*. Remember that the key words are marked in **bold**. Then see if you can translate just these words. Follow the model.

→ lines 4–5   *nōn est dubium quīn regat*   there is no doubt that (Rome) will rule

---

🔊 NUNTIĪ Ē GERMĀNIĀ

Lūcius, quī frātre absente sorōreque nuptā taedium habet, hodiē in culīnā cum coquō Sicōne sedet. Colloquuntur dē nuntiīs nūper Rōmam dē Germāniā relātīs.

Lūcius "Sicō," inquit, "audīvistīne dē Tiberiī victōriīs recentibus? **Nihil** nunc **prohibet** Augustum tōtōs fīnēs Germānōrum **capere. Nōn est dubium quīn** Rōma nunc
5 orbem tōtum terrārum **regat** et omnēs sciunt Tiberium proximum imperātōrem futūrum esse."

Sicō, quī semper maestus sollicitusque est, "Vērō," inquit, "**nēmō dubitat quīn** Tiberius imperātor proximus **fīat**. Sed cēna nōn iam parāta est et, sī cēna tarda fuerit, **nullum dubium est quīn** māter tua **faciat** ut vāpulem! Rogō ergō ut tū mē labōrāre sinās, domine parve."

Sōcratēs in brāchia mīlitis salit.

******

10   In aliīs urbis partibus aliī alia dē Tiberiō dīcunt. In Subūrā virī ōtiōsī prope officīnam tonsōris circumstantēs multa opīnātī sunt. Ūnus "Quae terra," rogat, "nunc legiōnibus capienda est?"

Alius "**Dubitō**," inquit, "**an** multae terrae **sint** quae nōn iam ā nōbīs captae sunt."

"Āh," respondet alius, "nōn rectē dixistī. Nōbīs Britannia in memōriā semper tenenda est. Iūlius Caesar ipse Britanniam capere nōn potuit et **dubitō num** Augustus ipse nunc id efficere **possit**."

15   "Attat!" alter subitō sollicitus clāmat. "Nihil nisi bonum dē imperātōre!"

******

In domō opulentō in Palātīnō, quattuor senātōrēs in cellā cuius iānuae ā servīs fidēlibus custōdiuntur quiētē colloquuntur.

Ūnus "Quid nunc," inquit, "dē Tiberiō agendum est? **Nōn dubitō quīn** ille triumphum dē Germāniīs agere **velit**. Drūsō mortuō, **nihil** nunc **impedit quīn** ille Augustō grātior **fīat** ut māter vult. Vereor nē rēs pūblica patrum

20 nostrōrum numquam restituātur."

Alius "Sed," inquit, "fortasse dīs volentibus rēs aliter ēvenient. Tiberius tam ambitiōsus est ut Augustus, quamquam hērēdis cupidissimus est, cautus esse dēbeat. Nepōtēs Augustī certē hērēdēs sunt."

******

Apud Valeriam, familia quoque post iānuās clausās sedēbat, et subitō aliquem iānuās pulsantem omnēs audīvērunt. Valeria et avia, semper incognita metuentēs, **dubitant an** iānuae **aperiendae sint**. Aelius autem ad

25 iānuās festīnāvit. Iānuīs apertīs Valeria mīlitem veterem, cicātrīcōsum et ūnum oculum habentem, aspexit et statim ad terram lapsa est. Valeriā ad terram collāpsā, parvus Maximus lacrimat, sed Sōcratēs, magnō cum gaudiō exclāmāns, ad mīlitem cucurrit et in brāchia eius salit.

Mīles, **nōn impediēns quīn** sīmia **saliat**, "Avē, Sōcrate," inquit. "Sīcut prōmīsī, revēnī."

🔊 VERBA ŪTENDA

Āh ha! ah!

aliter otherwise, else, in another way

ambitiōsus, -a -um ambitious

an whether

attat ah! (used to express surprise, fear, or warning)

cautus, -a, -um cautious, careful

cicātrīcōsus, -a, um scarred

circumstō, circumstāre, circumstetī stand around

collābor, collābī, collapsus sum fall in a faint, collapse

cupidus, -a, -um (+ gen.) longing for, eager for, desirous

dīs volentibus "if the gods are willing"

dubitō (1) doubt, hesitate

dubium est it is doubtful

dubius, -a, -um doubtful, uncertain

exclāmō (1) cry out, exclaim

gaudium, -ī n. joy

hērēs, hērēdis m./f. heir, heiress

impediō, impedīre, impedīvī/impediī, impedītum hamper, hinder, impede, stop from

incognitus, -a, -um not known

lābor, lābī, lapsus sum fall down

legiō, legiōnis f. legion, army

metuō, metuere, metuī, metūtum fear, be afraid of

opulentus, -a, -um rich, wealthy

ōtiōsus, -a, -um idle, unoccupied

Palātīnus, -a, -um Palatine (one of the hills of Rome)

prohibeō, prohibēre, prohibuī, prohibitum keep off; prevent; restrain; forbid

quīn that not (with subj. "from Xing"); indeed; why not?

referō, referre, rettulī, relātum carry, carry back, bring back

regō, regere, rexī, rectum rule, govern

replace, restore; give back

sollicitus, -a, -um uneasy, apprehensive, nervous, anxious that/lest

taedium, -ī n. boredom, weariness; *taedium habēre* to be bored

tardus, -a, -um late

tonsor, tonsōris m. barber

triumphus, -ī m. triumphal procession, military triumph

vāpulō (1) be beaten

vetus, veteris aged, old

POSTQUAM LĒGISTĪ

Answer all of the following questions in English. Also answer in Latin if the question is followed by (L).

1. What news does Lucius tell Sico? (L)
2. What is Sico's reaction to this news? (L)
3. How do the "men on the street" react to the news? (L)
4. How do the senators react to the news? (L)
5. Compare the reactions of the senators to those of the "men on the street." How are they similar? How are they different?
6. What do the senators think might happen in the future? (L)
7. Why are Valeria and her family afraid to open the door? (L)
8. Describe the physical appearance of the person at the door. (L)
9. Describe the reactions of Valeria, Maximus, and Socrates to this person. (L) What do their reactions suggest to you about his identity?

Grammatica A

Clauses of Doubting and Hindering/Preventing

Read the following dialogue, and notice how English uses different words in doubting clauses depending on the tense of the main verb.

Speaker 1:   I have no doubt that Tiberius was victorious in Germany.
Speaker 2:   He was. There is no doubt that Rome now rules the world!
Speaker 1:   Yes. I doubted that Tiberius would take Germany, but I was wrong.
Speaker 2:   Augustus did not doubt that he had chosen a strong leader.

Latin uses different tenses of the subjunctive as well. Here is the same dialogue in Latin:

Speaker 1:   *Nōn dubitō quīn Tiberius in Germāniā vīcerit.* (primary, time before)
Speaker 2:   *Vīcit. Nōn est dubium quīn Rōma nunc orbem terrārum regat.* (primary, near time)
Speaker 1:   *Habēs rectē. Dubitāvī num Tiberius Germāniam caperet, sed errāvī.* (secondary, near time)
Speaker 2:   *Augustus nōn dubitāvit quīn ducem fortem ēlēgisset.* (secondary, time before)

There is nothing new here. Every time you see a subjunctive in a subordinate clause, simply identify the tense and ask what time it shows in relation to the main verb. Here are the sample phrases for clauses of doubting we have already asked you to memorize.

Dubitō num/an	I doubt **that** ...
Nōn dubitō quīn	I do not doubt **that** ...

If you think about it, clauses of hindering and preventing are not conducive to "time before." A sentence like "I am stopping him from having done it" is most unlikely. We keep someone from doing something in the near or remote future. That is why you will see mostly present and imperfect subjunctive in such clauses.

Speaker 1:   Chiron **stopped** me from leaving!
Speaker 2:   No one is **keeping** you from leaving now!

As you might expect, the subjunctive is used for such expressions of hindering. Here is the same dialogue in Latin:

Speaker 1:   *Impedīvit Chīrōn nē/quōminus abīrem!* (secondary, near time)
Speaker 2:   *Nēmō nunc tē impedit quīn nunc abeās.* (primary, near time)

Make a point of memorizing these model phrases for clauses of hindering and preventing.

Impediō nē/quōminus	I keep someone **from Xing**
Nōn impediō quīn	I don't keep someone **from Xing**

Prohibeō

Nihil nunc prohibet Augustum tōtōs fīnēs Germānōrum capere.
Nothing now is prohibiting Augustus from conquering all the territory of the Germans.

This sentence appears in *Lectiō Prīma*, and you may have asked yourself where the *quīn* was. *Prohibeō* is a verb of preventing, but it tends to use an infinitive rather than a subjunctive clause.

Key Words in Clauses of Fearing, Doubting, and Hindering

Here is a summary of vocabulary you will find introducing Latin clauses of fearing, doubting, and hindering. Most are *Verba Discenda*.

> *dubitō* (1) doubt (39)
> *dubium est* it is doubtful
> *impediō, impedīre, impedīvī/impediī, impedītum* hamper, hinder, impede (39)
> *prohibeō, prohibēre, prohibuī, prohibitum* prevent, restrain (39)
> *teneō, tenēre, tenuī, tentum* hold, keep in check (6)
> *timeō, timēre, timuī* fear, be afraid (10)

EXERCEĀMUS!

39-2 **Doubting and Hindering**

Use the model phrases you memorized (*num/an, quīn,* or *nē/quōminus*) to find the right word to insert in the blank to introduce the clause. Then translate the sentence into English. Follow the model.

→ Dubitant *an* Tiberius Germāniam capiat. *They doubt that Tiberius will capture Germany.*

1. Nōn dubitant _____ Tiberius Germāniam capiat.
2. Impediunt _____ Tiberius Germāniam capiat.
3. Nōn impediunt _____ Tiberius Germāniam capiat.
4. Dubitābat _____ Tiberius Germāniam caperet.
5. Impediēbāmusne _____ Tiberius Germāniam caperet?
6. Nōn impedīmus _____ Tiberius Germāniam capiat.
7. Dubitāsne _____ Germānia ā Tiberiō capta sit?

Lectiō Secunda

Antequam Legis

Quinctilius Sevērus

In this *lectiō* you meet Quinctilius Severus, an old friend of Valeria's husband in Verona. Long ago Quinctilius was stationed in Spain, where he acquired Socrates, whom he brought home and gave to Valeria and her family. It was Quinctilius who had encouraged Valeria's son Licinius to join him in the army. As a result, when Valeria's husband died, there was no one left to run the family farm, causing Valeria to move to Rome. As luck would have it, Quinctilius ended up in the same legion as young Licinius in Germany, under Tiberius. Since he met his wife Licinia in Rome, Aelius has never met Quinctilius.

Relative Clauses in Indirect Constructions

Latin has as a general rule that, when a sentence containing a relative clause appears in an indirect construction, the verb in the subordinate clause goes in the subjunctive mood. Compare:

Direct Statement:
*Vir quem **vīdistī** dīves est.*   The man whom you saw is rich.

Indirect Statement:
*Sciō virum quem **vīderis** dīvitem esse.*   I know that the man whom you saw is rich.

EXERCEĀMUS!

39-3 **Relatives Clauses**

Make a line-by-line list of all the relatives marked in **bold** in *Lectiō Secunda*. Find the verb in the relative clause, and indicate whether it is indicative or subjunctive. Follow the model.

Line	Relative	Verb	Mood
→ 13	quam	portat	indicative

🔊 PECŪLIUM

Postquam Valeria lapsa est, Aelius, verēns nē hic advena molestus esset, pugnīs ēlevātīs mīlitī appropinquāvit ut familiam suam defenderet.

Licinia "Dēsiste!" clāmāvit. "Dēsiste, mī Aelī! Hunc cognōvimus. Hic est Quinctilius Sevērus, amīcus Vērōnensis cārissimus. Sevērus nōbīs Sōcratem dedit, quārē
5 sīmia Sevērum agnōvit. Cum Licinius in eādem legiōne esset, noster Sevērus nostrum Licinium tuēbātur."

Aelius, pugnōs summittēns, dextram Sevērō extendit, et "Mihi," inquit, "ignosce, amīce. Bene advēnistī."

Intereā Flāvia dominam suam adiūverat, et nunc Valeria lacrimāns stetit.
10 Quamquam lacrimābat, nihilōminus, sīcut Sōcratēs prius, Sevērum amplexa est.

Licinia "Māter," inquit, "nōnne adventus amīcī nostrī nōbīs laetitiae causa est? Cūr lapsa es et cūr iam lacrimās? Nōnne hic diēs ōminis bonī est?"

Valeria lacrimāns

Valeria, lacrimās dētergēns, rogat: "Vidēsne cistam **quam** Sevērus portat? Frātrī tuō ad Germāniam proficiscentī hanc cistam dedī. Ille mihi dixit cistam, **quae** ōlim patris tuī fuisset, sē numquam relictūrum esse. Cistā ā Sevērō
15 portātā, sciō frātrem tuum mortuum esse." Tālia dīcēns, iterum Valeria lūgēns ad terram collapsa est.

Paulō post omnēs calidum bibentēs et paulum dīcentēs sedēbant. Tandem Valeria lēniter dixit. "Sevēre, mī amīce, dīc nōbīs dē Liciniō."

Tunc, sōle occidente et diē vesperascente, Quinctilius Sevērus hunc narrātiōnem incēpit:

"Valeria," inquit, "rectē dīcis mē portāre cistam **quam** tū fīliō tuō Liciniō dederis. Et rectē aestimāvistī fīlium
20 tuum, **quī** mihi sīcut fīlius erat, mortuum esse. Recenter missiōnem honestam recipiēns atque praemia ferēns, Vērōnam reditūrus eram. Duōbus diēbus antequam abeundum est, Germānī castra nostra oppugnāvērunt. Illōs reppulimus, et Licinus multōs occidit, sed, maestum dictū, noster Licinus in proeliō graviter vulnerātus erat. Priusquam autem obiit, pauca verba mihi dixit **quae** vōbīs nunc referō.

"Licinius, manum meam prehendēns, dixit sē intellegere vītam suam **quae** nimis brevis fuisset, fīnītūram esse.
25 Rogābat pecūlium suum, quod est pecūnia **quam** mīlitēs sibi conservant, mihi ad vōs portandum esse. Prōmīsī mē id **quod** rogāret factūrum esse, et Licinius, exspīrāns, dixit suum nepōtem novum Maximum, **quem** nōn iam vīdisset, mihi osculandum esse.

"Licinius moriēns imperāvit nē lūgēret familia **quam** amāvisset et prō **quā** pugnāvisset."

🔊 VERBA ŪTENDA

advena, -ae m./f. foreigner,
    stranger
adventus, -ūs m. arrival
agnoscō, -ere, agnōvī,
    agnōtum recognize
amplector, amplectī,
    amplexus sum embrace
cista, -ae f. chest, box
**collābor, collābī,
    collapsus sum
fall in a faint, collapse**
conservō (1) preserve,
    keep safe
contentus, -a, -um content,
    satisfied
**collābor, collābī,
    collapsus sum
    fall in a faint, collapse**
**defendō, defendere, de-
    fendī, defensum defend**
dēsistō, dēsistere, destitī, dē-
    stitum stop, cease, desist
dētergeō, dētergēre, dētersī,
    dētersum wipe away, rub
    clean

ēlevō (1) raise up, lift up
exspīrō (1) breathe out
extendō, extendere, extendī,
    extentum/extensum
    stretch out, extend
ignoscō, ignoscere, ignōvī,
    ignōtum (+ dat.) pardon,
    forgive
laetitia, -ae f. happiness
labor, labī, lapsus fall down
lūgeō, lūgēre, luxī, luctum
    mourn, lament
missiō, -ōnis f. discharge
    (military); missiō honesta
    "an honorable discharge"
narrātiō, -ōnis f. narrative,
    story
nihilōminus nevertheless
nisi if ... not
obeō, obīre, obīvī/obiī,
    obitum go away, die
**occīdō, occīdere, occīdī,
    occīsum kill, slay**
ōmen, ōminis n. religious
    sign, omen

oppugnō (1) attack
osculō (1) kiss
pecūlium, -iī n. savings,
    private property
**praemium, -iī n. plunder;
    prize; reward; pl.
    discharge benefits**
pugnus, -ī m. fist
**repellō, -ere, reppulī,
    repulsum push back,
    repel, repulse**
summittō, summittere,
    summīsī, summissum
    lower, put down
Vērōna, -ae f. Verona, a town
    in northern Italy
Vērōnensis, Vērōnense
    Veronan, from Verona
vesperascō, vesperascere,
    vesperāvī grow toward
    evening

POSTQUAM LĒGISTĪ

1. Describe Aelius' behavior in this *lectiō*. What is your opinion of this behavior? Is it appropriate?
2. Use this *lectiō* to describe Quinctilius' character. Do you like him? Why or why not?
3. Use Licinius' last words to describe his personal values. What is most important to him in life? What do you think about Licinius as a person?

Grammatica B

Relative Clauses in Indirect Constructions

There are many, many rules that you could learn to try to understand which subjunctive is used when a subordinate clause occurs in an indirect statement. When you remember the basic concept of relative time in the sequence of tenses, it is easier than you think.

> *Sciō virum quem **videās** dīvitem esse.* (primary, near time)
> I know the man whom you see is rich.
>
> *Sciō virum quem **vīderis** dīvitem esse.* (primary, time before)
> I know that the man whom you saw is rich.
>
> *Scīvī virum quem **vidērēs** dīvitem esse.* (secondary, near time)
> I knew the man whom you were seeing was rich.
>
> *Scīvī virum quem **vīdissēs** dīvitem esse.* (secondary, time before)
> I knew that the man whom you had seen was rich.

You have seen tense charts several times in this book, but here is a simplified version that applies generally:

	IF THE MAIN VERB (INDICATIVE) IS	USE THIS SUBJUNCTIVE TO SHOW
Primary		
	present future future perfect (present perfect) (imperative)	present = near time perfect = time before FAP + *sim, sis,* etc. = time after
Secondary		
	imperfect perfect (usual) pluperfect	imperfect = near time pluperfect = time before FAP + *essem, esses,* etc. = time after

Indicatives in Relative Clauses in Indirect Statement

In Exercise 39-3, did you find the relative clauses inside an indirect statement that were in the indicative?

> *Mihi dixit pecūlium suum, quod est pecūnia quam mīlitēs sibi* **conservant**, *mihi ad vōs portandum esse.*
>
> *Et rectē aestimāvistī fīlium tuum, quī mihi sīcut fīlius* **erat**, *mortuum esse.*

When a relative clause is explaining something, as in the first example, and is not part of the direct statement, it stays in the indicative. Likewise, in the second example, Quinctilius is stating his own opinion and not that of Licinius. That is why the verb is indicative.

Relative Clauses in Other Indirect Constructions

So far we have been talking about relative constructions in indirect statement, but relative clauses in indirect commands and indirect questions work much the same way. Here is an example in an indirect command from *Lectiō Secunda*:

> *Licinius moriēns imperāvit nē lūgēret familia quam* **amāvisset** *et prō quā* **pugnāvisset**.

The next exercise is designed to help you recognize these constructions.

EXERCEĀMUS!

39-4 Subordinate Clauses

Each sentence contains a relative clause within an indirect statement, indirect command, or indirect question. Use your knowledge of the sequence of tenses to identify the sequence shown by the main verb and the time relationships shown by the subjunctive. Several sentences have more than one subjunctive. Follow the model.

→ Augustus scit deōs mīlitēs quī prō patriā pugnent amāre.

Main Verb	Sequence	Subjunctive	Time Relationship
scit	primary	pugnent	near time

1. Augustus scit deōs mīlitēs quī prō patriā pugnāverint amāre.
2. Augustus scīvit deōs mīlitēs quī prō patriā pugnārent amāre.
3. Augustus scīvit deōs mīlitēs quī prō patriā pugnāvissent amāre.
4. Mihi imperat ut pecūniam quam conservāverit ad familiam suam feram.
5. Mihi imperāvit ut pecūniam quam conservāvisset ad familiam suam ferrem.
6. Rogō ubi pecūnia quam conservāverit sit.
7. Rogāvī ubi pecūnia quam conservāvisset esset.

Mōrēs Rōmānī

Gemma Augustēa

Licinius' patriotic last words at the end of *Lectiō Secunda* are parallel to the grander-scale image on the *Gemma Augustēa* (Gem of Augustus), now in the Kunsthistorisches Museum in Vienna. This gem is a low-relief cameo cut from two layers of Arabian onyx. It was probably created by a craftsman named Dioscurides or one of his students in the second or third decade of the 1st century A.D. It is very likely that the scene deals, at least in part, with Tiberius' northern campaigns.

Gemma Augustēa

The cameo consists of two parallel panels. At the top, the emperor Augustus (identified with the god Jupiter) is seated on a throne and is being crowned by a figure representing the whole world. Behind him sit Neptune or Ocean and a figure representing either Italy or Mother Earth. On Augustus' right sits a personification of Roma, dressed in armor. At the right a winged victory is driving a chariot from which a male figure, perhaps Tiberius, is descending. The male figure standing between the chariot and Livia is perhaps Tiberius' brother, Drusus. This panel is celebrating Roman victories and associates the imperial family, especially Augustus, with the Roman pantheon of gods.

The lower panel depicts the conquered subjects. Here, at the far right, a war trophy is being erected as prisoners of war cower below. The scene at left is less certain. It may depict war captives begging for mercy.

Although the interpretation of this cameo is controversial in its details, the general impression created by the gem is Roman pride in its power and victories and the high status of the imperial family. As you saw in Chapter 38, it was important for Tiberius to gain some military experience, and, after the disaster of Varus, Tiberius was sent to Germany to try to secure the area. After a long series of campaigns, he did just that.

Here is how Tiberius' biographer Suetonius describes the campaign in Germany and its aftermath:

> Nam sub id ferē tempus Quinctilius Varus cum tribus legiōnibus in Germāniā periit, nēmine dubitante quīn victōrēs Germānī iunctūrī sē Pannoniīs fuerint, nisi dēbellātum prius Illyricum esset. Quās ob rēs triumphus eī dēcrētus est multī et magnī honōrēs.
>
> Suetonius. *Tiberius* 17

🔊 **VERBA ŪTENDA**

dēbellō (1) vanquish
ferē nearly, almost, about
Illyricum, -ī n. Illyricum, a
    Roman province in the
    Balkans
Pannonius, -a, -um
    Pannonian

Latīna Hodierna

Grammatica Latīna

It may come as no surprise to you that most English grammatical terms are derived from Latin. In fact, many of the terms come from Romans writing about their own language. Here are some terms you will surely recognize.

ablātīvus	*genetīvus*	*prōnōmen*
adiectum	*imperfectum*	*subiunctīvus*
coniugātiō	*indicātīvus*	*subordinātus*
coniunctum	*interiectum*	*verbum*
datīvus	*nōminātīvus*	*vocātīvus*
dēclīnātiō	*praesens*	
futūrum	*praepositum*	

Now use your knowledge of Latin to see how the literal Latin meanings of these terms refer to the grammatical concepts. For example, *praepositum* literally means "placed before." Isn't that where a preposition is usually found in relation to its object?

Thermae Aquincī Antīquī

Orbis Terrārum Rōmānus

Prōvinciae Dānuvinae

The Roman provinces near the Danube River were important in the career of Tiberius before he became emperor.

- **Raetia:** In 15 B.C., Tiberius subdued the Raetians and Vindelici in what is now eastern Switzerland, northern Italy, Bavaria, and the Austrian Tyrol. By the end of the 1st century A.D., the Roman province of Raetia (eastern Switzerland and northern Italy) had been combined with Vindelicia (Bavaria and the Austrian Tyrol), and Raetia became a strategically important part of a line of defense called the *līmes Germānicus.* These defensive fortifications along the Rhine and the Danube were started by Augustus after the defeat of Varus in 9 A.D. In 15 B.C., during Tiberius' Raetian campaigns, a garrison called *Augusta Vindelicōrum* (modern Augsburg, Germany) was founded. By 129 A.D. *Augusta Vindelicōrum* had become the capital of the province of Raetia.

- **Illyricum:** From 12 to 9 B.C., Tiberius led a successful campaign against the Pannonians in eastern Europe (modern Hungary, Austria, and the northern Balkans). This territory was incorporated into the province of Illyricum, which extended to the Adriatic Sea on the west and the Danube river on the east. In 6 A.D. the Pannonians joined with the Dalmatians, another Illyrian people, in a rebellion that was not crushed by Tiberius and his nephew Germanicus until 12 A.D.

- **Pannonia et Dalmatia:** After this revolt Illyricum was divided into the separate provinces of Pannonia and Dalmatia. Located in Pannonia were the cities of *Aquincum* (modern Budapest, Hungary) and *Vindobona* (modern Vienna, Austria). Both cities were founded as important military installations and became major trade centers on the frontier of the empire. The emperor Diocletian (ruled 284–305) retreated to *Spalatum* (modern Split, Croatia) in Dalmatia after he retired from the throne and built a major palace there.

- **Nōricum:** Located between Raetia and Pannonia, in what is now Austria and Slovenia, Noricum was conquered about the same time as those provinces, but here the campaign was led not by Tiberius but by a proconsul named Publius Silius.

Prōvinciae Dānuvinae

QUID PUTĀS?

1. Do we use any art objects today for propaganda in a way that recalls the *Gemma Augustēa*?
2. List three other grammatical terms not mentioned in the *Latīna Hodierna*, and use a dictionary to find out the words they are derived from. Watch out! Some English grammatical terms (like the word "grammar" itself) are derived from Greek, not Latin.
3. How important do you think their Roman heritage is to the residents of European cities like Budapest, Vienna, and Split? Browse the Internet to try to find an answer.

EXERCEĀMUS!

39-5 Scrībāmus

Using the events narrated by Quinctilius as a guide, write a brief letter from Quinctilius to Valeria describing what happened to Licinius. This is the letter he would have written had he not been able to come in person. Keep the sentences short. Begin with the German attack and end with Licinius' death.

39-6 Colloquāmur

Practice indirect statement by using Quinctilius' narrative. The first person takes one of his sentences, simplifies it, and then rephrases it aloud as an indirect statement introduced by *Quinctilius dixit* ... When he or she is done, the next person picks up the narrative by saying, *Et tunc Quinctilius dixit*. Follow the model.

Rēgia Diocletiānī Spalatī

→ Quinctilius dixit sē cistam Liciniī portāre.
   Et tunc Quinctilius dixit Licinium mortuum esse.

39-7 Verba Discenda

For each of the following perfect stems, provide the present stem of the *Verbum Discendum*. Then give the meaning of the verb. Follow the model.

Perfect Stem	Present Stem	Meaning
→ collaps-	collāb-	fall into a faint
1. conservāv-	5. laps-	9. reppul-
2. defend-	6. metu-	10. restit-
3. dubitāv-	7. occīd-	11. rettul-
4. impedīv-	8. prohibu-	12. rex-

🔊 VERBA DISCENDA

adventus, -ūs m. arrival [adventitious]

aliter otherwise, else, in another way

an whether

collābor, collābī, collapsus sum fall in a faint, collapse [collapsible]

conservō (1) preserve, keep safe [conservation]

cupidus, -a, -um (+ gen.) longing for, eager for, desirous [cupidity]

defendō, defendere, defendī, defensum defend [defensive]

dubitō (1) doubt, hesitate [indubitable]

dubius, -a, -um doubtful, uncertain [dubious]

impediō, impedīre, impedīvī/impedīī, impedītum hamper, hinder, impede, stop from [impediment]

lābor, lābī, lapsus sum fall down [lapse]

legiō, legiōnis f. legion, army [legionary]

metuō, metuere, metuī, metūtum fear, be afraid of

nihilōminus nevertheless

occīdō, occīdere, occīdī, occīsum kill, slay

oppugnō (1) attack

praemium, -iī n. plunder; prize; reward; pl. discharge benefits [premium]

prohibeō, prohibēre, prohibuī, prohibitum keep off; prevent; restrain; forbid [prohibitive]

quīn that not (with subj. "from Xing"); indeed; why not?

recens, recentis recent

referō, referre, rettulī, relātum carry, carry back, bring back [refer, relate]

regō, regere, rexī, rectum rule, govern [regent]

repellō, repellere, reppulī, repulsum push back, repel, repulse [repellent, repulsive]

restituō, restituere, restituī, restitūtum replace, restore; give back [restitution]

sollicitus, -a, -um uneasy, apprehensive, nervous, anxious that/lest [sollicitous]

tardus, -a, -um late [tardy]

vetus, veteris aged, old [veteran]

Angulus Grammaticus

Negatives in Subordinate Clauses

Clauses of Fearing

Negatives in some Latin subordinate clauses can appear confusing to English speakers. Look at how we express "not" with fear expressions in English:

I am **afraid not to** get married.
I am **afraid that** I will **not** get married.

English is straightforward. It uses "not" with the thing feared. In Latin, however, the rules are a bit more complicated and even seem backward from an English point of view:

If the Latin writer fears that something is NOT going to happen the sentence uses:

- *ut* + subjunctive. This can be confusing since, up until now, *ut* has most often been translated as "that."

  Vereor ut amīcī meī Rōmam eant.   I'm afraid that my friends are not coming to Rome.

- *nē ... nōn* + subjunctive

  Vereor nē amīcī meī nōn Rōmam eant.   (Same meaning as above.)

And the following is actually possible in Latin:

Nōn vereor nē amīcī nōn vēnerint.   I do not fear that my friends have not come.

Interestingly, in early Latin *ut* was the preferred usage, but by the time of Caesar, *nē ... nōn* was more prevalent.

Clauses of Preventing

English speakers face a similar challenge with subjunctive clauses following verbs of hindering or preventing. Look at these examples:

Chīrōn impedit nē (quōminus) puerī abeant!   Chiron is preventing "lest the boys go away."
Chiron is keeping the boys from going away.

Chīrōn nōn impedit quīn puerī abeant.   Chiron is not keeping the boys from going away.

Nēmō tē impedit quīn (quōminus) abeās.   No one is keeping you from going.

Quīn and *quōminus* have interesting origins. *Quīn* is actually a compound of an archaic form *quī* meaning "how" and *nē ... nōn*. The third example above could thus be translated literally, "**No one** is hindering **how** you should **not** go," or "**No one** is hindering **lest** you should go," but both sentences sound very odd in English. The conjunction *quōminus* can be used in both positive and negative clauses of preventing and is equivalent to the Latin *ut eō minus* (that thereby less).

40

Fīnēsque Initiaque

Lectiō Prīma

Antequam Legis

Roman Triumphs

A significant amount of time has passed since Tiberius' victorious campaign in Germany. We read about the future emperor's triumph in *Lectiō Prīma* and the burial of Licinius' ashes in *Lectiō Secunda*.

As you read, notice how you can build on your knowledge of Latin to understand unfamiliar words. If you know *triumphus, -ī* m. means "triumph," then you can easily sort out the meanings of *triumphātor, -ōris* m.; *triumphālis, -e*; and *triumphō* (1).

This reading is also designed to help you review the subjunctive mood and consolidate its uses in Latin.

EXERCEĀMUS!

40-1 Review of Uses of the Subjunctive

Find an example of each of the following types of subjunctive in *Lectiō Secunda*. All the subjunctives are marked in **bold** to help you.

1. purpose clause	4. hortatory	7. indirect command
2. result clause	5. relative clause of description	8. clause of doubt
3. wish	6. indirect question	9. condition

GRAMMATICA

Consolidation of Uses of the Subjunctive
Impersonal Use of Passive Verbs
Consolidation of Impersonal Expressions

MŌRĒS RŌMĀNĪ

Iō, Triumphe!

LATĪNA HODIERNA

Contractiōnēs Latīnae

ORBIS TERRĀRUM RŌMĀNUS

Mons Vāticānus

ANGULUS GRAMMATICUS

Quō Vādis?

LECTIŌNĒS:
TIBERIĪ TRIUMPHUS
and
MANIBUS IUNCTĪS

The day of Tiberius' triumph has come. Members of the Servilian family attend the triumph, while Valeria's family walks out to the Vatican Hill to bury Licinius' ashes.

TIBERIĪ TRIUMPHUS

Hodiē Tiberius, prīvignus Augustī, extrā pōmērium manet ut per viās Rōmae **triumphet.** Tot hominēs agmen exspectant ut tōtus orbis terrārum adesse **videātur.**

In aliquā viā et familia et clientēs Servīliī stant. Cum paedagōgus Hermēs
5   servus **sit,** tamen Lūciī cūrandī grātiā adest. Omnēs adsunt ut Servīlium, et patrem et patrōnum, nunc quoque praetōrem, in pompā **videant.**

"Ubi est pompa? Nihil aut vidēre aut audīre possum! Mē taedet. Utinam **inciperētur!** Iēiūnus sum!" clāmat Lūcius.

Māter "Fac," inquit, "ut patientior **sīs,** mī fīlī! Omnia in tempore suō fīent!

Ad triumphum spectandum

10   Mox sonitus tubārum hominumque plaudentium audītur et, nōn multō post, ingrediuntur magistrātūs Rōmānī inter quōs Servīlius conspicitur. Post magistrātūs senātus omnis venit et multī hominēs imāginēs splendidās portantēs et spolia bellī plaustrīs vecta prōcēdunt.

Lūcius imāginēs animadvertēns quaerit: "Quālēs illae imāginēs pictae sunt?"

Marcus, nūper ā Graeciā revertus et omnia familiae expōnēns, respondet: "Aliae imāginēs victōriās triumphātōris
15   Tiberiī aliae terrās populōsque Germāniae victōs dēmonstrant. In illā imāgine, exemplī grātiā ... Sed ecce! **Spectēmus!** Illīc, post illōs taurōs albōs, captōs Germānicōs videō."

Multī captīvī ad terram spectant sed ūnus, vīsū nōbilis et statūrā ērectus, superbus sōlusque prōgreditur. Nōn dubium est quīn ille, quī dux Germānōrum victōrum est, mox ad Tulliānum strangulandī causā **veniat,** sed vir est quī mortis floccum nōn **faciat.**

20   Lūcius impatiens rogātūrus est ubi Tiberius **sit** cum subitō triumphātor ipse adest! In quadrīgā eburneā atque aureā stat et post eum servus positus est quī corōnam auream super caput **tollat** iterum atque iterum repetēns in aure triumphātōris, "Respice post tē! Hominem tē mementō."

Tālibus audītīs vīsīsque Lūcius rogat: "Marce? Nōn intellegō quid haec verba **significent.**"

Marcus respondet: "Haec verba triumphātōrem, quisquis est, monet nē superbus **fīat.** In rē Tiberius hodiē
25   triumphātor est sed sī nimis in hāc rē **gaudeat,** fortūna mala eum **persequātur.**"

Lūcius "Quid," addidit, "dē faciē rubrā?"

Marcus "Dē faciē rubrā," inquit, "nihil sciō. Mōs māiōrum est."

Mox mīlitēs, laureās in capitibus gerentēs, praetereunt, "Iō Triumphe!" fortiter clāmantēs et carmina obscoena dē Tiberiō canentēs. Tālī diē, et sōlum diē tālī, sīc canere fās est. Mīlitibus praetereuntibus, nihil plūs videndō
30   dignum remanet et omnēs domum redeunt. Agmen autem iter facit ad Capitōlium ut taurī **sacrificentur** et senātōrēs cum triumphātōre dape sumptuōsā **fruantur.** Tanta est glōria atque māiestās Rōmae!

POSTQUAM LĒGISTĪ

Answer the following questions in English. Respond in Latin if the question is followed by (L).

1. Describe two significant features of a Roman triumph. (L)
2. Describe the leader of the Germans. (L) What is your opinion of his character? Why?
3. What would be the closest equivalent to a triumphal procession today? Do not confine your thinking to the United States.
4. In your opinion, what does the way the Romans treat the defeated Germans tell us about Roman civilization?
5. What does the last line of the *lectiō* suggest about ancient Rome? Do you agree? Why or why not?

🔊 VERBA ŪTENDA

addō, addere, addidī, additum add, give; say in addition

agmen, agminis n. column of troops, battle line; troops, army; herd, flock; crowd

albus, -a, -um white

animadvertō, animadvertere, animadvertī, animadversum observe, notice remark

aureus, -a, -um golden

canō, canere, cecinī, cantum sing, sing about

captīvus, -ī m. captive, prisoner

corōna, -ae f. crown

daps, dapis f. sacrificial feast, offering

dēmonstrō (1) point at, show, depict

eburneus, -a, -um ivory

ērectus, -a, -um upright

exemplum, -ī n. sample

expōnō, expōnere, exposuī, expositum set out; exhibit, explain

extrā (+ acc.) beyond, outside of

fās (indecl.) n. right, law

floccus, -ī m. tuft of wool; *nōn floccum facere* (+ gen.) to consider of no importance

glōria, -ae f. glory

imāgō, -inis f. image, likeness; statue

impatiens, impatientis impatient

in rē in fact

iō a shout of religious emotion

laurea, -ae f. laurel wreath

māiestās, -tātis f. majesty; grandeur

obscoenus, -a, -um obscene

patiens, patientis patient

persequor, persequī, persecūtus sum pursue, chase

pingō, pingere, pinxī, pictum paint

plaustrum, -ī n. cart, wagon

pōmērium, -iī n. open space surrounding the walls of a Roman city or town

prīvignus, -ī m. stepson

quadrīga, -ae f. chariot with four horses

quisquis, quodquod/quicquod/quidquid whoever, whatever

remaneō, remanēre, remansī remain, stay behind

repetō, repetere, repetīvī/ repetiī, repetītum repeat

respiciō, respicere, respexī, respectum take notice of

ruber, rubra, rubrum red

sacrificō (1) sacrifice

significō (1) mean

splendidus, -a, -um bright, shining, illustrious, splendid

spolium, -iī n. spoils (of war)

statūra, -ae f. stature

strangulō (1) choke, strangle

sumptuōsus, -a, -um expensive, costly

superbus, -a, -um proud, haughty

taedet, taedēre, taeduit, taesum est (impersonal + gen. or inf.) be tired (of), be sick (of), be bored (with); *mē taedet*, "I'm bored!"

taurus, -ī m. bull

tot (indecl. adj.) so many

Tulliānum, -ī n. Tullianum, the state prison in Rome

victōrum from *vincō*

Grammatica A

Consolidation of Uses of the Subjunctive

Here is an overview of the many uses of the subjunctive you have learned. It is a broad outline only. For complete information, refer to the chapter where this concept is taught.

Independent Subjunctives

The following subjunctives are used independently, i.e., as the main verb in a sentence:

- **Hortatory**   (Chapter 31)
  Spectēmus!   Let's watch!

- **Jussive**   (Chapter 31)
  Fīat!   Let it be done!

- **Deliberation**   (Chapter 31)
       (1st person subjunctive only)
  Quid faciam?   What should/might I do?

- **Negative Command**   (Chapter 36)
       nē + perfect subjunctive
  Nē rogāveris!   Don't ask!

- **Subjunctive of Wishing**   (Chapter 31)
       Utinam + subjunctive
  Utinam inciperētur.   Would that it would begin!
  Cordus sit!   May Cordus be there!

Dependent Subjunctives

The following subjunctives are used dependently, i.e., in subordinate clauses.

- **Purpose Clauses**   (Chapter 31)
  ut or *nē* + subjunctive

  Omnēs adsunt ut Servīlium in   All are present to see Servilius in the parade.
  pompā videant.

- **Result Clauses**   (Chapter 32)
  A "so" word (e.g., *tam, tot*) + *ut/ut nōn* + subjunctive

  Tam fortis est ut morī nōn timeat.   He is so brave that he is not afraid to die.

- **Indirect Commands**   (Chapter 33)
  verb of commanding + *ut/nē* + subjunctive

  Mihi imperat ut abeam.   He orders me to leave.

- **Indirect Questions**   (Chapter 34)
  head verb + interrogative word + subjunctive

  Nōn intellegō quid haec verba significent.   I don't know what these words mean.

- **Jussive Noun Clauses (noun clauses with *fac ut*)**   (Chapter 32)
  fac ut + subjunctive

  Fac ut patientior sīs!   Try to be more patient!

- **Negative Command**   (Chapter 33)
  cavē(te) + *nē* + subjunctive

  Cavē nē id faciās.   Beware of doing that. Don't do that.

- **Conditions (Future Less Vivid, etc.)**   (Chapter 37)
  sī + subjunctive

  Sī nimis gaudeat, fortasse fortūna   If he should rejoice too much, perhaps
  mala eum persequātur.   bad luck would follow him. (FLV)

- **Cum Clauses (Temporal, Concessive, Causal)**   (Chapter 36)
  cum + subjunctive

  Cum paedagōgus Hermēs servus sit,   Although Hermes the pedagogue is a slave,
  tamen ipse adest Lūciī   nevertheless he is present to watch over
  cūrandī grātiā.   Lucius. (concessive)

- **Fear Clauses**   (Chapter 38)
  verb of fearing + *nē* or *ut/nē … nōn* + subjunctive

  Timeō ut Cordus veniat.   I'm afraid Cordus is not coming.

- **Clauses of Doubting, Hindering, and Preventing**   (Chapter 39)
  verb of doubting, or hindering, or preventing + *num/an* or *quīn* + subjunctive

  Nōn dubium est quīn ille mox ad   There is no doubt that he will soon come
  Tulliānum strangulandī causā veniat.   to the Tullianum to be strangled.

- **Relative Clauses of Characteristic**   (Chapter 38)
  relative pronoun + subjunctive

  Vir est quī mortis floccum nōn faciat.   He the sort of man who considers
  death of no importance.

- **Relative Clauses of Purpose**   (Chapter 38)
  quī + the subjunctive

  Post eum stat servus quī corōnam   Behind him stands a slave to raise
  auream super caput tollat.   a golden crown over his head.

- **Relative Clauses in Indirect Constructions**   (Chapter 39)
  indirect statement or question + subordinate clause + subjunctive

  Marcus dīxit Tiberium, quī Germāniam   Marcus said that Tiberius, who had
  vīcisset, *mox ventūrum esse.*   conquered Germany, would come soon.

EXERCEĀMUS!

40-2 Review of Sequence of Tenses

Identify the type of the subjunctive clauses in each sentence. Identify the Latin word(s) that identify the subjunctive clause. Then translate the sentence into English. Follow the model.

→ Tam fortis est ut morī nōn timeat. *Result:* tam … ut
   He is so brave that he isn't afraid to die.

1. Nōn intellegō quī hī sint.
2. Cave nē Tiberius tē audiat!
3. Tiberius est vir quī bene imperet.
4. Nōn est dubium quīn Tiberius mox imperātor fīat.
5. Tiberius servō imperāvit nē corōnam āmitteret.
6. Tiberius servum ēlēgit quī corōnam tolleret.

Lectiō Secunda

Antequam Legis

Licinius' Funeral

Valeria's family cannot afford an elaborate burial and tomb for Licinius, whose ashes will be interred in a *columbārium* (a series of niches for funerary urns) outside the city of Rome on the Vatican Hill. While the family is there for the funeral, they come upon someone quite unexpected. His story is modeled on Roman plays and tales of adventure.

Columbārium Ostiae

As you read the *lectiō*, watch for passive verbs used impersonally. Impersonal verbs are most commonly found in the 3rd person singular. If the subject "it" seems to work for such a verb, it is probably an impersonal. You have seen such passives before. For example, in Chapter 22 you encountered the phrase *diū pugnātur*, literally, "it is fought for a long time," or "the fighting goes on for a long time." These impersonal passives lead to a consolidation of impersonal constructions in Latin.

EXERCEĀMUS!

40-3 Pre-Reading

Look closely at the following verbs marked in **bold** in the *lectiō*, and decide whether each verb is a regular passive, a deponent verb, passive used impersonally or a gerund(ive) used impersonally. Follow the model.

→ l. prōgrediēbātur (line 2)   *deponent*

1. sequuntur (line 4)	7. captī sunt (line 20)
2. portābātur (line 4)	8. datum erit (line 23)
3. adventum est (line 5)	9. mīrātī sunt (line 25)
4. persequitur (line 9)	10. locūta est (line 25)
5. caperētur (line 10)	12. abeundum est (line 27)
6. nātus sum (line 17)	

MANIBUS IUNCTĪS

In aliā urbis parte familia Valeriae (praeter Plōtiam quae aegra domī remanet) ad Vātīcānum **prōgrediēbātur**. Aelius, quī nunc pater familiās est, fīlium Maximum in umerīs portat. Valeria, Licinia et Flāvia, quae sīmiam Sōcratem per fūnem tenet, **sequuntur**. Olla, in quā cinerēs Liciniī sunt, ā Quinctiliō Sevērō amīcō familiae **portābātur**.

5 Ambulant nihil dīcentēs (quid dīcī potest?) dōnec ad columbāria **adventum est**.

Manibus iunctīs

Cum ad Vātīcānum advēnissent, Valeria ollam cinerēs Liciniī continentem in terrā dēposuit et Aelius Maximum, quī nunc paene trēs annōs nātus erat, quoque in terrā posuit. Flāvia fūnem Sōcratis in arbore fixit. Maximus, autem, nihil dē maestitiā fūneris sciēns et lūdere volēns, Sōcratem līberāvit. Mox, puer sīmiam per grāmina **persequitur**. Licinia iterum gravida fīlium currentem petere nōn
10 poterat et imperāvit Flāviae ut Maximus **caperētur**. Sed puer et sīmia post monumenta celeriter cucurrērunt.

Sed, mīrābile dictū, illīc post monumenta dormiēbat ille ipse servus fugitīvus, quī in insulā Valeriae in Subūrā salūtem petīverat. Prope aliqua fēmina quoque dormiēbat.

Aelius advēnit et, lēniter illum pede suō pulsāns, "Expergiscere," inquit, "expergiscere." Vir territus oculōs dētergēns stetit et "Vōs," inquit, "meminī! Nōnne mē meministis? Ego sum ille servus cui cibum dedistī. At, rectius
15 dīcam, servus fuī! Postquam vōs relīquī, ad Calabriam iter fēcī ubi uxōrem meam in pistrīnō labōrantem invēnī. Ille pistor, Faustus nōmine, hunc ānulum quem semper in digitō gerō aspexerit et statim mē cognōverat! Haud servus sed cīvis Brundisiī sum et Callistus C. Callistī fīlius **nātus sum**!

"Ille benignus Faustus, parentibus meīs morientibus, prōmīserat sē mē cūrātūrum esse et hunc ānulum, quī patris meī fuerat, mihi trēs annōs nātō dedit.

20 "Paulō post," Callistus addidit, "ego et Faustus ad Graeciam nāvigantēs ā pīrātīs **captī sunt**. Faustō in insulā relictō, mē sīcut servum vendidērunt. Ānulum, dē collō meō suspensum, nōn invēnērunt!

"Nunc, lībertāte acceptā, hanc epistulam ā Faustō scrīptam et ā magistrātibus signātam ferō ut dē Zēthō, quī ōlim dominus meus erat, pecūniam poscam. Sī nōn **datum erit**, eum magistrātibus trādam. Pecūniā acceptā ego et uxor pistrīnum nostrum condēmus."

25 Omnēs audientēs fābulam **mīrātī sunt** sed Valeria sōla **locūta est**. "Ambōbus vōbīs grātulātiōnēs offerō, cīvis Calliste. Fortūna vestra melior, nostra pēior facta est. Ut vidētis, lūgēmus et in hāc ollā cinerēs fīliī meī habēmus et nunc nōbīs ut fīlium sepeliāmus **abeundum est**. Fac ut valeātis!"

Tālibus dictīs, ad columbārium **adventum est**. Omnēs inscriptiōnem quae ibi scrīpta erat lēgērunt:

C LICINIO C F
30   LEGXIIXANNXXVI
CECIDIT
BELLGERMAN
VALERIA MATER
FILIO BM F

35 Licinia, quae valdē tristis est, "Māter," inquit, "mē miseret. Quōmodo pax Rōmāna bona esse potest? Quōmodo aliquid bonum esse potest cum tot iuvenēs cārī semper moriuntur? Semper sīc erit?"

Valeria ad terram oculōs dīmīsit et lēniter lacrimat. Quinctilius, vir bonī cordis, manum Valeriae prehendit. Vesperascit et, manibus iunctīs, Valeria et Quinctilius domum redeunt.

Gemma

Here is a transcription of Licinius' monument in simpler Latin:
Gāiō Liciniō Gāiī Fīliō
Legiōnis XVIII annīs XXVI
Cecidit Bellō Germānicō
Valeria māter
Fīliō bene merentī fēcit

POSTQUAM LĒGISTĪ

Answer all of the following questions in English. Also respond in Latin if the question is followed by (L).

1. Who is now *pater familiās* of Valeria's family? (L) Why?
2. How does Licinius' funeral compare to the funerals of Avus and Mendax in Chapter 33? How does it compare to a modern funeral?

3. Who is Callistus? (L) Where have you seen him before? (L)
4. How realistic do you think Callistus' story is? Why do you think Romans enjoyed such stories so much?
5. What does Callistus want from Zethus? (L) Do you think he will get it? Why or why not?
6. What do you think the future holds for Quinctilius and Valeria?

🔊 VERBA ŪTENDA

ānulus, -ī m. ring
Brundisium, -iī n. Brundisium, a city in Calabria
cinis, cineris m. ash
collum, -ī n. neck
columbārium, -iī n. a niche for a cinerary urn
condō, condere, condidī, conditum build, found
contineō, continēre, continuī, contentum contain, hold
dētergō, dētergere, dētersī, dētersum wipe away, rub clean

exclāmō (1) cry out, exclaim
extendō, extendere, extendī, extentum/extensum stretch out, extend
extrā (+ acc.) beyond, outside of
fīgō, fīgere, fīxī, fīxum fasten in place
fūnis, fūnis m. cord, rope
fūnus, fūneris n. burial, funeral
grāmen, grāminis n. grass
grātulātiō, -iōnis f. congratulations
inscriptiō, -iōnis f. inscription, writing on stone

lībertās, -tātis f. freedom, liberty
lūgeō, lūgēre, luxī, luctum mourn, lament
maestitia, -ae f. sadness, grief
mē miseret it distresses me
mīrābilis, mīrābile amazing, wondrous
monumentum, -ī n. tomb
olla, -ae f. pot, jar; urn
pīrāta, -ae m. pirate
prehendō, prehendere, prehendī, prehensum take hold of, seize

sepeliō, sepelīre, sepelīvī/sepeliī, sepultum bury
sepulchrum, -ī n. tomb
signō (1) mark, seal, stamp
suspendō, suspendere, suspendī, suspensum hang
umerus, -ī m. shoulder
Vāticānus, -ī m. Vatican, a hill on the right bank of the Tiber in Rome
vesperascit it is growing late
vīcīnus, -ī m. neighbor

Grammatica B

Impersonal Use of Passive Verbs

Did you find the three impersonal passive verbs used in *Lectiō Secunda?* Here is how they are translated, first literally and then more freely.

*dōnec ad columbārium **adventum est***
until there was an arrival at the columbarium ...
until they arrived at the columbarium ...

Sī nōn datum erit...
If there will not have been a giving ...
If he doesn't give it ...

Nōbīs abeundum est
There must be a going away by us.
We must go away.

Note that impersonal passive expressions are used especially with intransitive verbs (which, as you may remember, do not otherwise have passive forms). So in *Sīc ītur ad astra* (the motto of the Canadian Air Force mentioned in Chapter 22), the intransitive verb *eō, īre* is put into the 3rd person singular passive: literally, "there is a going to the stars" or "thus is the going to the stars" or, more freely, "thus we go to the stars."

Consolidation of Impersonal Expressions

Impersonal expressions are usually in the 3rd person singular neuter in Latin. Besides this impersonal use of intransitive verbs, Latin uses a variety of other impersonal expressions that you have seen in this book:

• Many future passive periphrastic constructions are impersonal.

Nunc est bibendum.   Now there must be drinking.

- Many impersonals, such as *constat* (it is decided, it is clear); *decet* (it is fitting); *licet* (it is permitted); and *oportet* (it is right) are used with an infinitive.

oportet pugnāre	it is right to fight
decet pugnāre	it is fitting to fight

- Some regular verbs, such as *placeō* and *videor*, can be used impersonally in the 3rd person, often with infinitive subjects.

placet librum bonum legere	it is pleasing to read a good book
vidēbātur librum bonum legere	it seemed good to read a good book

- Verbs like *parcō* (spare) and *persuādeō* (persuade), which take dative rather than accusative objects (see Chapter 12), are often used impersonally in the passive voice.

Tibi parcō.	I spare you.
Tibi parcitur.	You are spared. (Literally, "there is a sparing to you")
Tibi persuādeō.	I persuade you.
Tibi persuādētur.	You are being persuaded. (Literally, "there is a persuading to you")

- Many verbs of feeling are used impersonally. In this case the person who has this feeling is put in the accusative or dative case:

Mē miseret.	It grieves me.	I regret.
Mē paenitet.	It repents me.	I am sorry.
Mē piget.	It disgusts me.	I am disgusted.
Mē pudet.	It shames me.	I am ashamed.
Mē taedet.	It tires me.	I am tired. I am bored.
Mihi displicet.	It displeases me.	I don't like it.
Sī tibi placet.	If it pleases you.	Please.

- Finally, like English, Latin uses impersonal verbs for weather and time expressions:

Fulgurat.	It is lightning.
Ningit.	It is snowing.
Obscūrat.	It is getting dark.
Pluit.	It is raining.
Tonat.	It is thundering.
Vesperascit.	It is getting late.

EXERCEĀMUS!

40-4 Translating Impersonal Expressions

Match each impersonal expression in column A with its English translation in column B.

	A		B
_____ 1.	*Nunc est edendum*	A.	It is fitting
_____ 2.	*Oportet*	B.	It is getting dark
_____ 3.	*Mē paenitet*	C.	Now there must be eating
_____ 4.	*Nōbīs parcitur*	D.	I am sorry
_____ 5.	*Adventum est*	E.	It is permitted
_____ 6.	*Decet*	F.	They go
_____ 7.	*Licet*	G.	I am persuaded
_____ 8.	*Mihi persuādētur*	H.	It is right
_____ 9.	*Placet*	I.	It is pleasing
_____ 10.	*Obscūrat*	J.	We are spared

Mōrēs Rōmānī

Iō, Triumphe!

Triumphs were granted only to generals who had had a significant victory over foreign enemies. By 9 B.C. only the emperor himself, or a member of his family, could
conduct a triumph.

The triumphal procession began in the Campus Martius, proceeded through
the *Porta Triumphālis,* around the Capitoline Hill through the Circus Maximus,
then around the Palatine Hill to the *Via Sacra.* On the *Via Sacra,* the procession
moved through the Forum up the Capitoline Hill to the Temple of Jupiter Capitolinus, where the *triumphātor* conducted a sacrifice of thanksgiving.

Triumphus

The procession included higher magistrates (like the praetor Servilius), members of the Senate, plunder captured in the war, sacrificial animals, musicians, ban-
ners, and floats. Military captives like the German chieftain who marched in Tiberius' procession
were traditionally led from the triumph to the nearby Tullianum prison, where they were uncere-
moniously strangled. You have read that the victorious army also marched in the procession, shouting *iō, triumphe* and making ribald comments about their leader. The triumphant general rode in a
special *quadrīga* accompanied by a slave holding a laurel crown of victory over his head and whispering into his ear warnings like the "*Respice post tē! Hominem tē mementō.*" The general wore special clothing, including a gold and purple *tunica picta* and had his face smeared with red paint. The
origin of many of these customs, as Marcus explains to Lucius, are shrouded in the distant past.

Following the religious sacrifice on the Capitoline, the general provided a feast, not only
for the senators and for his army, but also for the common people. Gifts of coins from the
plunder were also often distributed to the soldiers and to the populace.

In his lifetime Tiberius celebrated six triumphs, including this one in 9 B.C. One of these
six triumphs is depicted on a famous silver cup found at a villa in Boscoreale near Pompeii, in
a silver horde buried in the eruption of Vesuvius in 79 A.D. This so-called Boscoreale cup, now
in the Louvre in Paris, depicts the emperor riding in his quadriga on one side, and the sacrifice
of bulls in front of the Temple of Jupiter Capitolinus on the other. You can see a picture of this
cup on the first page of this chapter.

Here is how Tiberius' biographer Suetonius described the triumph:

> Ā Germāniā in urbem post biennium regressus, triumphum ēgit prōsequentibus
> etiam lēgātīs, quibus triumphālia ornāmenta impetrāverat. Ac prius quam in Capitōlium
> flecteret, descendit ē currū sēque praesidentī patrī ad genua summīsit. Prandium dehinc
> populō mille mensīs et congiārium trecēnōs nummōs virītim dedit. Dēdicāvit et Concor-
> diae aedem, item Pollūcis et Castoris suō frātrisque nōmine dē manubiīs.
>
> Suetonius. *Tiberius,* 20

🔊 VERBA ŪTENDA

aedēs, aedis f. temple
Castor, -oris m. Castor, the
divine twin brother of
Pollux, one of the
Gemini
congiārium, -iī n.
largesse, gift
currus, -ūs m. chariot
dēdicō (1) dedicate,
devote

dehinc after this; next
*flectō, flectere, flexī,
flectum* turn
genū, -ūs n. knee
impetrō (1) obtain by
formal request
manubiae, -iārum f. pl.
general's share of
military plunder
mille (indecl.) 1000

ornāmentum, -ī n.
decoration
Pollūx, -ūcis m. Pollux, divine
twin brother of Castor,
one of the Gemini
*praesideō, praesidēre,
praesēdī* presiding (over)
prandium, -iī n. luncheon
*prōsequor, prōsequī,
prōsecūtus sum* follow

*(sē) summittō, summittere,
summīsī, summissum*
(+ dat.) lower oneself to
trecēnī, -ae, -a three
hundred
triumphus, -ī m. triumph,
triumphal procession
virītim man by man,
per person

Latīna Hodierna

Contractiōnēs Latīnae

Many abbreviations commonly used in English are derived from Latin. Here are just a few examples:

Scholarly Citations

ca., c.	*circa* (around, about, approximately)
et al.	*et aliī* (and others)
etc.	*et cētera* (and the others)
e.g.	*exemplī grātiā* (for the sake of example)
i.e.	*id est* (that is)
N.B.	*notā bene* (note well)
op. cit.	*opere citātō* (in the work cited)

Academic Degrees

D.D.	*Dīvīnitātis Doctor* (Teacher of Divinity)
J.D.	*Iūris Doctor* (Teacher of Law)
M.A.	*Magister Artium* (Master of Arts)
Ph.D	*Philosophiae Doctor* (Teacher of Philosophy)

Other Expressions

A.M.	*ante merīdiem* (before midday)
P.M.	*post merīdiem* (after midday)
lb.	*lībra* (pound)
percent	*per centum* (for each one hundred)
pro tem.	*prō tempore* (for the time being)
P.S.	*post scriptum* (after what has been written)
R.I.P.	*requiescat in pāce* (may he/she rest in peace)
A.D.	*Annō Domini* (in the year of the Lord)

Orbis Terrārum Rōmānus

Mons Vāticānus

Obeliscus Vāticānus

The Vatican Hill, where Licinius' ashes are laid to rest, was not one of the fabled seven hills of Rome. Like the Janiculum Hill (Iāniculum, -ī n.), the Vatican was not enclosed within the walls of the ancient city. Since the Romans buried their dead outside the city walls, it is not unreasonable to assume that Valeria would bury her son's ashes in a columbarium on the Vatican Hill. Can you find Licinius' columbarium marked on the map below? In the next century, Agrippina, the mother of the emperor Caligula, built gardens in the field between the hill and the river. In the same area, Caligula began the construction of a *circus*, which was finished by Nero. It was in this circus that Peter, the first pope, was martyred by crucifixion in 67 A.D. By tradition he was buried nearby, in a tomb located under the main altar of St. Peter's Basilica. The emperor Constantine built a basilica over the site in the 4th century. This basilica was replaced by the present church in the 16th century. At that time, the obelisk that once stood in the *spīna* of Nero's circus was moved into the center of St. Peter's Square, designed by Gian Lorenzo Bernini and built between 1656 and 1667.

Obeliscus Vāticānus dē caelō

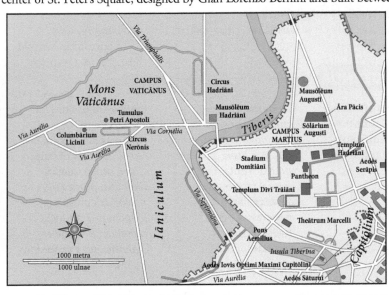

Vāticānus

QUID PUTĀS?

1. Why do you think the soldiers were allowed to make fun of their general during a triumph? Can you think of any equivalents to this sort of behavior today?
2. Compare a Super Bowl victory parade with a Roman triumph.
3. Why do you think Latin abbreviations are still used in English today?
4. Why do you think Bernini used the obelisk from Nero's circus in his design for St. Peter's Square?

EXERCEĀMUS!

40-5 Scrībāmus

Imagine you are a print journalist preparing a feature story on the life of Callistus, the runaway slave. Use the readings from Chapters 18 and 40 to make a list of questions in Latin that you want to ask Callistus, his wife, Faustus, and Zethus in an interview. Be sure to cover all the major events in his life, including his early childhood, his life as a slave, and more recent events.

40-6 Colloquāmur

Now team up with classmates to hold interviews in Latin with Callistus, Callistus' wife, Faustus, and Zethus. Use the questions you created in Exercise 40-5 as a basis for these interviews.

40-7 Verba Discenda

Find a word in the *Verba Discenda* that fits each of the following descriptors. You can use any *Verbum Discendum* more than once.

1. one noun in the first declension
2. one masculine noun
3. one 2-1-2 adjective
4. one indeclinable adjective
5. one deponent verb
6. one preposition
7. one 2nd declension neuter noun
8. two 3rd declension neuter nouns
9. two 3rd declension femine nouns
10. two verbs in the 2nd conjugation

🔊 VERBA DISCENDA

addō, addere, addidī, additum add, give; say in addition [addition]

agmen, agminis n. column of troops, battle line; troops, army; herd, flock; crowd

animadvertō, animadvertere, animadvertī, animadversum observe, remark, notice, understand [animadvert, animadversion]

canō, canere, cecinī, cantum sing, sing about [incantation]

captīvus, -ī m. captive, prisoner [captivate, captivity]

condō, condere, condidī, conditum build, found [condominium]

contineō, continēre, continuī, contentum contain, hold [continence, content, contentment]

dēmonstrō (1) point at, show, depict [demonstration, demonstrative]

exemplum, -ī n. sample [example, exemplar]

expōnō, expōnere, exposuī, expositum set out; exhibit, explain [exposition]

extrā (+ acc.) beyond, outside of [extraordinary, extraterritorial]

fās (indecl.) n. right, law

fūnus, fūneris n. burial, funeral [funereal]

glōria, -ae f. glory [glorify]

imāgō, -inis f. image, likeness; statue [imagine, imagination]

lībertās, -tātis f. freedom, liberty

persequor, persequī, persecūtus sum pursue, chase [persecution]

quisquis, quodquod/quicquid/quidquid whoever, whatever

remaneō, remanēre, remansī remain, stay behind

significō (1) mean [signification]

superbus, -a, -um proud, haughty [superb]

tot (indecl. adj.) so many

Angulus Grammaticus

Quō Vādis?

With the vocabulary and grammatical tools you have acquired in this program, you are ready to begin reading almost any Latin author. The Latin of each author varies greatly in style and vocabulary, but this is no surprise, because moving from Plautus to Cicero to Vergil to Seneca to Apuleius in Latin is in many ways like moving from Chaucer to Shakespeare to Coleridge to Mark Twain to T.S. Eliot in English.

Ergō, quō vādis? Where should you go from here? One direction is toward stocking your desk with more formal Latin grammars and larger lexicons, several of which are listed below. Such grammars will provide you with more detailed and technical information than you have found in this introductory book.

Another direction to consider is the study of ancient Greek, which is structured in many ways like Latin, with its inflected words, declensions, personal endings, etc.

If you enjoy Latin grammar you might also want to look at Latin in the context of other languages, in comparative grammars, especially studies of Indo-European languages.

Grammars and Lexicons

Lexicons

Andrews, E. A., William Freund, Charlton Thomas Lewis, and Charles Short. *A Latin Dictionary Founded on Andrews' Edition of Freund's Latin Dictionary. Rev., Enl., and in Great Part Rewritten*. Oxford: Clarendon Press, 1955. Long the classic, still very useful. Desktop reference.

Glare, P. G. W. *Oxford Latin Dictionary*. Oxford [Oxfordshire]: Clarendon Press, 1982. The most modern lexicon for serious students and scholars. Desktop reference.

Smith, William, and John Lockwood. *Chambers/Murray Latin-English Dictionary*. Edinburgh: Chambers, 1976. The best portable dictionary for a Classics major. Full definitions and examples from ancient authors.

Traupman, John C. *The New Collegiate Latin and English Dictionary*. New York: Bantam Books, 1966. A very basic but solid dictionary. Basic meanings but few examples from authors. There are various versions of this book under different publishers.

Grammars

Allen, Joseph Henry, J. B. Greenough, et al. *Allen and Greenough's New Latin Grammar for Schools and Colleges: Founded on Comparative Grammar*. Revised by Anne Mahoney. Newburyport, MA: Focus, 2001. Excellent desktop grammar with useful examples.

Gildersleeve, Basil L., and Gonzalez Lodge. *Gildersleeve's Latin Grammar*. Wauconda, IL: Bolchazy-Carducci Publishers, 1997. Very solid and in-depth.

Mahoney, Anne, and Charles E. Bennett. *Essential Latin Grammar: Bennett's Grammar Revised*. Newburyport, MA: Focus/R. Pullins, 2007. Another old standard brought up to date.

Appendix

Forms

Nouns

	1ST DECLENSION	2ND DECLENSION					
Singular	Fem.	Masc.	Masc.	Masc.	Masc.	Masc.	Neut.
Nom.	fēmina	discipulus	vir	fīlius	magister	puer	vīnum
Gen.	fēminae	discipulī	virī	fīliī	magistrī	puerī	vīnī
Dat.	fēminae	discipulō	virō	fīliō	magistrō	puerō	vīnō
Acc.	fēminam	discipulum	virum	fīlium	magistrum	puerum	vīnum
Abl.	fēminā	discipulō	virō	fīliō	magistrō	puerō	vīnō
Voc.	fēmina	discipule	vir	fīlī	magister	puer	vīnum
Plural							
Nom.	fēminae	discipulī	virī	fīliī	magistrī	puerī	vīna
Gen.	fēminārum	discipulōrum	virōrum	fīliōrum	magistrōrum	puerōrum	vīnōrum
Dat.	fēminīs	discipulīs	virīs	fīliīs	magistrīs	puerīs	vīnīs
Acc.	fēminās	discipulōs	virōs	fīliōs	magistrōs	puerōs	vīna
Abl.	fēminīs	discipulīs	vīrīs	fīliīs	magistrīs	puerīs	vīnīs
Voc.	fēminae	discipulī	virī	fīliī	magistrī	puerī	vīna

	3RD DECLENSION			I-STEMS	
Singular	Masc.	Fem.	Neut.	Masc./Fem.	Neut.
Nom.	frāter	soror	nōmen	ignis	mare
Gen.	frātris	sorōris	nōminis	ignis	maris
Dat.	frātrī	sorōrī	nōminī	ignī	marī
Acc.	frātrem	sorōrem	nōmen	ignem	mare
Abl.	frātre	sorōre	nōmine	igne or ignī	marī
Voc.	frāter	soror	nōmen	ignis	mare
Plural					
Nom.	frātrēs	sorōrēs	nōmina	ignēs	maria
Gen.	frātrum	sorōrum	nōminum	ignium	marium
Dat.	frātribus	sorōribus	nōminibus	ignibus	maribus
Acc.	frātrēs	sorōrēs	nōmina	ignēs	maria
Abl.	frātribus	sorōribus	nōminibus	ignibus	maribus
Voc.	frātrēs	sorōrēs	nōmina	ignēs	maria

4TH DECLENSION			
Singular	**Masc.**	**Fem.**	**Neut.**
Nom.	lacus	manus	genū
Gen.	lacūs	manūs	genūs
Dat.	lacuī	manuī	genū
Acc.	lacum	manum	genū
Abl.	lacū	manū	genū
Voc.	lacus	manus	genū
Plural			
Nom.	lacūs	manūs	genua
Gen.	lacuum	manuum	genuum
Dat.	lacibus	manibus	genibus
Acc.	lacūs	manūs	genua
Abl.	lacibus	manibus	genibus
Voc.	lacus	manūs	genua

5TH DECLENSION		
Singular	**Masc.**	**Fem.**
Nom.	diēs	rēs
Gen.	diēī	reī
Dat.	diēī	reī
Acc.	diem	rem
Abl.	diē	rē
Voc.	diēs	rēs
Plural		
Nom.	diēs	rēs
Gen.	diērum	rērum
Dat.	diēbus	rēbus
Acc.	diēs	rēs
Abl.	diēbus	rēbus
Voc.	diēs	rēs

Irregular Noun *Vīs*

	Singular strength, power	**Plural** troops, forces
Nom.	vīs	vīrēs
Gen.	vis	vīrium
Dat.	vī	vīribus
Acc.	vim	vīrēs
Abl.	vī	vīribus

Adjectives

2-1-2 ADJECTIVES

	2ND DECLENSION	1ST DECLENSION	2ND DECLENSION
Singular	**Masc.**	**Fem.**	**Neut.**
Nom.	bonus	bona	bonum
Gen.	bonī	bonae	bonī
Dat.	bonō	bonae	bonō
Acc.	bonum	bonam	bonum
Abl.	bonō	bonā	bonō
Voc.	bone	bona	bonum
Plural			
Nom.	bonī	bonae	bona
Gen.	bonōrum	bonārum	bonōrum
Dat.	bonīs	bonīs	bonīs
Acc.	bonōs	bonās	bona
Abl.	bonīs	bonīs	bonīs
Voc.	bonī	bonae	bona

	2ND DECLENSION	1ST DECLENSION	2ND DECLENSION
Singular	**Masc.**	**Fem.**	**Neut.**
Nom.	pulcher	pulchra	pulchrum
Gen.	pulchrī	pulchrae	pulchrī
Dat.	pulchrō	pulchrae	pulchrō
Acc.	pulchrum	pulchram	pulchrum
Abl.	pulchrō	pulchrā	pulchrō
Voc.	pulcher	pulchra	pulchrum
Plural			
Nom.	pulchrī	pulchrae	pulchra
Gen.	pulchrōrum	pulchrārum	pulchrōrum
Dat.	pulchrīs	pulchrīs	pulchrīs
Acc.	pulchrōs	pulchrās	pulchra
Abl.	pulchrīs	pulchrīs	pulchrīs
Voc.	pulchrī	pulchrae	pulchra

3RD DECLENSION ADJECTIVES

3 Terminations

Singular	Masc.	Fem.	Neut.
Nom.	celer	celeris	celere
Gen.	celeris	celeris	celeris
Dat.	celerī	celerī	celerī
Acc.	celerem	celerem	celere
Abl.	celerī	celerī	celerī
Voc.	celer	celeris	celere

Plural			
Nom.	celerēs	celerēs	celeria
Gen.	celerium	celerium	celerium
Dat.	celeribus	celeribus	celeribus
Acc.	celerēs	celerēs	celeria
Abl.	celeribus	celeribus	celeribus
Voc.	celerēs	celerēs	celeria

2 Terminations

Singular	Masc./Fem.	Neut.
Nom.	fortis	forte
Gen.	fortis	fortis
Dat.	fortī	fortī
Acc.	fortem	forte
Abl.	fortī	fortī
Voc.	fortis	forte

Plural		
Nom.	fortēs	fortia
Gen.	fortium	fortium
Dat.	fortibus	fortibus
Acc.	fortēs	fortia
Abl.	fortibus	fortibus
Voc.	fortēs	fortia

1 Termination

Singular	Masc./Fem./Neut.
Nom.	fēlix
Gen.	fēlīcis
Dat.	fēlīcī
Acc.	fēlīcem (m./f.) fēlix (n.)
Abl.	fēlīcī
Voc.	fēlix

Plural	
Nom.	fēlīcēs (m./f.) fēlīcia (n.)
Gen.	fēlīcium
Dat.	fēlīcibus
Acc.	fēlīcēs (m./f.) fēlīcia (n.)
Abl.	fēlīcibus
Voc.	fēlīcēs (m./f.) fēlīcia (n.)

Comparative Adjectives

Note: Comparatives are declined like 3rd declension regular (not i-stem) nouns.

Singular	Masc./Fem.	Neut.
Nom.	celerior	celerius
Gen.	celeriōris	celeriōris
Dat.	celeriōrī	celeriōrī
Acc.	celeriōrem	celerius
Abl.	celeriōre	celeriōre
Voc.	celerior	celerius
Plural		
Nom.	celeriōrēs	celeriōra
Gen.	celeriōrum	celeriōrum
Dat.	celeriōribus	celeriōribus
Acc.	celeriōrēs	celeriōra
Abl.	celeriōribus	celeriōribus
Voc.	celeriōrēs	celeriōra

Superlative Adjectives

REGULAR FORMATION

POSITIVE	SUPERLATIVE
laetus, -a, -um	laetissimus, -a, -um
fortis, forte	fortissimus, -a, -um
crūdēlis, crūdēle	crūdēlissimus, -a, -um

IRREGULAR FORMATIONS

A. All adjectives ending in -er in the masculine nominative singular:

POSITIVE	SUPERLATIVE
miser, misera, miserum	miserrimus, -a, -um
pulcher, pulchra, pulchrum	pulcherrimus, -a, -um
celer, celeris, celere	celerrimus, -a, -um

B. Some adjectives ending in *-lis* in the masculine nominative singular:

POSITIVE	SUPERLATIVE
facilis, facile	facillimus, -a, -um
difficilis, difficile	difficillimus, -a, -um
similis, simile	simillimus, -a, -um
dissimilis, dissimile	dissimillimus, -a, -um
gracilis, gracile	gracillimus, -a, -um
humilis, humile	humillimus, -a, -um

C. Irregular comparative and superlative adjectives:

POSITIVE	COMPARATIVE	SUPERLATIVE
bonus, -a, -um	melior, melius	optimus, -a,- um
malus, -a, -um	pēior, pēius	pessimus, -a, -um
magnus, -a, -um	māior, māius	maximus, -a, -um
multus, -a, -um	plūrēs, plūra	plūrimus, -a, -um
multī, -ae, -a	plūs (neuter form only)	plūrimī, -ae, -a
parvus, -a, -um	minor, minus	minimus, -a, -um
[no positive]	prior, prius	prīmus, -a, -um
superus, -a, -um	superior, superius	suprēmus, -a, -um
		summus, -a, -um

Personal / Reflexive Adjectives

PERSON	LATIN FORMS	TRANSLATION
Singular		
1st	meus, -a, -um	my
2nd	tuus, -a, -um	your
3rd	suus, -a, -um (reflexive)	his/her/its own
Plural		
1st	noster, -tra, -trum	our
2nd	vester, -tra, -trum	your
3rd	suus, -a, -um (reflexive)	their own

UNUS NAUTA Adjectives

Ullus, -a, -um any
Nullus, -a, -um no, none
Ūnus, -a, -um one
Sōlus, -a, -um alone, only

Neuter, neutra, neutrum—neither
Alius, -a, -ud another, other
Uter, utra, utrum either, which (of two)
Tōtus, -a, -um whole, entire
Alter, altera, alterum the other (of two)

	MASC.	FEM.	NEUT.
Singular			
Nom.	sōlus	sōla	sōlum
Gen.	sōlīus	sōlīus	sōlīus
Dat.	sōlī	sōlī	sōlī
Acc.	sōlum	sōlam	sōlum
Abl.	sōlō	sōlā	sōlō
Plural			
Nom.	sōlī	sōlae	sōla
Gen.	sōlōrum	sōlārum	sōlōrum
Dat.	sōlīs	sōlīs	sōlīs
Acc.	sōlōs	sōlās	sōla
Abl.	sōlīs	sōlīs	sōlīs

Adverbs

REGULAR

	POSITIVE	COMPARATIVE	SUPERLATIVE
Based on 2-1-2 adjective	laetē	laetius	laetissimē
Based on 3rd declension adjective	fortiter	fortius	fortissimē

PARTIALLY IRREGULAR

	POSITIVE	COMPARATIVE	SUPERLATIVE
3rd declension adjectives ending in -er	celeriter	celerius	celerrimē
Other 3rd declension adjectives	facile	facilius	facillimē

COMPLETELY IRREGULAR

bene	melius	optimē
male	pēius	pessimē
magnopere	magis	maximē
multum	plūs	plūrimum
parum	minus	minimē

Pronouns

	1ST PERSON	2ND PERSON	3RD PERSON		
Singular					
Nom.	ego	tū	is	ea	id
Gen.	meī	tuī	eius	eius	eius
Dat.	mihi	tibi	eī	eī	eī
Acc.	mē	tē	eum	eam	id
Abl.	mē	tē	eō	eā	eō
Plural					
Nom.	nōs	vōs	eī	eae	ea
Gen.	nostrī/nostrum	vestrī/vestrum	eōrum	eārum	eōrum
Dat.	nōbīs	vōbīs	eīs	eīs	eīs
Acc.	nōs	vōs	eōs	eās	ea
Abl.	nōbīs	vōbīs	eīs	eīs	eīs

RELATIVE PRONOUN AND INTERROGATIVE ADJECTIVE

	MASC.	FEM.	NEUT.
Singular			
Nom.	quī	quae	quod
Gen.	cuius	cuius	cuius
Dat.	cui	cui	cui
Acc.	quem	quam	quod
Abl.	quō	quā	quō
Plural			
Nom.	quī	quae	quae
Gen.	quōrum	quārum	quōrum
Dat.	quibus	quibus	quibus
Acc.	quōs	quās	quae
Abl.	quibus	quibus	quibus

INTERROGATIVE PRONOUN

	MASC./FEM.	NEUT.
Singular		
Nom.	quis	quid
Gen.	cuius	cuius
Dat.	cui	cui
Acc.	quem	quid
Abl.	quō	quō
Plural		
Nom.	quī	quae
Gen.	quōrum	quōrum
Dat.	quibus	quibus
Acc.	quōs	quae
Abl.	quibus	quibus

DEMONSTRATIVE: *hic haec hoc*

	MASC.	FEM.	NEUT.
Singular			
Nom.	hic	haec	hoc
Gen.	huius	huius	huius
Dat.	huic	huic	huic
Acc.	hunc	hanc	hoc
Abl.	hōc	hāc	hōc
Plural			
Nom.	hī	hae	haec
Gen.	hōrum	hārum	hōrum
Dat.	hīs	hīs	hīs
Acc.	hōs	hās	haec
Abl.	hīs	hīs	hīs

NUMBERS

Only the Latin words for the cardinal numbers 1, 2, 3 and 1000 are declinable:

	I			II			III			M
Nom.	ūnus	ūna	ūnum	duo	duae	duo	trēs	trēs	tria	mīlia
Gen.	ūnīus	ūnīus	ūnīus	duōrum	duārum	duōrum	trium	trium	trium	mīlium
Dat.	ūnī	ūnīus	ūnī	duōbus	duābus	duōbus	tribus	tribus	tribus	mīlibus
Acc.	ūnum	ūnam	ūnum	duōs	duās	duo	trēs	trēs	tria	mīlia
Abl.	ūnō	ūnā	ūnō	duōbus	duābus	duōbus	tribus	tribus	tribus	mīlibus

	ROMAN NUMERAL	CARDINAL NUMBER	ORDINAL NUMBER
1	I	ūnus, -a, -um	prīmus, -a, -um
2	II	duo, -ae, -o	secundus, -a, -um
3	III	trēs, -ēs, -ia	tertius, -a, -um
4	IIII or IV	quattuor	quartus, -a, -um
5	V	quinque	quintus, -a, -um
6	VI	sex	sextus, -a, -um
7	VII	septem	septimus, -a, -um
8	VIII	octō	octāvus, -a, -um
9	VIIII or IX	novem	nōnus, -a, -um
10	X	decem	decimus, -a, -um
11	XI	undecim	undecimus, -a, -um
12	XII	duodecim	duodecimus, -a, -um
13	XIII	tredecim	tertius decimus, -a, -um
14	XIIII or XIV	quattuordecim	quartus decimus, -a, -um
15	XV	quindecim	quintus decimus, -a, -um
16	XVI	sēdecim	sextus decimus, -a, -um
17	XVII	septendecim	septimus decimus, -a, -um
18	XVIII	duodēvīgintī	duodēvīcēsimus, -a, -um
19	XVIIII or XIX	undēvīgintī	undēvīcēsimus, -a, -um
20	XX	vīgintī	vīcēsimus, -a, -um
21	XXI	vīgintī ūnus	vīcēsimus prīmus, -a, -um
22	XXII	vīgintī duo	vīcēsimus secundus, -a, -um
30	XXX	trīgintā	trīcēsimus, -a, -um
40	XL or XXXX	quadrāgintā	quadrāgēsimus, -a, -um
50	L	quinquāgintā	quīnquāgēsimus, -a, -um
60	LX	sexāgintā	sexagēsimus, -a, -um
70	LXX	septuāgintā	sepuāgēsimus, -a, -um
80	LXXX	octōgintā	octōgēsimus, -a, -um
90	XC	nōnāgintā	nōnāgēsimus -a, -um
100	C	centum	centimus, -a, -um
500	D	quīngentī	quīngentēsimus, -a, -um
1000	M	mīlle mīlia	millēsimus, -a, -um

Regular Verbs

INDICATIVE MOOD

1st Conjugation   vocō, vocāre, vocāvī, vocātum

Active

PRESENT	IMPERFECT	FUTURE	PERFECT	PLUPERFECT	FUTURE PERFECT
vocō	vocābam	vocābō	vocāvī	vocāveram	vocāverō
vocās	vocābās	vocābis	vocāvistī	vocāverās	vocāveris
vocat	vocābat	vocābit	vocāvit	vocāverat	vocāverit
vocāmus	vocābāmus	vocābimus	vocāvimus	vocāverāmus	vocāverimus
vocātis	vocābātis	vocābitis	vocāvistis	vocāverātis	vocāveritis
vocant	vocābant	vocābunt	vocāvērunt	vocāverant	vocāverint

Passive

PRESENT	IMPERFECT	FUTURE	PERFECT (MASC.)	PLUPERFECT (FEM.)	FUTURE PERFECT (NEUT.)
vocor	vocābar	vocābor	vocātus sum	vocāta eram	vocātum erō
vocāris	vocābāris	vocāberis	vocātus es	vocāta erās	vocātum eris
vocātur	vocābātur	vocābitur	vocātus est	vocāta erat	vocātum erit
vocāmur	vocābāmur	vocābimur	vocātī sumus	vocātae erāmus	vocāta erimus
vocāminī	vocābāminī	vocābiminī	vocātī estis	vocātae erātis	vocāta eritis
vocantur	vocābantur	vocābuntur	vocātī sunt	vocātae erant	vocāta erunt

2nd Conjugation   moneō, monēre, monuī, monitum

Active

PRESENT	IMPERFECT	FUTURE	PERFECT	PLUPERFECT	FUTURE PERFECT
moneō	monēbam	monēbō	monuī	monueram	monuerō
monēs	monēbās	monēbis	monuistī	monuerās	monueris
monet	monēbat	monēbit	monuit	monuerat	monuerit
monēmus	monēbāmus	monēbimus	monuimus	monuerāmus	monuerimus
monētis	monēbātis	monēbitis	monuistis	monuerātis	monueritis
monent	monēbant	monēbunt	monuērunt	monuerant	monuerint

Passive

PRESENT	IMPERFECT	FUTURE	PERFECT (MASC.)	PLUPERFECT (FEM.)	FUTURE PERFECT (NEUT.)
moneor	monēbar	monēbor	monitus sum	monita eram	monitum erō
monēris	monēbāris	monēberis	monitus es	monita erās	monitum eris
monētur	monēbātur	monēbitur	monitus est	monita erat	monitum erit
monēmur	monēbāmur	monēbimur	monitī sumus	monitae erāmus	monita sumus
monēminī	monēbāminī	monēbiminī	monitī estis	monitae erātis	monita estis
monentur	monēbantur	monēbuntur	monitī sunt	monitae erant	monita sunt

3rd Conjugation Regular: scrībō, scrībere, scripsī, scriptum

Active

PRESENT	IMPERFECT	FUTURE	PERFECT	PLUPERFECT	FUTURE PERFECT
scrībō	scrībēbam	scrībam	scripsī	scripseram	scripserō
scrībis	scrībēbās	scrībēs	scripsistī	scripserās	scripseris
scrībit	scrībēbat	scrībet	scripsit	scripserat	scripserit
scrībimus	scrībēbamus	scrībēmus	scripsimus	scripserāmus	scripserimus
scrībitis	scrībēbātis	scrībētis	scripsistis	scripserātis	scripseritis
scrībunt	scrībēbant	scrībent	scripsērunt	scripserant	scripserint

Passive

PRESENT	IMPERFECT	FUTURE	PERFECT (MASC.)	PLUPERFECT (FEM.)	FUTURE PERFECT (NEUT.)
scrībor	scrībēbar	scrībor	scriptus sum	scripta eram	scriptum erō
scrīberis	scrībēbāris	scrībēris	scriptus es	scripta erās	scriptum eris
scrībitur	scrībēbātur	scrībētur	scriptus est	scripta erat	scriptum erit
scrībimur	scrībēbāmur	scrībēmur	scriptī sumus	scriptae erāmus	scripta erimus
scrībiminī	scrībēbāminī	scrībēminī	scriptī estis	scriptae erātis	scripta eritis
scrībuntur	scrībēbantur	scrībentur	scriptī sunt	scriptae erant	scripta erunt

3rd Conjugation -iō: capiō, capere, cēpī, captum

Active

PRESENT	IMPERFECT	FUTURE	PERFECT	PLUPERFECT	FUTURE PERFECT
capiō	capiēbam	capiam	cēpī	cēperam	cēperō
capis	capiēbās	capiēs	cēpistī	cēperās	cēperis
capit	capiēbat	capiet	cēpit	cēperat	cēperit
capimus	capiēbāmus	capiēmus	cēpimus	cēperāmus	cēperimus
capitis	capiēbātis	capiētis	cēpistis	cēperātis	cēperitis
capiunt	capiēbant	capient	cēpērunt	cēperant	cēperint

Passive

PRESENT	IMPERFECT	FUTURE	PERFECT (MASC.)	PLUPERFECT (FEM.)	FUTURE PERFECT (NEUT.)
capior	capiēbar	capiar	captus sum	capta eram	captum erō
caperis	capiēbāris	capiēris	captus es	capta erās	captum eris
capitur	capiēbātur	capiētur	captus est	capta erat	captum erit
capimur	capiēbāmur	capiēmur	captī sumus	captae erāmus	capta erimus
capiminī	capiēbāminī	capiēminī	captī estis	captae erātis	capta eritis
capiuntur	capiēbantur	capientur	captī sunt	captae erant	capta erunt

4th Conjugation   audiō, audīre, audīvī, audītum

Active

PRESENT	IMPERFECT	FUTURE	PERFECT	PLUPERFECT	FUTURE PERFECT
audiō	audiēbam	audiam	audīvī	audīveram	audīverō
audīs	audiēbās	audiēs	audīvistī	audīverās	audīveris
audit	audiēbat	audiet	audīvit	audīverat	audīverit
audīmus	audiēbāmus	audiēmus	audīvimus	audīverāmus	audīverimus
audītis	audiēbātis	audiētis	audīvistis	audīverātis	audīveritis
audiunt	audiēbant	audient	audīvērunt	audīverant	audīverint

Passive

PRESENT	IMPERFECT	FUTURE	PERFECT (MASC.)	PLUPERFECT (FEM.)	FUTURE PERFECT (NEUT.)
audior	audiēbar	audiar	audītus sum	audīta eram	audītum erō
audīris	audiēbāris	audiēris	audītus es	audīta erās	audītum eris
audītur	audiēbātur	audiētur	audītus est	audīta erat	audītum erit
audīmur	audiēbāmur	audiēmur	audītī sumus	audītae erāmus	audīta erimus
audīminī	audiēbāminī	audiēminī	audītī estis	audītae erātis	audīta eritis
audiuntur	audiēbantur	audientur	audītī sunt	audītae erant	audīta erunt

SUBJUNCTIVE MOOD

1st Conjugation   vocō, vocāre, vocāvī, vocātum

Active

PRESENT	IMPERFECT	PERFECT	PLUPERFECT
vocem	vocārem	vocāverim	vocāvissem
vocēs	vocārēs	vocāveris	vocāvissēs
vocet	vocāret	vocāverit	vocāvisset
vocēmus	vocārēmus	vocāverimus	vocāvissēmus
vocētis	vocārētis	vocāveritis	vocāvissētis
vocent	vocārent	vocāverint	vocāvissent

Passive

PRESENT	IMPERFECT	PERFECT (MASC.)	PLUPERFECT (FEM.)
vocer	vocārer	vocātus sim	vocāta essem
vocēris	vocārēris	vocātus sīs	vocāta essēs
vocētur	vocārētur	vocātus sit	vocāta esset
vocēmur	vocārēmur	vocātī sīmus	vocātae essēmus
vocēminī	vocārēminī	vocātī sītis	vocātae essētis
vocentur	vocārentur	vocātī sint	vocātae essent

2nd Conjugation   moneō, monēre, monuī, monitum

Active

PRESENT	IMPERFECT	PERFECT	PLUPERFECT
moneam	monēre	monuerim	monuissem
moneās	monērēs	monueris	monuissēs
moneat	monēret	monuerit	monuisset
moneāmus	monērēmus	monuerimus	monuissēmus
moneātis	monērētis	monueritis	monuissētis
moneant	monērent	monuerint	monuissent

Passive

PRESENT	IMPERFECT	PERFECT (MASC.)	PLUPERFECT (FEM.)
monear	monērer	monitus sim	monita essem
moneāris	monērēris	monitus sīs	monita essēs
moneātur	monērētur	monitus sit	monita esset
moneāmur	monērēmur	monitī sīmus	monitae essēmus
moneāminī	monērēminī	monitī sītis	monitae essētis
moneantur	monērentur	monitī sint	monitae essent

3rd Conjugation Regular: scrībō, scrībere, scripsī, scriptum

Active

PRESENT	IMPERFECT	PERFECT	PLUPERFECT
scrībam	scrīberem	scripserim	scripsissem
scrībās	scrīberēs	scripseris	scripsissēs
scrībat	scrīberet	scripserit	scripsisset
scrībāmus	scrīberēmus	scripserimus	scripsissēmus
scrībātis	scrīberētis	scripseritis	scripsissētis
scrībant	scrīberent	scripserint	scripsissent

Passive

PRESENT	IMPERFECT	PERFECT (MASC.)	PLUPERFECT (FEM.)
scrībar	scrīberer	scriptus sim	scripta essem
scrībāris	scrīberēris	scriptus sīs	scripta essēs
scrībātur	scrīberētur	scriptus sit	scripta esset
scrībāmur	scrīberēmur	scriptī sīmus	scriptae essēmus
scrībāminī	scrīberēminī	scriptī sītis	scriptae essētis
scrībantur	scrīberentur	scriptī sint	scriptae essent

3rd Conjugation -iō: capiō, capere, cēpī, captum

Active

PRESENT	IMPERFECT	PERFECT	PLUPERFECT
capiam	caperem	cēperim	cēpissem
capiās	caperēs	cēperis	cēpissēs
capiāt	caperet	cēperit	cēpisset
capiāmus	caperēmus	cēperimus	cēpissēmus
capiātis	caperētis	cēperitis	cēpissētis
capiant	caperent	cēperint	cēpissent

Passive

PRESENT	IMPERFECT	PERFECT (MASC.)	PLUPERFECT (FEM.)
capiar	caperer	captus sim	capta essem
capiāris	caperēris	captus sīs	capta essēs
capiātur	caperētur	captus sit	capta esset
capiāmur	caperēmur	captī sīmus	captae essēmus
capiāminī	caperēminī	captī sītis	captae essētis
capiantur	caperentur	captī sint	captae essent

4th Conjugation   audiō, audīre, audīvī, audītum

Active

PRESENT	IMPERFECT	PERFECT	PLUPERFECT
audiam	audīrem	audīverim	audīvissem
audiās	audīrēs	audīveris	audīvissēs
audiat	audīret	audīverit	audīvisset
audiāmus	audīrēmus	audīverimus	audīvissēmus
audiātis	audīrētis	audīveritis	audīvissētis
audiant	audirent	audīverint	audīvissent

Passive

PRESENT	IMPERFECT	PERFECT (MASC.)	PLUPERFECT (FEM.)
audiar	audīrer	audītus sim	audīta essem
audiāris	audīrēris	audītus sīs	audīta essēs
audiātur	audīrētur	audītus sit	audīta esset
audiāmur	audīrēmur	audītī sīmus	audītae essēmus
audiāminī	audīrēminī	audītī sītis	audītae essētis
audiantur	audīrentur	audītī sint	audītae essent

Infinitives

CONJUGATION	ACTIVE	PASSIVE
Present		
1st	vocāre	vocārī
2nd	monēre	monērī
3rd	scrībere	scrībī
3rd-iō	capere	capī
4th	audīre	audīrī
Perfect		
1st	vocāvisse	vocātus, -a, -um esse
2nd	monuisse	monitus, -a, -um esse
3rd	scripsisse	scriptus, -a, -um esse
3rd-iō	cēpisse	captus, -a, -um esse
4th	audīvisse	audītus, -a, -um esse
Future		
1st	vocātūrus, -a, -um esse	vocātum īrī
2nd	monitūrus, -a, -um esse	monitum īri
3rd	scriptūrus, -a, -um esse	scriptum īrī
3rd-iō	captūrus, -a, -um esse	captum īrī
4th	audītūrus, -a, -um esse	audītum īrī

Imperatives

CONJUGATION	ACTIVE		PASSIVE	
	Singular	Plural	Singular	Plural
Present				
1st	Vocā!	Vocāte!	Vocāre!	Vocāminī!
2nd	Monē!	Monēte!	Monēre!	Monēminī!
3rd	Cape!	Capite!	Capere!	Capiminī!
3rd-iō	Scrībe!	Scrībite!	Scrībere!	Scrībiminī!
4th	Audī!	Audīte!	Audīre!	Audīminī!
Future				
1st	Vocātō!	Vocātōte!		
2nd	Monētō!	Monētōte!		
3rd	Capitō!	Capitōte!		
3rd-iō	Scrībitō!	Scrībitōte!		
4th	Audītō!	Audītōte!		

Negative Imperative

CONJUGATION	SINGULAR	SINGULAR
1st	Nōlī vocāre!	Nōlīte vocāre!
2nd	Nōlī monēre!	Nōlīte monēre!
3rd	Nōlī scrībere!	Nōlīte scrībere!
3rd-iō	Nōlī capere!	Nōlīte capere!
4th	Nōlī audīre!	Nōlīte audīre!

Irregular Imperatives

	SING.	PL.
dīcō, dīcere	dīc	dīcite
dūcō, dūcere	dūc	dūcite
faciō, facere	fac	facite
ferō, ferre	fer	ferte

Participles

CONJUGATION	ACTIVE	PASSIVE
Present		
1st	vocāns, -antis	
2nd	monēns, -entis	
3rd	scrībēns, -entis	
3rd-*iō*	capiēns, -ientis	
4th	audiēns, -ientis	
Perfect		
1st		vocātus, -a, -um
2nd		monitus, -a, -um
3rd		scriptus, -a, -um
3rd-*iō*		captus, -a, -um
4th		audītus, -a, -um
Future		
1st	vocatūrus, -a, -um	
2nd	monitūrus, -a, -um	
3rd	scriptūrus, -a, -um	
3rd-*iō*	captūrus, -a, -um	
4th	audītūrus, -a, -um	

Declining Participles

Singular	Masc./Fem.	Neut.
Nom.	vocāns	vocāns
Gen.	vocantis	vocantis
Dat.	vocantī	vocanti
Acc.	vocantem	vocāns
Abl.	vocantī/vocante	vocantī/vocante
Plural		
Nom.	vocantēs	vocantia
Gen.	vocantium	vocantium
Dat.	vocantibus	vocantibus
Acc.	vocantēs	vocantia
Abl.	vocantibus	vocantibus

GERUND(IVE)S

Gerund

Nom.	(vocāre)	(monēre)	(scrībere)	(capere)	(audīre)
Gen.	vocandī	monendī	scrībendī	capiendī	audiendī
Dat.	vocandō	monendō	scrībendō	capiendō	audiendō
Acc.	vocandum	monendum	scrībendum	capiendum	audiendum
Abl.	vocandō	monendō	scrībendō	capiendō	audiendō

Gerundive

vocandus, -a, -um   monendus, -a, -um   scrībendus, -a, -um   capiendus, -a, -um   audiendus, -a, -um

Supines

ACC.	ABL.
vocātum	vocātū
monitum	monitū
scriptum	scriptū
captum	captū
audītum	audītū

Deponent Verbs

Deponent verbs use passive endings but are active in meaning. Note the presence of a present active participle.

> cōnor, cōnārī, cōnātus sum
> vereor, verērī, veritus sum
> sequor, sequī, secūtus sum
> patior, patī, passus sum
> potior, potīrī, potītus sum

Indicative Mood

INDICATIVE

Present

cōnor	vereor	sequor	patior	potior
cōnāris	verēris	sequeris	pateris	potīris
cōnātur	verētur	sequitur	patitur	potītur
cōnāmur	verēmur	sequimur	patimur	potīmur
cōnāminī	verēminī	sequiminī	patiminī	potīminī
cōnantur	verentur	sequuntur	patiuntur	potiuntur

Imperfect

cōnābar	verēbar	sequēbar	patiēbar	potiēbar

Future

cōnābor	verēbor	sequar	patiar	potiar

Perfect

cōnātus sum	veritus sum	secūtus sum	passus sum	potītus sum

Pluperfect

cōnātus eram	veritus eram	secūtus eram	passus eram	potītus eram

Future Perfect

cōnātus erō	veritus erō	secūtus erō	passus erō	potītus erō

Subjunctive

Present

cōnar	verear	sequar	patiar	potiar

Imperfect

cōnārer	verērer	sequerer	paterer	potīrer

Perfect

cōnātus sim	veritus sim	secūtus sim	passus sim	potītus sim

Pluperfect

cōnātus essem	veritus essem	secūtus essem	passus essem	potītus essem

INFINITIVES

Present	cōnārī	verērī	sequī	patī	potīrī
Perfect	cōnātus esse	veritus esse	secūtus esse	passus esse	potītus esse
Future	cōnātūrus esse	veritūrus esse	secūtūrus esse	passūrus esse	potītūrus esse

IMPERATIVES

Singular	cōnāre	verēre	sequere	patere	potīre
Plural	cōnāminī	verēminī	sequiminī	patiminī	potīminī

Participles

Present Active	cōnāns	verēns	sequēns	patiēns	potiēns
Perfect Passive	cōnātus, -a, -um	veritus, -a, -um	secūtus, -a, -um	passus, -a, -um	potītus, -a, -um
Future Active	cōnātūrus, -a, -um	veritūrus, -a, -um	secūtūrus, -a, -um	passūrus, -a, -um	potītūrus -a, -um

Gerund(ive)s

GERUND

Nom.	(cōnārī)	(verērī)	(sequī)	(patī)	(potīrī)
Gen.	cōnandī	verendī	sequendī	patiendī	potiendī
Dat.	cōnandō	verendō	sequendō	patiendō	potiendō
Acc.	cōnandum	verendum	sequendum	patiendum	potiendum
Abl.	cōnandō	verendō	sequendō	patiendō	potiendō

Gerundive

cōnandus, -a, -um	verendus, -a, -um	sequendus, -a, -um	patiendus, -a, -um	potiendus, -a, -um

Supines

ACC.	ABL.
cōnātum	cōnātū
veritum	veritū
secūtum	secūtū
captum	captū
potītum	potītū

Irregular Verbs
sum, esse, fuī

Indicative

PRESENT	IMPERFECT	FUTURE	PERFECT	PLUPERFECT	FUTURE PERFECT
sum	eram	erō	fuī	fueram	fuerō
es	erās	eris	fuistī	fuerās	fueris
est	erat	erit	fuit	fuerat	fuerit
sumus	erāmus	erimus	fuimus	fuerāmus	fuerimus
estis	erātis	eritis	fuistis	fuerātis	fueritis
sunt	erant	erunt	fuērunt	fuerant	fuerint

Subjunctive

PRESENT	IMPERFECT	PERFECT	PLUPERFECT
sim	essem	fuerim	fuissem
sīs	essēs	fueris	fuissēs
sit	esset	fuerit	fuisset
sīmus	essēmus	fuerimus	fuissēmus
sītis	essētis	fueritis	fuisssētis
sint	essent	fuerint	fuissent

Infinitives

	ACTIVE
Present	esse
Perfect	fuisse
Future	futūrus, -a, -um esse

Imperatives

	SINGULAR	PLURAL
Present	Es!	Este!
Future	Estō!	Estōte!

Participle

Future	futūrus, -a, -um

possum, posse, potuī

Indicative

PRESENT	IMPERFECT	FUTURE	PERFECT	PLUPERFECT	FUTURE PERFECT
possum	poteram	poterō	potuī	potueram	potuerō
potes	poterās	poteris	potuistī	potuerās	potueris
potest	poterat	poterit	potuit	potuerat	potuerit
possumus	poterāmus	poterimus	potuimus	potuerāmus	potuerimus
potestis	poterātis	poteritis	potuistis	potuerātis	potueritis
possunt	poterant	poterunt	potuērunt	potuerant	potuerint

Subjunctive

PRESENT	IMPERFECT	PERFECT	PLUPERFECT
possim	possem	potuerim	potuissem
possīs	possēs	potueris	potuissēs
possit	posset	potuerit	potuisset
possīmus	possēmus	potuerimus	potuissēmus
possītis	possētis	potueritis	potuisssētis
possint	possent	potuerint	potuissent

Infinitives

	ACTIVE
Present	posse
Perfect	potuisse

Participle

Present	potēns

volō, velle, voluī

Indicative

PRESENT	IMPERFECT	FUTURE	PERFECT	PLUPERFECT	FUTURE PERFECT
volō	volēbam	volam	voluī	volueram	voluerō
vīs	volēbās	volēs	voluistī	voluerās	volueris
vult	volēbat	volet	voluit	voluerat	voluerit
volumus	volēbāmus	volēmus	voluimus	voluerāmus	voluerimus
vultis	volēbātis	volētis	voluistis	voluerātis	volueritis
volunt	volēbant	volent	voluērunt	voluerant	voluerint

Subjunctive

PRESENT	IMPERFECT	PERFECT	PLUPERFECT
velim	vellem	voluerim	voluissem
velīs	vellēs	volueris	voluissēs
velit	vellet	voluerit	voluisset
velīmus	vellēmus	voluerimus	voluissēmus
velītis	velētis	volueritis	voluissētis
velint	vellent	voluerint	voluissent

nōlō, nōlle, nōluī

Indicative

PRESENT	IMPERFECT	FUTURE	PERFECT	PLUPERFECT	FUTURE PERFECT
nōlō	nolēbam	nōlam	nōluī	nōlueram	nōluerō
nōn vīs	nolēbās	nōlēs	nōluistī	nōluerās	nōlueris
nōn vult	nolēbat	nōlet	nōluit	nōluerat	nōluerit
nōlumus	nolēbāmus	nōlēmus	nōluimus	nōluerāmus	nōluerimus
nōn vultis	nolēbātis	nōlētis	nōluistis	nōluerātis	nōlueritis
nōlunt	nolēbant	nōlent	nōluērunt	nōluerant	nōluerint

Subjunctive

PRESENT	IMPERFECT	PERFECT	PLUPERFECT
nōlim	nōllem	nōluerim	nōluissem
nōlīs	nōllēs	nōlueris	nōluissēs
nōlit	nōllet	nōluerit	nōluisset
nōlimus	nōllēmus	nōluerimus	nōluissēmus
nōlitis	nōlētis	nōlueritis	nōluissētis
nōlint	nōllent	nōluerint	nōluissent

mālō, mālle, māluī

Indicative

PRESENT	IMPERFECT	FUTURE	PERFECT	PLUPERFECT	FUTURE PERFECT
mālō	mālēbam	mālam	māluī	mālueram	māluerō
māvīs	mālēbās	mālēs	māluistī	māluerās	mālueris
māvult	mālēbat	mālet	māluit	māluerat	māluerit
mālumus	mālēbāmus	mālēmus	māluimus	māluerāmus	māluerimus
māvultis	mālēbātis	mālētis	māluistis	māluerātis	mālueritis
mālunt	mālēbant	mālent	māluērunt	māluerant	māluerint

Subjunctive

PRESENT	IMPERFECT	PERFECT	PLUPERFECT
mālim	māllem	maluerim	maluissem
mālīs	māllēs	malueris	maluissēs
mālit	māllet	maluerit	maluisset
mālimus	māllēmus	maluerimus	maluissēmus
mālitis	mālētis	malueritis	maluissētis
mālint	māllent	maluerint	maluissent

Infinitives

Present	velle	nōlle	mālle
Perfect	voluisse	nōluisse	māluisse

Imperatives (only nōlō)

	SINGULAR	PLURAL
Present	Nōlī!	Nōlīte!
Future	Nōlītō	Nōlītōte

Present Participle:

volēns	nōlēns	—

eō, īre, īvī / iī, ītum

Indicative

PRESENT	IMPERFECT	FUTURE	PERFECT	PLUPERFECT	FUTURE PERFECT
eō	ībam	ībō	īvī	īveram	īverō
īs	ībās	ībis	īvistī	īverās	īveris
it	ībat	ībit	īvit	īverat	īverit
īmus	ībāmus	ībimus	īvimus	īverāmus	īverimus
ītis	ībātis	ībitis	īvistis	īverātis	īveritis
eunt	ībant	ībunt	īvērunt	īverant	īverint

Subjunctive

PRESENT	IMPERFECT	PERFECT	PLUPERFECT
eam	īrem	īverim	īvissem
eās	īrēs	īveris	īvissēs
eat	īret	īverit	īvisset
eāmus	īrēmus	īverimus	īvissēmus
eātis	īrētis	īveritis	īvissētis
eant	īrent	īverint	īvissent

Infinitives

Present	īre
Perfect	īvisse
Future	itūrus, -a, -um esse

Imperatives (only nōlō)

	SINGULAR	PLURAL
Present	Ī!	Īte!
Future	Ītō	Ītōte

	PARTICIPLES	GERUND	GERUNDIVE
Present	iēns, euntis	eundum, -ī, etc.	eundus, -a, -um
Future	itūrus, -a, -um		
Perfect	itum (impers.)		

fīō, fierī, factus sum

Indicative

PRESENT		IMPERFECT	FUTURE	PERFECT	PLUPERFECT	FUTURE PERFECT
fīō	[fīmus]	fīēbam	fīam	factus sum	factus eram	factus erō
fīs	[fītis]	etc.	etc.	etc.	etc.	etc.
fit	fīunt					

Subjunctive

PRESENT	IMPERFECT	PERFECT	PLUPERFECT
fīam	fierem	factus sim	factus essem

Infinitives

Present	fierī
Perfect	factus esse
Future	factūrus, -a,-um esse

Imperatives

SINGULAR	PLURAL
Fī!	Fīte!

PARTICIPLES		GERUND	GERUNDIVE
Future	factūrus, -a, -um	faciendī, -ō etc.	faciendus, -a, -um
Perfect	factus, -a, -um		

EDŌ, ESSE / EDERE "EAT"	
Present Indicative	
edō	edimus
ēs	ēstis
ēst/edit	edunt

Verba Omnia

Modus Operandī: Words in bold are *Verba Discenda* through Chapter 40. Bracketed numbers indicate the chapter in which this word became a *Verbum Discendum*. Definitions of *Verba Discenda* aim for comprehensiveness. The definitions of other words are not necessarily comprehensive but rather focus on the meanings in the context of the narrative.

abl. = ablative
acc. = accusative
adj. = adjective
dat. = dative
conj. = conjunction
excl. = exclamation
esp. = especially
f. = feminine
gen. = genitive
imp. = impersonal
imper. = imperative
indecl. = indeclinable

inf. = infinitive
interj. = interjection
interr. = interrogative
m. = masculine
n. = neuter
nom. = nominative
pl. = plural
prep. = preposition
subj. = subjunctive
v. = verb
voc. = vocative

A

ā/ab/abs (+ abl.) **from, away from; by (with persons) [5]**

abdō, abdere, abdidī, abditum **hide, conceal [19]**

abeō, abīre, abīvī/abiī, abitum **go away [7]**

abhinc from here; ago

abitus, -ūs m. departure

abluō, abluere, abluī, ablūtum wash, cleanse

absum, abesse, āfuī **be absent [19]**

abūtor, abūtī, abūsus sum (+ abl.) use up, waste

ac **and, and besides; than [33]**

acadēmia, -ae f. the academy

accēdō, accēdere, accessī, accessum **agree, assent; approach; attack [38]**

accendō, accendere, accendī, accensum light, burn

accidō, accidere, accidī, happen; fall at, fall near

accipiō, accipere, accēpī acceptum accept, receive

accumbō, accumbere, accubuī, accubitum recline at table

accurrō, accurrere, accurrī/accucurrī, accursum run, hasten to

ācer, ācris, ācre **sharp, violent, eager, swift [38]**

acervus, -ī m. heap

acētum, -ī n. vinegar

Achillēs, Achillis m. Achilles, the hero of the *Iliad*

acquiescō (1) quiet down, subside

Acrisius, -iī m. Acrisius (Perseus' grandfather)

ācriter sharply

Actiacus, -a, -um of Actium

Actium, Actiī n. Actium, site of Octavian's decisive battle with Marc Anthony and Cleopatra in 31 B.C.

actor, actōris m. actor

ad (+ acc.) **to, toward, for [3, 5]**

ad dextram to the right

ad lūnam by moonlight

ad sinistram to the left

adamō (1) fall in love, love passionately

addīcō, addīcere, addīxī, addictum consecrate

addō, addere, addidī, additum **add, give; say in addition [40]**

addūcō, addūcere, adduxī, adductum bring in, lead to

adeō so much, to such a degree

adeō, adīre, adīvī/adiī, aditum **go to [7]**

adeps, adipis m./f. fat

adhūc **to this point, still, yet [30]**

adiungō, adiungere, adiunxī, adiunctum join to, add to

adiūtor, -ōris m. helper

adiuvō, adiuvāre, adiūvī, adiūtum **help [16]**

adminiculum, -ī n. tool, support, aid

admīror, admīrārī, admīrātus sum **admire, wonder at [26]**

admoneō, admonēre, admonuī, admonitum warn strongly, admonish

adoleō, adolēre, adoluī, adultum burn
adoptō (1) adopt
adsum, adesse, adfuī be near, be present; (+ dat.) be
    "there" for someone, be of assistance, help, aid [19]
adulescens, -entis m./f. youth [15]
advena, -ae m./f. foreigner, stranger
adveniō, advenīre, advēnī, adventum arrive at,
    come to [11]
adventus, -ūs m. arrival [39]
adversārius, -iī m. opponent, enemy
adversus (+ acc.) opposite to, against
adversus, -a, -um adverse, contrary
aedēs and *aedis, aedis* f. temple, house of a god
aedificium, -iī n. building [38]
aedificō (1) build, make
aedīlitās, -tātis f. aedilship, office of aedile (public works)
aedes, see *aedēs*
aeger, aegra, aegrum sick [37]
aegrescō, aegrescere grow sick
Aegyptus, -ī f. Egypt, a province of Rome
Aelius, -iī m. Aelius, a male name
aēneus, -a, -um bronze [30]
aequē fairly
aequinoctiālis, aequinoctiāle equinoctal,
    of the equinox
aequor, aequoris n. (level surface of the) sea
aequus, -a, -um even, equal; fair, just; patient,
    calm [31]
āēr, āeris m. air, atmosphere; Greek acc. sing.,
    āera [32]
aes, aeris n. metal, especially copper or bronze
aestimō (1) value, estimate, consider [38]
aestuōsus, -a, -um hot [31]
aestus, -ūs m. heat
aetās, -tātis f. age, period of time
Aetia, -ōrum n. pl. "The Causes," title of a book
    by Callimachus
afferō, afferre, attulī, allātum bring to
afficiō, afficere, affēcī, affectum affect, move, influence
affinis, affine related by marriage
afflīgō, afflīgere, afflīxī, afflictum bother
affulgeō, affulgēre, affulsī (+ dat.) shine on, smile on;
    also spelled *adfulgeō,* etc.
Āfrica, -ae f. Africa, the Roman province of Africa
    (modern Tunisia)
Āfrus, -a, -um African
Agamemnōn, -nonis m. Agamemnon, king of Mycenae
age, agite come! well! all right! [36]
agedum come! well! all right!
ager, agrī m. field [14]
aggredior, aggredī, aggressus sum go to, approach
agitātor, -ōris m. driver, charioteer

agitātus, -a, -um shaken, disturbed, upset
agitō (1) agitate, disturb
agmen, agminis n. column of troops, battle line;
    troops, army; herd, flock; crowd [40]
agnoscō, agnoscere, agnōvī, agnōtum recognize, acknowledge
agō, agere, ēgī, actum act, do, lead, drive [4]
Agrippa, -ae m., Agrippa (M. Vipsanius Agrippa),
    Augustus' general and brother-in-law
Āh ha! ah!
aha ha! (in reproof, amusement, or denial)
āit, āiunt say (in present only)
albus, -a, -um white
Alcinous, -ī m. Alcinous, king of the Phaeacians and host
    of Odysseus
Alcmēna, -ae f. Alcmena, mother of Hercules
ālea, -ae f. die (singular of dice), dice-playing
Alexander, -ī m. Alexander (the Great), king
    of Macedonia
Alexandrēa, -ae f. Alexandria and Alexandriae
Alexandrēos, -ē, -on Alexandrian (Greek form
    of *Alexandrīnus*)
Alexandrīnus, -a, -um Alexandrian, pertaining
    to the city in Egypt
alibī elsewhere, in another place
aliōquī besides
aliquandō sometimes, at length, formerly, someday,
    hereafter [26]
aliquis, aliquid n. someone, something [18]
aliter otherwise, else, in another way [39]
aliunde elsewhere, from another person
alius, -a, -ud other, another [9]; *alius . . . alius*
    one . . . another; in pl. some . . . others [31]
allegō (1) deputize, commission, charge
alloquor, alloquī, allocūtus sum speak to, address
almus, -a, -um nourishing, kind, dear [18]
Alpēs, Alpium f. pl. Alps, the mountains of northern Italy
altē high
alter, altera, alterum the other (of two) [17]
altus, -a, -um high, deep [2]
alumnus, -ī m. foster son
alveus, -ī m. tub, basin
alvus, -ī m. belly, stomach
amābilis, amābile lovable
amārus, -a, -um bitter
amātōrius, -a, -um loving, pertaining to love, amatory
ambitiō, -ōnis f. canvassing (for votes), political
    campaign [37]
ambitiōsus, -a, -um ambitious, ostentatious
ambō, ambae, ambō both (of two); (dat./abl. pl.)
    ambōbus/ambābus [31]
ambulō (1) walk [2]
Amerīcānus, -a, -um American

amīca, -ae f. (female) friend, girlfriend [13]

amīcus, -ī m. friend [7]

āmittō, āmittere, āmīsī, āmissum lose,
send away [9]

amō (1) love [13]

amor, amōris m. love [15]

āmoveō, āmovēre, āmōvī, āmōtum remove, move away

amphitheātrum, -ī n. amphitheater [17]

Amphitrītē, -ēs f. Amphitrite, wife of Neptune.
Note Greek case endings.

Amphitruō, -ōnis m. Amphitryon, husband of Alcmena

amphora, -ae f. amphora

amplector, amplectī, amplexus sum embrace, cherish

amputō (1) cut off

amulētum, -ī n. charm, amulet

an or, whether [39]

ancilla, -ae f. female servant [8]

angiportum, -ī m. alley

angulus, -ī m. corner

angustiae, -ārum f. pl. trouble, difficulty

angustus, -a, -um narrow

anīlitās, -tātis f. old age (of a woman)

anima, -ae f. breath, soul, life

*animadvertō, animadvertere, animadvertī,
animadversum* observe, remark, notice,
understand [40]

animal, -ālis n. animal [17]

animus, -ī m. mind [29]

annō superiōre last year

annōna, -ae f. year's provision

annuō, annuere, annuī nod (in approval), agree with

annus, -ī m. year [12]

ante in front, before, ahead; (+ acc.) before, in front of

anteā previously

antehāc before this time, earlier

antequam before [34]

antiburschius, -iī m. someone who is anti-student,
a student hater

antīquitās, -tātis f. antiquity

antīquus, -a, -um old, ancient [10]

Antōnius, -iī m. Antonius, Antony

ānulus, -ī m. ring

anus, -ūs f. old woman [27]

anxius, -a, -um uneasy, anxious [29]

apage go! scram!

aper, aprī m. boar

aperiō, aperīre, aperuī, apertum open; discover; show

apiārius, -iī m. beekeeper

apodytērium, -iī n. dressing room

Apollō, Apollinis m. Apollo, god of prophecy

Appennīnī, -ōrum m. pl. Appennines, the mountains
along the spine of Italy

appetō, appetere, appetīvī/appetiī, appetītum seek,
grasp for, grasp after

applaudō, applaudere, applausī, applausum applaud

*applicō, applicāre, applicāvī/applicuī,
applicātum/applicitum* apply

appōnō, appōnere, apposuī, appositum serve,
put to [26]

appropinquō (1) (+ dat.) approach, come near to [11]

aprīcus, -a, -um sunny

aptus, -a, -um attached to, connected to; suitable,
fit [31]

apud (+ acc.) at the house of, with, at ____'s [16]

aqua, -ae f. water [2]

aquaeductus, -ūs m. aqueduct

āra, -ae f. altar [19]

arānea, -ae f. spider

arbitror, abitrārī, arbitrātus sum observe, perceive;
think [37]

arbor, arboris f. tree [29]

arca, -ae f. chest

Arcadia, -ae f. Arcadia, a region in Greece

arcānus, -a, -um secret

arcessō, arcessere, arcessīvī/arcessī, arcessītum fetch;
call for; summon; procure [32]

archierus, -ī m. chief priest

arcus, arcūs m. arch

ardeō, ardēre, arsī, arsum burn, glow

ardor, ardōris m. fire, flame

argentārius, -a, -um of silver, pertaining to silver [31];
faber argentārius silversmith

argentārius, -iī, m. banker

argenteus, -a, -um of silver, silvery [34]

argentum, -ī n. silver; money [31]

Argī, Argōrum m. pl. Argos, a city in Greece

Argīlētum the Argiletum, (a street leading into
the Roman Forum)

argūmentum -ī, n. plot, summary (of a play)

arguō, arguere, arguī, argūtum argue

arma, armōrum n. pl. arms, weapons

armō (1) arm [37]

ars, artis f. skill, art [16]

artifex, artificis m. artist, artisan, maker

Artorius, -iī m. Artorius, a male name

artus, -ūs m. limb

as, assis m. as, a small copper coin of minimal value

ascendō, ascendere, ascendī, ascensum climb,
ascend [24]

Asia, -ae f. Asia, a Roman province in what is now Turkey

Asinius, -iī m. Asinius

asinus, -ī m. donkey

aspectō (1) gaze, look at

asper, aspera, asperum rough, harsh

aspergō, aspergere, aspersī, aspersum sprinkle
aspiciō, aspicere, aspexī, aspectum
    look at [23]
assentior, assentīrī, assensus sum approve
assequor, assequī, assecūtus sum pursue, gain
assō (1) roast
assuētus, -a, -um accustomed
astō, astāre, astitī stand (up); stand by, assist
astrologia, -ae f. astrology
astrologus, -ī m. astrologer
astūtus, -a, -um smart
at but, and yet [20]
āter, ātra, ātrum black
Athēnae, Athēnārum f. pl. Athens, a city in Greece
atque and, and also, and even, yet [20]
atquī yet
ātrium, -iī n. atrium, public greeting room
    of a Roman house [33]
atrōciter fiercely
attat Ah! (used to express surprise, fear, or a warning)
attendō, attendere, attendī, attentum listen carefully
attonitus, -a, -um astonished, amazed
auctōritās, -tātis f. authority, power
audācia, -ae f. daring
audeō, audēre, ausus sum dare [9]
audiāmus "Let's listen!", subj.
audiō, audīre, audīvī/audiī, audītum
    hear, listen to [7]
Augēās, Augēae m. Augeas, king of Elis in Greece
Augēus, -a, -um Augean, pertaining to King Augeas
augustus, -a, -um revered
Augustus, -ī m. "the revered one," a title of Octavius, the
    emperor C. Julius Caesar Octavianus (63 B.C.–14 A.D.),
    known as *Augustus* ("Revered")
aura, -ae f. breeze
aureolus, -a, -um golden
aureus, -a, -um golden
auris, auris f. ear [29]
auscultō (1) listen
auspex, auspicis m. diviner, soothsayer
auspicium, -(i)ī n. sign, omen, auspices
aut or; **aut . . . aut** either . . . or [4]
autem however [20]
auxilium, -iī n. help, aid; pl. auxiliary forces [25]
Avē Greetings! [29]
aveō, avēre be eager
avia, -ae f. grandmother [30]
avidē eagerly
avidus, -a, -um eager
avis, avis f. bird [28]
āvolō (1) hasten away, fly away
avunculus, -ī m. maternal uncle
avus, -ī m. grandfather, ancestor [29]

B

Bacchus, -ī n. Bacchus, the god of wine;
    also known as Liber
Bāiae, Bāiārum m. pl. Baiae, a resort town near
    Naples, Italy
balneae, ārum f. pl. bath
barba, -ae f. beard
basilica, -ae f. basilica, courthouse
beātus, -a, -um blessed, happy
bellum, -ī n. war; **bellum gerere** wage war [23]
bellus, -a, -um handsome, pretty
bene well, nicely [4]
beneficium, -iī n. kindness, benefit, favor [38]
benevolens, benevolentis well-wishing, benevolent
benignē kindly
benignus, -a, -um kind, kind-hearted, bounteous
bestiārius, -iī m. animal fighter
bēta, -ae f. beet
bibliothēca, -ae f. library [27]
bibliothēcē, -ēs f. library (the Greek equivalent
    of *bibliothēca, -ae*)
bibō, bibere, bibī drink [2]
biennium, -iī n. a two-year period
bīga, -ae f. two-horse chariot
bis twice, two times [36]
bonus, -a, -um good [3]
bōs, bovis m./f. cow, bull, ox
brāc(c)hium, -iī n. arm [14]
brevī in a short time
brevis, breve short [18]
breviter briefly
Brundisium, -iī n. Brundisium, a city in Calabria
Brūtus, -ī m. Marcus Iunius Brutus (85–42 B.C.),
    one of the leading assassins of Julius Caesar
būbō, būbōnis m. owl
bulla, -ae f. bulla, a locket worn around
    a child's neck

C

cachinnātiō, -ōnis f. loud laughter
cachinnō (1) laugh loudly
cacūmen, cacūminis n. tree top
cadāver, cadāveris n. corpse, dead body
cadō, cadere, cecidī, cāsum fall (down); be slain;
    end [21]
Caecilia, -ae f. Caecilia, a female name
caelibāris, caelibāre unmarried
Caelius, -a, -um Caelian, pertaining to one
    of the seven hills of Rome
caelum, -ī n. sky
Caesar, Caesaris m. Caesar

Calabria, -ae f. region in the heel of Italy

caldārium, -iī n. hot bath

calidum, -ī n. a hot drink

calidus, -a, -um warm, hot [30]

Callimachus, -ī m. Callimachus, chief librarian at Alexandria and poet (c.280–243 B.C.)

calvus, -a, -um bald

calx, calcis f. goal, chalkline

Campānia, -ae f. Campania, region of southern Italy around Naples

campus, -ī m. field [33]

candidātus, -ī m. candidate

candidus, -a, -um dazzling white; bright

canis, canis m./f. dog [23]

canō, canere, cecinī, cantum sing, sing about [40]

cantō (1) sing [27]

cantus, -ūs m. song

cānus, -a, -um white-haired

capax, capācis spacious, roomy; "full of"

capillus, -ī m. hair

capiō, capere, cēpī, captum take, catch [3]

Capitōlīnus, -a, -um Capitoline, pertaining to the Capitoline hill

Capitōlium, -iī n. the Capitoline hill, one of the seven hills of Rome

captīvus, -ī m. captive, prisoner [40]

caput, capitis n. head; master [36]

carcer, carceris m. prison; starting gate

careō, carēre, caruī, caritum (+ abl.) lack, be without, lose [36]

cāritās, -tātis f. charity, generosity

carmen, carminis n. song, poem, poetry [17]

carō, carnis f. flesh; meat

carōta, -ae f. carrot

carpō, carpere, carpsī, carptum seize, pluck, enjoy

cārus, -a, -um dear [13]

Cassius, -iī m. C. Cassius Longinus (85–42 B.C.), one of the leading assassins of Julius Caesar

Castor, -oris m. Castor, the divine twin brother of Pollux, one of the Gemini

Castōrum of the Castors, i.e., Castor and Pollux

castra, -ōrum n. pl. camp [23]

cāsus, -ūs m. event; misfortune

catēna, -ae f. chain, fetter

catulus, -ī m. puppy

caudex, caudicis m. piece of wood, as an oath "blockhead!"

causa, -ae f. cause, reason; *causā* (+ gen.) on account of, because of [30]

causidicus, -ī m. lawyer

cautus, -a, -um cautious, careful

cavea, -ae f. cage

caveō, cavēre, cāvī, cautum take care, beware [33]

cēdō, cēdere, cessī, cessum go, walk; (+ dat.) yield to, give way to; succeed; allow, grant [35]

celeber, celebris, celebre frequent, famous

celer, celeris, celere fast, swift [15]

celeriter quickly, swiftly

cella, -ae f. room [18]

cēlō (1) hide

celsus, -a, -um high, lofty, tall

cēna, -ae f. dinner [12]

cēnō (1) dine [12]

censeō, censēre, censuī, censum be of the opinion

centaurus, -ī m. centaur, half-human and half-horse

centum (indecl.) one hundred [37]

centuria, -ae f. century, i.e., a division of the Roman citizenry based on wealth; the two highest such centuries were the senators and the *equitēs* (knights)

centuriō, -ōnis m. centurion [23]

Cephallenia, -ae f. Cephallenia (modern Kefalonia), an island on the west coast of Greece

certāmen, certāminis n. contest, race [35]

certē certainly

certiōrem facere make more certain, inform; *sē certiōrem facere,* make oneself more certain, learn, learn about

certus, -a, -um sure, certain

cēterum besides, for the rest

Chaldaeus, -a, -um Chaldaean, an inhabitant of Mesopotamia

Charōn, Charōnis m. Charon, the ferryman of the Underworld

Chīrōn, -ōnis m. Chiron, a schoolmaster who shares his name with a centaur who taught various heroes.

cibus, -ī m. food [2]

cicātrīcōsus, -a, -um scarred

cicātrix, cicātrīcis f. scar

cingō, cingere, cinxī, cinctum gird, put a belt around; tie

cingulum, -ī n. belt

cinis, cineris m./f. ash

circā, round about

circulus, -ī m. circle

circum (+ acc.) around [6]

circumambulō (1) walk around

circumcingō, circumcingere, circumcinxī, circumcinctum gird around, surround

circumcurrō, circumcurrere run around

circumeō, circumīre, circumīvī/circumiī, circumitum go around

circumsiliō, circumsilīre leap around

circumspectō (1) look around

circumstō, circumstāre, circumstetī stand around, surround

circus, circī m. circle, circus; racetrack

cista, -ae f. chest, box

cisterna, -ae f. cistern, well

cīvis, cīvis m./f. citizen [27]

cīvitās, -tātis f. citizenship, the state

clādēs, clādis f. defeat
clāmō (1) shout, cry out [5]
clāmor, clāmōris m. shout, cry, uproar [20]
clāmōsus, -a, -um noisy
clārus, -a, -um clear, bright; loud, distinct; famous [36]
Claudius, -iī m. Claudius, *nōmen* of an old Roman family
claudō, claudere, clausī, clausum shut, close [38]
clēmentia, -ae f. mercy, clemency
Cleopatra, -ae f. Cleopatra, the last Ptolemaic ruler of Egypt
cliens, clientis m. client [31]
cloāca, -ae f. sewer
cōdex, cōdicis m. book
coepī, coepisse, coeptum begin
coetus, -ūs m. assembly, band
cōgitō (1) think, think about [10]
cognātus, -a, -um relative; kinsman
cognōmen, cognōminis n. cognomen, a name added after the *nōmen* for a Roman male
cognoscō, cognoscere, cognōvī, cognitum learn, get to know, observe; in the perfect: "know" [29]
cōgō, cōgere, coēgī, coactum drive together, force [23]
cōliculus, -ī = cauliculus,-ī m. small cabbage, cabbage sprout
collābor, collābī, collapsus sum fall in a faint, collapse [39]
collāre, collāris n. collar
collēgium, -iī n. club, group, corporation, association
collis, collis m. hill [32]
colloquium, -iī n. talk, conversation
colloquor, colloquī, collocūtus sum talk together, converse [25]
collum, -ī n. neck
colō, colere, coluī, cultum cultivate, take care of; honor, pay court to, worship; haunt
colōnia, -ae f. colony
color, -ōris m. color, complexion
columbārium, -iī n. a niche for a cinerary urn
coma, comae f. hair
combūrō, combūrere, combussī, combustum burn, burn up [30]
cōmoedia, -ae f. comedy
comes, comitis m./f. companion
comitia, -ōrum n. pl. elections
comitō (1) accompany, attend
comitor, comitārī, comitātus sum accompany, attend
commentāriolum, -ī n. small handbook, short essay
committō, committere, commīsī, commissum entrust
commodus, -a, -um pleasant, comfortable, convenient, suitable
commūnis, commūne common
commutō (1) change
comoedia, -ae f. comedy

compescō, compescere, compescuī confine, restrain
compitālis, compitāle of the crossroads
complector, complectī, complexus sum embrace
comprehendō, comprehendere, comprehendī, comprehensum seize, grasp, understand
compressus, -a, -um squeezed together, narrow
comprimō, comprimere, compressī, compressum press, squeeze together
computō (1) count up, calculate
concalescō, concalescere, concaluī to warm up
concēdō, concēdere, concessī, concessum go away; (+ dat.) yield to, withdraw, allow, grant
concīdō, concīdere, concīdi, concīsum cut, chop up
concilium, -iī n. council = Roman senate
conclāve, conclāvis n. room
conclūdō, conclūdere, conclūsī, conclūsum conclude, finish
concordia, -ae f. concord, harmony
Concordia, -ae f. the goddess of Concord
concordō (1) be in agreement
condīmentum, -ī n. spice, seasoning
condō, condere, condidī, conditum build, found [40]
condūcō, condūcere, condūxī, conductum rent
conferō, conferre, contulī, collātum bring together, collect; sē conferre go (betake oneself), [28]
conficiō, conficere, confēcī, confectum do, accomplish, complete [28]
confirmō (1) reassure, strengthen, confirm, encourage
congiārium, -iī n. largesse, gift
congregō (1) gather
cōniciō, cōnicere, cōniēcī hurl, cast
coniunctiō, -iōnis f. joining together, union
coniungō, coniungere, coniunxī, coniunctus join, connect, ally
coniunx, coniugis m./f. spouse
cōnor, cōnārī, cōnātus sum try, undertake [24]
consacrō (1) dedicate, consecrate
conscendō, conscendere, conscendī, conscensum ascend; embark
conscrībō, conscrībere, conscripsī, conscriptum enlist
consentiō, consentīre, consensī, consensum consent, agree
consequor, consequī, consecūtus sum obtain, procure
conservō (1) preserve, keep safe [39]
conservus, -ī m. fellow slave
consīderō (1) consider, inspect
consilium, -iī n. plan, advice, counsel, reason, judgment [23]
consistō, consistere, constitī, constitum stop, halt; (+ ā or ex + abl.) consist of
consōbrīna, -ae f. female first cousin (on the mother's side)
consōlor, consōlārī, consōlātus sum console
conspiciō, conspicere, conspexī, conspectum catch sight of, see, look at, observe [9]

constat imp. "it is known (that)"; it is agreed

consternō (1) confuse, terrify, shock

constituō, constituere, constituī, constitūtum put, appoint, decide, establish

consto, constāre, constitī, constātum stand still; cost [10]; *satis constat* it is agreed that, it is an established fact that

constringō, constringere, constrinxī, constrinctum bind fast; compress

construō, construere, construxī, constructum build

consuētūdō, -inis f. companionship

consul, consulis m. consul

consulāris, consulāre consular, of consular rank

consulātus, -ūs m. consulship

consūmō, consūmere, consumpsī, consumptum use up, eat, consume [38]

contemnō, contemnere, contempsī, contemptum scorn

contemplor, contemplarī, contemplātus est reflect on, contemplate

contendō, contendere, contendī, contentum make one's way toward

contentus, -a, -um content, satisfied

contineō, continēre, continuī, contentum contain, hold [40]

continuus, -a, -um successive

contrā (+ acc.) against, facing, opposite (to) [19]

contractiō, -ōnis f. contraction

contrahō, contrahere, contraxī, contractum draw together, gather

conventus, -ūs m. gathering, assembly

convīvium, -iī n. feast, banquet [25]

convocō (1) call together

cōpiōsus, -a, -um plentiful

coquō, coquere, coxī, coctum cook [26]

coquus, -ī m. cook [25]

cor, cordis n. heart [17]

Corcyra, -ae f. Corcyra (modern Corfu), an island on the west coast of Greece.

Cordus, -ī m. Cordus, a male name

coriandrum, -ī n. coriander

Corinthiacus, -a, -um Corinthian, pertaining to Corinth

Corinthus, -ī f. Corinth, a city in southern Greece

Corinthus, -ī f. Corinth, a city in Greece

cornicen, -cinis m. horn blower

corōna, -ae f. crown, garland

corpus, corporis n. body [15]

corrumpō, corrumpere, corrūpī, corruptum spoil, destroy

cortex, corticis m./f. skin, bark, rind

cōtīdiē (cottīdiē) daily, every day

crās tomorrow [6]

crassus, -a, -um crass, less polite

crēbrō frequently

crēdō, crēdere, crēdidī, crēditum (+ dat.) believe, trust [25]

crepitus, -ūs m. rattling

crepundia, -ōrum n. pl. rattle

Crescens, -entis m. Crescens, a male name

crescō, crescere, crēvī, crētum grow, arise, appear, increase [32]

Crēta, -ae f. Crete, an island in the eastern Mediterranean

crīmen, crīminis n. crime

crīnis, crīnis m. hair

crocodīlus, -ī m. crocodile

crūdēlis, crūdēle harsh, cruel [18]

cruentus. -a, -um bloody, gory

cruor, cruōris m. gore, blood

crūs, crūris n. leg, shin

cubiculum, -ī n. bedroom [12]

cubō (1) lie down (in bed) lie asleep, sleep

culīna, -ae f. kitchen [25]

culpa, -ae f. fault, blame

cultellus, -ī m. knife

cultūra, -ae f. agriculture

cum (+ abl.) with [6]

cum prīmum as soon as

cum when [15]

cumīnum, -ī n. cumin

cūnae, cunārum f. pl. cradle

cunctor, cunctārī, cunctātus sum tarry, linger, hesitate [25]

cupidus, -a, -um (+ gen.) longing for, eager for, desirous [39]

cupiō, cupere, cupīvī/cupiī, cupītum wish, want to [4]

cupressus, -ī f. cypress tree

cūr why [11]

cūra, ae f. worry, concern, care, anxiety

cūrātor, -ōris m. caretaker, manager

cūria, -ae f. curia, senate house

cūrō (1) care for [13]

currō, currere, cucurrī, cursum run [5]

currus, -ūs m. chariot

cursor, cursōris m. runner

cursum amittere to go off course

cursus, -ūs m. course; voyage; journey; race; march; career [35]

custōdia, -ae f. custody

custōdiō, custōdīre, custōdīvī/custōdiī, custōdītum watch, guard [30]

custōs, custōdis m./f. guard [30]

D

Damascus, ī f. Damascus, city in Roman province of Syria

damnātus, -ī m. condemned criminal

Danaē, Danaēs f. Danaë, mother of Perseus

daps, dapis f. sacrificial feast, offering

dē (+ abl.) **away from, down from; concerning, about** [7]

dea, -ae f. **goddess** [11]

dealbātor, -ōris m. whitewasher, someone charged with whitewashing walls either to cover up graffiti or to prepare the wall for new graffiti

dealbō (1) whitewash

dēbellō (1) vanquish

dēbeō, dēbēre, dēbuī, dēbitum owe, ought, have to [7]

dēbilis, dēbile weak

decem (indecl.) **ten** [12]

dēcernō, dēcernere, dēcrēvī, dēcrētum judge, award

decet, decēre, decuit (+ dat. + inf.) **imp. it is fitting** [24]

dēcipiō, dēcipere, dēcēpī, dēceptum cheat

decōrus, -a, -um fitting, noble

dēdicō (1) dedicate, devote

dēdūcō, dēdūcere, dēdūxī, dēductum lead down, bring away; conduct, escort; *uxōrem dēdūcere* take a wife, marry [38]

dēductiō, -ōnis f. transportation

defendō, defendere, defendī, defensum defend [39]

dēfluō, dēfluere, dēflūxī, dēfluxus flow away; disappear

dēfungor, dēfungī, dēfunctus sum die

dehinc after this, next

deinceps in succession

deinde then

dēlectābilis, dēlectābile delicious

dēlectō (1) **amuse, delight, charm** [38]

dēleō, dēlēre, dēlēvī, dēlētum destroy, wipe out

dēlīberō (1) debate, deliberate

dēliciae, -ārum f. pl. delight, darling; pet

dēligō, dēligere, dēlēgī, dēlectum pick out, choose

Delphī, -ōrum m. pl. Delphi, a major oracular shrine of the god Apollo in Greece

Delphicus, -a, -um Delphic, pertaining to Delphi (a shrine of Apollo)

delphīnus, delphīnī m. dolphin

dēlūbrum, -ī n. temple, shrine

dēmānō (1) flow out, spread out

dēmittō, dēmittere, dēmīsī, dēmissum send down

dēmonstrō (1) **point at, show, depict** [40]

Dēmosthenēs, -is m. Demonsthenes, a famous Greek orator of the 4th century B.C.

dēmum finally, at length, at last [26]

dēnārius, -iī m. denarius, a silver coin

dēnique finally, at last, in fact [32]

dēplōrō (1) lament

dēpōnō, dēpōnere, dēposuī, dēpositum leave, lay down; commit; entrust, deposit

dēprecor, dēprecārī, dēprecātus sum beg pardon from

descendō, descendere, descendī, descensum go down, descend [31]

describō, describere, descripsī, descriptum describe, draw

dēserō, dēserere, dēseruī, dēsertum desert, abandon

dēsīderium, -iī n. desire, wish

dēsīderō (1) wish for

dēsinō, dēsinere, dēsīvī/dēsiī, dēsitum (+ gen.) cease, desist (from)

dēsistō, dēsistere, dēstitī, dēstitum stop, cease, desist

dēsperō (1) despair (of)

destituō, destituere, destituī leave

destruō, destruere, destruxī, destructum destroy [34]

dēsuper from above

dētergeō, dētergēre, dētersī, dētersum wipe away, rub clean

dētrīmentum, -ī n. loss, damage; defeat

deus, -ī m. **god; *dī*** (alternate nom. pl.) [14]

dēvertō, dēvertere, dēvertī, dēversum turn aside, stop to visit

dēvorō (1) devour, consume

dexter, dext(e)ra, dext(e)rum right, *dext(e)ra (manus)*, -ae f. right hand [38]

dī m. nom. pl. gods = *deī*

diabolus, -ī m. devil

Diāna, -ae f. Diana, goddess of the hunt and of the moon; the moon itself

dīcō, dīcere, dīxī, dictum say, tell [7]

dictum, -ī n. word

Dictys, -yos m. Dictys, brother of the king of Seriphos

diēs, diēī m. **day** [24]

differō, differre, distulī, dīlātum delay

difficilis, difficile hard, difficult [15]

difficultās, -tātis f. **trouble, difficulty** [23]

diffugiō, diffugere, diffugī flee from

diffundō, diffundere, diffūdī, diffūsum pour forth, spread out

digitus, -ī m. **finger** [38]

dignitās, -tātis f. **worthiness, merit; dignity; office; honor** [35]

dignus, -a, -um worthy, deserving

dīligens, dīligentis careful, diligent, frugal [30]

dīligenter carefully

dīmidium, -iī n. half

dīmittō, dīmittere, dīmīsī, dīmissum let go, send out; dismiss; release; divorce [35]

Dioclēs, Dioclis m. Diocles, a male name

dīrectē directly

dīrectus, -a, -um straight, direct

dīrigō, dīrigere, direxī, dīrectum direct, guide

dīs dat./abl. pl. of *deus*

discēdō, discēdere, discessī, discessum leave, depart

discernō, discernere, discrēvī, discrētum separate, distinguish

disciplīna, -ae f. instruction, knowledge

discipula, -ae f. **(female) student** [2]

discipulus, -ī m. **(male) student** [2]

discō, discere, didicī learn [6]

disertus, -a, -um eloquent

dispergō, dispergere, dispersī, dispersum scatter, disperse

dispiciō, dispicere, dispexī, dispectum consider

displiceō, displicēre, displicuī, displicitum (+ dat.) displease; **displicet** imp. it is displeasing [26]

disputō (1) argue

disserō, disserere, disseruī, dissertum discuss

dissimilis, dissimile unlike [37]

diū for a long time [16]

diūtius (comparative of *diū*) for a bit longer

dīversus, -a, -um different, varied

dīvēs, dīvitis rich, talented [24]

dīvidō, dīvidere, dīvīsī, dīvīsum divide

dīvitiae, -ārum f. pl. wealth, riches

dīvus, -a, -um divine [29]

dīvus, -ī m. god = *deus*

dō, dare, dedī datum give [2]

doceō, docēre, docuī, doctum teach; show [35]

doctus, -a, -um learned

documentum, -ī n. instruction, warning

dolor, dolōris m. pain, grief [21]

dolōsus, -a, -um clever, crafty

domī at home

domicilium, -iī n. home

domina, -ae f. mistress (of the house), the woman in charge, ma'am [25]

dominus, -ī m. master [18]

domus, -ī f. home, house; domum home, to a house [4]

domus, -ūs f. house [24]

dōnec as long as, until [27]

dōnum, -ī n. gift [23]

dormiō, dormīre, dormīvī/dormiī, dormītum sleep [12]

dorsum, -ī n. back

dōtālis, dōtāle pertaining to a dowry

Drusus, -ī m. Drusus, *cognōmen* in the Claudian *gens*; Tiberius and his descendants were members of this family

dubitō (1) doubt, hesitate [39]

dubius, -a, -um doubtful, uncertain [39], *dubium est*, it is doubtful

dūcō, dūcere, duxī, ductum lead [4]

dūdum just now, a little while ago

dulcis, dulce sweet [23]

dulciter sweetly

dum while, as long as; until [33]

dummodo provided that, as long as

dumtaxat only up to

duo, duae, duo two [7]

duōbus two

duodecim (indecl.) twelve [12]

duodēvīgintī (indecl.) eighteen

dūrus, -a, -um hard, harsh, difficult

dux, dūcis m. leader [27]

E

ē, ex (+ abl.) out of, from [5]

Eborācum, -ī n. Eboracum, city in Roman province of Britannia (modern York, England)

ēbrius, -a, -um drunk [27]

eburneus, -a, -um ivory

ecce Behold! Look! [11]

edax, edācis devouring

Edepol! By Pollux! [37]

ēditor, ēditōris m. organizer; *Ēditor ludōrum* public official in charge of the games

ēdō, ēdere, ēdidī beget

edō, ēsse/edere, ēdī, ēsum eat [7]

ēdūcō, ēdūcere, ēduxī, ēductum rear, raise

efficiō, efficere, effēcī, effectum execute, accomplish, do [32]

effrēnātus, -a, -um unbridled

effugiō, effugere, effūgī escape, flee

effugium, -iī n. flight, escape

effundō, effundere, effūdī, effūsum pour out

effūsē a lot

effūsus, -a, -um poured forth; widespread

ēgelidus, -a, -um warm

egēnus, -a, -um in need of, in want of, destitute [22]

ego I [7]

ēgredior, ēgredī, ēgressus sum march out, go out

ehem ha! aha! (in pleasant surprise)

ēheu alas! oh no! [16]

eho here you! hey! (often followed by *tū* or a vocative)

ei/hei ah! oh! (in fear or dismay)

ēia/hēia ah! ah ha! good! yes, indeed!; (+ *age*) quick! come on then!

ēiciō, ēicere, ēiēcī, ēiectum throw out

ēlāborō (1) take pains, exert oneself

elephans, elephantis m. elephant

ēlevō (1) raise up, lift up

ēligō, ēligere, ēlēgī, ēlectum pick out, choose

Ēlis, -idis f. Elis, a region in the Greek Peloponessus

ēlixus, -a, -um boiled

ēloquor, ēloquī, ēlocūtus sum speak out, declare [24]

ēlūdō, ēlūdere, ēlūsī, ēlūsum mock, escape

Emerita Augusta, Emeritae Augustae, f. city in Roman Spain (modern Merida)

emō, emere, ēmī, emptum buy [18]

ēn/ēm (+ dat.) come on! (in commands); really? (in questions)

enim for, because [20]

ensis, ensis m. sword

eō, īre, īvī/iī, itum go [7]

Epaphrodītus, -ī m. Epaphroditus, a Greek name for a man

Ephesus, -ī f. Ephesus, city in the Roman province of Asia (modern Turkey)

epistula, -ae f. letter [23]

epulae, -ārum f. pl. food, dishes of food; banquet, feast [26]

epulor, epulārī, epulātus sum feast, dine

eques, equitis m. horseman, knight; pl. cavalry; order of knights [34]

equus, -ī m. horse [34]

ergō therefore [8]

ērigō, ērigere, ērexī, ērectum erect, raise

errō (1) wander

error, errōris m. mistake

ērubescō, ērubescere, ērubuī redden, blush

ērudītus, -a,-um skilled

ērumpō, ērumpere, ērūpī, ēruptum erupt

ēruptiō, -ōnis f. eruption

Erymanthius, -a, -um Erymanthian

Erymanthos, -theī n. Erymanthus, a mountain in Greece

Esquiliae, -ārum f. pl. the Esquiline hill, one of the seven hills of Rome

Esquilīnus, -a, -um Esquiline, one of the seven hills of Rome

est is [1]

ēsuriō, ēsurīre, ēsurītum be hungry

et and [2]; also, even; *et . . . et* both . . . and [4]

etiam still; also, even, too, and also, even now [17]

etsī although, even if

eu fine! great! (sometimes ironic)

euax hurray!

eugae/euge/eugepae terrific! bravo! [36]

Eumolpus, -ī m. Eumolpus, a character in the *Satyricon*

Eurystheus, -eī m. Eurystheus, king of Mycenae in Greece

ēveniō, ēvenīre, ēvēnī, ēventum come about; happen [35]

ēvītō (1) shun, avoid

ēvoluō, ēvoluere, ēvoluī, ēvolūtum unroll, unfold

exāminō (1) examine

excipiō, excipere, excēpī, exceptum receive, welcome

excitō (1) awaken, excite, raise [32]

exclāmō (1) cry out, exclaim

excubiae, -ārum f. pl. guard, watch

exemplar, exemplāris n. copy, model

exemplum, -ī n. sample [40]

exeō, exīre, exīvī/exiī, exitum go out

exerceō, exercēre, exercuī, exercitum practice

exercitus, -ūs m. army [38]

exhibeō, exhibēre, exhibuī, exhibitum show, exhibit

exīlis, exīle thin, small

eximō, eximere, exēmī, exemptum take out, remove

existō, see *ex(s)istō*

exitiābilis, exitiābile deadly, desctructive

exornō (1) adorn

exōticus, -a, -um strange, exotic, foreign

expallescō, expallescere, expalluī turn very pale

expellō, expellere, expulī, expulsum throw out

expergiscor, expergiscī, experrectus sum awake, wake up [32]

expiō (1) atone for

explicō (1) unfold, display; explain

explōrō (1) test, try

expōnō, expōnere, exposuī, expositum set out; exhibit, explain [40]

expositus, -a, -um exposed

ex(s)istō, ex(s)istere, ex(s)titī arise, appear

exspectō (1) await, wait for [16]

exspīrō (1) breathe out

ex(s)tinguō, ex(s)tinguere ex(s)tinxī, ex(s)tinctum quench, extinguish

exsultō (1) exult in

extendō, extendere, extendī, extentum/extensum stretch out, extend

extimescō, extimescere, extimuī be alarmed, dread

extinguō see *ex(s)tinguō*

extrā (+ acc.) beyond, outside of [40]

extrahō, extrahere, extraxī, extractum draw out, drag out

extrēmus, -a, -um final, last; *extrēmās poenās habēre* die

exuō, exuere, exuī, exūtum strip, undress

exūrō, exūrere, exussī, exustum burn up

F

faber, fabrī m. craftsman, artisan; smith; workman [28]; *faber argentārius* silversmith

Fabius, -iī m. Fabius, a Roman *praenōmen*

fabrica, -ae f. workshop; art, craft [37]

fabricō (1) forge, make, shape, build, construct [30]

fābula, -ae f. story, play [9]

faciēs, faciēī f. face, appearance, beauty [24]

facilis, facile easy [20]

faciliter easily

faciō, facere, fēcī, factum make, do [6]

factiō, -ōnis f. team

factum, -ī n. deed [20]

faenum, -ī n. hay

Falernum, -ī n. Farlernian wine

Falernus, -a, -um Falernian, referring to a region in Italy producing a particularly good kind of wine

fāma, -ae f. fame, rumor, report [20]

famēs, famis f. hunger

familia, -ae f. family [4]

fāmōsus, -a, -um famous, well known

famulus, -ī m. servant, attendant

farreus, -a, -um of grain, grain

fās (indecl.) n. right, law [40]

fatīgō (1) weary, tire

fatīgātus -a, -um weary, tired

fātum, -ī n. fate, destiny

Faustus, -ī m. Faustus, a male name

faveō, favēre, fāvī, fautum (+ dat.) favor, support, cheer for

favor, -ōris m. favor, goodwill

fax, facis f. torch

febris, febris f. fever

fēlēs, fēlis f. cat

fēliciter luckily, with luck

fēlix, fēlīcis lucky, fortunate [18]

fēmina, -ae f. woman [2]

fenestra, -ae f. window

ferē nearly, almost, about; in general

feriō, ferīre strike, hit; kill, slay

ferō, ferre, tulī, lātum bear, carry, lead [23]; *sē ferre* go ("betake oneself")

ferox, ferōcis fierce, savage

ferrum, -ī n. iron, sword [22]

ferus, -a, -um wild, savage

fervidē heatedly, fervently, hotly

fervidus, -a, -um boiling, hot; fervent

Fescinnīnus, -a, um Fescinnine, pertaining to the Fescinnine verses sung at weddings

fessus, -a, -um tired [8]

festīnō (1) hasten [9]

festus, -a, -um festal, solemn, religious

Festus, -ī m. Festus, a man's name

fētidus, -a, -um filthy, foul smelling

ficus, -ī f. fig; fig tree

fidēlis, fidēle faithful, trustworthy [33]

fidēs, fideī f. faith, trust; credibility

fidius see *medius*

figō, figere, fixī, fixum fasten in place

figūra, -ae f. shape, figure [10]

filia, -ae f. daughter [8]

filiola, -ae f. little daughter (affectionate), dear daughter

filiolus, -ī m. little son (affectionate), dear son

filius, -ī m. son [4]

fingō, fingere, finxī, fictum shape, form, fashion

finiō, finīre, finīvī/finiī, finītum finish, end [8]

finis, finis m. end; pl. country, territory [14]

fiō, fierī, factus sum be made, be done; happen, become [26]

firmāmentum, -ī n. support

firmus, -a, -um firm, strong [36]

flagrans, flagrantis glowing, blazing, ardent

flamma, -ae f. flame

flammeum, -eī n. bridal veil

Flāvia, -ae f. Flavia, a female name

flectō, flectere, flexī, flexum turn, bend

fleō, flēre, flēvī, flētum weep, cry

flō (1) blow

floccus, -ī m. tuft of wool; *nōn floccī facere* to consider of no importance

flōrus, -a, -um bright, rich

Flōrus, -ī m. Florus, a male name

flōs, flōris m. flower, bloom

fluitō (1) flow, float

flūmen, -inis n. river [33]

focus, -ī m. fireplace, hearth

fodicō (1) nudge, prod; stab

folium, -iī n. leaf

fons, fontis m. spring, fountain

forās outdoors, out

foris, foris (commonly forēs, -ium pl.) f. door, gate; forīs out of doors, outside; abroad [34]

forma, -ae f. shape, form; beauty; ground plan [24]

formīdō (1) dread

formōsus, -a, -um beautiful, handsome, pretty [35]

fornax, fornācis f. forge

forsitan perhaps

fortasse perhaps [11]

fortis, forte strong, brave, loud [15]

fortiter strongly, bravely, loudly

fortūna, -ae f. fortune, chance, luck; wealth, prosperity [33]

fortūnātus, -a, -um lucky, fortunate [22]

forum, -ī n. forum, city center [5]

fossa, -ae f. ditch

frangō, frangere, frēgī, fractum break; crush; conquer [36]

frāter, frātris m. brother [13]

frāterculus, -ī m. little brother [36]

fremō, fremere, fremuī, fremitum growl, groan

frequens, -entis frequent, usual

fricō, fricāre, fricuī, frictum rub, rub down

frīgidārium, -iī n. cold water bath

frīgidus, -a, -um cold

frons, frontis f. forehead, brow

fructus, -a, -um enjoyed

Fructus, -ī m. Fructus, a male first name

fruor, fruī, fructus/fruitus sum (+ abl.) enjoy, profit by [24]

frustrā in vain

frustum, -ī n. morsel, scrap

frutex, fruticis m. bush, shrub

fuga, -ae f. flight

fugiō, fugere, fūgī, fugitum flee, run away [12]

fugitīvus, -ī m. runaway, fugitive

fulgeō, fulgēre, fulsī shine, gleam

fulgur, -uris n. lightning

fullō, -ōnis m. fuller, launderer

fullōnica, -ae f. laundry

fūmōsus, -a, -um smokey

fūmus, -ī m. smoke

fundus, -ī m. farm

fūnebris, fūnebre funereal

fungor, fungī, functus sum (+ abl.) perform, discharge [24]

fūnis, fūnis m. cord, rope

fūnus, fūneris, n. burial, funeral [40]

furcifer, furciferī m. scoundel

furnus, -ī m. oven, bakehouse

furor, -ōris m. fury, rage

furtīvē secretly
furtīvus, -a, -um secret
fūrunculus, -ī m. petty thief
fuscus, -a, -um dark
Fuscus, -ī m. Fuscus, a male name
fustis, fustis m. staff, club, stick
futūrum, -ī n. future [14]
futūrus, -a, -um, future

G

Gāia, -ae f. Gaia, ceremonial name of a Roman bride
Gāius, -iī m. Gaius, ceremonial name of a Roman bridegroom
Gallia, -ae f. Gaul, the Roman province now known as France
gallīna, -ae f. hen
garriō, garrīre, garrīvī/garriī, garrītum chatter
garrulus, -a, -um chattering, blabbing
garum, -ī n. fish sauce
gaudeō, gaudēre, gavīsus sum rejoice, be glad [38]
gaudium, -iī n. joy
gelidus, -a, -um icy, cold
geminus, -a, -um twin
gemma, -ae f. gem
gemō, gemere, gemuī, gemitum moan, groan
gener, generī m. son-in-law [30]
geniālis, geniāle marriage; merry, festive
gens, gentis f. famly, tribe
genū, -ūs n. knee
genus, generis n. race, type
Germānī, -ōrum pl. Germans, the German people
Germānia, -ae f. Germany
Germānicus, -a, -um German
Germānicus, -ī m. Germanicus, the son-in-law of the emperor Tiberius
gerō, gerere, gessī, gestum bear, carry [22]; bellum gerere wage war [23]; sē gerere act, conduct oneself [28]
gerūsia, -ae f. a council building for elders, senate house
gestiō, gestīre, gestīvī/gestiī, gestītum exult
gladiātor, -ōris m. gladiator [17]
gladius, -iī m. sword [17]
glīs, glīris m. dormouse
glōria, -ae f. glory [40]
gracilis, gracile thin, slender, scanty
gradus, -ūs m. step, pace, tier (of a theater) [24]
Graecia, -ae f. Greece
Graecus, -a, -um Greek
grāmen, grāminis n. grass
grandis, grande great, old
grātiā (+ gen.) for the sake of, for the purpose of [30]
grātia, -ae f. grace, favor; (pl.) thanks; *grātiās agere* give thanks [19]

grātiōsus, -a, -um agreeable
grātulātiō, -ōnis f. congratulations
grātus, -a, -um pleasing, thankful [23]
gravidus, -a, -um pregnant [25]
gravis, grave heavy, serious, deep [15]
graviter severely
gremium, iī n. lap [27]
grex, gregis m. flock, herd (of animals); company, group (of people), troop (of actors)
grūs, gruis, m./f. crane (a bird)
gubernō (1) steer (a ship); govern

H

habeō, habēre, habuī, habitum have, hold [5]
habitō (1) live in, inhabit [12]
habitus, -ūs m. dress, clothing
haereō, haerēre, haesī, haesum cling to, stick
hahae hah!
Halicarnassus, -ī f. Halicarnassus, city in Roman province of Asia (modern Turkey)
hama, -ae f. fire bucket
harēna, -ae f. sand; arena [22]
hasta, -ae f. spear
haud not, by no means [16]
haudquāquam by no means
hauriō, haurīre, hausī, haustum drink, swallow, drain
Hephaestus, -ī m. Hephaestus, slave named after the blacksmith god
herba, -ae f. herb
Herculaneum, -eī n. Herculaneum, city destroyed by eruption of Vesuvius in 79 A.D.
Hercule by Hercules! [28]
Herculēs, Herculis m. Hercules, the Greek hero Heracles
hērēs, hērēdis m./f. heir, heiress
heri yesterday [19]
Hermēs, -ae m. Hermes, a slave named after the Greek messenger god
Hermēs, -ēs m. Hermes, the Greek messenger god
hērōs, herōis m. hero
heu (often + acc.) oh! (in pain or dismay) [36]
heus say there! hey! you there! (to draw attention)
hic, haec, hoc this [19]
hīc here, in this place [10]
Hierosolyma, -ōrum n. pl. Jerusalem, city in Roman province of Judaea (modern Israel/Palestine)
hilaris, hilare cheerful
hinc from here
hiō (1) yawn
hippopotamus, -ī m. hippopotamus
Hispānia, -ae f. Spain
Hispānus, -a, -um Spanish
historia, -ae f. history

hodiē today [4]

hodiernus, -a, -um today's, modern

holus, holeris n. vegetables

homō, hominis m. human being, person, man [13]

honestus, -a, -um worthy, decent, of high rank [29]

honor, -ōris m. honor, office, dignity

honōrō (1) esteem, honor

hōra, -ae f. hour, time [8]

Horātius, -iī m. Horace (Q. Horatius Flaccus),
    a Roman poet

hōrologium, -iī n. clock

horrendus, -a, -um horrible, terrible

horribilis, horribile rough, terrible, horrible [37]

hortor, hortārī, hortātus sum urge [33]

hortus, -ī m. garden

hospes, hospitis m. guest, host, stranger [26]

**hostis, hostis m./f. stranger, foreigner, enemy;
    (pl.) the enemy [14]**

hūc (to) here, to this place [36]

huī (exclamation of astonishment or admiration) wow!

humilis, humile low; humble

humus, -ī f. earth, soil

hyaena, -ae f. hyena

Hydra, -ae f. Hydra, a many-headed serpent-like monster
    with poisonous blood

Hymēn, only found in nom. m. Hymen, the god of
    marriage; also, the wedding song or the marriage itself

Hymenaeus, -ī m. Hymenaeus = Hymen

Hymettus, -ī m. Hymettus, a mountain near Athens,
    famous for its honey

hypocauston, -ī n. hypocaust; heating system for a bath

I

iaceō, iacēre, iacuī lie, lie still, lie dead [21]

iaciō, iacere, iēcī, iactum throw, hurl [22]

iactō (1) hurl, throw; (with *se*) boast

iam dūdum for a long time now

iam now, already [8]; *nōn iam* not any longer

Iāniculum, -ī n. Janiculum, a hill on the west side of the
    Tiber at Rome

iānitor, -ōris m. doorman, porter [34]

iānua, -ae f. door [25]

ibi there [21]

īdem, eadem, idem the same [21]

identidem again and again

idōneus, -a, -um (+ dat.) fit, suitable [36]

iēiūnus, -a, -um hungry [13]

ientāculum, -ī n. breakfast [31]

igitur therefore [20]

ignāvus, -a, -um idle, cowardly

ignis, ignis m. fire [14]

ignōminia, -ae f. dishonor

ignōrō (1) be ignorant of

ignōscō, ignoscere, ignōvī, ignōtum (+ dat. of person, +acc.
    of offense) forgive, grant pardon to, pardon

ignōtus, -a, -um unknown

Iliacus, -a, -um Trojan

ille, illa, illud he, she, it; they; that, those [17]

illīc there, over there [8]

illīdō, illīdere, illīsī, illīsum strike against

illūc to there [36]

illūminō (1) brighten

Illyria, -ae f. Illyria (modern Croatia)

Illyricum, -ī n. Illyricum, a Roman province in the Balkans

imāgō, -inis f. image, likeness; statue [40]

imbuō, imbuere, imbuī, imbūtum wet, soak

imitātiō, -ōnis f. imitation, copy

immānis, immāne huge, vast

immineō, imminēre (+ dat.) be on the watch for

immittō, immittere, immīsī, immissum send to

immō rather, more precisely

immōbilis, immōbile immovable, unmoving

immolō (1) offer as a sacrifice

immortālis, immortāle immortal

impatiens, impatientis impatient (of)

**impediō, impedīre, impedīvī/impediī,
    impedītum hamper, hinder, impede, stop from [39]**

**imperātor, -ōris m. commander, general, ruler,
    emperor [25]**

imperium, -iī n. command, order, rule, empire, supreme
    command

imperō (1) (+ dat.) command, order, rule [26]

impetrō (1) obtain by formal request or petition

impetus, -ūs m. attack, assault

impleō, implēre, implēvī, implētum fill

implōrō (1) plead, beg

impōnō, impōnere, imposuī, impositum
    (+ dat.) put on, put upon, assign, impose upon

**improbus, -a, -um disloyal, shameless, morally
    unsound [23]**

īmus, -a, -um inmost, deepest, bottommost

in (+ abl.) in, on, at [2]; (+ acc.) into, onto, against [5]

inānis, ināne poor, useless, vain

inaurēs, inaurium f. pl. earrings

incautus, -a, -um uncautious, not careful

incendium, -iī n. fire, conflagration [32]

**incendō, incendere, incendī, incensum set fire to, inflame,
    burn [32]**

incertus, -a, -um uncertain, illegitimate [35]

incidō, incidere, incidī, incāsum fall (into); meet (with);
    occur, arise

incipiō, incipere, incēpī, inceptum begin [18]

incitō (1) incite; spur on

inclīnō (1) bend, tilt

inclūdō, inclūdere, inclūsī, inclūsum shut in, enclose

incognitus, -a, -um not known

incola, -ae m./f. inhabitant [38]

incolō, incolere, incoluī inhabit

incommodus, -a, -um disagreeable

incurrō, incurrere, incurrī/incucurrī run into

indecōrē sē gerere misbehave

indecoris, indecore shameful

indicō, indīcere, indīxi, indictum declare publically

indīviduus, -a, -um indivisible

induō, induere, induī, indūtum put on

industria, -ae f. pl. industry

Īdūs, Īduum f. pl. the Ides of the month (either the 13th or 15th day)

industrius, -a, -um industrious, diligent

inertia, -ae f. idleness

infāmia, -ae f. dishonor

infāmis, infāme disreputable

infans, infantis m./f. infant [14]

infēlix, infēlīcis unhappy, unfortunate [36]

inferior, inferius lower

infernus, -a, -um infernal, pertaining to the underworld

inferō, inferre, intulī, illātum bring, serve

inferus, -a, -um below; *in inferōs locōs* into "the places below," i.e., hell

infortūnātus, -a, -um unlucky, unfortunate [22]

infrā below, underneath, under [32]

ingenium, -iī n. talent

ingens, ingentis huge, great

ingenuus, -a, -um freeborn

ingredior, ingredī, ingressus sum enter, go in [24]

iniciō, inicere, iniēcī, iniectum throw in

inīquus, -a, -um unequal

initium, -iī n. beginning

inquīrō, inquīrere, inquīsīvī/inquīsiī, inquīsītum inquire

inquit, inquiunt say [2]

insānia, -ae f. madness, insanity

inscriptiō, -ōnis f. inscription, writing on stone

insequor, insequī, insecutus sum pursue

insignis, insigne conspicuous, famous, notable

insiliō, insilīre, insiluī leap into

inspectō (1) look closely at [19]

inspiciō, inspicere, inspexī, inspectum look (closely) at; inspect [10]

instar (indecl. + gen.) equal

instrūmentum, -ī n. tool, instrument [27]

insula, -ae f. island, apartment block [9]

insum, inesse, infuī be in

intactus, -a, -um intact

intellegens, intellegentis smart, intelligent [15]

intellegō, intellegere, intellēxī, intellectum understand [13]

intendō, intendere, intendī, intentum stretch, direct

intentō (1) point (at), threaten

intentus, -a, -um intent, eager

inter (+ acc.) between, among [5]

intercēdō, intercēdere, intercessī, intercessum come between; interrupt

interdiū by day

interdum occasionally

intereā meanwhile [35]

interficiō, interficere, interfēcī, interfectum kill [14]

interiaceō, interiacēre, interiacuī lie between

interim meanwhile

interpellō (1) interrupt

interrogō (1) ask, question; examine [34]

intrā (+ acc.) within [25]

intrepidus, -a, -um fearless

intrō (1) enter [8]

introductiō, -ōnis f. introduction

intueor, intuērī, intuitus sum look at, gaze at, consider [25]

inūtilis, inūtile useless, profitless

inveniō, invenīre, invēnī, inventum find, discover [14]

invictus, -a, -um unconquered

invideō, invidēre, invīdī, invīsum (+ dat.) envy, hate, grudge; refuse [38]

invidiōsus, -a, -um arousing hatred or envy

invidus, -a, -um envious

invīsus, -a, -um hated

invītō (1) invite

iō a shout of religious emotion

iocor, iocārī, iocātus sum (1) joke

iocōsus, -a, -um funny

iocus, - ī m. joke

Iphiclēs, -eī m. Iphicles, Heracles' brother

Iphigenīa, -ae f. Iphigenia, daughter of Agamemnon

ipse, ipsa, ipsum he, she, it; they; himself, herself, itself, themselves (emphatic) [17]

īra, -ae, f. anger

īrācundē angrily

īrascor, īrascī, īrātus sum be angry at

īrātus, -a, -um angry [6]

irreparābilis, irreparābile irrecoverable, irreparable

irrīdeō, irrīdēre, irrīsī, irrīsum laugh at, mock [37]

irrīsor, -ōris m. mocker, "one who mocks"

irrītō (1) upset, annoy, aggravate

irrumpō, irrumpere, irrūpī, irruptum burst, break open

is, ea, id he, she, it; they [17]

Īsēon, -ī n. temple of the goddess Isis

iste, ista, istud that one of yours (derogatory) [17]

ita so, thus; yes [22]

Italia, -ae f. Italy

Italus, -a, -um Italian

itaque therefore [20]

item similarly, likewise [35]

iter, itineris n. road, journey [21]; *iter facere* to make a journey, to journey

iterō (1) repeat, do again

iterum **again [4]**

Ithaca, -ae f. Ithaca, island home of the Greek hero
  Ulysses, located in western Greece

iubeō, iubēre, iussī, iussum **order [28]**

iūcundus, -a, -um **pleasant, agreeable [35]**

Iūdaea, -ae f. Judaea, the Roman province in what is now
  approximately Israel

Iullus, -ī m. Jullus, Servilia's intended husband

iunctiō, -ōnis f. joining

iungō, iungere, iunxī, iunctum **join [38]**; *sē iungere*
  (+ dat.) to join oneself (with), to ally oneself (with)

Iūnō, Iūnōnis f. Juno, queen of the gods

Iuppiter, Iovis **m. Jupiter, king of the gods [24]**

iūrō (1) swear

iūs, iūris n. law

iussus, -ūs m. order, command (only used in abl.) "by
  order of"

iustus, -a, -um legal

iuvenis, iuvenis **m./f. youth [15]**

iuventūs, -tūtis f. young men collectively, youth

iuvō, iuvāre, iūvi, iūtum **help [25]**

iuxtā (+ acc.) near to

K

Kalendae, -ārum f. pl. kalends, the first day of the month

L

L. = Lūcius

lābor, lābī, lapsus sum **fall down [39]**

labor, labōris **m. work, labor [16]**

labōriōsus, -a, -um working, laborious, tedious

labōrō **(1) work [9]**

labrum, -ī n. basin; lip

Labyrinthus, -ī m. maze, labyrinth, especially the one
  in Crete in which the Minotaur was imprisoned

Lachesis, -is f. Lachesis, one of the three goddesses of Fate

Lacō, -ōnis m. Laconian, Spartan

lacrima, -ae f. tear

lacrimō **(1) cry, shed tears [17]**

lactō (1) nurse

lacus, -ūs **m. lake [28]**

laedō, laedere, laesī, laesum hurt, damage

laetitia, -ae f. happiness

laetor, laetārī, laetātus sum be happy, rejoice

laetus, -a, -um **happy [3]**

lalla excl. calming sound

lambō, lambere, lambiī lick

lāneus, -a, -um woolen

lanista, -ae m. trainer, manager of a gladiatorial troop

lanius, -iī m. butcher, butcher shop

lanx, lancis f. dish, place

lapsō (1) slip

laqueus, -ī m. snare, noose

Lār, Laris m. Lar, a household god

lateō, latēre, latuī hide

latericius, -a, -um brick, made of brick

lātifundium, -iī n. large country estate

lātrīna, -ae f. public toilet

latrō, latrōnis m. thief, robber

lātus, -a, -um **wide, broad [31]**

latus, lateris n. side, ribs; *latus fodicō* poke in the ribs

laurea, -ae f. laurel wreath

laus, laudis f. praise

lavō, lavāre, lāvī, lautum/lavātum/lōtum **wash [31]**

lectīca, -ae f. litter, a sedan chair

lectīcārius, -iī m. litter bearer

lectiō, -ōnis f. reading

lectus, -ī **m. (dining) couch, bed [18]**

lēgātus, -ī m. lieutenant; legate

legiō, legiōnis **f. legion, army [39]**

legitmus, -a, -um real, lawful, right

legō, legere, lēgī, lectum **gather, choose; read [15]**

lēniō, lēnīre, lēnīvī/lēniī, lēnītum ease, put at ease;
  allay, mitigate

lēnis, lēne **smooth, soft, mild, gentle [27]**

lēniter smoothly, softly, midly, gently

lentē slowly, calmly

lentus, -a, -um slow, calm; tough

leō, leōnis m. lion

lētum, -ī n. death

levis, leve **light, gentle [23]**

levō (1) lift, lighten

libellus, -ī m. little book

libens, libentis **cheerful [35]**

libenter freely, willingly

līber, lībera, līberum **free [14]**

liber, librī **m. book [14]**

līberī, -ōrum **m. pl. children [33]**

līberō **(1) (+ abl.) free, free from [36]**

lībertās, -tātis **f. freedom, liberty [40]**

lībertīnus, -ī **m. freedman (used as defining social
  status) [37]**

lībertus, -ī m. freedman (in relation to his master)

libet, libēre, libuit, libitum est (+ dat.) imp. it is pleasing
  (to someone)

libitīnārius, -iī m. undertaker

librārius, -iī m. bookseller, book copier

lībum, -ī n. special holiday cake or pancake

licet, licēre, licuit **or** **licitum est** **imp. (+ dat.) it is
  permitted [29]**

Licinia, -ae f. Licinia, a female name

Licinius, -iī m. Licinius, a male name

ligneus, -a, -um wooden

lignum, -ī m. wood, firewood
ligō (1) tie
līmen, līminis n. threshold
līmus, -ī m. mud, slime
lingua, -ae f. tongue, speech [33]
liquāmen, liquāminis n. liquid, especially fish sauce
liquor, -ōris m. fluid, liquid
līs, lītis f. lawsuit
littera, -ae f. letter of the alphabet
lītus, lītoris n. shore
Līvius, -iī m. Livy, the historian
locō (1) put in place, contract for, rent
locus, -ī m. place [19]; also *locum, -ī* n.
longē far off, far, a long distance, for a long time [11]
longinquus, -a, -um far away, far off
longus, -a, -um long [19]
loquēla, -ae f. speech, utterance
loquor, loquī, locūtus sum speak, talk, say [24]
lōtium, -ī n. urine
lubet = libet (+ dat.) imp. it is pleasing (to someone)
lūceō, lūcēre, luxī shine
lucerna, -ae f. (oil) lamp
lūcifer, lūcifera, lūciferum light-bearing (an epithet or nick-name for the goddess Diana); *Lūcifera Diana* "the light-bearer"
Lūcius, -iī m. Lucius, son of Servilius and Caecilia
lucrum, -ī n. profit
luctātor, luctātōris m. wrestler
lūdia, -ae f. a gladiator's girl
lūdō, lūdere, lūsī, lūsum play, tease [30]
lūdus -ī m. school, game [4]
lūgeō, lūgēre, luxī, luctum mourn, lament
lūgubris, lūgubre mourning
lūmen, lūminis n. light, torch
lupa, -ae f. she-wolf
lūteus, -a, -um yellow, saffron
lutum, -ī n. mud, dirt
lux, lūcis f. light

M

M. = *Marcus*
macellum, -ī n. (grocery) market, store
maculō (1) spot, stain, pollute
madefaciō, madefacere, madefēcī, madefactum make moist, soak
madidus, -a, -um moist, wet
Maecēnās, Maecēnātis m. Gaius Clinius Maecenas (70–8 B.C.), Augustus' close friend and advisor
maestās, -tātis sadness
maestitia, -ae f. sadness, grief
maestus, -a, -um sad, gloomy [18]
magis more, rather [16]
magister, -trī m. teacher (male), schoolmaster [2]

magistra, -ae f. teacher (female), schoolmistress [2]
magistrātus, -ūs m. office, magistracy; magistrate [37]
magnificus, -a, -um noble, elegant, magnificent
magnitūdō, -inis f. greatness
magnopere much, greatly, especially [23]
magnus, -a, -um large, great, loud [8]
magus, -ī m. magician
māiestās, -tātis f. majesty, authority
māior, māius older; m. pl. ancestors, elders [15]
male badly
malefactor, -ōris m. evil-doer, criminal
maleficus, -a, -um wicked, criminal, harmful
malleum, -ī n. hammer, mallet
mālō, mālle, māluī prefer [7]
mālum Pūnicum, -i f. pomegranate (lit., "Punic apple")
malus, -a, -um bad [6]
mamma, -ae f. breast
māne early in the morning [4]
maneō, manēre, mansī, mansum stay, remain, endure, await [23]
manifestus, -a, -um clear, evident
mansuētus, -a, -um gentle
manubiae, -ārum f. pl. general's share of an army's military plunder
manus, -ūs f. hand [24]
mappa, -ae f. table napkin; starting flag
Marcus, -ī m. Marcus, son of Servilius and Cornelia, brother of Lucius
mare, maris n. sea [14]
marītus, -ī m. husband [16]
marmor, -oris n. marble
marmoreus, -a, -um marble, made of marble
Mars, Martis m. Mars, god of war
Martius, -a, -um of Mars
mās, maris male
mastīgia, -ae m. rascal, someone worthy of a whipping
māter, mātris f. mother [13]
matercula, -ae f. dear mother
mātcria, -ae f. material
mātertera, -ae f. aunt, mother's sister
mātrimōnium, -iī n. marriage, matrimony [37]
mātrōna, -ae f. married woman
mātūrus, -a, -um timely, early, mature, ripe
mātūtīnus, -a, -um of or belonging to the early morning
mausōlēum, ēī n. mausoleum, tomb
maximē, with *cum* especially
maximus, -a, -um greatest [20]
mē me [3]
Mēdēa, -ae f. Medea, the midwife
medicus, -ī m. doctor, physician
medius fidius/mediusfidius by the gods of truth! most certainly!

medius, -a, -um midway, in the middle (of), the middle
of [22]

medulla, -ae f. marrow

Megara, -ae f. Megara, wife of Hercules

mehercle by Hercules! (as an oath to express strong feeling)

meī of me

mel, mellis n. honey [31]

melior, melius better [19]

membrum, -ī n. limb (arm or leg), body part; member

**meminī, meminisse remember; mementō, -tōte (imper.)
remember! [32]**

memor, memoris mindful (of), remembering

memoria, -ae f. memory [37]

mendax, -dācis untruthful; *Mendax*, a beggar living
in Valeria's *insula*

mendīcus, -a, -um beggar

mens, mentis f. mind; reason; mental disposition [31]

mensa, -ae f. table [16]

mensis, mensis m. month [14]

mentior, mentīrī, mentītus sum lie, deceive [24]

mercātor, -ōris m. trader, merchant

mercātōrius, -a, -um mercantile, commercial

Mercurius, -iī m. Mercury, the messenger god

mereō, merēre, meruī, meritum deserve

merīdiē at noon

merīdiēs, -ēī f. midday, noon

merum, -ī n. pure (unmixed) wine

merx, mercis f. a commodity; (pl.) goods, merchandise

Mesopotamia, -ae f. Mesopotamia, the
land between the Tigris and Euphrates rivers

mēta, -ae f. turning post

**metuō, metuere, metuī, metūtum fear,
be afraid of [39]**

metus, -ūs m. fear [36]

meus, -a, -um my [5]

mī = mihi to me; my (vocative of *meus*)

mihi to me, my, [1]

mīles, mīlitis m. soldier [23]

mille indecl. thousand; *mīlia* n. pl. thousands

Minerva, -ae f. Minerva, Roman goddess of wisdom
and crafts

minimus, -a, -um smallest [20]

minor, minus smaller [19]

Mīnōtaurus, -ī m. Minotaur, half-human, half-bull
imprisoned in the Labyrinth

mīrābilis, mīrābile amazing, wondrous

mīrāculum, -ī n. miracle

mīror, mīrārī, mīrātus sum wonder at, admire [25]

mīrus, -a, -um astonishing, wonderful

misceō, miscēre, miscuī, mixtum unite, blend, mix, stir up

miser, misera, miserum wretched, miserable [35]

miserābilis, miserābile miserable

miserābiliter miserably

misereor, miserērī, miseritus sum pity; *mē miseret* it distresses me

miseria, -ae f. misery

misericordia, -ae f. pity

missiō, -ōnis f. discharge (military); permission
(for gladiators) to cease fighting; *ad missiōnem* to a
draw; *missiō honesta* an honorable discharge

mītis, mīte soft

mittō, mittere, mīsī, missum send [20]

modicum moderately

modicus, -a, -um a moderate amount of

modo only, just now, but [23]

modus, -ī m. way, manner

molae, -ārum f. pl. mill

molestus, -a, -um troublesome, tiresome [29]

mollis, molle soft

molliter softly

mōmentum, -ī n. importance, (important) moment; effort

moneō, monēre, monuī, monitum warn, advise [33]

monīle, -is n. necklace, collar

mons, montis m. mountain

monstrō (1) show, display, point out

monstrum, -ī n. monster

monumentum, -ī n. memorial, monument; tomb

morbus, -ī m. illness, sickness [34]

mordax, mordācis biting

mordeō, mordēre, momordī, morsum bite

morior, morī, mortuus sum die [29]

mors, -tis f. death

morsum, -ī n. morsel

morsus, -ūs m. bite, nibble

mortuus, -a, -um dead [22]

mōs, mōris m. custom; (pl.) character [15]

mōtus, -ūs m. movement, motion

moveō, movēre, mōvī, mōtum, move, affect [30]

mox soon [9]

mūla, -ae f. mule

mulceō, mulcēre, mulsī, mulsum soothe, stroke, pet

mulier, mulieris f. woman, wife

mulsum, -ī n. warm drink of honey and wine

multitūdō, -inis f. great number, multitude

multō much, by far, long [26]

multum a lot, much [16]

multus, -a, -um much; (pl.) many [2]

mūlus, -ī m. mule

mundō (1) clean

mundus, -a, -um clean, refined, elegant

mundus, -ī m. world

mūnicipium, -iī n. town under Roman rule but governed
by its own local laws

**mūnus, -eris n. function, duty; gift; pl. games, public
shows, spectacles [17]**

murmillo, murmillōnis m. murmillo, a heavily armed
gladiator

murmur, -uris n. whispering, murmur, growling

murmurō (1) mutter

mūrus, -ī m. wall [28]

mūs, mūris m. mouse

musca, -ae f. fly

musculus, -ī m. muscle

mūsicus, -ī m. musician

mussitō (1) mutter

mustāceus, -ī m. a grape-cake, a wedding cake baked with
    must on bay leaves

mūtō (1) alter, change

mūtus, -a, -um speechless, mute

mūtuus, -a, -um shared, mutual

N

Naevia, -ae f. Naevia, Servilia's friend

Naevius, -iī m. Naevius, Q. Naevius Cordus, object
    of Servilia's love

nam for [23]

nānus, -ī m. dwarf

nārēs, -rium f. pl. nostrils

narrātiō, -ōnis f. narrative, story

narrō (1) say, tell [14]

nascor, nascī, nātus sum be born [37]

Nāsō, -ōnis m. Naso, Ovid's *cognomen*

nāsus, -ī m. nose

natiō, -ōnis f. nationality

natō (1) swim

nātū by birth

nātūra, -ae f. nature, character [32]

nātus, -a, -um born; *xx annōs nātus* = xx years old [12]

naufragium, -iī n. shipwreck, crash (of chariots),
    collision, wreck

nāvicula, -ae f. little boat

nāvigō (1) sail [36]

nāvis, nāvis f. ship [34]

nāvus, -a, -um active, industrious

-ne asks a yes/no question [4]

nē not, that not, in order that not, lest [31]

Neāpolis, f. Naples, a city in southern Italy

nec and not; *nec . . . nec* neither . . . nor [15]

necessārius, -a, -um necessary, indispensable [34]

necesse est imp. (+ dat. + inf.) it is necessary (to) [12]

necō (1) kill, slay [21]

negō (1) deny

negōtium, -iī n. business, task [8]

Nemausus, -ī f. Nemausus, a city in Roman Gaul
    (modern Nīmes)

nēmō, -inis m./f. nobody, no one [13]

**nepōs, -ōtis m. grandson, grandchild, descendant,
    nephew [27]**

neptis, -is f. granddaughter

Neptūnus, -ī m. Neptune, god of the sea

neque and not; *neque . . . neque* neither . . . nor [28]

**nesciō, nescīre, nescīvī/nesciī, nescītum
    not know [34]**

neuter, neutra, neutrum neither [17]

nī, -nisi unless

Nicopolis, -is f. Nicopolis, city in western Greece founded
    by Augustus after the battle of Actium in 31 B.C.
    Nicopolin Note Greek accusative ending.

niger, nigra, nigrum black

nihil (indecl.) nothing [3]

nihilōminus nevertheless [39]

Nīlōticus, -a, -um of the Nile (river)

nimbus, -ī m. cloud

nimis too much

nimium too, too much, excessively [16]

nisi unless [30]

niteō, nitēre, nituī shine, glitter

nitidus, -a, -um gleaming, shiny

nītor, nītī, nīsus/nixus sum lean on, rest on; endeavor,
    exert oneself, strain, struggle

nōbilis, nōbile noble [15]

**noceō, nocēre, nocuī, nocitum (+ dat.) harm,
    hurt, injure, do injury to [12]**

nocte for the night (abl.)

noctū at night

nocturnus, -a, -um nocturnal, of the night

nōdus, -ī m. knot

nōlō, nōlle, nōluī not want to, be unwilling [7]

nōmen, -inis n. name [1]

nōmenclātor, -ōris m. nomenclator, one who announces
    the names of people

nōminō (1) name [22]

nomisma, -atis n. coin

nōn iam not any longer

nōn not [3]

nōn sōlum . . . sed etiam not only . . . but also [18]

nōndum not yet [32]

nōnne asks a question expecting a yes answer [5]

nōnnullī, -ae, -a some, several [9]

nōnus, -a, -um ninth

nōs, nostrum/nostrī, nōbīs, nōs, nōbīs we, us [21]

noscō, noscere, nōvī, nōtum know, get to know [11]

noster, nostra, nostrum our [9]

nota, -ae f. sign, word

notō (1) mark, note; write down

nōtus, -a, -um known, familiar

novitās, -tātis f. newness, freshness

novus, -a, -um new [8]

nox, noctis f. night [14]

nūbēs, nūbis f. cloud

nūbō, nūbere, nupsī, nuptum marry [31]

nūdus, -a, -um naked, nude, unarmed

nūgae, -ārum f. pl. trifles, nonsense
nullus, -a, -um no, not any, none [17]
num asks a question expecting a no answer [5]
nūmen, nūminis n. divine presence; god
numerō (1) count, include
numerus, -ī m. number
nummus, -ī m. coin, money [27]
numquam never [17]
nunc now [3]
nuncupō (1) name
nuntiō (1) announce, report [37]
nuntius, -iī m. messenger; news [33]
nūper recently, not long ago [25]
nupta, -ae f. bride
nuptiāe, -ārum f. pl. wedding, marriage
nuptiālis, nuptiāle nuptial, marriage for a wedding
nūtriō, nūtrīre, nūtrīvī/nūtriī, nutrītum nurse, nourish, raise
nūtus, nūtūs m. nod
nux, nucis f. nut

O

ō oh! hey!
ob (+ prep.) in the direction of, towards
obeō, obīre, obīvī/obiī, obitum go away, die
obēsus, -a, -um fat
oblāta, -ōrum n. pl. "that which has been served"
oblīviscor, oblīviscī, oblītus sum (+ gen.) forget [36]
obscēnus, -a, -um obscene
obscūrō (1) darken, obscure, conceal
obscūrus, -a, um dark, shady; gloomy; uncertain [38]
obsecrō (1) implore, beg
obserō (1) block, obstruct
observō (1) pay attention (to)
obstetrix, -icis f. midwife
obtineō, obtinēre, obtinuī, obtentum hold, support, gain [9]
occāsiō, -ōnis f. opportunity, appropriate time
occīdō, occīdere, occīdī, occīsum kill, slay [39]
occlūdō, occlūdere, occlūsī, occlūsum shut, close
occupō (1) occupy, busy
occurrō, occurrere, occurrī/occucurrī, occursum (+ dat.) run toward; encounter, run into [36]
ocrea, -ae f. metal greave
Octāviānus, -ī m. Octavian
octāvus, -a, -um eighth
octō (indecl.) eight [12]
octōgintā (indecl.) eighty
oculus, -ī m. eye [23]
ōdēum, -ī n. odeum, a building for musical performances
ōdī, ōdisse hate
odor, odōris m. scent, odor [21]
Oedipus, -ī m. Oedipus, king of Thebes

oenogarum, -ī n. a sauce made of garum and wine
offerō, offerre, obtulī, oblātum (+ dat.) bring before, offer
officīna, -ae f. workshop [34]
officium, -iī n. task, duty
oleō, olēre, oluī smell, stink
oleum, -ī n. oil
ōlim once, formerly [19]
olīva, -ae f. olive
olla, -ae f. pot, jar; urn
Ollus archaic form of *ille* That (man)
ōmen, ōminis n. religious sign, omen
omnīnō utterly, altogether, completely [32]
omnis, omne each, every; (pl.) all [15]
onus, oneris n. load, burden
opera, -ae f. work, pain, labor [36]
operam dare (+ dat.) pay attention to
operiō, operīre, operuī, opertum cover
opīmus, -a, -um rich, plentiful
opīniō, -ōnis f. opinion, belief; reputation [34]
opīnor, opīnārī, opīnātus sum think, believe [30]
oportet, oportēre, oportuit imp. (+ inf.) one ought [12]
oppidum, -ī n. town [28]
oppugnō (1) attack [39]
optimus, -a, -um best [20]
optō (1) wish [37]
opulentus, -a, -um rich, wealthy
opus, operis n. work, effort; structure, building; (pl.) goods [23]; *opus est* imp. (+ dat.) there is need for
ōrāculum, -ī n. oracle, divine pronouncement
ōrātiō, -ōnis f. speech [16]
ōrātiōnem habēre give/deliver a speech
ōrātor, -tōris m. speaker
orbis, -is m. circle, ring; *orbis terrārum* **circle of the lands, the world [20]**
ordinō (1) put in order
ordō, -inis m. row, line, order; rank; class of citizens [34]
oriens, orientis m. east
orīgō, -inis f. origin, beginning, source [38]
orior, orīrī, ortus sum rise, get up, be born [33]
ornāmentum, -ī n. decoration, mark of distinction
ornātrix, ornātrīcis f. hairdresser
ornātus, -a, -um decorated
ornō (1) adorn, decorate [35]
ōrō (1) pray [33]
ōs, ōris n. mouth, face [13]
os, ossis n. bone [28]
osculō (1) kiss
Oscus, -a, -um Oscan
ōsor, -ōris m. hater
ostendō, ostendere, ostendī, ostentum/ostensum show, display [38]
ostentātiō, -ōnis f. display, flashiness

Ostia, -ae f. Ostia, the harbor of Rome; *Ostiam* "to Ostia"
Ostiensis, Ostiense pertaining to Ostia, Ostian
ōtiōsus, -a, -um useless, unoccupied
ōtium, -iī n. leisure
Ovidius, -iī m. Ovid (P. Ovidus Naso)
ovis, -is m./f. sheep
ōvum, -ī **n. egg [10]**

P

p. = *pūblicus, -a -um*
paedagōgus, -ī **m. a slave assigned to a young boy,
    a tutor [5]**
paene **almost [18]**
paeniteō, paenitēre, paenitui to cause dissatisfaction:
    **paenitet paenitēre, paenituit imp. it gives reason for
    regret; mē paenitet I am sorry [29]**
pāgus, -ī m. country district
Palātīnus, -a, -um Palatine, of the Palatine
Palātium, -iī n. the Palatine hill, one of the seven hills
    of Rome
palma, -ae f. palm frond (of victory)
Palmȳra, -ae f. Palmyra, city in Roman province
    of Syria
palpitō (1) beat, throb
palpō (1) stroke, caresss
pānis, pānis **m. bread [31]**
Pannonius, -a, -um Pannonian, member of a Balkan tribe
pannus, -ī m. cloth, garment, rag
papāver, -eris n. poppy; poppy-seed
papȳrus, -ī **f. papyrus [27]**
pār, paris equal
pār, paris n. pair, couple
parātus, -a, -um prepared
parcō, parcere, pepercī/parcuī/parsī, parsūrus
    (+ dat.) spare, pardon, show mercy to [12]
Pardalisca, -ae f. Pardalisca, a female name
parens, parentis **m./f. parent [16]**
pariēs, parietis m. wall
pariō, parere, peperī, paritum/partum **bring forth,
    give birth (to), bear, create [25]**
parma, -ae f. small shield carried by a Thrax gladiator
parō **(1) prepare, make ready [12]**
pars, partis **f. part, piece [19]**
parturiō, parturīre, parturīvī/parturiī be pregnant,
    be in labor, give birth
partus, -ūs m. childbirth, birth
parum little, too little, not enough
parvulus, -a, -um very small, tiny, little
parvus, -a, -um **small [10]**
passer, -eris m. sparrow
passus, -a, -um spread out, dried
pastināca, -ae f. parsnip

pater familiās, patris familiās **m. pater familias
    head of the family [29]**
pater, patris **m. father [13]**
patiens, patientis patient
patientia, -ae f. patience
patior, patī, passus sum **suffer, allow [24]**
patria, -ae **f. country, fatherland [27]**
patricius, -a, -um noble, patrician
patrōnus, -ī **m. patron [26]**
pātruus, -ī m. paternal uncle
paucus, -a, -um **few, little [9]**
paulisper for a little while
paulō **a little, somewhat, by a little [25]**
paulō post a little later, somewhat later
paulum **a little, somewhat [28]**
pauper, pauperis **poor [25]**
paupertās, -ātis f. poverty
pavīmentum, -ī n. ground, floor, pavement
pax quiet! enough!
pax, pācis **f. peace [27]**
pectus, pecoris n. breast, chest
pecus, pecoris n. herd
pecūlium, -iī n. savings, private property
pecūnia, -ae **f. money [3]**
pecus, pecoris n. herd
pēior, pēius **worse [19]**
pellō, pellere, pepulī, pulsum banish
Penātēs, -ium m. pl. Penates, household gods
penna, -ae f. feather, wing
per **(+ acc.) through [5]**
peragō, peragere, perēgī, peractum finish, complete
perditus, -a, -um ruined, lost
perdō, perdere, perdidī, perditum lose, destroy
perdūcō, perdūcere, perduxī, perductum conduct, bring
    through, lead through
peregrīnor, peregrīnārī, peregrīnātus sum travel,
    travel abroad
pereō, perīre, perīvī/periī, peritum **perish,
    vanish [32]**
perfectus, -a, -um perfect
perferō, perferre, pertulī, perlātum convey
pergō, pergere, perrexī, perrectum **go ahead, advance,
    proceed [37]**
pergrātus, -a, -um very agreeable
perīculōsus, -a, -um **dangerous [25]**
perīculum, -ī n. danger
peristȳlium, -iī **n. peristyle, courtyard, colonnaded
    garden [26]**
perītus, -a, -um experienced (in), skilled (in) + gen.
perlaetus, -a, -um **very happy [27]**
perlegō, perlegere, perlēgī, perlectum scan, survey
permaximus, -a, -um very great, very loud
permultus, -a, -um very many

perpetuus, -a, -um continuous, uninterrupted;
   in perpetuum forever
persequor, persequī, persecūtus sum pursue, chase [40]
Perseus, -eī m. Perseus, the Greek hero who decapitated
   Medusa
perstō, perstāre, perstitī, perstātum stand firm, stand around
persuādeō, persuādēre, persuāsī, persuāsum (+ dat.)
   persuade [33]
perterritus, -a, -um very frightened, terrified [21]
pertimescō, pertimescere, pertimuī become very scared
pertineō, pertinēre, pertinuī belong to
perturbātus, -a, -um disturbed, confused, very frightened
perturbō (1) disturb, trouble greatly [26]
pervehō, pervehere, pervexī, pervectum carry, bear
perveniō, pervenīre, pervēnī, perventum arrive at, reach [21]
pervigilō (1) be awake all night, "to be up all night"
pēs, pedis m. foot [28]
pessimus, -a, -um worst [20]
petītiō, -ōnis f. candidacy, petition; lawsuit [37]
petō, petere, petīvī/petiī, petītum seek; look for; attack;
   run for political office [21]
philosophia, -ae f. philosophy
philosophus, -ī m. philosospher
Pholus, -ī m. Pholus the centaur
pictor, -ōris m. painter, professional artist paid to write
   (political) graffiti on public wall
pictūra, -ae f. picture
Pieridēs, -um f. pl. the inhabitants of Pieria, i.e., the Muses
pietās, -tātis f. reverence, respect
piger, pigra, pigrum low, sluggish, lazy
piget imp. it displeases
pigmentum, -ī n. color, pigment
pila, -ae f. ball
pilleus, -eī m. felt cap worn by a freed slave
pingō, pingere, pinxī, pictum paint
pīpiō (1) chirp
pīrāta, -ae m. pirate
piscātor, -ōris m. fisherman
piscīna, -ae f. fishpond
piscis, -is m. fish [26]
pistor, -ōris m. miller
pistrīnum, -ī n. mill
pius, -a, -um pious, devout
placenta, -ae f. a flat cake (Roman cakes looked more
   like pancakes)
placeō, placēre, placuī, placitum (+ dat.) please,
   be pleasing to; _placet_ imp. (+ dat. + inf.)
   it is peasing to [12]
placidus, -a, -um calm, peaceful
plānē clearly
planta, -ae f. sole of the foot
plānus, -a, -um plane, flat; even; obvious [34]
Platō, -ōnis m. Plato, a Greek philosopher

plaudō, plaudere, plausī, plausum clap, applaud [26]
plaustrum, -ī n. cart, wagon
plausus, -ūs m. applause, recipient of applause
plēbēius, -a, -um plebian, pertaining to the common people
plēnus, -a, -um (+ abl.) full, full of [22]
plōrō (1) weep, cry
Plōtia, -ae f. Plotia, Valeria's mother
pluō, pluere, plūvī to rain; *pluit* imp. it is raining
plūrēs, plūra more (in number) [19]
plūrimus, -a, -um most [20]
plūs more (in amount) [19]
pōculum, -ī n. cup
poena, -ae f. punishment, penalty
poēta, -ae m. poet [14]
poliō, polīre, polīvī, polītum polish
polliceor, pollicērī, pollicitus sum promise [24]
Polliō, -ōnis m. Aginius Pollio, a wealthy patron of Vergil
   and advisor of Augustus
Pollux, -ūcis m. Pollux, divine twin brother of Castor,
   one of the Gemini
Polydectēs, -ae m. Polydectes, king of the island of Seriphus
pōmerium, -iī n. open space surrounding the walls
   of a Roman town
pompa, -ae f. ceremonial procession
Pompēiānus, -a, -um Pompeian
Pompēiī, -ōrum m. pl. Pompeii, city in Campania
   destroyed by eruption of Mt. Vesuvius in 79 A.D.
pōmum, -ī n. fruit, apple
pōne behind; (+ acc.) behind
pōnō, pōnere, posuī, positum put, place [4]
pontifex, -icis m. priest
populus, -ī m. people [4]
porrō and besides, further
porrus, -ī m. leek
porta, -ae f. door, gate [23]
portitor, -ōris m. ferryman
portō (1) carry [8]
portus, -ūs m. gate
poscō, poscere, poposcī ask for, demand, request [5]
possum, posse, potuī be able, can [7]
post (+ acc.) after, behind [5]
posteā afterward, then [30]
posterus, -a, -um following, next
postis, -is f. doorpost
postquam after, since [21]
postrēmō at last, finally
postrīdiē the next day [35]
postulō (1) ask for, beg, demand, require, request [33]
potens, potentis powerful [15]
potestās, -ātis f. power, authority
potior, potīrī, potītus sum (+ abl. or gen.)
   take possession of, get, acquire [24]
pōtō (1) drink [31]

pōtus, -ūs m. (a) drink [29]

praecipiō, praecipere, praecēpī, praeceptum order

praecipuus, -a, -um special, particular [27]

praeclārus, -a, -um very clear, famous, noble,
excellent, beautiful [16]

praecox, praecocis naïve, premature

praefectus, -ī m. director, supervisor

praefica, -ae f. hired female mourner

praegredior, praegredī, praegressus sum go before, precede

praemium, -iī n. plunder; prize; reward; (pl.)
discharge benefits [39]

Praeneste, -is n. Praeneste, a town in Latium

Praenestīnus, -a, -um of Praeneste, a town in in Latium

praenōmen, praenōminis n. praenomen, the first name
of a Roman male

praeparō (1) prepare

praesentiō, praesentīre, praesensī, praesensum to perceive
beforehand

praesertim especially, particularly [25]

praeses, -idis m. guardian, warden

praesideō, praesidēre, praesēdī preside (over)

praestō, praestāre, praestitī, praestātum (+ dat.)
be superior to; stand out from; surpass [10]

praeter (+ acc.) along, beyond; except [8]

praetereā besides, moreover [34]

praetereō, praeterīre, praeterīvī/praterīī, praeteritum
go past; escape notice of; neglect [35]

praetextus, -a, -um bordered; *toga praetexta* a toga
with a purple border

praetor, -ōris m. judge, praetor [35]

praetōriānus, -ī m. a man who has been praetor but
has not yet become consul

praetrepidō (1) be nervous in ancitipation

praetūra, -ae f. praetorship, judgeship [36]

prandium, -ī n. noon meal, luncheon

prasinus, -a, -um green

precor, precārī, precātus sum pray

prehendō, prehendere, prehendī, prehensum take hold
of, seize

prēlum, -ī n. wine- or oil-press

pretiōsus, -a, -um valuable, expensive

pretium, -iī m. price

prex, prēcis f. prayer

prīdiē on the day before [35]

prīmigenius, -a, -um original

prīmō at first [32]

prīmum first, at first [28]

prīmus, -a, -um first [18], *prīmum digitum* fingertip

princeps, -cipis m. head, leader, chief; title of Augustus
and his imperial successors

principium, -iī n. beginning

prior, prius former, in front [19]

priscus, -a, -um old, ancient

prius formerly, before, in the past

priusquam before [10]

prīvātus, -a, -um private (citizen)

prīvō (1), to deprive of

prīvignus, -ī m. stepson

prō (+ abl.) before, in front of, for, instead of [6]

proavus, -ī m. great-grandfather, remote ancestor

probus, -a, -um good, honest [30]

procax, procācis pushy, undisciplined

prōcēdō, prōcēdere, prōcessī, prōcessum proceed,
advance [10]

prōcreō (1) procreate, create

procul far, far away, from far away [36]

prōcūrātor, -ōris m. administrator, procurator

prōdigus, -a, -um wasteful, extravagant

proelium, -iī n. battle [34]

profectō without question, undoubtedly [32]

professor, -ōris m. professor

proficiscor, proficiscī, profectus sum set out, depart [28]

prōgeniēs, -ēī f. family, children, progeny

prōgredior, prōgredī, prōgressus sum go to, advance,
march forward, proceed [24]

prohibeō, prohibēre, prohibuī, prohibitum keep off;
prevent; restrain; forbid [39]

prōiciō, prōicere, prōiēcī, prōiectum throw down

prōmittō, prōmittere, prōmīsī, prōmissum send forth;
promise [34]

promptus, -a, -um ready

pronepōs, -ōtis m. great-grandson

proneptis, -is f. great-granddaughter

prōnuba, -ae f. matron-of-honor

prōnuntiō (1) proclaim, announce, say, recite, report

propāgō (1) increase, enlarge

prope (+ acc.) near [5]

prōpellō, prōpellere, prōpulī, prōpulsum drive, push forward

properō (1) hasten

Propertius, -iī m. Propertius (S. Aurelius Propertius),
a Roman elegiac poet of the 1st century A.D.

propinquus, -a, -um neighboring, nearby

propitius, -a, -um favorable, propitious

proprius, -a, -um one's own, personal, unique

propter (+ acc.) on account of [9]

prōra, -ae f. prow

prorsus straight ahead; forward

proscaenium, -iī n. stage

prōsequor, prōsequī, prōsecūtus sum accompany, follow

prospectus, -ūs m. view

prōsum, prōdesse, prōfuī (+ dat.) benefit, profit, be useful to

prōtegō, prōtegere, prōtexī, prōtectum cover, protect

prōvincia, -ae f. province

prōvocō (1) challenge

proximus, -a, -um nearest, next [30]

prūdens, prūdentis foreseeing, prudent

prūnum, -ī n. plum
pūblicus, -a, -um public, common [30]
pudeō, pudēre, puduī, puditum be ashamed; *mē pudet*
    I am ashamed
pudor, -ōris m. shame, modesty, decency
puella, -ae f. girl [6]
puellāris, puellāre pertaining to a girl
puer, puerī m. boy [6]
pugna, -ae f. fight [22]
pugnō (1) fight [12]
pugnus, -ī m. fist; a handful
pulcher, pulchra, pulchrum pretty, handsome [13]
pullus, -a, -um dingy, somber; *toga pulla* a dark gray
    toga worn in mourning
pulsō (1) strike, beat; push, drive [23]; "strike the
    ground with feet," i.e., dance
pulvīnar, -āris n. cushioned couch (used for a religious statue)
pūmiliō, -ōnis m./f. dwarf
pūpa, -ae f. doll, girl
puppis, puppis f. stern (of a ship)
purgō (1) clean, cleanse [22]
pūrus, -a, -um pure, plain, without an iron tip
puteus, puteī m. well, pit
Puticulī, -ōrum m.pl. a nickname for a burial area outside
    the Esquiline hill
putō (1) think
Pȳthia, -ae f. Pythia, oracular priestess of Apollo at Delphi

Q

quā dē causā? for what reason? why? [34]
quā where, in so far as
quadrāgēsimus, -a, -um fortieth
quadrātus, -a, -um square
quadrīga, -ae f. pl. chariot with four horses
**quaerō, quaerere, quaesivī/quaesiī, quaesītum seek
    ask [18]**
quaestiō, -ōnis f. question
quaestūra, -ae f. quaestorship, treasurer [36]
quālis, quāle? what kind of? what sort of? [34]; see also
    tālis
quam how! [13]
quam than [10]
quamdiū for how long
quamquam although, yet [27]
quamvīs although
quandō when [29]
Quantī constat? How much does it cost?
quantus, -a, -um how much, how many [10]
quārē for, because [30]; interr. in what way? how?;
    whereby; wherefore, why
quartus, -a, -um fourth [38]
quasi as if, practically [37]

quater four times [36]
quatiō, quatere, quassī, quassum shake, wave about
quattuor (indecl.) four [10]
-que and; -que . . . -que both . . . and [4]
queror, querī, questus sum complain
quī, quae, quod who, which [18]
quia since, because [18]
quid what? [1]
Quid agis? How are you? How are you doing? [4]
Quid fit? What is going on? What's happening?
Quid plūra? Why say more?
**quīdam, quaedam, quoddam certain (indefinite, as in
    "a certain person") [21]**
quidem certainly
quiēs, -ētis f. quiet, calm, rest, peace
quiescō, quiescere, quiēvī, quiētum rest [14]
quiētus, -a, -um calm, quiet [25]
quīlibet, quaelibet, quidlibet/quodlibet whoever, whatever
**quīn that not (with subj. "from X'ing"); indeed; why
    not? [39]**
Quinctilius, -iī m. Quinctilius, a male name
quindecim (indecl.) fifteen
quinquāgintā (indecl.) fifty
quinque (indecl.) five [10]
quintum for the fifth time
quintus, -a, -um fifth
Quirīnālis, -Quirīnāle Quirinal, pertaining to one of the
    seven hills of Rome
Quirīs, -ītis m. (archaic) citizen
quis = aliquis after *sī*
quis, quid who? what? [6, 18]
quisquam, quicquam any
**quisque, quaeque, quodque/quicque/quidque
    each, every [21]**
**quisquis, quodquod/quicquid/quidquid whoever,
    whatever [40]**
quīvīs, quaevīs, quidvīs anyone, anything
quō? where (to)?
quod because [3]
quōmodo how [17]
quondam someday
quoque also [8]
quot? (indecl.) how many? [34]
quōusque how long

R

rādō, radere, rāsī, rasum scrape, scratch, shave, erase
rāmus, -ī m. branch
rapiō, rapere, rapuī, raptum snatch, seize [20]
rārō rarely, seldom
rārus, -a, -um rare; thin [27]
rāsilis, rāsile smooth, well-polished

ratiō, -ōnis f. account, transaction; *ratiōnem habēre*
    "to have a sense of"
recēdō, recēdere, recessī, recessum retire, withdraw
recens, recentis recent [39]
recenter recently [37]
**recipiō, recipere, recēpī, receptum accept, receive, take
    back; *se recipere* retreat (take oneself somewhere) [31]**
recordor, recordārī, recordātus sum remember
recreō (1) relax, restore
rectē straightly, correctly
rectus, -a, -um straight, correct
recumbō, recumbere, recubuī lie down, recline
reddō, reddere, reddidī, reditum give back
**redeō, redīre, redīvī/rediī, reditum come back, go
    back, return [21]**
redigō, redigere, redēgī, redactum drive back, restore
reditus, -ūs m. return
**referō, referre, rettulī, relātum carry, carry back, bring
    back [39]**
refrīgerō (1) make cool
refugiō, refugere, refūgī run away
rēgia, -ae f. palace
rēgīna, -ae f. queen
regiō, -ōnis f. region, district [21]
regnō (1) reign, hold power over
regnum, -ī n. kingdom [36]
regō, regere, rexī, rectum rule, govern [39]
regredior, regredī, regressus sum return
rēiciō, rēicere, rēiēcī, rēiectum throw
religiōsissimē most piously
religiōsus, -a, -um pious, devout
**relinquō, relinquere, relīquī, relictum leave, leave
    behind [21]**
reliquus, -a, -um remaining [21]
remaneō, remanēre, remansī remain, stay behind [40]
remittō, remittere, remīsī, remissum send back
**removeō, removēre, remōvī, remōtum move back;
    remove [32]**
**repellō, repellere, reppulī, repulsum push back, repel,
    repulse [39]**
repetō, repetere, repetīvī/repetiī, repetītum repeat
repleō, replēre, replēvī, replētum fill up, fill again
reportō (1) bring home
repōtia, -ōrum n. pl. celebration on the day following
    a festivity like a marriage
repugnō (1) fight back; resist
requiescō, requiesere, requiēvī, requiētum rest
requīrō, requīrere, requīsīvī/requīsiī, requīsītum seek,
    look for, search for
rēs gestae f. pl. deeds
rēs pūblica, reī pūblicae f. republic
rēs, reī f. thing, matter; business, affair; reason [24]
resideō, residēre, resēdī sit, remain in a place

respiciō, respicere, respexī, respectum take notice of,
    read (omens)
respīrō (1) breathe
**respondeō, respondēre, respondī, responsum (+ dat.)
    reply, answer [3]**
**restituō, restituere, restituī, restitūtum replace, restore;
    give back [39]**
restitūtus, -a, -um restored
rēte, rētis n. net
rētiārius, -iī m. gladiatorial fighter with a net
**retineō, retinēre, retinuī, retentum hold fast, retain;
    cling to [37]**
**reveniō, revenīre, revēnī, reventum come back,
    return [31]**
revertō, revertere, revertī come back, turn back, return;
    also *revertor, revertī, reversus sum* turn back, return
revocō (1) call back
rex, rēgis m. king [14]
rhētor, rhētoris teacher of rhetoric (public speaking) [16]
rhētorica, -ae f. rhetoric
rhētoricus, -a, -um rhetorical [16]
rīdeō, rīdere, rīsī, rīsum laugh [7]
rīdiculōsus, -a, -um laughable, riduculous
rigor, rigōris m. straight line; *Rigor Valī Aelī* Hadrian's
    Wall in Britain
rixa, -ae f. (loud) quarrel, violent quarrel, brawl
rōbustus, -a, -um strong
rogō (1) ask (for) [10]
Rōma, -ae f. Rome [11]
Rōmānus, -a, -um Roman [11]
Rōmulus, -a, -um of Romulus (the founder of Rome);
    Roman
rostra, -ōrum n. pl. speaker's platform
rostrum, -ī n. beak
rota, -ae f. wheel
ruber, rubra, rubrum red
Rūfus, -ī m. Rufus ("Red"), one of Servilius' slaves
**rumpō, rumpere, rūpī, ruptum break, burst, break
    down [28]**
ruō, ruere, ruī rush, rush at; fall to ruin [22]
rursus again [16]
rūs, rūris n. country, country estate; abroad [36];
    rurī "in the country" (note the lack of a prep.)
russātus, -a, -um red
rusticus, -a, -um rural, rustic

S

S.D. = *salūtem dīcit*
Sabīnus, -a, -um Sabine, pertaining to the Sabines,
    neighbors of Rome
saccus, -ī m. wallet, bag sack, pocket book [11]
sacer, sacra, sacrum sacred, holy

sacrāmentum, -ī n. oath, sacred obligation (especially one sworn by soldiers)

sacrificō (1) sacrifice

saeculum, -ī n. age, era

saepe often [6]

saevus, -a, -um raging, violent, savage, cruel, furious

sagax, sagācis wise, sharp

sagitta, -ae f. arrow [28]

sāl, salis m./n. salt

Saliāris, Saliāre of the Salii (priests of Mars, god of war)

saliō, salīre, saliī/saluī, saltum leap, jump [11]

saltātor, -ōris m. dancer

saltem at least

salūs, -ūtis f. health, safety [32]

salūtātiō, -ōnis f. greeting, formal morning visit by a client to a patron [31]

salūtō (1) greet [4]

Salvē/Salvēte! Hello. Hi. Be well! [3]

salvus, -a, -um safe, well [25]

sanguis, sanguinis m. blood [22]

sānitās, -ātis f. health, sanity

sānō (1) restore to health

sānus, -a, -um healthy [25]

sapiō, sapere, sapīvī/sapiī show good sense

satis enough, sufficient [30]

satura, -ae f. satire

scālae, -ārum f. pl. stairs, staircase

scalpō, scalpere, scalpsī, scalptum scratch

scelerātus, -a, -um wicked

scelus, -eris n. crime [20]

sciō, scīre, scīvī/sciī, scītum know, know about [28]

Scorpus, -ī m. Scorpus, a male name

scrība, -ae m. scribe, secretary

scrībō, scrībere, scripsī, scriptum write [6]

scriptor, -ōris m. writer [27]

scrūta, -ōrum n. pl. trash

scutum, -ī n. shield

Scybalē, -ēs f. Scybale, a female name

schola, -ae f. school, leisure

sē (see *suī*)

secō, secāre, secuī, sectum cut, cut off, cut up

secundus, -a, -um second; favorable

Secundus, -ī m. Secundus, a male name

sed but [3]

sēdecim (indecl.) sixteen [8]

sedeō, sedēre, sēdī, sessum sit [5]

sēdēs, -is f. seat, home, residence [14]

sēligō, sēligere, sēlēgī, sēlectum select, choose

sella, -ae f. chair [25]

semel once

semper always [3]

senātor, -ōris m. senator, member of the senate [29]

senātus, -ūs m. senate [29]

senectūs, -tūtis f. old age

senex, senis m. old man [29]

senex, senis old, aged

sensus, -ūs feeling

sententia, -ae f. proverb, saying

sentiō, sentīre, sensī, sensum feel, hear, see, sense, perceive [21]

sepeliō, sepelīre, sepelīvī/sepeliī, sepultum bury

septimum for the seventh time

septuāgintā indecl. seventy

sepulcrum, -ī n. tomb

sepultūra, -ae f. burial, grave

sequor, sequī, secūtus sum follow [24]

serēnitās, -tātis f. cheerful tranquility

sērius later, too late, rather late [17]

sermō, -ōnis m. speech, talk

sermōcinor, sermōcinārī, sermōcinātus sum converse, talk, chat [31]

sērō late, too late

serpens, serpentis f. snake, serpent

servātor, -ōris n. savior

Servīlia, -ae f. Servilia, daughter of Servilius

Servīliānus, -a, -um Servilian, of the Servilii

Servīlius, -iī m. Servilius, head of the *Servīliī*

serviō, servīre, servīvī/serviī, servītum serve, be a slave to

servitūs, -ūtis f. slavery, servitude

servō (1) save, protect; observe, pay attention to [27]

servus, -ī m. slave, servant [7]

Sevērus, -ī m. Severus, a male name

sex (indecl.) six [10]

sextus, -a, -um sixth [37]

Sextus, -ī m. Sextus, a male *praenōmen*

sī if [7]

sī placet Please! lit., "if it pleases" [7]

sī vōbīs placeat Please!

sīc so, thus, in this way; yes [11]

siccus, -a, -um dry

Sicō, Sicōnis m. Sico, a male name; Servilius' cook

sīcut just as, like [7]

significō (1) mean [40]

signō (1) mark, seal, stamp

signum, -ī n. mark, token, sign, seal [38]

silenter silently

silentium, -iī n. stillness, silence, tranquility [23]; *silentium tenēre* to keep silent

silescō, silescere, silescuī grow quiet

silva, -ae f. woods, forest [21]

sīmia, -ae m./f. monkey [5]

similis, simile similar, like to [37]

simplex, simplicis simple, naïve

simul atque also **simul ac** as soon as [21]

simul together, altogether, at the same time, all at once [24]

Sinae, -ārum f. pl. China
sināpis, sināpis f. mustard
sine (+ abl.) **without [6]**
singulāris, singulāre single
singulātim one by one
singulī, -ae, -a individual, one to each (in a group);
    one by one; *singulō* one by one
sinister, sinistra, sinistrum left; ***sinistra (manus), -ae*** f.
    the left hand [38]
sinō, sinere, sīvī/siī, situm allow, permit [33]
sīnus, -ūs m. lap; gulf
sīp(h)ō, -ōnis m. siphon, water hose
sistō, sistere, stetī/stitī, statum stand still [8]
sitiens, sitientis thirsty
sitiō, sitīre, sitīvī/sitiī be thirsty [31]
sitis, sitis f. thirst
situs, -a, -um located, buried
sīve or
soccus, -ī m. loose-fitting slipper
socer, soceris m. father-in-law
socius, -iī m. partner, companion [36]
Sōcratēs, -is m. Socrates, 5th century B.C. Athenian philosopher
socrus, -ūs f. mother-in-law
sodālis, -is m. companion
sōl, sōlis m. sun; day [33]
sōlāciolum, -ī n. relief, comfort
sōlārium, -iī n. sundial
soleō, solēre, solitus sum be accustomed (to) [29]
solidum, -ī n. something firm, solid; "a substantial sum"
sollemnis, sollemne solemn, holy
sollicitus, -a, -um uneasy, apprehensive, nervous,
    anxious that/lest [39]
sōlum only [3]
solum, -ī n. earth, soil
sōlus, -a, -um only, alone [6]
solvō, solvere, solvī, solūtum loosen, unbind; fulfil,
    perform; pay, deliver; *nāvem solvō* set sail [36]
sollemnis, sollemme solemn, holy
sollicitō (1) upset, shake up
sollicitus, -a, -um uneasy, apprehensive, nervous,
    anxious that/lest
somniculōsus, -a, -um sleepy
somnus, -ī, m. sleep, rest; laziness
sonitus, -ūs m. sound [24]
sonus, -ī m. sound
sordidus, -a, -um filthy [28]
soror, sorōris f. sister [13]
spargō, spargere, sparsī, sparsum spread, scatter, sprinkle
spatiōsus, -a, -um wide
spatium, -iī n. space [28]
speciālis, speciāle individual, particular, special
speciēs, -ēī f. appearance, look, type [24]

spectāculum, -ī n. sight, spectacle, game
spectātor, -ōris m. spectator, observer [24]
spectō (1) look at, watch [10]
speculum, -ī n. mirror [30]
spēlunca, -ae f. cave
spernō, spernere, sprēvī, sprētum reject, scorn, disregard
spērō (1) hope, hope for, look forward to [9]
spēs, speī f. hope, expectation [33]
spīna, -ae f. thorn; spine; center barrier of the circus
spiritus, -ūs m. soul
spīrō (1) breathe [32]
splendidus, -a, -um bright, shining, illustrious,
    splendid, shiny
spolium, -iī n. spoils (of war); *spolia opīma* spoils taken
    by one general from another in single combat
sponsa, -ae f. a woman engaged to be married
sponsiō, -ōnis f. bet, wager; *sponsiōnem facere* to
    make a bet
sportula, -ae f. little basket; gift of money or food from
    patron to client
squālidus, -a, -um dirty, filthy
squālor, squālōris m. filth
st shh! shush!
stabulum, -ī n. stable
stāmen, stāminis n. thread
statim immediately [20]
statiō, statiōnis f. post (military); pl. barracks
statuō, statuere, statuī decree
statūra, -ae f. stature
status, -ūs m. condition, position
stercus, -oris n. dung, excrement
sternō, sternere, strāvī, strātum spread out
stertō, stertere, stertuī snore
stilus, -ī m. stilus, pen
stīpendium, -iī n. tax, contribution, pay
stirps, stirpis f. offspring, children
stō, stāre, stetī, statum stand [5]
strangulō (1) choke, strangle
strēnuē actively, vigorously [26]
strēnuus, -a, -um active, vigorous, hard, strenuous
strepitus, -ūs m. noise
struō, struere, struxī, structum build, construct
studeō, studēre, studuī (+ dat.) devote one's self to,
    be eager for, study [12]
studiōsus, -a, -um (+ gen.) eager (to), devoted (to)
studium, -iī n. study, eagerness, zeal [6]
stultus, -a, -um stupid
stuprum, -ī n. dishonor, shame
Stygius, -a, -um Stygian, pertaining to the River Styx
    in the Underworld
Stymphālus, -ī m. Stymphalus, a Greek lake and town
    of the same name

Styx, Stygis f. river Styx, river bordering the Underworld

suāsōria, -ae f. persuasive speech

suāvis, suāve pleasant, agreeable, delightful

sub (+ abl.) under, from under; (+ acc.) under [6]

sūbiciō, sūbicere, sūbiēcī, sūbiectum throw from beneath, put under foot.

subitō suddenly [11]

sublevō (1) lift, raise, support, lighten, alleviate

submissus, -a, -um low (voice)

submittō = summittō

subsīdō, subsīdere, subsēdī crouch

Subūra, -ae f. Subura, a neighborhood in Rome

succēdō, succēdere, successī, successum go below, go under; come to; succeed (to) [37]

sūdo (1) sweat, perspire

suffrāgātiō, -ōnis f. public espression of support

suī, sibi, sē, sē himself, herself, itself, themselves [21]

sum, esse, fuī be [2]

summittō, summittere, summīsī, summissum lower, put down (with *sē* + dat.) lower oneself to

summus, -a, -um highest, greatest [20]

sumptuōsus, -a, -um expensive, costly

sunt (they) are [2]

super above; (+ acc. or abl.) over, on top of [10]

super left over

superbus, -a, -um proud, haughty [40]

superēmineō, superēminēre stand out over

superficiēs, -ēī f. surface

superior, superius higher [19]

superō (1) surpass, conquer

supersum, superesse, superfuī be left over; survive; have strength (for) [35]

superus, -a, -um "above"; *in superōs (locōs)* = in heaven

suppetō, suppetere, suppetīvī/suppetiī, suppetītum be available for

suprā (+ acc.) over, above [32]

suprēmus, -a, -um highest, final [20]

surdus, -a, -um deaf

surgō, surgere, surrexī, surrectum get up, rise up [32]

sūs, suis m./f. pig, sow

suscipiō, suscipere, suscēpī, susceptum accept

suspendō, suspendere, suspendī, suspensum hang

suspīrium, -iī n. sigh, heartthrob

suspīrō (1) sigh

sustineō, sustinēre, sustinuī, sustentum hold up, support, withstand [37]

susurrō (1) whisper

suōpte = stronger form of *suō*

sūtor, -ōris m. cobbler, shoemaker

suus, -a, -um his/her/its/their own [9]

Syria, -ae f. Syria, a Roman province located approximately where modern Syria is today

T

T. = *Titus*

taberna, -ae f. (snack) shop [2]

tabula, -ae f. counter, slate, tablet

tabulārium, -iī n. office

taceō, tacēre, tacuī, tacitum be quiet, be silent [13]

tacitus, -a, -um silent, secret

taeda, -ae f. pine-torch

taediōsus, -a, -um boring

taedit, taedēre, taesum est (+ gen. or + inf.) imp. be tired (of), be sick (of), be bored (with)

taedium, -iī n. boredom, weariness; object of weariness, boring thing; *taedium habēre* to be bored

Talassiō, -ōnis m. Talasio! an ancient wedding cry

tālis, tāle such, of such a kind, of such a sort [21]; *tālis, -e . . . quālis, quāle* of such a sort . . . as

tam so, so much (as) [11]

tamen nevertheless [20]

tamquam just as, just like

tandem at last, at length, finally [20]

tangō, tangere, tetigī, tactum touch; reach; affect; move; mention [32]

tantum so much, to such a degree

tantus, -a, -um so great, so much [28]

tardus, -a, -um late [39]

taurus, -ī m. bull

tectum, -ī n. roof, house

tegō, tegere, texī, tectum to protect, hide, conceal, cover

tēla, -ae f. loom, web

tellūs, tellūris f. earth, ground, land

tempestās, -ātis f. time, weather, season, storm [36]

tempestīvē on time

tempestīvus, -a, -um opportune, seasonable, timely

templum, -ī n. temple

temptō (1) feel; try; test [32]

tempus, -oris n. time, season [13]; forehead

teneō, tenēre, tenuī, tentum hold [6]

tener, tenera, tenerum soft, delicate

tenuis, tenue thin, mild

tepidārium, -iī n. warm bath

tepor, -ōris m. warmth, heat

ter three times [36]

tergum, -ī n. back; *ā tergō* behind

terminō (1) conclude, end

terra, -ae f. land [8]

terreō, terrēre, terruī, territum frighten, terrify

terribilis, terribile frightening, terrible [27]

terrificus, -a, -um terrifying
territus, -a, -um afraid, scared [14]
tertius, -a, -um third [38]
tessellātus, -a, -um mosaic
testor, testārī, testātus sum bear witness to, testify to
theātrum, -ī n. theater
Thēbae, Thēbārum f. pl. Thebes, a city in Greece
thermae, -ārum f. pl. public baths
Thracia, -ae f. Thrace, a Roman province located in what is now part of Greece, Bulgaria, and Turkey
Thrax, Thrācis m. Thracian; a gladiator with lighter armor, including a helmet and greaves on both legs
Tiberis, -is m. Tiber, the river running through Rome
Tiberius, -iī m. Tiberius, Augustus' stepson, adopted son, and successor
tibi your, to you [1]
tībīcen, -inis m. piper
timeō, timēre, timuī fear, be afraid [10]
timidē timidly
timidus, -a, -um afraid, timid
timor, timōris m. fear; object of fear
tintinnō (1) ring
Tīrō a male name, especially the slave and trusted scribe of Cicero
tīrō, -ōnis m. recruit
Tīryns, -nthos f. acc. *Tīryntha* f. Tiryns, a Greek city in the Argolid
Tītus, -ī m. Titus, a male name
toga, -ae f. toga [33]
togātus, -a, -um dressed in a toga [33]
tolerō (1) bear, endure
tollō, tollere, sustulī, sublātum lift, raise [11]
tonō (1) thunder, make to resound
tonsor, -ōris m. barber
torpeō, torpēre, torpuī grow numb
torreō, torrēre, torruī, tostum bake
tortus, -a, -um twisted, crooked
torus, ī m. marriage bed
tot (indecl. adj.) so many [40]
tōtus, -a, -um whole, all, entire [17]
tractō (1) treat, handle
trādō, trādere, trādidī, trāditum hand down, entrust, deliver [33]
tragicōmedia, -ae f. tragicomedy
tragoedia, -ae f. tragedy
trahō, trahere, traxī, tractum drag, haul, draw, remove [22]
tranquillitās, -tātis f. calmness, stillness; fair weather [31]
tranquillus, -a, -um calm, still, peaceful [31]
trans (+ acc.) across [5]
transeō, transīre, transīvī/transiī, transitum go over, go across [32]
transfigō, transfigere, transfixī, transfixum pierce through

transportō (1) carry (across), convey, transport [27]
trecentī, -ae, -a three hundred
tremō, tremere, tremuī tremble [34]
tremulus, -a, um trembling
trepidus, -a, -um nervous, anxious
trēs, tria three [6]
tribūnicius, -a, -um m. belonging to a tribune
tribūnus, -ī m. tribune; *tribūnus militum* military tribune
tribūtim by tribes
trīclīnium, -iī n. triclinium, dining room [26]
tridens, tridentis m. trident
triennium, -iī n. a three-year period
trietēris, -idis f. triennial, unit of three years
trīgintā (indecl.) thirty
tristis, triste sad [15]
tristitia, -ae f. sadness
triumphālis, triumphāle triumphal
triumphātor, -ōris m. one who celebrates a triumph
triumphō (1) triumph, celebrate a triumph
triumphus, -ī m. triumph, triumphal procession, military triumph
trivium, triv(i)ī n. an intersection, a place where three roads meet
Trōia, -ae f. Troy, city in the Roman province of Asia (modern Turkey)
tropaeum, tropaeī n. trophy, victory monument
tū [2], *tuī*, tibi [1], *tē, tē* you (sing.) yourself [4]
tuba, -ae f. horn, trumpet [35]
tubicen, tubicenis m. trumpeter
tueor, tuērī, tuitus sum look at, watch over, look after, protect [29]
Tulliānum, -ī n. Tullianum, the state prison in Rome
tum then [20]
tumeō, tumēre swell
tumultus, -ī m. uproar, disturbance
tunc then [3]
tunica, -ae f. tunic
turba, -ae f. disorder, confusion; crowd [35]
turbō (1) disturb, disorder
turbō, turbinis m. whirlwind
turpis, turpe ugly, foul, loathsome [38]
Tuscus, -a, -um Etruscan
tūtus, -a, -um safe [14]
tuus, -a, -um your (sing.) [6]
Tyrius, -a, -um from Tyre; purple
Tyrus, -ī f. Tyre, city in Roman province of Syria (modern Lebanon)

U

ubi where; when [5]
ubīque everywhere

ūdus, -a, -um wet

Ulixēs, -is or *-eī* m. Ulysses, the hero of Homer's *Odyssey*, known in Greek as Odysseus

ūllus, -a, -um any [17]

ulna, -ae f. yard (unit of measurement)

ulula, -ae f. screech owl

ululō (1) wail, weep

umbilīcus, -ī m. navel, belly button, center, umbilical cord

umbra, -ae f. shade, soul

umerus, -ī m. shoulder

umquam at any time, ever [28]

unda, -ae f. wave

unde from where

unguentārius, -iī m. perfume seller

ūnicus, -a, -um one and only, sole

ūnus, -a, -um one [7]

urbānus, -a, -um polished, refined; witty; of the city

urbs, urbis f. city, esp. the city of Rome [20]

ūrīna, -ae f. urine

urna, -ae f. large water jar

ūrō, ūrere, ussī, ustum burn

usque as far as

ut in order that, so that; how; as; when [31]

uterus, -ī m. womb, belly

utilis, utile useful [30]

utinam if only! would that! [37]

ūtor, ūtī, ūsus sum (+ abl.) use, employ, enjoy, experience [24]

utrum whether

ūva, -ae f. grape; *ūva passa* dried grape, raisin

uxor, -ōris f. wife [18]

V

vādō, vādere, vāsī go, advance, proceed

vae (often + dat.) woe! (in pain or dread) [36]

vāgītus, -ūs m. cry, wail

vagor, vagārī, vagātus sum wander

vah/vaha ah! oh! (in astonishment, joy, anger)

val(l)um, val(l)ī n. a line of palisades

valdē very (much), a lot [11]

valeō, valēre, valuī be strong, be well; *Valē/Valēte!* Farewell. Good-bye. Be well! [3]

Valeria, -ae f. Valeria, owner of the snack shop

vāpulō (1) be beaten

varius, -a, -um various, changeable, mixed [30]

vastō (1) plunder, lay waste

vastus, -a, -um huge

Vatia, -ae f. Vatia, a Roman *nōmen*

Vaticānus, -ī m. Vatican, a hill on the right bank of the Tiber in Rome

vehemens, -entis violent, strong, intense, vehement

Veiī, Veiōrum m. pl. Veii, a very old Etruscan city north of Rome

vēlōciter quickly

velut just as, just like

vēnātiō, -ōnis f. hunt

vēnātor, -ōris m. hunter [29]

venditiō, -ōnis f. sale

venditor, -ōris m. merchant

vendō, vendere, vendidī, venditum sell [30]

venēnātus, -a, -um poisonous

venēnum, -ī n. poison

venetus, -a, -um blue

veniō, venīre, vēnī, ventum come [2]

venter, -tris m. belly, abdomen, womb

ventus, -ī m. wind [36]

Venus, -eris f. Venus, goddess of love

venustus, -a, -um charming, attractive

vēr, vēris n. springtime

verber, verberis n. lash, blow

verberō (1) assail, flog, batter, lash, scourge, beat

verbum, -ī n. word [11]

vērē truly [15]

verēcundus, -a, -um modest

vereor, verērī, veritus sum be afraid of, fear, show reverence to [24]

Vergilius, -iī m. Vergil, the poet

vēritās, -ātis f. truth

vērō indeed, in truth, truly

Vērōna, -ae f. Verona, a town in northern Italy

Vērōnensis, -ense Veronan, from Verona

verrō, verrere, versum sweep clean

versō (1) keep turning around, spin, whirl

versor, versārī, versātus sum come and go, frequent

versus, -ūs m. verse, line of poetry [27]

vertō, vertere, vertī, versum turn, overturn [26]

vērus, -a, -um true [15]

vescor, vescī (+ abl.) take food, feed devour

vesper, -eris m. evening

vesperascō, vesperascere, vesperāvī grow towards evening

Vesta, -ae f. Vesta, goddess of the hearth

Vestālis, Vestālis f. Vestal virgin

vester, vestra, vestrum your (pl.) [6]

vestīmentum, -ī n. garment, clothing

vestiō, vestīre, vestīvī/vestiī, vestītum dress, clothe [33]

vestis, vestis f. garments, clothing [33]

Vesuvius, -iī m. Vesuvius, volcanic mountain in Campania

vetō, vetāre, vetuī, vetitum forbid, prohibit [33]

vetus, veteris aged, old [39]

vexātus, -a, -um upset

vexillum, -ī n. standard, banner
vexō (1) agitate, harry, upset, disturb
via, -ae f. road, street, way [5]
Vibius, -iī m. Vibius, a male name
vīcennālis, vīcennāle made for a period of twenty years, 20th anniversary
vīcīnitās, -tātis f. neighborhood
vīcīnus, -ī m. neighbor
victor, -ōris m. victor, conqueror [35]
victōria, -ae f. victory [35]
victrix, -īcis f. female conquerer
videō, vidēre, vīdī, vīsum see, perceive [3]
videor, vidērī, vīsus sum seem, appear; be seen; *vidētur* imp. (+ inf.) it seems good [27]
vigeō, vigēre, viguī be strong, thrive
vigescō, vigescere become strong
vigil, -is m./f. sentry, guard; firefighter; (pl.) fire brigade [29]
vigilō (1) watch, keep watch; stay awake, stay awake all night; wake up
vīgintī (indecl.) twenty [12]
villa, -ae f. villa, country estate
Vīminālis, Vīmināle Viminal (hill in Rome), pertaining to the Viminal
Vīminālis, Vīminālis m. Viminal (hill), one of the seven hills of Rome
vinciō, vincīre, vinxī, vinctum tie up, fetter, bind
vincō, vincere, vīcī, victum conquer [12]
vindicō (1) protect
vīnum, -ī n. wine [3]
violentia, -ae f. force, violence
Vipsānius, -iī m. Vipsanius
vir, virī m. man [2]; husband
virga, -ae f. rod
virgō, -inis f. young girl
virītim, man by man, per person
vīs, vis f. strength, power, force; (pl.) *vīrēs, vīrium* strength, troops, forces [21]
vīscera, -um n. pl. internal organs, entrails

vīsitō (1) see frequently, visit
vīta, -ae f. life [13]
vitta, -ae f. ribbon
vīvo, vīvere, vīxī, victum live [29]
vīvus, -a, -um alive, living [35]
vix scarcely, hardly [32]
vōbīs dat./abl. you (all) [17]
vōcālis, vōcāle speaking, vocal
vōciferor, vōciferārī, vōciferātus sum yell, cry out
vocō (1) call [8]
Volcānus, -ī m. Vulcan, the god of fire and smiths
volō (1) fly; hasten [36]
volō, velle, voluī want to, be willing to [7]
vōs, vestrum/vestrī, vōbīs [17], *vōs, vōbīs* [17] **you all**
vōtum, -ī n. vow; votive offering
voveō, vovēre, vōvī, vōtum vow
vox, vōcis f. voice [15]
vulnerō (1) wound [22]
vulnus, -eris n. wound [22]
vult (s)he wants, wishes [5]
vulturīnus, -a, -um of a vulture
vultus, vultūs m. face; also spelled *voltus*
vulva, -ae f. womb

X

Xerxēs, Xerxis m. Xerxes, king of Persia
Xanthus, -i m. Xanthus ("Blondie"), one of Servilius' slaves

Z

Zakynthus, -ī f. Zakynthus, an island in western Greece
Zephyrus, -ī m. the West Wind, which brings mild weather
Zēthus, -ī, m. Zethus ("Westy"), a male name

Verba Discenda
English-Latin Glossary

English-Latin Lexicon: This English-Latin Lexicon is based on the *Verba Discenda* in Chapters 1–40. Numbers in brackets indicate the chapter in which the Latin word becomes a *verbum discendum*. Before you use a word in a Latin sentence, it is a good idea to check its entire meaning in the *Verba Omnia*.

abl. = ablative
acc. = accusative
adj. = adjective
dat. = dative
conj. = conjunction
esp. = especially
excl. = exclamation
f. = feminine
gen. = genitive
imp. = impersonal
imper. = imperative
indecl. = indeclinable

inf. = infinitive
interj. = interjection
interr. = interrogative
m. = masculine
n. = neuter
nom. = nominative
pl. = plural
prep. = preposition
subj. = subjunctive
v. = verb
voc. = vocative

A

a lot *multum* [16]; *valdē* [11]
about *dē* (+ abl.) [7]
abroad *rūs, rūris* n. [36]
above *suprā* (+ acc.) [32]
abroad *forīs* adv. [34]
accept *recipiō, recipere, recēpī, receptum* [31]
accomplish *conficiō, conficere, confēcī, confectum* [28]; *efficiō, efficere, effēcī, effectum* [32]
acquire *potior, potīrī, potītus sum* (+ abl. or gen.) [24]
across *trans* (+ acc.) [5]
act *agō, agere, ēgī, actum* [4]
actively *strēnuē* [26]
add *addō, addere, addidī, additum* [40]
admire *admīror, admīrārī, admīrātus sum* [26]; *mīror, mīrārī, mīrātus sum* [25]
adorn *ōrnō* (1) [35]
advance *pergō, pergere, perrēxī, perrectum* [37]; *prōcēdō, prōcēdere, prōcessī, prōcessum* [10]; *prōgredior, prōgredī, prōgressus sum* [24]
advice *consilium, -iī* n. [23]
advise *moneō, monēre, monuī, monitum* [33]
affect *moveō, movēre, mōvī, mōtum; tangō, tangere, tetigī, tactum* [32]

affair *rēs, reī* f. [24]
afraid of (be) *metuō, metuere, metuī, metūtum* [39]
afraid *territus, -a, -um* [14]
after (conj.) *postquam* [30]
after (prep.) *post* (+ acc.) [5]
afterwards *posteā* [30]
again *iterum* [4]; *rursus* [16]
against *in* (+ acc.) [5]; *contrā* (+ acc.) [19]
aged *vetus, veteris* [39]
agree *accēdō, accēdere, accessī, accessum* [38]
agreeable *iūcundus, -a, -um* [35]
aid (n.) *auxilium, -iī* n. [25]
aid (v.) *adsum, adesse, adfuī* (+ dat.) [19]
air *āēr, āeris* m. [32]
alas! *ēheu* [16]
alive *vīvus, -a, -um* [35]
all at once *simul* [24]
all right! *age* [38]
all *omnēs, -ia* [15]; *tōtus, -a, -um* [17]
allow *cēdō, cēdere, cessī, cessum* (+ dat.) [35]; *patior, patī, passus sum* [24]; *sinō, sinere, sīvī/siī, situm* [33]
almost *paene* [18]
alone *sōlus, -a, -um* [6]
along *praeter* (+ acc.) [8]
already *iam* [8]

alright *salvus, -a, -um* [16] cf. "correct"

also *et* [4]; *etiam* [17]; *quoque* [8]

altar *āra, -ae* f. [19]

altogether *omnīnō* [32]; *simul* [24]

always *semper* [3]

am *sum* [2]

among *inter* (+ acc.) [5]

amphitheater *amphitheātrum, -ī* n. [17]

amuse *dēlectō* (1) [38]

ancestor *avus, -ī* m. [29]

ancestors *māiōrēs, māiōrum* m. pl. [15]

ancient *antīquus, -a, -um* [10]

and *ac* [33]; *et* [2]; *atque* [20]; *-que* [4]

and also *atque* [20]; *et* [2]; *etiam* [17]

and besides *ac* [33]

and even *atque* [20]

and not *nec* [15]; *neque* [28]

angry *īrātus, -a, -um* [6]

animal *animal, -ālis* n. [17]

announce *nuntiō* (1) [37]

another *alius, -a, -ud* [9]; another (of two) *alter, altera, alterum* [17]

answer *respondeō, respondēre, respondī, responsum* (+ dat.) [3]

anxious *anxius, -a, -um* [29]

anxious that/lest *sollicitus, -a, -um* [39]

any *ūllus, -a, -um* [17]

apartment block *insula, -ae* f. [9]

appear *crescō, crescere, crēvī, crētum* [32]; *videor, vidērī, vīsus sum* [27]

appearance *faciēs, faciēī* f. [24]; *speciēs, speciēī* f. [24]

applaud *plaudō, plaudere, plausī, plausum* [26]

apprehensive *sollicitus, -a, -um* [39]

approach *accēdō, accēdere, accessī, accessum* [38]; *appropinquō* (1) (+ dat.) [11]

are (they) *sunt* [2]

arena *harēna, -ae* f. [22]

arise *crescō, crescere, crēvī, crētum* [32]

arm (n.) *brāc(c)hium, -iī* n. [14]

arm (v.) *armō* (1) [37]

army *agmen, agminis* n. [40]; *exercitus, -ūs* m. [38]; *legiō, legiōnis* f. [39]

around *circum* (+ acc.) [6]

arrival *adventus, -ūs* m. [39]

arrive at *adveniō, advenīre, advēnī, adventum* [11]; *perveniō, pervenīre, pervēnī, perventum* [21]

arrow *sagitta, -ae* f. [28]

art *ars, artis* f. [16]; *fabrica, -ae* f. [37]

artisan *faber, fabrī* m. [28]

as if *quasī* [37]

as long as *dōnec* [27]; *dum* [10]; *ut* [31]

as soon as *simul ac* [21]; *simul atque* [21]

ascend *ascendō, ascendere, ascendī, ascensum* [24]

ask (for) *poscō, poscere, poposcī* [5]; *rogō* (1) [10]

ask *interrogō* (1) [34]; *quaerō, quaerere, quaesivī/quaesiī, quaesītum* [18]

asking a question expecting a no answer *num* [5]

asking a question expecting a yes answer *nōnne* [5]

asking a simple question *-ne* [4]

assent *accēdō, accēdere, accessī, accessum* [38]

at *in* (+ abl.) [2, 5]

at ____ 's *apud* (+ acc.) [16]

at first *primō* [32], *prīmum* [28]

at last, *dēmum* [26]; *dēnique* [32]; tandem [20]

at length *aliquandō* [26]; *dēmum* [26]; *tandem* [20]

at the house of *apud* (+ acc.) [16]

at the same time *simul* [24]

atmosphere *āēr, āeris* m. [32]

atrium (public greeting room of a Roman house) *atrium, -iī* n. [33]

attached to *aptus, -a, -um* [31]

attack *accēdō, accēdere, accessī, accessum* [38]; *oppugnō* (1) [39]; *petō, petere, petīvī/petiī, petītum* [21]

auxiliary forces *auxilia, -iōrum* n. pl. [25]

await *exspectō* (1) [16]

awake, awaken *expergiscor, expergiscī, experrectus sum* [32]; *excitō* (1) [32]

away from *ā/ab/abs* (+ abl.) [5]; *dē* (+ abl.) [7]

B

bad *malus, -a, -um* [6]

bag *saccus, -ī* m. [11]

banquet *convīvium, -iī* n. [25]; *epulae, -ārum* f. pl. [26]

battle *proelium, -iī* n. [34]

battle line *agmen, agminis* n. [40]

be *sum, esse, fuī* [2]

be able *possum, posse, potuī* [7]

be absent *absum, abesse, āfuī* [19]

be accustomed (to) *soleō, solēre, solitus sum* [29]

be afraid of *vereor, verērī, veritus sum* [24]

be afraid *timeō, timēre, timuī* [10]

be born *nascor, nascī, nātus sum* [37]; *orior, orīrī, ortus sum* [29]

be done *fīō, fierī, factus sum* [26]

be eager for *studeō, studēre, studuī* (+ dat.) [12]

be glad *gaudeō, gaudēre, gavīsus sum* [38]

be made *fīō, fierī, factus sum* [26]

be near *adsum, adesse, adfuī* (+ dat.) [19]

be of assistance to *adsum, adesse, adfuī* (+ dat.) [19]

be pleasing to *placeō, placēre, placuī, placitum* (+ dat.); esp., it is pleasing *placet* (+ inf.) [12]

be present *adsum, adesse, adfuī* (+ dat.) [19]

be quiet, silent *taceō, tacēre, tacuī, tacitum* [13]

be slain *cadō, cadere, cecidi, cāsum* [21]

be strong *valeō, valēre, valuī, valitum* [3]

be superior to *praestō, praestāre, praestitī, praestitum/ praestātum* (+ dat.) [10]

be "there" for someone *adsum, adesse, adfuī* (+ dat.) [19]

be thirsty *sitiō, sitīre, sitīvī/sitiī* [31]

be unwilling *nōlō, nolle, nōluī* [7]

be well *valeō, valēre, valuī, valitum* [3]

Be well! *Salvē/Salvēte!* [3]; *Valē/Valēte!* [2]

be willing to *volō, velle, voluī* [7]

be without *careō, carēre, caruī, caritum* + abl. [36]

bear *ferō, ferre, tulī, lātum* [23]; *gerō, gerere, gessī, gestum* [22]; *pariō, parere, peperī, paritum/partum* [25]

beat *pulsō* (1) beat [23]

beautiful *formōsus, -a, -um* [35]; *pulcher, pulchra, pulchrum* [13]; *praeclārus, -a, -um* [16]

beauty *faciēs, faciēī* f. [24]; *forma, -ae* f. [34]

because *enim* [20]; *quia* [18]; *quod* [3]

because of *causā* + gen. [30]

become *fīō, fierī, factus sum* [26]

bed *lectus, -ī* m. [18]

bedroom *cubiculum, -ī* n. [12]

before (conj.) *antequam* [34], *priusquam* [10]

before (prep.) *prō* (+ abl.) [6]

begin *incipiō, incipere, incēpī, inceptum* [18]

beginning *orīgō, originis* f. [38]

behind *post* (+ acc.) [5]

Behold! *Ecce!* [11]

belief *opīniō, -iōnis* f. [34]

believe *crēdō, crēdere, crēdidī, crēditum* (+ dat.) [25]; *opīnor, opīnārī, opīnātus sum* [30]

below *infrā* [32]

benefit *beneficium, -iī* n. [38]

be seen *videor, vidērī, vīsus sum* [27]

besides *praetereā* [34]

best *optimus, -a, -um* [20]

better *melior, melius* [19]

between *inter* (+ acc.) [5]

beware *caveō, cavēre, cāvī, cautum* [33]

beyond *extrā* (+ acc.) [40]; *praeter* (+ acc.) [8]

bird *avis, avis* f. [28]

blood *sanguis, sanguinis* f. [22]

body *corpus, corporis* n. [15]

bone *os, ossis* n. [28]

book *liber, librī* m. [14]

born *nātus, -a, -um* [12]

both (of two) *ambō, ambae, ambō* [31]

both . . . and *et . . . et* [4]; *-que . . . -que* [4]

boy *puer, puerī* m. [6]

brave *fortis, forte* [15]

bravo! *eugae/euge/eugepae* [36]

bread *pānis, pānis* m. [31]

break *frangō, frangere, frēgī, fractum* [36]

break down *rumpō, rumpere, rūpī, ruptum* [28]

breakfast *ientāculum, -ī* n. [31]

breathe *spīrō* (1) [32]

bright *clārus, -a, -um* [36]

bring away *dēdūcō, dēdūcere, dēdūxī, dēductum* [38]

bring back *referō, referre, rettulī, relātum* [39]

bring together *conferō, conferre, contulī, collātum* [28]

broad *lātus, -a, -um* [31]

bronze *aēneus, -a, -um* [30]

brother *frāter, frātris* m. [13]

build *condō, condere, condidī, conditum* [40]; *fabricō* (1) [37]

building *aedificium, -iī* n. [38]; *opus, operis* n. [23]

burial *fūnus, fūneris,* n. [40]

burn *incendō, incendere, incendī, incensum* [32]

burn, burn up *combūrō, combūrere, combussī, combustum* [30]

burst *rumpō, rumpere, rūpī, ruptum* [28]

business *negōtium, -ī* n. [8]; *rēs, reī* f. [24]

but *at* [20]; *modo* [23]; *sed* [3]

but also *sed etiam* (with *nōn sōlum* . . . not only . . .) [18]

buy *emō, emere, ēmī, emptum* [18]

by (with persons) *ā/ab/abs* (+ abl.) [5]

by a little *paulō* [25]

by far *multō* [26]

By Hercules! *Hercule* [28]

by no means *haud* [16]

By Pollux! *Edepol!* [37]

C

call *vocō* (1) [8]

call for *arcessō, arcessere, arcessīvī/arcessī, arcessītum* [32]

calm *aequus, -a, -um* [31]; *lentus, -a, -um; quiētus, -a, -um* [25]; *tranquillus, -a, -um* [31]

calmness *tranquillitās, -tātis* f. [31]

camp *castra, -ōrum* n. pl. [23]

campaign (political) *ambitiō, -iōnis* f. [37]

can *possum, posse, potuī* [7]

candidacy *petitiō, -iōnis* f. [37]

canvassing (for votes) *ambitiō, -iōnis* f. [37]

captive *captīvus, -ī* m. [40]

care for *cūrō* (1) [13]

career *cursus, -ūs* m. [35]

careful *dīligens, dīligentis* [30]

carpenter *faber, fabrī* m. [28]

carry *ferō, ferre, tulī, lātum* [23]; *gerō, gerere, gessī, gestum* [22]; *portō* (1) [8]; *referō, referre, rettulī, relātum* [39]

carry (across) *transportō* (1) [27]

cause *causa, -ae* f. [30]

cavalry *equitēs, equitum* m. pl. [34]

centurion *centuriō, -iōnis* m. [23]

certain (indefinite, as in "a certain person") *quīdam, quaedam, quoddam* [21]

chair *sella, -ae* f. [25]

chance *fortūna, -ae* f. [33]

changeable *varius, -a, -um* [30]

character *mōrēs, mōrum* m. pl. [15]; *nātūra, -ae* f. [32]

charm *dēlectō* (1) [38]

chase *persequor, persequī, persecūtus sum* [40]

chat *sermōcinor, sermōcinārī, sermōcinātus sum* [31]

cheerful *libens, libentis* [35]

children *līberī, -ōrum* m. pl. [33]

choose *legō, legere, lēgī, lectum* [15]

circle *orbis, orbis* m. [20]

citizen *cīvis, cīvis* m./f. [27]

city, esp. the city of Rome *urbs, urbis* f. [20]

city center *forum, -ī* [5]

clap *plaudō, plaudere, plausī, plausum* [26]

class of citizens *ordō, -inis* m. [34]

clean, cleanse *purgō* (1) [22]

clear *clārus, -a, um* [36]

client *cliens, clientis* m. [31]

climb *ascendō, ascendere, ascendī, ascensum* [24]

cling to *retineō, retinēre. retinuī, retentum* [37]

close *claudō, claudere, clausī, clausum* [38]

clothe *vestiō, vestīre, vestīvī/vestiī, vestītum* [33]

clothing *vestis, vestis* f. [33]

coin *nummus, -ī* m. [27]

collapse *collābor, collābī, collapsus sum* [39]

collect *conferō, conferre, contulī, collātum* [28]

colonnaded garden *peristȳlium, -iī* n. [26]

column of troops *agmen, agminis* n. [40]

come *veniō, venīre, vēnī, ventum* [2]

come about *ēveniō, ēvenīre, ēvēnī, ēventum* [35]

come back *redeō, redīre, rediī, reditum* [21]; *reveniō, revenīre, revēnī, reventum* [31]

come near to *appropinquō* (1) (+ dat.) [11]

come to *accēdō, accēdere, accessī, accessum* [38]; *adveniō, advenīre, advēnī, adventum* [11]; *succēdō, succēdere, successī, successum* [37]

come! *age* [36]

command *imperō* (1) (+ dat.) [26]

commander *imperātor, -ōris* m. [25]

common *pūblicus, -a, -um* [30]

companion *socius, -iī* m. [36]

complete *conficiō, conficere, confēcī confectum* [28]

completely *omnīnō* [32]

conceal *abdō, abdere, abdidī, abditum* [19]

concerning *dē* (+ abl.) [7]

conduct *dēdūcō, dēdūcere, dēdūxī, dēductum* [38]

conflagration *incendium, -iī* n. [32]

confusion *turba, -ae* f. [35]

connected to *aptus, -a, -um* [31]

conquer *frangō, frangere, frēgī, fractum* [36]; *vincō, vincere, vīcī, victum* [12]

conqueror *victor, victōris* m. [35]

consider *aestimō* (1) [38]; *intueor, intuērī, intuitus sum* [25]

construct *fabricō* (1) [30]

consume *consūmō, consūmere, consumpsī, consumptum* [38]

contain *contineō, continēre, continuī, contentum* [40]

contest *certāmen, certāminis* n. [35]

converse *colloquor, colloquī, collocūtus sum* [25]; *sermōcinor, sermōcinārī, sermōcinātus sum* [31]

convey *transportō* (1) [27]

cook (n.) *coquus, -ī* m. [25]

cook (v.) *coquō, coquere, coxī, coctum* [26]

cost *constō, constāre, constitī, constātūrum* [10]

couch (dining) *lectus, -ī* m. [18]

counsel *consilium, -iī* n. [23]

country *fīnēs, fīnium* m. pl. [14]; *patria, -ae* f. [27]; *rūs, rūris* n. [36]

country estate *rūs, rūris* n. [36]

course *cursus, -ūs* m. [35]

courtyard *peristȳlium, -iī* n. [26]

craft *fabrica, -ae* f. [37]

craftsman *faber, fabrī* m. [28]

create *pariō, parere, peperī, paritum/partum* [25]

crime *scelus, sceleris* n. [20]

crowd *agmen, agminis* n. [40]; *turba, -ae* f. [35]

cruel *crūdēlis, crūdēle* [18]

crush *frangō, frangere, frēgī, fractum* [36]

cry *lacrimō* (1) [17]

cry out *clāmō* (1) [5]

custom *mōs, mōris* m. [15]

D

dangerous *perīculōsus, a, -um* [25]

dare *audeō, audēre, ausus sum* [9]

dark *obscūrus, -a, -um* [38]

daughter *fīlia, -ae* f. [8]

day *diēs, diēī* m. [24]; *sōl, sōlis* m. [33]

day before *prīdiē* [35]

dead *mortuus, -a, -um* [22]

dear *almus, -a, -um* [18]; *cārus, -a, -um* [13]

deceive *mentior, mentīrī, mentītus sum* [24]

decent *honestus, -a, -um* [29]

decorate *ornō* (1) [35]

deed *factum, -ī* n. [20]

deep *altus, -a, -um* [2]; *gravis, grave* [15]

defend *defendō, defendere, defendī, defensum* [39]

declare *ēloquor, ēloquī, ēlocūtus sum* [24]

delight *dēlectō* (1) [38]

deliver *solvō, solvere, soluī, solūtum* [36]; *trādō, trādere, trādidī, trāditum* [33]

demand *poscō, poscere, poposcī* [5]; *postulō* (1) [33]

depart *proficiscor, proficiscī, profectus sum* [28]

depict *dēmonstrō* (1) [40]

descend *descendō, descendere, descendī, descensum* [31]

descendant *nepōs, nepōtis* m. [27]

desirous *cupidus, -a, -um* (+ gen.) [39]

destitute *egēnus, -a, -um* [22]

destroy *destruō, destruere, destruxī, destructum* [34]

devote one's self to *studeō, studēre, studuī* (+ dat.) [12]

die *morior, morī, mortuus sum* [29]

difficult *difficilis, difficile* [15]

difficulty *difficultās, -tātis* f. [23]

dignity *dignitās, -tātis* f. [35]

diligent *dīligens, dīligentis* [30]

dine *cēnō* (1) [12]

dining couch *lectus, -ī* m. [18]

dinner *cēna, -ae* f. [12]

discharge *fungor, fungī, functus sum* (+ abl.) [24]

discharge benefits (military) *praemia, -iōrum* n. pl. [39]

discover *inveniō, invenīre, invēnī, inventum* [14]

dishes of food *epulae, -ārum* f. pl. [26]

disloyal *improbus, -a, -um* [23]

dismiss *dīmittō, dīmittere, dīmīsī, dīmissum* [35]

disorder *turba, -ae* f. [35]

displease *displiceō, displicēre, displicuī, displicitum* [26]

distinct *clārus, -a, -um* [36]

district *regiō, regiōnis* f. [39]

disturb *perturbō* (1) [26]

divine *dīvus, -a, -um* [29]

divorce *dīmittō, dīmittere, dīmīsī, dīmissum* [35]

do *agō, agere, ēgī, actum* [4]; *conficiō, conficere, confēcī, confectum* [28]; *efficiō, efficere, effēcī, effectum* [32]; *faciō, facere, fēcī, factum* [6]

do injury to *noceō, nocēre, nocuī, nocitum* (+ dat.) [12]

dog *canis, canis* m./f. [23]

Don't! *Nōlī* + inf. (sing.)/ *Nōlīte* + inf. (pl.)

door *foris, foris* f. [34]; *iānua, -ae* f. [25]; *porta, -ae* f. [23]

doorman *iānitor, -ōris* m. [34]

doubt *dubitō* (1) [39]

doubtful *dubius, -a, -um* [39]

down from *dē* (+ abl.) [7]

drag *trahō, trahere, trāxī, tractus* [22]

dress *vestiō, vestīre, vestīvī/vestiī, vestītum* [33]

dressed in a toga *togātus, -a, -um* [33]

drink (n.) *pōtus, -ūs* m. [29]

drink (v.) *bibō, bibere, bibī* [2]; *pōtō* (1) [31]

drive *agō, agere, ēgī, actum* [4]; *pulsō* (1) [23]

drive together *cōgō, cōgere, coēgī, coactum* [23]

drunk *ēbrius, -a, -um* [27]

duty *mūnus, mūneris* n. [17]

E

each *omnis, omne* [15]; *quisque, quaeque, quodque/quicque/quidque* [21]

eager *ācer, ācris, ācre* [38]

eager for *cupidus, -a, -um* (+ gen.) [39]

eagerness *studium, -iī* n. [6]

ear *auris, auris* f. [29]

early in the morning *māne* [4]

easy *facilis, facile* [20]

eat *consūmō, consūmere, consumpsī, consumptum* [38]; *edō, ēsse/edere, ēdī, ēsum* [7]

effort *opus, operis* n. [23]

egg *ōvum, -ī* n. [10]

eight *octō* (indecl.)

either . . . or *aut . . . aut* [4]

elders *māiōrēs, māiōrum* m. pl. [15]

else *aliter* [39]

emperor *imperātor, -ōris* m. [25]

employ *ūtor, ūtī, ūsus sum* (+ abl.) [24]

encounter *occurrō, occurrere, occurrī/occucurrī, occursum* (+ dat.) [36]

end (n.) *fīnis, fīnis* m. [14]

end (v.) *cadō, cadere, cecidi, cāsum* [21]; *fīniō, fīnīre, fīnīvī/fīniī, fīnītum* [8]

endure *maneō, manēre, mansī, mansum* [23]

enemy *hostis, hostis* m./f.; pl. the enemy *hostis, hostis* m./f. [14]

enjoy *fruor, fruī, fructus/fruitus sum* (+ abl.) [24]; *ūtor, ūtī, ūsus sum* (+ abl.) [24]

enough *satis* [30]

enter *ingredior, ingredī, ingressus sum* [24]; *intrō* (1) [8]

entire *tōtus, -a, -um* [17]

entrust *dēpōnō, dēpōnere, dēposui, dēpositum*; *trādō, trādere, trādidī, trāditum* [33]

envy *invideō, invidēre, invīdī, invīsum* (+ dat.) [38]

equal *aequus, -a, -um* [31]

escape notice of *praetereō, praeterīre, praeterīvī/praterīī, praeteritum* [35]

escort *dēdūcō, dēdūcere, dēdūxī, dēductum* [38]

especially *magnopere* [23]; *praesertim* [25]

estate *rūs, rūris* n. [36]

estimate *aestimō* (1) [38]

even *aequus, -a, -um* [31]; *plānus, -a, -um* [34]

even *et* [2]; *etiam* [17]

even now *etiam* [17]

every *omnis, omne* [15]; *quisque, quaeque, quodque/quicque/quidque* [21]

examine *interrogō* (1) [34]

excellent *praeclārus, -a, -um* [16]

except *praeter* (+ acc.) [8]

excessively *nimium* [16]

excite *excitō* (1) [32]

execute *efficiō, efficere, effēcī, effectum* [32]
exhibit *expōnō, expōnere, exposuī, expositum* [40]
expectation *spēs, speī,* f.
experience *ūtor, ūtī, ūsus sum* (+ abl.) [24]
explain *expōnō, expōnere, exposuī, expositum* [40]
eye *oculus, -ī* m. [23]

F

face *faciēs, faciēī* f. [24]; *ōs, ōris* n. [13]
facing *contrā* (+ acc.) [19]
fair *aequus, -a, -um* [31]
fair weather *tranquillitās, -tātis* f. [31]
faithful *fidēlis, fidēle* [33]
fall down *cadō, cadere, cecidi, cāsum* [21]; *lābor, lābī, lapsus sum* [39]
fall in a faint *collābor, collābī, collapsus sum* [39]
fall to ruin *ruō, ruere, ruī, rutum* [22]
fame *fāma, -ae* f. [20]
family *familia, -ae* f. [4]
famous *clārus, -a, -um* [36]; *praeclārus, -a, -um* [16]
far, far away *procul* [36]
far, far off *longē* [11]
Farewell! *Valē/Valēte!* [3]
fast *celer, celeris, celere* [15]
father *pater, patris* m. [13]
fatherland *patria, -ae* f. [27]
favor *beneficium, -iī* n. [38]; *grātia, -ae* f. [19]
fear (n.) *metus, -ūs* f. [36]
fear (v.) *metuō, metuere, metuī, metūtum* [39]; *timeō, timēre, timuī* [10]; *vereor, verērī, veritus sum* [24]
feast *convīvium, -iī* n. [25]; *epulae, -ārum* f. pl. [26]
feel *sentiō, sentīre, sensī, sensum* [21]; *temptō* (1) [32]
female servant *ancilla, -ae* f. [8]
fetch *arcessō, arcessere, arcessīvī/arcessī, arcessītum* [32]
few *paucī, -ae, -a* [9]
field *ager, agrī* m.[14]; *campus, -ī* m. [33]
fight (n.) *pugna, -ae* f. [22]
fight (v.) *pugnō* (1) [12]
figure *figūra, -ae* f. [10]
filthy *sordidus, -a, -um* [28]
final *suprēmus, -a, -um* [20]
finally *dēnique* [32]; *dēmum* [26]; *tandem* [20]
find *inveniō, invenīre, invēnī, inventum* [14]
finger *digitus, -ī* m. [38]
finish *fīniō, fīnīre, fīnīvī/fīniī, fīnītum* [8]
fire *ignis, ignis* m. [14]; *incendium, -iī* n. [32]
fire brigade *vigilēs, vigilum* m. pl. [29]
fire fighter *vigil, vigilis* m./f. [29]
firm *firmus, -a, -um* [36]
first (adj.) *prīmus, -a, -um* [18]
first(adv.) *prīmum* [28]

fish *piscis, piscis* m. [26]
fit *aptus, -a, -um* [31]; *idōneus, -a, -um* [36]
fitting (it is) *decet, decēre, decuit* (+ dat. + inf.) [24]
five *quinque* (indecl.) [10]
flat *plānus, -a, -um* [34]
flee *fugiō, fugere, fūgī, fugitum* [12]
flock *agmen, agminis* n. [40]
fly *volō* (1) [36]
follow *sequor, sequī, secūtus sum* [24]
food *cibus, -ī* m. [2]; *epulae, -ārum* f. pl. [26]
foot *pēs, pedis* m. [28]
for (conj.) *enim* [20]; *nam* [23]
for (prep.) *ad* (+ acc.) [2, 5]; *prō* (+ abl.) [6]
for a long time *diū* [16]; *longē* [11]
for a second time *iterum* [4]
for the purpose, for the sake of *grātiā* (+ gen.) [30]
for what reason? *quā dē causā?* [34]
forbid *prohibeō, prohibēre, prohibuī, prohibitum* [39]; *vetō, vetāre, vetuī, vetitum* [33]
force (n.) *vīs, vis* f. [21]; force (n.) *vīrēs, vīrium* f. pl. [21]
force (v.) *cōgō, cōgere, coēgī, coactum* [23]
forehead *tempus, temporis* n. [13]
foreigner *hostis, hostis* m./f. [14]
forest *silva, -ae* f. [21]
forge *fabricō* (1) [30]
forget *oblīviscor, oblīviscī, oblītus sum* [36]
form *forma, -ae* f. [34]
former *prior, prius* [19]
formerly *aliquandō* [26]; *ōlim* [19]
fortunate *felix, felicis* [18]; *fortūnātus, -a, -um* [22]
fortune *fortūna, -ae* f. [33]
forum *forum, -ī* [5]
foul *turpis, turpe* [38]
found *condō, condere, condidī, conditum* [40]
four *quattuor* (indecl.) [10]
four times *quater* [36]
free (adj.) *līber, lībera, līberum* [14]
free, free from (v.) *līberō* (1) (+ abl.) [36]
freedman *lībertīnus, -ī* m. [37]
freedom *lībertās, -tātis* f. [40]
friend (female) *amīca, -ae* f. [13]
friend (male) *amīcus, -ī* m. [7]
frightening *terribilis, terribile* [27]
from *ā/ab/abs* (+ abl.) [5]; *ē/ex* (+ abl.) [5]
far away *procul* [36]
from under; *sub* (+ abl.) [6]
frugal *dīligens, dīligentis* [30]
fulfil *solvō, solvere, soluī, solūtum* [36]
full, full of *plēnus, -a, -um* [22]
function *mūnus, mūneris* n. [17]
funeral *fūnus, fūneris,* n. [40]
future *futūrum, -ī* n. [14]

G

gain *obtineō, obtinēre, obtinuī, obtentum* [9]

game *lūdus -ī*, m. [4]; public games *mūnera, mūnerum* n. pl. [17]

garden (colonnaded) *peristȳlium, -iī* n. [26]

garments *vestis, vestis* f. [33]

gate *foris, foris* f. [34]; *porta, -ae* f. [23]

gather *legō, legere, lēgī, lectum* [15]

gaze at *intueor, intuērī, intuitus sum* [25]

general *imperātor, -ōris* m. [25]

gentle *lēnis, lēne* [27]; *levis, leve* [23]

get *potior, potīrī, potītus sum* (+ abl. or gen.) [24]

get to know *cognoscō, cognoscere, cognōvī, cognitum* [29]; *noscō, noscere, nōvī, nōtum* [11]

get up *orior, orīrī, ortus sum; surgō, surgere, surrēxī, surrectum* [32]

gift *dōnum, -ī* n. [23]; gift (public) *mūnus, mūneris* n. [17]

girl *puella, -ae* f. [6]

girlfriend *amīca, -ae* f. [13]

give *dō, dare, dedī, datum* [2]; *addō, addere, addidī, additum* [40]

give back *restituō, restituere, restituī, restitūtum* [39]

give birth (to) *pariō, parere, peperī, paritum/partum* [25]

give reason for regret *paenitet, paenitēre, paenituit* imp. [29]

give thanks *grātiās agere* [19]

give way to *cēdō, cēdere, cessī, cessum* (+ dat.) [35]

gladiator *gladiātor, -ōris* m. [17]

gloomy *maestus, -a, -um* [18]; *obscūrus, -a, -um* [38]

glory *glōria, -ae* f. [40]

go *accēdō, accēdere, accessī, accessum* [38]; *cēdō, cēdere, cessī, cessum* (+ dat.) [35]; *eō, īre, īvī/iī, itum* [7]; *prōgredior, prōgredī, prōgressus sum* [24]; go ("betake oneself") *sē conferre* [28]

go across *transeō, transīre, transīvī/transiī, transitum* [32]

go ahead *pergō, pergere, perrēxī, perrectum* [37]

go away *abeō, abīre, abīvī/abiī, abitum* [7]

go back *redeō, redīre, rediī, reditum* [21];

go below *succēdō, succēdere, successī, successum* [37]

go down *descendō, descendere, descendī, descensum* [31]

go in *ingredior, ingredī, ingressus sum* [24]

go over *transeō, transīre, transīvī/transiī, transitum* [32]

go past *praetereō, praeterīre, praeterīvī/praeteriī, praeteritum* [35]

go to *adeō, adīre, adīvī/adiī, aditum* [7]

go under *succēdō, succēdere, successī, successum* [37]

god *deus, -ī* m.; *dī* (alternate nom. pl.) [14]

goddess *dea, -ae* f. [11]

good *bonus, -a, -um* [3]; *probus, -a, -um* [30]

Good-bye! *Valē/Valēte!* [3]

goods *opera, operum* n. pl. [23]

govern *regō, regere, rēxī, rectum* [39]

grace *grātia, -ae* f. [19]

grandfather *avus, -ī* m. [29]

grandmother *ava, -ae* f. [30]

grandson, grandchild *nepōs, nepōtis* m. [27]

grant *cēdō, cēdere, cessī, cessum* (+ dat.) [35]

great *magnus, -a, -um* [8]

greater *māiōr, māiōris* [15]

greatest *maximus, -a, -um* [20]; *summus, -a, -um* [20]

greatly *magnopere* [23]

greet *salūtō* (1)

greeting (formal morning visit by a client to a patron) *salūtātiō, -ōnis* f. [31]

Greetings! *avē* [29]

grief *dolor, dolōris* m. [21]

ground plan *forma, -ae* f. [34]

grow *crescō, crescere, crēvī, crētum* [32]

grudge *invideō, invidēre, invidī, invisum* (+ dat.) [38]

guard (n.) *custōs, custōdis* m./f. [30]; *vigil, vigilis* m./f. [29]

guard (v.) *custōdiō, custōdīre, custōdīvī/custōdiī, custōditum* [30]

guest *hospes, hospitis* m. [26]

H

hamper *impediō, impedīre, impedīvī/impediī, impedītum* [39]

hand *manus, -ūs* f. [24]

hand down *trādō, trādere, trādidī, trāditum* [33]

handsome *formōsus, -a, -um* [35]; *pulcher, pulchra, pulchrum* [13]

happen *accidō, accidere, accidī; ēveniō, ēvenīre, ēvēnī, ēventum* [35]; *fīō, fierī, factus sum* [26]

happy *laetus, -a, -um* [3]

hard *difficilis, difficile* [15]

hardly *vix* [32]

harm *noceō, nocēre, nocuī, nocitum* (+ dat.) [12]

harsh *crūdēlis, crūdēle* [18]

hasten *festīnō* (1) [9]; *volō* (1) [36]

hate *invideō, invidēre, invidī, invisum* (+ dat.) [38]

haughty *superbus, -a, -um* [40]

haul *trahō, trahere, trāxī, tractus* [22]

have *habeō, habēre, habuī, habitum* [5]

have strength (for) *supersum, superesse, superfuī* [35]

have to *dēbeō, dēbēre, dēbuī, dēbitum* [7]

he *ille, illīus* [17]; *is, eius, eī, eum, eō* [17]

he wants, he wishes *vult* [5]

head *caput, capitis* n. [36]

head of the family *pater familiās, patris familiās* m. [29]

health *salūs, salūtis* f. [32]

healthy *sānus, -a, -um* [25]

hear *audiō, audīre, audīvī/audiī, audītum* [7]; *sentiō, sentīre, sensī, sensum* [21] heart *cor, cordis* n. [17]

heavy *gravis, grave* [15]

Hello! *Salvē/Salvēte!* [3]

help (n.) *auxilium, -iī* n. [25]

help (v.) *adiuvō, adiuvāre, adiūvī, adiūtum* [16]; *adsum, adesse, adfuī* (+ dat.) [19]; *iuvō, iuvāre, iūvi, iūtum* [25]

her own *suus, -a, -um* [9]

herd *agmen, agminis* n. [40]

here *hīc* [10]; (to) here *hūc* [36]

hereafter *aliquandō* [26]

herself *suī, sibi, sē, sē* [21]

herself (emphatic) *ipsa* [17]

hesitate *dubitō* (1) [39]

Hi! *Salvē/Salvēte!* [3]

hide *abdō, abdere, abdidī, abditum* [19]

high *altus, -a, -um* [2]

higher *superior, superius* [19]

highest *summus, -a, -um* [20]; *suprēmus, -a, -um* [20]

hill *collis, collis* m. [32]

himself *suī, sibi, sē, sē* [21]

himself (emphatic) *ipse* [17]

hinder *impediō, impedīre, impedīvī/impediī, impedītum* [39]

his own *suus, -a, -um* [9]

hold *contineō, continēre, continuī, contentum* [40]; *habeō, habēre, habuī, habitum* [5]; *obtineō, obtinēre, obtinuī, obtentum* [9]; *teneō, tenēre, tenuī, tentum* [6]

hold fast *retineō, retinēre. retinuī, retentum* [37]

hold up *sustineō, sustinere, sustinuī, sustentum* [37]·

home *domus, -ī* f. [24]; *sēdēs, sēdis* f. [14]

home, to a house *domum* [4]

honest *probus, -a, -um* [30]

honey *mel, mellis* n. [31]

honor *dignitās, -tātis* f. [35]

hope (n.) *spēs, speī,* f. [33]

hope, hope for (v.) *spērō* (1) [9]

horn *tuba, -ae* f. [35]

horrible *horribilis, horribile* [37]

horse *equus, -ī* m. [34]

horseman *eques, equitis* m. [34]

host *hospes, hospitis* m. [26]

hot *aestuōsus, -a, -um* [31]; *calidus, -a, -um* [33]

hour *hōra, -ae* f. [8]

house *domus, -ī* f. [4]l; *domus, -ūs* f. [24]

how (conj.) *quōmodo* [17]

How are you? How are you doing? *Quid agis?* [4]

how many? *quot?* (indecl.) [34]

how many, how much *quantus, -a, -um* [10]

how (conj.) *quōmodo* [17]; *ut* [31]

how! (interj.) *quam* [13]

how? (interr.) *quārē* [30]

however *autem* [20]

human being *homō, hominis* m. [13]

hundred (one) *centum* indecl. [37]

hungry *iēiūnus, -a, -um* [13]

hunter *vēnātor, -ōris* m. [29]

hurl *iaciō, iacere, iēcī, iactus* [22]

hurt *noceō, nocēre, nocuī, nocitum* (+ dat.) [12]

husband *marītus, -ī* m. [16]

I

I *ego* [7]

I am sorry *mē paenitet* [29]

if *sī* [7]

if only! *utinam* [37]

illegitimate *incertus, -a -um*

illness *morbus, -ī* m. [34]

image *imāgō, -inis* f. [40]

immediately *statim* [20]

impede *impediō, impedīre, impedīvī/impediī, impedītum* [39]

in *in* (+ abl.) [2, 5]

in another way *aliter* [39]

in front *prior* [19]

in front of *prō* (+ abl.) [6]

in need of *egēnus, -a, -um* [22]

in order that *ut* [31]

in order that not *nē* [31]

in the middle (of) *medius, -a, um* [22]

in this place *hīc* [10]

in this way *sīc* [11]

in want of *egēnus, -a, -um* [22]

in what way? *quārē* [30]

increase *crescō, crescere, crēvī, crētum* [32]

indeed *quīn* [39]

indispensable *necessārius, -a, -um* [34]

infant *infans, infantis* m./f. [14]

inflame *incendō, incendere, incendī, incēnsum* [32]

inhabitant *incola, -ae* m./f. [38]

injure *noceō, nocēre, nocuī, nocitum* (+ dat.) [12]

inspect *inspiciō, inspicere, inspexī, inspectum* [10]

instrument *instrūmentum, -ī* n. [27]

intelligent *intellegens, intellegentis* [15]

into *in* (+ acc.) [5]

iron *ferrum, -ī* n. [22]

is *est* [1]

island *insula, -ae* f. [9]

it *id, eius* [17]; *illud, illīus* [17]

it is necessary (to) *necesse est* (+ inf.) [12]

it is pleasing to *placet* imp. + inf.

its own *suus, -a, -um* [9]

itself *suī, sibi, sē, sē* [21]

itself (emphatic) *ipsum* [17]

J

join *iungō, iungere, iunxī, iunctum* [38]
journey *cursus, -ūs* m. [35]
judge *praetor, praetōris* m. [35]
judgeship *praetūra, -ae* f. [36]
judgment *consilium, -iī* n. [23]
jump *saliō, salīre, saliī/saluī, saltum* [11]
Jupiter (king of the gods) *Iuppiter, Iovis* m. [24]
just *aequus, -a, -um* [31]
just as *sīcut* [7]
just now *modo* [23]

K

keep off *prohibeō, prohibēre, prohibuī, prohibitum* [39]
keep safe *conservō* (1) [39]
kill *interficiō, interficere, interfēcī, interfectum* [14]; *necō* (1) [21]; *occīdō, occīdere, occīdī, occīsum* [39]
kind *almus, -a, -um* [18]
kindness *beneficium, -iī* n. [38]
king *rex, rēgis* m. [14]
kingdom *regnum, -ī* n. [36]
kitchen *culīna, -ae* f. [25]
knight *eques, equitis* m. [34]
know *cognoscō, cognoscere, cognōvī, cognitum [29]*; *noscō, noscere, nōvī, nōtum* [11]
know, know about, know how to *sciō, scīre, scīvī/sciī, scītum* [28]

L

labor *labor, labōris* m. [16]; *opera, -ae* f. [36]
lack *careō, carēre, caruī, caritum* + abl. [36]
lake *lacus, -ūs* m. [28]
land *terra, -ae* f. [8]
lap *gremium, iī* n. [27]
large *magnus, -a, -um* [8]
late *tardus, -a, -um* [39]
later *sērius* [17]
laugh at *irrīdeō, irrīdēre, irrīsī, irrīsum* [37]
laugh *rīdeō, rīdere, rīsī, rīsum* [7]
law (it is) *fās* [40]
lawsuit *petitiō, -iōnis* f. [37]
lead down *dēdūcō, dēdūcere, dēdūxī, dēductum* [38]
lead *agō, agere, ēgī, actum* [4]; *dūcō, dūcere, dūxī, ductum* [4]; *ferō, ferre, tulī, latum* [23]
leader *dux, ducis* m. [27]
leap *saliō, salīre, saliī/saluī, saltum* [11]
learn *cognoscō, cognoscere, cognōvī, cognitum* [29]; *disco, discere, didicī* [6]
learn to know *noscō, noscere, nōvī, nōtum* [11]

leave *dēpōnō, dēpōnere, dēposui, dēpositum; relinquō, relinquere, relīquī, relictum* [21]
leave behind *relinquō, relinquere, relīquī, relictum* [21]
left *sinister, sinistra, sinistrum* [38]
left hand *sinistra (manus), -ae* f. [38]
left over (be) *supersum, superesse, superfuī* [35]
legion *legiō, legiōnis* f. [39]
lest *nē* [31]
let go *dīmittō, dīmittere, dīmīsī, dīmissum* [35]
letter *epistula, -ae* f. [23]
liberty *lībertās, -tātis* f. [40]
library *bibliothēca, -ae* f. [27]
lie *mentior, mentīrī, mentītus sum* [24]
lie, lie still, lie dead *iaceō, iacēre, iacuī* [21]
life *vīta, -ae* f. [13]
lift *tollō, tollere, sustulī, sublātum* [11]
light *levis, leve* [23]
like *sīcut* [7]
like to *similis, simile* [37]
likeness *imāgō, -inis* f. [40]
likewise *item* [35]
line *ordō, -inis* m. [34]
line of battle *agmen, agminis* n. [40]
line of poetry *versus, -ūs* m. [27]
linger *cunctor, cunctārī, cunctātus sum* [25]
little brother *frāterculus, -ī* m. [36]
little (adj.) *paucus, -a, -um* [9]
little (adv.) *paulō* [25]; a little *paulum* [28]
live *habitō* (1) [12]; *vīvo, vīvere, vīxī, victum* [29]
living *vīvus, -a, -um* [35]
loathsome *turpis, turpe* [38]
long (adj.) *longus, -a, -um* [19]
long (adv.) *multō* [2]
long distance *longē* [11]
longing for *cupidus, -a, -um* (+ gen.) [39]
look (n.) *speciēs, speciēī* f. [24]
look after *tueor, tuērī, tuitus sum* [29]
look at *aspiciō, aspicere, aspexī, aspectum* [24]; *conspiciō, conspicere, conspexī, conspectum* [9]; *intueor, intuērī, intuitus sum* [25]; *spectō* (1) [10]; *tueor, tuērī, tuitus sum* [29]
look closely at *inspectō* (1) [19]; *inspiciō, inspicere, inspexī, inspectum* [10]
look for *petō, petere, petīvī/petiī, petītum* [21]
look forward to *spērō* (1) [9]
Look! *Ecce!* [11]
loosen *solvō, solvere, soluī, solūtum* [36]
lord *dominus, -ī* m. [18]
lose *āmittō, āmittere, āmīsī, āmissum* [9]; *careō, carēre, caruī, caritum* + abl. [36]
loud *clārus, -a, -um* [36]; *fortis, forte* [15]; *magnus, -a, -um* [8]

love (n.) *amor, amōris* m. [15]
love (v.) *amō* (1) [13]
luck *fortūna, -ae* f. [33]
lucky *felix, felicis* [18]; *fortūnātus, -a, -um* [22]

M

ma'am *domina, -ae* f. [25]
magistracy, magistrate *magistrātus, -ūs* m. [37]
make *fabricō* (1) [30]; *faciō, facere, fēcī, factum* [6]
make ready *parō* (1) [12]
man *homō, hominis* m.; *vir, virī* m. [2]
many *multī, -ae, -a* [2]
march (n.) *cursus, -ūs* m. [35]
march forward *prōgredior, prōgredī, prōgressus sum* [24]
mark *signum, -ī* n. [38]
marriage *matrimōnium, -iī* n. [37]
marry a husband *nūbo, nūbere, nupsī, nuptum* [31]
marry a wife *uxōrem dēdūcere* [38]
master *dominus, -ī* m. [18]; *caput, capitis* n. [36]
matrimony *matrimōnium, -iī* n. [37]
matter *rēs, reī* f. [24]
me *mē* (acc., abl.) [3]; *mihi* (dat.) [1]
mean *significō* (1) [40]
meanwhile *intereā* [35]
memory *memoria, -ae* f. [37]
mental disposition *mens, mentis* f. [31]
merit *dignitās, -tātis* f. [35]
messenger *nuntius, -iī* m. [33]
middle of, midway *medius, -a, -um* [22]
mild *lēnis, lēne* [27]
mind *animus, -ī* m.; *mens, mentis* f. [31]
mirror *speculum, -ī* n. [30]
miserable *miser, misera, miserum* [35]
mistress (of the house) *domina, -ae* f. [25]
mixed *varius, -a, -um* [30]
mock *irrīdeō, irrīdēre, irrīsī, irrīsum* [37]
money *argentum, -ī* n. [31]; *nummus, -ī* m. [27];
    pecunia, -ae f. [3]
monkey *sīmia, -ae* m./f. [5]
month *mensis, mensis* m. [14]
morally unsound *improbus, -a, -um* [23]
more *magis* [16]; (in amount) *plūs* [19];
    (in number) *plūres, plūra* [19]
moreover *praetereā* [34]
most *plūrimus, -a, -um* [20]
mother *māter, mātris* f. [13]
mouth *ōs, ōris* n. [13]
move *moveō, movēre, mōvī, mōtum* [30];
    tangō, tangere, tetigī, tactum [32]
move back *removeō, removēre, remōvī, remōtum* [32]
much (adj.) *multus, -a, -um* [2]

much (adv.) *magnopere* [23]; *multō* [26]; *multum* [16]
my *meus, -a, -um* [5]
my, to me *mihi* [1]

N

name (n.) *nōmen, nōminis* n. [1]
name (v.) *nōmīnō* (1) [22]
nature *nātūra, -ae* f. [32]
near *prope* (+ acc.) [5]
nearest *proximus, -a, -um* [30]
necessary *necessārius, -a, -um* [34]
neglect *praetereō, praeterīre, praeterīvī/praterīī, praeteritum* [35]
neither . . . nor. . . *nec . . . nec . . .* [15];
    neque . . . neque . . . [28]
neither *neuter, neutra, neutrum* [17]
nervous *sollicitus, -a, -um* [39]
never *numquam* [17]
nevertheless *nihilōminus* [39]; *tamen* [20]
new *novus, -a, -um* [8]
news *nuntius, -iī* m. [33]
next day *postrīdiē* [35]
next *proximus, -a, -um* [30]
night *nox, noctis* f. [14]
no *nūllus, -a, -um* [17]
no one *nēmō, nēminis* m./f. [13]
noble *nōbilis, nōbile* [15]; *praeclārus, -a, -um* [16]
nobody *nēmō, nēminis* m./f. [13]
none, not any *nūllus, -a, -um* [17]
not *haud* [16]; *nōn* [3]; *haud* [16] *nē* [31]
not know *nesciō, nescīre, nescīvī/nesciī, nescītum* [34]
not long ago *nūper* [25]
not only . . . but also *nōn sōlum . . . sed etiam* [18]
not want to *nōlō, nolle, nōluī* [7]
not yet *nōndum* [32]
nothing *nihil* (indecl.) [3]
notice *animadvertō, animadvertere, animadvertī, animadversum* [40]
nourishing *almus, -a, -um* [18]
now *iam* [8]; *nunc* [3]

O

observe *animadvertō, animadvertere, animadvertī, animadversum* [40]; *arbitror, abitrārī, arbitrātus sum* [37]; *cognoscō, cognoscere, cognōvī, cognitum* [29]; *conspiciō, conspicere, conspexī, conspectum* [9]; *servō* (1) [27]
observer *spectātor, spectātōris* m. [24]
obvious *plānus, -a, -um* [34]
odor *odor, odōris* m. [21]
of high rank *honestus, -a, -um* [29]

of such a kind, of such a sort *tālis, tāle* [21]

office *dignitās, -tātis* f. [35]; *magistrātus, -ūs* m. [37]

often *saepe* [6]

oh no! *ēheu!* [16]

oh! (in pain or dismay); *heu* (often + accusative) [36]

old *antiquus, -a, -um* [10]; *senex, senis; vetus, veteris* [39]

old man *senex, senis* m. [29]

old woman *anus, -ūs* f. [27]

older *māior, māiōris* (often with *nātū*) [15]

on *in* (+ abl.) [2, 5]

on account of *causā* (+ gen.) [30]; *propter* (+ acc.) [9]

on top of *super* (+ acc.) [10]

once *ōlim* [19]

one *ūnus, -a, -um* [7]

one hundred *centum* (indecl.) [37]

one ought, must *oportet, oportēre, oportuit* (+ acc. + inf.) [12]

one . . . another . . . *alius . . . alius . . .* [31]

only (adj.) *sōlus, -a, -um* [6]

only (adv.) *modo* [23]; *solum* [3]

opinion *opīniō, -iōnis* f. [34]

or *an* [39]; *aut* [4]

order (v.) *imperō* (1) (+ dat.) [26]; *iubeō, iubēre, iussī, iussum* [28]

order (n.) *ordō, -inis* m. [34]

order of knights *equitēs, equitum* m. pl. [34]

origin *orīgō, orīginis* f. [38]

other *alius, -a, -ud* [9]

otherwise *aliter* [39]

ought *dēbeō, dēbēre, dēbuī, dēbitum* [7]; *oportet, oportēre, oportuit* (+acc. +inf.) [12]

our *noster, nostra, nostrum* [15]

out of *ē, ex* (+ abl.) [5]

out of doors, outside *forīs* adv. [34]

outside of *extrā* (+ acc.) [40]

over *super* (+ acc.) [10]; *suprā* (+ acc.) [32]

over there *illīc* [8]

overturn *vertō, vertere, vertī, versum* [26]

owe *dēbeō, dēbēre, dēbuī, dēbitum* [7]

P

pace *gradus, -ūs* m. [24]

pain *opera, -ae* f. [36]; *dolor, dolōris* m. [21]

papyrus *papȳrus, -ī* f. [27]

pardon *parcō, parcere, pepercī/parsī/parcuī, parsūrus* (+ dat.) [12]

parent *parens, parentis* m./f. [16]

part *pars, partis* f. [19]

particular *praecipuus, -a, -um* [27]

particularly *praesertim* [25]

partner *socius, -iī* m. [36]

pater familias *pater familiās, patris familiās* m. [29]

patient *aequus, -a, -um* [31]

patron *patrōnus, -ī* m. [26]

pay *solvō, solvere, soluī, solūtum* [36]

pay attention to *servō* (1) [27]

peace *pax, pācis* f. [27]

peaceful *tranquillus, -a, -um* [31]

people *populus, -ī* m. [4]

perceive *arbitror, abitrārī, arbitrātus sum* [37]; *sentiō, sentīre, sensī, sensum* [21]

perceive *videō, vidēre, vīdī, vīsum* [3]

perform *fungor, fungī, functus sum* (+ abl.) [24]; *solvō, solvere, soluī, solūtum* [36]

perhaps *fortasse* [11]

perish *pereō, perīre, perīvī/periī, peritum* [32]

peristyle *peristȳlium, -iī* n. [26]

permit *sinō, sinere, sīvī/siī, situm* [33]

permitted (it is) *licet, licēre, licuit, licitum* imp. (+ dat.) [29]

person *homō, hominis* m. [13]

personal *proprius, -a, -um*

persuade *persuādeō, persuādēre, persuāsī, persuāsum* (+ dat.) [33]

petition *petitiō, -iōnis* f. [37]

piece *pars, partis* f. [19]

place (n.) *locus, -ī* m. [19]

place (v.) *pōnō, pōnere, posuī, positum* [4]

plan *consilium, -iī* n. [23]

plane *plānus, -a, -um* [34]

play (n.) *fābula, -ae* f. [9]

play (v.) *lūdō, lūdere, lūsī, lūsum* [30]

pleasant *iūcundus, -a, -um* [35]

please *placeō, placēre, placuit* (+ dat.) [12]

Please! *sī tibi placet/sī vobis placet* [7]

pleasing *grātus, -a, -um* [23]

plunder *praemium, -iī* n. [39]

pocketbook *saccus, -ī* m. [11]

poem *carmen, carminis* n. [17]

poet *poēta, -ae* m. [14]

point at *dēmonstrō* (1) [40]

political campaign *ambitiō, -iōnis* f. [37]

poor *pauper, pauperis* [25]

porter *iānitor, -ōris* m. [34]

power *vīs, vis* f. [21]

powerful *potens, potentis* [15]

practically *quasī* [37]

practice *exercereō, exercēre, exercuī, exercitum* [40]

praetor *praetor, praetōris* m. [35]

praetorship *praetūra, -ae* f. [36]

pray *ōrō* (1) [33]

prefer *mālō, malle, māluī* [7]

pregnant *gravidus, -a, -um* [25]

prepare *parō* (1) [12]

preserve *conservō* (1) [39]

pretty *formōsus, -a, -um* [35]; *pulcher, pulchra, pulchrum* [13]

prevent *prohibeō, prohibēre, prohibuī, prohibitum* [39]

prisoner *captīvus, -ī* m. [40]

prize *praemium, -iī* n. [39]

proceed *pergō, pergere, perrēxī, perrectum* [37]; *prōcēdō, prōcēdere, prōcessī, prōcessum* [10]; *prōgredior, prōgredī, prōgressus sum* [24]

procure *arcessō, arcessere, arcessīvī/arcessī, arcessītum* [32]

profit by *fruor, fruī, fructus/fruitus sum* (+ abl.) [24]

prohibit *vetō, vetāre, vetuī, vetitum* [33]

promise *polliceor, pollicērī, pollicitus sum* [24]; *prōmittō, prōmittere, prōmīsī, prōmissum* [34]

prosperity *fortūna, -ae* f. [33]

protect *servō* (1) [27]

proud *superbus, -a, -um* [40]

public *pūblicus, -a, -um* [30]

public show *mūnus, mūneris* n. [17]

pursue *persequor, persequī, persecūtus sum* [40]

push *pulsō* (1) [23]

push back *repellō, repellere, reppulī, repulsum* [39]

put *pōnō, pōnere, posuī, positum* [4]

put to *appōnō, appōnere, apposuī, appositum* [26]

Q

quaestorship *quaestūra, -ae* f. [36]

question *interrogō* (1) [34]

quiet *quiētus, -a, -um* [25]

R

race *certāmen, certāminis* n. [35]; race *cursus, -ūs* m. [35]

raise *excitō* (1) [32]; *tollō, tollere, sustulī, sublātum* [11]

rare *rārus, -a, -um* [27]

rather *magis* [16]

rather late *sērius* [17]

reach *perveniō, pervenīre, pervēnī, perventum* [21]; *tangō, tangere, tetigī, tactum* [32]

read *legō, legere, lēgī, lectum* [15]

reason *causa, -ae* f. [30]; *consilium, -iī* n. [23]; *mens, mentis* f. [31]; *rēs, reī* f. [24]

receive *recipiō, recipere, recēpī, receptum* [31]

recent *recens, recentis* [39]

recently *nūper* [25]; *recenter* [37]

refuse *invideō, invidēre, invīdī, invīsum* (+ dat.) [38]

region *regiō, regiōnis* f. [39]

rejoice *gaudeō, gaudēre, gavīsus sum* [38]

release *dīmittō, dīmittere, dīmīsī, dīmissum* [35]

remain *maneō, manēre, mansī, mansum* [23]; *remaneō, remanēre, remansī* [40]

remaining *reliquus, -a, -um* [21]

remark *animadvertō, animadvertere, animadvertī, animadversum* [40]

remember *meminī, meminisse* [32]

Remember! *Mementō* imper. [32]

remove *trahō, trahere, trāxī, tractus* [22]; *removeō, removēre, remōvī, remōtum* [32]

repel *repellō, repellere, reppulī, repulsum* [39]

replace *restituō, restituere, restituī, restitūtum* [39]

reply *respondeō, respondēre, respondī, responsum* (+ dat.) [3]

report (n.) *fāma, -ae* f. [20]

report (v.) *nuntiō* (1) [37]

reputation *opīniō, -iōnis* f. [34]

request *poscō, poscere, poposcī* [5]; *postulō* (1) [33]

require *postulō* (1) [33]

residence *sēdēs, sēdis* f. [14]

rest *quiescō, quiescere, quiēvī, quiētum* [14]

restore *restituō, restituere, restituī, restitūtum* [39]

restrain *prohibeō, prohibēre, prohibuī, prohibitum* [39]

retain *retineō, retinēre, retinuī, retentum* [37]

retreat *sē recipere* [31]

return *redeō, redīre, rediī, reditum* [21]; *reveniō, revenīre, revēnī, reventum* [31]

reward *praemium, -iī* n. [39]

rhetorical *rhētoricus, -a, -um* [16]

rich *dīves, dīvitis* [24]

right (it is) *fās* [40]

right *dexter, dext(e)ra, dext(e)rum* [38]

right hand *dext(e)ra* (manus), *-ae* f. [38]

ring *orbis, orbis* m. [20]

rise *orior, orīrī, ortus sum* [33]

rise up *surgō, surgere, surrēxī, surrectum* [32]

river *flūmen, -inis* n. [33]

road *iter, itineris* n. [21]; *via, -ae* f. [5]

Roman *Rōmānus, -a, -um* [11]

Rome *Rōma, -ae* f. [11]

room *cella, -ae* f. [18]

rough *horribilis, horribile* [37]

row *ordō, -inis* m. [34]

rule *imperō* (1) (+ dat.) [26]; *regō, regere, rēxī, rectum* [39]

ruler *imperātor, -ōris* m. [25]

rumor *fāma, -ae* f. [20]

run *currō, currere, cucurrī, cursum* [5]

run for political office *petō, petere, petīvī/petiī, petītum* [21]

run towards *occurrō, occurrere, occurrī/occucurrī, occursum* (+ dat.) [36]

rush, rush at *ruō, ruere, ruī, rutum* [22]

S

sack *saccus, -ī* m. [11]

sad *maestus, -a, -um* [18]; *tristis, triste* [15]

safe *salvus, -a, -um* [16]; *tūtus, -a, -um* [14]

safety *salūs, salūtis* f. [32]

sail *nāvigō* (1) [36]

same *īdem, eadem, idem* [21]

sample *exemplum, -ī* n. [40]

sand *harēna, -ae* f. [22]

save *servō* (1) [27]

say *dīcō, dīcere, dīxī, dictum* [7]; *inquit, inquiunt* [2]; *loquor, loquī, locūtus sum* [24]; *nārrō* (1) [14]

say hello *salūtō* (1) [4]

say in addition *addō, addere, addidī, additum* [40]

scarcely *vix* [32]

scared *territus, -a, -um* [14]

scent *odor, odōris* m. [21]

school *lūdus, -ī* m. [4]

schoolmaster *magister, -trī* m. [2]

schoolmistress *magistra, -ae* f. [2]

sea *mare, maris* n. [14]

seal *signum, -ī* n. [38]

season *tempestās, tempestātis* f. [36]; *tempus, temporis* n. [13]

seat *sēdēs, sēdis* f. [14]; *sella, -ae* f. [25]

see *conspiciō, conspicere, conspexī, conspectum* [9]; *sentiō, sentīre, sensī, sensum* [21]; *videō, vidēre, vīdī, vīsum* [3]

seek *petō, petere, petīvī/petiī, petītum* [21]

seem *videor, vidērī, vīsus sum* [27]

seem good, seem like a good idea *vidētur* imp. + inf. [27]

seize *rapiō, rapere, rapuī, raptum* [20]

sell *vendō, vendere, vendidī, venditum* [30]

senate *senātus, -ūs* m. [29]

senator *senātor, -ōris* m. [29]

send *mittō, mittere, mīsī, missum* [20]

send away *āmittō, āmittere, āmīsī, āmissum* [9]

send forth *prōmittō, prōmittere, prōmīsī, prōmissum* [34]

send out *dīmittō, dīmittere, dīmīsī, dīmissum* [35]

sense *sentiō, sentīre, sensī, sensum* [21]

sentry *vigil, vigilis* m./f. [29]

serious *gravis, grave* [15]

servant (female) *ancilla, -ae* f. [8]

servant (male) *servus, -ī* m. [7]

serve *appōnō, appōnere, apposuī, appositum* [26]

set fire to *incendō, incendere, incendī, incensum* [32]

set out *expōnō, expōnere, exposuī, expositum* [40]; *proficiscor, proficiscī, profectus sum* [28]

set sail *nāvem solvere* [36]

several *nōnnūllī, -ae, -a* [9]

shady *obscūrus, -a, -um* [38]

shameless *improbus, -a, -um* [23]

shape (n.) *figūra, -ae* f. [10]; *forma, -ae* f. [34]

shape (v.) *fabricō* (1) [30]

sharp *ācer, ācris, ācre* [38]

she *ea, eius* [17]; *illa, illīus* [17]

shed tears *lacrimō* (1) [17]

ship *nāvis, nāvis* f. [34]

shop *taberna, -ae* f. [2]

short *brevis, breve* [18]

shout (noun) *clāmor, clāmōris* m. [20]

shout (v.) *clāmō* (1) [5]

show *dēmonstrō* (1) [40]; *doceō, docēre, docuī, doctum* [35]; *monstrō* (1); *ostendō, ostendere, ostendī, ostentum/ostensum* [38]

show mercy to *parcō, parcere, pepercī/parsī/parcuī, parsūrus* (+ dat.) [12]

show reverence to *vereor, verērī, veritus sum* [24]

shut *claudō, claudere, clausī, clausum* [38]

sick *aeger, aegra, aegrum* [37]

sickness *morbus, −ī* m. [34]

sign *signum, -ī* n. [38]

silence *silentium, -iī* n. [23]

silver *argentum, -ī* n. [31]

silver, pertaining to silver *argentārius, -a, -um* [31]

silver, silvery *argenteus, -a, -um* [31]

similar *similis, simile* [37]

similarly *item* [35]

since *postquam* [30]; *quia* [18]

sing, *canō, canere, cecinī, cantum* [40]; *cantō* (1) [27]

sing about *canō, canere, cecinī, cantum* [40]

sister *soror, sorōris* f. [13]

sit *sedeō, sedēre, sēdī, sessum* [5]

six *sex* (indecl.) [10]

sixteen *sēdecim* (indecl.) [8]

sixth *sextus, -a, -um* [37]

skill *ars, artis* f. [16]

slave assigned to a young boy *paedagōgus, -ī* m. [5]

slave *servus, -ī* m. [7]

slay *necō* (1) [21]; *occīdō, occīdere, occīdī, occīsum* [39]

sleep *dormiō, dormīre, dormīvī/dormiī, dormītum* [12]

small *parvus, -a, -um* [10]

smaller *minor, minus* [19]

smallest *minimus, -a, -um* [20]

smith *faber, fabrī* m. [28]

smooth *lēnis, lēne* [27]

snack shop *taberna, -ae* f. [2]

snatch *rapiō, rapere, rapuī, raptum* [20]

so *ita* [22], *tam* [11]

so great *tantus, -a, -um* [28]

so many *tot* indeclinable adj. [40]

so much *tantus, -a, -um* [28]

so much (as) *tam* [11]

so that *ut* [31]

soft *lēnis, lēne* [27]
soldier *mīles, mīlitis* m. [23]
some *nōnnūllī, -ae, -a* [9]
some . . . others . . . . *aliī . . . aliī* [31]
someday *aliquandō* [26]
someone, something *aliquis, aliquid* n. [18]
sometimes *aliquandō* [26]
somewhat *paulō* [25]; *paulum* [28]
son *fīlius, -iī* m. [4]
song *carmen, carminis* n. [17]
son-in-law *gener, generī* m. [30]
soon *mox* [9]
sound *sonitus, -ūs* m. [24]
source *orīgō, orīginis* f. [38]
space *spatium, -iī* n. [28]
spare *parcō, parcere, pepercī/parsī/parcuī,*
    parsūrus (+ dat.) [12]
speak *loquor, loquī, locūtus sum* [24]
speak out *ēloquor ēloquī, ēlocūtus sum* [24]
special *praecipuus, -a, -um* [27]
spectator *spectātor, spectātōris* m. [24]
speech *lingua, -ae* f. [33]; *ōrātiō, ōrātiōnis* f. [16]
stand *stō, stāre, stetī, statum* [5]
stand out from *praestō, praestāre, praestitī,*
    praestitum/praestātum (+ dat.) [10]
stand still *cōnstō, cōnstāre, cōnstitī, cōnstātum* [10];
    sistō, sistere, stetī/stitī, statum [8]
statue *imāgō, -inis* f. [40]
stay *maneō, manēre, mansī, mansum* [23]
stay behind *remaneō, remanēre, remansī* [40]
step *gradus, -ūs* m. [24]
still (adj.) *tranquillus, -a, -um* [31]
still (adv.) *adhūc* [30]; *etiam* [17]
stillness *silentium, -iī* n. [23]; *tranquillitās, -tātis* f. [31]
storm *tempestās, tempestātis* f. [36]
story *fābula, -ae* f. [9]
stranger *hospes, hospitis* m. [26]; *hostis, hostis* m./f. [14]
street *via, -ae* f. [5]
strength *vīs, vis* f. [21]
strike *pulsō* (1) [23]
strong *firmus, -a, -um* [36]; *fortis, forte* [15]
structure *opus, operis* n. [23]
student (female) *discipula, -ae* f. [2]
student (male) *discipulus, -ī* m. [2]
study (n.) *studium, -iī* n. [6]
study (v.) *studeō, studēre, studuī* (+ dat.) [12]
succeed (to) *succēdō, succēdere, successī, successum* [37];
    cēdō, cēdere, cessī, cessum (+ dat.) [35]
such *tālis, tāle* [21]
suddenly *subitō* [11]
suffer *patior, patī, passus sum* [24]
sufficient *satis* [30]

suitable *aptus, -a, -um* [31]; *idōneus, -a, -um* [36]
summon *arcessō, arcessere, arcessīvī/arcessī, arcessītum* [32]
sun *sōl, sōlis* m. [33]
support *obtineō, obtinēre, obtinuī, obtentum* [9];
    sustineō, sustinere, sustinuī, sustentum [37]
surpass *praestō, praestāre, praestitī, praestātum* (+ dat.) [10]
survive *supersum, superesse, superfuī* [35]
sweet *dulcis, dulce* [23]
swift *ācer, ācris, ācre* [38]; *celer, celeris, celere* [15]
sword iron *ferrum, -ī* n. [22]; *gladius, -iī* m. [17]

T

table *mensa, -ae* f. [16]
take *capiō, capere, cēpī, captum* [3]
take a wife *uxōrem dēdūcere* [38]
take back *recipiō, recipere, recēpī, receptum* [31]
take care *caveō, cavēre, cāvī, cautum* [33]
take possession of *potior, potīri, potītus sum*
    (+ abl. or gen.) [24]
talented *dīves, dīvitis* [24]
talk *loquor, loquī, locūtus sum* [24]; *sermōcinor, sermōcinārī,*
    sermōcinātus sum [31]
talk together *colloquor, colloquī, collocūtus sum* [25]
tarry *cunctor, cunctārī, cunctātus sum* [25]
task *negōtium, -iī* n. [8]
teach *doceō, docēre, docuī, doctum* [35]
teacher (female) *magistra, -ae* f. [2]
teacher (male) *magister, -trī* m. [2]
teacher of rhetoric (public speaking) *rhētor, rhētoris* [16]
tease *lūdō, lūdere, lūsī, lūsum* [30]
tell *nārrō* (1) [14]
ten *decem* (indecl.) [12]
terrible *horribilis, horribile* [37]; *terribilis, terribile* [27]
terrific! *eugae/euge/eugepae* [36]
terrified *perterritus, -a, -um* [21]
territory *fīnēs, finium* m. pl. [14]
test *temptō* (1) [32]
than *ac* [33]; *quam* [10]
thankful *grātus, -a, -um* [23]
thanks *grātiae, -ārum* f. pl. [19]
that man *ille, illīus* [17]
that not (with subj. "from X'ing") *quīn* [39]
that not *nē* [31]
that one of yours *iste, ista, istud* (derogatory) [17]
that thing *illud, illīus* [17]
that woman *illa, illīus* [17]
their own *suus, -a, -um* [9]
themselves *suī, sibi, sē, sē* [21]
themselves (emphatic) *ipsī, ipsae, ipsa* [17]
then *posteā* [30]; *tum* [20]; *tunc* [3]
there *ibi* [21]; *illīc* [8]; (to) there *illūc* [36]

therefore *ergō* [8]; *igitur* [20]; *itaque* [20]

they *eī, eae, ea* [17]; *illī, illae, illa* [17]

thin *rārus, -a, -um* [27]

thing *rēs, reī* f. [24]

think *arbitror, abitrārī, arbitrātus sum* [37]; *cogitō* (1) [10];
    opīnōr, opīnārī, opīnātus sum [30]

third *tertius, -a, -um* [38]

thirsty (be) *sitiō, sitīre, sitīvī/sitiī* [31]

this *hic, haec, hoc* [19]

those *illī, illae, illa* [17]

three times *ter* [36]

three *trēs, tria* [6]

through *per* (+ acc.) [5]

throw *iaciō, iacere, iēcī, iactus* [22]

thus *ita* [22]; *sīc* [11]

tier (of a theater) *gradus, -ūs* m. [24]

time *hōra, -ae* f. [8]; *tempestās, tempestātis* f. [36];
    tempus, temporis n. [13]

tired *fessus, -a, -um* [8]

tiresome *molestus, -a, -um* [29]

to *ad* (+ acc.) [2, 5]

to me *mihi* [1]

to this place *hūc* [36]

to this point *adhūc* [30]

to you *tibi* [1]

today *hodiē* [4]

toga *toga, -ae* f. [33]

together *simul* [24]

token *signum, -ī* n. [38]

tomorrow *crās* [6]

tongue *lingua, -ae* f. [33]

too (also) *etiam* [17]

too late *sērius* [17]

too, too much *nimium* [16]

tool *instrūmentum, -ī* n. [27]

touch *tangō, tangere, tetigī, tactum* [32]

toward *ad* (+ acc.) [2, 5]

town *oppidum, -ī* n. [28]

tranquility *silentium, -iī* n. [23]

transport *transportō* (1) [27]

treasurer *quaestūra, -ae* f. [36]

tree *arbor, arboris* f. [29]

tremble *tremō, tremere, tremuī* [34]

triclinium *trīclīnium, -iī* n. [26]

thirsty (be) *sitiō, sitīre, sitīvī/sitiī* [31]

troops *agmen, agminis* n. [40]; *vīrēs, vīrium* f. pl. [21]

trouble *difficultās, -tātis* f. [23]

trouble greatly *perturbō* (1) [26]

troublesome *molestus, -a, -um* [29]

true *vērus, -a, -um* [15]

truly *vērē* [15]

trumpet *tuba, -ae* f. [26]

trust *crēdō, crēdere, crēdidī, crēditum* (+ dat.) [25]

trustworthy *fidēlis, fidēle* [33]

try *cōnor, cōnārī, cōnātus est* [24]; *temptō* (1) [32]

turn *vertō, vertere, vertī, versum* [26]

tutor *paedagōgus, -ī* m. [5]

twelve *duodecim* (indecl.) [12]

twenty *vīgintī* (indecl.) [12]

twice *bis* [36]

two *duo, duae, duo* [7]

two times *bis* [36]

type *speciēs, speciēī* f. [24]

U

ugly *turpis, turpe* [38]

unbind *solvō, solvere, soluī, solūtum* [36]

uncertain *dubius, -a, -um* [39]; *incertus, -a, -um* [35];
    obscūrus, -a, -um [38]

under (adj.) *sub* (+ abl.) [6]; *sub* (+ acc.) [6]

under (adv.) *infrā* [32]

underneath *infrā* [32]

understand *animadvertō, animadvertere, animadvertī,*
    animadversum [40]; *intellegō, intellegere, intellēxī,*
    intellectum [13]

undertake *cōnor, cōnārī, cōnātus est* [24]

undoubtedly *profectō* [32]

uneasy *anxius, -a, -um* [29]; *sollicitus, -a, -um* [39]

unfortunate *infēlix, -icis* [36]; *infortūnātus, -a, -um* [22]

unhappy *infēlix, -icis* [36]

unique *proprius, -a, -um*

unless *nisi* [30]

unlike *dissimilis, dissimile* [37]

unlucky *infortūnātus, -a, -um* [22]

until *dōnec* [27]; *dum*

urge *hortor, hortārī, hotātus sum* [33]

us *nōs, nōstrum/nōstrī, nōbīs, nōs, nōbīs* [21]

use *ūtor, ūtī, ūsus sum* (+ abl.) [24]

use up *consūmō, consūmere, consumpsī, consumptum* [38]

useful *utilis, utile* [30]

utterly *omnīnō* [32]

V

value *aestimō* (1) [38]

vanish *pereō, perīre, perīvī/periī, peritum* [32]

various *varius, -a, -um* [30]

verse *versus, -ūs* m. [27]

very (much) *valdē* [11]

very frightened *perterritus, -a, -um* [21]

very happy *perlaetus, -a, -um* [27]

victor *victor, victōris* m. [35]

victory *victōria, -ae* f. [35]

vigorously *strēnuē* [26]
violent *ācer, ācris, ācre* [38]
voice *vox, vōcis* f. [15]
voyage *cursus, -ūs* m. [35]

W

wage war *bellum gerere* [23]
wait for *exspectō* (1) [16]
wake up *expergiscor, expergiscī, experrectus sum* [32]
walk *ambulō* (1); *cēdō, cēdere, cessī, cessum* (+ dat.) [35]
wall *mūrus, -ī* m. [28]
wallet *saccus, -ī* m. [11]
want to *cupiō, cupere, cupīvī/cupiī, cupītum* [4]; *volō, velle, voluī* [7]
wants (he, she, it) *vult* [5]
war *bellum, -ī* n. [23]
warm *calidus, -a, -um* [33]
warn *moneō, monēre, monuī, monitum* [33]
wash *lavō, lavāre, lāvī, lautum/lavātum/lōtum* [31]
watch *custōdiō, custōdīre, custōdīvī/custōdiī, custōditum* [30]; *spectō* (1) [10]
watch over *tueor, tuērī, tuitus sum* [29]
water *aqua, -ae* f. [2]
way *via, -ae* f. [5]
we *nōs* [21]
wealth *fortūna, -ae* f. [33]
weather *tempestās, tempestātis* f. [36]
well (adj.) *salvus, -a, -um* [16]
well (adv.) *bene* [4]
well! *age* [36]
what? *quid* [1, 18]
whatever *quisquis, quodquod/quicquod/quidquid* [40]
what kind of? what sort of? *qualis, quale?* [34]
when *cum* [15]; *quandō* [29]; *ubi* [5]
where *ubi* [5]
whereby, wherefore *quārē* [30]
whether *an* [39]
which *quī, quae, quod* [18]
while *dum* [10]
who *quī, quae, quod* [18]
who? *quis* [6, 18]
whoever, whatever *quisquis, quodquod/quicquod/quidquid* [40]
whole *tōtus, -a, -um* [17]
why *cūr* [11]; *quārē* [30]; *quā dē causā* [34]
why not? *quīn* [39]
wide *lātus, -a, -um* [31]
wife *uxor, uxōris* f. [18]
willing *libens, libentis*
wind *ventus, -ī* m. [36]
wine *vīnum, -ī* n. [3]

wish *cupiō, cupere, cupīvī/cupiī, cupitum* [4]; *optō* (1); *volō, velle, voluī* [7]
with *apud* (+ acc.) [16]; *cum* (+ abl.) [6]
within *intrā* (+ acc.) [25]
without *sine* (+ abl.) [6]
without question *profectō* [32]
withstand *sustineō, sustinere, sustinuī, sustentum* [37]
woe! (in pain or dread) *vae* (often + dative) [36]
woman *fēmina, -ae* f. [2]
woman in charge *domina, -ae* f. [25]
woman (old) *anus, -ūs* f.
wonder at *admīror, admīrārī, admīrātus sum* [26]; *mīror, mīrārī, mīrātus sum* [25]
woods *silva, -ae* f. [21]
word *verbum, -ī* n. [11]
work (n.) *labor, labōris* m.; *opera, -ae* f. [36]; *opus, operis* n. [23]
work (v.) *labōrō* (1) [9]
workman *faber, fabrī* m. [28]
workshop *fabrica, -ae* f. [37]; *officīna, -ae* f. [34]
world *orbis terrārum* [20]
worse *pēior, pēius* [19]
worst *pessimus, -a, -um* [20]
worthiness *dignitās, -tātis* f. [35]
worthy *honestus, -a, -um* [29]
would that! *utinam* [37]
wound *vulnerō* (1) [22]
wound *vulnus, vulneris* n. [22]
wretched *miser, misera, miserum* [35]
write *scrībō, scrībere, scripsī, scriptum* [6]
writer *scriptor, -ōris* m. [27]

Y

year *annus, -ī* m. [12]
years old *annōs nātus, -a, -um* [12]
yes *ita* [22]; *sīc* [11]
yesterday *heri* [19]
yet *adhūc* [30]; *at* [20]; *atque* [20] *quamquam*
yield to *cēdō, cēdere, cessī, cessum* (+ dat.) [35]
you (all) *vōs, vestrum, vōbīs, vōs, vōbīs* [21]
you (all) *vōbīs* (dat./abl.) [17]
you (sing.) *tū* [3]
your (sing.) *tuus, -a, -um* [6]; (pl.) *vester, vestra, vestrum* [6]
your *tibi* [1]
youth *adulescens, -entis* m./f. [15]; *iuvenis, iuvenis* m./f. [15]

Z

zeal *studium, -iī* n. [6]

Photo Credits

Index

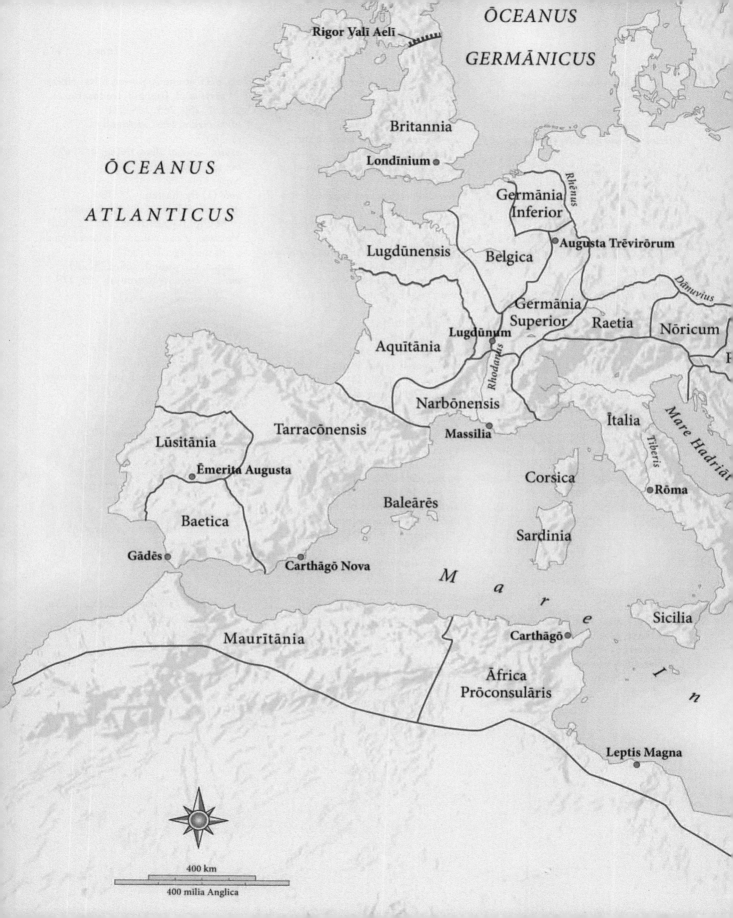

ŌCEANUS
GERMĀNICUS

ŌCEANUS

ATLANTICUS

Rigor Valī Aelī

Britannia

Londīnium

Germānia
Inferior

Rhēnus

Lugdūnensis

Belgica

Augusta Trēvirōrum

Dānuvius

Germānia
Superior

Raetia

Nōricum

Aquītānia

Lugdūnum

Rhodanus

Narbōnensis

Ītalia

Mare Hadriāt

Massilia

Tarracōnensis

Lūsitānia

Corsica

Tiberis

Rōma

Ēmerita Augusta

Baleārēs

Baetica

Sardinia

Gādēs

Carthāgō Nova

Mare

Sicilia

Maurītānia

Carthāgō

Āfrica
Prōconsulāris

I
n

Leptis Magna

400 km

400 mīlia Anglica

Roman Empire

ncum

Dācia

Dānuvius

Moesia
Superior

Moesia
Inferior

Thrācia

Macedonia

Constantinopolis

pīrus

Pergamum

Achaea

Athēnae

Pontus Euxīnus

Bithȳnia
et Pontus

Galatia

Asia

Cappadocia

Armenia

Cilicia

Lycia et
Pamphȳlia

Syria

Tigris

Mesopotamia

Euphrātēs

Crēta

Cyprus

Damascus

Iūdaea

Jerusalem

r

n

u

m

ica

Alexandrīa

Cȳrēnē

Arabia

Aegyptus

Sinu

Imperial Rome

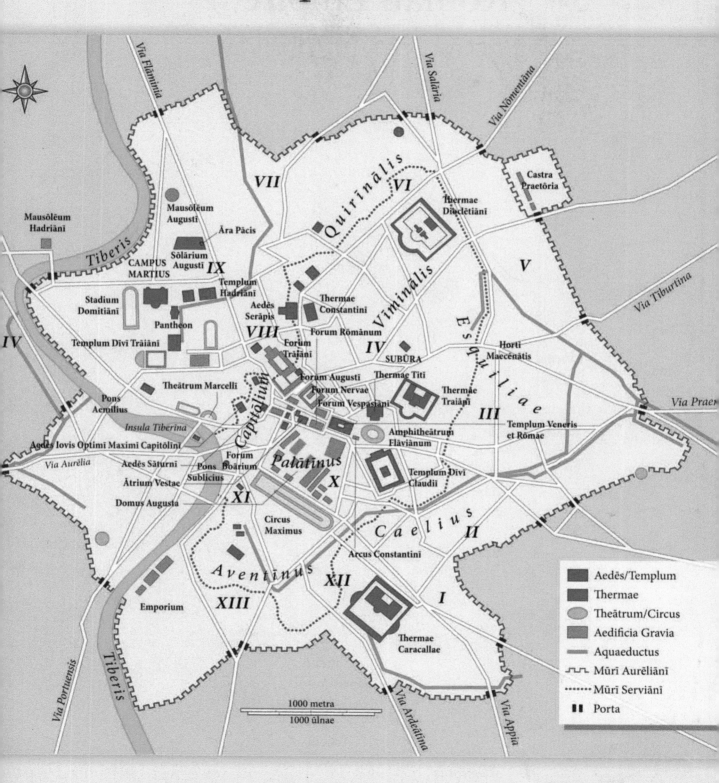

Via Flāminia

Via Salāria

Via Nōmentāna

Mausōlēum Hadriānī

Tiberis

CAMPUS MARTIUS

Mausōlēum Augustī

Āra Pācis

Sōlārium Augustī

VII

Quirīnālis

VI

Thermae Dioclētiānī

Castra Praetōria

V

Via Tiburtīna

IX

Templum Hadriānī

Aedēs Serāpis

VIII

Thermae Constantīnī

Vīminālis

Stadium Domitiānī

Pantheon

Templum Dīvī Trāiānī

Forum Rōmānum

Forum Trāiānī

IV

SUBŪRA

Esquiliae

Horti Maecēnātis

Via Praer

IV

Forum Augustī
Forum Nervae
Forum Vespasiānī

Thermae Titī

Thermae Trāiānī

III

Templum Veneris et Rōmae

Theātrum Marcellī

Capitōlium

Pons Aemilius

Insula Tiberīna

Amphitheātrum Flāviānum

Aedēs Iovis Optimī Maximī Capitōlīnī

Via Aurēlia

Aedēs Sāturnī

Ātrium Vestae

Domus Augusta

Forum Boārium

Pons Sublicius

Palātīnus

X

Templum Dīvī Claudiī

XI

Circus Maximus

Caelius

II

Arcus Constantīnī

Aventīnus

XII

I

Emporium

XIII

Thermae Caracallae

Tiberis

Via Portuensis

Via Ardeātīna

Via Appia

1000 metra

1000 ūlnae

■	Aedēs/Templum
■	Thermae
●	Theātrum/Circus
■	Aedificia Gravia
—	Aquaeductus
⌐⌐	Mūrī Aurēliānī
····	Mūrī Serviānī
▮▮	Porta